THE ONTARIO HISTORICAL STUDIES SERIES

The Ontario Historical Studies Series is a comprehensive history of Ontario from 1791 to the present, which will include several biographies of former premiers, numerous volumes on the economic, social, political, and cultural development of the province, and a general history incorporating the insights and conclusions of the other works in the series. The purpose of the series is to enable general readers and scholars to understand better the distinctive features of Ontario as one of the principal regions within Canada.

THE BIOGRAPHIES OF THE PREMIERS

J.M.S. Careless, ed., *The Pre-Confederation Premiers: Ontario Government Leaders, 1841–1867*

Charles W. Humphries, *'Honest Enough to Be Bold': The Life and Times of Sir James Pliny Whitney* (Premier, 1905–1914)

Charles M. Johnston, *E.C. Drury: Agrarian Idealist* (Premier, 1919–1923)

Peter Oliver, *G. Howard Ferguson: Ontario Tory* (Premier, 1923–1930)

Roger Graham, *Old Man Ontario: Leslie M. Frost* (Premier 1949–1961)

A.K. McDougall, *John P. Robarts: His Life and Government* (Premier, 1961–1971)

FORTHCOMING

A. Margaret Evans, SIR OLIVER MOWAT (Premier, 1872–1896)
Robert J.D. Page, SIR GEORGE W. ROSS (Premier, 1899–1905)
John T. Saywell, HON. MITCHELL F. HEPBURN (Premier, 1934–1942)

Leslie Frost, 1953

ROGER GRAHAM

Old Man Ontario: Leslie M. Frost

Published by University of Toronto Press
Toronto Buffalo London
for The Ontario Historical Studies Series

ISBN 0-8020-3459-4

Printed on acid-free paper

Canadian Cataloguing in Publication Data

Graham, Roger, 1919–1988
Old man Ontario : Leslie M. Frost, 1895–1973

(Ontario historical studies series)
Includes bibliographical references.
ISBN 0-8020-3459-4

1. Frost, Leslie M. (Leslie Miscampbell), 1895–1973.
2. Ontario – Politics and government – 1923–1943.*
3. Ontario – Politics and government – 1943–1985.*
4. Prime ministers – Ontario – Bibliography.
5. Politicians – Ontario – Bibliography.   I. Title.   II. Series.

FC3075.I.F7G7 1990   971.3'04'092   C90-093046-2
FI058.F7G7 1990

This book has been published with funds provided by the Government of
Ontario through the Ministry of Culture and Communications.

TO KAY

Contents

The Ontario Historical Studies Series

For many years the principal theme in English-Canadian historical writing has been the emergence and the consolidation of the
Canadian nation. This theme has been developed in uneasy awareness of the persistence and importance of regional interests and
identities, but because of the central role of Ontario in the growth
of Canada, Ontario has not been seen as a region. Almost uncon-
sciously, historians have equated the history of the province with
that of the nation and have depicted the interests of other regions
as obstacles to the unity and welfare of Canada.

The creation of the province of Ontario in 1867 was the visible
embodiment of a formidable reality, the existence at the core of
the new nation of a powerful if disjointed society whose traditions
and characteristics differed in many respects from those of the
other British North American colonies. The intervening century
has not witnessed the assimilation of Ontario to the other regions
in Canada; on the contrary it has become a more clearly articulated
entity. Within the formal geographical and institutional framework
defined so assiduously by Ontario's political leaders, an increasingly
intricate web of economic and social interests has been woven and
shaped by the dynamic interplay between Toronto and its hinter-
land. The character of this regional community has been formed
in the tension between a rapid adaptation to the processes of modernization and industrialization in modern Western society and a
reluctance to modify or discard traditional attitudes and values.
Not surprisingly, the Ontario outlook is a compound of aggressive-
ness, conservatism, and the conviction that its values should be the
model for the rest of Canada.

From the outset the objective of the Board of Trustees of the
series has been to describe and analyse the historical development

of Ontario as a distinct region within Canada. The series as planned will include thirty-two volumes covering many aspects of the life and work of the province from its original establishment in 1791 as Upper Canada to our own time. Among these will be biographies of several premiers, numerous works on the growth of the provincial economy, educational institutions, minority groups, and the arts, and a synthesis of the history of Ontario, based upon the contributions of the biographies and thematic studies.

In planning this project, the Editors and the Board have endeavoured to maintain a reasonable balance between different kinds and areas of historical research, and to appoint authors ready to ask new questions about the past and to answer them in accordance with the canons of contemporary scholarship. Nine biographies have been commissioned, because through biography the past comes alive most readily for the general reader as well as for the historian.

Old Man Ontario: Leslie M. Frost is the sixth biography to be published. It depicts the life and times of a premier whose values and attitudes epitomized those of the small-town Ontario of his youth. He held office longer than any premier except Sir Oliver Mowat. He presided over a crucial phase in the modernization of provincial society – a process in which the distinctive features of Old Ontario began to crumble and disappear.

This study illuminates clearly, honestly, and yet sympathetically the character, the objectives, and the actions of the man who governed this province with authority from 1949 to 1961. It will add very substantially to our understanding of the formation of contemporary Ontario.

The Editors and the Board of Trustees are deeply grateful to Roger Graham for undertaking this immense task. We regret profoundly that he did not live to see the fruit of his devoted labours.

Goldwin French
Peter Oliver
Jeanne Beck
Maurice Careless, Chairman of the Board of Trustees

Toronto
6 December 1989

Preface

This book has two purposes: to delineate Leslie Frost's character and personality by telling of his ancestry, upbringing, and experience as soldier, small-town lawyer, politician, and elder statesman; and to shed a little light on the history of Ontario during the period when he was prominent, and for more than a decade dominant, in its public affairs. Every political biographer has to grapple with the problem of striking a proper balance between the 'life' and the 'times.' This proved to be especially difficult in Frost's case because, at a time when the ambit of provincial government action was expanding very rapidly, he was so much a 'hands on' leader, concerning himself actively with almost every aspect of policy. As I have had to be highly selective in choosing which subjects to write about of all those that occupied his mind, there is in his papers and related collections a wealth of material about those which are here ignored or touched upon only lightly that is worthy of study by those interested in provincial politics and government. This, let me add, by no means implies that the aspects of his life and times which do find a place in this volume will not bear further examination.

Some of the matters that did engage his close attention, among them federal-provincial relations, the financial problems of municipalities and school boards, and the development of additional energy sources to fuel Ontario's burgeoning economy, clearly were of fundamental significance. Others, liquor licensing and control, let us say, may seem to many readers in the late 1980s to have been of less consuming importance than he and many of his contemporaries thought. The seriousness with which Frost regarded still others, for example whether night harness racing ought to be permitted, at times mystified his aides, colleagues, and supporters, but some such issues have been dealt with because their proper disposition seemed to him vital to the welfare of the province and its people.

Although important strides were made under his leadership in modernizing provincial administration and building an expert, professional civil service, Frost's style of government was distinctly personal. His politics were not, however, as much oriented toward rural Ontario as is sometimes thought, even though he thoroughly understood its political power. The touchstone was promotion of economic development. In the main this meant facilitating a rapid industrialization which would have gone on apace willy-nilly but which his measures were intended to and did encourage. Ironically, rejoicing in the statistics of growth which to him spelled progress, he thus presided over the comparative weakening of Old Ontario's rural and small-town society, to which he felt a strong affinity, and over the ushering in of an essentially urban, industrial New Ontario, some of whose values and mores he instinctively mistrusted and disliked.

In my research and writing I have incurred a great many debts. I gratefully acknowledge the encouragement and constructive suggestions offered by Goldwin French, Peter Oliver, and Jeanne Beck, as well as the exemplary, not to say superhuman, patience with which they awaited a manuscript that took far longer to complete than they (and I) would have preferred. The staff of the Archives of Ontario uncomplainingly (at least in my hearing) fetched me a seemingly endless succession of file boxes and assisted me materially in other ways. They made spending a great deal of time in the precincts of that institution a pleasure. To Ken Johnston, former archivist of Trent University, and to Bernadine Dodge, the present archivist, I am indebted for many courtesies extended in using the important collection of Frost Papers held by Trent. The staffs of the Queen's University Archives, the Douglas Library of Queen's University, the Orillia and Lindsay Public Libraries, and the *Lindsay Post* all gave assistance that is greatly appreciated.

The book is based chiefly on written sources: the voluminous Frost papers and other personal collections, government documents, newspapers and periodicals, and the available secondary literature which, while rather slight in quantity, is very useful in substance. But I have benefited as well from oral testimony, much of it in the excellent interviews assembled by the Ontario Historical Studies Series' oral history program, and from correspondence with a number of persons. Peter Oliver and I planned to conduct a series of interviews with Mr Frost but his final illness prevented all but the first of these, about his early life, from taking place. I owe a special debt of gratitude to the late Hugh D. Latimer, who figures quite prominently in the following pages and to whom Leslie Frost was a hero. In conversation and by mail, Mr Latimer supplied me with information, some of it in copies of documents from his own papers, and with explanations of certain events which I could not have found elsewhere. In addition, at my instance he recorded his reminiscences, which add significantly to one's understanding of Ontario politics during the Frost era. It is a matter of great regret to me that he died before the book was finished.

I am conscious of my failure to draw on the knowledge of many people still living who knew, and in some cases worked with, Mr Frost. There are, however, some to whom I am indebted for agreeing to be interviewed or for answering my queries by letter. I am grateful to Mr Frost's niece, Marjorie Porter, and his cousin, Dorothy Swallow, who were especially helpful in this way. Others, some now deceased, to whom I am similarly obliged are Hon. J.N. Allan, Elmer Bell, Ray Farrell, Hon. the Rev. J.W. Foote, v.c., Hon. W.E. Hamilton, and Right Hon. Roland Michener.

Last but far from least, my wife, to whom the book is lovingly dedicated, assisted in the early stages of research, listened patiently to much of the first draft, and offered numerous constructive criticisms. More than that, her encouragement bolstered my flagging spirits in the all too numerous moments when completion of the work seemed beyond attainment.

Roger Graham
24 August 1988

This preface and the manuscript of *Old Man Ontario* were completed by Roger Graham in August 1988. At the time of his death in November of that year, we were about to discuss with him some suggestions for editing his account of Leslie Frost's life and political career. Subsequently we were obliged to assume direct responsibility for preparing the manuscript for consideration by the University of Toronto Press and for seeing it through all stages of the publishing process. In editing the text we have sought scrupulously to ensure that the spirit and content of Professor Graham's narrative were not altered in any way. We are most grateful to Professor J.M.S. Careless for his generous and wise assistance and counsel in carrying out this difficult task. We wish also to thank warmly Diane Mew for her careful and conscientious work as copy-editor of the Frost manuscript and Riça Night for preparing the index.

Roger Graham was a very dear friend and one of Canada's most distinguished historians. We and all those who knew him well greatly mourn his untimely death. We believe that his biography of Leslie Frost will be acknowledged as a fitting conclusion to Roger Graham's scholarly achievements. We earnestly hope that it will be a source of profound pride and consolation to Kathleen Graham and her family.

Goldwin French
Peter Oliver
Jeanne Beck

Leslie Frost, c. 1953

Gertrude Frost at 17 Sussex Street North, Lindsay

William Sword Frost

Margaret Barker Frost (Mater)

Cecil Frost

Grenville Frost

The cottage at Pleasant Point, Sturgeon Lake

Leslie and Cecil Frost, 1914

17 Sussex Street North, Lindsay

Gertrude Frost and other Tory women

Leslie Frost and Prime Minister Louis St Laurent

Election night in Lindsay

Leslie Frost meeting the people

Official opening of Robert H. Saunders–St Lawrence Generating Station,
5 September 1958. From left to right: Hon. W. Averell Harriman, Governor,
New York State; Hon. Leslie M. Frost, Premier, Province of Ontario; James
S. Duncan, Chairman, Ontario Hydro; Robert Moses, Chairman, Power
Authority of the State of New York

Leslie Frost with Donald C. MacDonald at historical plaque unveiling at Queen's Park, 25 October 1956

Frost unveils an historical plaque at Port Carling, 26 September 1956. From the left: Mr Robert J. Boyer, newspaper publisher; Miss Penson, who was Leslie Frost's teacher in Orillia; Leslie Frost; Hon. Bryan Cathcart, minister of tourism and publicity; Hon. William Griesinger, minister of public works; Reeve Robert Bennett, Port Carling

Frost meets the press

OLD MAN ONTARIO: LESLIE M. FROST

1

Growing up in Mariposa – and in France

Amidst the festivities of 1 July 1867, the first Dominion Day, a certain family of Scottish immigrants arrived unnoticed in Toronto, completing a journey begun more than two weeks earlier in Wemyss Bay, a short distance west of Glasgow. Descending from the railway coach, they stood uncertainly on the station platform, a husband and wife with three small children, looking as presentable as could be expected after a fortnight's travel. John Frost was wearing a good broadcloth suit with grey topper set firmly on his head; Janet Frost wore a clean dress and bonnet, a Paisley shawl around her shoulders; and the youngsters were in their best bib and tucker. Frost was a miller and baker by trade, a Presbyterian and Freemason by conviction, but above all a Scot to the marrow of his being.

John Frost soon decided to move to Orillia, then a ramshackle village of eight hundred people subsisting mostly on the timber trade. Arriving there in 1868, Frost opened the Glasgow Bakery, in which he practised his trade with modest success until his death in 1883.[1] William Sword Frost, the second child of John and Janet and father of Leslie, was four when his family settled in Orillia. A man who would receive little formal education but possessing lively intelligence and great enthusiasm, he founded his own jewellery business in 1892, with the financial help of Andrew Miscampbell, a fellow Presbyterian and a member of the Ontario legislature. Although he was apparently more interested in public affairs than in making money, his shop prospered sufficiently to enable him and his family to live comfortably.[2]

On New Year's Day 1890, William Frost married Margaret Jane Barker of London, Ontario, until her marriage an adherent of the Salvation Army, and like her future husband an ardent advocate

of temperance.[3] William and Margaret Frost had three sons, Grenville Barker, Leslie Miscampbell, and Cecil Gray. Leslie, the second
son, was born on 20 September 1895 in a modest two-storey house
on Mississaga Street, a few blocks from the jewellery store.[4] Two
years later the family moved to a house known as 'Highlands' on
the northern outskirts of Orillia, overlooking the splendid expanse
of Lake Couchiching. Leslie Frost and his brothers grew up in this
home of happy memories.

The Frosts were a close-knit, affectionate family, united by strict
but not unreasonable parental discipline dutifully accepted by the
three sons, and by a routine of life that stressed common family
interests and the faithful performance by each member of tasks
assigned. Religious precept and practice exercised a pervasive influence. Each day before breakfast they gathered in the library,
together with the servant or two who normally lived in, for morning
prayers; the head of the household would read a chapter from the
Bible and, Leslie remembered, 'it was pretty dry going.'[5] Attendance at Sunday school and church was obligatory, but the boys
accepted this duty as part of the order of their lives. Naturally, too,
they had instilled in them their parents' abhorrence of liquor.
Christian abstinence, total and uncompromising, was demanded.[6]

Due observance of the Sabbath was also required, although the
Frosts were a little less severe about this than some, as they were
about card-playing and dancing. They permitted newspapers to be
read on Sundays, something prohibited in many Presbyterian
homes. The Sunday afternoon practice, weather permitting, was to
hitch up the horse, Prince, and go for a drive; many of their fellow
church people frowned upon them for this regrettable lapse from
proper Christian conduct. The family customarily camped on the
shore of Lake Couchiching for part of each summer, Leslie's introduction to the outdoor life to which he would remain addicted. On
these outings, and after their father built a summer home which
they dubbed 'the Beach' in 1910, the boys virtually lived on the
lake, sailing the dinghy before a spanking breeze, or waiting in the
rowboat for the fish to strike, or skimming over the water in their
canoe like the voyageurs of old. Unfortunately, boating on the Sabbath was against the rules and this caused much anguish. A family
discussion, however, produced a compromise: 'It wasn't any sin to
put the boat in the water and sit in it but we just couldn't paddle
around in it.'[7]

There was much discussion of public affairs at the family dinner
table, as William Frost was active in Orillia politics and would

become mayor. As they grew old enough to have an intelligent interest, the boys were encouraged to take part in these conversations and to prepare themselves by reading the various publications that came into the house. The *Orillia Packet*, of course, was read avidly for its coverage of local issues. From Toronto the *Globe* and the *Mail and Empire* arrived regularly, while the *News*, the *World*, and the *Telegram* were often brought home by William. He also subscribed year after year to *Saturday Night*, despite his distaste for certain opinions advanced by E.E. Sheppard, its founder and editor until 1906. 'It was a wet paper,' Leslie remembered, 'and my father used to frown on it and have a great deal to say about Sheppard but he still subscribed to it.'[8] Disagreements were not ruled out in the Frosts' table talk and were quite common, the youngsters sometimes disputing even their father's vigorously expressed views. But he 'could always beat us ... by putting a few of the arguments in his graces which were inordinately long, and we couldn't dispute it. He would put in a few relevant things and we used to accuse him of that, of using his prayers and graces to get back at us.'[9]

The boys' parents maintained a lively interest in British affairs and there was, if anything, more discussion at the table of old country politics than of Canadian. William Frost was a spirited supporter of home rule for Ireland and frequently waxed eloquent about the stupid Unionists who opposed it. But holding that belief in no sense weakened his loyalty to the British Empire or his faith in its enlightened mission. Both Margaret and he were typical of Old Ontario society in being swept up on a wave of imperial sentiment that seemed to carry all before it in those prosperous antebellum years. They were perhaps less typical in maintaining an independent outlook on Canadian politics; their general inclination appears to have been increasingly Conservative, but when it came to making intelligent judgments, party affiliations were less instructive than the individual qualities of public men, how they stood on the questions of the day or, where East Simcoe politics was concerned, their personal relationships with the Frosts.

Thus the Frosts supported the Conservative Andrew Miscampbell, who represented Simcoe East at Queen's Park for a dozen years beginning in 1890, and later the Liberal J.B. Tudhope, who held the seat from 1905 to 1911 and who was Orillia's leading businessman. In provincial affairs Frost was strongly attracted to Newton Rowell, the Liberal leader whose strong temperance views agreed exactly with his own, but was won over by Sir William

Hearst, whose Conservative government brought the dream of outright prohibition close to reality during the Great War. When Hearst's Tory successor, Howard Ferguson, went back on that some years later and decided to legalize beverage alcohol under government control, Frost's fidelity to the Conservative cause provincially was severely strained. Certainly he was by then firmly wedded to the Tory party nationally. In earlier times he had warmly admired and supported Sir Wilfrid Laurier but the latter's abortive reciprocity agreement with the United States had aroused serious misgivings in his mind. As the Great War dragged on and with two of his sons fighting overseas, Frost became an advocate of conscription, and on that issue his attachment to Laurier came definitely to an end. In the khaki election of 1917 he served as vice-president of the Union Government Association in East Simcoe; that was a duty all the more worth discharging because his friend Tudhope, one of many Liberals supporting conscription, was the government candidate. From then on Frost never wavered in supporting the Conservative party, even though he still liked to affect an air of jaunty independence.

Leslie's preparation for public life began with exposure to all the lively talk around the family table, with his father's many discussions with his cronies he had listened to in the back room of the jewellery store or the Frost living room, and with the numerous political meetings which their parents encouraged the boys to attend. Leslie's earliest memory of such an occasion was a speech by Laurier during a campaign tour in 1908, and he recalled accompanying his father to hear such other notables as Sir James Whitney, R.L. Borden, and George P. Graham. In 1911 they were treated to a withering attack on the reciprocity agreement by Stephen Leacock, whose mother lived across the street from the Frosts and who, though not a native of Orillia, was on his way to becoming its most famous son.[10]

In his early years Leslie's prospects did not seem at all promising. He was a sickly child, plagued by bouts of pneumonia and pleurisy; there was some doubt whether he would survive childhood. So delicate was his health that he missed the first two years of schooling. As a result, he and Cecil proceeded through the lower grades together, trudging the mile or more to school and home again for lunch. When the winter weather was severe they would walk the shorter distance to the store, to be taken by their father to lunch at the Orillia House across Mississaga Street. Leslie and Cecil were always to be very close. They went almost everywhere and did almost everything together as children, youths, and grown men, and had in common their friends and ambitions, their recreations and concerns. Each had a deep affection for the other and their lives intertwined with a harmony rare even between brothers. With Grenville it was rather different. Being almost five years older than Leslie and nearly seven years Cecil's senior, he went his own way, making his friends and pursuing his distinctive interests. Unlike the younger boys, he had a scientific bent and natural musical talent. While attending high school he played the organ in St James Anglican Church and later supported himself as a student at the University of Toronto by serving as organist at Wycliffe College and then at Knox College. When Ernest MacMillan was interned in Germany upon the outbreak of war in 1914, Grenville capped his Toronto musical career by filling in as organist at Convocation Hall. Such talent was wholly missing from the other two. 'My dear mother,' Leslie later confessed ruefully, 'sent my brother Cecil and I [sic] to Miss Jessie Dickson for three years in Orillia and we never learned to play a note.' There was, though, a fleeting trace of his father's artistic gift in Leslie. At the age of thirteen he won a drawing contest sponsored by the Toronto *Globe* with a picture of the family's grandfather clock and was rewarded with a copy of Jules Verne's *The Castaways*.[11]

By the time he reached the later stages of public school, Leslie's health had improved and he was able to skip the third year of high school. In fact he became robust enough to be named top athlete at the Orillia Collegiate and Vocational Institute in 1913, to be appointed captain of the school cadet corps, and to play on the YMCA basketball team. It was beginning to look as though his life expectancy was not so meagre as had been feared. Whatever he lacked at first in physical robustness was made up for by an iron hardness of will. His cousin Dorothy Swallow remembered her mother often saying that 'he was a very strong willed little boy, who went after what he wanted and generally achieved it.'[12] The determination to succeed was instilled at home, of course, and on top of that his active brain and lively curiosity stood him in good stead. So did the ministrations of a few fondly remembered teachers, especially George A. Cole, who taught the high school entrance class and had a marked gift for stimulating the minds of his charges. 'I never was a star, you understand,' Leslie explained, 'but I did used [sic] to top the class there.'[13] He also did well at the collegiate. A classmate, Floyd Chalmers, reminisced years later that Les and he had vied for the honour of being top boy in the class.[14] Frost's overall standing upon graduation in the spring of 1915 earned him admission to the University of Toronto the following autumn. That greatly pleased his parents, who set much store by a sound education and were determined to see their sons better served in that way than they had been. Grenville had gone through the university and was on his way to an academic career in chemistry. It was expected that his brothers would follow in his tracks and obtain a degree before embarking on careers of their own. That was not to be. The war intervened, rescuing Leslie from a university stint that was both brief and unenjoyable, and diverting Cecil entirely from this course.

Growing up comfortably middle class in a small Ontario town had more to it, of course, than assiduous attention to school work. Certain assigned household tasks had to be routinely performed. Once they were big enough to handle the job, Leslie and Cecil every Saturday morning would head for the pile of logs at the far end of the back yard to saw and split a week's supply of wood for the fireplaces and the kitchen stove. They also divided the labour of keeping the family conveyances polished and in good order, of feeding and grooming the horse, and of cleaning out the stable. At the end of each weekday one of them would hitch Prince to the phaeton or the sleigh, depending on the season, and drive the mile and a half into town to bring their father home.

Doing such tasks and the nightly homework took time but much was left over for other things such as reading, not only the newspapers and other periodicals on hand but literature more attuned to the interests of growing boys. Most of this was of British origin, although there were exceptions – Horatio Alger's stories were avidly consumed – and it strongly reinforced the British imperial sentiments and loyalties in which the youngsters were steeped both at home and at school. G.A. Henty's tales were staple fare, as were *Chums* and the *Boy's Own Annual*. In Leslie's case such reading was supplemented by his discovery at a fairly young age of Samuel de Champlain and the early history of Huronia. This was the start of his never-ending love affair with the history of Ontario, especially of that area he knew best, from Georgian Bay eastward through Victoria and Haliburton counties. No matter how immersed he later became in the complexities of public affairs, he could find time to read a book, write a letter, or, occasionally, give a speech about some aspect of Ontario's romantic past.

One's memories of childhood in long retrospect are normally a collection of separate, unrelated snapshots, some more sharply focused than others, rather than a continuously unfolding reel of moving pictures. This was true of Leslie Frost's recollections in later years as he turned his mind back to the Orillia days. But thinking back, he found, had therapeutic value, affording relief from the cares of public office, 'a quiet anchorage in these days of a multitude of stresses.'[15] Not that all the childhood incidents he recalled had been free of momentary stress. He remembered, for instance, getting the strap for some forgotten misdemeanour, observing matter of factly, 'I got it along with the rest of them. This was just part of the nature of things. But it was never really serious.'[16] Other memories were more pleasant, such as the delight occasioned when Cecil was given a bugle and he and Leslie marched up and down the road in front of 'Highlands' taking turns at making ear-splitting and lamentably unmusical noises with this splendid new toy. That must have been distressing, Leslie realized later, to their long-suffering but uncomplaining next-door neighbour, but there was no escaping it; Cecil simply had to do his practising as a member of the school cadet corps bugle band.[17]

Growing up in Orillia had much to recommend it and the Frost boys were not at all unhappy with their lot. Nevertheless, they were fortunate that their parents were able to give them the chance of venturing every so often beyond its familiar scenes. There were frequent excursions to Beaverton or Barrie on one of the Lake Simcoe steamers; getting to such unexciting places by boat must have been more than half the fun. Then, too, there were visits by rail to Midland, thirty miles away, where William Frost's sister Emily lived with her husband J.C. Swallow, also a jeweller, and their daughter Dorothy. The two families had the custom of celebrating Christmas together, the Swallows coming to spend a few days at 'Highlands' one year, the Frosts returning the favour the next. More venturesome were Margaret Frost's periodic visits to London with the boys to see their Grandmother Barker, and even more so the odd trip to Buffalo. The real mecca, though, was Toronto. William Frost quite often had business there and sometimes took the family with him as a treat. They would catch 'the greatest express in the world, the 4.40 train to Toronto,' and for three or four days put up at the Prince George Hotel, 'a very nice hotel, really, in those days.'

As a small lad Leslie had informed Dr Wilfred Grenfell that he wanted to be a soldier. That proved to be no mere childish whim. One of his earliest memories was of hearing his parents talk worriedly about the South African war and the setbacks encountered by the imperial forces. Leslie believed that this was the beginning of his interest in the military. The Frosts' loyal, patriotic attitude to the Boer War was typical of the townspeople and many other Ontarians.[18] They became if anything more devoted to the cause, as the tide of imperial sentiment swelled in the early years of the twentieth century. None of this would diminish the appeal of the military life to a vigorous teenage boy who read the newspapers and listened to his elders, or moderate his sympathetic feelings about the empire, its glories, its needs, the dangers it faced in an increasingly hazardous world. Neither would the literature of martial exploits and stirring adventure – the Henty, the *Chums*, and the rest – in which the young male minds of that generation were steeped. And such sentiments were strongly reinforced during Frost's progress through public and high school: by curriculum, ceremony, and communal activity; by the robust British teachings of the *Third Reader*, the annual celebration of Empire Day, and the make-believe drills and exercises of the cadet corps. Playing soldier was one thing; that being a soldier in battle was quite another – agonizing, unglamorous, horrible – was a lesson yet to be learned.

The imagined glory of soldiering was most vividly depicted for the youths of Orillia by the sight of C and G companies of the 35th Regiment Simcoe Foresters, the Orillia companies, parading along Mississaga Street, as they did on special occasions. Resplendent in their red tunics, blue trousers, and white helmets, the officers' swords gleaming in the sun, they were a sight to stir the blood. Each summer the cadet corps joined the regiment at Niagara-on-the-Lake for a short training session, 'learning to defend their country in the very locality where their forefathers had fought with the British to repel invaders.' The spirit of remembrance was pervasive there; 'brooding over Niagara was that atmosphere of the Empire and the defence of the Empire and of Brock and of the York Volunteers and all that sort of thing. Those were great thrills to us in those days.'[19] For Leslie, who enjoyed male company, and the camaraderie of men working in a common cause then relaxing together at the end of the day, the summer camps at Niagara were the high spots of his collegiate years.

It was thus not surprising that when war broke out the itch to enlist became almost irresistible. His parents, however, strongly objected. He was not yet nineteen and still had a year of high school to complete. They hoped and expected that he would then follow Grenville to the university, a prospect without allure for Leslie. He was a dutiful son and would go to almost any length to avoid a serious breach in the family; but he could not believe that he belonged out of harm's way on the university campus when so many others of his age were preparing to fight in France. He eventually resolved this conflict of loyalties in the spring of 1915 when he enlisted as a provisional lieutenant in the Simcoe Foresters. He had taken the first step toward realizing his ambition and establishing his independence.

Leslie Frost, natty in his new uniform ('the very latest cut,' he noted with satisfaction), set off for military training at Niagara-on-the-Lake in August 1915. All the family were on hand to see him off. In a way this goodbye was not so different from seeing the two younger boys leave with the cadet corps for summer camp; after all, Les was only going for a few weeks to take a course. Still, there *was* a world of difference. The war was raging; the names Ypres, Festubert, Givenchy, and the heavy Canadian casualties they signified were by then imprinted on people's minds. Leslie would shortly turn twenty and, while his parents had not relinquished all authority, they must have recognized that he, to say nothing of Cecil, was determined to get himself overseas, that this trip to Niagara was but a step towards that goal. Lying ahead was something infinitely more terrible to contemplate than a mere officers' training course. Tucked away in Leslie's luggage was a Bible his mother had given him just before this departure. It was inscribed with Paul's admonition to Timothy; 'endure hardness as a good soldier.'[20]

Leslie was soon installed at camp along with about eight thousand others. Writing to his Aunt Sadie Barker, he described the regimen there in a long, unbroken sentence arousing doubt that English composition had been one of his best subjects in school. 'We roll out here at 5.30 and have coffee & rolls and parade at 6.15 when we have physical drill and a lecture then we have breakfast and parade at 9.00 & have drill till 12, then a lecture till one and luncheon at 1.15 then from 2 till 2.45 we have company drill then we are free.' The other important feature of camp life about which an aunt would naturally want to be informed was the food. 'We certainly get great meals, for tea (dinner they call it here) we had soup & Fish stuffed lamb, thimble berries, ice cream, fruit cake, oranges, bananas, apples and coffee.' To this he added superfluously, 'that's not starvation rations.'[21]

Leslie completed his stint in mid September and returned home briefly, knowing that, like it or not, his next immediate destination was the university. Probably that die had been cast before his departure for Niagara. His parents did not object to military service as such, but they thought Leslie still too young for active service. In this they were strongly supported by Grenville, who seems to have been entirely without martial spirit and whose advice that Leslie be enrolled at the university in mathematics and physics was accepted. How much Leslie himself had to say about this or what arguments may have disturbed the interior peace of 'Highlands' one can only guess; he later implied that the decision had been imposed upon him. In any event, he went to the university reluctantly and his stay there was brief and academically unrewarding. 'Academic studies with me were futile,' he admitted long afterward. 'Of all the courses for which I would be totally unsuited, mathematics and physics would head the list ... I had positively no interest in it.' 'I must confess my thoughts were entirely related to the military.' He discovered that students who volunteered for active service would receive credit for that scholastic year. 'Driven partly by patriotism and my own yearning to be in the military and partly because it was the only way I knew to get my year,' Leslie decided to take advantage of this opportunity and to bring his university career speedily to a close.[22]

After attending the School of Infantry in Toronto to earn his captaincy, Leslie was appointed assistant adjutant of the First Simcoes with a temporary posting to battalion headquarters at Barrie. His duties there took him about a good deal and he 'met with most of the dignitaries around Simcoe County.' Among others he met William Finlayson, a Midland lawyer twice his age, who took a liking to the young man. He set out to persuade Frost that, once the current fuss and bother was over, he should make a career in the law. 'Finlayson advised me that a lot of young fellows like myself were wasting their lives and that the war would not last forever.' Leslie should decide now to become articled to him and thereby prepare himself for the return to normalcy that was bound to come. This argument did not impress Leslie. 'I didn't think I was wasting my life. I thought I was having a pretty good time and all the rest of it – the war would last indefinitely and so I didn't need to worry about anything.' Finlayson eventually secured the documents that would bind Frost to him as an articled clerk, and one day at Camp Borden produced them to be signed. 'I wasn't too sure what was in them,' Frost remembered, 'but I signed those papers and then ... I didn't know where I was going to get the $51 to pay him for the fees to register. However, I did.'[23]

In the mean time Leslie happily served at Barrie and even more happily at Orillia, to which he was posted as commander of C Company of the First Simcoes. Nothing could have seemed more agreeable to Captain Frost than this appointment, pending departure to camp for final battalion training before going overseas. He would remain in the cherished family circle, and enjoy the comfort of living at home. And to be an officer commanding, even if only of a company, was a feather in the cap of one who less than a year earlier had been a callow student. If he felt any trepidation about his new duties, he was not the kind to show it.

One glaring truth helped to keep such disquiet at bay. The new c.o. of C Company was no more ignorant of the ways of war than his fellow officers, except one who had served in the Boer War, or than the rank and file. What they did not know about waging war, however, they made up for by due attention to ceremony. For all their lack of military experience and tradition, they endeavoured, Frost recalled many years later, 'to observe the traditional rules of conduct and etiquette of the old British army.' Occasional lapses were to be expected; 'they easily reverted to their free and easy, ordinary customs of life. When they were off duty they called one another by their first names as a matter of course, regardless of rank.'24

It had been expected that the First Simcoes would go to Niagara-on-the-Lake for more advanced training in the spring of 1916. Instead it became the first battalion to set up tents at the newly created Camp Borden southwest of Barrie. For C Company the move took place on Sunday, 2 July. Marching through the streets in a steady rain, the band leading the way and the ranks carrying their dummy rifles, they made their way toward the depot, watched admiringly by townspeople who lined the route despite the inclement weather. As the column reached the corner of West Street and the Coldwater Road, the skies opened in a torrential downpour. Without hesitation, Captain Frost wheeled the company into a conveniently situated garage, whence they emerged when the rain subsided to find onlookers still lining the streets and packing the railway station yard. Some of Orillia's dour Sabbatarians interpreted the storm as divine punishment for staging the troop movement on a Sunday, but none of those present seemed worried by that possibility. Among the marchers was Cecil Frost, whose eagerness to serve could not be contained once his brother had joined up; where the one went the other was sure to follow. Without completing his senior matriculation, Cecil had enlisted and earned his lieutenancy. So the two sons, the younger not yet nineteen, paraded together off to war.

For the time being, of course, it was only off to Camp Borden. For the first few days after its arrival the battalion worked in extremely hot, dry weather at burning stumps and preparing the enormous parade ground in readiness for the official inauguration of the camp on 11 July, when the minister of militia, Sir Sam Hughes, would review the troops in the kind of mass martial display he loved so well. Once Hughes had come and gone, the further training of the men could commence. Leslie's battalion was assigned to the Second Infantry Brigade and before long C Company was able to dispense with its dummy rifles as more real ones became available, though only enough for about every other man.

At the end of September, at long last, all ranks were ordered to make their wills – a sure if ominous sign that a move was at hand – and early in October the battalion went on final leave. On the eve of its return to Camp Borden to await orders to entrain for Halifax, C Company was tendered a farewell banquet in the Presbyterian Sunday school room. A great banner had been hung up bearing the words, 'God bless you, boys in khaki; here's Orillia's love to you.' The mayor delivered a speech dilating on that sentiment and Captain Frost responded. Then some of the company marched through the streets to the music of the Citizens' Band to board the waiting train, while others walked the route in the moonlight with relatives or friends. Several thousand townfolk were on hand, but this time there was little cheering and none of the exuberance that had marked other departures. By now everyone was all too aware of the war's dark, cruel side and knew in their hearts that some, perhaps many, of these fine young men would not return.

On 13 October 1916 the 157th Battalion left Camp Borden for Halifax. For Leslie only one fly in the ointment marred this long anticipated event: somehow his predecessor as company commander, Major Mainer, had wangled a transfer to resume command of C company as its men set foot on the train. Frost was thus deprived of his status but, so it turned out once they reached Britain, was expected to go on performing the duties of the position. Mainer 'is nominally c.o.,' he explained to his parents from Bramshott, where the battalion was encamped in England, 'but his wife is at Liphook 3 miles away, and between that and his natural laziness we see very little of him. So for all intents and purposes I am the same as before.'[25]

Upon reaching Halifax, the battalion boarded ss *Cameronia*, which sailed out of the great harbour under the protection of the French cruiser *Montcalm*. The crossing was uncomfortable, with crowded conditions, of course, and rough weather. 'We appeared to be walking on the walls and ceiling most of the time,' Leslie wrote as the crossing neared its end, adding, 'I will never be guilty of taking a sea voyage for my health.'[26] Disembarking with relief at Liverpool, the Simcoes immediately entrained for Witley Camp in Surrey. At last they were getting close to where the action was.

They had hoped to retain their identity and bring glory to Simcoe County as part of the 5th Canadian Division, the formation of which had been promised by Hughes. Vain hope! The unit was soon being dismantled without ever coming under enemy fire. The military authorities in England looked upon the battalion, as upon many others, as a pool of reinforcements to be dispersed as needed in a seemingly capricious fashion. A piecemeal erosion began almost as soon as the Canadians arrived in England. The battalion's death knell was officially sounded early in December when, as Leslie was to express it in his book *Fighting Men* with understandable testiness, 'Simcoe County's proud contribution to Canada's war effort was finally and summarily broken up ... within two months of the great farewells given by practically every Simcoe community.'[27]

Chagrin over the breakup of the First Simcoes found expression in one of Leslie's early letters home, written shortly after Sam Hughes's resignation from the Borden government. As he saw it from his lowly vantage point, the Canadian forces were 'in a very disorganized state' and seething with dissatisfaction. Large numbers of officers like himself, separated from their men drafted to other units, were 'left with nothing to do but draw their pay and see England.' But a day of reckoning would come. 'When the war is over the Canadian troops will pay the political grafters who are making the soldiers' lot almost ten times as heavy ... Between Hughes & Borden I would choose Hughes because he was apparently on the right track and Borden has never shown ... anything but ... "Watchful waiting." '

The grafters and incompetents at home, though, were not the only evils. The Canadian force should be 'run by Canadians. Imperial officers do not understand us and it will cause perpetual friction to have it go on.' There was great respect for Irish and Scottish regiments but dislike of the English, not including 'old "Imperial" officers who are soldiers and gentlemen from the ground up ... Let Canada raise her own army, feed it, and officer it and it will be better than having Englishmen who think we are backwoodsmen, run us.' Having let loose this blast, Leslie added a cautionary word: 'Don't give anyone my views on the above because we are not supposed to think these things.'[28] Evidently, however, the military censor was not unduly alarmed by the outburst.

For what seemed an interminable time, the Frost brothers were stuck with little to do but 'draw their pay and see England,' and this they were not slow to do. Not long after settling down at Bramshott Camp, Leslie and Cecil had several days' leave together and decided to visit their ancestral homelands, Scotland and Yorkshire, after first spending a day in London. There, after a morning tour of some of the sights, they spent the afternoon in the gallery of the House of Commons ('I think I was more interested in that than anything,' wrote Leslie). Edinburgh seemed to excite him less than the side trip he and Cecil took to the Firth of Forth, where they saw Sir David Beatty's battle cruiser squadron at anchor. After visiting Melrose Abbey, the two Canadians headed south to York.

Back in London for a few more days, Leslie went again to the House of Commons. Many a conversation around the family dinner table must have come to mind as he listened to Reginald McKenna, Andrew Bonar Law, Edward Carson, and Arthur Henderson. He also had a new picture taken to send home. 'I never much fancied the other and for goodness sake if they want to put my picture in the paper again use one of these new ones.' As one would expect, home and family were much on his mind those days, especially as the first Christmas overseas approached. He did his best, however, not to show his homesickness and to keep his parents' spirits high. Late in November he wrote: 'I hope you are not downhearted, we are not ... Now remember this – especially Mater – don't be sad because we are away.' When the war was finally won, 'those who did not go and parents who did not let their sons go will not be able to look you in the face.'[29] It was not enough merely to have enlisted and then be content, as Leslie suspected some of his fellows were, to return home after a sojourn in England or to go on frittering the war away there. 'I firmly believe,' he declared, 'that a lot of officers ... enlisted with no intention of going to the front.' He was still determined to get there; simply going home would be 'enough to ruin any man's reputation.'[30]

Nevertheless, when he sat down on Christmas Day to write another letter, his mind filled with recollections of Christmases past, he penned some nostalgic lines. 'It doesn't seem like Christmas at all. The weather is very mild just like a fall day at home. No sign of snow or ice. It seems to rain all the time and the camp is very muddy but it doesn't dampen our spirits at all. We are surely not downhearted in the least ... The thing I miss as much as anything here is the snow. I can just imagine stepping out of the front door today and feeling the nice crisp air and feel the boards of the verandah creak with the cold.' As he wrote he noticed that it was about 5:30 p.m. and he imagined the noontime scene at that moment in 'Highlands.' 'You will be about sitting down for dinner. I'll bet Dad will be in the bathroom, Gren on the couch reading the Globe, and Aunt and Mater sitting at the table, protesting vigorously in unison about the defects of the masculine sex ... All that will be needed will be Cec to swipe grapes off the table before we sit down and me to pull Mater's hair.'[31]

Towards the end of January 1917 the wearying inactivity of Bramshott came to an end when the Frosts were posted to a Canadian military school at Crowborough, Sussex, to take an advanced eight weeks' course. Neither their quarters nor the food came up to Bramshott standards. After 'doing absolutely nothing at Bramshott for so long ... it was quite a hardship to get down to work again.'[32] But at least the work had some reference to the war, even though the course, very like one both had taken in Toronto, was less advanced than they had expected.

By the late winter of 1916–17, fourteen months after enlisting to serve the king, Frost had become somewhat disillusioned with the soldier's life he had been so eager to embrace. A cynical note, shallower and less worldly wise than he probably thought it was, crept into some of what he wrote home. Early in March he wrote:

Serving the country may be all very well but it does not in most cases help you to live. Generally there is nobody more ungrateful than the people whom you serve and give your best to. In times of trouble they are generally the very first to desert you and cast you aside for somebody else. Like Dad I like to do things and serve my country but I am glad that I have been able to learn at my young age that the best way to serve people is to serve yourself first and give them the surplus and if that doesn't suit them they can 'lump it.' ... History shows almost invariably that the man who gives his best to his town or country in the end gets a raw deal ... if I get back ... from this job I will most certainly look after myself and my people first and anybody else when I have time and means. I will never regret joining the 'Expeditionary Force' because I have learned more of human nature and gained more experience than I could have otherwise in a great many years.[33]

For the erstwhile commander of C Company the war seemed to mean taking one officers' training course after another. In March

1917 he finished his stint at detestable Crowborough and was sent to the Hythe School of Musketry at West Sandling, Kent. Cecil went too but shortly had to report back to Crowborough, the transfer to the Machine Gun Corps for which he had applied having come through. 'Naturally I am sorry to see him go,' Leslie wrote, doubtless understating the truth, 'but otherwise I was tickled to death because the Machine Gun work is very good ... considered a fairly safe job at the front. Cec is lucky.' His own luck had also taken a turn for the better. The course at the Hythe musketry school, he told his parents with new-found satisfaction, 'is no doubt one of the most up to date in the world if not the most ... In the British army it is an authority on all musketry matters and I consider myself very lucky to be chosen to attend it ...' Furthermore, the British knew how to provide quarters fit for officers and gentlemen – those at Sandling were reputed to be the best in England – and Frost was assigned 'a large room all to myself with every convenience in it ... quite elegantly furnished with old fashioned furniture.' He was one of few Canadians there. The rest were mostly 'imperial officers from nearly all of the British line regiments and they seem to be a fine bunch of fellows.'[34]

The course at Hythe was completed late in April and Leslie again waited for a posting, this time to the front, he hoped, but the weeks dragged by while he cooled his heels. With some others he offered to take a reduction in rank in order to get to France but nothing happened.

While he continued to bide his time, there were certain exciting developments to occupy his mind. Most noteworthy was the entrance of the United States into the war, which Leslie thought 'absolutely seals the doom of Kaiserism.' But he was too optimistic about the short-term prospect. 'The war news has been very good,' he wrote early in May, perhaps having in mind especially the capture of Vimy Ridge by the Canadians, 'and I ... would not be surprised if the show ended at not a very distant date.'[35] Affairs in Canada, though, did not please him. For one thing, Ontario had granted women the provincial franchise, a concession mooted for some time and probably discussed in the Frost household before his departure. 'Needless to say,' he remarked, 'I was heartily disgusted when I heard about "votes for women." I think it was an entirely needless "reform"? and I would certainly have voted against the Liberals if the Conservatives had not adopted it. I agree as never before with the "Packet" for standing out against it and if it is the only paper in Ontario not in favour of women's suffrage then it is the only paper that is right.'[36]

Much more disturbing than that was the controversy in Canada over conscription, resort to which was announced by Sir Robert Borden in May. Frost favoured compulsory military service but was well aware that there would be intense, possibly violent, opposition in some quarters, Quebec in particular. He vented his feelings on the subject early in June. Both parties had fanned the flames of political and racial prejudice in Quebec but there was little sympathy among the men overseas for French-Canadian sentiment. 'If they think they can gain anything by opposing military service and conscription they are vastly mistaken.' Canada would be a different place after the war. No longer would the 'whims' of Quebec be considered before the desires of any of the other provinces. Bourassa and his lieutenants had been 'allowed to shoot holes in the flag with their mouths in order to get a "breath of freedom" and nobody molested them.' In the future Canada would be governed by those who had fought overseas 'and the men who have endured the bitterness and hardships of the war will be very different than when you saw them go away. They will not be at all afraid of threats of revolts and what Quebec will do and what she won't do.'[37]

A few days later he returned to the subject, venturing also to refute the 'socialistic' view of the war that Grenville had expressed, the gist of which may be inferred from Leslie's comments. He was glad that the *Globe*, a Liberal paper, objected to Laurier's proposal of a referendum before conscription took effect. 'Party politics should no longer take any part. Anything and everything should be for the Empire. I admire Laurier as a statesman but I do not believe in pampering a French Canadian minority while the Empire trembles in the balance ... Conscription is the only way to reinforce our men at the front and it should be enforced regardless of politics.' He was surprised by his older brother's opinions about the real meaning of the struggle in Europe. Contrary to Gren's belief, American capitalists could best make money by selling to the belligerents while their country remained neutral. 'Has the war made Great Britain rich? No!' The 'average capitalist' must long for the end of the war. 'The allied cause is the cause of freedom and democracy ... I believe that Emperor Wilhelm and his government are responsible wholly for the war.'[38]

Secure in this faith, Frost continued to hope for an assignment in France. Three weeks before he at last crossed the Channel, he let fly another verbal blast about the political situation in Canada, unleashing some of his contempt for his country's miserable politics and its practitioners.

After three years of bungling the same ministry stays in power with hardly a change in its personel [*sic*]. I say it's time ... that business men and statesmen guided the destinies of our country instead of a lot of politicians who have little more ability than to ask for votes. I must say Canadian 'statesmen' such as Borden, Laurier and the whole outfit have done admirable work; with hundreds of thousands of men away from the country they bungle and mismanage things till the country is in a state of rebellion. It makes very fine reading for a soldier overseas to hear of Quebec talking of breaking away from the confederation. I would kick the Borden government bag and baggage out – not necessarily to pick a government from the opposition but ... from the brains of the country and get rid for a while of the curse of politics.[39]

Anyone watching Frost in action forty years later might have found it hard to believe that he had once so roundly denounced politics and politicians.

When his posting to the 20th Infantry Battalion at the front finally came through at the end of July, Leslie's mood improved distinctly. In fact, on top of that good news there was a delicious twist of fate to savour. A few hours after his orders for France arrived, word came that all senior officers who had not been to France must revert to lieutenant or go home. Moreover, all infantry officers who had not served at the front would go into a training battalion, as distinct from a reserve battalion such as the one to which Leslie had been attached since the breakup of the Simcoes, until they were needed. 'They will have to live like the men,' he chortled, 'clean their own boots and buttons etc. – not that that will hurt them at all but it is an awful come down ... I expect they will have a horrible time. About 25 went from this Reserve and I certainly gave them the hee-haw – me going to a fighting battalion and they to a "labour" unit in England.'[40]

So on 7 August 1917, almost exactly two years after he had set off from Orillia as a provisional lieutenant bound for Niagara-on-the-Lake, Leslie at last stepped on French soil, a lieutenant once again. Cecil remained behind in England, much to his disappointment. It was another three months before Cecil went to the 2nd Machine Gun Battalion at the front, not far from where Leslie was stationed.

When Leslie, accompanied by Lieutenant Ernest Walker, another leftover from C Company, joined the 20th Battalion as a platoon officer, the Canadian Corps, under its newly appointed commander, Lieutenant-General Sir Arthur Currie, was preparing for an assault on Hill 70, an important German stronghold some miles north of Vimy Ridge. The battalion was part of the 2nd Division, one of two which were to make a frontal attack on the hill. Leslie did not have to wait long for his baptism of fire, for he was almost at once put in charge of a work party carrying small-arms ammunition to the front lines. He soon learned to take cover at the sound of an approaching shell or from the light of enemy flares. At first he was disconcerted to find himself suddenly standing alone in the open, the ammunition on the ground and his men out of sight under any available shelter, from which they emerged after a detonation to pick up the boxes and proceed. This was a trick of the trade that had to be mastered quickly for survival's sake.[41]

The struggle for Hill 70, 'altogether the hardest battle in which the Corps has participated,' Currie concluded when it was over,[42] began just before daybreak on 15 August and C company was in the thick of it. That evening, though, after a successful day's work, it was pulled back to a reserve position and Leslie had time to write a letter home. It gave no inkling of what he had seen and done that day and, indeed, contained a passage quite incongruous, considering the battle still raging a short distance away. 'Walker and I are together in one room,' he wrote. 'We have a big feather bed etc. and are very comfortable. The mess here is the best I have been in since I joined the army. Seems funny in view of the fact that we are so close to the front.'[43] By and large, his letters from the front were remarkably devoid of references to dangers faced, to actual fighting, and the day-by-day experiences of a front-line soldier.

Late in August Leslie received two pieces of welcome news from home. One was that Grenville had moved from his position with the Imperial Munitions Board in Quebec to a munitions factory in Trenton, Ontario. 'French Canadians are not a healthy crowd at present and I am very glad that he is again in an English place,' Leslie remarked.[44] 'Gren,' he added later, 'can do a thousand times more good where he is than ... in the army in any capacity and I have written him a strong letter telling him under no circumstances to enlist or do any foolish thing ... To waste his talent in such a barren desert as the army would be a crime.'[45] The other good news was that 'Highlands' had been sold, as Leslie had been urging. With the boys grown up and away, the elder Frosts decided that it was unwise to go on maintaining two large homes. 'The Beach' was too delightful a place to let go, with its lake frontage and pleasant surroundings, so they decided instead to renovate and winterize it, rechristen it 'Lochbrae,' and use it as their year-round residence.[46]

Judging by his letters home, regarding all these matters Leslie felt a thoughtful, almost single-minded concern about the welfare of the family back in Canada, while betraying no apprehension about his own immediate prospects. One gets the impression that he thoroughly enjoyed playing the role of wise counsellor, offering out of the ripeness of his experience much-needed warning and advice. As it did many men, the war aged him before his time. From the tone of some of his letters one might imagine him to have been in his forties, not going on twenty-two, and the eldest, not the second, son. One might suppose that his parents were almost in their dotage, depending on him to tell them what to do, instead of a couple in their early fifties, in the prime of life and fully possessed of their faculties.

Not long after Hill 70, Leslie was appointed musketry officer, as befitted a graduate of the Hythe school, in charge of 'battalion training and building musketry ranges and the like.' It was a welcome turn of events for its effect was 'that while my duties in the line were still as a Junior Lieutenant I had some staff status when out of the line.'[47] This improvement may have prompted him in mid September to assure those at home that, 'so far in France I have had a very good time ... I pity those who went back to Canada without coming over here first.'[48]

The early fall of 1917 was a comparatively peaceful time for the Canadian Corps, a lull before the storm which all knew must sooner or later break upon their heads. It broke in October, on the Ypres sector of accursed memory. Over Currie's strenuous objections, and finally by a direct order which he had no option but to obey, the Corps was moved there to help bolster a flagging British offensive. Its particular assignment was to capture a ridge of land and a village on its crest which both bore the name of Passchendaele. The name is synonymous with agony and death in a muddy wasteland devastated by previous battles.

The Canadian action at Passchendaele consisted of a series of well-prepared forward thrusts, strongly supported by artillery. The assault role of the 20th Battalion was confined to assisting in the last of these, on 10 November, in order to secure additional high ground north of Passchendaele village, captured by other units a few days earlier. C Company was in the centre of the battalion's section of the front line, so Leslie must have been very much in the action. The official history of the battalion, however, does not mention him, and in his own book, *Fighting Men*, he deliberately omitted any reference to his experiences at the front. The letters he wrote at the time gave no hint that he was present during part of one of the most gruesome operations of the entire war, although he did permit himself the remark, in apologizing for his inability to send Christmas presents home, that 'we are and have been for several weeks quite away from civilization.'[49]

The period of calm which for Leslie ensued after Passchendaele afforded a chance for recovery and relaxation, and for savouring the news from home. In mid February he learned with delight that the jewellery shop had done a remarkably successful Christmas trade. 'The debts which used to loom so high,' he noted with satisfaction, 'are now disappearing rapidly and the assets are accordingly increasing. As soon as everything is clear you will be independent and able to devote yourselves to your hobbies.' He assumed that his mother's hobbies would be the same as always, her girls' Bible class and home missions. But what evil would his father wage war against now that prohibition had been adopted in Ontario?[50] That there would be some burning issue Leslie took for granted. Having outgrown his parents' obsession with temperance, he enjoyed having a bit of teasing fun at their expense. Shortly before the move to Flanders in the fall of 1917, he had written: 'Just one year ago today Ontario went dry – will it ever be wet again? I bought a bottle of beer to commemorate the occasion. I wonder what became of it.'[51]

Leslie Frost's interest in Canadian politics remained high, but it was not exactly the same after he had been in France for a time. One who had done battle where the stake was life itself could not view political battles back home with quite the same seriousness as formerly, or as one would again in the future. Not that he suddenly lost interest by any means. He thought that in 1917 Laurier had 'made a big mistake, if he had come out straight for conscription he would have swept the country including Quebec and there would have been no need of union.' His failure to do so had made the coalition 'necessary at present to offset the French-Canadian menace – if menace is the word.' But he was not very sanguine, for 'history has yet to show a coalition government that was a success,' not excepting the Lloyd George regime by which he had once set such store.[52]

He still believed that the size of the anti-conscription vote, even among the soldiers, would surprise many people; he still had reservations about Borden and about politicians as a breed. The new government, however, was the best of the available alternatives and when the time came he gave it the first ballot he ever cast. Not long after it was all over a batch of letters arrived, and he learned that his father had been serving as vice-president of the East Simcoe Union Government Association. This pleased Leslie for practical no less than patriotic reasons. 'Being a strong Unionist supporter and leader will do no harm I expect from the stand point of business and municipal politics if [Dad] desires to run again in the future. I am awaiting anxiously the later papers telling of the rest of the campaign and the results in detail.'[53]

As 1918 dawned, however, none of the Frosts could imagine how harrowing this year would be for them. Margaret, suspecting a cancer, entered Toronto's Wellesley Hospital early in February; her fears were confirmed and one breast was removed. Some weeks later Leslie was severely wounded, how seriously was not at first realized. In October Cecil was wounded in the head, though only slightly, and in the same month Grenville came down with the dreaded Spanish influenza, from which, however, unlike many others, he made a good recovery. Only the head of the family got through the year physically unscathed, though sorely afflicted by the worry these misfortunes caused. Leslie's reaction to his mother's illness was characteristic – a letter admonishing 'Mater' to be very careful and a separate note to his father, offering money from the cherished bank account should it be needed.[54] Unfortunately this was not the end of Margaret Frost's ordeal. A few years later the cancer was found to have spread; the other breast was removed and she had a hysterectomy as well. But she was not beaten by this. The surgeon, Dr Marlowe, told Leslie that in such cases the patient might be expected to live for two or three years. 'My mother lived for 24 years and died of old age and outlived Marlowe, the nurses and everyone else.'[55]

Leslie's brush with death occurred on Easter Sunday, ten days after the German armies launched a great offensive on the western front. With its onset the 2nd Division was detached from the Canadian Corps and sent to reinforce the British 3rd Army near Arras. The 20th Battalion was located near the village of Neuville-Vitesse, south of Arras, but it had no well-entrenched positions or clearly defined line. As the Germans advanced, the situation became fluid and confused, making it hard to know where the enemy were. On the last day of March, C Company was deployed in an assortment of shell craters and fox holes. Toward dusk there was a lull in the action. Leslie and his company commander, Major George Musgrove, ventured out to do a little reconnoitring in the hope of locating the enemy's position more exactly. Suddenly there was a burst of small-arms fire and Leslie was struck, the bullet passing through a field message book he carried in his left hip pocket. Stretcher bearers moved him to a nearby field dressing station, whence he was taken to a hospital in Doullens, well behind the lines. It was so crowded with casualties that for the better part of two days he lay on a stretcher in the courtyard with a number of others, while the harried medical staff did their best to cope with the influx of wounded men streaming westward from the front.[56]

Unhappily the seriousness of the wound was badly underestimated. The first news his parents received about it, apart from the official cabled notification and a reassuring cable from Leslie himself, came from a chaplain, Captain Ernest Pugsley of the 5th Battalion, formerly the Methodist minister in Orillia. Visiting the Doullens hospital, he came upon Leslie in the courtyard, 'stretched out wounded but quite happily enjoying a bowl of soup.' Pugsley's information was that the upper fleshy part of both legs had been struck, 'a good clean bullet wound which will heal splendidly. Leslie was feeling fine.'[57]

He was soon moved from Doullens to the Prince of Wales Hospital, London, an old hotel, 'and a swell one at that,' he informed those at home. 'My ward is in the ball room which is very swell – marble walls and guilded [sic] ceiling.' Patients who were on the mend, he explained, were put in the bedrooms upstairs but those who still needed watching were kept in wards. 'I guess they think I might get up if they let me upstairs so they keep me here for the time being.'[58] To his dismay, an x-ray revealed a bone fracture in the pelvic region, requiring him to lie still in bed for weeks on end while it mended. But his letters were generally cheerful and optimistic. By the close of June he could report that he was walking on crutches and doing fine.

In view of the generally encouraging news about his condition, his parents must have been shocked to be informed at the end of July that he was seriously ill, and must undergo further surgery.[59] His wound had become badly infected and his fractured pelvis had not properly healed. There ensued a number of operations in August and September, from which Leslie made a slow recovery until at length he was well enough to be invalided home in December. Back in Canada, he was sent to Christie Street Hospital in Toronto, from which he emerged finally in August 1919. He had spent twice as long recuperating from the wound as he had in the field. In fact, he never completely got over its effects, being left with a permanent limp which he did his best to conceal but which became noticeable when he was physically tired. Severe pain plagued him periodically for the rest of his days, occasionally sending him to hospital for treatment.

Cecil's wound, inflicted a month before the armistice, was much less serious. A machine gun bullet pierced his steel helmet, struck his right temple a glancing blow and bounced off to clip his batman on the chin. He made light of the incident. Refusing to stay in hospital more than a couple of days, Cecil, now a captain, rejoined his unit and took part in the march to the Rhine following the armistice, before returning to Canada in the spring of 1919. That was the end of his military career.

For Leslie, despite what he had been through, soldiering had not entirely lost its attraction. Now that the war was over, though, it could be no more than a part-time occupation. He had written jocularly from hospital in London, 'I don't know what I am going to do. I guess get a job ... in the Bank or perhaps sell shoe laces on the bank corner ... Caretaker at the armouries wouldn't be bad.'[60] There was at least one other possibility, the undertaking he had given to article with William Finlayson as a student-at-law. Should he decide to stick to that, it was almost certain that Cecil would want to follow suit.

2

Living by the Law in Lindsay

What to do next? The question confronted a horde of returned men as a rapid demobilization proceeded following the armistice. There seems to have been little hesitation on Leslie's part in deciding to honour his undertaking to Finlayson and seek admission to the bar, or on Cecil's in choosing the same destination. For Cecil, though, an impediment stood in the way. Senior matriculation was required for admission to Osgoode Hall, which monopolized legal education in Ontario, and he had enlisted before completing it. A big, strapping man of twenty-two, an army captain with more than two years' service overseas, he could not bear the thought of returning to high school. Fortunately the day was saved by his father's acquaintanceship with H.J. Cody, minister of education in the Hearst government. Together with Cecil and Leslie, newly released from hospital, he drove down to Queen's Park to see what might be done. As Leslie told the story long afterward, 'I sat outside and my father and my brother went in to see Canon Cody. Well, my father must have given the Canon quite a pep talk ... Cody looked at them and said, "Mr. Frost you're a fine looking young man, an officer in His Majesty's Forces ... You ought to be in law school and I'll fix it up!" '[1] Whatever Cody did, Cecil was spared the ignominy of going back to the collegiate and, along with his older brother, enrolled at Osgoode Hall in September 1919. Cody's intervention was in the nick of time. Two months later the government suffered a stunning defeat by the United Farmers of Ontario.

The course the two entered at Osgoode was an accelerated one, intended primarily for war veterans, and would be completed in the spring of 1921. Taking rooms on Carlton Street, they settled down to a routine of hard work, relieved by occasional vacations and a round of parties and dances, more engrossing to the handsome Cecil with his light-hearted spirit than to his more sober-minded brother. Both graduated with honours, Leslie standing quite a few places higher than Cecil in the class. But there was no sibling rivalry and Cecil was not downhearted. Writing to Leslie, who had returned to Orillia after the examinations while he stayed on in Toronto to article with the firm of Allan Cassels and Defries, he offered congratulations and confessed: 'I consider myself very fortunate in my results. It just convinces me, however, how far a little "bull" will go when you don't know anything.'[2]

The burning question now was where they should practise after articling and admission to the bar. It was probably not expected that they would go into partnership. Then Leslie, who had seriously considered practising law in Toronto, was offered the command of his old army C Company in the reorganized 35th Regiment Simcoe Foresters in Orillia. The prospect of returning to his home town looked pleasing and he was able to arrange his articling under William Finlayson so that he was able also to attend to his military duties.[3] But a legal practice in Orillia was not to be his or Cecil's fate. Their future was determined by a tragedy that befell a total stranger in another place.

Leigh R. Knight was a well-respected lawyer in Lindsay, about forty miles southeast of Orillia. In July 1921 Knight and his young son drowned while on vacation,[4] and his widow advertised his practice for sale. Leslie Frost was interested, for he preferred to acquire an existing practice rather than start from scratch or as a junior in another's firm. So he and his father drove down to Lindsay to look the situation over and Cecil, still with Allan Cassels and Defries, joined them from Toronto. The two young men were interviewed by Mrs Knight, whom they impressed favourably. They liked the look of the town, which they were seeing for the first time. It was the same size as Orillia, with slightly more than 7,500 inhabitants, and had the same small-town atmosphere they found congenial. The Kawartha Lakes to the north and the Haliburton district beyond afforded attractive opportunities for the outdoor life, the camping and fishing, of which both were so fond. The price settled upon was ten thousand dollars, with a small down payment which the brothers were able to make up from what was left of their war gratuities.[5] On 18 August they made the move to Lindsay, partners in a firm that would for some years be known as Knight, Frost and Frost.

Situated astride the Scugog River about half way between Lake Scugog and Sturgeon Lake, Lindsay had originally been a lumber mill site. When the Frosts came there, lumber milling was still the most important of its several industries. The yards of the largest such establishment, the John Carew Lumber Company, stretched for a mile along the west bank of the river from the sawmill at one end to a box factory at the other. The townsite had been carved out of part of Ops Township, with street names reflecting the origins and loyalties of its planners.[6] The original streets running north and south had been called after the reigning queen, her consort, and an assortment of her uncles – York, William, Cambridge, and Sussex. Those laid out on the east-west axis bore the names of various British statesmen and colonial governors – Durham, Melbourne, Glenelg, Russell, Peel, Wellington, Bond Head, Colborne – with one important exception: the main thoroughfare running westward from the river, Kent Street, honoured Queen Victoria's father and was an impressive one hundred feet wide as compared with the mere sixty feet allowed the lesser avenues. As the main business street, Kent was bordered by several blocks of shops and offices, including those of Knight, Frost and Frost.

In addition to lumber milling, some thirty locally owned manufacturing industries gave employment to nearly five hundred people. These included a carriage works and wheel factory, a machine shop and foundry, flour and woollen mills, a knitting company, a concrete products plant, a seed house, a creamery, and a marble and granite works. That was not all. Lindsay was a railway hub, served by both the Canadian Pacific and Canadian National systems; eight lines of track radiated from the town, bearing nearly thirty passenger trains and even more freight trains in and out each day.[7] It was also the centre for the surrounding agricultural area, marketing the products and supplying the needs of the farmers. Five chartered banks had branches and Lindsay boasted its own Victoria Trust and Savings Company, which in the early 1920s had assets of $4 million. It was never a boom town but its activity had a steady, settled pulse. As the souvenir booklet expressed it, 'Lindsay has escaped the great depressions which have been felt in other centres. As a consequence there is an air of prosperity prevailing throughout the Town ... The population is almost wholly of British descent, tending towards a citizenship that respects law and order and makes for settled conditions. Labour troubles are practically unknown in Lindsay.'[8] Six law firms, with fifteen or so lawyers in all, were kept busy attending to the needs of the community.

The lawyers, especially the established ones, ranked fairly high in the town's social pecking order. Social position was largely de-

pendent on wealth and function, though to a degree also on the
length of one's connection with Lindsay. The proprietors of the
most successful industrial and commercial concerns ranked at the
top and occupied many of the finest houses. These were large, solid
brick structures, often with broad front porches, some with turrets
and cupolas, dating from the late Victorian or Edwardian eras. The
professional people, doctors and lawyers, ranked next, along with
the bank managers who came and went but whose position gave
them a kind of ex officio importance and respectability.

The predominantly Protestant character of the population was
shown by the presence of two Methodist churches and one each
for the Presbyterians, Anglicans, Baptists, and Salvationists, while
for the Roman Catholics one church sufficed. The same imbalance
was reflected in the four public schools as against a single separate
school, all of which, along with the collegiate and the private Roman Catholic academy for children whose parents could afford its
fees, took care of Lindsay's educational requirements. Teachers
and clerics were respected, but the low stipends they were paid,
especially the teachers (the clergymen were at least given roofs over
their heads), rather set them apart socially from the successful and
well-to-do. Measured on the scale of income alone, they probably
ranked below many of the shopkeepers and somewhat above the
skilled tradesmen of the mills and factories.

Snobbery, affectation, pride of place, and the concentration of
power in a local élite were no doubt to be found in Lindsay, as
everywhere. But its citizens shared a civic loyalty and community
pride, a belief in honest toil and fair dealing, and a feeling of
satisfaction with things as they were. Lindsay was a conservative
town whose residents were prepared to accept newcomers and
judge them on their merits. It was thus very like Orillia and a place
in which the Frost brothers almost immediately felt at home.

As usual in small town practices, the one they took over in the
late summer of 1921 consisted mainly of settling estates, handling
real estate transactions, looking after the legal needs of some of
the town's business concerns, and representing clients in various
civil actions and minor criminal cases. In addition, the firm was
agent for a number of insurance companies whose commission payments constituted a significant part of its income. The two young
lawyers brought to their profession rather different, though complementary, qualities. While Leslie was proficient in courtroom
work and did a lot of it, his special strength lay in doing the homework of the solicitor. Cecil's more extroverted personality made the

courtroom with its adversarial atmosphere more congenial to him than to Leslie. By working closely together, seeking one another's opinion and advice, and from their unqualified reciprocal trust, they made a very effective team. The practice prospered.

To carve out a place for themselves in the community, it was not enough merely to practise law. One had to engage in the larger life of the town. They joined St Andrew's Presbyterian Church and the local service clubs. Leslie became a Rotarian and by 1926 was president of the Lindsay club. Leslie and Cecil also came out of the war fully committed to the Conservative party as a result of Laurier's rejection of conscription.

Leslie Frost's political allegiance to the Conservative party was shown by an incident shortly after the move to Lindsay. The country was in the throes of a general election in which a new generation of leaders were vying for public favour. Arthur Meighen had succeeded Borden at the head of the Conservative party and as prime minister in the summer of 1920. He was attempting to focus the campaign on preserving the National Policy of tariff protection against attack by the Liberals under Laurier's successor, Mackenzie King, and the organized farmers in the National Progressive party led by Thomas A. Crerar. Frost shared Meighen's belief that King would adopt an unacceptably far-reaching change in tariff policy in order to bring the Liberals and Progressives together. Furthermore, like many returned men, he held King in contempt for having, as was widely if unfairly believed, shirked his duty during the war.

Frost learned that a small group of veterans attending the Liberal nominating convention for East Simcoe had pledged the support of soldiers in the riding to the Liberal candidate. The news so incensed him that he went up from Lindsay to be at an indignation meeting in Orillia attended by between fifty and sixty furious veterans – a gathering the not altogether impartial *Packet* assured its readers 'thoroughly representative of the returned men of all ranks and branches of the service.' Frost addressed the angry protesters, stressing that no one could speak for the veterans without a mandate from a properly constituted soldier convention and that he was speaking only for himself. The *Packet* reported him as declaring: 'To say that the soldiers generally were going to support a man [Mackenzie King] who when the war was on went off to the United States, and then came home to oppose necessary war measures at a critical time was a lie – absolutely ... The men who were opposing the Meighen Government were the same men who, when the war was on, were opposed to every war measure.' There 'was only one fiscal policy for Canada, and that was protection.' The soldiers had gone 'to war to keep Canada a nation within the British Empire, and the same issue was still before them.' He knew there were differences of opinion about how well the government had treated the returned men. 'He could speak for himself. He had spent 17 months in the hospital ... Everything possible had been done for him, and after he got out of hospital, the Government had set him on his feet.' As a veteran he was going to support Meighen for all these reasons and he hoped others would do the same.[9] His audience may have gone away convinced, but his effort was in vain as far as the result in East Simcoe was concerned. Reflecting the verdict of the country as a whole, where the Conservatives suffered a crushing defeat, the Tory candidate, a war veteran, ran a poor second behind his Liberal opponent.

In addition to this appearance in Orillia, Leslie campaigned extensively through Victoria and Haliburton, as did Cecil, in support of T.H. Stinson, a prominent Lindsay lawyer. Even though they were recent newcomers to the district and might have been expected to prefer attending to their law practice, the call of politics was irresistible and they volunteered their services. Getting around the constituency to give speeches, knock on doors, and shake hands was not easy, especially in the Haliburton country where the roads were primitive, often impassable, and the population sparse and scattered. Motor trips there were not undertaken lightly. But interest was high everywhere. Packed houses greeted them at most of the meetings, as did a lot of lively heckling of the Meighen government and its supporters.[10] The heckling was an omen, for Stinson lost by a narrow margin to his only opponent, J.J. Thurston of the United Farmers of Ontario.

The loss of Victoria, like the downfall of the party nationally, was disappointing but not altogether unexpected. The Frosts, in company with many other Conservatives, regarded it as a temporary setback which good organization and hard work would do a lot to overcome. In the spring of 1923 they helped form the Conservative Club of Lindsay, of which Leslie was elected vice-president and Cecil a director, and a year afterward the latter became secretary-treasurer of the newly organized East Central Ontario Conservative Association. By that time the Tories had scored a striking success in Ontario, ousting the farmers' government of E.C. Drury and sweeping into power under Howard Ferguson. 'Cecil and myself,' Leslie told his former mentor Finlayson, who had won East Simcoe for the Conservatives, 'were deeply engaged in the election in these parts ... Unfortunately our own work fell into considerable arrears,' but that was made up for by the satisfaction of having aided in redeeming both North and South Victoria from the UFO. 'The Party is most enthusiastic here,' he assured Finlayson, 'and there is no question that Victoria and Haliburton will be Conservative in the next Dominion election.'[11] The prediction was correct. Stinson won the seat handily in the 1925 election.

It did not take Leslie and Cecil long to find a way of satisfying their fondness for the outdoor life. For three summers beginning in 1922 they and their friend Bill Page, who boarded at the same house in town, rented an old cottage at Pleasant Point on Sturgeon Lake, a few miles north of town. It was an unspoiled area where they could again share the simple pleasures of boating and fishing. The place was easily accessible, and this enabled them to live there continuously in the summertime. After closing the office they would walk over to the Scugog and board the SS *Lintonia*, sole survivor of a once numerous fleet of river steamboats. It set out from the government wharf at Sturgeon Point each weekday morning, stopping at Pleasant Point on the way to Lindsay. Later in the day it returned with mail and provisions for the lakeshore residents, and then steamed back to Lindsay to await the commuters at the end of their day's work.[12] Leslie was so taken with the Pleasant Point property that he bought it in 1925. For nearly fifty years thereafter it was a refuge whose enlargement, improvement, and enjoyment gave him untold pleasure.

Among the others who had summer places on that part of the shore were the Carew family, who owned a farm at Sturgeon Point. Before long the two young lawyers, partners in courtship as in war, business, and politics, were canoeing across the lake together on a Sunday afternoon or in the long twilight of a warm summer evening to pay court to two of the Carew daughters, Gertrude and Roberta. The girls' father, John Carew, was one of Lindsay's most prominent businessmen whose ancestors had come to Upper Canada from County Cork in 1825. His major enterprise was the lumber company bearing his name, but he was president or vice-president of several other firms. In addition, he displayed the public spirit expected of a leading citizen by taking a special interest in the Lindsay Central Exhibition, which advertised itself as the fourth largest in Canada,[13] and which he served for some years as chairman of the board. In 1914 he had been elected to represent Victoria South at Queen's Park but did not seek re-election in 1919 when, like many other

Conservative seats, Victoria South fell to the United Farmers.[14] Gertrude was the fourth and Roberta the youngest of his seven children.

Leslie Frost had already met Gertrude before coming to Lindsay, although that had nothing to do with his moving there. She had been a close friend of Arthur Ardagh, the only son of Dr and Mrs Edward Ardagh of Orillia, and it had been expected by their families and friends that they would marry. Arthur was older than Leslie but their school careers overlapped. Like Leslie, he yearned to take up soldiering. Going off to war in 1915, he joined the 20th Infantry Battalion in France as a company commander and was killed in action not long after the Battle of Vimy Ridge. Thereafter the Ardaghs treated Gertrude, who visited them from time to time, as an adopted daughter; when Leslie returned from overseas, having served in the same unit as Arthur, he too was received in the Ardagh household almost as one of the family. It was there that he and Gertrude Carew met for the first time.

The Ardagh connection gave Leslie and Gertrude something in common when they met again in Lindsay. It was a seed that grew into friendship and then blossomed into love. At the same time Cecil was smitten with Roberta and in due course they, as well as the other two, became formally engaged. These were not whirlwind romances leading quickly to the altar. One had to achieve a competency sufficient to support a wife in a style not too far below that to which she was accustomed. The debt to Mrs Knight had to be paid off and the practice built to a level where it produced an income adequate for two married couples. That took time, so while they courted, the brothers strove to improve their prospects and increase their resources.

Cecil and Roberta were married in 1925, and on 2 June 1926 Leslie and Gertrude were married and acquired their own house on Victoria Street, less than two blocks from where Cecil and Roberta lived. Thereafter, though each couple moved to other addresses, they were never separated by more than a five-minute walk. They shared Pleasant Point in the summertime and on many a spring or autumn weekend. Both brothers enjoyed fishing but they did not venture on fishing trips up north together because one of them always remained in Lindsay to attend to office matters.

Leslie and Gertrude were childless, so they lavished their love of children on nieces and nephews. It took a while for the latter to realize that Uncle Les's propensity for swearing under stress need

not be taken too seriously, and also to learn to understand his sense
of humour. 'Well, Gert,' he would say with a touch of mock menace
in his voice and look as he gazed at the youngsters, 'get the salt
and pepper, I'm going to eat them up.' And they would run off
frantically, not sure whether he meant it, until at last they saw that
this was simply his favourite joke for such moments, one that years
later he trotted out for his niece Marjorie's own children.[15] Although his temper had a rather short fuse and the small folk might
momentarily resent the authority over them which he sometimes
asserted, there could be no doubt of his affection or kindliness.

Gertrude Carew, 'Det' as she was called by her little nephew
Jack Beal and was ever afterwards known in the family, was a
remarkable young woman. Dynamic and strong-willed, her mind
sharp and decisive, she was a capable manager with a flair for
organization and a disposition to command. Marjorie Frost recalled
that she ran the whole family, her mother and father included.[16]
Although her three sisters had attended boarding school, she had
preferred to stay home for her education and to work part-time at
her father's lumber company. During the war, with her brother
Frank overseas, she became the office manager, keeping the accounts and directing the staff. In addition, she virtually ran the
Carew household.

These traits naturally survived her wedding. She chose Leslie's
clothes, managed their personal finances, dealt with the tradesmen
about repairs to the house, and controlled her own domestic domain. Her opinions were numerous, definite and unequivocally
stated, and she frequently disagreed, on occasion publicly, with her
equally strong-willed husband, who in later times sometimes referred to her as 'leader of the opposition.' But for all the dominance
of her personality, she possessed enormous charm and presence,
as well as a gift for stimulating conversation. She was genuinely
interested in people, considerate of their needs, and eager to help
them through their troubles. Above all, she devoted herself completely to Leslie with a devotion perhaps intensified by their not
having children.

Cecil and Roberta were equally happy and the four of them made
an effective partnership. The two couples were in constant consultation; many of the decisions affecting their lives and fortunes in
the town were made in concert. Thus, for example, if one brother
bought a Ford car, the other bought a Dodge, while their wives
patronized different stores and tradespeople, spreading their cus-

tom around.[17] This was as good for the law business as it was politically astute, and for the two men, business and politics were what life was all about.

By 1926 the law firm of Knight, Frost and Frost had acquired some recognition beyond the Lindsay community, thanks to three murder cases in which it acted for the defence. While these were less remunerative than the comparatively humdrum matters which produced the bulk of its revenue, they earned the headlines and made the Frosts more widely known. In two of them Cecil did the courtroom work, thus receiving most of the publicity, but in all three he and Leslie pooled their brains and energy to do the best they could for their clients. Leslie's efforts in the one of these cases in which he appeared for the defence lasted six months. The McGaughey affair, one in a series of 'sweetheart murders' in 1924, attracted province-wide attention and made the name of Leslie Frost more widely known.

There was no doubt that Frederick William McGaughey, who farmed near Omemee, had shot his fiancée, Beatrice Fee, during a lovers' quarrel one night in a parked car on a lonely road, that in the struggle two of his fingers had been shot off, or that he had then taken the woman to his house and called a doctor. The question was whether he was sane at the time. There had been a disagreement over the date of their wedding and some hard words about McGaughey's drinking habits. 'He was in a fit of temper and crazy drunk,' the victim told a friend before her death. 'Without any warning he turned on me and put four bullets in me.'[18] Having interviewed him at the Lindsay jail at the prisoner's request, Frost was convinced that McGaughey was not only a drunkard but mentally unsound, not incapable of instructing him but subject to some serious disorder of the brain.

Frost at once arranged to have the prisoner seen by the superintendents of the Ontario mental asylums at Kingston, Mimico, and Hamilton. All agreed that McGaughey suffered from catatonic dementia praecox at the time of the murder. Frost also turned up evidence of mental instability in the accused's grandmother and mother, as well as in McGaughey himself as a child, all of which was attested to by doctors who had attended them. He found out that McGaughey had done poorly in school, ending his formal education at the age of seventeen after repeatedly failing the high school entrance examinations. His farm had fallen into disrepair and his fields were overgrown with weeds, indicating serious irresponsibility. He had taken to drinking heavily, his demeanour was uncouth, and, except on rare occasions when he cleaned himself up, his appearance was slovenly. On top of all this, as his imprisonment continued, the jailer and others reported that he was threatening suicide and had once consumed paris green. Everything seemed to support the diagnosis of the three psychiatrists.

Of the three, Frost found Dr Edward Ryan of Kingston the most interested and helpful, and wanted to have him examine McGaughey again. But the crown attorney, J.E. Anderson, had instructed the jailer to let no one except his clergyman and counsel see the prisoner without his consent. Frost reported to Ryan that he found the crown attorney 'most hostile to the accused ... we have heard of no other case in which the defence of a man whose life is at stake has been hampered in this manner.'[19] Anderson refused the request for another visit by Ryan, informing Frost that he was acting on instructions from the attorney general's department. So Frost wrote to W.F. Nickle, attorney general in the Ferguson government, politely protesting the obstacles Anderson seemed determined to raise and soliciting the desired favour. Nickle's reply was not the one hoped for. He had no objection to McGaughey's being examined by any alienist his counsel chose, but 'I cannot permit employees of the state to act as experts for the defence; chaos would result.'[20]

Nickle later relented, courting chaos by allowing the three doctors to appear for the defence after all. The crown, meanwhile, had found two experts of its own who concluded that McGaughey was faking a mental disorder. Knowing that the medical witnesses would disagree with each other and that insanity was difficult to prove in a court of law, Frost had qualms about thus basing his case. He decided to seek advice from an experienced expert in criminal law. Two consultations with S.H. Bradford, KC, in Toronto convinced Frost that the plea of not guilty by reason of insanity offered the best, probably the only, hope for his client. Having done all he could to prepare, he awaited the start of the trial.

It was a cold, rainy morning as hundreds of would-be spectators lined up outside the Lindsay court-house. The few spectators' rows were quickly filled, and the remaining crowd stood in the rain anyway, hoping for a glimpse of the prisoner as he was brought to his trial. The next day the crowds returned, jamming not only the courtroom but the corridors. The trial lasted four days, with Peter White, KC, a prominent Toronto lawyer, representing the crown and Mr Justice W.A. Logie presiding. That the latter had drawn this assignment was not reassuring. 'The judges of the 1920's and thereabouts,' Frost wrote many years later, 'were never sympathetic to insanity defences,' and Logie's 'main qualification for his position on the Bench was that he had commanded the troops in Camp Borden in 1916 and was noted for his abrasive character. He became known as a judge noted for his harsh sentences.'[21]

A lengthy parade of witnesses took the stand while McGaughey sat in the dock expressionless and with downcast eyes, listening to divergent opinions about his mental condition. Then it was time for closing addresses by counsel. Frost's lasted nearly two hours and struck one listener as impressive. He had 'marshalled his facts in excellent order. He presented them with measured precision, calmly, cooly [sic], collectedly and deliberately. At times he waxed eloquent and at times struck the sympathetic chord with a convincing pathos.'[22] But all Frost's eloquence went for naught; McGaughey, found guilty, was sentenced to be hanged.

The real nemesis in this case was the M'Naghten rules, a judicial dictum arising from a nineteenth-century English case and incorporated into the Canadian criminal code, which stated that unless the accused had been incapable of understanding the nature and quality of his crime and of knowing it to be wrong, the plea of insanity must be rejected. The onus of proving such incapacity was on the defence. Bradford advised Frost that there were no good grounds for appeal, but was there any hope of clemency? Mr Justice Logie had unbent sufficiently to confide to Frost that he thought so. Bradford agreed, while cautioning that 'you may have to get some pressure to bear to bring that about. It might be difficult ... having regard to the circumstances, but after all there are not many people who like to see a man hanged.'[23]

Clemency is granted by the governor general in council, so the minister of justice, Ernest Lapointe, would have to be petitioned to reduce McGaughey's sentence to life imprisonment. Frost was determined to try, but how to approach Lapointe? Since 'pressure' would be needed and since Frost feared that politics might enter in, he thought it prudent to enlist the aid of someone 'on the other side of the House ... I am myself opposite in politics to the present Government and I think it would be well to consider that point.'[24] Senator George McHugh of Lindsay, a Liberal who knew the McGaughey family well, agreed to help, but Frost desired the assistance of someone even more influential. He finally decided on Senator F.F. Pardee of Sarnia, a lawyer and a powerful Liberal. The senator proved willing to assist, but his high fee obliged Frost not to employ him.[25]

Accompanied by Senator McHugh and Dr Ryan, he presented himself at Lapointe's office on 14 November. The minister greeted them cordially and a discussion with him and some of his officials ensued in an agreeably informal atmosphere. Ryan read a report he had prepared about McGaughey's mental state and Frost was urged to offer whatever additional argument he wished. He did so in a lengthy letter to Lapointe, and followed that up with a petition signed by a number of Victoria County's leading citizens. It was all to no avail. A final appeal to the governor general was denied and McGaughey was executed on 5 December.

Having devoted so much time and labour to the case, and having become emotionally as well as professionally involved, Frost was sick at heart and agreed with Ryan that the refusal of clemency was 'a terrible arraignment of our whole system ... The unfortunate part of a matter of this sort is that a few men who are not responsible [mentally] have to be hanged before public opinion becomes educated to the fact that this is a futile method of dealing with a man of this sort.'[26] Clearly there was something seriously wrong with the M'Naghten rules. In 1931 Frost presented a paper on the subject to the 20 Club, a group of Lindsay's business and professional men who met convivially to hear discourses by one another or by a guest. 'Our law-makers,' he declared, 'have never had the courage as yet to change the impossible law which at present exists.' The law ought to embody the contention of 'the most eminent authorities that the rule should include not only the *knowledge* of good and evil, but the power to *choose* the one and *refrain* from the other.' It 'should be a good defence to establish that an accused's insanity prevented him from controlling his actions' and 'from doing the act, although he knew it was wrong.'[27]

On this issue the partners in Frost and Frost were not so much of the same mind as they were about most things. Cecil wrote to a Calgary lawyer: 'It is my belief that if the law were changed murders would increase rather than decrease. My brother does not hold this view, but perhaps I am a little old fashioned.'[28]

These trials attracted the attention of the legal fraternity as well as widespread public interest and brought the Frosts' law firm out of the obscurity normally surrounding its small-town and country practice. The publicity, even in cases lost, was welcome but not financially beneficial, for the defendants were invariably poor and the costs of defending them high. Still, these cases may have helped open the door to a more certain, if intermittent, source of income from their employment as special crown prosecutors. Here William

Finlayson's assistance was invaluable. At his suggestion, Nickle had given Cecil Frost some of this work in Kingston and Belleville, and when Nickle was succeeded as attorney general by William Price, Cecil asked Finlayson, now minister of lands and forests, to use his good offices again. 'I do not know Col. Price so well,' he wrote early in 1927, 'but would feel very much indebted to you if you would be good enough to speak to him and see if he would put both Leslie's name and my own down for an assize this spring.'[29] The brothers each did a good deal of prosecuting work in the later 1920s and early 1930s. It was useful experience and payment was assured. Leslie saw a lot of the province in this capacity, visiting such towns as Sault Ste Marie, Belleville, Milton, Sudbury, and Welland, and made many new friends.

Apart from their legal practice, Leslie and Cecil Frost found there was no lack of opportunity in Lindsay to satisfy their appetite for political organizing and electioneering. Three provincial and four national general elections took place during their first ten years there, culminating in the great Tory victory under R.B. Bennett in 1930. The Frosts worked hard in all of them, although they carefully arranged their commitments so that one of them was at the office every working day. In the federal contests, their efforts contributed to T.H. Stinson's victories in 1925, 1926, and again in 1930. Provincially, however, the results were more mixed. In 1923 both North and South Victoria were regained from the UFO as part of the wholesale rejection of the Drury government. When Howard Ferguson sought re-election three and a half years later and again swept most of Ontario, the Conservatives lost in Victoria.

The overriding provincial issue was the liquor traffic. The Ontario Temperance Act of 1916 had prohibited the sale though not the manufacture, importation, or consumption of alcoholic beverages. Ferguson now proposed replacing it with a system of government-controlled sales. The prohibitionists, having advanced their cause during the war, were outraged at this prospective surrender to the forces of debauchery. The object of the Conservatives, in Victoria County at any rate, was to wither the prohibitionist case with ridicule; their arguments may be gathered from the notes on which Leslie Frost based his standard campaign speech. Ontario, he argued, was not really dry under the Temperance Act and it was hypocritical to pretend otherwise. The bar might have disappeared but bootleggers abounded. The act allowed permits for home brewing, and in Victoria alone about eleven hundred of these had been issued. Everyone knew that there were many illicit stills in operation. It was also common knowledge that certain doctors abused their right to prescribe elixirs with alcoholic content – in Lindsay alone roughly six hundred gallons of such medicines were prescribed annually – and some doctors had been disciplined by the Board of Licence Commissioners. There were druggists, too, who were amiably generous in dispensing liquor to their customers for 'therapeutic' use. Prohibition prevailed only in name, not in fact.

Conservatives such as Frost always asked what proportion of the adult public thought it wrong to take a drink? Various plebiscites in recent years, Frost claimed, showed that the proportion had steadily diminished, so much so that in the latest vote, in 1924, barely 51 per cent of the ballots supported prohibition. A law backed by so slim a majority was unjust, and enforcement of such a law was impossible. Government-controlled sale was the only realistic means of dealing with the problem. The majority of Victoria voters, however, did not support this position. The Conservatives, Frost remembered long afterward, 'got all the cheers but not enough votes in dry Victoria.' The two Victoria seats were won by Liberal-Progressives pledged to temperance and the Tories were left to await another day.[30]

That day arrived less than three years later when Ferguson went to the polls for the last time. The 1929 election, with the Frost brothers again active on the hustings, was also largely fought over the liquor question, the Tories defending the Liquor Control Act of 1927 which repealed the Temperance Act and brought in government control. But now attention was paid also to the general record of the Ferguson government. This time, in the south riding of Victoria, the Conservative candidate, W.W. Staples, was elected comfortably, part of a landslide which gave the party ninety-two of the 112 seats. North Victoria, though, was one of the holdouts. There, thanks largely to factional rivalry in Tory ranks, the Liberal incumbent, William Newman, managed to survive by a mere thirty-one votes.[31]

By the time Ontario voters again went to the polls in 1934, political circumstances had radically altered. Howard Ferguson was now Canadian high commissioner in London and his remarkable political mastery was noticeably lacking in his successor, George Henry. More than that, the prosperity of the late 1920s had come to a sudden, devastating end in the great stock market crash of October 1929, and the country was suffering from a deep and prolonged depression. It was a time better suited to critics than defenders, to oppositions than incumbents, and this was especially true in Ontario, where the outlook for the Henry administration was not at all promising. The premier put off the election as long as he could, but by 1934 it was inescapable. For the party in power, winning seats – perhaps even finding good candidates – was not going to be as easy as it had been for the past ten years.

In Victoria County, however, there was no shortage of Tory aspirants; among others, both partners in Frost and Frost were interested. They had paid their dues to the party. For a decade or more, they had spoken at many meetings, shaken countless hands, sat in on strategy sessions, and contributed money as well as time and effort. Both desired the nomination, both were encouraged to try, and neither lacked confidence in his ability to be a good member. But it had to be one or the other. A redistribution of seats had merged North and South Victoria as the riding of Victoria-Haliburton. It was therefore impossible for the brothers to seek nomination in two neighbouring constituencies where they were well known. In any event, it would be out of the question for both to be away from the office while the legislature was in session. They would not run against each other for the nomination. Thus a way had to be found, without giving offence to either, of deciding which one would seek the nomination at the convention scheduled for April. There was much discussion between them, each deferring to the other, not wanting to say or do anything to damage their close and cherished relationship, yet not quite willing to admit that the other had a superior claim. In the end they agreed on a sporting way out of their dilemma: they tossed a coin and Leslie won the toss.[32]

3

Low Tide for 'the Government Party'

The Ontario Liberal party entered the 1934 election campaign with a long record of failure behind it. Out of power continuously since 1905, its performance at the polls ranged from disappointing to dismal. It had lost to the powerful Conservative administrations of Sir James Whitney, Sir William Hearst, and Howard Ferguson, and it failed to thwart the transitory phenomenon of the UFO. Would it be different this time? Under their dynamic new leader, Mitchell F. Hepburn, the party hoped to achieve political ascendancy after losing eight elections in a row. Since their devastating defeat by Ferguson in 1929, the party's circumstances had changed, however, in some significant ways.

It was no longer the earnest but ineffectual William Sinclair, 'temporary' Liberal leader since 1923, against the masterful Ferguson. George Henry, Ferguson's well-meaning but colourless, often maladroit successor, now faced Mitch Hepburn. A successful Elgin County farmer, Hepburn had been elected to the House of Commons in 1926 at the age of thirty, and four years later, instead of falling like many Liberals before the Tory surge under R.B. Bennett, had increased his majority. His record in the House, however, was undistinguished. Annoyed by Mackenzie King's failure to be suitably impressed by his talent, and unhappy with the prospect of prolonged insignificance as an opposition back-bencher, he had sought and had captured the leadership of the provincial party at the end of 1930, promising to supply the 'pep and ginger' so lacking in Sinclair.[1]

Hepburn was not regarded as an unmixed blessing by all his fellow Liberals, and knowledge of this may have caused the Tories to underestimate him as the 1934 campaign approached. Yet there was no denying his personal charm and magnetism, or his vote-getting ability. On the hustings he knew how to carry the war to the enemy. George Henry, doggedly defending his government's record, was badly outmatched as Hepburn campaigned skilfully in the rural areas where relatively few votes could elect relatively many members.

Nevertheless, Frost sought the Conservative nomination in Victoria-Haliburton with high hopes. W.W. Staples, winner of Victoria South in 1929, retired, and J.R. Marks, loser in the last two contests in Victoria North to the Liberal-Progressive William Newman, was not interested in another try. Newman, a creamery operator widely known as 'Buttermilk Bill,' was again the Liberal candidate. As he was popular in the rural and especially the northern districts, his opponent would face a tough fight, even though Lindsay, the largest urban centre by far, was traditionally a Tory stronghold.

At 'a huge and enthusiastic' convention in the Academy Theatre, Frost won the nomination handily on the first ballot. He modestly admitted that 'the party is far greater than I am' but as a mere 'cog in the wheels' he was 'willing to serve you as long as there is a united party behind me.'[2] The supporters, particularly his brother Cecil, were initially optimistic.[3] But, as Leslie remembered it later: 'It was soon apparent that the situation was bad and I was determined to fight a good fight, make friends of all, and wait for better political weather.'[4]

Despite Frost's qualms, he wasted no time in getting organized. The Women's Institute rooms in the Lindsay town hall were rented for headquarters and a heavy program of engagements was arranged for the candidate. His campaign was centred on the record of the Henry government, which he did his best to defend, while belittling the exaggerated charges and extravagant promises that he thought were Hepburn's stock-in-trade. Naturally Frost stressed what the government had done for his constituency, where a great deal of money had been spent on roads, much of it to open up territory in the north, as well as on new bridges and other public works. In addition the government had expended large sums in Victoria-Haliburton on aid to education, northern development, old age pensions, mothers' allowances, workmen's compensation, and low-interest loans to farmers for which the province had had to increase the public debt. Newman charged that this was evidence of mismanagement. Frost retorted that the debt could be paid off when there were no longer needy farmers or unemployed workers. As he told one audience, 'he preferred to look after the people and let the Provincial debt look after itself.'[5]

His platform was simple: 'Help solve the difficulties of the day' and 'provide what people want,' namely, 'Better agricultural conditions, work & wages for the people.' He had 'no private interests to serve, no axe to grind. I have only the people *to serve. If you elect me I promise* I will *unselfishly represent these two great counties.*'

Although Frost asserted that issues were what mattered, the crowds who came to hear him expected entertainment as well as speeches and they were not disappointed. In Lindsay the meetings usually wound up with a frolic, including square dancing, amateur musical performers and recitations, and dance music provided by the Young Canada Conservative orchestra. On occasion, the politicians were not heard until the local musicians and elocutionists had displayed their talents.

The high point of Frost's campaign was a monster gathering at which Premier Henry addressed a capacity crowd at the Lindsay Armouries. With much blaring of trumpets and beating of drums, Henry was escorted from the Benson House Hotel by the Lindsay Boys' Band, and the indispensable Young Canada Conservative group provided both a musical prelude to the oratory and a dancing finale to the evening. The affair seemed to go well and the premier was pleased with it. 'That was a wonderful gathering in Lindsay,' he wrote to Frost on the morrow of the election. 'I do not think I should ever forget it.'

Even so, in Victoria-Haliburton Frost was beaten by about twenty-seven hundred votes, and in Lindsay his majority was only one-tenth of Staples's in 1929. The help of such prominent Conservatives as Henry, Leopold Macaulay, and H.H. Stevens had been of no avail, nor had Frost's extensive advertising in the *Lindsay Daily Post*. Newman had placed but one advertisement in the *Post*, on the day before the election, and had no campaign support from Liberal headquarters. To be beaten so badly after expending all that effort and money was sorely disappointing. 'I could not believe my eyes last night when I saw you chopped up among the slain,' Premier Henry commiserated: 'I did not think there was a new candidate in the field in whom I had more hopes of getting by than yourself.'[6] In fact, Frost had plenty of company in the host of slaughtered Tories. In contrast to the great sweep of 1929 which had given the party all but twenty of the one hundred and twelve seats, in the next, numerically diminished, assembly it would have only seventeen out of ninety. The tumultuous Hepburn era had dawned.

The Tories, in a state of shock, now began to reassess the future of what they had been inclined to think of as 'the government party' in Ontario. Inevitably, demands for new leadership were raised. Henry, a survivor of the débâcle, continued as leader, although he was under strong pressure to retire. The caucus confirmed him as chief, and he remained so for the next session, but by then it had been decided to hold a leadership convention in May 1936.

The Frost brothers shared the opinion that Henry should give way, and that it was time for fresh blood and new faces. They thought the party's recovery required a man free from the stigma of defeat, someone untainted by the suspicion, assiduously encouraged by Hepburn and his attorney general, Arthur Roebuck, of corruption in the Tory old guard. After the election, Leslie and Cecil maintained their political interest. The former had every intention of running again, but for the time being was quite overshadowed by his younger brother. Cecil had gone into municipal politics. After an earlier stint on the town council, he was elected mayor of Lindsay in January 1936, on a platform of 'Reduced Taxes – More Industry,' defeating the incumbent who undertook, less specifically but more grandly, to provide 'Fearless Administration.'[7] Yet Cecil undoubtedly aspired to a larger stage. His name frequently cropped up in speculation about who would succeed George Henry, who now announced his own retirement from the convention race.

When the convention was about to open in May, Cecil Frost did not stand for leader, deciding to seek the party presidency instead. He failed in that, but was elected first vice-president. For the leadership he and Leslie favoured Earl Rowe, American by birth but raised in Simcoe County and, along with George Drew, one of the two leading candidates among the seven nominated. Rowe had sat in the legislature from 1923 to 1925, when he resigned to run successfully for the House of Commons, and had served briefly in Bennett's cabinet. A breeder, trainer, and driver of standardbred horses, he was favourably known to many Ontario farmers for whom harness racing was an avocation, if not an addiction. The Frosts had no interest in the sport but they liked Rowe's down-to-earth, no-nonsense approach to things. He was chosen leader on the second ballot, not by swaying the convention with eloquence, according to Toronto's *Evening Telegram*, but because he was backed by the party machine. 'Mr. Rowe did not make the best speech,' the paper remarked candidly, 'but he polled the best vote. Conventions and elections are seldom won by speeches.'[8]

Hepburn had introduced controversial legislation to satisfy Roman Catholic demands that their separate schools be given a larger share of tax revenue. Shortly before the convention, promising that the party 'will give fair play to minorities, but we will restore a square deal to majorities,' Rowe announced that if he became premier the measure would be repealed. A motion to this effect was endorsed by the convention amid 'unprecedented scenes of enthusiasm,' as a *Telegram* reporter saw it, 'that have never been equalled in a political convention.'[9] Public opinion on this issue was tested after the convention when a by-election was called for 9 December 1936 in East Hastings, one of the deepest-dyed Protestant and Orange districts in the province.

The East Hastings seat had been continuously Conservative since 1908, save when a renegade Tory captured it for the UFO in 1919. Judging by the money and effort they expended, though, the Liberals thought they had a fighting chance to win it. Hepburn took up residence in the riding for much of the last few weeks of the campaign, waged in the snow and cold of an unusually early winter. He was joined by a procession of cabinet ministers, back-benchers and other luminaries, and supported by an outlay of $33,000, an almost unheard of sum in those days for a single constituency.[10] The Tories were no less energetic, if much more parsimonious. Rowe made several appearances assisted by a troop of supporters, among them Cecil Frost, the party's chief organizer for central Ontario. But the most active Conservative was George Drew. An ambitious, vigorous, eloquent, and strikingly handsome lawyer from Guelph, of which for a time he was mayor, Drew had made a name for himself as head of the Ontario Securities Commission until his dismissal by Hepburn in one of the latter's money-saving moves, a wholesale purge of civil servants. He had hoped to be leader after Henry but willingly took on the task of reviving the party machinery when Rowe made him chairman of the party's campaign organization. East Hastings was his first electoral test.

Despite inclement weather, meetings everywhere in the constituency were packed. Drew's attacks on the government concentrated on Catholic influence on Hepburn and the alleged iniquities of his separate schools' policy. In the end the Conservatives won by a massive majority. On election night Rowe, Drew, and Harold Welsh, the newly elected member, paraded triumphantly in Madoc. But the unity of that giddy moment was to be of brief duration and the result in East Hastings did not prove to be a portent of better things to come for the Conservatives.[11]

The legislature convened in January 1937 for a new session, the last before another general election. Some weeks following its close, on 27 April Hepburn invited an incredulous Earl Rowe, with only seventeen elected followers and no seat of his own, to join him in a coalition government. Half of its members would be named by Rowe, who should become premier if he wished. The usual and most persuasive explanation of this proposition, which Rowe dismissed as 'just out and beyond,' is that it came from George McCullagh, publisher of the *Globe and Mail*.[12] An eager, handsome and successful young Toronto stockbroker, McCullagh had made a good deal of money by investing in gold mining stocks and had formed close relationships with people in the mining business. In 1936, using money largely furnished by one of his mining friends, William H. Wright, he acquired and merged two Toronto newspapers, the Liberal *Globe* and the Tory *Mail and Empire*. His influence over Hepburn, whom he had supported in 1934, was thought to be visible, not only in the surprising overture to Rowe, but also in the premier's willingness to repeal his separate schools legislation and in his vigorous intervention in a strike at the General Motors plant in Oshawa.[13] There the Congress of Industrial Organizations, recently formed in the United States to promote industrial unionism and widely feared by businessmen, in that country and Canada as a crypto-communist body, was attempting to organize the workers. Hepburn found in events at Oshawa a new issue which he was to exploit with consummate skill in the general election soon to come.

Hepburn's offer to Rowe was consistent with McCullagh's disdain for party politics and politicians. Like many businessmen he scorned the bickering between the two established parties over minor issues which were not relevant to the true needs and interests of society. Coalition would effect an efficient, businesslike approach to public questions and provide a united front against a common radical foe. A coalition and its inevitable sweeping victory at the polls would demonstrate that the people of Ontario were united against subversion from the left.

Rowe's refusal of the offer was apparently approved of by most Tories who were aware of it.[14] But there were exceptions. The most prominent objector was Drew, whose resignation as chairman of the party's campaign committee was announced ten days after Hepburn made his overture. Drew and McCullagh were close friends and they shared, as did Hepburn, an intense dislike of Mackenzie King, a fear of communism as they thought it was manifested in the CIO, and a belief that the welfare of Ontario required the two old parties to join against both those enemies.

Drew's stated reason for resigning as chief organizer was that he fully supported Hepburn's attempt to prevent the CIO 'from exploiting Canadian labour.'[15] Rowe felt that Drew's real reason for quitting was that he favoured union with the Grits.[16] But since one of the chief purposes of such a union was supposed to be creation of a solid, bipartisan front against the CIO and labour 'radicalism,' it is doubtful that Drew was satisfied with the position on labour policy his leader had decided to take.

Rowe set forth the party's stand in a speech at Arthur, the day before Drew announced his resignation, and what he said put him at some distance from the government. He affirmed the right of employees to belong to and bargain collectively through a union of their choice, whether 'Canadian or international, craft or industrial,' provided that the laws of Canada, including prohibition of sit-down strikes such as had occurred at Oshawa, were observed and that the right to work not be dependent on union membership. The duties of the state in industrial disputes were to 'take no sides and to maintain law and order without the display of unnecessary or provocative force' and to 'enact and impartially administer adequate legislation' for conciliating disputes. His party, declared Rowe, stood for 'freedom of association within the law,' believing 'that the essence of democracy is to trust in the people and to rely on freedom and not on dictatorship, that public opinion may be led but not driven and that the greatest safeguard of orderly progress and reform is the sound common sense of all classes of the Canadian people.'[17]

Drew having left his organizer's job with a general election expected before long, an energetic, committed successor was urgently required. Rowe decided that he wanted Cecil Frost, who promptly accepted, thus leaving his brother more than ever alone in charge of the law practice. Leslie was used to this, for Cecil's duties as chief organizer for central Ontario, although less onerous than those he was now assuming, required him to spend a lot of time away from home. Leslie did not complain, being content to take up the slack at the office while seizing every opportunity to 'make friends of all' with an eye to his own political future. Cecil's vigour and prowess as a stump speaker during the East Hastings by-election had recommended him to Rowe, to say nothing of his unquestioned loyalty to the leader and his unqualified endorsement of the labour policy proclaimed at Arthur, which in all likelihood he had helped to formulate.

Shortly after succeeding Drew, Cecil addressed a letter to officers of Conservative riding associations, asking for their co-operation and extolling Rowe's virtues, but more especially defending the Arthur speech. The right of Canadian workers to organize in unions, he pointed out, had been enjoyed for many years and most of their unions were affiliated with American counterparts. 'When one remembers that capital is international, it naturally follows that labor also has the right of international affiliation.' The two types of unions, representing separate trades or, as in the CIO, embracing all workers in a given industry, were 'both legal, and it is for the workman to decide which, if either, of these plans he prefers ... Our Party can only succeed if its policies are founded on truth, and in my judgment the stand of the Hon. Mr. Rowe is impregnable.'[18]

Despite having to shoulder much of the work of the practice, Leslie was off and running well before the election was called in October 1937. He was acclaimed as candidate in Victoria-Haliburton at a convention in June. The chief speaker that evening was Earl Rowe, who treated the enthusiastic crowd to a hard-hitting indictment of Hepburn's performance and an exposition of Conservative policy, including the stand on labour relations. Accepting the nomination, Frost modestly described himself as 'a very ordinary sort of a chap and not too fond of making speeches.' He played down the labour question, perhaps sensing that the party's position would not be wildly popular with many voters in his district, and dismissed it with an offhand remark: 'I doubt if there is a labour issue in Ontario. I think it is just a child of Mr. Hepburn's imagination.'[19]

It was an issue, though, in fact the overriding one – Hepburn saw to that – and the Tories found themselves very much on the defensive over it. They were not helped by Drew, who announced that he would run as an independent Conservative in his home riding of Wellington South. Not content with the confines of his constituency, he stumped through the province, proclaiming the dangers of communism and his approval of Hepburn's stand against the CIO. This smacked of tacitly encouraging Conservatives to vote Liberal, or at least to stay home, and Rowe found it intolerable. He retaliated, as he later put it, by sending 'some money and some campaigners up to see that he [Drew] was defeated ... which he was.'[20]

The press publicized the Drew-Rowe controversy and virtually ignored the Victoria campaign in which Leslie Frost again faced William Newman. Frost undertook the same gruelling round of appearances in the same assortment of town halls, Orange lodges, theatres, and school houses where one sat uncomfortably, feigning enjoyment, through the customary musical selections, juggling acts, tap dance routines, recitations, and warm-up speeches before standing up and taking from one's pocket the notes for the speech delivered so often already.

Frost's two major rallies, naturally, were in Lindsay. In mid September a giant crowd, only slightly smaller than had heard Hepburn the night before, listened to a thumping attack on the government by Denton Massey, MP, an active Tory speaker around the province. And a few days before the election, Rowe reappeared to give a speech, thus demonstrating his opinion that Victoria could be won.

Apart from the routine of meetings, problems of organization absorbed much of Frost's time and energy. It was essential to keep tabs on the activities of the carefully chosen poll chairmen, to supervise the preparation and distribution of literature, and to help account for expenditures down to the last three cent stamp.

None of this was new, but some things had changed. Frost no longer had to defend an unpopular regime but could attack its successor as 'the worst dictatorship that has ever ruled in Ontario,' whose actions had stirred up 'animosities and bad feelings.'[21] In the main, however, Frost's campaign speeches avoided indignant condemnation of his opponents. As a true believer in the constructive power of positive thinking, he preferred to propose policies in an equable, even-tempered manner. Through his tireless canvassing, he was now much better known throughout the riding, and this greatly assisted him to create a more complete, efficient organization. Gertrude's nephew, Jack Beal, acted as his driver, and together they travelled twenty-five hundred miles, much of it before the election was called, without ever leaving the two counties. They would go up one concession road and down another while Frost called at every farm, shop, and village house, chatting with the occupants about their problems, needs, and hopes.[22] From these encounters he made lists of possible supporters and poll captains who would be responsible for getting out the vote. He excelled at such grass-roots political work and in this way acquired many new friends and followers, some of them former supporters of the provincial Liberals. There were, he told the Lindsay rally at which Rowe spoke, Mackenzie King Liberals and Hepburn Liberals, and the former 'seem to be supporting the Conservative party.'[23]

This time he sensed that things were going his way. His only campaign advertisement was inserted in the *Lindsay Post* just before polling day. In it he enumerated under nine headings what he would try to achieve if elected. Heading the list was an undertaking to urge an easing of property taxation, 'which is rendering the ownership of land unprofitable.' At the end came his approach to labour relations, which hewed to the Rowe line. By putting this at the bottom of the list and avoiding mention of the CIO, industrial unionism, world communism, or Hepburn's handling of the Oshawa strike, he probably hoped to discourage excitement over the issue. The advertisement declared in conclusion: 'Our people are not interested in petty party politics but ... in things designed to bring good to all of our people.'[24] It was a characteristic statement by one who would prove to be one of Ontario's shrewdest practitioners of party politics.

In giving priority to property tax reform, Frost's strategy was in harmony with the reforms being proposed by Earl Rowe. Speaking at Brockville, Rowe had committed the Conservatives to a revamped municipal tax system, proposing a non-political body to study real estate taxation and municipal administration. It should co-operate with the Royal Commission on Dominion-Provincial Relations recently appointed by Mackenzie King and chaired by the chief justice of Ontario, Newton W. Rowell. Property tax relief, Rowe argued, would stimulate the construction industry and reduce business operating expenses, thus encouraging expanded economic activity.

On the morrow of the Hastings by-election, Cecil Frost had begun to impress on Rowe that municipal tax reform should be prominent in the Tory platform. As mayor of Lindsay he had observed at first hand the ill effects of the tax burden on individuals and municipalities. To ease it would be 'a "vote-getter" ... *even if the same people pay the taxes in other forms*.'[25] Cecil must have discussed this matter with his brother. It was the kind of campaign issue that most appealed to both Frosts, and once Cecil succeeded Drew as campaign chairman, he was in a stronger position to influence party policy.

For whatever reasons, Leslie Frost's victory by over three hundred votes could hardly have been more pleasing, considering that Newman had had a majority nearly nine times as large in 1934. Frost made substantial gains in Haliburton County, while his own town, barely carried before, gave him a margin of about nine hundred. In the province as a whole it was a sadder story for the

Tories. They had gained six seats but without increasing their share of the vote, while the Liberals, though winning four fewer seats than before, had raised their proportion of the popular vote. In the new House there would be sixty-six government members and only twenty-three in opposition. Rowe's failure to win a seat, coupled with the disappointing result overall, inevitably roused doubts that he would be leader much longer.

What had gone wrong? There was a variety of explanations. 'The real reason for our defeat,' the party's publicity chairman told Cecil, 'was the lack of press for nearly a year past. The G. & M. & Tely had thoroughly poisoned the public mind so that our leader never had a real chance.'[26] A different explanation, more persuasive, was that Rowe's stand on labour relations had been the fatal chink in the party's armour. As one Lindsay businessman grumbled, Rowe 'could have said ... that he backed Hepburn 100% on his C.I.O. policy, but he did not, but side-stepped or straddled the issue, which ... played into the hands of Hepburn.'[27] Still another view was that Drew's defection had done great harm, causing many Conservatives to stay home and weakening the party's standing among uncommitted voters. But perhaps the fundamental reason, which the losers were understandably loath to admit, was that most people had no very compelling reason to be dissatisfied with the Hepburn government.

In view of all these faults and weaknesses in the party's strategy, for Leslie Frost to have bucked the trend successfully made his capture of Victoria-Haliburton all the sweeter. Of course he regretted the poor showing of the party generally and the personal defeat of Rowe, whom he greatly respected. With his usual industriousness and the self-confidence, that seldom if ever deserted him, he set about to prepare for his first attendance at the legislative assembly where he was destined to sit for nearly a quarter of a century.

The divisions now exposed in Tory ranks, natural to a party that had governed with only one interruption for thirty years and had now been ignominiously beaten in two successive elections, were so deep-seated that it was hard to believe that less than a year had elapsed since Rowe and Drew had linked arms on the roof of the car at Madoc while their followers celebrated victory in East Hastings.

Evidence of disunity and bad feeling emerged from a caucus of Conservative MPPs, which Cecil Frost attended also, at the Albany Club in Toronto late in October. It met amidst much speculation about Rowe's intentions. Would he, as some predicted, resign the provincial leadership and contest a by-election for his old federal House of Commons seat? That he might was given credence by his going to Ottawa shortly before the caucus to consult people there, in particular R.B. Bennett, about his future. Or would he accept the offer of some MPPs to open a seat and make another try (which Hepburn had said would be unopposed) to enter the legislature? The caucus met at 11:00 a.m. and was expected to be over in fairly short order. Rowe would announce his decision, and there would be discussion of the state of the party. It was not so simple. The meeting dragged on until 2:30 the following morning, with breaks for lunch and dinner, while the press corps cooled their heels and waited impatiently for something to report.

What eventually came out, pieced together from things said to newsmen by some of the politicians, was a story of harsh words and bitter recriminations, with Rowe's decision still pending. Everyone blamed everyone else for the election disaster. Rowe reportedly stated that the party had been at rock bottom when he became leader and there had not been enough time to reorganize it properly before the election. He pointed to the indifference of some 'who thought they saw a shortcut to the seats of the mighty.' This was obviously a reference to Drew and others who had wanted to accept Hepburn's coalition proposal. Rowe also attacked the 'old gang.' Indeed, according to one account he went so far as to say that 'continuation of his leadership was predicated on the retirement from his support of at least three "old gang" members.' Chief among the three, it seemed, was George Henry who, Rowe was reported as insisting, must resign his seat. Henry, having easily gained re-election in East York, refused this extraordinary and (as he must have viewed it) impertinent demand by one who had failed to win a seat for himself. Members of the old gang had struck back, arguing that lack of organization, poor publicity and Rowe's tactical error in unfolding the platform piecemeal day by day instead of issuing a proper election manifesto, had been to blame. After sixteen hours, the meeting had ended inconclusively.

Some had strongly urged Rowe to stay on and accept the offer of either William Finlayson or Leopold Macaulay to resign in his favour. He had declined to commit himself, which strengthened the belief that he preferred to re-enter national politics. On the day after the caucus he announced that he had decided to do so and offered a mystifying 'explanation': 'Under the present circumstances I can best reorganize the Conservative Party in Ontario from the outside.' That sounded like a rationalization of his desire to go back to Ottawa without suddenly leaving the provincial Tories in the lurch.[28]

As he sat through the stormy marathon at the Albany Club, Leslie Frost may well have reflected that never had a political career commenced under less promising conditions. The party was torn and demoralized. If its leader regained his old federal seat his preoccupation with national affairs would be detrimental to the provincial party he still nominally led. It simply was not feasible to direct the Ontario operation from the House of Commons. Rowe had tacitly recognized this in suggesting that serious consideration be given to holding a leadership and policy convention. A further meeting of elected and defeated candidates late in November warned him, according to the *Globe and Mail*, that he could not 'continue indefinitely to present 'remote control' leadership' and that before the proposed convention he must choose between Toronto and Ottawa.[29] In effect, Rowe had already made his choice by deciding to run in the Dufferin-Simcoe by-election. But until the convention met, the party would be in a state of suspended animation.

Frost's initiation into the life of an MPP occurred at a short special session of the legislature that opened on 1 December 1937. A day or two beforehand he checked into the Royal York Hotel, which was to be his home away from home for the next twenty-five years, settled into his office at Queen's Park, and at the appointed hour was seated in the chamber observing the opening formalities. The Conservative caucus had chosen Leopold Macaulay as house leader in place of George Henry. It was hoped that his spirited, aggressive style would give the opposition an effectiveness that would partly compensate for damaged morale and numerical weakness. The sole purpose of that session was to strengthen the province's hand in countering resistance to the assessment and collection of estate taxes. The Conservatives found nothing wrong with that but objected to a companion bill, an amendment to the Judicature Act making servants of the crown immune from prosecution for actions taken in performance of their public duties. Macaulay denounced this in principle, warning of its implications. He was joined by Leslie Frost who, on his second day in the House, argued fruitlessly that the government should withdraw this measure 'and trust to the courts to determine what was right and what was not.'

Once his first regular legislative session began in February 1938,

Frost quickly became a conspicuous figure in an opposition which consisted of only twenty-three members. He was one of the two or three most vocal, next to Macaulay and Henry. He found the public business engrossing and enjoyed the hard work of mastering it. Since he had never lacked opinions, been reticent about expressing them, or suffered from the slightest loss for words, he had no difficulty in acclimatizing himself to the atmosphere of the legislative forum.

When Frost was about to make his maiden speech, he received a nice little note from Hepburn: 'Good luck on your first big try.'[30] His speech was devoted mainly to two subjects, labour policy and property tax reform. Indulging in some good natured ribbing of Hepburn for his overblown anti-CIO rhetoric in the election campaign, he recalled the premier, 'beneath Samuel de Champlain's monument on the shores of Lake Couchiching,' promising to 'stop the C.I.O. at the Detroit River, and ... keep them there and keep the fingers of the C.I.O. out of the pockets of the workingmen of this Province.' That sounded good on the hustings but where was the legislation to make it possible? None was forecast in the throne speech, even though the CIO was still actively engaged in organizing workers. One must therefore conclude that Hepburn's promise and his emotional talk about the threat to law and order were empty bombast. That was just as well because, while the government was obliged to preserve public order, 'labour was capable of conducting its own housecleaning, if and whenever that was required.' The fact was, Frost contended, that the workers' 'common sense will kill the radical element in any movement, whether it is the C.I.O., One Big Union or any other,' for labour realized that its own democratic rights depended on law and order being upheld. On real estate taxes, however, he stuck to the line Rowe had laid down before the election: senior governments must give more help to municipalities in diminishing the burden on property owners; there should be a commission to study the problem.

The issue of municipal tax reform was related to the serious structural imbalance in the Canadian federal system between the financial capacity of the provinces and their constitutional responsibility. With their limited taxing power under the British North America Act, the provinces lacked – some more than others – the financial resources to perform duties laid on them by the act or deemed within their jurisdiction. On the other hand, with its unlimited power to tax, its control of monetary policy, and the greater ease with which it could borrow if it chose, Ottawa was debarred constitutionally from intervening in provincial economic affairs. Hoping for a cure, the King government in 1937 had appointed the Royal Commission on Dominion-Provincial Relations, chaired by Newton Rowell, which invited the provinces to co-operate by submitting their views on the nature and causes of the problem and how it might be solved.

Hepburn's solution was to enlarge provincial tax revenues so as to permit, among other things, greater assistance to the municipalities, which were a provincial responsibility. Specifically, he claimed that the provinces had a constitutional right to impose direct taxation, especially the income tax, a lucrative source of funds which Ottawa had improperly invaded. In 1938 he moved in the legislature a resolution asserting that right, with assurances that if it were conceded, Ontario would assume the entire burden of direct relief payments. This was passed unanimously. Leslie Frost agreed that provinces were entitled to a share of income tax revenue commensurate with the cost of functions they were expected to perform, but suggested that the only realistic solution to the dislocation of Canadian federalism would lie in a more far-reaching 'readjustment of the taxes or a readjustment of Government responsibilities.' But he cautioned that the provinces, 'in the spirit that brought about Confederation, must have a due sense of responsibility in the national sense and not lend themselves to a situation that would bring about nine separate and strong Provinces and one weak Federal Government.'[31]

Considering its small size, the Tory opposition made a creditable showing in the 1938 session, but the party remained in disarray. One cause of the malaise continued to be Rowe's absentee leadership for, as winter gave way to spring and spring to summer, he had still not announced his retirement. Many felt that his return to the House of Commons and his closeness to the national party establishment encouraged the latter to interfere in provincial party affairs. In March the Queen's Park caucus decided to accept 'no more dictation from Federal Ottawa,' and Macaulay, then attending a Conservative meeting in the capital, was expected to 'speak his mind on the matter of alleged interference by the Federal machine in Ontario party affairs.'[32]

After a long delay arising from objections by the national Conservatives, the annual meeting of the provincial association was held at the Royal York in July. Three candidates for the provincial party presidency were in the field, including Cecil Frost. The one-day session produced acrimonious wrangling and even a brief scuffle on the platform. An eloquent valedictory by Earl Rowe, who now announced his resignation, and a call to arms by Dr R.J. ('Fighting Bob') Manion, newly elected national chief, only momentarily overcame the distemper provoked by the day's events.

There were three chief items of business: reorganization, the draft constitution, and the election of officers. No clearly formulated plans were presented for the reorganization. A start was made on examining the constitution, but parts of it caused so much dispute that discussion had to be suspended to leave time for the election of officers. A disagreement over voting rights aroused the most commotion. The draft constitution stipulated that only accredited delegates to an annual meeting, rather than all paid-up party members, could vote on resolutions and the choice of officers. This reflected a widespread feeling that giving all members the franchise conferred an unfair advantage on Toronto, where the meetings were invariably held, because its residents could attend more conveniently and inexpensively than others. But A.D. McKenzie, a Toronto lawyer and president of the York South Conservative Association, who would later become a major figure in the provincial party, moved that this clause be deleted. He argued that disenfranchising the rank and file would make the party an undemocratic closed corporation. His motion was defeated. When Ontario party president W.H. Ireland ruled that its defeat would stand despite a scrutineer's dissatisfaction with the vote count, there was a howl of protest from one section of the hall. Two delegates leaped to the platform, shouting that it was 'dirty, rotten railroading.' One of them wrested the microphone from the chairman and spoke heatedly into it but his words were drowned out in 'a bedlam of shouts, cheers and catcalls in which the entire meeting indulged.' In the midst of this unedifying rampage another man came to Ireland's rescue, tussling with the angry delegate for possession of the microphone, and shouting 'Disgraceful!' above the din, while the crowd howled with mirth at this comic relief.

After that hullabaloo, the election of officers was an anti-climax. Cecil Frost won easily on the first ballot. He 'was cheered to the echo when he rose to speak,' a reporter wrote, 'cheered again and again as he spoke in a rapid flow of oratory, in which he pictured the party marching to success behind a new Leader and a new President.'[33] He posed for a picture with the outgoing president, Ireland, the outgoing leader, Rowe, and down from Orillia for the occasion, his father, looking trim and spry at seventy-five and smiling from ear to ear at the tribute paid his youngest son. The other politician son, unobtrusively present at the meeting, was not in the picture; this moment belonged to Cecil. His career seemed at that time to be rising toward its zenith.

Some weeks before the leadership convention in early December, one of the two favourites, Leopold Macaulay, withdrew. At once there was speculation that Cecil Frost would become the candidate of the faction, disdainfully termed by the *Globe and Mail* 'the former Rowe machine,' wanting to bar the door to Drew, the principal candidate. Cecil first announced that he would not stand, then that he would consider doing so.

The chief cause of the anti-Drew feeling was undoubtedly his resigning as organizer shortly before the election and running as an independent Conservative. Many believed, correctly, that he was really less interested in provincial politics than in national and international affairs. Since his break with Rowe he had spoken widely in Canada on the major issues of the day and especially on the dangers of communism at home and abroad, going so far as to claim in one speech that 4 per cent of the people of greater Toronto were Communists.[34] In addition, some mistrusted his judgment, especially in the light of his allegations of corruption in the awarding of a federal contract with the John Inglis Company to manufacture Bren guns.[35]

For ten days after agreeing to consider seeking the leadership, Cecil Frost wrestled with the pros and cons. There was his sense of duty to the party, his belief that Drew should not have a clear field without competition, and his confidence that he was up to the job. But weighty personal reasons made him decline to stand. One of his two daughters, eight years old, suffered seriously from epilepsy. She required constant care at home and there was little chance of improvement. The party leadership would add greatly to the burdens of his wife, who would also face heavy social and other obligations, many of which could be discharged only in Toronto. There were also several other constraints to be considered. As leader Cecil would have to hold a seat in the legislature, which would mean that both he and Leslie would be absent from the law office during the sessions. Finally, several experienced political figures advised him that Drew had enough support to secure the leadership.[36]

Having weighed these factors, Cecil decided not to run, citing personal reasons, especially his daughter's poor health, and so informed one of his principal sponsors, J.M. Macdonnell, general manager of the National Trust Company in Toronto. Macdonnell was understanding, if regretful,[37] as were others who had come to know Cecil and the Frost family.

At the convention, which began on 8 December 1938, three men in addition to Drew were candidates for the leadership, but only one, J. Earl Lawson, MP, regarded as the latest choice of the Rowe faction, was taken seriously. Four members of the caucus were said to be Lawson supporters, but Leslie Frost was not one of them. Drew scored an impressive first ballot victory which, in accordance with custom, was formally made unanimous. Addressing him after this had been done as the two men stood together at the microphone, Cecil declared: 'George, we have had a great convention. You are our unanimous choice. Every Conservative is behind you. We dedicate our forces in support of you and this historic party.' And Drew, magnanimous in victory, responded: 'The past is past. We look to the future now.'[38]

4

A Private in the Ranks

While the cracks in the Ontario Conservative party were thus being stuccoed over, the Liberals were encountering serious internal problems, which sprang mainly from Hepburn's mounting hatred of Mackenzie King. Hepburn had made common cause against Ottawa with Maurice Duplessis, a onetime Conservative who had become premier of Quebec in 1936 as leader of the newly formed Union Nationale. But party labels counted for little when it came to choosing sides in the never-ending game of dominion-provincial relations.[1] It was that game, chiefly, that pitted the two Liberal leaders against each other until the outbreak of war in 1939 gave Premier Hepburn new grounds on which to attack the prime minister. But how were the Tories to benefit from this? For the time being their best course seemed to be to refrain from all-out attacks on Hepburn, which might unite his party behind him, and let the Grits go on bickering among themselves.

The opposition could not, however, afford to let itself appear as an uncritical accomplice of the government. It found much to object to, especially in public finance, which Leslie Frost made his major interest. Acting as opposition financial critic, he challenged the characteristically optimistic tone of Hepburn's 1939 budget in a carefully prepared, if pedestrian, speech whose moderate tone and language prompted an appreciative compliment from Hepburn. After the sharp-tongued strictures of Macaulay the year before, Frost's comparatively bland and amiable style must have come as a welcome relief. In fact both the ability and demeanour of the member for Victoria impressed the premier, who was said to have remarked more than once, 'I wish we had that fellow on our side.'[2] In this speech Frost sounded a note of faith and hope that was to become his hallmark. Calling it 'a tragedy that in a young country

such as Canada we should have one-tenth of our population unemployed,' he asserted, 'There should be no unemployment in this
country. We are the natural location for the industrial centre of a
great Empire ... Nothing is beyond our grasp if we act with real
courage and imagination. This presents the real challenge to government and leadership.'[3]

An even greater tragedy and challenge lay in the offing, but
before that was precipitated, Canadians were treated to a royal
visit in the spring of 1939. Nowhere was this first visit by a reigning
monarch hailed more ardently than in Ontario, where loyalty to
the crown found effusive expression among a population still predominantly of British origin. Elaborate plans had been made for
as many people as possible to see King George VI and Queen
Elizabeth, and it was deemed especially desirable that children be
assembled. That aspect of the visit involved Leslie Frost in the kind
of organizing work at which he excelled. The royal train was to
proceed overnight from Ottawa to Toronto, where it was arranged
to have school children from the city and neighbouring counties
congregate on 22 May. Frost helped to organize the junket of his
young constituents from Victoria and Haliburton, and reserved
space for two thousand youngsters at the Riverdale Park parade
site. He enthusiastically oversaw plans to have the children brought
to Toronto by special trains and contributed thirty dollars to help
defray expenses in Haliburton. Among the horde of cheering,
singing small fry from Toronto and the counties of central Ontario
who were herded into the park to greet their sovereign, the contingent from Victoria-Haliburton was the largest from outside the
metropolis.[4]

Two days after Germany invaded Poland on 1 September, Great
Britain declared war on the Third Reich and a week later Canada
followed suit. George Drew at once pledged his party's full support
in furthering Ontario's war effort, and was several times invited by
Hepburn to confer with the cabinet about possible war measures.
At a brief special session of the legislature a War Resources Committee was created, comprising the premier, the leader of the opposition, and the lieutenant-governor. The committee, a 'bizarre
delegation,' Mackenzie King's secretary, J.W. Pickersgill, called it,
was granted a meeting with the prime minister early in October.
There were conflicting versions of what was said at this meeting
but apparently the visitors from Toronto offered Ontario's entire
resources to the cause, along with advice about specific actions
Ottawa should take and complaints that it was not mobilizing the

nation's strength with sufficient vigour.[5] The response from King satisfied neither Hepburn nor Drew, who rejected the doctrine that war preparations were exclusively the federal government's business, although they acknowledged that it must make the crucial decisions. They felt that provincial leaders must goad Ottawa into playing its proper leading role in a situation bound to get much worse.

Frost was entirely in accord with this view of the duty of provincial spokesmen. In September 1939, he wrote: 'this is a much graver crisis for us and for the democratic powers including the United States than that of 1914 ... we cannot afford to contribute less to the defence than our last dollar and our last machine and the last ounce of man-power that we possess ...' Mr. King has always worked on the principle of letting tomorrow cure today's ills and in the present situation this is only emulating the old Asquith policy of "wait and see" which almost made us too late in the last war.' The requirement was 'a National Government ... which would combine the best talents of this country, regardless of politics, with the object of making effective every bit of our national power.'

This objective would be difficult to achieve, given King's overwhelming majority in the House of Commons and the fact that the Tories were 'weak in numbers at Ottawa and I am afraid ... too much actuated by political considerations.' In these circumstances Frost did 'not know where we are to get the public sentiment which will be necessary to make the necessary change and indeed, outside of R.B. Bennett, I do not know where we can get the type of National leadership required.' Perhaps 'a political upheaval in both of the old Parties for a union in Federal politics of people of like mind is the only way.' Only the pressure of public opinion could make that possible and the impetus would have to come from Ontario. 'At the moment Hepburn and Drew appear to be the only ones who would have the slightest chance of effecting such a Dominion movement.' Much depended on whether Robert Manion could be induced to come out for national government. It was politically risky, but Frost asked: 'What does his political life or indeed the life of the Conservative Party matter if the Empire goes down to defeat? Perhaps both Federal and Provincial Conservatives should get together in urging Dr. Manion to give the country the leadership it has to have.'[6]

The idea of a national government was not new. Most recently it had been taken up by the Leadership League, founded by George McCullagh, owner of the *Globe and Mail*, and extravagantly publicized by his paper. It was a well-intentioned manifestation of political fundamentalism directed in part against the corruption and divisiveness of conventional democratic politics. The war made the idea even more attractive to its proponents and undoubtedly added to their numbers. This was notably so in Ontario where many, like Frost, supported it to rescue the nation from the petty partisanship that war conditions made intolerable.

When the Ontario legislature met in January 1940, Hepburn and Drew both expressed regret that Canadians were not taking the struggle seriously enough and implied that Mackenzie King was to blame. 'So far as the leader of the Canadian Government is concerned,' said Hepburn, 'I have not yet been able to provoke him into an open quarrel, although I have tried to do so with great dexterity on frequent occasions.' This caused Drew to comment, 'My only regret is that the Premier has not succeeded in arousing the Prime Minister of Canada ... and I can only wish him better luck next time.'[7] During the session both men berated King for Canada's inadequate war preparations.

Although Frost later complained that Drew showed more interest in national and international issues than in the affairs of Ontario which were his primary responsibility, he fully supported the efforts of Drew and Hepburn early in the war to work up public demand for more energetic direction by Ottawa. He found nothing sinister or unnatural in the Hepburn-Drew alliance. He explained their relationship to his friend Harold Hale, the editor of the *Orillia Packet*:

Hepburn, of course, hates King. The result is that when George enters dominion affairs he finds himself thrown in with Hepburn and ... is accused of ganging up.

The other side of the picture receives but little publicity ... Hepburn and Drew are not in any way personally close together although the people think they are. Drew takes the position that despite the fact that he is accused of conniving with Hepburn ... which, in fact, he is not ... he cannot refrain from taking part in things which he thinks are vital to the welfare of the country.[8]

Frost's one reservation about their attack on the federal government concerned its style, not its purpose; he thought some of their language needlessly personal and strident. This struck him as a poor way of trying to win over those still inclined to trust Mackenzie King. As well, public abuse of the prime minister was apt to boomerang by deepening partisan divisions, whereas the objective was to overcome them.

Frost did believe, however, that thus far there had been a distressing failure to summon the will, energies, and resources of the country effectively. He felt deep emotional ties to the enlisted men, recalling affectionately their fathers with whom he had served in France and readily identifying himself with their needs and problems. On the more intimate, personal level and privately as a lawyer, he did his own small bit to smooth their way. When the war had entered its fourth year he confided to Judge J.A. McGibbon of Lindsay that since September 1939 he had made it a rule not to charge soldiers or returned men for doing their legal work.[9]

Although concerned about Canada's commitment to the war, Frost left public pronouncements on it to others. The one exception was in a 1940 debate when a remark by Colonel Fraser Hunter, MPP, a much-decorated war veteran who sat for one of the Toronto ridings, provoked him. Hunter, a Liberal with a low opinion of Mackenzie King, had declared that 'our people will stand no more Lindsay hierarchies with their trail of graft and waste of young life, its ham and Ross rifles.' Frost rose to defend Lindsay's most famous son, whom he much admired. 'I take strong exception,' he declared with more vehemence than he normally displayed in the House 'to your reference to the Lindsay hierarchies and its obvious implications with regard to the regime of Sir Sam Hughes.' That man's 'courage, vision and vigor of outlook stand like mountain peaks compared to the temperament of those in authority today.' Hunter protested that he had not been thinking of Hughes, whose efforts he agreed had far outshone those of the present federal government, but of Sir Joseph Flavelle, widely regarded as one of the Great War profiteers. It was an implausible disclaimer. Flavelle was a native of Peterborough who became a Toronto meat packer. If he had something to do with ham, he did not with the Ross rifle, to which Hughes was devoted, and Hughes was not 'into' ham other than the kind usually found in the theatre.

Anyway, Hunter continued, Hughes was by no means above reproach. Frost should seek any professional soldier's judgment of him as minister of militia and defence. 'Let me remind you,' Frost retorted, rather stretching the truth, 'that I was a professional soldier.' Sir Sam had at least organized the production of munitions in the early stages of his war, more than could be said for his successors of the present day.[10] The lesson was clear: 'Until we get rid of the Asquiths at Ottawa there will be a shortage of arms.'

This prompted applause from both sides of the aisle in which, however, certain Liberals conspicuously did not join.

Hepburn wound up the debate with a motion that the House associate itself with the premier and the leader of the opposition 'in regretting that the Federal Government ... has made so little effort to prosecute Canada's duty in the war in the vigorous manner the people of Canada desire to see.' As he read, a number of Liberal members, realizing what he was up to and hoping to avoid the expected voice vote at this moment of truth, hurriedly left the chamber. To foil them, Hepburn demanded a formal division, but more than a score of his party refused to heed the summoning bells. Drew could hardly dissociate himself from Hepburn's motion, nor did he or any of his followers want to. When the question was put, ten of the Liberals voted against the motion, while all eighteen Conservatives present, Frost among them, joined with twenty-six Liberals to carry it.[11]

Hepburn's efforts to provoke Mackenzie King had at last succeeded. Parliament was to meet a few days later for the session King had promised Manion would take place to debate war plans and policies. King seized upon the Ontario resolution as a pretext for cancelling that commitment. An immediate dissolution of Parliament was announced in the speech from the throne. Manion led a badly divided party during the resulting election campaign[12] in which the Liberal juggernaut swept all before it. On polling day in March 1940, all but forty of Manion's candidates, running under the banner of National Government, were rejected by the voters.

The electors of Victoria riding voted Liberal by a large majority. It was a rebuke, not only for Cyril MacAlpine, the candidate, but for Frost, who had confined his electioneering to that one constituency. The 1940 verdict was obviously also a severe censure of both Hepburn and Drew who had badly miscalculated the temper of Ontario voters. The Liberals took fifty-seven of the province's eighty-two seats.

Frost did not judge Drew's political error harshly. In response to one observer who urged that Drew should be replaced he wrote: 'I have never felt that political warfare should be so bitter as to create divisions in our people. I do not feel that it is necessary ... I think that any political leader must be prepared to credit his opponents with at least some sincerity. I think our friend, [Drew] whom you mention, is learning this ... I believe that when he combines some of the diplomacy of Sir John A. and Sir Wilfred [sic]

Laurier with his own undoubted ability ... he will make a real contribution to the life of this country.'[13]

Although Manion was soundly beaten and soon retired from the leadership a disillusioned man, the idea of a national government did not die. Its supporters still regarded party politics as divisive and dangerous, particularly after the disastrous collapse of France in June 1940. King's secure political position did not deter the supporters of national government in their pursuit of this will-o'-the-wisp. 'I feel,' Frost wrote to Drew in June, 'that King should at once form a National Government which would be representative of the very best brains and leadership of the country regardless of party colour. We must act as a united people ... if we are to survive at all.'[14]

Many Ontario advocates of national government believed that for the time being it would be prudent to refrain, provincially and nationally, from open partisan warfare. Drew's plan to convene a meeting of the Ontario Conservative Association shortly after the election was put on hold when he saw how badly the national party had fared. He told Cecil Frost: 'The public does not want to hear any arguments as between Liberals and Conservatives at the present time ... The question of the moment is not so much whether we are to be ruled by Liberals or Conservatives but whether we are to be governed by the democratic form of government.' Drew wanted the party organization kept ready for the next provincial election, but it was equally important to avoid 'being charged with playing party politics at the moment of the country's greatest danger.' The party executive agreed with Drew and decided that the annual meeting would be indefinitely postponed.[15] Drew and his supporters would return to the attack at an opportune time.

This declaration of a temporary closed season on Mackenzie King made little or no difference to Leslie Frost's demeanour. As a relatively unknown provincial politician, he knew he would command little attention were he to criticize the conduct of the war. However, Frost still supported the idea of a national government. Steps must be taken, he remarked to Drew, 'to arouse our people from the apathy and complacency into which the Dominion Government has lulled them ... we must impress each one of our citizens of the duty he or she owes to this country.'[16]

Frost supported the creation of a volunteer corps of Home Guards as a psychological weapon with which apathy could be effectively combatted. The spring of 1940 brought the formation of a Home Guard lobby. Lindsay was one of the many centres where agitation for this policy developed, an outcry which had Frost's enthusiastic backing.

While the Department of National Defence dithered about implementing such a scheme, Hepburn, doubtless sensing a chance to embarrass King, announced in June that his government would assist municipalities to form and train a body of civil guards 'to protect property and persons from enemies within and without.' A few days later Hepburn was claiming that 'many Nazi and Fascist sympathizers in the United States are training ... They are only waiting for orders from across the Atlantic to act; to sweep in upon us and lay waste our land.' He appealed to Ontario's able-bodied men 'to act for the protection of their homes and their factories, of their wives and children,' since he had 'no confidence in the Dominion Government being of help to us in the event of such an invasion of our fair province.'[17]

Within a week, however, the King government made such projects superfluous. Its National Resources Mobilization bill provided for the compulsory registration of the citizenry and the conscription of men for home defence, with enlistment for overseas service remaining voluntary. Frost was convinced that Ontario's initiative had hastened Ottawa's decision to depart from its business-as-usual attitude. Although the mobilization bill was good as far as it went, more was needed. 'A war cannot be conducted as a matter of fact business altogether,' he remarked to Drew, who needed no convincing, 'and there has to be patriotism and enthusiasm aroused. In this King is failing and we have to await such dreadful events [the defeat of France by the German army] as the last few weeks before our people are prepared to do anything.'[18]

Frost did not aspire to cut a figure on the national stage. He was content to be a provincial politician whose interests were focused on Queen's Park, not on Parliament Hill. The political truce at Toronto and Drew's warning against the appearance of playing partisan politics in wartime did not obviate the need to keep the provincial party organization in a state of readiness, especially considering Hepburn's mercurial temperament and the constant uncertainty about what he would do next. 'Cecil has undertaken work on the organization throughout the Province,' Drew wrote in the summer of 1941 to Leslie (to whom it would scarcely be news); 'already he has had extraordinarily successful meetings of representatives of the various ridings ... and will be spending his full time on this work and we are confident that by the end of October everything will have been done which can be done in wartime to prepare for whatever may happen.'[19]

While Cecil's frequent absences on party business must have added to the load carried by his brother in the offices of Frost and Frost, Leslie cheerfully did double duty because he acknowledged the importance of good organization. Preparations for the next election had begun in his own district as soon as the ballots were counted in 1937, and he had assiduously kept his fences mended. Like every elected politician, he was bombarded by his constituents with their problems, complaints, and requests for assistance. Much of his time was spent in answering letters from anxious, angry, or hopeful correspondents and in interceding on their behalf with the bureaucracy in Toronto. As well he appeared around the riding at a seemingly endless succession of functions: fall fairs, school concerts and graduations, flower shows, church picnics, service club luncheons, and the like. When he spoke at these affairs it was in the informal, folksy manner of a neighbour among friends. He avoided partisan rhetoric at such gatherings and dwelt on patriotic themes such as the high moral purpose of the war and the need for unremitting effort.

Frost's effectiveness in these activities was aided by his ability to remember faces and to make the association between the name and the place. His friendliness and unassuming manner were not artificial or cultivated for political advantage. He enjoyed meeting people and was genuinely interested in them, where they lived, what they did, whom they knew or were related to, and what concerned them. Jonathan Manthorpe has graphically, if not without a trace of exaggeration, described what it was like to be encountered by Frost.

Meeting Leslie Frost was a physical experience that can be compared to receiving the ministrations of a chiropractor. In a conversation Frost never relied on the pull of his words to keep his audience with him, he preferred to trust the grip of his large bony hands, which maintained their grasp until everything to be said had been said. His cue was the simple introductory handshake, and while his right hand was vigorously squeezing and pumping away, his left hand had taken a firm hold on the upper arm or shoulder of the already slightly bemused person he had met. As the one-sided conversation progressed, Frost, still keeping a firm hold on the right hand, would drape his left arm around his companion's shoulders and start working away at the muscle with his strong blunt fingers. And all the while the kindly, confidential words would come tumbling smoothly out ...

When it was over and Frost had moved on, you felt from your aching muscles that you had done a day's work, and that you had met someone rather extraordinary.[20]

Often he was accompanied by Gertrude, whose manner was in its own way no less engaging than his own. Dropping a kind word here, buying a raffle ticket there, everywhere she showed interest and concern. Occasionally she was tangibly rewarded, as when she won a live lamb in a draw at the Bobcaygeon fair. Even more important, she kept track, especially in Lindsay and its immediate environs, of who was in distress and needed assistance, who deserved and must have some minor patronage. She knew the town and its people intimately and her knowledge was of inestimable value to her husband in keeping him up to date on the local political situation.

These personal contacts enabled him to attract potential party workers, whose names were included in the lists of people, not all of them Conservatives, who might be depended upon to help or whose affiliations were significant. The lists which he compiled were periodically revised to take account of deaths, departures, the discovery of new recruits, or the discarding of doubtful supporters. For example, in the summer of 1941 he wrote to 'Brother' R.J. Smith, secretary of the Haliburton County Orange Lodge, to ask a favour. Frost had joined the lodge in Lindsay, probably for practical political reasons because, although a Protestant and proud of it, he was as devoid of anti-Catholic prejudice as a committed Protestant could be. Would Smith supply him with a list of the Haliburton brethren? 'I always like to keep in touch with our friends in the Order and for some years have kept a pretty accurate list. I find that this is a bit out of date now and I thought perhaps you could send me a list in order that I might correct mine.'[21] A few months later he wrote to a number of the all-important foot soldiers in the constituency, including Arthur Gamble of Lindsay:

Following our telephone conversation, I beg to enclose herewith the following with stamped and addressed envelopes for return when you have completed the same. 1. – Part 1 of the voters' list for South Ward No. 2. 2. – Key list of fifty-nine names of people I can generally count on to help me. These people are not necessarily all Conservatives but include some who would do things for me on personal grounds.

For some time past I have been preparing a list of key people in each sub-division in the riding with the idea that in event of an election I could write to them a personal letter pointing out the difficulty of getting out a vote and asking them as a personal favour if they would vote early and do the best they can to get their friends and neighbours out to do the same thing. This is only an experiment but my belief is that if we were to enlist a large circle of people we would very much minimize work at election time, and at the same time it would put up to a large number of people their duty to take part in political affairs. I believe this is necessary if we are to improve government in Canada.

With the above in view, I wish you would go over this voters' list and place a mark in front of the names of one hundred or more heads of households whom we can reasonably count on to support us. If you would return this to me shortly it would help.[22]

Frost's political strategy encompassed much more than his own riding or even the counties of central Ontario. He was always on the lookout for ways in which the party could improve both its stand on important policy matters and its organization and image throughout the province. Early in 1941 more than two thousand farmers from southwestern Ontario assembled at London in response to an invitation from the federal agriculture minister, J.G. Gardiner, to discuss certain policies of his department which were known to be unpopular. Frost made it his business to be on hand. 'My object,' he told Drew, 'was just to look and listen and see what I could pick up.' The visit confirmed what he had observed in his own district. 'The farmers of the Province are seething with discontent and, of course, they have a lot of real grievances.' Agricultural prices were depressed, partly because of wartime price-fixing by Ottawa; it was almost impossible to hire farm labour because of the higher wages paid in other industries and the diversion of manpower into military service; prices of farm equipment and supplies and taxes had risen substantially. Politically, the farmers' plight was important as it involved an industry which employed or affected 'the largest number of people.'

Frost worried that the Conservative party was ignoring the potential support to be found in rural Ontario. 'There were not very many of our fellows at London,' he noted. 'Most of the farm organizations were represented by people who were not our men.' Such neglect was very short-sighted. 'It seems to me that the agricultural members of the Opposition should be doing everything possible to get into those meetings and organizations and take part in them. Such a course would make a great difference to the future of the Party.' Drew ought to raise the matter at a forthcoming caucus for it 'was out of a similar situation that the U.F.O. came. We may find ourselves in the same boat.'[23]

Frost's advice to Drew was coloured by the problems posed by the recommendations of the Royal Commission on Dominion-Provincial Relations (the Rowell-Sirois Report) to which the Conservative party had to react. Established by the King government, the commission had held public hearings, received research papers and consulted experts before submitting a list of remedies designed to solve the constitutional and financial deadlock between the federal and provincial governments.

The final recommendations were controversial: the commission had proposed that the provinces surrender their fixed annual subsidies and their right to impose personal and corporate income taxes and succession duties. In return, responsibility for unemployment relief and the burden of existing provincial debt should be assumed by the dominion and a system of national adjustment grants created. But Ontario, Alberta, and British Columbia would not receive what they considered their fair share of the adjustment grants. To Drew, however, Frost deplored the public ignorance of the recommendations in the report, which in turn made it difficult to inform Drew on current public opinion. But he pointed out that the Ontario farmers were one group which had exploded indignantly at the pegging of agricultural prices, particularly butter, and here political gains could be made.

In view of the shifting public mood, Frost advised Drew that open opposition to the Rowell-Sirois proposals should be avoided. Instead of passing adverse judgment, 'express willingness while safe-guarding the Ontario tax payer to discuss ... to use your own words "reduction of unnecessary government costs, the avoidance of duplicating services, practical co-operation between all governing bodies and a substantial increase in efficiency." This coupled with better allocation of taxing powers ... would probably be the answer.'[24] Drew withheld his comments and awaited Hepburn's response to the report.

This came immediately following King's opening remarks at the conference in which he recommended approval of the report. Hepburn condemned and ridiculed the scheme and was joined by William Aberhart of Alberta and T.D. Pattullo of British Columbia. That same day King terminated the conference. Drew then asked Frost for his assessment of Lindsay opinion concerning Hepburn's performance. Frost replied that he still believed 'that the attitude of reasonable co-operation is the best.' The problems disclosed by the report could form the basis of discussions. This approach would seem reasonable to the public in Lindsay whose opinions he summarized as follows:

1. The man on the street does not know anything about the Sirois Report.
2. Hepburn's wisecracks have taken hold to a considerable extent and have influenced the large body of the public, both liberal and conservative, against the Report.
3. As always sectional and immediate interests seem to have more sway with people than the long view. Mowat always carried the Province on Provincial Rights.
4. Everyone recognizes that there are problems although they do not know clearly what they are. They can see no reason why these should not be discussed and to this extent I think Hepburn's attitude may react against him.
5. There is a great appeal at the present time in talking to the people about cutting out duplications, avoiding needless taxation. Strange to say, however, the public mind does not view the Sirois Report as a method of attaining this, but is rather inclined to the point of view that Ontario is going to get soaked.[25]

Frost's reservations about the report and his opinion that it nevertheless deserved more considerate examination than Hepburn had been willing to give it were shared by much of Ontario's press. The bitter reaction of the *Globe and Mail*, which at one time had expected a lot of Hepburn, was especially noteworthy and reflected George McCullagh's general disillusionment with politicians. Alas, the *Globe* summed up gloomily, 'we are led by pygmies whose minds are perpetually occupied with calculations concerning the wet vote, the dry vote, the Orange vote, the Catholic vote, the labor vote, the farm vote or some scheme for redistributing seats so that the popular will may be misrepresented instead of truly represented in the legislatures.'[26]

After the Ontario CCF denounced Hepburn for scuttling the conference, it was Drew's turn to speak out on behalf of his party. For several days, though, he refrained. To attack Hepburn's conduct might threaten the political truce in Ontario and provoke an election which Drew preferred to avoid at that time. If the assessment of public opinion provided by Frost (and presumably others) was correct, it might be unwise, if not fatal, to criticize Hepburn openly or appear to be aligned against him with Mackenzie King, for whom Drew felt a contempt equal to Hepburn's own. Since federal and provincial Grits seemed eager to make war on each other, what advantage would the Tories derive from coming down firmly on one side or the other? When Drew did at last, a week after the conference, make passing reference to the subject in a speech devoted mainly to the need for universal military training, it was so oblique as to leave everyone in the dark as to what he thought of the report and Hepburn's cavalier dismissal of it. 'Let us,' he said, 'show our friends and our enemies as well that in this hour of trial Canada is united and strong for the task which lies ahead. The pitiful disputes which have diverted our attention from the supreme task of preparing for war should be forgotten as quickly as possible.'[27]

Speculation that Hepburn might call a snap election over provincial rights was rife once he and his attendants had packed their bags and left Ottawa. He quickly tried to squelch such talk. The province could not afford the 'luxury' of a general election, which would cost as much as seven or eight squadrons of Spitfires. When the House met in February Drew chided Hepburn for his parochial stand at Ottawa. He was not arguing for adoption of the Rowell-Sirois proposals, Drew stressed, only that the conference could have 'done a great deal of good and laid the foundations for future co-operation by agreeing on some method of tackling our problems.' Ontario should request a new meeting for that purpose. Frost endorsed Drew's proposal when it was his turn to speak. Characteristically leavening criticism with flattery, he observed that the premier had missed 'a great opportunity to give leadership to the people of Canada. If he had used his personality, and he has a great personality, he would have done a lot towards improving conditions.'[28]

As usual, however, Frost had devoted most of his attention in preparing for the session to the state of Ontario's finances. Hepburn was in the habit of presenting budget statements purporting to show yearly operating surpluses and the benefits of sound, economical administration. These were prepared by Chester Walters, the deputy provincial treasurer. Walters was not an economist – there were no professional economists in the full-time employ of the government at that time – but an accountant who had formerly held a senior position in the income tax branch of the federal Revenue Department. When it became known after the 1929 stock market crash that he had incurred large debts by over-extending himself in speculative investments, he was forced out of that position. For this he blamed Mackenzie King, against whom he developed an intense animus that made him a natural ally of Hepburn as the latter's deputy.[29]

Hepburn's basic assertion was that prudent husbandry made Ontario's position secure, and that since his province was well able to manage under the existing division of taxing powers, others ought to be able to do the same. Frost was convinced that the actual situation, hidden from view, was a great deal less sanguine. Getting at the facts was not easy, and in this he had by 1941 come to rely less on the small civil service in the Treasury Department than on a private agency, the Citizens' Research Institute of Canada. Responding to an invitation to subscribe to its 'Source-Brief Service,' a compilation of tax and financial information, Frost had inquired whether it could supply him with some comparative statistics and these were soon forthcoming with a covering letter from George A. Gathercole. This was apparently his first contact with a man upon whom he was later, as premier and provincial treasurer, to rely for advice on economic and financial policy.[30] He found the data from the institute very useful in buttressing his conviction that Ontario's actual financial position was rather different from that depicted in the yearly Hepburn-Walters presentations.

Frost felt frustrated that the major metropolitan newspapers accepted the government's accounting at face value. 'It is amazing,' Frost complained to Harold Hale, 'the extent to which Mr. Hepburn is permitted to misrepresent things to the public ... Any criticisms which the Opposition advance are usually either not printed or are so obscurely printed by the large Toronto papers that the public never gets them ... The Toronto dailies have taken Mr. Hepburn's talk about pay as you go and economy for gospel. This may be because they want to place him in the best light possible. Personally I think it is because they simply do not know.' Nor, evidently, could they be bothered finding out. 'The majority of Ontario newspapers have made little or no study of Ontario's financial position with the result that Hepburn is able to get away with his glib and inaccurate statements to the most amazing extent ... generally they are only interested in wise-cracks and smart statements.'

Current provincial taxes, Frost pointed out to Hale, were the highest since Confederation, and Hepburn had imposed heavier new taxation than any of his predecessors. Because of this, annual net revenue had risen by 75 per cent since 1934. During the same period, though, owing to greatly increased cost of government, the net dead-weight debt of the province, which must be serviced and would eventually have to be discharged out of tax revenues, had mounted by more than 40 per cent. It now stood at over $500 million, a record high. In the light of this, for Hepburn to talk smoothly about Ontario balancing its budget and paying its own way, as he had at Ottawa, was nonsense.

There would be a sunshine budget in 1941, Frost predicted. Thanks to buoyant revenues, lower relief costs, and cutting highway construction and maintenance to the bone, Hepburn would probably be able to show an operating surplus and announce a reduction in net debt. The people, Frost remarked glumly, 'will think that Hepburn is doing a wonderful job ... the fact is he is just about as bad as [George] Henry and goodness knows that was bad enough.' Perhaps Hale would like to take up the cudgels in his *Packet and Times* against these misrepresentations. This might encourage other small-town papers to follow suit and thus offset the unbalanced treatment of financial matters by the big city dailies.[31] Frost himself did his best to assist in this, drafting an editorial on the Ontario budget which was printed in Lindsay's *Watchman-Warder* soon after Hepburn brought down his latest bundle of good news in the middle of March.[32]

It was truly a sunshine budget which reported surpluses and promised that there would be no new taxes and no borrowing, other than to refinance debts coming due. During the budget debate Frost read a speech of eleven foolscap pages, but his criticism did not impress the media and a somnolent public did not react at all.[33]

J.L. Ilsley, the federal finance minister, brought down his own budget at the end of April. Thwarted in his hope of having the most lucrative direct taxes assigned exclusively to the dominion, and rejecting as ruinously inflationary the notion that Ottawa's revenue needs could be met by increasing the money supply, as Hepburn had argued, Ilsley persisted in his efforts to have the provinces relinquish for the duration of the war their right to levy personal and business income taxes. He proposed that in return they be paid subsidies equal to the amounts those tax fields had produced in 1940. All provinces save Ontario quickly accepted the offer.[34]

There was speculation that Hepburn might decide to call an election on this issue. Frost believed, however, that Hepburn had been neatly boxed into a corner from which his only escape lay in signing the agreement. This was not going to be a popular election issue when the international situation was uppermost in people's minds. Although Hepburn might not like having to forgo income taxes, the alternative was to subject taxpayers to both provincial and sharply increased federal levies, a course which would antagonize the voters. 'It is going to be pretty hard,' Frost noted, 'for Hepburn to raise a Provincial Rights cry in view of the fact that it will mean that we will have in effect double taxation if this should prevail.'[35] Hepburn read the situation in much the same way. In the summer of 1941 he reluctantly accepted the tax rental agreement in principle, and after protracted and acrimonious discussions between Toronto and Ottawa about its precise terms, the matter was at last settled in the late winter of 1942.

Meanwhile, the legislature unanimously agreed to extend its own life for one year, thus avoiding the dissolution that would otherwise have had to take place in 1942. On the whole this was a relief to government and opposition alike, and not only because their respective leaders had so often stated their aversion to the distraction of a wartime election. Frost had earlier cabled Drew, then visiting England, urging him to make it known that 'while Hepburn goverment open to serious criticisms ... war effort demands Ontario be spared election. Consent if necessary to extension [of legislative term] offering constructive criticism meantime.'[36]

The war was not, however, all that made avoiding an election seem desirable to the Conservatives; so did their own prospects. Their national party was in disarray, projecting an image of confused, aimless impotence that might prove a detriment in an Ontario election. Moreover, there was little reason to think that the Tories could defeat Hepburn. They lacked a compelling issue on which to attack the government. As the *Globe and Mail* accurately put it shortly before the extension was approved, the Ontario Tories 'would prefer to see the Liberal regime remain in office for one more year rather than face an immediate general election with the more than likely prospect of seeing the Liberals go back to power for another five years.'[37]

5

'Something to Fight and Cheer For'

With the lull on the provincial front, a great deal of theoretical talk was going on about the future of Canadian politics and the place the Conservative party should occupy in the political life of the country. The leading spirit in this inquiry was J.M. Macdonnell, who along with both Frost brothers, believed that a significant shift to the left in public attitudes was being signalled by a marked rise in the popularity of the CCF. In various magazine articles and speeches, Macdonnell tried to stimulate discussion and to point the way to a new Conservatism which would address new issues.

Leslie Frost was also reassessing the party's objectives. His thoughts, expressed in a number of letters and pertaining in part to the national scene, in part to the provincial, reflected what he thought most important, the feelings of the 'ordinary' citizen. His views were not very fully or systematically developed. Political theory was not his long suit and there were practical as well as theoretical difficulties in his ideas that do not seem to have occurred to him. His support of a national government reflected an abhorrence of artificial divisions among the people. This could lead to a state dominated by a massive 'government party' controlling the broad centre of the spectrum, with room on the fringes for splinter parties representing dissenting minority opinions. In some ways they foretold the course he pursued after 1949 as leader of his party (which he liked to think of as 'the people's party') and as premier. He wrote to Harold Hale in February 1942 that 'we are living in a new world in which straight thinking and courageous action is [*sic*] needed.' He had 'rather come to the conclusion that the days of the Liberal and ... Conservative Parties, as at present constituted, are numbered' and that 'a new party alignment is imminent.' In Ontario there was 'actually no difference between the ordinary Liberal and the ordinary Conservative; both are becoming supremely disgusted and they are beginning to realize that they are cancelling each others [sic] votes and allowing one minority or another always to dominate the situation. I think a real shake-up is overdue.'¹ It was to become clear that the minorities he had chiefly in mind were the socialists of the CCF and the French Canadians.

In early July 1942 Frost elaborated on these thoughts in another letter to Hale and two long missives to George Drew. His opinions about French-Canadian influence were confided to Harold Hale:

In this country we are faced with a very difficult situation with the Quebec people. This centres around the language difficulty and their unreasonable isolationist position ... I really wonder as to where their sympathies lie and ... whether they think victory or defeat [in the war] would help most in the creation of a French state ... I have come to the conclusion that there has been enough appeasement in that direction and that it has reached the stage where so-called national unity will be harmed if there are further concessions. Taking the broad view, the North American continent is English speaking and it is in that mold that our ways are cast. The language difficulty if extended beyond Quebec is bound to create friction and trouble in the future.

If political leaders would act 'in the proper way' in developing Canada, the country could support thirty or forty million people in prosperity for the next century.

We are so hampered by timidity, log-rolling and compromise on the part of our political parties that there is not much direction, just apology. Without strong direction ... this country may break up and the western part go in with the States ... even in the Province of Ontario and in high places there is an amazing change of sentiment along these lines. The events of the last few years have brought the British and American people so closely [sic] together that there can be little doubt now that American and British international policies are going to be identical and about the only place in the North American continent where isolationism will continue will probably be the Province of Quebec.²

In writing to Drew in mid July, Frost concentrated more on the threat from the CCF, arguing that its growing popularity made a reordering of Conservative policy imperative. Ordinarily he would agree that an opposition party should avoid enunciating a detailed specific platform but 'a new world is going to come out of the present war.' The CCF was 'going to be extremely radical and as a new movement they are going to have a very definite appeal, particularly in view of the present dissatisfied state of the public mind.' For the man in the street there is a feeling 'that there are many things in our democratic system which need changing and that we have not been making the best of our opportunities.' The old parties would be blamed for this, to the benefit of the CCF, but it afforded 'an excellent field for a new, moderate party brought about by a fusion of the best elements' of both the old ones. 'The fact is that the sound people of the Dominion are divided by politics with the result that one minority or another usually runs things.' In any event, 'the Conservative Party must bring itself in line with new world conditions. Many of the old policies of the past have gone by the boards.'

Frost then sketched for Drew the kind of platform he would like to see. It touched a lot of bases. Farmers wanted and should be promised 'some control over processing and marketing their products.' Labour and capital ought to be thought of as partners, labour organization be encouraged, collective bargaining be recognized, and workers be free to join the union of their choice. Individual enterprise must be stimulated but 'extremes between wealth and poverty ... leveled by means of taxation,' which would furnish social capital for housing and other needed public works. 'Every person should not only have the opportunity but the duty to engage in useful work. But the non-contributory nature of social service programs 'has an undermining effect on public morals. One could not say this too openly for fear of being misunderstood, but ... through non-contributory old age pensions, mothers' allowances, unemployment relief, etc. we have tended to instill into people the feeling that the country owes them a living.'

There was more. Education should inculcate 'a national point of view ... in the minds of our young people,' and 'national rights should be above the rights of the individual ... I fail to see how Canada can exist in the world if her people are not determined to regard the country's interest on every standpoint as being paramount. We have to very considerably alter our democratic view in this regard.' After mentioning public health insurance, public housing, and low-interest government loans as other items worth including in a platform, Frost concluded by expressing doubt that 'we can afford to wait. The country is looking for dynamic leadership.' There had to be 'a new idea of the development of this country ... which will give the people something to fight and cheer for and the feeling that they are not fighting for a return to the old conditions of unemployment, depression ... political log-rolling and incompetency which mark the course of things in the past.'[3]

There was no response from Drew to this letter, so a fortnight later Frost renewed his argument for a realignment of parties. In the mean time, Macdonnell had published three articles in *Saturday Night* about the future of the Conservative party.[4] His prescription was not a fusion of right-minded Grits and Tories, but a reformed, updated, and rejuvenated Conservatism pledged to restore and safeguard individual freedom and parliamentary government which, paradoxically, were undermined in a war to preserve freedom. The party must become an attractive, credible alternative government that did not 'propose to deal with new and formidable problems by a mere prescription of old remedies.' In particular, Conservatives would have to admit the need for an expanded state role in economic planning and social security.

Frost perused these articles with intense interest but, although at some points there was a meeting of minds, he was not greatly impressed by their approach. After reading them he wrote another long letter to Drew, the fullest exposition of his ideas so far. Overshadowing all else was 'the possibility of absolute defeat in this war ... In addition, however, we face the tremendous task of reconstructing this country in a new world.' Many people doubted whether this could be done without a new alignment of parties. 'In this province, for instance, Liberals and Conservatives, Catholics and Protestants alike think practically in the same way; our interests are in common, but we are divided by party tags and old prejudices ... with the result that we cannot pull with our full weight.' In Ottawa, there was 'compromise of all kinds in an effort to satisfy ... minorities, racial, financial, class, etc.'

Frost was inclined to regard as nonsense talk about reviving 'the old Conservative Party with its present representation at Ottawa and the jealousies which divide it.' The party had some good men in Parliament, such as Howard Green and John Diefenbaker, 'but I doubt whether there is anyone there who can fire the imagination of this country in a way which will be sufficient.' Should the Tories gain power, it would 'be because they have elected sufficient French Canadian followers to pretty well dominate things, and I fail to see where that will improve things very much.' In Ontario, the provincial Tories and Grits should unite in a government that would include 'the best representatives of labour, agriculture and business with policy somewhat more radical' than Macdonnell had suggested and a 'new party organization which would take the place of both the Liberal and Conservative organizations.' Such a solidly based regime in Ontario would be able to press effectively for changes federally 'and start at once organizing for a new state of affairs in Ottawa.'

Drew would not find it easy, Frost conceded, to propose such a plan but it would attract widespread support. The *Globe and Mail* and *Telegram* were sympathetic to the idea and 'the rank and file of people would welcome it.' The national Conservative party was too ridden with jealousies, too lacking in purpose and leadership, to give Canada the kind of direction it needed. The CCF was 'too much founded on class' and anyway most of its 'ammunition ... would be taken by a new centre or unionist party.' He would not turn a blind eye, Frost wrote, to any practicable alternative to his proposal, but 'I cannot see one that is remotely feasible.' The impracticability of his own plan seems not to have occurred to him![5]

This time Drew responded, but only in general terms. 'Thank God,' he wrote, 'there are those like yourself who are seeing and thinking ... Your letter was one of the most refreshing I have read after the disappointing evidence of utter incompetence which has come to us from Ottawa. There seems to be no appreciation whatever of the point which you make ... that we do face the possibility of defeat in this war.' As for Frost's ideas about the changed shape of things to come, Drew agreed 'that we must accept a complete revolution in thinking and attitude of our people. An epoch has ended. These are not idle words.' He would prefer to leave until they met a detailed discussion of the points raised by Frost, who should not hesitate to put his thoughts on paper.[6] But nothing came of Frost's plan. He would have to await another day to apply his ideas in his own way.

Frost's concerns about the war led him to write many letters on national themes, but generally, as he explained to Harold Hale, he took the position that he was 'a provincial member ... I find that people are not interested in provincial matters very much, although I have endeavoured to confine myself largely to these things.'[7] Drew, however, was embroiled in a fierce row with the King government during the spring and summer of 1942, which illustrated what Frost termed the principal difficulty with Drew – 'getting him to at least largely confine himself to the sphere in which he should be interested, provincial politics.'[8]

The furor began when Drew charged in a radio talk that the two Canadian battalions sent to bolster the defence of Hong Kong, all

of whose members were either killed or captured in the spectacular
Japanese sweep around the perimeter of southeast Asia, had been
untrained and improperly exposed to danger. The King government
appointed Sir Lyman Duff, chief justice of Canada, to investigate
the charge. His report, made public in the spring of 1942, largely
exonerated the government, which was promptly attacked by Drew
for having denied the chief justice 'very serious information' and
withholding some 'blood-curdling facts.'

The government's response to this was severe. The minister of
justice, Louis St Laurent, ordered Drew charged with violating the
Defence of Canada Regulations on the ground that his remarks
were likely to discourage recruiting. An astounded Cecil Frost assured Drew that the words complained of were 'not subversive,
(only critical),' but he offered a bit of advice: 'In all future statements be sure to make it clear that your words of criticism were
uttered for the purpose of preventing future mistakes and inefficiency and ... not for the purpose of adding worry to the parents of
the boys in Hong Kong. The term "blood curdling" is but another
way of saying "appalling" and I presume you had every reason to
be appalled.'⁹ To Leslie Frost the incident suggested that 'George
is something like Sir Charles Tupper. He is lacking in humour and
is altogether too severe with his political opponents. He should
follow Sir Robert Borden's advice and generally speaking never
treat a political opponent so roughly as to prevent him some day
from being a friend ... Politics makes strange bed-fellows and in
the course of time new alignments are made and oftimes [sic] political enemies on one day become allies later on.'¹⁰

Drew was never tried, much less convicted. Three weeks after
laying the charge, the government withdrew it. Seeing this retreat,
Drew renewed his offensive. He fired off a blistering letter to the
prime minister, 'a perfectly appalling communication,' King complained in his diary. 'I have never read a more extreme or dangerous type of letter.'¹¹ King and his cabinet were not alone in being
put off by the tone and substance of Drew's attack. The 'doves' in
the Ottawa Conservative caucus, comprising probably a majority,
shied away from supporting his strictures on the government and
the Duff report, and were inclined to view the Hong Kong disaster
simply as part of the tragic but unavoidable fortunes of war. The
'hawks' in the caucus held a decidedly different view; they wanted
Drew supported to the hilt.¹²

Those internal caucus divisions were, however, more profound
than mere personal jealousies or disagreements over the proper

conduct of an opposition in wartime. They concerned also what the party should be, and where it should stand when next presenting itself to the electorate. To resolve this dilemma, J.M. Macdonnell quietly promoted holding a 'laymen's' conference, and was supported by a group consisting of Dana Porter, Roland Michener, David J. Walker, and Donald Fleming, all good Conservatives holding no public office. They enlisted the help in organizing it of R.K. Finlayson, who had been executive assistant to Prime Minister Bennett, and later of Cecil Frost. The conference, Macdonnell wrote with exaggerated but becoming modesty to Leslie Frost long after the event, 'owed everything to these two.'[13] It was decided to stage it at Trinity College School, Port Hope.

Although it was somewhat irregular for a group outside the Conservative parliamentary establishment to organize such an event, the conference proceeded on schedule. After three days of strenuous discussion, the laymen approved a program that tried to reconcile faith in free enterprise with recognition of the need for a more active government role in economic planning and regulation, and in the achievement of social security. It called for conscription for overseas service, mutual toleration by French- and English-speaking Canadians, a close post-war relationship between the British Commonwealth and the United States, and international economic co-operation. It undertook to update Conservative positions, especially on agriculture, industrial relations, and social welfare. It advocated agricultural credits and debt adjustment, aid to east and west coast fisheries, compulsory collective bargaining, and recognition of labour's right to free association. It demanded guaranteed employment with wages sufficient to support a home and family; and supported low-cost housing, slum clearance, and federal aid to education; unemployment and retirement insurance, more generous old age pensions, adequate allowances for mothers and widows, and a contributory national health plan. The social security proposals outraged old-fashioned Conservatives, for they implied rejection of the individualist ethic and a growing disposition to rely upon action by the state.

The Port Hope manifesto accorded in some ways with the policy suggestions Leslie Frost had put to Drew, although his eye had been mainly on the provincial field. 'What is needed,' Frost observed to Hale not long after Port Hope, 'is some leader with the imagination, fervour and personal appeal who will really believe in the general principles and be prepared to carry them into effect ... King drifts along behind public opinion as he has always done with very considerable success. The other people are providing no inspiration or leadership and the man does not seem to be in sight. At the time of this great crisis this may be fatal to our country.'[14]

On the provincial front during the summer of 1942, Hepburn seemed to be sailing a more and more erratic course. His attacks on Mackenzie King and the federal government grew increasingly violent and unrestrained. From the Tories' viewpoint this was not unwelcome, partly because they thought the chiding of Ottawa largely deserved, partly because the cleavage in their opponents' ranks was becoming ever deeper. Hepburn's attacks on King for his handling of the legal status of the Communist party did cause some disquiet, however, on the Conservative side, especially for Drew.

In June 1940 the federal government by order-in-council had banned the Communist party. A number of its prominent figures were arrested and interned but some others escaped, either by going underground or, like their leader, Tim Buck, fleeing to the United States. Following the German invasion of Russia in 1941, there were mounting demands by people of widely differing political persuasions that, inasmuch as Canada and the Soviet Union were now allies, the ban should be lifted and the imprisoned communists freed. The government refused, and warrants for the arrest of the fugitives remained in force. In September the wanted men suddenly gave themselves up to the RCMP and were lodged in Toronto's Don Jail. At this juncture Hepburn joined the chorus urging removal of the ban and release of the prisoners. This caused a good deal of puzzlement. Had he simply seized a new stick with which to belabour Mackenzie King, or was he now overcome by the pro-Russian sentiment which the heroic defence of Stalingrad had aroused? Was he posing as a civil libertarian and friend of labour in the hope of countering the rising popularity of the CCF?

Drew, a fierce foe of communism, did not know what to make of this but it bothered him. It looked to him, he told Frost, as though Hepburn was 'trying to curry favour with strange companions.' Possibly the ban on the Communist party should be lifted but it would be foolish to suppose that Buck and his friends would be of help in the war effort or that the demand for their release would gain general approval. Still, it would be unfortunate 'if sympathy and admiration for the Russian people carried itself to the point of believing that Communism itself is any different to what it was before Germany attacked Russia.'

Frost's view was that Buck and his followers were trying to capitalize on Canadians' ambivalent feelings about communism and Russia. 'I think that Hepburn is opposed to allowing these people to make martyrs of themselves and to be proud in the publics [*sic*] eyes. Therefore, he requested that they be released and I must admit that I am inclined to that view.' It would be better to free them than to permit them 'to make martyrs of themselves and thus cause a great division in public feeling here as well as misunderstanding in Russia.' In fact, Frost did not consider communism as dangerous as Drew did.

Drew indicated that he would not comment publicly on this issue. Were he to land on Hepburn's side, it would be interpreted as an effort to embarrass the minister of justice, 'something which I shall certainly do in a more direct way when the time comes.' St Laurent was in a tough spot, it seemed to Drew. If he freed the men and rescinded the ban on their party, he would antagonize his own province; a refusal to do so would be widely regarded as a surrender to Quebec opinion.[15] In any event, the immediate problem was presently resolved by an illogical compromise: the prisoners were released but the legal prohibition of their party remained.

Public surprise over the Buck affair was tempered by its astonishment a few weeks later when, without warning his caucus or consulting most of his cabinet, Hepburn resigned the premiership and advised the lieutenant-governor to call on the attorney general, Gordon Conant, to take his place. After a short interval he agreed to Conant's request that he stay on for a time as provincial treasurer. There was much resentment of the high-handed way in which he had chosen his successor and suspicion, as the *Toronto Star* unkindly put it, 'that he had it in mind to play Bergen to Mr. Conant's Charlie McCarthy.' Two ministers, Harry Nixon and Farquhar Oliver, both of whom had earlier rejected Hepburn's offer of the premiership, promptly registered their objections by resigning from the cabinet.

Frost was amazed by this turn of events. Only a month previously he had introduced Hepburn to an audience at the Lindsay Central Exhibition as 'a generous opponent,' a 'swell fellow,' a 'great showman,' and 'great Canadian' who 'told us fearlessly – early – that this [war] was a fight for survival.'[16] The premier had given no inkling then of an intention to step down. Upon learning that he had done so, Frost addressed a friendly note to 'Dear Mitch,' describing what he prematurely considered a retirement from politics as 'a great loss to Canada.' From the outset Hepburn had been 'one of the few who had the war situation properly sized up.' Canadians would some day thank him for having the 'courage and forcefulness ... to tell people the truth.'[17]

The same mail that carried Frost's compliments to Hepburn also conveyed his congratulations to Conant. He had had more to do with the new premier than most on the opposition side. Conant had invited him to serve on a law revision committee, and Frost had been Conant's chief ally in getting one of the select committee's proposals, that women be allowed to do jury duty, approved by the legislature against objectors in both parties.[18]

Frost's good wishes to Conant were sincere for he respected his good intentions and devotion to duty. He accompanied them, however, with some gratuitous remarks about which there was an unmistakable air of self-importance.

In our party set-up I, of course, am on the other side of things as an opposition member in these extremely difficult and trying days. I have endeavoured to be a constructive critic. I have opposed those things that I did not agree with but I have supported every measure in which I thought there was merit. I promise you that this will be my attitude in the future. We are living in most difficult times and it is going to need the best efforts of us all to bring Canada through. The leader of a government in this province has very great and onerous responsibilities. I shall certainly support legislation which may be sponsored by your administration or by anyone else which I believe to be in the best interests of the people. In opposition I shall endeavour to be constructive. I think this is the position an opposition member should take in these days when everything is at stake.[19]

Frost's goodwill to his opponent did not blunt his determination to advance the Conservative party's interests. 'The Grits,' he wrote to his friend George Challies, 'have certainly got themselves into a queer fix.' Drew 'would be well advised to disregard their quarrelling and fighting and come out with a very fine platform which would give our people something to hope for. With their party divided as it is it should be no trick to win the next election.'[20]

Frost's attention was diverted from the provincial scene by the national Conservative convention which was to begin in Winnipeg on 9 December 1942. Cecil was the chairman of the resolutions and policy committee for this gathering, a task which took up much of his time in the autumn of 1942. Leslie must have been aware that John Bracken was the favoured candidate of the party establishment to succeed Arthur Meighen. But when a Gallup poll indicated that Drew was the most popular candidate, Frost wrote to the latter that he 'was very glad indeed to see the result of the gallop [sic] poll as far as you were concerned ... if you decide to let your name go before the Convention I will most certainly support you. I would hate, however, to see you leave the Ontario field.'[21] Drew, however, declined to run.

Although Leslie was concerned about neglecting his legal work, he decided to attend the convention in Winnipeg. As it turned out, it was an exciting affair. Bracken's intentions were still far from clear when the proceedings opened. He held back even after seeing in advance the resolutions drafted by Cecil's committee, which adhered faithfully to the Port Hope declaration. Bracken's nomination papers were filed at the last minute, and on the second ballot a majority of delegates, including Leslie Frost, voted for him. The convention then approved Bracken's demand that the party's name be changed to Progressive Conservative.[22] Equipped with a new title, a new chieftain, a forward-looking platform, and a revised organizational structure, the party optimistically awaited the next national election.

Having assisted inconspicuously in all this, Leslie Frost hastened home to concentrate on his immediate political objective – victory in the provincial contest that seemed sure to take place before long. Drew now appeared ready to devote himself to his duties as provincial leader and Frost was eager to help prepare for the fray.

The Liberals' problems did not diminish after Gordon Conant assumed the premiership. The movement to supplant him gained momentum, and it was decided to hold a leadership convention in late April of 1943. Harry Nixon was the choice of the anti-Hepburn, anti-Conant element in the party's provincial and federal wings. In this beleaguered state, Conant summoned the legislature in February. When Conant, after consulting his caucus, introduced a motion extending the legislature's life for a further year, it was carried, with all the Conservatives and eight Liberal bolters opposing it. How long it would remain in effect depended, of course, on the actions of the new Liberal leader. As expected, Nixon was the convention's choice at the April meeting and shortly after he became premier. He was the only one never to meet the House while holding that office, as late in June he announced an election for 4 August 1943.

Drew at once attacked this decision. Dissolving the legislature in such haste, he charged, had been done on orders from Ottawa and at the worst possible time. Intimations had come from various sources, including Winston Churchill, of an imminent Allied invasion of Europe, which in fact began in Sicily with Canadian troops participating less than a fortnight after the election was called. It was wrong, said Drew, to cause turmoil 'while the families and friends of our fighting men and women overseas wait anxiously, hour by hour, for word of the mighty offensive in which so many of them will be engaged,' and also at a time when farmers 'will be working to the breaking point and beyond so that our war requirements of food may be supplied.'[23] There was a slightly hollow ring in much of this since, as Nixon quickly pointed out, the Tories had opposed a second extension of the legislative term. Drew's statement contained, however, a claim that was to figure prominently in his party's campaign: that Nixon was a puppet of the federal government.

As the campaign developed, the Conservatives attacked the Liberal regime on that and numerous other counts, but their main thrust was their new platform, which Drew unveiled in a radio talk on 8 July. Here was the very fine platform Frost had so much wanted, a twenty-two point manifesto which, as the *Toronto Star* observed in giving parts of it grudging approval, promised something for everyone.[24] The length and comprehensiveness of the document as published in full suggested that it had been in preparation for some time.

Yet, despite Frost's claim in a radio broadcast that the platform was based on resolutions moved in the House and reviewed by the caucus, he and the other MPPs appear to have played no real part in putting it together. It was Drew's handiwork, possibly in consultation with a few of his trusted friends outside the House. According to Fred Gardiner, Cecil Frost, still provincial party president, knew nothing of it until the two of them, driving to a nomination meeting, heard Drew announce it over the radio. If that was true, Leslie, one of Drew's principal caucus lieutenants, was either similarly uninformed or had refrained from discussing it with his brother, a scarcely credible possibility.[25] But he left no complaint on the record about being excluded from the drafting process and embraced the platform in his public remarks as warmly as if he had composed it single-handed. The declaration would not have been very different had he done so.[26]

The platform touched upon almost all subjects within provincial jurisdiction. There would be co-operation with other governments in the prosecution of the war and, while insisting on the province's constitutional rights, in creating a 'sound basis of social security, health insurance and protection in their old age for all our people.' A Conservative government would assist all sectors of the economy to increase employment at good wages. 'In every field of employment individual initiative will be encouraged and hard work rewarded by reducing taxes and removing bureaucratic restrictions.' Stockyards would be brought under public ownership and farming 'organized in every county under committees of outstanding farmers who will be given authority to plan production ... processing and distribution of their output.' Labour's right to collective bargaining was to be guaranteed and a labour relations committee formed to advise in framing 'the fairest and most advanced' legislation in that field. Mining and forestry were not forgotten. The former would benefit from lower taxes and other assistance, and be 'placed under the direction of a Minister with practical knowledge of mining.' A forest resources commission was promised to oversee conservation, reforestation and soil control. Another commission would plan a housing program to improve standards and stimulate employment in the construction industry once the war ended.

One of the most attractive and widely discussed commitments concerned property taxes: 'There will be a sweeping revision of our whole system of real estate taxation so that the owning and improvement of homes and farm land ... will not be discouraged by excessive taxation. As an initial step in that direction the Provincial Government will assume at least 50% of the school taxes now charged against real estate. It is however to be clearly understood that this change will not affect the authority of the local school boards.' Moreover, under a Drew government all children would be educated 'to the full extent of their mental capacity no matter where they live or what the financial circumstances of their parents may be.'

There was more. Removal of the Hydro-Electric Power Commission from political control was promised, as were equitable power rate adjustments, the acceleration of rural electrification, and elimination of the service charge to rural customers. Representative citizen committees representing labour and veterans would assure 'adequate supplies at reasonable prices' of fuel, milk, and other basic necessities. Finally, there would be a rehabilitation and social security committee to draft plans for affording social security to all, and to assist in retraining veterans and munitions workers for peacetime employment.[27]

It was hoped that such an attractive platform would attract good candidates in constituencies where nominations were still to be made. No less important was a smoothly functioning organization. In the spring of 1943 Drew had made A.D. McKenzie, long active in the party, chief organizer, a duty Cecil Frost had until then combined with those of association president. Blessed with a sharp mind, a lively wit, an impressive command of language, and a thorough knowledge of the works of Shakespeare, McKenzie was essentially a shy man, an avid buyer and reader of books, who shunned the limelight, refused to be interviewed, never gave a speech if he could help it, and hardly ever ventured outside Toronto on party business. He preferred to use the mail, and even more the telephone, working from his office at party headquarters on Richmond Street or from a room he kept at the Royal York Hotel, not to sleep in but for the private discussion of political matters that occupied so much of his time.

Although McKenzie belonged to the Albany Club, gathering place of prominent Tories, he seldom went there, choosing instead to lunch at Simpson's cafeteria and then spend a little time in the book department where more often than not he found new titles that had to be bought. Because of his *modus operandi*, he was virtually unknown to the general membership of the party across the province. But until his death in 1960, as chairman of organization and, from the fall of 1943, as provincial party president, he was the friend, confidant, and adviser of a large roster of MPPs, candidates, riding association presidents, and others of significance in Conservative affairs. Drew relied implicitly on his shrewd judgment and clear-eyed understanding of human nature. And, following an initial period of uncertainty, so did Leslie Frost after he became leader in 1949.[28] Because of McKenzie's and Cecil Frost's work, the party went into this election with a more effective grassroots organization than six years earlier.

As an incumbent with an efficient organization of his own, Leslie Frost had little need of help from McKenzie or others on the small staff of the party's Toronto office. His campaign began officially with an uncontested nomination in the Academy Theatre, Fred Gardiner doing the honours as guest speaker. In his remarks Frost, dismissing Nixon as Mackenzie King's puppet, promised that the Progressive Conservatives would give people the 'long-promised new deal they have been looking for.'[29]

As gasoline was rationed, Frost suggested a series of joint meetings with his two opponents but that was not accepted. Thus, he and his committee contented themselves for Lindsay with a modest party affair in the committee rooms, instead of the customary large rally with bands and entertainment which might seem inappropriate in time of war. But political meetings seemed to have lost their appeal: 'It is awfully difficult to get attendance at meetings,' Frost wrote to a friend in Haliburton village, advising him that there would be one there, 'and I wish you would do what you can to drum up a crowd.'[30] Hence, other means were used to reach his constituents: four talks over radio station CHEX, Peterborough; advertisements in all the riding's newspapers; and letters through the mail, two to the key people he and his workers had identified and one to every household in the two counties. Most of the time, he told Cyril McAlpine who had offered to help, 'I am spending in straight visiting and organizing. I am going to try and visit everywhere I can. This of course takes time. On the other hand I find that I can cover more ground and see more people by simply going along the road and in the factories etc., than I can by holding meetings each night.'[31]

His hard work, coupled with a strong anti-Liberal tide in the province as a whole, served Frost well. He was re-elected handily over Liberal and CCF opponents with a margin six times that of 1937. He had expected to win but the size of his victory surprised him, he admitted to Gardiner.[32]

Throughout the province the Liberal party had been decisively rejected. Counting Hepburn, who was returned as an independent Liberal, only sixteen of its ninety candidates were successful, and seven of Nixon's ministers were among the losers. Thirty-eight Conservatives were elected, fifteen more than in 1937, but this was no cause for unrestrained jubilation. The most stunning feature of the election was the strong showing of the CCF, which came from nowhere to elect thirty-four members. Hardly less surprising were the victories in Toronto of two communists. Five former Tory seats fell to the CCF, which with four fewer candidates not only outpolled the Liberals but came within less than 5 percentage points of equalling the Conservative popular vote.

In 1937 the Conservatives had not won in any constituency in the southern part of the province west of Peel County and in the north had taken but one seat, Fort William. The loss of the latter to the CCF in 1943 was part of a rejection of both old parties in the vast northern region. In the traditional heartland of Liberalism, the area west of Toronto, the Tories gained eleven seats. In some of these their pluralities were substantial, and in some they failed to win, the large Liberal majorities of 1937 were greatly reduced. Although this was a notable advance, Conservatism still had a long way to go to match the grip it had had on the southwest in Howard Ferguson's day. Nevertheless, these gains, added to those in such central Ontario ridings as Durham, Northumberland, Peterborough, and Simcoe Centre, were evidence of a significant broadening of the party's base from its traditional stronghold in eastern Ontario and the Toronto region. The loss of four seats in Toronto and the Yorks was a severe disappointment but was partly compensated by the capture of two other districts in the city from the Liberals.

The division of seats and votes on class, ethnic, and religious lines is more difficult to determine than these simple geographical distributions but clearly the Progressive Conservative party was not yet the broadly based people's party that Frost hoped it would become. In its campaign publicity much had been made of the varied occupations of its nominees, all of them male, with twenty-four farmers, thirty professionals, and (lumped together) thirty-six representing business and labour. In fact, only three could be counted from the ranks of labour, and none was elected. While a number of constituencies with a large working-class electorate did return Conservatives, the successful CCF and Communist candidates were from worker-dominated ridings. Urban Tory support continued to come from the Protestant middle class. The party did not do well in areas dominated by a large Roman Catholic element or in pockets of French-Canadian settlement. The exceptions were Renfrew North and Stormont, where a previous Liberal majority of nearly five thousand was turned into a modest Tory plurality.[33]

Frost sent Drew a note of congratulation as soon as the election result was known:

I can only say that starting out in 1938 you have fought along against odds which sometimes were pretty nearly overwhelming. Your courage has been justified by the utter defeat of the government which ... was so overbearing in the early days of our opposition.

It is, of course, unfortunate that we have not got a clear majority. This, however, may work out for good. The Progressive Conservative Party is undoubtedly now the rallying point for moderate opinion. The result of this election has shown great changes in political alignments. Now it would appear that our Party is going to become the alternative to Socialism.[34]

As the leader of the party with a plurality of both seats and votes, Drew was summoned by the lieutenant-governor to form a government. It seemed to be taken for granted that Frost would be given a major portfolio. Although he later recalled that when first elected in 1937, 'I always planned with my wife that I should never be any more than a private member,'[35] when Drew summoned him to be something more he does not seem to have seriously considered refusing it. His six years in the House had established him as one of its most active, hard-working members, and as one of Drew's two or three chief lieutenants. With Leopold Macaulay's retirement before the election, Frost became a natural choice for provincial treasurer in view of the special attention he had paid to public finance.

Like some of the others, he assumed a double responsibility, being named to the Mines portfolio as well. This raised eyebrows because of the assurance in the election platform that the department would be put in charge of a man with practical knowledge of mining, to which Frost could lay no claim. Drew explained that this arrangement would remain in effect only until adjustments in the tax system had been made 'in keeping with the great changes that have taken place in the mining industry in the past few years.' But Frost was still in his position six years later when Harry Nixon indulged in some good-natured ribbing about it. Drew, he reminded the House, had promised that 'we would have a Minister of Mines who was an outstanding authority on mines.' 'Have you not?' asked Frost, enjoying the joke. 'He appointed a Lindsay lawyer,' Nixon went on, 'who did not know a mine from a rat hole. Nevertheless he is such a fine gentleman.'[36]

With the important exception of the north, whose voters had denied themselves the advantage of a minister, the new cabinet was fairly representative geographically. Drew, who in addition to becoming president of the council took on the Education department, and Leslie Blackwell, attorney general, were from Toronto. The eastern Ontario Tory bastion was given three spokesmen: George Challies, without portfolio but representing the government on the Hydro Commission; George Doucett, in charge of both Highways and Public Works; and George Dunbar as provincial secretary and minister of municipal affairs. The central region had, in addition to Frost, T.L. Kennedy in Agriculture and R.P. Vivian in the two departments of Health, and Public Welfare. Charles Daley as minister of labour and W.G. Thompson, assigned to Lands and Forests, hailed from southwestern Ontario. It was a small cabinet, purposely so, with half of its members, if the premier was included, handling two departments.

Frost's appointment as treasurer pleased the townsfolk of Lindsay. Not since the departure of Sam Hughes from the Borden government in 1916 had one of their own occupied such high public office. When Frost returned from the swearing-in ceremony in Toronto he was given a civic welcome. Throngs met his train and then formed a parade to Victoria Park for speeches and a presentation.[37] The celebration was a gratifying prelude to the important responsibilities which Frost had accepted.

As guardian of the public purse Frost would have a great deal to say about how to make the Conservative alternative to socialism work, and he would help the Conservative party establish itself again as a great force not only in Ontario but in the whole country – tasks which would concern him for the rest of his career.

Resisting the Centralist Tide

Unlike some new regimes, impatient to wield the broom in a flurry of reform and renovation, the Drew government displayed no great haste to implement its program. Calling the House could be left until the normal time in February while groundwork was laid and the cabinet became acquainted with their tasks. Their party having been out of office for nearly a decade, there was an understandable shortage of administrative experience among them. Two, Kennedy and Challies, had previously been ministers under George Henry, but only Kennedy found himself presiding over his old department. Of the others, Drew, Frost, and Doucett had been elected to the House previously. The remaining five were novices yet to be initiated into both departmental management and parliamentary debate. Prudence dictated that they be given time before confronting the opposition.

The government was very much aware of its minority position, although it was unlikely that the opposition groups would soon combine to bring it down. The CCF was encouraged by its astonishing breakthrough, but the third-place finish of so many of its candidates on 4 August was a sobering fact, and it could not afford another election so soon after the last one. The Liberals, divided and demoralized, had everything to lose in precipitating another vote. Early in October their caucus, over the objections of some, decided to co-operate with the Conservatives in the next session.[1] That was all Drew and his ministers could expect. It was their task to demonstrate a capacity to govern, to avoid serious missteps, and to carry out the platform on which their party had been returned to office.

As Frost set out to master the business of his two departments and to develop a set of policies early in November, Cecil announced his retirement as provincial party president, giving as his reasons the demands of his law practice and the belief that 'young blood' should now take charge. Drew's relations with Cecil, while friendly enough, had never been close. That Cecil had been favoured as a rival candidate for the leadership by some instigators of the 'stop Drew' movement in 1938 was presumably known to Drew. So undoubtedly was the fact that Cecil was on the opposite side when he and Earl Rowe had had their falling out in 1937. There was no actual animosity between them, only a coolness in marked contrast to the warm friendship and reciprocal confidence of Drew and McKenzie.

Knowledge of the leader's wishes may have had a lot to do with Cecil's decision to retire; he was well aware also that the law practice would require his own undivided attention now that Leslie had two portfolios to look after. So he bowed out gracefully, his star in eclipse at the very moment Leslie's had begun to shine more brightly.

One of Frost's first major decisions as provincial treasurer was to keep Chester Walters as his deputy, despite his closeness to Hepburn and his Liberal proclivities. The story went around Queen's Park that not long after the election Hepburn dropped into Walters's office and said, 'Well Chester, I guess we're going,' to which Walters replied, 'No, Mitch, you're going, I'm staying.'[2] His long experience and practical knowledge, to say nothing of his political acumen, were assets to the new ministry too valuable to be discarded at once. Moreover, he could be counted on as a strong defender of the provincial interest against the King government. Walters was soon to discover, however, that working under Frost, whose invariable practice was to keep his subordinates under a tight rein, would be very different from the relatively free and easy relationship with Hepburn, where he acted on occasion like a de facto premier. For the most part he accepted this change with good grace, but occasionally his impatience forced Frost to remind him that he was a deputy minister, not the acting premier, and that making major decisions was not his prerogative.[3] In time his role became less influential as Frost relied increasingly on younger men for advice on economic and financial matters.

As Frost settled into the treasurer's chair, certain distinct and interrelated characteristics of his approach became evident. His immediate desire, not unheard of in new finance ministers, was to restore fiscal responsibility and prudence – which meant in effect that Ontario must live more within its means than in recent years.

He put it to Walters, incidentally implying criticism of the Hepburn-Walters performance, that the net provincial debt, which had risen steeply during the past decade, 'has been created largely due to our failure to tax for services rendered.' This appeared to be at variance with Frost's frequent charge that taxes had increased more under Hepburn than in any previous comparable period. 'Our financial plan for the future,' he insisted, 'cannot overlook the retirement of this class of debt.'[4] But he knew that simple parsimony was not the answer when the prospect was burgeoning government activity.

Frost's careful plans for the post-war period were based on the assumption that when peace came Ottawa would relinquish its grip on the powers it had usurped from the provinces. The cost of these restored constitutional responsibilities would undoubtedly exceed the revenues to be obtained through their limited taxing powers. The first step therefore was to devise means to cut the cost of servicing the provincial debt. But Frost believed that the budget must do more than lay out anticipated revenues and expenditures for the coming year; it should express the broad objectives of government over a longer term, especially the encouragement of economic growth. He recognized that in devising new fiscal measures in the context of an expanding range of government activity, he would have to look beyond the limited resources of the civil service for those with useful expert knowledge. He would begin by modernizing the administration of the Treasury Department and giving it a more central role in making policy.

A press release issued a few months after the new government was sworn in indicated the changes Frost was planning to implement. The accounting system would be thoroughly overhauled, centralized, and operated with the most up-to-date equipment. The public accounts would be simplified to make them more accessible to legislature and the public. Members would be able to scrutinize data for the current fiscal year instead of having to wait for the session following its close, to which Frost had objected when in opposition. More significant, and in keeping with the decision to create a new department of planning and development, was the proposed establishment within the Treasury of a Bureau of Statistics and Research. This, said Frost, would be in line 'with the need for scientific analysis of public affairs upon which the Government can rely in its efforts to make progressive measures effective.' The bureau would be 'available and qualified to investigate all matters relating to social and economic problems in which the Government is interested,' as well as the organization of all government departments.[5]

It proved impossible to bring in all these reforms immediately, as Frost was forced to admit in his first budget speech in March 1944. Modernization of the accounting system would require additional space, staff, and technology which under wartime conditions could not be had. Members of the House should feel free to ask questions about current revenues and spending but the publication of interim accounts, which he had hoped to have available, would have to await the day when those improved facilities were in place. The Bureau of Statistics and Research was established, however, with the appointment of Harold Chater, an accountant, as provincial statistician. Later in 1944 George Gathercole became his assistant. Within a few years the latter took Walters's place as the most influential civil servant, and eventually became provincial economist reporting directly to Frost. Gathercole worked especially, though by no means solely, as an adviser on the highly complex issue of dominion-provincial financial relations, which loomed larger than any other throughout Frost's years as treasurer and as premier.

Scientific analysis was equally a need of Frost's other department, Mines, which received hardly less of his attention than the Treasury. The two were closely related because the health of the mining industry was seen as a key to the growth and prosperity of Ontario's economy. Two chief needs were considered pressing: tax reform to remove disincentives to mining investment, exploration, and development; and encouragement of carefully planned research by mining companies and universities to assist discovery of new ore bodies and improve techniques for extracting mineral wealth. The universities were expected to play a vital role in furnishing the desired expertise, not only for mining but for resource industries generally. Neither Drew nor Frost regarded academics, as did some politicians, as strange beings, learned in their specialties but not wholly reliable, and given to fine-spun theories acquired through arcane research which was not in touch with practical realities. Since the universities were publicly funded, they should and could make a contribution to economic development. 'Research is of tremendous importance in wartime,' Frost said in his budget speech. 'After the war it will be of even greater importance ... The Government has determined that to the extent of its powers it will make available to our workers and our industries the advantages of scientific research ... our universities should be freed from the burden of debt ... and ... grants should be made to them which would permit them now in time of war to organize for peace.'[6]

Early in 1944 the government decided to give the three provincially supported institutions at Toronto, London, and Kingston special research grants that might produce results useful to government and the resource industries. This decision appears to have grown, at least in part, out of discussions Frost had with his older brother, now a professor of chemistry at Queen's University, about the feasibility of enlisting academic scientists. Grenville had suggested that he write to R.C. Wallace, principal of Queen's, as a logical first step. Accordingly, Frost explained to Wallace his idea 'that we might in some way unite the efforts of the Mines Department here with those of the Science Departments' of the universities. He had in mind a moderate research grant 'which might immediately assist the prospector in his task.' The research, he added, need not be confined to mining but might embrace natural resources generally.

This tentative offer called for a modest proposal in response. Wallace obliged by outlining three projects, two related to mining, the other to eastern Ontario fisheries, which promised material benefits at a cost of about $30,000. This was needlessly modest, for Drew informed J.M. Macdonnell, chairman of Queen's board of trustees, that his institution would receive a special grant of $250,000, the same as the University of Western Ontario, with a larger sum earmarked for the University of Toronto.[7]

Tax reform, Frost's second main approach to the needs of mining, required for its success the co-operation of other governments, dominion and provincial. One serious disincentive to investment, in his opinion, was that in the absence of reciprocal tax agreements, the estate of a person investing in one province but resident in another would have to pay succession duties to both. Shortly after taking office, he launched an effort to eliminate such double taxation but met with only limited success. 'At that time,' he later recalled, 'there was an almost complete lack of communication between provinces, perhaps other than on a very arm's length basis.' Closer contact between provincial mines departments was desirable for the exchange of technical information and Frost was instrumental in forming a Mines Ministers Association, of which he became first president and which met annually with the ministers and their senior officials in attendance. He used those new contacts to re-open negotiations on the provincial tax reciprocity he was so eager to obtain.[8] In 1944 a death duties agreement was reached with Quebec, and one with Nova Scotia a little later. With the other provinces Frost fared less well; in any case, all except Quebec and Ontario before long entered into a new tax rental agreement with Ottawa under which they relinquished the right to levy succession duties.[9]

In fact, correcting most of what Frost saw as defects in the tax system, including some adversely affecting mining operations, would require changes in federal policy, as he explained in addressing the Canadian Institute of Mining and Metallurgy a month before the legislature convened in 1944. 'Mining taxation,' he told an audience that needed no convincing, 'must be placed on a different basis from that of other industry ... A mine is a wasting asset ... Only about 1 per cent of the properties are an economic success.' Thus the industry depended on discovery of fresh ore bodies, and consequently on a supply of new capital. Taxation should be designed to attract investment in what were unavoidably risky ventures. Ottawa should permit more generous tax deductions and depletion allowances in order to stimulate activity.[10] Since the changes he proposed would diminish both dominion revenue and provincial expenditure, while adding to provincial income, the likelihood of their being enacted was not great.

A new government's first budget is always a focus of general interest, and this one would be all the more so because the many pledges which Drew had given in 1943 would have to be redeemed. Frost wanted this initial presentation to be, as he instructed Walters, 'a full, fair, impartial statement of our financial position and difficulties ... Now, I believe, is a real opportunity to lay the foundations for reforms which will have a very lasting effect ... to accomplish much we must have an informed public opinion.'[11] Frost's speech and its accompanying statistics reflected his determination to reduce the debt and to some extent belied his warnings about Ontario's financial condition. In fact, the good news he reported was strongly reminiscent of Hepburn's sunny budgets about which he had been so sceptical. For the fiscal year drawing to a close there would be a net debt reduction of $12 million, the largest in history, and a surplus on ordinary account of more than $8.5 million. On the other hand, he predicted, revenues would be sharply reduced in the coming year, for which he forecast a small surplus. This prompted A.A. MacLeod, one of the two Communist members, to claim that Frost was too pessimistic and 'close to being a peregrinating apostle of gloom.' Perhaps, MacLeod shrewdly added, the treasurer was 'packing away a little sunshine for next session to make the welkin ring with the surplus he will announce.'[12]

The only new tax was an additional 5 per cent impost on racetrack bets, less to discourage than to profit from this activity. On the expenditure side there would be substantial new outlays: the special research grants to the three universities; an extra $3.6 million for old age pensions, mothers' allowances, and health services; and $1 million more for municipal road work. Of greater interest to most people was the fulfilling of the government's pledge to assume half of the cost of schooling. Here Drew scooped his treasurer by his statement on the eve of budget day. The promise, he said, would be honoured to the letter but not until a royal commission had studied the question. Meanwhile, as a temporary measure the government would pay an extra $3.5 million to assist in meeting the direct cost of education. It was left for Frost to explain that the sum was made up of a $3.1 million grant to municipalities, equivalent to one mill on their tax bills, the balance going into the teachers' superannuation fund. That was far short of the promised 50 per cent and was derided by Edward Jolliffe of the CCF who was now the leader of the opposition.

Frost then turned to some more general observations. The province would incur very large expenses after the war; it must carefully husband its resources so as to avoid heavy additional taxation, which would stifle enterprise and growth, or a burdensome enlargement of the net debt, now standing at roughly $500 million and costing about $20 million annually to carry. He never accepted that a growing debt should be a legitimate feature of public finance. He therefore proposed a rather complicated plan of debt retirement over fifty years, whose objective would be to ensure that all future borrowings 'will be retired within the lifetime of the works for which they were incurred.' Equally important was 'termination of the present Dominion-Provincial [tax rental] agreement and the vacation of our taxing fields.'[13] Frost's ministerial counterpart in Ottawa, J.L. Ilsley, could take that as notice that a strenuous tussle over the division of taxing power lay ahead.

The budget passed easily, as did everything proposed by the government in that first session. Under the lacklustre leadership of Harry Nixon the Liberals made sure of that. The CCF also did not oppose vigorously measures which for the most part would be well regarded by the majority of voters. The other ministers had made a businesslike start at implementing the twenty-two points of the election manifesto with a wide range of bills concerning labour, health, agriculture, education, municipal affairs, public welfare, Hydro, and forest management. Their first test of governing from a minority position had been passed without serious difficulty.

There were, however, difficulties enough on another front – the all-important one of dominion-provincial relations in which Frost, as treasurer, had a special interest. As the budget had indicated, Drew's government was committed to careful post-war planning. To avert the recession which, in the past, had seemed always to follow a war, there must be jobs available for the thousands of soldiers and war workers who required redirection and absorption into the peacetime labour force. This necessitated both interim and long-term planning, in which financial responsibilities and resources would have to be clearly allocated between the federal and provincial governments. If joint projects were undertaken, their respective fiscal and legal powers must be clearly defined.

Early in 1944 Drew proposed a conference of all ten Canadian governments to consider the problems which would arise once the temporary tax rental arrangement of 1942 came to an end. Drew feared that the King government, while agreeing with co-operation in principle, was preparing to ignore in practice any suggestions to achieve true consultation and consensus with the provinces. Drew emphasized that 'where it will be necessary to obtain the agreement of the Provincial Governments in regard to the joint occupation of fields ordinarily under their exclusive jurisdiction there should be previous discussion so that any measures introduced will be on a basis agreed upon in advance.' He cautioned that no such measures should be put before Parliament or the legislatures until a conference had settled 'the present and future relationship of the various governments.'[14]

Parliament met three weeks after Drew sent his letter. The throne speech made it abundantly clear that the King government intended to continue its activist and directing role after the war, and that Drew's misgivings had some foundation. Three new departments, Veterans' Affairs, Reconstruction, and Social Welfare, were to be established. To the first of these there could be no objection; the dominion's responsibility in that field was long and well established. But the proposal for a Social Welfare Department which was 'to organize and to assist in administering activities of the federal government in the fields of health and social insurance,' seemed to Drew an intrusion into provincial jurisdiction in the matter of family allowances. The speech did recognize, however, that a comprehensive national scheme of social security, 'in which federal and provincial activities will be integrated and which will include nation-wide health insurance, will require further consultation and close co-operation with the provinces. My Ministers will welcome opportunities for such consultation.'[15] Shortly, King reported that the other premiers agreed, as he did, that a conference should be held. All that remained was to assemble the necessary statistical data, settle the agenda, and find a time suitable to all.[16]

In the protracted and at times short-tempered correspondence between Prime Minister King and Premier Drew in which these arrangements were discussed, it was evident that on the subject of provincial rights the new Drew was but old Hepburn. Part of the difficulty was the intense dislike of each man for the other. Drew was still angry at the attempt to use the Defence of Canada Regulations against him over the Hong Kong affair, while King could not forget or forgive Drew's many brutal attacks or his having made common cause with Hepburn.

In addition, the Ontario ministers were annoyed by what they considered the federal ministers' blatant usurpation of provincial responsibilities when early in March the minister of pensions and national health unveiled a health insurance plan which, Drew pointed out, 'was reported throughout Canada as though it was the proposed plan of the Dominion Government.' Why so, when the throne speech had promised consultation?[17] Even more objectionable to Drew was the family allowances bill which was presented to Parliament a few months later as settled federal policy after formidable opposition in King's cabinet and caucus had been overcome.

Heightening these aggravations was the fact that the East Block and Queen's Park could not agree on the objectives of the proposed conference. Ontario wanted an agreement on general principles which would restore its legislative and fiscal powers and lay down ground rules for joint action where that was called for. Indeed, Drew urged a preliminary first ministers' meeting to settle these matters in advance of specific plans and policies being considered. King saw no need for a separate discussion of such general questions. Nor was he in any hurry to discuss the details of his government's post-war plans, for they were still incomplete. Moreover, when perfected, those plans could be made the basis of his next appeal to the voters. If he won on such a platform, he would be in a stronger position to contend with troublesome provincial upstarts like Drew. As he did not intend to call an immediate election (indeed he did not go to the people until the spring of 1945), he let the discussions drag on, all the while maintaining the pretence of willingness to confer.

At length, in Drew's absence, Frost wrote to King late in September, reiterating the need for a conference and 'a clear understanding concerning our taxing powers and other matters.' Without that, the plans made in Ontario by government and industry to prepare for the coming of peace would be seriously hampered. The meeting should be convened immediately. 'We have been ready for months.'[18] Apparently this elicited no reply but in effect King had given his answer some weeks earlier in the Commons, where he read into the record a sentence from a recent radio talk by Drew: 'My one ambition in the political field outside of Ontario is to see an end as soon as possible of the weak and incompetent government in power at Ottawa to-day, and to assist in every way I can to assure that John Bracken is the next Prime Minister of Canada.' Said King: 'Such being the declared aim of the Premier of Ontario, it must be apparent that any conference held before a federal election would have little or no hope of success, and would almost certainly prejudice the success of a subsequent conference.'[19]

This statement was the dénouement to seven months of argument, and Frost's letter may have been written more for the record than with any hope of changing the prime minister's mind. Drew decided, however, to make one more try. The following February he telegraphed King that the increasing hope of victory in Europe that year made at least a preliminary gathering of first ministers urgently necessary. 'No matter what differences of opinion have existed between the heads of any governments in the past I believe that the welfare of Canada demands that these be forgotten.' King did not bother answering this himself; he had the Clerk of the Privy Council inform Drew that the prime minister had nothing to add to his statement in Parliament that there would be no conference before a national election.[20]

Drew's attention now turned to preparations for the next session of the legislature. The ease with which his government had sailed through its first one proved to be the calm before the storm, for by the spring of 1945 a marked sea change had occurred, thanks largely to the re-emergence of Mitch Hepburn as a would-be power in the land. Hepburn had been untypically docile in the House the year before, remaining silent for the most part. But the bronco still had a few kicks left. Late in 1944 he began to attack Drew as the embodiment of a reactionary toryism which it was his mission to destroy. He no longer had, he proclaimed, any quarrel with the federal Liberal party or its leader.

He was especially disturbed by Drew's objections to the family allowances plan, which he denounced as prejudice against French Canadians with their large families, and an attempt to foment racial strife.[21] Although Drew had stated that 'one isolationist province' could not be allowed 'to dominate the destiny of a divided Canada,' the charge of racism ignored his main points: first, that the plan was an unconstitutional infringement of provincial rights; and second, that Ontario, if the tax fields surrendered in 1942 were recovered, could itself provide the more ample family allowances he favoured and at vastly less cost to its people.[22]

The dispirited Liberal caucus at Toronto was convinced that Hepburn's outburst was proof that the political magic of 1934 was still there. Late in 1944, in a remarkable act of abnegation, Harry Nixon nominated Hepburn as House leader, which led to his becoming full-fledged party leader once again. If he was truly intent on bringing down the ministry and could carry the caucus with him, the government's defeat in the House was almost certain, for the CCF, despite evidence that its popularity was waning, now seemed willing to face a test at the polls. Hepburn, however, contended that a change of government without an election could be engineered through a coalition of Liberals, Communists, and the CCF which would command the confidence of the existing House and permit the lieutenant-governor to deny Drew a dissolution. This fanciful plan was supported by A.A. MacLeod, whose Communist party nationally and provincially had expediently aligned itself with the Liberals. But Jolliffe and others in the CCF rejected it as a political trap.[23]

Nevertheless, defeat in the legislature was probable, and for the forthcoming election the government had to gain the political upper hand. It was Frost's responsibility to present an attractive budget, which in particular would make good on the famous promise to assume half the cost of education. In order to bring the budget down before a possible defeat at the end of the throne speech debate, that debate was interrupted to allow him to announce his good news. There would be no new taxes for the splendid reason that, having greatly underestimated revenue, he could report a surplus of nearly $9 million. Almost all of this would go to municipalities, on top of regular payments, to fulfil the undertaking about school costs. In the twelve preceding months the gross provincial debt had been cut by almost $18.5 million, the net debt by more than $1 million. Ontario would persist in its pay-as-you-go policy. As much of the increased provincial bill for education was to go on being paid out of surpluses, buoyant revenues and strictly controlled expenditures would obviously be necessary. The only way to balance the two sides of the ledger in the long run, he argued, was to convene the dominion-provincial conference for which Queen's Park had been pressing, so as to restore to the provinces their full taxing powers. The collection of Ontario's rightful revenues, coupled with an end to the inhibiting effects of federal taxes on business investment, would set things right.[24]

This declaration was shrewd politics, for it set Ottawa up as the real adversary; as Frost reminded his leader, Oliver Mowat always won elections on the issue of provincial rights. In late March 1945 the opposition parties, not at all to the dismay of the cabinet, combined on a CCF want of confidence motion to defeat the government. Drew was granted a dissolution and announced that polling would be on 11 June. When Mackenzie King immediately chose the same day for his own election, Drew advanced the Ontario date by one week; casting ballots in two elections on the same day would be too confusing, while waiting until after the national poll might be damaging to the provincial Tories.

For some time the Ontario campaign was a quiet one, despite efforts by opposition spokesmen to breathe fire into it. Their chief stock-in-trade was personal abuse of Drew and his alleged lust for power and arrogance. Drew responded in kind, disdainfully dismissing Hepburn as an irresponsible, erratic has-been and lumping CCFers and Communists together as a sinister threat to the traditions and institutions of the province. For the most part, though, the Tories concentrated on the government's good record and on other benefits it would bring if it continued in office. But it was evident that there was little public interest in provincial politics. Other events and issues – the concurrent federal campaign, the end of the war in Europe and plans for peace, the death of Franklin D. Roosevelt and Harry Truman's accession to the White House – were more absorbing than a mere provincial election.

This indifference was abruptly shattered toward the end of May when Jolliffe charged in a radio talk that Drew was conducting a secret political spying operation by a special branch of the Ontario Provincial Police against left wing elements, in particular the CCF. The strategy of this 'gestapo,' Jolliffe claimed, was to spread slanders which were designed by reactionaries to whip up public opinion and make the electors fear the forces of reform. The special branch, headed by a certain William J. Osborne-Dempster (who in the time-honoured manner of espionage agents employed a code name, D. 208), was hand-in-glove, according to Jolliffe, with various notorious anti-socialists. Most notable of these were Gladstone Murray, former general manager of the CBC and now a well-known publicist, and M.A. Sanderson, a minor Toronto businessman. The latter was manager of a company called Reliable Exterminators; with reckless enthusiasm he was devoting his expertise to rooting out the 'vermin' of the political left. Under the name and presumably at the expense of his company, the 'bug man' regularly advertised in the Toronto papers, excoriating all left wingers over the slogan, 'You Bet I'm a Vet.'

Shortly after taking office, Jolliffe alleged, Drew had resurrected and reorganized the special branch, which had recently been closed down. Furthermore, he not only knew of but encouraged its nefarious activities in compiling dossiers and writing reports on numerous individuals who could not possibly be considered subversive. Jolliffe's allegations were promptly denied by Drew, who appointed Mr Justice A.M. LeBel of the Ontario Supreme Court a royal commissioner to investigate. Provincial politics became front page news for the remainder of the campaign.

Having made this his chief election issue, Jolliffe could not be expected to back down from his charges in deference to a royal commission inquiry yet to begin. But it seems probable that his increasingly shrill attacks on the premier damaged his own credibility. The public did not believe the extravagant charge that under Drew's leadership Ontario was in danger of becoming a reactionary police state, nor did Mr Justice LeBel, who reported after the voters had handed down their own verdict. He corroborated many of Jolliffe's specific allegations about Osborne-Dempster, exonerated Drew, who had misled the commissioner in testifying that he was only slightly acquainted with Gladstone Murray and unaware of D. 208's activities,[25] from complicity, and administered a mild rebuke to the only other minister directly implicated, Attorney General Blackwell. In the meantime Jolliffe and his party were overwhelmingly crushed at the polls. There had turned out to be a lot less political mileage than they had hoped for in the 'gestapo' revelations.

Frost seems to have been entirely untouched by the affair. In all probability he had never heard of Osborne-Dempster, perhaps not even of the OPP's special branch, before Jolliffe's sensational radio talk. It is even more probable that, once he did, he regarded the goings-on of D. 208 as not only misguided but downright silly, especially when it became known that reports had actually been compiled on such notorious 'revolutionaries' as B.K. Sandwell of *Saturday Night* and Principal Wallace of Queen's, whom the government was shortly to appoint chairman of a new Ontario Research Commission.

At the same time, the scurrilous, inflammatory charge that a 'gestapo' was operating in Ontario was preposterous, in his view, and had to be countered in no uncertain fashion. During the closing phase of the campaign Frost did what he could to disparage it. In his scribbled notes for use on the hustings he declared that, while Osborne-Dempster might have exceeded his authority, 'There is *No Gestapo* & will be none under a P.C. Gov't.' Anyway, he told his listeners, this was a case of people in glass houses throwing stones, as two clippings before him clearly showed. One reported a statement by Nelson Alles, a left-wing CCFer and former member for Essex North who was not running this time, that he and his wife had been spied on by CCF functionaries who prepared detailed evidence, with which he was then confronted, that they had been seen consorting with non-CCFers in their home. The other clipping quoted two former CCF Manitoba MLAS who had bolted: 'We accuse the C.C.F. party of deliberately spying on our private affairs and movements and using material gathered in this way to misrepresent our views.' This, said Frost righteously, was the party accusing Drew, a wounded veteran of the last war, and his ministers, seven of them also veterans and a number wounded, of gestapo methods.[26] It was not exactly high political discourse; it was about equal to the oratory on the other side. And it was good enough for his constitutents; Frost easily routed his Liberal and CCF opponents, winning by a considerably greater margin than in 1943.

The CCF elected only eight, a drop of twenty-six, while its share of the popular vote declined by nearly 10 per cent. Jolliffe was beaten in York South and all but one of his party's victories were in northern Ontario. The CCF's hold on the industrial sections of the province, so marked in 1943, had been severely weakened. The Liberals fared slightly better, enough to become the official opposition, but their portion of the votes shrank marginally and their fourteen seats, including two won under a Liberal-Labour banner, were two shy of their previous total. Most humiliating of all, their resurrected leader, Hepburn, was defeated in Elgin, the final event in his tempestuous public career.

The *Toronto Star*, which had conducted an especially venomous editorial campaign against Drew, announced the general result in a banner headline: 'Minority Vote Wins for Drew.' That was factually true, as it usually is when more than two parties are in the field; fewer than 45 per cent of the ballots were cast for Conservatives and the *Star*'s interpretation of this was that over half of the electorate voted against Drew. But the Tory share of the vote had risen by well over 8 per cent and it gave them sixty-six of the ninety seats, a smashing victory. These included all the Toronto and York ridings except the two retained by the Communists, MacLeod and J.B. Salsberg. In a two-way fight against a CCFer, Drew kept his own seat much more comfortably than in 1943, despite the *Star*'s eloquent appeals to the voters of High Park to turn him out.[27] Elsewhere, except in the north, the Conservatives scored striking gains in a number of largely rural constituencies formerly Liberal, and in many urban districts that had gone to the CCF two years earlier. On the morrow of the contest Frost dropped A.D. McKenzie a note: 'I think your organization ... was one of the main factors in our success ... you did a swell job and ... we all owe you a very great deal. George and yourself have made a great team. I think this campaign was pretty well the perfect campaign, that is for the Tories.'[28] It was a different story nationally a week later. Mackenzie King remained in the saddle astride a slightly wounded steed, a reduced majority at his back.

Ten days later Mackenzie King informed the premiers that the dominion-provincial conference would open in Ottawa on 6 August. Shortly after, Frost visited Maurice Duplessis in Quebec City. There were various things he wanted to discuss, but chief among them was dominion-provincial relations. The meeting was part of an unobtrusive effort by the Drew government to drum up support for its position; and Quebec, along with Alberta and British Columbia, whose leaders had joined with Hepburn in rejecting the Rowell-Sirois Report, was counted on for help. In the autumn of 1944, Frost had called on John Hart, leader of British Columbia's minority Liberal government. 'Saw Hart with reasonable success,' he wired Drew. 'He agrees with reservations which I shall explain on return.' Frost planned to see Ernest Manning, Aberhart's political disciple and heir, in Edmonton, 'where I believe there is approval.' Less could be hoped for from T.C. Douglas, Saskatchewan's new CCF premier, so no mention was made of stopping off in Regina. Similarly, Frost did not try to see Stuart Garson, Bracken's successor as premier of Manitoba, who was believed to be closer than any other to the King government and the least likely to sympathize with Ontario's views.[29]

These western soundings were useful, but special importance was attached to Quebec and Duplessis. He was an unknown personality to Ontario's ministers, but enough was known of his outlook and that of his province to make him seem the most promising ally against Ottawa's centralizing ambitions. And Quebec's support was crucial to the national Liberal party.

Frost was not dissatisfied with this meeting with Duplessis, although he gained the distinct impression that the Quebeckers had given a lot less thought to the specific issues than these had received in Toronto. 'Mr. Duplessis,' he wrote afterwards, 'made it clear that Quebec was opposed to centralization, and he indicated many dangers in continuing the present trend ... the Quebec people are extreme provincial rightists. They would go much further along that line than we would. Our attitude towards the Dominion and the other provinces has been and is much more generous.' Frost had made a point of telling Duplessis 'that we did not want a repetition of the 1941 Sirois fiasco ... and that we were prepared to use all sorts of patience' to avoid it. Perhaps some aspects of policy traditionally in the provincial orbit had now become national in scope and character. Nevertheless, 'a continuation of the present trend at Ottawa in concentrating power there would certainly not "Make Ontario strong," but actually make us weak and impotent.' It would mean a lower standard of living and less money to develop the province. 'In the end, as far as the Dominion Government is concerned, it would kill the goose that lays the golden egg because we are contributing about one half of all Dominion revenues.'

The immediate question was how best to counter the centralizing tendency. 'As a matter of strategy at the Conference,' Frost advised, 'it might be well to let some of the others throw the balls at the outset, enabling us not to offend anyone until such time as we think we can get the maximum good. Manitoba will probably lead in the centralization attitude. Quebec, and perhaps British Columbia, probably will be quick to take the other point of view.'[30] Drew and Duplessis had not met before the delegations assembled in Ottawa early in August and it was there that Frost introduced them. This, he remarked many years later, 'was the commencement of what became known as the Drew-Duplessis axis which I must admit I never intended to be, in any way, the author of and which [term] in many other ways was quite unjustified by what took place subsequently.'[31]

Mackenzie King opened the Dominion-Provincial Conference on Reconstruction[32] with some pleasantly reassuring generalities about the federal system. 'We do not believe,' he said, 'that unity is to be found in uniformity, in standardization or in centralization. We believe the unity and strength of Canada is [sic] equally dependent upon the soundness and strength of the provinces, and their capacity to discharge their functions effectively.'[33] Responding, Drew elaborated on that theme. His manner and tone were unprovocative but the substance of his discourse was a strong, well-reasoned affirmation of provincial rights. 'The power to legislate and to govern,' he asserted, 'rests upon the power to raise funds by taxation.' A government that surrendered to another its fiscal autonomy was bound to become a client of the other and cease to be an equal partner in Confederation.[34]

The Ontario delegation's apprehension was not allayed while they listened to a succession of King's ministers expound the federal proposals. These, said J.L. Ilsley in concluding the presentation, were 'neither revolutionary nor disruptive' but designed to permit both levels of government to exercise their powers more fully and effectively.[35] But what were these powers? The plan, conceived by the Ottawa mandarinate, was an elaborate attempt to translate Keynesian economic theory into practice. It breathed high purpose; it glowed with stunning confidence. If the provinces agreed (initially for three years) to continue the rental of corporate and personal income taxes and to surrender their right to collect succession duties, the King government would replace the existing subsidies with larger unconditional per capita grants geared to the gross national product but irreducible below their original size. These would give the provinces larger revenues, it was claimed, than would the tax fields they were being asked to vacate.

With those fields at its command, the central government could act as the balance wheel of the economy; it would smooth out the peaks and valleys of the business cycle by contra-cyclical budgeting; it would greatly broaden its responsibility for social security, health care, public works, development of natural resources, and co-ordination of public investment policy; and it would both mitigate regional economic disparities and contribute to the achievement of full employment far more successfully than if ten governments were to go more or less their separate ways. It was a dazzling prospect, not the least of whose attractions was that it could be attained without formal constitutional amendment. But despite Ilsley's assurance, some provinces, Ontario prominent among them, were quick to see that, as Donald Creighton later put it, 'acceptance of the federal proposals would result in a revolutionary change in the Canadian constitution. A monopoly of all the great modern taxes would enable the federal government to control the entire population. It was the greatest advance ever yet planned towards the centralized administration of all phases and aspects of Canadian life.'[36]

Drew was the first to express an opinion. He thought the proposals so far-reaching that ample time must be allowed for reflection on their meaning and implications. The provinces' objections resulted in the establishment of a joint co-ordinating committee consisting of the prime minister, three of his colleagues, and the nine premiers, along with a fact-finding body of officials. The former would organize and oversee detailed study by committees when the time came for that and meet periodically to assess the results. Meanwhile, the provincial delegations would take the plan home for analysis, prepare their responses, and frame whatever alternative suggestions they might wish to offer.

Because only the premiers spoke for their respective governments, Frost said nothing at the plenary sessions. He agreed with Drew about the issues involved but was less given to political theory and more to counting dollars and cents. He expressed his opinions when the Ontario contingent huddled for evening strategy sessions in their quarters at the Chateau Laurier, and even more in the long-drawn-out subsequent process, which he was instrumental in conducting, of framing a detailed response to the plan and providing some counter-proposals. In addition to Drew and himself, those chiefly engaged in this were Attorney General Blackwell, Dana Porter of Planning and Development, and a number of senior officials, in particular some of Frost's subordinates in the Treasury. It meant an almost endless succession of meetings and numberless informal discussions as they plumbed the implications of Ottawa's scheme and tried to determine its probable financial impact on Ontario. In the midst of this, the joint co-ordinating committee gathered in November without conclusive results. By the end of the year Ontario's objections to the federal offer and a statement of its own proposals were ready for despatch to the other capitals to be considered before being formally presented when the co-ordinating committee met again late in January.

Ontario's statement was not well received by the other governments. Those provinces less advantageously situated than Ontario, or lacking the defensive outlook of Quebec with its distinctive culture to protect from the assimilative force of centralism, were less impressed by theoretical arguments on behalf of provincial autonomy than by their prospective financial gain if Ottawa's proposition went into effect. An important exception to this was Nova Scotia with its deep-rooted sense of identity and with a strong defender of its rights in Angus L. Macdonald, who had recently resumed the premiership after an unhappy interlude as one of King's wartime ministers.

Still, neither he nor any of the others, not even the premiers of the two biggest provinces, could dismiss from their minds one basic possibility: that the irreducible annual grant of $12 per capita (later in the negotiations raised to $15) would be adequate compensation for relinquishing the major direct tax fields. The prevailing disposition was to agree that it would, although the spokesmen for some acquiescent governments, notably Macdonald, had objections to certain features which led to eventual modification of the plan. Most premiers found it difficult to resist the persuasive contention that post-war reconstruction required more concentration of power at the centre, a view directly challenged by Ontario's brief.

The brief examined the effects that acceptance of the proffered grants in exchange for taxing rights would have on provincial governments and legislatures. The broad conclusion was bluntly stated: 'No matter what the intention may be, the almost inevitable result ... would be the ultimate abandonment of the Federal System in favour of a Unitary System.' With the return of peace, the provinces would incur much greater costs in performing their unquestioned constitutional functions. Their revenue requirements would undoubtedly go on rising. But under the scheme laid before them by Ottawa, the power to order their own priorities and decide upon their own revenue needs would be seriously impaired. The 'steady whittling down of provincial rights of taxation would produce a limitation of legislative independence which could only have the effect of rapidly increasing the centralized power of the Dominion Government.'[37]

The fundamental point of the brief was that each province should retain flexibility in setting its taxation instead of having to appeal to the dominion for funds. Access to major sources would be essential should minor direct taxes such as those on gasoline and liquor prove at times less productive than anticipated. The federal plan would force the provinces to resort more extensively to nuisance consumer taxes, which would both increase collection costs and erect barriers to interprovincial trade. The subsidies offered were inadequate. Adjustments based on the gross national product would not benefit Ontario as much as the major direct taxes with their progressive rates. Reliance on subsidies for so large a proportion of its income would compel the province to resort to deficit financing. Moreover, unconditional grants were wrong in principle because 'a government ... autonomous within its assigned jurisdiction should be charged with the responsibility of raising the money which it spends.'

Although the agreement was limited initially to three years it would not be easy to terminate. 'As the centralized levying of taxes took deep root, it would become difficult ... to resist the pressure of the Dominion to accept whatever terms were offered,' especially in a time of economic distress. Finally, 'decentralization of services provides the best assurance that the flexibility, vigour and efficiency of public administration will be preserved,' a fact that was particularly relevant in a country such as Canada. Thus the government of Ontario felt compelled to reject the federal program.[38]

So much for objections, but was there a better way? As Drew, Frost, and the others saw things from Toronto, there assuredly was. It was outlined in their submission, the only one, as Ilsley later remarked, that might be called an alternative to the dominion's proposals. It has been said that in 1945 Drew took the lead in an effort by some provinces 'to turn the clock right back to the thirties.'[39] That is not borne out by Ontario's brief or by the general attitude of Drew and his colleagues to the operation and structure of Canada's federal system. The brief suggested, to start with, certain instrumental innovations. There should be a continuing joint economic board of technical experts to digest statistics and advise the co-ordinating committee, which should also be made permanent. The two bodies together would help achieve a genuine co-operative federalism. Both levels of government should tax corporate and personal earnings at their own rates, with the dominion acting as collection agent for the provinces. Only the latter might impose succession duties. There must be provision for equalization, for assisting financially weaker provinces, a principle enshrined in the Rowell-Sirois Report but virtually abandoned in Ottawa's 1945 plan. To this end, 10 per cent of provincial revenues from the three large direct taxes should be placed in a national adjustment fund, from which disbursements would be made by the co-ordinating committee on the basis of fiscal need. Ontario claimed that this would provide an amount greater than the adjustments grants recommended by the Rowell-Sirois Commission. As further compensation for provinces which, unlike Ontario and Quebec, had few corporate head offices, a readjustment of corporation tax revenues was suggested. The federal government should discontinue imposing taxes on gasoline, amusements, pari-mutuel betting, security transfers, and consumption of electricity, and also accept the provinces' prior right to tax mining and logging operations. It was, to say the least, open to doubt that these ideas could be reconciled with those advanced by Ottawa.

The same was true of public investment policy, in which the King government offered to play a more leading role as initiator and co-ordinator in periods of economic slackness when the private sector might be unable to maintain adequate gainful employment. In Ontario's view, while financial contributions by Ottawa would be welcome, indeed essential, public investment should be planned by the proposed permanent co-ordinating committee and economic board, rather than by delegating responsibility for 'extremely important decisions within the sphere of exclusive provincial jurisdiction.' To Queen's Park it seemed obvious 'that decisions as to when, where and to what extent activities should proceed ... in the forests, in the mines, in the construction of highways, in conservation of soil and in practically every aspect of production can be made very much better by those who are constantly in touch with these very subjects.'

The two plans were equally far apart respecting social welfare and security. Heavy additional financial obligations on the federal government were proposed for mothers' allowances, children's aid, old age pensions, and assistance to the unemployed. At the same time it was argued that, as welfare services 'require considerable local supervision and care,' their administration should be handled by the provinces. That did not seem consistent with the principle implicit in Ontario's general position, that the government supplying the funds should control their expenditure.

The brief closed with comments on the proposed jointly financed health insurance plan. Ottawa intended to raise the money for this largely from a special social security tax and recommended that the provinces finance their share by a uniform head tax on all over sixteen years of age. Queen's Park rejected a head tax unrelated to income and whether the taxpayer was employed, and contended that the enormous complexity of the project demanded further study.[40] This argument at least was accepted; twenty years were to pass before a full national health insurance plan was operative.

When the co-ordinating committee met in January it was evident that there was less provincial support for Ontario's point of view than had been hoped for. Faced with that reality, Drew intimated, as he reminded the reassembled conference in April 1946, that 'the

Ontario Government was prepared to vacate and to rent for an annual cash payment ... the fields of corporation and personal income taxes for the term of a Transition Tax Agreement.' Considering the vehemence of his earlier opposition to such a concession, this was a significant move. But it was accompanied by a number of stipulations, some of which, by denying Ottawa the right of direct taxation in other than those two fields and by demanding that it make additional financial commitments, would almost certainly be unacceptable to the federal government. Furthermore, the formula Ontario now proposed for calculating annual rental would, Ilsley complained, be much more costly to his treasury than adjustments geared to the GNP from a base of $15 per capita. After a heated argument in which Drew, with some support from Duplessis, was pitted against various federal ministers and some provincial spokesmen, Garson most prominently, the conference broke up without reaching agreement.

Frost had made it clear to Duplessis in the summer of 1945 that the Drew cabinet were prepared to be very patient for the sake of preventing another 'Sirois fiasco.' Certainly they had been a lot more patient, more willing to negotiate, than Hepburn in 1941. Not only had they come to Ottawa again and again for further discussion, they and their officials had devoted countless hours, with Frost co-ordinating the work, to accumulation of data, analysis of the federal scheme, and preparation of an alternative. Even so, the end result was much the same, except that instead of Alberta and British Columbia, Ontario's only real ally now was Quebec.

7

Resolving Problems Old and New

Another troublesome issue that refused to go away was that hardy perennial of Ontario politics – the liquor problem. During the Great War Ontario had joined the other provinces in adopting a policy of prohibition which was embodied in the Ontario Temperance Act. Similarly, the province had followed the post-war trend away from such restrictions with the Liquor Control Act of 1927. This provided, subject to local option, for the exclusive sale of beverage alcohol in government stores, under the supervision of a Liquor Control Board, and at brewers' warehouses. There was to be no licensing of public gathering places and advertising of alcoholic products was forbidden.

In 1934 the Henry government brought in amendments to the 1927 act, on the understanding that they would not take effect until after the forthcoming election. These allowed, at the discretion of the Control Board, the sale of wine and beer in hotel dining-rooms ('hotel' being defined as a place with at least six bedrooms) and of beer in hotel beverage rooms, as well as in private clubs. The sale of spirits except in sealed bottles at government stores for private consumption was still forbidden. The Hepburn government quickly implemented these changes, and thereafter the Liquor Control Board, according to its critics of whom Frost was one, granted licences, especially for beverage rooms, in an alarmingly indiscriminate manner. Complaints abounded about conditions in badly run, poorly equipped beer parlours and about the rising incidence of public drunkenness in these dank, dark, odoriferous premises.

In 1946 the Drew government decided to grasp the nettle of the liquor question in its own way. Two years earlier it had created a separate licensing body, the Liquor Authority Control Board (later renamed the Liquor Licence Board), and appointed a redoubtable county court judge, W.T. Robb, its chairman. But widespread abuse and violation of the law persisted, and this the new policy of 1946 was intended to curb. Buried deep in the speech from the throne was one seemingly innocuous sentence: 'The Liquor Authority Control Act (1944) will be amended to improve the licensing and controlling of licensed premises.' When Leslie Blackwell introduced the amendments a few weeks later, it was evident that in fact a marked liberalization of the law was in store.

The legislation was admittedly founded on the government's reading of majority public opinion. As the five major cities (Toronto, Ottawa, Hamilton, London, and Windsor) were deemed to be firmly in favour of liberalization, they would be permitted forthwith to operate under the new rules. Elsewhere opinion seemed less certain, so a three-fifths majority in local option votes would be required for approval of any of the five types of licensed establishments defined in Blackwell's bill. These ranged from lowly public houses – a euphemism for the familiar beverage rooms – in which only beer could be sold, through dining-rooms (including restaurants), lounges, taverns, and hotels, the requirement for these last being a number of bedrooms larger than previously and in proportion to the population of the municipality concerned. The legislation not only increased the variety of licensed premises, it seemed bound to lead to their proliferation. The most startling innovation of all was that some of them would be permitted to dispense spirits by the glass, which had not been lawful for thirty years.

The newspapers reported that when Blackwell completed his outline of the bill on first reading, 'the House burst into applause.'[1] Either that approval was confined to the government benches or some who applauded had sober second thoughts, for all three opposition groups spoke and voted against the bill on second reading. Nor was opposition confined to the legislative chamber. The temperance organizations and many concerned church people were much disturbed by what one objector, with inspired alliteration, called this 'lounge liquor lapping legislation.'[2] Ironically, complaints came also from some of their opponents. Brewers disliked the subjection of their retail outlets to the authority of the Liquor Control Board; proprietors of certain hotels feared that when they were surveyed and rated they would, if granted licences at all, continue to be limited to selling beer as mere public houses.

Frost took no part in debating the bill. It was outside the sphere of his two departments, except insofar as the Treasury might derive added revenue from increased sales and higher licence fees. An additional reason for silence may have been that the measure caused him some discomfort personally and politically. It was not because of his upbringing; as he remarked to a clergyman friend in Haliburton, he and his father had long ago parted company on the issue, the son preferring true temperance to strict abstinence.[3] But he had escaped parental influence only to find himself married to one whose prohibitionist ardour was equal to that of the elder Frost, and whose talent for stating her views in forceful language was, if anything, superior. (In later years she relented sufficiently to take an occasional drink of Canadian whiskey.)[4]

Gertrude Frost had been incensed by the earlier successive relaxations of the liquor laws. She was furious when she read in the paper about Blackwell's revelation of this latest step. She was in Toronto at the time, and when Frost got back to his lodgings at the Royal York after the House rose, she 'proceeded without reservation,' he confessed, 'to give me blazes.' After suffering this scolding, 'I had Gert fairly well pacified ... but, unfortunately, I left the radio on this morning, which provoked another all-out attack, although I believe it was not quite as strong as last night. I recognize that in a matter of this sort you have to ride out the storm.'[5]

In his own riding of Victoria-Haliburton he tried to forestall agitation by issuing a reassuring statement about the effects of the changes and by writing letters to some probable critics. These were not couched in defensive language. 'I do not want you to think,' he told the Anglican rector in Lindsay, Clinton Cross, 'that I am in any way making excuses – I am asserting.' His pragmatic stance was that there must be 'laws that will work in the Province of Ontario. One of the factors which you must face is ... that people do not think it is wrong to drink.' Frost was convinced that Lindsay people, like those of many other small towns, did not want spirits sold by the glass there. He found it, however, 'amazing ... how many of them ... have no objection to coming to Toronto ... and to taking liquor in dining rooms and putting it on the table. They do not think it is wrong and they close their eyes to the fact that it is against the law.'

In any case, he argued, local option regulation protected the rights of those opposed to an increase in drinking establishments: they need only muster 40 per cent of the votes plus one to prevent it. Residents of the major centres, too, could by local option, after a trial period, prohibit any or all of the types of licences allowed by the legislation. The police would enforce the law. 'The liabilities [to licence holders] for allowing drunkenness ... are the most severe ever introduced in any jurisdiction,' for the incorruptible Judge Robb and his Liquor Authority Control Board had the power to grant, withhold, or rescind licences. 'The people have asked us to clean up a rotten situation. It is for us therefore to pass a law which ... is enforceable and to enforce it. That we intend to do.'[6]

This more permissive approach did not solve the problem. The management of the sale and use of liquor remained a divisive issue which would bedevil Frost in the coming years.

His main business in the 1946 session was, as usual, the budget.

This one was a mixture of glad tidings about the fiscal year drawing to a close and, in one respect, a disturbing forecast for the one about to begin. Higher than expected revenues had produced a surplus which allowed nearly $6 million in aid to school boards, in addition to the continued one mill subsidy to municipalities for education purposes. Refinancing had reduced interest and capital payments to American lenders by well over $6 million. On the other hand, the estimated gross ordinary expenditures on a variety of desirable undertakings would cause a deficit for fiscal 1946–7 of over $21 million. Deficit financing had little appeal to Frost with his ingrained preference for a pay-as-you-go policy. But he depicted it as only a temporary expedient, going so far as to pledge that the deficit 'will be overtaken from future ordinary revenue.'[7]

That optimistic promise apparently rested on the expectation that Ontario's latest financial proposal would be favourably received by the federal government. It included acceptance of tax rental in principle but made it subject to certain conditions and the adoption of a formula for calculating subsidies different from Ilsley's. But most of the other provinces did not find Ontario's proposal very attractive and Frost feared that the federal government could afford to ignore Ontario's concerns. He pointed out later to Drew: 'I have reason to believe that the Dominion feels that the large forecast deficit brings us that much closer to the end of our rope.'[8] When the Reconstruction Conference met for its final plenary sessions in the spring of 1946, there appeared in fact to be a general disposition to let Ontario twist in the wind.

At the conference, Ottawa came up with modifications of its original proposals which each province could accept or not. Separate agreements would be made with all consenting governments, but the provisions regarding taxing powers remained essentially unchanged. For a term of five years a province would relinquish the three much-debated direct tax fields. One significant concession was offered: provincial income taxes on mining and logging operations would be permitted and be wholly deductible from federal tax. There was no promise to abandon the numerous minor direct taxes, which Ontario and Nova Scotia had demanded. Ottawa would pay a minimum rental of $15 per capita, adjustable upwards in proportion to a rising gross national product. In any province rejecting this, Ilsley noted, there would necessarily be double taxation of incomes and estates. To mitigate this he offered a credit of up to 5 per cent of the tax on income payable to federal coffers. Figures were produced to show that every province would receive larger amounts than under existing arrangements, Ontario at least $14 million more in 1947 and probably, given the expected growth of the Gross National Product (GNP), $20 million more.[9]

At Queen's Park the ministers began at once to analyse this latest proposition, and to decide whether to accept it. They were not convinced that Ilsley's figures showing benefits to Ontario were reliable, and they did not like some features of the plan. They soon decided that Frost and Roland Michener, who had become provincial secretary following his election to the House the year before, should visit Ottawa in the hope of persuading John Bracken and J.M. Macdonnell, the opposition budget critic, to attack these features in the House of Commons. Frost assembled statistical data and ventured to coach them about how to tackle the subject. 'All oppositions in order to emphasize, have to exaggerate to some extent,' he advised Bracken. But he cautioned against going too much into precise figures in debating the matter. 'From an Opposition standpoint, I believe principles are more important than figures, [which] often ... are very misleading.'

Frost wanted them to emphasize that the King government should forsake its 'uncompromising rigidity' in refusing to give up succession duties and minor direct tax fields. It should be content with a monopoly of personal and corporate income taxes, for which a minimum $15 per capita was not an excessive price. If Ilsley objected that such a settlement was too costly, then Bracken should simply reply that 'if they feel they cannot run the country's business efficiently they should resign and that when you take office you will show them how it can be done.'[10] The two federal spokesmen tried to assist but did not make much of an impression. Macdonnell accused the cabinet of violating the spirit of Confederation with its inflexible, take-it-or-leave-it attitude. Bracken made an aggressive speech, as Frost had suggested, but neither his nor Macdonnell's objections had much practical effect.[11] There was not the slightest chance that Ilsley's new plan would be rejected by Parliament, or even significantly amended; rejection was for any province that wished to do so.

A fortnight after the plan was unveiled, Frost received a long handwritten letter from Drew, who had gone home to Guelph for a vacation. Drew believed that the federal-provincial squabble over taxing powers should be viewed as a specific instance of a larger problem – the federal government's attempt to circumvent the constitutional foundations of the federal system. The King government was seeking to impose changes in the British North America Act, 1867, without consulting the provinces. They were starting with the tax structure but 'they will follow as a matter of course with the occupation of legislative and administrative fields as well on the ground that their over-all tax powers demand over-all administrative powers.' (An example of this tactic was the St Laurent redistribution motion.) The premier stressed that the Ontario government must defeat this invasion of its position by planning a counter-attack, and he urged Frost to 'get all our experts thinking on this problem from the aggressive and not the defensive point of view.'[12]

Frost answered this in a discursive twelve-page letter which characteristically dwelt more on practicalities than on the larger issues of federalism. He agreed, of course, that the 'maintenance of the Federal system is of immense importance to our people' and also that the dominion's proposals would in the long run destroy it. 'Certainly they would prevent the Province from doing those things which, by the Constitution, it is our job to do.' But these were dangers that had to be explained in concrete terms.

From an academic standpoint, it is difficult to get the man on the street interested ... His view changes, however, when he begins to see how it will affect him personally ... I have no doubt that when we get away from the academic approach to this matter and discuss the same with our people in the terms of dollars and cents, that [sic] Old Man Ontario will bestir himself ... The long term solution will be illustrated by each one of our voters by the effect on himself personally and on his community. This was Mowat's method ... I think, quite properly, we have refrained from emphasizing this angle because other parts of Canada would say we were selfish. When we are putting the same to our own people, however, it is proper that we should use this argument to the limit.

The ordinary citizen must be convinced that he would not be worse off if Ontario turned down Ottawa's terms and continued to levy all its own direct taxes. After studying the figures with his officials, Frost concluded that 'with the rejection of the Dominion proposals, we can reasonably see our way clear for the period of the agreement.' It would be essential, even at the cost of considering higher and new direct taxes, to keep the provincial levies on personal and business income within the 5 per cent range deductible for federal tax purposes, thus avoiding double taxation. But taking all things together, and assuming even a modest economic expansion and frugal administration, it should be possible to make ends meet.

While recommending that Ontario go its own way, at least for the present, Frost obviously hoped that Drew would not make a big issue of it or burn all his bridges. 'At the moment it seems to me that everything is in favour of going slowly and saying nothing.' The die need not be cast until the close of fiscal 1946 at the end of the following March. There were rumours that Ilsley, would shortly retire. 'This may make it possible to make a deal.' If only Ottawa would offer a fair rental for the two types of income tax and 'vacate the other fields to us, with the possible exception of succession duties, upon which there might be a compromise,' the whole problem could be resolved. 'I feel that, with patience, provided we keep our negotiating position ... we can achieve this.'[13]

The rumours about Ilsley's impending departure from Finance were well founded. In December he moved to Justice and was succeeded by Douglas Abbott, who came over from National Defence. Abbott took charge at a rather awkward moment. Three provinces – Manitoba, Saskatchewan and New Brunswick – had accepted the deal offered in Ilsley's last budget. Then British Columbia managed to extract much better terms. This provoked a private protest from Stuart Garson and a public one from J.B. McNair of New Brunswick. Two days after Abbott's move to Finance, McNair sent to the Prime Minister and released to the press a strongly worded telegram condemning such favouritism and repudiating the agreement he had signed. 'the whole business,' King wrote grumpily in his diary, 'is certainly a terrible muddle and all because of the rigidity of the Finance Department in not yielding a few minor taxes in the last Conference.'[14] Having sweetened the pot for the three original signatories, Abbott announced a revised and more complex offer to those still outside the fold which increased considerably the subsidies they would receive.

Although Frost did not advocate acceptance of the new offer as it stood, he favoured a positive response as a basis of further negotiation. It was, he argued in an analysis prepared for Drew, very close to, and in some respects an improvement on, what Ontario had suggested some months earlier. Of course it entailed surrender of income and corporation taxes but that had already been accepted in principle. On the other hand, it offered joint rather than exclusive federal levying of succession duties, as well as abandonment by Ottawa of its gasoline tax. Frost thought Abbott could be persuaded to give up the other minor direct taxes as well. His officials had calculated that, in addition to these advantages, Ontario would receive higher subsidies under the Abbott scheme than under its own, their actual size being dependent, of course, on the GNP during the five-year span of the agreement. The same would be true for Quebec. Shortly before Abbott made the new offer, the two central provinces had been talking with a view, at least on Ontario's part, to making their tax policies as similar as possible in the practically certain event that both refused the last Ilsley proposition.[15] At Queen's Park, maintaining a common Ontario-Quebec front was thought to be highly desirable and Frost evidently hoped that Duplessis could be persuaded not to reject the new offer out of hand and to engage in amicable discussion about its possible improvement.

That it needed improvement Frost readily admitted, stressing one of its major defects. The federal government had earlier mooted the prospect that it would assume responsibility for assisting the unemployed and would introduce universal old age pensions at age seventy. But those inducements had been withdrawn when the collapse of the conference made it necessary to seek agreements with the provinces individually, and Abbott had intimated that Ottawa could not afford both them and the larger subsidies it was now proffering. '*Before Ontario could give consideration to the Abbott Proposals*,' advised Frost, '*a definite statement would have to be made by the Dominion in connection with social securities, and particularly, Old Age Pensions and Relief for Employables.*'[16] The provinces should seek such an undertaking and not close the door to further negotiation.

This analysis was backed up in talks with Drew, and it appears that he found the premier less favourably impressed than he by what Abbott had brought forth, and in some need of persuasion. He had been around a lot and listening, said Frost. Conversations with people in Ottawa, on the train, at a Victoria County council meeting, at a large dinner in Toronto, with various party supporters, some Tory MPPs, and his brother Cecil had convinced him that 'Ontario is not Quebec and is only mildly interested in the D.P.

controversy.' People feared that there would be double taxation if the federal proposals were turned down, so much so that Frost wondered whether a provincial income tax would ever again be politically possible. Furthermore, the 'average man is in favour of O.A.P. at 70 and does not want us to obstruct,' while municipalities dreaded the cost of large-scale unemployment which neither they nor the province could bear.

To Frost, this all meant that 'now is the time to negotiate ... Our people are war weary. They have had 10 years of turmoil. They want what Bonar Law referred to as *Tranquillity*.' ...The public wanted development of Hydro, natural resources and tourism, immigration, especially into the north, new hospitals, and educational and municipal reform. 'To this end I believe we should devote all energies ... with an eye to an election in autumn 1948 or perhaps spring of 1949. With such a plan we could put the opposition out of business.' Patient persistence had paid dividends in the form of Abbott's offer. 'Is now the time to *drive a bargain*? *I think it is. I believe we can negotiate for everything we want. It can be a victory for us.*'[17]

Frost's sympathetic assessment of the Abbott proposals and his plan of action for further negotiation did not come to fruition. As one by one the other provinces accepted the federal terms, it became evident that Ontario and Quebec would receive short shrift from the Ottawa negotiators. Editorials in the Liberal *Montreal Star* castigating Duplessis and Drew as selfish obstructionists were an indicator to Frost that there would be no further concessions from the King government. Thus, he warned J.M. Macdonnell that to accept Abbott's terms 'would be putting Ontario and Quebec, who have been paying the bills [for the other provinces] in a financial strait-jacket ... Anything approaching a fixed subsidy with us is simply poison.'[18]

Frost summarized the Ontario government's objections in his budget speech. The two main shortcomings of the federal proposals were the withdrawal of the earlier social security plans and the plan's inherent discrimination against Ontario and Quebec. Quebec would receive the lowest and Ontario the second lowest per capita subsidy, despite the fact that their people paid the lion's share of income and corporation taxes to the dominion. 'This is illogical and discriminatory,' Frost declared. 'To this the Province of Ontario could not possibly agree.' It 'has no option therefore but to reject these proposals, the acceptance of which would have been a betrayal of the interests of this province.'

Having chosen to go it alone and raise its own revenue, the Drew government had had to decide what use to make of the three main direct taxes at its disposal. It would, announced Frost, continue to collect succession duties at the same rates (lower than the dominion's which had recently been doubled) and with the same exemptions for estates of $25,000 or less and for charitable bequests. It would also reinstate the tax on business profits at 7 per cent. No personal income tax would be imposed by the province in the coming fiscal year. Frost's advice to Drew that it would be political folly to impose income tax was accepted.

He justified the decision, however, on the ground of the public interest. 'Heavy income taxes imposed without regard to sound principles of taxation, destroy initiative, damage the national economy and, in the long run, dry up those sources of revenue from which a nation should derive the financial strength necessary to provide for expansion and development ... There should be a sweeping reduction in personal income rates.' By deciding not to tax incomes itself and by abstaining from the tax rental agreement, thus saving Ottawa large subsidy payments, Ontario was facilitating such a reduction, and Frost invited the federal government to do the right thing.[19]

Frost anticipated that the lost revenue from income tax would be replaced in part by the yield from the levy on business profits and by an addition to the gasoline tax, for which the way was paved by Ottawa's abdicating that field. Frost exuded optimism. The predicted deficit for the current year had turned into a surplus of nearly half a million dollars; a slightly smaller surplus was forecast because of a considerable increase in expenditure in the coming year. There had been and would be further reductions in the public debt. Special grants were being given to universities and the Ontario College of Education for capital equipment, from a long-accumulating reserve fund that had grown larger than need be. Frost's message was clear: under this government's careful stewardship, Ontario was well able to resist the pressure from Ottawa, preserve its financial autonomy, and take care of its own needs. 'We do not intend to undermine the strength of our province or of Confederation by consenting to the centralization of powers which will leave the development of our great heritage in other hands. We do not ask any other authority to do our job for us.'[20]

A year later Frost reported that going it alone had kept Ontario's finances strong and healthy. Contrary to the prophecies of opposition critics in 1947, the province had derived almost as much revenue from its own taxes as it would have by renting them. There was a large surplus for 1947–8, although spending on health and highways had been higher than anticipated. The net debt had been diminished during the past year by the largest amount ever. No income tax, no increase in existing taxes, and no new taxes would be imposed in the coming year. Ontario's buoyant economy would provide a small surplus in spite of a further rise in spending. The province was poised on the threshold of a great economic development that would bring a more abundant life to all.[21]

A fundamental requirement for future prosperity was an assured, expanding supply of energy. Booming wartime production had caused shortages of fuels in Ontario, and one effect had been to force the Hydro Commission to ration electricity. The difficulty remained after the war as demands for more energy to meet industrial and other needs continued. In the latter half of 1947 a crisis developed in the supply of natural gas to parts of southwestern Ontario. Frost, wearing his Department of Mines hat, was responsible for producing a solution.

While an Alberta oil and gas boom was being fuelled by the discovery of the Leduc field in 1947, Ontario's natural gas was produced in part locally and in part imported from Texas by Union Gas Company of Chatham. The immediate problem as the winter of 1947 approached was an anticipated shortfall in supplies available to the Dominion Natural Gas Company serving London and district. Many of its residential customers occupied premises lacking proper chimneys, which made conversion to other fuels impossible. It was imperative to find more gas somewhere, but where and how to make it available were questions without easy answers. There were a few possible expedients: temporary diversion from another utility, Union Gas, whose market lay in an adjoining area to the west; substitution of propane or butane to be furnished by the federally owned Polymer plant at Sarnia; or the manufacture of gas from oil, which in fact Dominion Gas intended to do at a plant it intended to build at Port Stanley.

Any of these options would require assistance by Ottawa, so Frost got in touch with C.D. Howe, the federal minister of reconstruction, who wielded large powers over production and allocation of supplies and equipment. Diversion from Union Gas might necessitate an expanded flow through its pipeline from Texas; this could not be had without consent of the American authorities which it would be up to Howe to obtain. The transport of substitute gases would require railway tank cars, whose disposition was subject to his authority. And construction of the Port Stanley plant depended on the availability of steel, which again was under his control. Howe was sympathetic but unable to be very helpful. He would try to have the Texas allotment to Union Gas increased, he assured Frost, but there was strong opposition in the United States to larger exports. The assignment of enough tank cars to carry propane or butane from Sarnia was problematic at best. As for the proposed Port Stanley oil conversion facility, the required steel could simply not be spared for the time being.[22]

Faced with this discouragement, Frost turned to another possible solution. He initiated discussions with Union Gas and its local supplier, Imperial Oil Limited, about the latter providing an additional amount sufficient to permit Union to lend Dominion Natural Gas one million cubic feet daily between 1 December and 30 April. Imperial was willing but Union was not. Its general manager politely but firmly refused Frost's request, explaining that its supply situation was becoming progressively worse in relation to demand and that it therefore could not 'voluntarily agree to supply any gas for distribution in the markets of other companies.' Since voluntary compliance was denied, the force of law would have to be invoked and Frost did not hesitate. Under authority of the Natural Gas Conservation Act, he signed a ministerial regulation directing Union to fall in line. With ill-concealed displeasure the company did so. Its manager informed Frost that, rather than buy extra quantities from Imperial Oil, it would obey the order 'by manufacturing high cost gas from oil at our Windsor plant and enriching it with purchased propane.' Presumably this assertion of the right to decide how it would co-operate made up in part for the indignity of being forced to do so.[23]

Frost realized that averting one immediate crisis was not going to solve Ontario's pressing problem of an inadequate supply of a popular and economical fuel in a booming economy. Fortuitously, at a meeting of the Mines Ministers' Committee he met Alberta's minister, Nathan E. Tanner, and a possible long-term solution began to emerge. Tanner explained that, thanks to new discoveries, Alberta was reconsidering its ban on exports of natural gas. It was being pressed to relax the ban by certain American gas companies interested in supplying the northwestern coastal region of the United States. Frost reported to Howe that Tanner had suggested three options for consideration. The first was construction of a pipeline across the prairies and northern Ontario to serve the market north of the lower Great Lakes. 'It would,' Frost remarked realistically, 'involve a very large expenditure and thousands of miles of pipe, which for some time may not be possible.' The second option was to connect the Alberta fields with pipelines in the American middle west, on condition that the requirements of Ontario companies be met by an enlarged flow from Texas. Or, finally, Alberta might supply the northwestern states, with the same *quid pro quo* for southern Ontario. 'All of this,' wrote Frost, 'is interesting and very well worth considering.'

Howe agreed; he too had been investigating methods of conveying Alberta gas to Ontario through American pipelines but could find no practicable way of doing so. Exports from Alberta to the United States could not be allowed unless an equivalent amount of American gas were obtained for another part of Canada. He would gladly try to secure such reciprocity, should the Manning government apply for an export licence, but there was little prospect of getting a greater quantity from south of the line during the winter when it was most needed. 'The most practical suggestion is the one you gave me over the telephone today,' he told Frost, 'namely, that Alberta use its natural gas to manufacture propane, which could then be shipped to Ontario ... I will do what I can to promote this arrangement.' How facilities for its manufacture and shipment might be secured he did not explain, nor did he mention Tanner's first option, an all-Canadian pipeline.[24]

Working away in Toronto at the business of his two departments, at the never-shrinking pile of correspondence, the never-ending round of discussions, at problems to be grappled with and decisions made, Frost was burdened in 1947 with the profound personal sorrow of a family tragedy which came close to causing his departure from public life. Ever since returning from the war, his brother Cecil had been plagued by problems with his eyes, a susceptibility to severe strain and headaches, and an over-sensitivity to light. He had had to have shutters mounted on his office windows to keep out the glare and none of a succession of eye glass prescriptions satisfactorily corrected the condition. He had learned to live with this handicap uncomplainingly, and obviously it had not stood in the way of his leading a very active life.

One day in the autumn of 1946, however, Cecil was suddenly seized by an excruciating pain in the right side of his head and in his right eye. Eventually Dr K.G. McKenzie, a Toronto neurosurgeon, concluded that Cecil was suffering from a brain tumour and that surgery was imperative. Two days later the right front portion of his brain, containing a malignant tumour, was removed, and in a gloomy prognosis the surgeon informed Leslie and Grenville, standing by anxiously for word, that death might be no more than six months away. He thought there was a remote chance, though, that for the time being Cecil would have a reasonably comfortable and active existence. He was taken home and for a while seemed better, getting out to church on Sundays and even doing a little legal work. But in February of 1947 his health began to deteriorate noticeably and from then on he seldom ventured outside the house. He died in early June 1947, before his fiftieth birthday.

This was a devastating blow to Leslie. He had grieved, of course, over his father's sudden death in 1940, but William Frost had enjoyed a full, active lifetime of nearly eighty years. The beloved Mater had succumbed six years later, and that affected Leslie even more deeply, but the wonder was that she had survived for a quarter of a century her drastic surgery for cancer. It was much more difficult to be reconciled to the passing of Cecil in his prime: the dynamic, handsome, eloquent, charming Cecil with whom Leslie had gone to school and then to war, his companion in courtship, his partner in law, his tireless ally in political campaigns and confidant in so many discussions of matters personal, professional, and public. Seldom can the lives of two brothers have been so closely intertwined with such warm rapport.

Leslie convinced himself that his brother's war wound, the superficial bullet laceration over the right temple, had taken its long-delayed toll. Feeling keenly his responsibility for the financial security of Cecil's widow and her two girls, he tried to persuade the Canadian Pensions Commission of this, but his persistent efforts, unsupported by medical testimony, met with no success. The needs of Cecil's family would have to be provided for in other ways. In practical terms that meant, in part, carrying on the law practice, and his feeling that he must commit himself to this nearly led Leslie to retire from the government and from politics. Indeed the belief that he should do so had settled in his mind before Cecil died. He later explained, 'I was then oppressed by the fact that my brother was fatally ill. I had a very considerable practice and all of Cec's work on hand, to say nothing of two Portfolios. It was at that time I decided to leave public life.'

This inclination, encouraged by Gertrude, remained with him as he worked at settling Cecil's estate and, with the help of Thomas Carley, an old friend (and staunch Liberal) who practised in Peterborough, at clearing away the backlog of litigation and other business that had accumulated. 'I'd be more interested and much more happy,' he told a reporter the following spring, 'if I could devote all my time to practising law in Lindsay. The way of life in a town like Lindsay has a tremendous appeal to me.'[25] And yet, the more he thought of the future, the less sure he became that he should or could leave Queen's Park. There was another duty to consider, to Drew and his other colleagues, and to the party. No one was indispensable, he knew that, but his retirement would be a serious blow to the government.

Moreover, ten years in the legislature had created many valued friendships and a comfortable, wholly agreeable familiarity with the corridors of power. Four years in office had accustomed him to the satisfaction of working out solutions, of giving directions and making important decisions that influenced provincial affairs. He was regarded as the number two man in the cabinet, whose judgment was sought, whose influence counted. He felt no consuming desire to control or dominate, no overweening ambition to advance his own interests on the public stage, but he could not at that moment bring himself to turn his back on all this for the life of a small-town lawyer. So he found a new partner to look after the firm, William Richardson, the first of several who came and went in the ensuing years. Frost gave what assistance he could, visiting the office when in Lindsay and doing some work, mainly in settling estates, but he was too busy in Toronto to spend much time on legal business.[26] The idea of returning to private life was not for the present entirely abandoned; from time to time the temptation was strong. Important political changes in the offing at both Toronto and Ottawa, however, resulted in his career as an active practising lawyer never being resumed.

Frost had remarked more than once on George Drew's greater interest in national and international than in provincial affairs. Early in 1948, as dissatisfaction with John Bracken's performance mounted and intensifying pressure was exerted on him to retire, it became probable that Drew would soon have a chance to go after the leadership he wanted in place of the one he already had. None could deny that Bracken had worked hard at the job of opposition leader in the unfamiliar domain of national politics, but he lacked the charisma to win elections.

It was widely believed that Bracken's prospective retirement, advised by even some of his closest friends,[27] prompted Drew's surprise announcement as the legislature was about to prorogue in

April 1948 that there would be a provincial election on 7 June. Drew's explanation for going to the people only three years after the last appeal was that he wanted popular sanction for a projected large-scale expansion and modernization of the Hydro system, including the conversion of those areas of southern Ontario served with 25 cycle power to the standard 60 cycle. Although the bill authorizing the conversion had been passed unanimously by the House and the planned borrowings approved, Drew professed to see evidence of serious opposition.[28]

Drew's argument struck many as laboured and caused suspicion that he had some ulterior motives in calling an early election. Liberal critics, in particular, asserted that Drew intended to use a provincial electoral victory as the weapon to knock Bracken off his shaky pedestal.

If Drew did plan to use the election as a springboard to the national leadership, things did not turn out quite as he hoped. After a comparatively quiet campaign, the voters returned his government but with a sharply reduced majority. Drew suffered personal defeat in Toronto High Park at the hands of William Temple, a former airforce officer and now a prohibitionist CCFer, who inveighed eloquently against the recent demoralizing liquor legislation. Two other ministers, Roland Michener and William Wallace, likewise lost their seats. The CCF, which Drew had gone out of his way to attack in customary fashion as largely a collection of crypto-communists, took altogether eleven seats in Toronto and the Yorks from the Tories. Jolliffe recaptured York South, and the two Communist members, MacLeod and Salsberg, were re-elected. The Conservatives also gave up seats to the CCF and Liberals in other urban ridings in Hamilton, Brantford, London, Waterloo, and Ontario County. On the other hand, they improved their position in the north and took two substantially French-speaking constituencies, Russell and Stormont, from the Grits. The final tally showed the Conservatives with fifty-three seats, a drop of thirteen from 1945, the CCF, which displaced the Liberals as the official opposition, with twenty-one, a gain of thirteen, and the Liberals holding steady at fourteen. These totals roughly reflected changes in the distribution of the popular vote. It all amounted to a reverse that marred the premier's winning image.

Frost, who easily held off two opponents in Victoria, one of them his old rival William Newman, appraised the general result in a letter to Harold Hale, remarking that the election contained many lessons. One in particular, a question of manner, not policy, impressed him: 'The party's misfortunes were largely within a dozen or so miles of Toronto City Hall and this situation was much aggravated by intemperate statements and attitudes ... This I personally very much regret ... Personally I think that abuse and sarcasm, except in most exceptional cases, do more harm than good.'[29]

Bracken's resignation was submitted in July 1948. Before long Drew, undaunted by his recent setback, announced he would be a candidate at the leadership convention to be held in Ottawa at the beginning of October. When that time came his personal defeat in High Park and the party's reduced majority in Ontario proved to be no detriment. He won easily, routing John Diefenbaker and Donald Fleming on the first ballot. This result had generally been taken for granted by Ontario Conservatives and thus during the summer of 1948 Frost came under some pressure to stand as his successor. Both Hale's *Orillia Packet and Times* and the Lindsay *Watchman-Warder*, neither an entirely unbiased voice, declared flatly that he was the man for the job. Although 'a rather retiring disposition has kept him from seeking the limelight,' he had been, Hale proclaimed, a 'conspicuous success' as treasurer and mines minister. 'He has shown sound judgment, firmness and progressiveness, and at the same time a kindly and diplomatic disposition that enabled him to get his way with a minimum of friction ...' As a speaker he displayed 'a sincere and convincing style of argument, which wins a tolerant and sympathetic hearing.' Also to his credit from the perspective of Simcoe County was that he 'has not cultivated the political nabobs of Toronto. But on his record he has won the confidence and good will of the rank and file throughout the province.'[30] Frost definitely did not consider himself a candidate, and informed a Tory MPP: 'Concerning myself, as you know, Cecil's passing a year ago made a very great difference. I am not in a position to "burn my bridges" as I once was and I really think that it would be impossible for me to take on any further committments [sic]. The fact is I have too many now.'[31]

Other ministers were ready to take Drew's place. Indeed, Leslie Blackwell hastily announced his aspirations for the provincial job and began pressing for a convention before the end of the year. That smacked to many of a power play that must be resisted, an attempt to stampede the party before other possible contenders had enough time to consider their position and organize in their own interests. Among those opposed to an early convention was Drew. To that end, and possibly to head off Blackwell, whose relations with Drew were believed to be less than friendly and who was considered the front runner should a convention be held soon,

Drew recommended that Thomas L. Kennedy be appointed as his successor.[32]

It was clear, though, that the Kennedy appointment could be no more than a stopgap; there would have to be a convention as the party constitution required. No one seriously objected to the new premier designate, who was universally popular, but obviously a septuagenarian in rather frail health could be only a caretaker, and for not too long a time. Hence it was agreed in cabinet, and subsequently approved unanimously at a caucus meeting in Drew's home, that Kennedy would become interim leader and premier pending a convention, at which he would not be a candidate. The party executive chose the following April and the Royal York Hotel as the time and place. In short order Drew resigned the premiership, Kennedy was summoned by the lieutenant-governor, a cabinet shuffle occurred which left Frost's responsibilities unaltered and the new administration began to prepare for summoning the House.

The contrast between old premier and new was stark. Kennedy had a relaxed, informal, homespun, rather casual manner, and a gift for gentle, ironic humour. When the House met, A.A. MacLeod felicitated the government's new leader and remarked on the contrast between old and new. Noting that in the absence of Drew (the 'Big Chief'), Kennedy had customarily been acting premier, MacLeod remarked: 'I always like to think of that particular partnership as "arsenic and old lace" ... and having suffered through four years of "arsenic," I feel very sure that "old lace" will be welcome, it is softer, and ... will help to relieve the tensions which have existed here since 1944.'[33]

But the really fascinating subject for speculation was who would succeed Kennedy at the April convention. In the assembly MacLeod indulged his distinctive wit in some predictions about that. He discussed the chances of the most prominent contenders and dismissed all of them, particularly Blackwell, for the *Globe and Mail* and the *Telegram* had not supported him. Jovially he then considered his final contestant: 'I suppose I should refer to him as "the Reluctant Dragon," the hon. Provincial Treasurer ... If I were asked to make a prophecy and point my finger at the next Prime Minister of this province after the present Prime Minister has laid down his burden, that man would be the hon. Provincial Treasurer.'

MISS A. MACPHAIL (York East): He is good looking, too.
SOME HON. MEMBERS: Hear, hear.
MR. MACLEOD: That is quite true.

AN HON. MEMBER: Take a bow.

HON. LESLIE M. FROST ... : Mr. Speaker, do not take that too seriously. My hon. friend [Mr. MacLeod] is wrong in nearly everything he prophesies, you know.

MR. MACLEOD: Now, now. If he becomes the Prime Minister of Ontario we shall be in the happy position of being able to claim that we have in this province the best looking Prime Minister that any province in Canada has ever had in its history.

SOME HON. MEMBERS: Hear, hear.

MR. MACLEOD: But, of course, that may hurt your chances, because who believes for a moment that 'Gorgeous George' would ever permit a better looking man than himself to be the Prime Minister of Ontario. I predict that when Dr. McCullagh goes into high gear and lays down the law and says: 'It has got to be the hon. member for Lindsay,' you will be just like Barkis, you will be willing to step in.[34]

Thus, while exaggerating the power of 'Dr.' McCullagh, MacLeod accurately foretold, not for the first time, the unfolding of events. Barkis would indeed be willing.

Front and Centre

The short life of the Kennedy government was marked by one explosive episode in which Frost, for the first time in his public career, found himself at the centre of bitter controversy. The Toronto *Telegram* described him as 'mild-mannered,' the 'most tranquil man in the Ontario legislature.'[1] Those who worked with him knew well that there was much more to him than tranquillity, that he could be strong-willed, tough-minded, short-tempered, commanding, and unafraid of a fight if there had to be one. But head-on collisions in public were not to his taste. He preferred smoothing things over with a kind word, a glad hand, a homely joke, reconciling rather than exposing and aggravating differences. So it suited him to leave confrontations and slanging matches in the House or on the hustings to others, especially Drew, who revelled in and conducted them with a panache that helped to make and keep him the focus of attention.

Drew, indeed, had so dominated the scene and monopolized the headlines, had been so much the target of opponents in the House and the press, that in public his ministers were comparatively inconspicuous figures. Of course they were noticed, some more than others, as they sponsored their bills, answered for their departments, attended meetings, met delegations, gave speeches – in short, did the things expected of ministers. None, however, rivalled 'the Big Chief' in prominence. In the theory of the cabinet system, Drew may have been only first among equals, but he enjoyed the leadership role and he had no equals.

Tom Kennedy was not the dynamic force Drew had been. His age, indifferent health, and lack of driving temperament made him less eager to assert his authority, however transitory, and put his stamp on the administration. He was frequently away from his office, and from the House when it was sitting, and at those times Frost filled in for him. 'I am not sure of getting back to the buildings this week or perhaps next,' Kennedy wrote in a typical note. 'I wonder if you would carry on for me.'[2] With this added responsibility, Frost's own retirement, a course still lingering in the back of his mind, was out of the question.

Until now Frost's one major performance each session had come on budget day. Of course, he was in charge of numerous other measures year by year and had always taken an active part in debate. But the budget address was the big moment, an occasion for reviewing the past with pride and projecting optimism about the foreseeable future. His sixth budget was the familiar recitation of rising revenues and higher outlays for worthy purposes. He pledged that Ontario was not about to enter a tax rental accord with Ottawa or reinstate its own personal income tax. As on previous budget days, Frost reviewed dominion-provincial relations, and produced figures to prove the advantages to Ontario of retaining its taxing power. Things had gone so well, in fact, that for yet another year there would be no new taxes and a few existing ones would be either reduced or repealed. The one tiny cloud in the sky was a marked rise in the net debt but that would soon go away. It was largely indirect, Frost explained, resulting from heavy, provincially guaranteed borrowings by the Hydro Commission. 'This debt will be liquidated without cost to the general taxpayer of Ontario.' The opposition parties disputed some of his assertions, questioned his figures, doubted his forecasts, but his successes refuted their arguments.[3]

Three weeks later, however, Frost had a first-class quarrel on his hands when, leading the government in Kennedy's absence, he introduced a bill relating indirectly to estate taxes. There had been no specific mention of this legislation in the throne speech or in the budget. Notice had been given of intention to amend the Succession Duty Act to broaden exemption for religious bodies and for widows and children, nothing more. But when Frost moved first reading of an 'Act respecting certain charitable and other gifts,' it was evident that the government was bent on more far-reaching action. In essence the bill stipulated that a charitable trust or foundation would be permitted to own no more than 10 per cent of the capital stock of any business, and must within three years divest itself of excess holdings in one of two ways: by sale, subject to the proviso that the proceeds could not be invested in more than 10 per cent of the shares of any one company; or by outright gift to specific charities, on condition that no charitable organization hold more than one-tenth of the stock.

What prompted this measure? Frost's explanation, widely disbelieved, was that steps must be taken to prevent the duplication in Ontario of a tax evasion device already causing problems in the United States. He remarked that bequests to charity were in the public interest and should be encouraged, as they were by the Succession Duty Act. Exemptions from death duties were in effect 'a gift from the public' and thus 'the largest contributor to charitable and religious organizations ... is the government and the people of this province.' It was essential that the stated intent of charitable trusts and foundations be carried out; to assure this, tighter regulations under the Charitable Accounting Act would be adopted. But a troubling situation arose when outright ownership of a business or a controlling stake in it was bequeathed to a charitable trust. In that case the trustees, a self-perpetuating body, could appoint themselves officers, directors, and managers of the business, pay themselves such remuneration as they chose, and operate the business in perpetuity.

And why should they not? Because, Frost contended, it might have undesirable results. For one thing, support of charity could become secondary to the operation of the business, especially if the testator had neglected to prescribe which charities should be assisted. In that event, the foundation would turn out to be a cloak for the conduct of a business solely for the profit of the trustees who controlled it. Such a business would enjoy an unfair competitive advantage. Frost described an ostensibly hypothetical case: 'The business is operated as a charitable trust. It has been relieved of succession duty. Very large sums of public money indeed are invested in the foundation by means of the exemption referred to. The trustees are under no obligation to pay dividends. They may provide goods and services at such prices as to constitute unfair competition to the detriment of other businesses which are ... endeavouring to pay the claims which the public impose by way of taxation.'[4]

The bill imposed no new or additional taxes, Frost pointed out, nor would it apply to the stock of any company vested in a religious denomination. Frost had studiously avoided referring to any particular foundation, but most people connected the measure with the estate of Joseph E. Atkinson, founder and, until his death in May 1948, owner of the *Toronto Daily Star* and the *Star Weekly*, in their combined circulation the largest newspaper enterprise in Canada. Atkinson's will, reflecting the wish that his newspapers be protected from private outside control, bequeathed the Toronto Star Limited, the company operating them, and the Toronto Star Realty Limited, in which ownership of the *Star* building at 80 King Street West was vested, to the Atkinson Charitable Foundation, established in 1942 but with no notable charitable donations to its credit. The directors of the two companies were also trustees of the foundation. The formidable opposition to the Charitable Gifts Act, which emerged in and out of the legislature, assumed that it was a vengeful means of destroying the *Star*, inveterate foe of the government and the Conservative party, by forcing dispersal of the parent companies' shares. The *Star* denounced the bill as vicious, 'violent in its destruction of one of the primary rights of man.' It was 'a general measure with a particular purpose ... to vitiate and annul the disposal of his wealth' by Atkinson.[5]

The *Star* was soon joined by newspapers of almost every stripe across the province, as well as an array of individual critics. It was not surprising that the Liberal *Ottawa Citizen* attacked the bill as a device 'to destroy the largest newspaper in Canada because of its long-standing feud with Mr. George Drew ... and because of the *Star*'s aggressive opposition to Tory policies.'[6] More disconcerting was the judgment of Brockville's *Recorder and Times*, a paper which had little sympathy with the *Star*'s editorial views. It called the act 'a thoroughly iniquitous and odoriferous method of dealing with a political foe.'[7] Still worse was the regretful but emphatic condemnation by the *Ottawa Journal*, than which no more ardent press supporter of the Conservative party existed. Even Frost's devoted champion, the *Packet and Times*, while approving the principle of the bill, urged that its retroactive application be removed. In fact the only unequivocal support came from the other two Toronto papers, the *Globe* and the *Telegram*, both now owned by George McCullagh.

Frost had stressed the alleged advantage over its competitors that a business owned by a charitable foundation would enjoy. As McCullagh's newspapers could suffer the greatest loss it was widely believed that he had engineered the bill, probably with the connivance of his friend Drew. The former was reputed to have great influence at Queen's Park and he assuredly had scores to settle with the *Star*. McCullagh admitted, 'Personally, I relish the blame,' adding 'Knocking out that rag is my only passion.'[8]

Was there not reason, nevertheless, to think that the Conservatives, with McCullagh's encouragement, were out to 'get' the *Star* and thwart the late Mr Atkinson's desires? The *Brockville Recorder and Times* revealed that before the bill was introduced it had 'actually heard in Tory circles boasts to the effect that the ... Government of Ontario is "going to fix the *Toronto Star*." '[9] Kelso Roberts later recalled a conversation with Ralph Cowan, the *Star*'s circulation manager, who recounted that McCullagh had urged him to join the newly acquired *Telegram*. His objective, said McCullagh as Roberts reported Cowan's version, was to out-strip the *Star* and, McCullagh assured Cowan, 'the charitable trust set up by Mr. Atkinson would be torn to shreds.' So Cowan formed the definite opinion 'that Mr. McCullagh was in on the discussions leading to the Charitable Gifts Act.'[10]

Frost categorically denied this allegation then and afterward. But once the act was announced, McCullagh, by giving credence to the suspicion that it had a malicious political motivation, was more hindrance than help. 'His interpretation of the Act which was not mine,' Frost reminisced, 'made it extremely hard for me, and as a matter of fact, in the first instance turned all the Ontario press against me.' The measure had originated in the Treasury Department, nowhere else. 'I never had it in mind, and I am sure the Treasury people did not, to be vindictive towards Mr. Atkinson.'[11]

In the fall of 1948 Frost had instructed Chester Walters to set up an interdepartmental committee of civil servants to look into the tax implications of charitable trusts. He wanted it to examine patents already issued and applications pending in order to discover general trends in their character and purposes, and what effect their exemption from succession duties would have on provincial revenues. It should also answer another question: 'Are these foundations being used for actual charitable purposes or are they a subterfuge, or are they capable of becoming a subterfuge to provide for hidden bequests and benefactions free of succession duties?' He added: 'I [do not] desire to do anything which would deter people from setting up truly charitable foundations. As a matter of public policy it seems to me ... advisable to encourage such things ...' It was equally important, however, that trusts not be created 'for the purpose of evasion of our taxation laws; otherwise the situation would become such that governments could not operate.'[12]

The committee drafted a one-page summary of its findings which did not satisfy Frost, who asked for more information. He wanted a list of all private Ontario charitable trusts, indicating which had been incorporated during the past year, and a review of the two estates he evidently had chiefly in mind, of J.E. Atkinson and W.E.

Mason. 'What if any differences are there and how should it [*sic*] be dealt with?'¹³ Mason, a strong Conservative, had died at about the same time as Atkinson. The bulk of his property, including the *Sudbury Star*, was willed to a foundation bearing his name, with instruction that its funds be devoted mainly to assisting the Sudbury General Hospital. Ordinarily the Mason estate would have paid about $3 million in death duties, the Atkinson estate about $8 million.

There was no doubt that Atkinson had hoped to escape such duties on the major part of his wealth or of his fear that, failing this, the *Star* might have to be sold for the money to pay them. Application had been made to Queen's Park to have the Atkinson Foundation recognized as charitable but this had not been granted when he died. In addition he had tried, partly through personal appeals to Mackenzie King, to persuade the federal government to amend its law so as to make all instead of only half of large charitable bequests tax free. The King government was receptive but the change was not enacted until after Atkinson's death, sufficiently retroactive to apply to his estate.¹⁴

In moving second reading of the bill, Frost insisted that no trust honestly created for charitable ends need have any fear. The only complaint would come 'from those who intend to rackateer and to subvert the high purposes of charity.' Upon being asked whom he had in mind in using that language, Frost told his questioner not to be so 'touchy,' but it became clear that he was thinking of the Atkinson Foundation. Thus far he had not mentioned it by name in the House but now, confronted with the *Star*'s allegations of sinister motives and bad faith, he felt constrained to do so. Quoting the will, he tried to show that in Atkinson's mind philanthropy was secondary to operation of the newspaper business, with, in the language of the document, 'the profit motive, while still important, subsidiary to ... the chief functions of a metropolitan newspaper' and propagation of 'the doctrines and beliefs which I have promoted in the past.' Inasmuch as funds for worthy causes were to come out of earnings, this subordination of the profit motive, Frost contended, showed that the charitable objective was incidental. 'Is this government on behalf of the people of this province ... justified in allowing a contribution of ... the taxpayers' money for this purpose?' And what did that contribution in the form of uncollected death duties amount to? Tacitly admitting that his estimate lacked a firm basis, he thought that it was more than $5 million.

The amount in any event was academic, since no effort was being made to tax the estate. The only aims of the Charitable Gifts Act were to see that charity was served and to prevent unfair business competition. Respecting this latter point, the weakest in his case, he left the impression that a business controlled by a trust or foundation would not be taxed like an ordinary company. A typical profit-making company 'pays taxes to the state,' while one owned by a foundation 'is largely relieved of the profit motive and competes most unfairly.' But the truth was, as the *Star* was at pains to point out, that the Toronto Star Limited would be taxed on its income by both levels of government like any other enterprise, with earnings after taxes going to the foundation for philanthropic disbursement. Moreover, nothing other than suspicion was adduced to back up the claim that the new proprietors of the two newspapers would be less strongly motivated to maximize profits than Atkinson himself had been.[15]

Frost was followed in the debate on second reading by Jolliffe, who delivered a remarkable speech of more than seven hours' duration stretching over portions of two days. That he went on so long was partly owing to frequent interruptions from across the aisle, in particular by Frost who was allowed unusual latitude by the Speaker. During its later stages Jolliffe's set discourse gave way to a running argument between the two, to the accompaniment, in the face of warnings by the Speaker that they would not be tolerated, of displays from the gallery of support for Jolliffe. As the latter talked on, Frost became convinced, and said so, that he was attempting a filibuster and had made himself the agent of the *Star*, 'your sponsor downtown,' which the opposition leader hotly denied. On Jolliffe's first day, a Wednesday, there was discussion among the ministers about how to deal with the incipient filibuster. 'Blackwell wanted to go ahead,' Frost recalled, 'and sit night and day and force the legislation through. I disagreed. I knew that the CCF ... were bringing in blankets, food etc., to their fortress in the opposition rooms.'[16] Better to foil them by cooling things down than continue the engagement in such an overheated atmosphere. Therefore he moved the adjournment of the House at II p.m. and on the ensuing two days it devoted itself to other bills and to passing estimates. The Charitable Gifts Act was set aside until the following Monday, when Jolliffe led off with the balance of his speech. The debate continued with a good deal of warmth for another four days.

There *was*, indeed, something odd about the CCF, and equally the two Communists – all champions of equality, foes of privilege, intent on destruction of a capitalist system that encouraged accumulation and retention of great personal riches – defending a testamentary contrivance such at Atkinson's. For the obvious aim of the will was not only perpetual control of valuable properties by a favoured few, but avoidance of estate taxes which the CCF praised as an indispensable means of sharing the wealth.

In his effective attack on the bill, Jolliffe was able to show that the act had little or nothing to do with collecting estate duties or ensuring that a professed charitable purpose was fulfilled. Had those been its objects, powers already at the government's disposal, notably in the Charities Accounting Act, were sufficient to achieve them. The true object, he asserted, was clearly political and calculated to assist (if it was not inspired by) George McCullagh: to destroy the government's most formidable journalistic opponent. Moreover, Jolliffe reminded the House, for years the *Telegram* had been owned and operated by a trust created by its founder, John Ross Robertson, with the directive that its profits go to assisting the Hospital for Sick Children. For some mysterious reason the government had seen nothing wrong in that.[17]

Concluding the debate after Jolliffe and others from all four parties had had their say, Frost announced that in the light of various representations some amendments to the legislation would be proposed. The maximum time allowed a foundation to dispose of its excess stock in a company would go up from three to seven years, with further extensions being granted by the Supreme Court of Ontario as particular circumstances might make proper. During that period companies operated by charitable trusts would be required to file with the public trustee their balance sheets and statements of profit or loss, along with disclosure of directors' fees and executive salaries over $8,000. In that interim, trustees of a foundation controlling more than half the shares of a business would meet annually with the public trustee to determine the profits in the previous calendar year and the amount to be turned over to the foundation, with the Supreme Court to adjudicate in case of disagreement. Finally, and significantly from the standpoint of the *Star*, while a foundation as such would be debarred from owning more than one-tenth of a company, its trustees could in their own right purchase a controlling interest.[18] Thus they or their successors could acquire and operate the *Star* and *Star Weekly*, as in due course they did, and continue if they wished to disseminate the views and support the causes dear to the heart of J.E. Atkinson. These amendments were approved and the bill received third reading, forty-seven votes to thirty-four, on the day before the House was prorogued. In its final form the policy was less repugnant to the trustees of the Atkinson Foundation than as originally drafted, but the *Star* would continue to denounce it.

The session ended little more than a fortnight before the leadership convention was to open on 25 April 1949. Much uncertainty remained about who the candidates would be. Two, Leslie Blackwell and Kelso Roberts, had long since declared themselves. There was speculation that five others would run: Robert Saunders, chairman of Hydro, Toronto mayor Hiram McCallum, Dana Porter, George Doucett, and Frost. Saunders, whom Drew reputedly wanted to be his successor after a Kennedy interregnum, professed indifference. 'I have enough to do at Hydro today looking after horsepower,' he said, 'without thinking of dark horses.' That did not rule him out and a few days before the convention he was still being mentioned in the rumour market.[19] McCallum appeared unsure until in his welcoming remarks at the convention he announced that he would not run.[20] The three ministers were considered the principal contenders and shortly after prorogation first Porter and then Frost announced that they were in the race. But the popular, respected Doucett kept his own counsel.

Frost had been under pressure for months to get into the race. He was sometimes depicted as lacking ambition, but that was not entirely accurate. He was not obviously ambitious, but he was not wanting in self-confidence or fondness for playing a directing role. By the time arrangements for Kennedy's temporary succession were made, he was prepared to consider seriously the prospect of moving to the top. 'The political situation ... has caused me a great deal of concern from my own personal standpoint,' he wrote to Harold Hale at the end of October. 'You can quite realize that Cec's passing has made this very, very difficult for me. Under the circumstances, I have just been letting things take their course ... This does not alter the fact, however, that I am confronted with a very big problem.'[21]

Of course the problem could have been at once removed had Frost simply ruled himself out. He did not. His failure to deny a press report in February 1949 that he would 'definitely' run did nothing to discourage those who wanted him,[22] nor did the manner in which he piloted the Charitable Gifts Act through the House. Whatever they thought of the measure, most Tories were impressed by a performance that made him suddenly much the most prominent minister. He had faced the criticisms of the policy firmly but not inflexibly, and for the most part with patience and good humour. Even its severest critics such as Jolliffe had made a point of expressing regard for him personally. Frost finally ended the speculation on 12 April with a two-sentence press release stating that since the end of the session five days earlier he had considered the matter and decided to stand.[23] Obviously he had thought about it for longer than that, but exactly when he made up his mind only he knew for sure. Once the decision was made, a rudimentary campaign apparatus was hurriedly created. It was less embryonic than a remark attributed to Frost after the convention would lead one to think: 'Hell, Gert and I just stood in the lobby of the Royal York and shook hands with the delegates.' But compared with what some of the others had working for them, especially Blackwell with his long head start, it was simplicity itself, with no resemblance to the elaborate, expensive organizations of a later generation.

A small committee of advisers was set up but there were no media consultants, no public relations experts, no privately commissioned polls. And lack of time ruled out trips around the province to meet delegates, even had there been the inclination to make them and funds to pay the costs. The total expenses of his campaign came to less than three thousand dollars[24] and consisted mainly of charges for printing and postage, and for thirty-five hundred buttons and three banners bearing the message 'Frost for Leader.' The same slogan appeared on the back of a four-page pamphlet, with his photograph on the cover and inside a thumb-nail biographical sketch which, as Frost saw it, 'gives the delegates all of the information in a concise way without any high-pressuring. This, I think, is most desirable.' The sketch stressed the trait that was his hallmark, one natural to him but carefully nurtured as the image he wanted to project: 'He has never allowed his public responsibilities to completely detach him from living the simple country life which he has always lead [sic]. He enjoys his hobbies of fishing and hunting but his greatest hobby is "people".'[25]

The only other piece of written material figuring in Frost's run for the leadership, although he did write personally to a number of individuals soliciting support, was a brief letter to all delegates and alternates with a promise to 'give my very best efforts [if] you feel that I merit your support.' Afterwards he remarked that this letter 'was about all the organization – the rest was goodwill.'[26] And goodwill he received; offers of help came from all over the province.

This support was indicative of both fondness for the man and a view of him as representing the non-metropolitan element in the party. Dislike of Toronto, of the power and pretensions that had earned it the name of 'Hogtown,' was as much in evidence elsewhere in Ontario as in the rest of Canada. The three others, Blackwell, Roberts, and Porter (Doucett at length decided to stay out), were all residents of the city and could be identified with it despite efforts to broaden their base. Frost and his advisers were careful to play up his small-town background and affiliations: the letter to the delegates was deliberately postmarked Lindsay; the twelve scrutineers selected to represent him at the balloting were carefully chosen to personify the different sections of Ontario, with but one from Toronto. At the other extreme, Porter's were all from the city.[27]

The convention was to open on a Monday afternoon. Frost spent the weekend in Lindsay and drove down to Toronto on Monday morning with Gertrude. She was thought to have discouraged him from seeking the leadership,[28] to have hoped, in fact, for his retirement after Cecil's death. But now that he was in the race she was prepared to give her all for victory. They found the lobby of the Royal York crowded with the party faithful. Nearly seventeen hundred voting delegates and over twelve hundred alternates were registered, and the crowd was swollen by many other enthusiasts who had come to talk up their favourite candidate and enjoy the fun. This was the largest assemblage to which the hotel had played host since opening for business twenty years before.

It was a cross-section of provincial society. Farmers from the back concessions in their Sunday suits rubbed shoulders with business and professional men from the cities, full of *savoir-faire*. Merchants and tradesmen, doctors, lawyers, and salesmen from across Old Ontario mingled with their counterparts from the distant northern regions visiting a centre of power from which they felt a certain estrangement. The largest contingent of women ever to attend a Conservative convention, nearly three hundred and fifty, was in the hall, and one of them, Mrs Robert Cumming, a vice-president of the party, was to second Frost's nomination.

The Royal York's main ballroom, serving as the convention hall, reminded one reporter of a midway. Booths for all the candidates, each bedecked with a blown-up photograph of its man, had been set up around the room as focal points dispensing literature, buttons, and sound advice. Large signs urging support for the contestants covered the walls, and placards were propped up in every corner. A troubadour strolled around the hotel strumming a guitar and singing the praises of Dana Porter. The Frost committee had engaged three pipers and a drummer, who strode through the lobby, the ballroom, and other public areas emitting sounds that would have warmed the blood of their man's Scottish grandfather. Away from this carnival atmosphere a suite of rooms had been reserved for each contender; there the delegates were urged to repair for a handshake, a few friendly words, and, in Porter's case, entertainment by a girl accordionist. Frost was said to be keeping 'banker's hours' in his suite, and these were posted all over the hotel with an invitation to 'come up and talk it over.'[29]

Many did so, but one delegate found himself there unintentionally. James Maloney, a young man from Renfrew County, well known as a Blackwell supporter and worker, was lodged down the hall from the Frost suite. One evening, making for his room, he passed the door to the suite just as it was opened by Gertrude to accept a telegram from a bellhop. Spying him, she said, 'Jim Maloney, come in here.' It was as much a command as an invitation. He entered to find the Frosts entertaining a group of friends. Being from an enemy camp, Maloney felt ill at ease, despite being warmly greeted by the host, and his embarrassment was not lessened when Gertrude began introducing him around the room as Mr James Maloney, KC. After the third such introduction he felt bound to set the record straight. 'But Mrs. Frost,' he objected, 'I am not a K.C.' 'What, you're not a K.C.,' she exclaimed in a voice all could hear. 'Les, I want you to attend to that.' Perhaps Les did, because before very long Maloney's name appeared in a list of new King's Counsel.[30]

During the two days preceding the voting on Wednesday afternoon, certain preliminaries had to be got through. Mayor McCallum's welcoming address, a few remarks by A.D. McKenzie, the chairman, and various committee reports. But the audience had come chiefly to hear speeches by Kennedy and Drew. The former spoke briefly, dwelling on how in the last session of the House 'our Liberal friends – God bless them – ... voted 32 [times] with the C.C.F. and 31 votes they voted with the Communists and the C.C.F. – not with us ... I'd like to run an election platform on that record alone.' Drew held forth at greater length in a characteristically well-composed and well-delivered oration, on a favourite theme, the dangers of international communism. But all these were mere appetizers before the main course, the speeches of the four candidates.

Speaking in alphabetical order as the party constitution stipulated, they were allowed fifteen minutes each. Blackwell started off first. A native of Lindsay, two years younger than Frost, he had successfully practised law in Toronto until appointed attorney general in 1943. By common consent, allowing for the dislike by many of the liquor legislation to which his name was attached, Blackwell had performed well in that office. Being a somewhat combative, blunt-spoken man, however, he was regarded by some as less 'safe' than Frost. Relations between him and Drew were reputed to have become less than harmonious and shortly before the latter's retirement from provincial politics Blackwell submitted his resignation from the cabinet. It had not taken effect, though, and upon Drew's departure he changed his mind, becoming the first declared aspirant for the succession. But Blackwell was believed to be out of favour with the party establishment.

Leslie Blackwell was known to have strength and influential backers across the province. His speech, a ringing appeal for party unity and a lucid exposition of his approach to economic development that made a bow to every important interest group, did not disappoint those committed to him. Whether it changed any minds or swayed the uncommitted was the question.

Frost spoke next. Each nominee was presented by two advocates. Frost had chosen Sam Hughes of Welland, grandson of the redoubtable Sir Sam, and Mrs Cumming, a leading northern Conservative from Haileybury. Both made much of Frost's small town and rural associations. 'Bearing the name I do,' said Hughes, 'the words Victoria and Haliburton have for me the sound of trumpets.' He reminded the audience that the enduring roots of the party lay in the soil of Ontario and affirmed that never 'since the days of Howard Ferguson have we been able to vote a minister in as premier who speaks with such authority for ... rural Ontario.' Mrs Cumming echoed that in praising the accomplishments of Frost, 'a product of Ontario life outside the big cities.'[31] Frost himself made no allusion to this but dwelt upon the many achievements of Conservative governments since 1943 and the promise of still better things ahead. He also picked up the cue from the speeches of Kennedy and Drew in giving the back of his hand to 'Socialists and Communists and weak people who go along with them. They would change our way of life [and] undermine and destroy our fundamental beliefs.' The party must reaffirm its devotion to the principles and policies that had made Ontario great. 'Personal initiative, vision, development. From these things have come the fine standards of life we enjoy to-day.' Almost half of provincial outlays were now spent on human services, and the means to pay for them must come from further economic growth. 'Jobs, new wealth, development, expansion, industry and population are the answers to better and fuller standards of life and security.'[32] As after Blackwell's speech, a noisy demonstration erupted at the close of Frost's. When it subsided the chairman called on those presenting Dana Porter. The mild-mannered, soft-spoken Porter was also a lawyer and like two of them he practised in Toronto. At forty-seven he was the youngest of the four and he bore a distinctive air of suavity and refinement. He had gone through the private University of Toronto Schools before proceeding to the university and then to Oxford, whence he returned to Osgoode Hall to do his law. He had had a more varied ministerial experience than either Blackwell or Frost as the first minister of planning and development in 1944, then as provincial secretary since 1948, and adding to that the education portfolio when Drew left for Ottawa. But he was regarded as the rankest long shot in the field and was thought to be running this time more with an eye to future consideration than with any expectation of winning. His speech was as bland and non-controversial as the two preceding it.

Kelso Roberts was last to the podium. A backbench MPP from 1943 to 1948, before settling in Toronto he had practised law for some years in Cobalt, developing a specialty in mining law, and much of his campaign was directed to gaining strength in northern Ontario. As the only contestant without a seat in the House, indeed the only one not a minister of the crown, Roberts was at a disadvantage. He tried, however, to make an asset of this by picturing himself as a non-establishment candidate who would bring a fresh, more independent approach to the job. A few days before the convention he raised a flurry of excitement by intimating that he had a 'secret weapon.' This turned out to be a promise to call a special caucus to reconsider 'the objectionable and contentious retroactive features' of the Charitable Gifts Act. To attack a major piece of government policy in a governing party convention was simply not the thing to do. He caused an uproar. A loud chorus of boos and cries of 'Sit down' greeted his announcement, and was countered by cheers from his followers as he struggled to be heard. He had committed the unpardonable indiscretion of giving comfort to the common foe.[33]

With an ease that surprised even him, and which was believed to be the result in part of George Doucett's influence, Frost won a decisive majority on the first ballot, with well over two hundred more votes than the other three combined and nearly twice as many as Blackwell.* A thunderous roar of approval went up when this was announced. Gertrude Frost so far forgot herself as to throw her arms around Leslie's neck and give him a resounding kiss, while the press photographers jostled for position and their flashbulbs popped. Fiorenza Drew followed suit, running 'the length of the platform, and it was a long run, to throw an arm across his shoulder. If she didn't kiss him she gave a good imitation.' At that moment the Frost pipers strode into the ballroom in full, splendid cry, followed by a group of celebrants holding aloft large photographs of their hero. When the noise died down, Blackwell moved, seconded by Roberts, that the election be made unanimous.[34]

Frost's acceptance speech was a typical Frost speech, rambling in style, genial in manner, appreciative in spirit, modest in tone, in which he insisted that 'my wife has more political aptitude than I have,' and reminisced fondly about his childhood home. In his peroration he urged his listeners 'to carry the enthusiasm of this great convention ... to every corner of this Province' and for good measure invoked God's blessing on its people.[35]

Once the convention was over, Lindsay beckoned, an inviting refuge from commotion. Frost intended to go there for a little relaxation before his ministry was sworn in on 4 May. Escape was impossible, however, until the composition of his cabinet was settled, and the most important of those decisions concerned the future of Leslie Blackwell. The day after the convention Frost visited Blackwell and offered him any position he would like. Blackwell had made up his mind to retire. He wrote to the new leader in a friendly letter, 'I think ... you realized that the conclusion of the Convention would mark the end of a chapter in my life.' He would return to the practice of law. 'I regret your decision,' Frost responded, 'but I quite understand your point of view ... I shall miss you very greatly.'[36]

With Blackwell removed, Dana Porter was chosen as attorney general and retained the Education portfolio for the time being. Frost, keeping the Treasury for himself, relinquished Mines to Welland Gemmell of Sudbury, the only newcomer. Arthur Welsh was to add to his duties as provincial secretary the chairmanship of the Liquor Control Board. Otherwise the cabinet remained the same

---

* No figures were announced but unofficially the tally was Frost 834, Blackwell 442, Roberts 121, Porter 65.

as under Kennedy,* except that George Doucett was designated deputy premier. Full-time ministers of Education and Reform Institutions would be named later; until then the latter would continue under the care of George Dunbar, along with Municipal Affairs.

The Frosts now made their getaway to Lindsay. Apparently by prearrangement between Frost and the newspaper, they were accompanied by a *Globe and Mail* reporter with a camera who provided the kind of image-making publicity which delights any politician. Thus it became known that the Frosts were up early the next morning because Gertrude wanted to catch up on her unavoidably neglected baking and produce some of Les's favourite butter tarts (a picture showed her in the kitchen), while her husband refilled the goldfish pond in the back yard and readied his gear for an assault on some less fortunate fish. They really were, it appeared, just plain folks. With the reporter tagging along, Frost visited the minister of Cambridge Street United Church, the Reverend Harold Neal, to invite him to offer prayers at the swearing-in ceremony. Neal, interrupted in the middle of a Young People's meeting, pumped Frost's right arm vigorously and said, 'Les, we're proud of you. There isn't a man, woman or child in Lindsay who isn't thrilled.' Finally, the Frosts, with reporter in tow, spent Saturday afternoon at the beloved Pleasant Point cabin.[37]

Frost returned to Toronto early Monday morning, not forgetting to take along his father's well-worn Bible upon which he intended to swear his oath of office. Arrangements had to be completed for his move into the large corner office on the second floor of the old sandstone pile, and for the ceremony on Wednesday afternoon. At the appointed hour the ministers assembled in the office of Lieutenant-Governor Ray Lawson, and reporters, photographers, and a few invited guests filed in, among them Grenville Frost. After Mr Neal's opening prayer, the clerk of the executive council read the oath and Frost swore to be 'vigilant, diligent and circumspect.' The ritual was repeated for each colleague in turn and the Frost era was formally begun.

---

* The cabinet was: L.M. Frost, President of the Council and Treasurer; T.L. Kennedy, Agriculture; George Doucett, Highways and Public Works; Dana Porter, Attorney General and Education; George Dunbar, Municipal Affairs and Reform Institutions; Charles Daley, Labour; Arthur Welsh, Provincial Secretary and chairman, LCBO; William Goodfellow, Public Welfare; William Griesinger, Planning and Development; Harold Scott, Lands and Forests; Louis Cecile, Travel and Publicity; Welland Gemmell, Mines; Russell Kelley, Health; George Challies, without portfolio and vice-chairman of Hydro.

The festive celebration in Lindsay that evening was typical of an old Ontario now reaching its twilight time. The Frost's train was met at the depot by a welcoming committee; they were seated in an open car and driven to their place in a parade formed to escort them to Victoria Park. And what a parade! It stretched for fully a mile, with a Canadian Legion colour party leading the way and a Legion honour guard of more than one hundred men accompanying the guests of honour. There were bands – from the Salvation Army, Lindsay Collegiate, and the village of Little Britain; the Bobcaygeon Boys and Girls band, and the Canadian General Electric Pipes from Peterborough, and the Orillia Pipes skirled their way along the route. Between the bands were contingents of marchers, Rotarians and Kinsmen, Boy Scouts and Girl Guides, and hundreds of children from the town and a wide area around, many bearing banners and large portraits of the conquering hero. Delegations of their elders had come from Orillia and Peterborough, as well as from all over Victoria and Haliburton counties: from Coboconk and Minden, Norland and Omemee and Janetville; from Little Britain, Dorset, and Haliburton village. The members of the Lindsay Motorcycle Club rode en masse, their throttled-back engines sounding a subdued, throaty roar, while numerous bicycles, streamers flying from their handlebars and fenders and festooning their wheels, added to the kaleidoscope of colour. Onlookers thronged the sidewalks and peered from windows and other vantage points, an estimated ten thousand in all, more than the entire population of the town. At Victoria Park the Frosts were greeted with a deafening cannon salute, courtesy of the Fourth Field Regiment, and then mounted the bandstand. There the new premier was presented with an illuminated address by Mayor R.I. Moore, on behalf of the town council, and President Jasper Forman of the local Canadian Legion branch. Scipio, returning from his triumph over Hannibal, could not have been more joyfully welcomed by the citizens of Rome.

New Directions

Winning the leadership meant for Frost a descent from the treasurer's office on the third floor of the legislative building to the premier's office directly below. But, still being treasurer, he did a good deal of shuttling up and down. A pair of retired colonels who had served Frost's two immediate predecessors continued in the senior administrative positions, Lorne McDonald as deputy minister to the premier, and Ernest J. Young as executive assistant. Before long, however, the staff began to expand, thanks in part to the transfer of the cabinet secretariat from the provincial secretary's department, but also because of a growing specialization of function as Frost recruited new men to perform particular tasks. That reflected not only the increasing complexity of government business, but also his tendency, to a more marked degree than Drew, to direct and keep on top of what was being done in the various departments.

As was to be expected, some other changes from the Drew regime were soon evident. At Frost's request the office furniture, grouped on a blue floral rug and backed by blue velvet drapes, was rearranged. It consisted of an assortment of tables and blue leather chairs, complemented by a Philco console radio and a collection of statuary, likenesses of Queen Victoria, Sir Isaac Brock, Tecumseh, and Sir John A. Macdonald. He also ordered a new, conventional desk to replace the old-fashioned one used by his predecessors – at least as far back as George Henry.

Drew had kept his desk neat as a pin, clear of paper; there was a place for everything and everything was in its place. Frost's desk was always strewn with papers, but not so much so as to prevent its surface becoming scratched from his habit of putting his feet up while he talked on the telephone or indulged in rumination. Drew, sitting alone in his office and having decided what he wanted to say, generally used the dictaphone when composing letters or memoranda in his lucid prose. Frost preferred, especially in his early years as premier, to have his secretary come in to take dictation. And if the subject concerned government policy, he liked to have one or two others present so that he could ask questions or bounce ideas off their heads as he went along, in case – a remote possibility – this might expose some serious flaw in his thinking. At these sessions, or while simply talking something over with a minister or official, his habit, one too disorderly for Drew to indulge in, was to wad up pieces of paper that had served their purpose and, causing anyone sitting in the line of fire to duck, throw them at the walnut waste basket, located at some distance from his chair and usually an elusive target.

At the convention Frost had promised that his door would be open. There were necessary limits to that, of course, and occasions when he wished, sometimes aloud and profanely, that he could be better protected from unwanted delegations and the like. But he did make himself more readily available than Drew. If a minister wanted to see Drew he had his secretary telephone for an appointment. With Frost, ministers could and did simply knock on his door and walk in. Not that liberties could be taken or that he encouraged undue familiarity; his authority as commander of the ship was quickly established and unfailingly maintained. He was, though, more approachable than Drew and more naturally inclined to approaching others.

Hugh Latimer remarked that Drew's 'very manner suggested action. He would rush from his office to the Legislature chamber,' striding down the halls 'pre-occupied in thought and would very rarely recognize anyone as he passed. There was always a sense of urgency with Mr. Drew.' Frost's style was less hurried, more relaxed. 'It was natural for him to speak to you or nod a greeting to nearly every person he met on his way ... civil servants who had only known Mr. Drew to see him were most impressed and pleased with the friendly way they were recognized by Mr. Frost.' The new premier was as apt to seek the opinion of a total stranger wandering the halls or standing on the building's steps as that of a minister, MPP or senior official (without necessarily according the stranger's views the same weight) and always had time for a few friendly words or a little joke with any member of his staff, however junior.[1]

These were a few of the minor contrasts noted by those who had served with Drew. In the realm of high policy a much more fundamental change was in the offing, awaiting the right moment to be adopted. That moment would not arrive until after the dominion general election on 27 June, in fact would not come at all, in the way Frost had in mind, should the Conservatives win. It amounted to a more conciliatory approach to the federal government, now headed by Louis St Laurent who had succeeded Mackenzie King in 1948. Such an overture in the midst of an election campaign would seem a betrayal of Drew, a tacit admission that the Conservative premier of Ontario did not expect a Tory victory.

In his acceptance speech at the convention Frost had urged those present to 'stand behind our former leader and our great chief, George Drew, in the big battle that lies ahead.' One might thus have expected him to ensure as far as he could that the party organization was thrown into the fray without stint and to set an example himself. A.D. McKenzie and his headquarters staff supported Drew enthusiastically,[2] as no doubt many workers throughout the province did, but Frost seems not to have offered the kind of vigorous lead that Drew had given four years earlier on Bracken's behalf. Frost in 1949 was more restrained, less noticeable, as though going through the motions without his heart being in it. He did give a few speeches, at Tweed, Huntsville, Bracebridge, and Midland, and showed every outward appearance of hoping that Drew would be the next prime minister. But his appearances in those four small towns were perhaps largely prompted by a feeling of obligation to the local candidates. He was on the platform at Drew's Massey Hall rally near the close of the campaign – his staying away would have been a pointed snub – but he neither introduced Drew nor spoke to the gathering. Conceivably he was not invited to do either but, if not, almost certainly could have been, by giving the word. Drew took occasion in his speech to deny reports that there were divisions between himself and other Conservative party leaders.[3] Strictly speaking, that was true as far as Frost was concerned; he felt no estrangement from Drew, only a lack of warm friendship and a strong suspicion that the federal Tories were doomed to lose.

In any event, to the extent that he and the organization rolled up their sleeves and went to work, the results did not say much for their influence. The Conservatives came out of it with half of the forty-eight Ontario seats they had taken in 1945 and with less than half as many as the Grits. In all but three of those they did win the margin was cut, in some cases drastically, and they defeated not a single Liberal incumbent. The three ridings in which Frost spoke remained, incidentally, more solidly Liberal than before. The Tories' share of seats was diminished almost everywhere else in Canada, too, but nowhere so calamitously as in Ontario. But no black crepe was hung from Frost's office windows. Two days later, on 30 June, he made his overture to St Laurent.

Publicly over the years, in and out of the House, Frost had been as critical as Drew, though in less provocative language, of Ottawa's intransigence in dealing with the provinces. He was equally insistent on defending provincial rights against encroachment and at pains to stress the advantage to Ontario of shunning the tax rental plan by which the feds set such store. Devouring Grits was not for him, however, the appetizing diet it was for Drew, especially as they were, once he became premier, his 'favourite recruiting ground,' as he sometimes said. Confrontations with Ottawa, he now believed, had simply proved not to be the way to achieve desired results. He explained his reasoning in a memorandum after his retirement in 1961.

With the experiences of the past Conferences in which Ontario was represented by Mr. Hepburn and Mr. Drew, I was of the opinion that a new approach had to be made to the Dominion Government based upon as much understanding and co-operation as could be achieved. An arm's length attitude was completely impossible from the standpoint of getting anything done and, in my opinion, it had no political strength owing to the fact that the people were completely tired of the bickering and dickering between the Provincial and Federal Governments. This thinking was borne out in the federal election of 1949 when the people of Ontario decisively rejected the Drew point of view.[4]

Consequently Frost decided to write St Laurent a friendly letter as soon as the election was past, should the government be sustained as expected, suggesting that they talk matters over. So, shortly after this latest Liberal sweep he despatched a note expressing his personal good wishes and congratulations on the outcome, which 'was undoubtedly a tribute to you personally.' There followed what he most wanted to say. Upon assuming office, he had determined, once the federal election was past, 'to offer to the Prime Minister of Canada the co-operation of the Government of Ontario in matters of common interest ... While the governments are of different political complexions, I do not think it either necessary or desirable that our relations should be what I might term "at arm's length." I take the view that when the people in their wisdom determine who shall form the governments, we, as Canadians, should all co-operate in the public cause. In that spirit ... I express the view that it would be well if we could have an informal and private conversation in which we could review, in a preliminary way, a number of matters of common interest. I should be glad indeed to call and see you.'[5]

St Laurent was more than willing to talk and the funeral early in July of P.D. Ross, the venerable publisher of the *Ottawa Journal*, afforded an unforeseen opportunity. An exchange of pleasantries with Mackenzie King and St Laurent after the service led to an invitation to the prime minister's office for some further talk. There, Frost recalled, 'we had a very informal, off-the-cuff chat ... This was really the commencement of a completely new day and out of this grew the exchanges that resulted in much more rational Federal-Provincial relations.'[6] Frost followed up this initial meeting with another letter and a memorandum that might serve as the basis for further informal discussions which they had agreed should take place. Suggestions in the memorandum were 'not to be regarded as hard and fast and incapable of such changes as may be deemed necessary in order to reach agreement.'[7] That evinced a quite different spirit from what Ottawa had grown accustomed to in George Drew.

As Frost saw it, his overture to St Laurent opened the door to epoch-making results: universal pensions at age seventy, supplementary pensions with a means test at age sixty-five, health insurance, the Trans-Canada Highway agreement, the St Lawrence Seaway, and a natural gas pipeline from Alberta, to name but a few. It did not, however, meet with universal approval in his own party. When it became evident that he was adopting a more flexible, less combative stance than Drew, there was apprehension in some quarters that he would unduly sacrifice provincial rights and perhaps undercut the federal Tories. 'I might say,' George McCullagh told him bluntly, 'I have a suspicion that you share the feeling of many others that your predecessor was constantly warring with Ottawa too much. My own viewpoint is that, due to that feeling, you are over-compensating and not standing up to them enough.' But Frost made no apologies. After disarmingly thanking McCullagh for the forthright but fair way in which he had always addressed him, he wrote: 'I cannot say that George's methods have ever influenced me very greatly. When I was with him I always endeavoured to give him loyal support, even though he knew that many times I was in disagreement with his methods. I never hesitated to tell him that. I have never attempted to be anything but myself. For better or for worse, my methods are my own. George no doubt in given situations would do much better than I. On the other hand, in some cases the converse perhaps will apply. Time alone will tell.'[8]

Misgivings similar to McCullagh's were expressed by Drew himself concerning the federal government's decision in the summer of 1949 to proceed by unilateral action of Parliament to abolish appeals from Canadian courts to the Judicial Committee of the British Privy Council, and to seek from Westminster an amendment to the British North America Act giving Parliament power to amend those sections of the act pertaining to subjects exclusively within federal jurisdiction. These actions did not in themselves trouble Frost but they were opposed by the Conservatives at Ottawa. In keeping with his general view of Canadian federalism, Drew believed that the Fathers of Confederation had not doubted that there should be consultation with the provinces 'prior to establishing the pattern by which any amendments were to take place.' This was especially important because the division of powers depended in practice so much on judicial interpretation. He feared that with a Canadian court having the final judicial say, previous decisions forming part of the fundamental law might be disturbed. He also worried that as the process of patriating the constitution went ahead in the step-by-step manner on which St Laurent had determined, with its ultimate goal a completely Canadian amending procedure, the provinces might concede too much for the sake of reaching agreement. Drew hoped that Frost would confidentially keep him posted on Ontario's views. 'It may not be possible for us to see eye to eye at all times but this is a subject on which it is most important that we keep as close together as possible.'[9] Seeing eye to eye on this matter, as on many others, was not going to be easy for the two Conservative leaders. Replying, Frost agreed that changing the method of constitutional amendment 'should be handled with great care and precipitous [sic] action could very easily create situations which would prevent any general agreement ... I shall be glad indeed to discuss the same with you from time to time.' Nevertheless, 'we should be able to amend our Constitution ourselves ... on the general principle that we are grown up and the solution of these matters would be in line with our status. I do not think anyone quarrels with this.' Drew 'should be careful to avoid having opposition to procedure confused with opposition to the principle involved ... On the other hand, the Government's decision to proceed with this very complicated problem piecemeal may create misunderstandings which will be difficult to bridge.'[10] But building bridges was Frost's strong suit. Peace had been declared between Toronto and Ottawa, or at any rate an armistice opening the way to peace negotiations and a more harmonious relationship. The federal election, he was convinced, demonstrated that the people of Ontario wanted that and he was going to see that they got it.

In the fall of 1949 there was a by-election in Leeds following the death of the sitting member. Ordinarily provincial by-elections caused little excitement, except locally, and those in distant rural areas rarely received much attention in the metropolitan press. The Tories had won all four they had faced since assuming office in 1943 and Leeds seemed the least likely of places to break the string, since it had always voted Tory, except in the 1934 Hepburn sweep. When the by-election was called for 31 October there seemed no reason to expect a change. The Conservative candidate was a Brockville coal merchant, Hugh Reynolds, a cousin of the deceased member. In addition to the labours of local party workers, he had the benefit of the presence of Hugh Latimer, down from party headquarters in Toronto to lend his unsurpassed political skills to the cause. Given the county's tradition, the chances of the Liberal standard-bearer (the CCF stayed out) seemed slight indeed.

That estimate, though, did not take into account the mentality of the *Toronto Star*'s proprietors, who decided to make the by-election the stage for an all-out assault on the Charitable Gifts Act. The *Star*'s resources were poured into the battle with a lavish hand. Every day a semi-trailer truckload of papers arrived from Toronto for free distribution to each household in the constituency; it was estimated that 300,000 copies were given away. Arrangements were made with the post office for rural delivery and one rural mailman was heard to say that he would be relieved when the election was over.[11]

Despite the Liberals' frenetic efforts, the Leeds Tories and their candidate had every reason to be satisfied when the by-election finally closed. With almost 80 per cent of the electorate having gone to the polls, Hugh Reynolds defeated Ernest Miller, the Liberal candidate, by nearly 2,700 votes. The Conservatives could be excused for thinking that Frost understated the truth in calling it a dandy victory.

Nevertheless, there were disturbing signs of sagging morale and bitter intra-party dissension while the Leeds campaign was going on and afterwards. Ten days before the by-election, the *Star* came out with some startling intelligence: a movement to displace Frost had begun in recent weeks among government MPPs, at least six of whom were privy to it. One of them, who like the others was unidentified, had assured the *Star* that a poll of the caucus 'would reveal a surprising unanimity' of dissatisfaction. One complaint was Frost's 'disregard' in not calling a caucus since becoming leader, another his 'inability' to dispense with the yes-men chosen for the cabinet by Drew. There was, it was claimed, a distinct opinion that 'the strongest men ... are in the back benches gathering moss.' The situation was so bad, according to another member of the anonymous cabal, that the government was 'tottering' as badly as the Liberals had following Hepburn's sudden resignation in 1942.[12]

This story followed on the heels of another which quoted a former Conservative cabinet minister, who of course would not speak for attribution, about a 'decided feeling in the party opposed to the present party directorate.' Dissatisfaction was said to be centred among rural MPPs, who complained that patronage, including the granting of liquor licences, was being handled almost exclusively by a coterie of Toronto lawyers who were not members of the legislature. But it was not essentially an anti-Toronto feeling in the view of Kelso Roberts, apparently the only one the *Star* spoke to who did not mind being quoted by name and who explained: 'It is not a protest against city party supporters so much as against individuals and groups who happen to live in Toronto and who exercise control which should be held only by those chosen in election by the people to represent them.' The two Toronto lawyers against whom this sentiment had crystallized were, according to the *Star*, party president A.D. McKenzie and F.G. Gardiner, who no longer held an executive position but was believed to wield much influence in patronage decisions.[13]

Making due allowance for the *Star*'s intensified desire to cause mischief for the Tories during the by-election, there was more than a kernel of truth in its reports. The bad publicity provoked a wrathful letter to Frost from J.G. White, MPP for Kenora, angrily denying rumours he had heard that he was among the malcontents interviewed by the *Star* and denouncing those who were. White did not deny, however, that there was unrest and that he shared the disaffection of many he had talked to 'about some phases of the way things are being run.' Frost should ask someone he trusted to visit all the members privately. This 'would reveal a lot of beefs which might never be revealed anywhere else and the sooner you find out what the members think the better. They won't talk out in caucus as they do in private.'

One prevalent grievance was 'the lackadaisical attitude of the civil servants generally and the time it takes to get things done,' another that some of the ministers were weak, still another 'that we are tied to the federal apron strings too tightly.'[14] In a subsequent letter White raised the issue of control over patronage. The MPPS were 'very jealous of their rights in this matter' but he did not wholly agree that control was too centred at party headquarters. Many members, not to speak of defeated candidates who thought they should dispense patronage in their constituencies, could not be trusted to make these decisions alone. They should be consulted but needed the guidance of the chief party organizer and his assistants in Toronto to ensure that the greatest political advantage was gained. There was, though, one grievance with which White was in full agreement; he explained in a passage which illuminates what grass roots politics was all about.

One of the worst shellackings I have ever taken was administered to me this past week on several occasions in regard to local purchases. Instead of purchasing locally, most of the departments we are concerned with have a central purchasing agency where batteries, tires, cars, shovels, and many other items are purchased. Our people are wild about this. We may be saving the people of the province generally a few thousand dollars but we are doing ourselves incalculable harm politically ... Not long ago a dept. of Lands & Forests truck had a set of spark plugs changed right here in Dryden. It was charged to the department. Three days later the driver brought in a set of plugs sent up from Port Arthur and said that they were supplied by the central purchasing agency and the garage here had to take them and cancel the charge against the department. Truck purchases by some of the departments are made from a central pool and our local dealers see these new trucks coming into their territory without any commission going to them ... We may be saving a little money but I doubt this, while we are cutting our own throats politically.[15]

Frost was fully alive to the importance of such minor patronage; he dispensed it in his own riding. In the summer of 1949 he reminded George Doucett that commissions on the sale of a few Highways Department trucks to be used in his district had been allotted several months earlier to certain dealers in Lindsay and Haliburton. He had so advised the dealers, who now informed him

that the commissions had not been paid. Doucett looked into it
and the dealers got their money. One of them wrote to Frost, 'Since
receipt of this cheque is entirely due to your efforts on our behalf
we are deeply appreciative. Should any occasion arise in the future
where we can be of any assistance to you we shall be only too happy
to cooperate.'[16] Just so; that was the point of the whole system. No
less important than commissions were contracts. Concerning one
of these, Frost was told by a party worker in his riding that Morgan
Prentice, a Minden contractor, had put in a bid. It was not too high
and he should get the contract. Frost agreed, jotting on the letter,
'Morgan Prentice. Give him job if possible.' He then asked his
executive assistant to attend to the matter. Colonel Young reported
that Prentice's bid was two hundred dollars above the lowest but
the deputy minister of public works was 'going to ask Mr. Prentice
to come in & see him with a view to the tenders being brought
closer together.' Before long Young was able to append a further
notation: 'Mr. Prentice got the job.'[17]

It was no doubt easier for one in Frost's position to obtain satisfaction in decisions of this sort than for a back-bencher. Recognizing this, Frost was not deaf to the complaints about patronage
voiced by White and others. Nor did he entirely lack sympathy with
some of the other grievances that surfaced in the *Star*'s interviews
with disgruntled Tories. He was too sensitive to currents of opinion
not to realize that there was a bubbling cauldron of discontent
which the Leeds fight and Reynolds's victory did nothing to cool.
In fact it looked as though it might boil over during the party's
annual meeting at the Royal York early in November, when there
would be an election of officers and a chance to carry out the
housecleaning being demanded by the dissidents. At their head was
a leading cabinet minister, Doucett, and at his elbow – indeed the
brains behind the movement, some believed – was Harry Robbins,
public relations officer at party headquarters.

The chief target of these two was Alex McKenzie, their objective
to gain control of the organization by ousting him from the presidency. In cabinet Doucett was regarded by most as an ambitious
loner, but one who had to be taken seriously as a political force
because of his extensive connections in rural Ontario. He had been
active for years in the municipal politics of Lanark County and
become widely known to the wardens and reeves of the province.
These contacts had been enlarged and strengthened during his
term as president of the Ontario Good Roads Association, and
even more since his appointment as minister of highways in 1943.

As such he travelled a great deal, discussing road and highway matters with municipal politicians. In these ways he had made a lot of friends and acquired a feel for political and party sentiment in the local districts. It was thus not surprising that he was viewed as a formidable prospective leadership candidate in the spring of 1949, or that his decision to back Frost was considered instrumental in securing the latter's lopsided win.

Robbins, a highly placed civil servant in the Ferguson and Henry administrations, was hired by the Conservative party after Drew became leader as a publicist and speech writer. He exemplified the political animal and had a close familiarity with government operations. His political instincts were sharpened by constant exercise and one staff member in the premier's office recalled admiringly that there 'was nothing about politics that Mr. Robbins didn't know.'[18] With an ingratiating personality and talent as a writer, he enjoyed good rapport with the Queen's Park press corps. Some of McKenzie's supporters suspected as the annual meeting approached that Robbins was feeding to reporters much of the raw material for their stories about dissension in the party. He and Doucett became close friends. Robbins also grew well acquainted with many of the contractors and suppliers doing business with the Highways Department; their representatives were frequently observed coming in to see him by Hugh Latimer in the office next door. Presumably they were not there simply to pass the time of day but for their own and Robbins's advantage.[19]

Doucett did not hide his intention of displacing McKenzie and it was widely expected that he would run for the office himself. He shared the opinion said to be widespread in rural Ontario that the party apparatus was too tightly controlled from Bay Street in a secretive manner which excluded MPPs and riding association officers from decisions about patronage and other important affairs. He did not dispute the feeling among many of the foot soldiers that the organization, personified by McKenzie, was to blame for the loss of strength in the last provincial election and the dismal showing in the recent federal contest. Nor did Doucett attempt to quell the nasty whispering campaign impugning McKenzie's honesty that was much in evidence prior to the annual meeting. In fact he and Robbins, along with the six or eight caucus members known to support Doucett, and who presumably were the ones sounding off to the *Star*, almost certainly fomented it. The gossip went that McKenzie made a practice of trafficking in liquor licences and accepting rake-offs from those doing business with the government.

Hugh Latimer, who by 1949 had been employed at headquarters for nearly two years, conceived an immense admiration for McKenzie's intellect and integrity, and did not believe him the sort to use his office for feathering his own nest. Latimer found in his travels around the province that his judgment was that of most influential people in the party. So, he recalled, 'I spoke to a number of these people on the phone and told them that Mr. McKenzie was likely to be opposed and related some of the preposterous stories being circulated.' Robbins may have got wind of this because about ten days before the annual meeting he called Latimer into his office. He 'intimated to me that there would likely be interesting developments ... and cautioned that it would be best for me if I didn't get involved.' Undeterred by this thinly veiled threat, Latimer persisted in his lobbying.[20]

In trying to exploit the restiveness in party ranks, Doucett may have had a more personal motive than a desire to open up and democratize the management. McKenzie was regarded by some as Drew's man. One of the complaints mentioned to Frost by J.G. White was that the organization was too tightly tied to federal apron strings; it was suspected – without reason according to Harry Price who shortly became party treasurer – that in order to help the federal Tories in 1949, the coffers were emptied, to the detriment of the provincial wing.[21] It was assumed that Drew, who was going to attend the annual meeting, would use his influence on McKenzie's behalf and Doucett, who had been known to speak disparagingly of the former leader, had his own private reason for wanting to thwart him. In the first Drew cabinet Doucett, in addition to his duties as highways minister, was put in charge of buying insurance on government properties; having for years owned an insurance business in Almonte, he had the necessary expertise. Before long Drew began to receive complaints from various companies that their policies had been cancelled, and he appointed a two-man committee to examine the status of the government's coverage. It was soon discovered that not long after the Conservatives took office, Doucett had transferred the business to a company for which his firm was the agent. Drew promptly countermanded this action and ordered Doucett to reinstate the original policies.[22] It was a humiliating rebuke, not easy to forget or forgive.

At length Doucett decided not to run for president and prevailed upon James N. Allan, a Dunnville dairyman, to do so in his stead. The popular and respected Allan was a former warden of Haldimand County and, like his good friend Doucett, a one-time president of the Good Roads Association. He agreed that there was need for change in the party. Some constituency organizations, he thought, 'are just in a plain mess.' A defeated candidate 'is useless which was probably the reason for his defeat and the county organization is like him.' Furthermore, there was 'a lot of sloppy work by the cabinet in handling patronage. Executives & defeated members know nothing of appointments until they see them in the paper.' Ministers tended to 'forget that boosting of Liberals is not admired,' a reference to the feeling that some opposition MPPs were being allowed to claim credit for work done or patronage dispensed in their ridings.

Allan was therefore in a mood to co-operate with Doucett and Robbins; but he had no idea when he got to the Royal York for the meeting that he was about to be made a candidate for the presidency. Accompanied by Bert Edgecombe, president of the Haldimand-Norfolk Conservative Association, he arrived unsuspecting in Toronto on opening day, believing that Doucett would run against McKenzie. That belief was dashed when, as Edgecombe later recounted, they 'met Doucett and Harry Robbins and some others. They put it up to Jim so strongly and he being such a friend of Doucette [sic] could hardly back up.' Allan's own explanation was that 'I consented to run with the thought that I was doing the party a good turn because there was [sic] ... a great many wanting a change ... I think a lot of Geo. Doucett and really I just couldn't let him down ... I felt I could take a trimming with results that would be trivial in comparison to Geo taking one.'[23]

Where did Frost stand in all this? Uncomfortably in the middle. Newspapermen covering the meeting assumed that he and Drew, with a vested interest in maintaining the status quo against an untoward uprising in the ranks, were working together to keep McKenzie in office. But E.A. Goodman, a Toronto lawyer active at the centre of party affairs, was in a better position to know and saw the situation differently. 'Frost just stood by and wouldn't lift a finger to help him [McKenzie],' Goodman remembered many years later. 'He thought it was in his own political best interests to stay out of that fight and he stayed out ... I never forgave him for that [because he] owed everything to McKenzie.'[24] That overstates the truth, but certainly McKenzie in his own fashion, quietly behind the scenes, had backed Frost for the leadership. Why, then, would the latter not return the favour when the opportunity arose? Frost had given no hint that he wanted McKenzie to step aside and, in fact, had reappointed him chairman of organization for the next election, although for some reason this was not made public until a week before the annual meeting.[25] That vote of confidence made the more surprising Frost's failure to indicate a preference for the incumbent. Equally puzzling, one incident during the meeting suggests that he not only did not raise a finger to help but was prepared to discourage those who did.

Hugh Latimer was on hand working hard for McKenzie when William Goodfellow, cabinet minister and lifelong friend and neighbour of Latimer in Northumberland County, brought a message to him from the premier. Frost wanted Latimer to absent himself from the meeting forthwith, conceivably to protect him from the possible loss of his job should the Doucett-Robbins-Allan effort be successful. Latimer, however, put a different interpretation on it – that Doucett had complained to the premier about a member of headquarters staff being involved. Of course, the same rule ought to have applied to Robbins, who was walking about unmolested, openly advertising his allegiance to Allan. Latimer at once related to McKenzie what Goodfellow had told him and said, as he recollected, that 'if I lose my job tomorrow I will stay [at the meeting] and work for you if you want me to.' McKenzie replied, 'I want you to stay.' Busy canvassing delegates the next morning, Latimer was approached by Doucett and Allan. The former said to Allan, rather ominously, 'This is the chap I was speaking to you about,' and then to Latimer, 'I thought you weren't supposed to be around here,' a remark indicating that Frost had accepted Doucett's demand that Latimer be told to leave. 'When I hear people telling lies about McKenzie,' answered Latimer, 'I don't intend to let them get away with it.'[26]

Why would Frost not only accede to the demand but decline to endorse McKenzie, under whom as president and organizer the party had come to power and retained it in two general elections? For one thing, he was beholden to Doucett for assisting his election as leader. Then too, McKenzie was closely identified with Drew, whose lingering authority in the provincial party Frost may well have wanted to see diminished in the process of establishing his own. More important, Frost shared some of the dissatisfaction with the organization and believed that the prevalence of this feeling might jeopardize his own position, to say nothing of the party's fortunes, if changes were not made. He had been promoted at the convention as personifying rural Ontario and implicitly symbolizing resistance to the big city's baneful domination. The organization of 'the people's party,' he thought, should be reformed so as to give the local associations and MPPs more say, to get more people involved, and to destroy the perception that a few power-brokers at the centre were in control. Later on, in the presence of others, he and McKenzie got into a heated altercation in which the latter was accused of running a hole-in-the-wall type of organization.[27] Thus Frost had a feeling for the complaints which Doucett, Robbins and friends were nourishing in their effort to push McKenzie out of the picture.

That effort was very nearly crowned with success; McKenzie was re-elected with a majority of only twenty-five of the more than four hundred votes cast. Allan was ahead until the final ballot box was opened, from the area in the hall where the ministers and other MPPs were sitting, and it made the difference. When McKenzie died in 1960, Frost grieved to Latimer that he had lost his right arm. Possibly he thought back to how close the arm had come to being severed eleven years earlier and how, had it been, his own failure to lift a finger would have been partly to blame. In 1949, it seemed, Frost had not yet fully grasped the truth that in McKenzie the party had the most adroit political manager in the province, if not the country, or learned to appreciate the consummate skill and judgment with which he did his work.

McKenzie now proceeded to demonstrate that, whatever else might be thought of him, he was not a vindictive man. Robbins retained his position at headquarters until after McKenzie's death, while Allan and McKenzie became close friends when the former was later elected to the House and then appointed to the cabinet. Allan accepted his defeat for the presidency in good part and put the best possible face on it. 'I believe the effect of the contest,' he wrote, 'will be to impress upon the present organization that they should be more active in assisting local organizations and work generally more closely with them.'[28]

A month after the annual meeting Frost wrote to W.E. Hamilton, whom he had brought into the cabinet as minister of reform institutions. The first institution Frost wanted Hamilton's help in reforming was the party organization. Reverses in the 1948 provincial and 1949 federal elections showed the need for a fresh approach. It was 'essential that the direction of organization should lie with our elected membership. They are the persons who have the carriage of our Party's activities in the Province and being on the firing line their knowledge, interest and control is [sic] very essential indeed.'

The memorandum, reflecting in part Frost's own experience and way of doing things in Victoria-Haliburton, enumerated the matters that should be investigated by the committee of three MPPS he proposed to appoint and which he wanted Hamilton to chair. After discussing with McKenzie and his executive the way in which the organization currently functioned, the committee ought to report on each constituency, bearing in mind that in some of them 'there is really no provincial organization' apart from the federal one. Perhaps there should be one in each riding. In some cases constituency associations had not held annual meetings for years and the committee should ascertain the facts about this. Organization at the very bottom, the poll or subdivision level, was of key significance, but indications were that it was in very bad shape in the recent federal election. Because it did double duty, the conclusion must be that it was not in good condition for provincial purposes either. It was necessary to have up-to-date lists of key workers in each subdivision and Frost wanted the committee to find out whether this was being attended to. The catalogue of faults continued. 'There has been the utmost dissatisfaction with our advertising in the last three provincial elections.' Moreover, a membership drive in 1948 'was probably much too late in the day to be of any real good. Now is the time to strengthen the membership of the Party.' Ways needed to be found, also, of encouraging party members to play an active part on municipal councils, local power commissions, school boards, and other community bodies, although it would be unwise 'that there be party intervention in any of these fields.'

Frost then turned to McKenzie's establishment in Toronto and to the roles of the party association, MPPS and the leader. He desired a thorough investigation by Hamilton's committee of the paid organization in Ontario and offices maintained by the party with respect 'to the efficiency of these offices, what the personnel are doing, what their duties are and what changes should be made.' Inquiry should be made 'into ways and means of having our membership in the House actively engaged in organization,' and how improvements could be made in ridings not then held by the party. Last, but by no means least, was the relationship of the party association to the MPPS, in particular to their leader. 'The general direction should come from the Party Leader who is in consultation with the elected members. At the same time the ... Association represents the active membership of the Party and ... should be an integral and effective part of Party activities as directed by the Leader.'[29] The significance of all this lay less in what it led to in the way of immediate practical results than in its revelation of Frost's desire to subject McKenzie's operations much more to his own control. The Hamilton committee soon died after meeting twice without accomplishing anything. Its demise did not, however, end the tug-of-war between those who wanted reform, which they tended to equate with reducing McKenzie's power, and those who believed that he had earned his wings and should be left to fly the craft in his own way.

The discussions dragged on through most of 1950 until early October, when the association executive was summoned to prepare for another annual meeting. Frost then tried a new move, announcing that he had named Hamilton and Fred Cawthorne, association secretary, joint chairmen of a committee on basic organization. But Cawthorne declined to assume the chairmanship, joint or otherwise. Faced with this rejection, which apparently caught him off guard, Frost departed, leaving the subject, as the minutes put it, 'in a bit of a confused state.' Hamilton presently removed himself from the picture. He resigned as minister of reform institutions to accept a position with an insurance company and though remaining in the cabinet without portfolio, ceased to be involved in party organization.[30]

As a result, then, this new committee on basic organization was headed by McKenzie, with Hugh Latimer as secretary. Recognizing his value to the party, Frost had forgiven Latimer's refusal to depart the annual meeting the year before. Evidently wanting to discuss things privately and not in office hours, Frost invited him to a hockey game at Maple Leaf Gardens. There he explained what he had in mind and gave Latimer the draft of a letter which was to go out on association letterhead over the premier's signature to the presidents and secretaries of all riding associations. A second letter from Latimer was to follow a few days later. The Frost missive ended on a note of exhortation: 'Our party as the people's party must attract to itself men and women of all walks of life who are impressed with the fact that our policies are right and that the party is a real means to good government in our province.'[31]

Latimer's letter outlined three steps which it was hoped all constituency executives would take: elect an organizing committee, appoint a riding organizer, and choose a full complement of poll chairmen, the names of all these people to be sent to the party office in Toronto. Further suggestions by the basic organization committee would be forthcoming from time to time, 'the appropriateness of which each riding will have to decide having regard to its own local conditions and present state of its organization.'[32] That, of course, was a nod to local sensitivities to combat the feeling that conduct of party business was too centralized. No more tender toes were to be stepped on if it could be avoided.

Frost's initiative obviously did not produce exactly the results intended; he found it easier to claim the leader's primacy in organizational matters than to remove the obstacles to it. Nevertheless, the initiative had a salutary effect. More people started to become active in the local districts and many of the moribund riding associations began to be revived. Greater efforts were made to consult constituency executives, as well as MPPs about patronage and other matters, and complaints about the undue concentration of decision-making diminished in number and bitterness. In short, a marked rise in morale could be seen as the party looked forward with mounting confidence to the next election. McKenzie retained the job of chief organizer along with the presidency but was now to find himself in more constant contact with the leader than he was accustomed to. While at first his relations with Frost were at times a bit stormy, before long the two formed a close and mutually admiring partnership, an unbeatable combination. The Royal York became their regular meeting place, a kind of unofficial party headquarters. Frost lived there, as did several other ministers and about forty Tory back-benchers when the House was in session. As a result, Latimer recalled, 'in the evening the lobby ... could very well be likened to a party caucus.' Many of the members would be entertaining constituents and if Frost chanced to cross the lobby they would seize the opportunity to introduce their friends to him. McKenzie kept a room as a private meeting place a few floors down from Frost's suite. It was there or in the suite that they made their plans and settled party business, rather than at Frost's corner table for eight in the Venetian Room where McKenzie, having come down from his home, would often join the premier and various ministers for breakfast and some good political conversation.[33] By offering a convenient meeting place for intimate discourse, the Royal York became the place where the symbiotic relationship of party and government was most visibly shown.

10

Growing Pains

A strong 'people's party,' growing in numbers and vibrant with activity from top to bottom, was vital to success. But, it went without saying, much depended on the leadership given both party and government. Since the leader more than any other would be held responsible for the performance of both, his authority must be firmly established and clearly recognized. Although Frost's early moves to reform the organization so as to circumscribe McKenzie's power and enhance his own led to no real structural change, in the following years, as one electoral triumph followed another, his preeminence in the party became unchallengeable. As for public governance as apart from party management, any initial impression that he was too amiable, unassuming, and lacking in ambition ever to be truly master of the administration was soon dispelled. Much more than Kennedy, of course, and in some ways even more than Drew, he was the 'take charge' kind of leader. Not that there had ever been the slightest doubt that Drew was in charge; he was not a man to play second fiddle to anyone. His opinions, often controversial, were usually more clearly stated and more unequivocally defined than Frost's, at least in public, and his enjoyment of open combat was much more exuberant. Frost epitomized the patient, pragmatic willingness to accept the limits of what was possible for the time being; Drew, more the idealist, bent his energies towards pursuing what he thought true, right, and desirable.

In these ways Frost was unlike his seemingly more direct, decisive, and authoritarian predecessor. It would be wrong, however, to overdraw the contrast, to exaggerate Drew's inflexibility or leave the impression that Frost had an almost infinite capacity for compromise, procrastination, and the avoidance of contentious decisions. Allan Grossman, minister without portfolio in the closing phase of Frost's premiership, has accurately observed: 'Contrary to the myth that grew up about him, George Drew was one of the most democratic of political leaders. Certainly if you compare him to Leslie Frost, who had the reputation of being a kindly, humble Premier, there was a great difference but not the way most people have been led to believe. Leslie Frost ran a one-man show and he would brook no interference from anyone. George had the greatest respect for the democratic process and ... was certainly anything but a Colonel Blimp as some parts of the media pictured him.'[1]

Thus appearances were to some extent deceiving. While preferring to wait for a consensus to develop among ministers, backbenchers, and senior civil servants, and then to act, Frost never held back from imposing his own judgment if he thought the consensus wrong in principle or politically unwise. He was less disposed than Drew to delegate authority to his ministers and give them a more or less free hand, especially those (probably the majority) in whom he lacked entire confidence. He kept them under a tight rein, often bypassing them altogether to deal directly with their deputies or other officials. Nor did Frost hesitate when the House was sitting to relegate a minister to the sidelines unceremoniously in answering questions or engaging in debate. His colleagues sometimes had the impression that Big Brother was watching them, as indeed he was.

Farquhar Oliver of the Liberals chided him for this on one occasion. Acknowledging that Frost had carried a very heavy load in the session then in progress, Oliver said: 'There are some dangers which are inherent of [sic] the exalted position the Hon. Prime Minister now occupies. One of them is, and it has become very evident during this session of the House, that [he] is taking too much responsibility on his own shoulders ... It is an excellent thing for a Prime Minister to be able to divide ministerial responsibilities and to allow those Ministers – yes, to expect that those Ministers accept that responsibility. There has been a tendency in this Legislature, I feel, to depart from that very basic principle. The sooner we get back to it, the better for all concerned.'

Because Frost was taking too much on himself, Oliver went on, he sometimes lost both his patience and his temper, as when he had recently accused an opposition member of cowardly behaviour. He 'is far from his best when he loses his temper' and did not improve his standing 'in the estimation of the hon. members of the House or in the estimation of the public generally.' Frost confessed that now and then he showed irritation and for this 'I very humbly apologize ... I think, on the other hand, it will be agreed that, with all the worth of the hon. members of the Opposition, there are times they would try the patience of a saint, and I am not a saint.' The charge that he was running a one-man show seemed to astonish him and he denied that 'I am in any sense a dictator or that I, myself, do all the jobs of work done in this Assembly. That is not the case. It is not my nature to crack the whip ... By nature I am not a dictator.'[2]

Of course Oliver had not accused him of being one, only of tending to dominate proceedings. He did, even though the head of a government was expected to play a conspicuous part. The index of the *Debates* in 1951, to take it as an illustration, contains eleven pages of entries under Frost's name, far more than for any other minister and a good deal more than for opposition leader Jolliffe, the next most talkative member. Frost took part, often at length, in discussing nearly forty bills, mostly government measures in charge of one or other of his ministers and not all of prime importance by any means. His colleagues must have sometimes chafed under this regimen, even when his interventions saved them from their own ineptitude. But there were others who admired his dominance in the House. At the end of one session a back-bencher wrote to compliment him on his 'real leadership' and to say, 'It was a grand feeling to sit back with every confidence that if the going got a bit rough you were on the job and completely on top of the situation.'[3] There was never the slightest doubt that Frost *was* on the job and no less the supreme commander than Drew had been. Gripped by a consuming interest in almost every aspect of life in Ontario and how it was affected by government action, he once told the House that 'every day I am in these buildings I am more impressed with the amount there is to learn about the business of our Province.'[4] Thanks to indefatigable labour on his part, a constant insistence on being kept informed, a retentive memory and good staff work by his subordinates, he appeared to have an almost encyclopedic knowledge of what had been and was going on under the aegis of Queen's Park.

The scope and variety of what was going on were increasing rapidly everywhere in Canada, at all levels of public authority, as governments sought to satisfy rising expectations and a growing reliance on action by the state. In general Frost readily, even eagerly, accepted this expanding activist role. His willingness to take on new obligations and embark on new paths was always tempered, though, by his reading of what 'the people' wanted or could be persuaded to stand for, by what was affordable politically as well as financially. His assessments of public opinion, usually exhibiting an uncanny feel for the mood of the electorate, were made with much confidence. It was not always clear how they were arrived at – he did not rely on commissioned polls – but more often than not they happened to coincide with his own opinion of what was best or expedient for Ontario, and therefore for government and party. He never allowed himself, however, to get too far ahead of what he perceived to be majority sentiment.

The obvious fact that the accelerating rate and rising volume of government activity were matched by an escalation of costs frequently gave him pause but did not upset him too much, as long as the price could be paid without excessive borrowing or unduly high taxation. The touchstone of it all was economic development, the adoption of public investment and fiscal policies that would create a favourable environment for material growth and thus contribute to the good life for more and more Ontarians. That the good life could not be measured by the gross provincial product alone he understood very well. It required, too, higher standards of education, public health, and social services. But these were unattainable without wealth and that in turn demanded hard work, improved productivity, and encouragement of the private economic sector by the state.

At the annual meeting of the provincial party in November 1950, Frost offered a distinctly up-beat depiction of Ontario's recent history, current conditions, and probable future. Great were the wonders to contemplate after seven years of beneficent Conservative guidance, greater still the ones yet to unfold. Ontario's population, growing by nearly ten thousand a month, comprised about one-third of all Canadians but contributed fully 40 per cent of the gross national product, equalling the whole country's output of goods and services a decade earlier. This expansion had been and would continue to be assisted by intelligent public policy in the managed exploitation of natural resources, the provision of such necessities as abundant cheap power and improved highways, and fiscal measures designed to promote development. Certain facts on which, said Frost, 'I could elaborate indefinitely,' illustrated the success already achieved. Mineral production was at a record high value and the extraction of long-neglected iron ore deposits was 'going ahead full steam.' That, combined with mounting steel production, would 'change the industrial outlook of Ontario.' The growth of Hydro's generating capacity would soon end the shortage of electric power which had been a troublesome problem for some years. Manufacturing output was expanding apace. As an indicator of this, he observed proudly that more stoves and refrigerators had been turned out in the province during the first half of 1950 than in the whole of Canada during 1938 and 1939 combined.

Frost reported that unemployment was low, the demand for workers great and growing, the total of wages and salaries was over three times that of 1939, and Ontario had 'the best labour relations legislation ... in Canada.' New housing was available not only for the affluent but for those of modest means. In education 'we lead America in both our curriculum and in our provincial financial assistance to education.' Grants to municipalities had risen by 400 per cent during the same period, while rural electrification had been so speeded up that 'we have built more lines and taken on more customers than ... in the previous 23 years.' There had been similar progress in public health, with the introduction for the first time in Canada of capital and maintenance grants to hospitals and the formation of community health units, of which there were now twenty-four compared with the one existing in 1943.

Frost conceded that there were difficulties which resulted from these rapid changes on so many fronts. The economy was affected by an unwelcome price inflation, which no provincial government had the means to control, and there were still shortages, for example of power and low cost housing, as well as deficiencies in a highway system unavoidably neglected during the war. But efforts to cope with these problems had already shown improved results and these had been achieved with balanced budgets and 'our debt position well in hand.' This was no mean feat, Frost claimed, considering the impact of high federal taxation, which was now taking 67 cents of every tax dollar as against 47 cents in 1939.[5]

Part of the solution was making sure that government operated economically. At his request the provincial statistician, Harold Chater, conducted in 1951 a survey of the provincial budget with an eye to cutting costs. Frost acknowledged Chater's report with a letter the length and detail of which showed the importance he attached to the subject. Chater had managed to effect a reduction of an unspectacular $1.5 million overall, but Frost thought this 'by no means an insignificant sum and the moral effect will be good ... In these days of high cost and free spending the value of a dollar is overlooked ... I am not looking for the spectacular. I am looking for sound results over the long pull.' It might be well to have the deputy ministers meet every couple of months 'to constantly keep before them the necessity of sound economy and avoiding unnecessary duplication and expense.'

The premier felt that strict controls should be maintained in the area of job overlapping and classification so that staff increases in the civil service could be minimized. Chater was to proceed to arrange the first meeting of deputies. Frost stated he would 'drop in at some time to each one and perhaps say a little, which will indicate my interest and the importance of the work undertaken.'[6]

The need to find more money, which such minor economies alone would certainly not satisfy, was not, of course, the only familiar problem facing Frost as he took over the premiership. For all the expanding role of the provincial government in the 1950s, its entry into new fields of policy, its growing civil service and proliferating boards and commissions, there was a distinct sense of *déjà vu*. Certain old standbys remained the predominant issues: dominion-provincial relations, natural resource management, the liquor traffic, Hydro Commission affairs, highway construction and improvement, educational policy, and municipal government. These had been Ontario's chief concerns historically and nothing had happened to change that.

Frost's optimistic speech to the 1950 annual meeting preceded by less than a month the opening of a new round in the seemingly endless sparring match over the division of taxing powers between Ottawa and the two provinces outside the rental agreement. Early in December yet another gathering of first ministers began in the House of Commons chamber, this one officially called a Federal-Provincial Conference in line with the St Laurent government's ambition to expunge the word 'Dominion' from the Canadian vocabulary. In corresponding with the prime minister following their encounter at P.D. Ross's funeral, Frost had sent him a memorandum outlining some proposals but stressing that these were not carved in stone. They were backed by comparative figures based on projections to the end of March 1952, when the present rental arrangement would expire. They showed that Ontario would receive less by entering an agreement under existing terms than if it went on collecting its own business income tax and succession duties and introduced its own modest levy on personal incomes. Two basic principles underlay Ontario's case: that joint federal-provincial occupancy of certain of these major fields should continue; and that the rental for any field surrendered should reflect its true value and not be merely a per capita payment geared to the gross national product.

This last implied willingness to give a little ground, and such there was. Ontario would relinquish its right to impose a personal income tax (which it had not been doing in any case) in return for 5 per cent of what the tax yielded to Ottawa in the province. That was a limited retreat from the principle, often enunciated by Drew and Frost, that taxing and spending powers should go hand in hand. It also implicitly belied the claim that Ontario was doing very well on its own and presumably had no need to surrender any of its taxing rights. It did not propose to give up either death duties or the corporation income tax, of which the latter was by far the more productive. Frost contended that large industrial growth in Ontario imposed onerous public obligations to provide facilities and services not required of most other provinces or their municipalities. A higher corporate tax than elsewhere was therefore both necessary and justified. He invited the federal government to allow the whole of a provincial tax, and also of estate duties, to be deductible federally, instead of the limited percentage permitted as things stood. Of course, a province would have to agree not to raise its own rates for the duration of the agreement.[7]

All this could hardly have been as well thought of in Ottawa as it was in Toronto. Apart from its conciliatory tone, which accorded with the friendly spirit of Frost's accompanying letter to St Laurent, and its token offer to vacate the personal income tax field, it contained little to appeal to the federal cabinet and the mandarins of the Finance Department. Ontario seemed to be asking the federal government to accept diminished revenues without much of a *quid pro quo*. Presumably the mixture of renting one tax source and jointly occupying the other two was much less appealing to them than the kind of lease, including all three and embracing all provinces, on which they had long trained their sights. Possibly the memorandum simply stated a negotiating position from which there might be some departure; its tenor and that of Frost's letter suggested as much. It remained, however, the substance of Ontario's position when the conference opened on 4 December.[8]

Frost arrived in Ottawa with much the largest provincial contingent, five ministers in addition to himself, a galaxy of senior officials and four academic advisers, W.P.M. Kennedy, E.E. Reilly, F.A. Knox, and D.C. McGregor. More than any of his predecessors, he was eager to benefit from the specialized knowledge such experts possessed. The prime minister opened the proceedings and was followed by external affairs minister L.B. Pearson, who painted a sombre picture of a world deeply divided by the cold war and by hostilities in Korea. Then it was the turn of Douglas Abbott, with a promise of a revised tax rental plan and a plea to the provinces to help dampen the threatening fires of inflation by refraining from large public investment not needed for defence purposes.

In accordance with custom at those affairs, Ontario's premier spoke first for the provinces. His speech exuded a spirit of co-operation and goodwill.[9] There was no verbal assault on the central power of the kind that Drew, and Hepburn before him, had indulged in. Ontario would do everything possible to help meet the perils of the world situation described by Pearson. Apart from that, said Frost, two subjects were chiefly on all their minds, financial arrangements and welfare. Old age pensions were the main item under the latter heading and he came out strongly for a universal, federally paid pension at age seventy, with a jointly financed supplement for needy citizens at age sixty-five. At the close of the conference, contentedly riding the wave of the future, he committed his province to support these reforms.

There was no important disagreement on that but the other subject was much thornier. Ontario would take to heart Abbott's admonition about the need to curb inflation, Frost promised. But his administration faced large capital outlays for Hydro development, highway construction, and other public works from which there could be no turning back without serious damage to the provincial economy, and therefore to the people not alone of Ontario but of the whole country. Those commitments had to be honoured to satisfy requirements dictated by rapid population growth and industrial expansion. It was regrettable that historically this kind of development had been concentrated so heavily in the two central provinces. The conference would be wise to consider ways (he did not suggest what they might be) of reducing such disparities because the 'more even the development of this country, the better it will be for all of us.'

As matters stood, however, the provinces were differently situated; many had needs and problems quite unlike Ontario's and for this reason it was impossible, Frost argued, to devise a single formula for tax rental or tax sharing suitable to all. There could be no question now, he readily admitted, of the federal government getting out of personal and corporate income taxation. 'What is needed is the frank recognition that there must be a joint occupation of these fields' for provinces wishing it 'and with this recogniton an active spirit of cooperation.' It was still Ontario's view 'that the most efficient use of the tax dollar can only be gained in a system ... which provides that the government which spends the money is responsible to the people for raising it.' Not all agreed with that. Since some preferred federal subsidies to provincial taxes, a flexible plan was needed to allow each province to choose between the two.

Abbott's revised scheme did reflect an effort to be flexible. It offered two options, the first simply an upward adjustment of rents, the other avowedly tailored to satisfy Frost by attempting to embrace his contention that remittances should reflect the true current value of the tax fields. Prescribed percentages of the yield from personal and business incomes in a province would be paid, plus a province's average annual revenue from succession duties during a defined period. Adding to these the regular subsidies required by the constitution, it was estimated that under this option Ontario would receive about $102 million per annum.[10] While a welcome signal of Ottawa's wish to be accommodating, the offer had some drawbacks for Queen's Park, one of them that it was still a pure rental plan without provision for joint occupancy. This, however, might have been overlooked had it not been that, according to computations by Frost's advisers, for the life of the agreement Ontario would derive about $5 million more by collecting its own revenues than by accepting Abbott's second option.

Not surprisingly, the only conclusion reached at the conference was that each province would study both options and report its decision at a later date. No doubt Frost was gratified by the federal government's willingness to be less intransigent than he had often accused it of being in the past. Warren Baldwin, the *Globe and Mail*'s knowledgeable Ottawa correspondent, predicted that 'further negotiations in an attempt to arrive at agreement are assured and there are a good many indications that it will be reached.' He reported the opinion of an informed source in Ontario's delegation that Abbott's second option provided 'for the first time a common ground. It shows that the federal government was approaching the federal-provincial tax relationship with reality [sic].'[11] That may well have summed up Frost's view. Although the option was not entirely acceptable as it stood, he hoped that a mutually satisfactory solution could be hammered out and the protracted, wearisome dispute be at last resolved.

It was business as usual, however, when it came time to unveil his newest budget early in March 1951. He made but passing reference to the recent conference, saying only that the federal cabinet had offered proposals which 'will be examined on their merits.'[12]

As Frost wanted neither to slam the door in Ottawa's face nor endorse the offer as it stood, for the time being the less said about it the better while discussions went on. In the main the budget address drew the usual attractive picture: a healthy surplus, declining net per capita debt, no new or increased taxes, and more generous grants to municipalities, education (including free text books in the first eight grades), public health, and welfare programs. The one cloud in the sky was inflation, which if unchecked would have a seriously detrimental effect on provincial finances, but as yet heroic remedies were not called for. Nor, as far as listeners could tell, was Ontario in pressing need of a tax agreement.

Nonetheless, negotiations to that end were proceeding. Frost had meetings with both the prime minister and Abbott, arguing for a further change in their position. This would not only enable Ontario to enter the fold but (and in some ways even more important) might overcome the objections of Maurice Duplessis. To leave Quebec alone outside would harm national unity, and Frost was convinced that some revision of federal policy would prevent that. Duplessis, who had made a career out of battling Ottawa, had seemed in an unusually agreeable humour at the December conference. He had not rejected Abbott's proposal outright and had joined the other premiers in approving a universal federal old age pension. Not too much significance could be read into that, of course, much less into the fact that he had been photographed in a jovial mood clasping hands with St Laurent and Frost in a rare display of camaraderie. From so canny and mercurial a politician as 'le grand Maurice' it would be foolish to expect a miracle of repentance.

Still, Frost was hopeful. He had established a friendly relationship with Duplessis since their first encounter in 1945, and also with Quebec's treasurer, Onesime Gagnon. There had been quite frequent telephone conversations and some meetings in Quebec City or Montreal to discuss matters of common interest. Frost's objective was to have the two provinces march to the same drum beat on as many topics as possible; to him this meant that Quebec, like Ontario, should modify its defence of provincial rights and seek an acceptable compromise, were Ottawa to make the right move.

What should that move be? Frost couched his answer in terms calculated to appeal to the Liberals' conviction that theirs was the party of national unity. It was fundamentally important, he pointed out to Abbott, who may well have thought to himself that he needed no instruction about this, that Quebec 'not be isolated or indeed feel that it was isolated.' A new offer should be made of the sort set out in the statement he was enclosing. This began with two assertions Abbott had heard before: Ontario had earned more revenue from its own taxes than it would have by renting them; and the demand for large new provincial expenditures arising from industrialization created a pressing need for even greater revenue. There was nothing new there. But there was another salient fact, that Quebec did not favour discontinuing its business income tax, even temporarily. If Ontario should do so, 'corporations in Quebec would be ... paying higher ... taxes than those in the rest of Canada.' That would not be a good thing for national unity.

To get around these difficulties, the federal government should offer a third option. As Frost described it, this was in essence a slightly modified version of Ontario's 1950 memorandum, supported by the same arguments, with the added claim that 'Quebec would undoubtedly find this proposal satisfactory.' Abbott was noncommittal, promising only to consider the suggestions carefully and have his staff 'do a little pencil work to see what they amount to.'[13]

By the time Douglas Abbott undertook in the summer of 1951 to work on Ontario's tax proposals, Frost had made up his mind to call an election for the fall. He was very conscious of the fact that since the spring of 1949 the premier-in-office had 'been filling someone else's shoes and [had] not had an actual mandate.'[14] He must seek one, and conditions for doing so looked propitious. Walter Thomson, who had become the vociferous and peripatetic leader of the Liberal party late in 1950, was peppering the administration with criticisms from outside the legislature, of which he had not yet tried to become a member, and demanding an election. He sounded full of confidence but Frost was inclined to discount that as either bluster or a serious misreading of political realities. The government had to its credit a record of balanced budgets and, he believed, of progressive legislation. The economy was prospering, the long dispute with Ottawa over taxing powers seemed on the way to being settled and, as he saw it, neither opposition party posed a serious threat.

Contentious issues arousing bitter controversy existed, to be sure. One was liquor policy, an everlasting burden from which no real relief could be found. Equally explosive potentially was the recently submitted report of a royal commission on education, appointed by Drew, with some controversial recommendations affecting separate schools. The report dismayed Frost, who prayed that it could be swept under the rug.

Drew had appointed a large, representative commission, chaired by Mr Justice Hope of the Ontario Supreme Court, to conduct a comprehensive inquiry into education. The commission reported in December 1950 with over three hundred recommendations.[15] The most controversial was that the system below the university level be made over into a three-tier structure. The elementary schools would include the first six grades, the secondary, grades seven to ten inclusive. The top tier of further education would comprise junior colleges (grades eleven through thirteen), technical institutes, apprentice training, and part-time studies.

Whatever might be said for this reform on pedagogical grounds, it caused outrage among Roman Catholics. The distinction between public and separate schools would cease at the end of grade six instead of later, thus reducing the denominational element in the system. The Catholics' temper was not improved by the suggestion that corporation and public utility school taxes be devoted exclusively to secondary and further education, rather than be assigned to public or separate elementary schools at the option of the company. These recommendations were made little more palatable by the proposal that, in addition to religious teaching continuing to be compulsory in the elementary grades, it be required in secondary schools with clerics of the various churches giving instruction. Nor did two further suggestions – that school boards be authorized to offer French as a subject of study in the lower grades and that instruction in French be offered where appropriate – assuage the worry of those who detected an attack on separate schools. No sooner was the report released than James Cardinal McGuigan of Toronto declared that it would cause 'astonishment and consternation' among Roman Catholics.[16] At the same time many on the opposite side began to urge Frost to introduce the reorganization without delay.

The raising of so divisive a subject was most unwelcome to him. He had, he told Harold Hale in Orillia, 'disagreed with George Drew at the time of the appointment of this Commission on the grounds that the reference was altogether too broad. It should have been limited to specific things and certainly a matter as controversial as the Separate School issue going back a hundred years in our history is something upon which we can get nothing but a statement of differences from a Commission of this sort ... The great difficulty with this Report is that in many respects it lacks any real relationship to reality.' He added: 'I very much question the Hope recommendations from a Constitutional standpoint.' Furthermore, as provincial treasurer he had 'to deal with the complicated tax system as it is, and it is all very well to suggest sweeping revisions but who is to pay for them and where is the money to come from and what is the impact on individual tax-payers.' Expecting him to implement the report 'holus-bolus is simply fantastic.' In recent years there had been 'tremendous advances in education, and I am Scotch enough to want to see something better before I do something which displeases people and gets them walking on the opposite sides of the street.'[17]

That Scotch point of view had typified Frost's statement when the Hope report was tabled in the House. Not wanting to touch off a debate about separate schools, he carefully avoided referring to its recommendations and dwelt upon the high quality of the existing system. Thanks to reforms in the last half dozen years – vastly higher grants, improved teacher training, curriculum revisions, and improvements in school buildings and facilities – 'we can say with surety that we have made the greatest and most forward changes in education in all of our history ... we have not created division among our people. We have been walking on the same side of the street and proceeding with amity.' The commission's proposals were only that, proposals: 'the Government in no way considers itself bound by the Report either in whole or in part ... In no sense has there been any delegation of policy to the Commission.'[18]

This intimation of inaction displeased many Protestants, but Frost was unyielding. The real menace, in his mind, was an entirely needless revival of old sectarian animosities.

However, should the government find itself facing growing demand for action, a fresh popular mandate would strengthen his hand. Moreover, some other important undertakings were in the offing and these could be better carried out by a newly elected administration. The structure of government in greater Toronto was going to be reformed, for example, and a large commitment of funds made to electric power development in conjunction with the much delayed St Lawrence Seaway, construction of which, it was hoped, would begin before long. For these reasons, Frost decided to go to the polls in late November 1951.

The election announcement drew a mixed reception from opposition party leaders. Walter Thomson welcomed it, promising to avoid personal attacks and stick to the issues. E.B. Jolliffe, in contrast, thought it idiotic, a case of bad taste because the campaign would coincide with a visit by Princess Elizabeth and Prince Philip, of bad judgment because the probably inclement November weather would reduce voter turnout, and bad luck for the Frost government, which the electorate would seize this opportunity to reject. The *Canadian Forum*, voice of the intellectual left, agreed that it was no time for an election but for different reasons. 'Nothing could be more irresponsible and contrary to the spirit of the constitution than for a government to hold an election for no other reason than that the voters are unlikely to want a change.'[19]

The politicians, in fact, would have found it next to impossible to compete with the royal couple for the attention of press and public. The visitors were greeted everywhere by large, enthusiastic crowds and newspapers devoted much space to recounting in word and picture the happenings of the tour. For the most part Frost stayed out of the scene, leaving the lieutenant-governor or local functionaries to do the honours. He was, however, one of those greeting the couple on their arrival in Toronto. At a banquet in the Royal York tendered by the province, Frost presented gifts, both fashioned by Ontario craftsmen from Ontario precious metals, one of sterling silver for the prince, and for Elizabeth a gold and platinum brooch bearing the inscription, 'Loyal She Began; Loyal She Will Ever Remain.'[20]

When the election was called, most candidates for all parties had yet to be nominated. Theoretically this was done in open conventions where party members freely made their choice, but with the Tories at least, *laissez-faire* did not wholly prevail. Close attention was paid at party headquarters, and by Frost himself, to the identity and characteristics of probable aspirants and to who would be the best nominee in each constituency. Lists were drawn up containing frank, detailed comments by an unidentified author about all those who were or might be going after nominations. Ridings in which a desirable outcome seemed in doubt were called to the notice of Frost, A.D. McKenzie, George Doucett, or William Griesinger, presumably so that they could make it clear to local party officers that such-and-such a person was preferred by the leadership.[21] This had to be done delicately, of course, for fear of offending sensitivities and some egos were bound to be bruised. But save for the constituencies of Carleton and Prescott, where rejected warriors entered the lists as independent Conservatives and trailed the field, it was apparently accomplished without provoking serious ill-feeling.

Late in October Frost took to the road and for the next three weeks was a travelling salesman, living out of a suitcase and becoming acquainted with more hotel rooms than ever before. As leader he was in demand everywhere and felt obliged to show himself in as many places as humanly possible. It was a gruelling grind, enough to try the stamina and good humour of any man, especially in a cold, snowy season. Sundays he rested, repairing to Lindsay to catch his breath, but otherwise he was constantly on the go by plane, train or automobile, usually speaking two or three times a day. On 29 October he flew to Timmins for an evening appearance and the next day was driven to New Liskeard and then to North Bay for another evening meeting before boarding the night train to Toronto. The following afternoon he was in the air to Fort William and, after staying there overnight, flew back to Toronto, whence he drove to Galt to strut his stuff once more. During the week of 12 November he visited Kitchener, Hamilton, Simcoe, Welland, Niagara Falls, Bowmanville, Belleville, Napanee, Cornwall, Eastview, Ottawa, Renfrew, and Pembroke before coming thankfully to rest in Lindsay for a day off. Sault Ste Marie and Sudbury saw him, as did Brantford, London, Windsor, Goderich, and many places in between. There was no big Toronto rally, but Frost, while leaving the campaign in the metropolitan area mostly to others, did not neglect it entirely. On 20 November, two days before the ballots were cast, he appeared and spoke briefly at the committee rooms in all seventeen of its constituencies and that night addressed meetings in three collegiate institutes. Even for someone with his energy and fondness for talking, that was quite a feat.[22]

The message in all these speeches was much the same: a defence of the Tories' record since 1943, especially under his leadership; an outline of the good works in progress and to be carried on if the government was re-elected; and a plea to all fair-minded citizens of whatever political affiliation to support a party which knew no boundaries of class, creed, race, or region and wanted only to see all work together for the common good. His speeches were reminiscent of the rhetoric of Mackenzie King, whose oratorical style on the hustings was in some ways not unlike, and may have influenced, Frost's own. In fact, another passage in all of Frost's utterances on the 1951 campaign trail was pure, unadulterated King: 'This government does not stand before the electorate ... with an armful of promises nor upon a platform of assurances constructed expressly for the purpose of a general election.'

On the whole the campaign was quiet with few dramatic moments. With one major exception, the newspapers, while dutifully covering events and offering some editorial comment, gave the election rather low-key coverage, understandably since there was no outstanding issue. The *Globe and Mail*, which to no one's surprise strongly supported Frost, professed worry over the lack of serious challenge to the Conservatives. One danger was complacency, from which Jolliffe was convinced the Tories suffered badly. He complained to one of his audiences that the Conservative party was bankrupt of able manpower, 'a shadow of its former self.'[23] Jolliffe strove manfully to inject some adversarial spirit into the proceedings but his efforts resembled those of a big game hunter armed with a pea shooter. Most of the noise was made by Liberal leader Walter Thomson, whose safari crashed through the jungle while he fired off his double-barrelled shotgun in all directions.

Frost paid little attention to his opponents. At his nomination meeting he paid his jocular compliments to the Liberals. 'They give me little to say. In the House they usually agree with us. When we bring in legislation they rush to vote for it.' After poking fun at some of Thomson's claims and promises without naming him, which he refrained from doing throughout the campaign, Frost turned to the CCF. 'There are some nice fellows there,' he said. 'Sometimes I tell them that they should come over and join a party that is going somewhere. But they talk blue ruin, the country going to pot.' Jolliffe challenged him to a public debate but he ignored this, causing the challenger to accuse him of running away. Like any sensible front-runner, Frost was having none of that kind of confrontation.[24]

Thomson, unkindly called by the *Globe and Mail* a 'part-time farmer, part-time stockbroker, part-time lawyer, part-time member of Parliament, part-time leader of the Ontario Liberal Party,'[25] practised law in Toronto and had represented the riding of Ontario at Ottawa since 1949. Upon becoming provincial leader in November 1950, he devoted most of his attention to the provincial field while retaining his seat in the House of Commons. The federal Liberals, according to Blair Fraser of *Maclean's*, had no great fondness for Thomson. The 'Ottawa machine' had opposed him at the leadership convention and had now written off his chances of winning the Ontario election. They may have feared that Thomson would be another Mitch Hepburn, while in their eyes Frost was both competent and well-behaved, merits confirmed by the acid test: the premier and prime minister 'have got on famously.'[26]

Thomson was distinctly more optimistic than they about his prospects, as he had to be for the sake of credibility. In his campaign, he concentrated on what he considered the paramount issue, health care. He promised that he would at once establish a universal, prepaid hospitalization plan, financed partly by a small premium and partly out of general revenue. The government had had this subject under consideration but Frost decided that it would be premature to create the kind of system Thomson had in mind, whatever its attractions; there would have to be more hospitals, beds, nurses and equipment to make it feasible.

On this issue of free hospital services, the *Toronto Star* unleashed its crusading fervour, affording the one major exception to the blandness with which the press treated the election. The more worked up it got about the merits of Thomson's plan and the unspeakable hardships it would banish, and the angrier it became at the Tories for heartlessly disregarding the welfare of the common people, the more the *Star* seemed to be fighting the Leeds election all over again. Of course at stake now was preserving health rather than disposing of wealth and Frost was pictured as almost a murderer. There was, indeed, an echo of the Leeds fight when Thomson pledged to repeal the Charitable Gifts Act. Conservatives immediately charged that he had been forced into this commitment as the price of the *Star*'s support but the paper, disavowing any such bargain, stated what everyone knew was true: 'The Star has always supported Liberal leaders. It is a Liberal newspaper.'[27] Not only so, the health question was ideally suited to its progressive predilections, its advocacy of social reform and the need to protect the little man, the powerless citizen, from the predatory instincts of the rich and highly placed.

In its last appearance before voting day the *Star* pulled out every stop.[28] It devoted its seven editorials to the election and endorsed all Liberal candidates save those running against two estimable CCFers, Jolliffe and C.H. Millard, in 'ridings where Liberal chances are small.' Its front page was topped by a three-line banner in letters two inches high:

SUPPORT HOSPITAL PLAN
AND INSURE YOUR HEALTH
ELECT WALTER THOMSON

Judging by the final result, the electorate were not persuaded that Thomson's hospital care proposal was the dominant issue he and the *Star* mightily strove to make it. Nor did his other inducements, such as promises to reduce the gasoline tax and to pay a subsidy on fluid milk, seem to catch the fancy of enough voters. The same was true of the various grounds on which the opposition parties attacked the alleged failings of the government, in its housing and forest conservation measures, its lack of control over the free-spending proclivities of the Hydro Commission, the looseness of liquor law administration, and inadequate assistance to municipalities. And the explosive subject of the status and future of separate schools, probably to the relief of most politicians in all parties, and certainly to Frost's relief, did not loom as large or affect the outcome as might have been expected.

Following his whirlwind tour of Toronto on 20 November, and presumably thankful that the health and schools issues had not changed his position, Frost made for Lindsay. On the morning of election day he and Gertrude went to the polls, pausing to pick up Harry Marland, an octogenarian Great War veteran whom the *Globe and Mail* obligingly pictured standing proudly with the premier. That afternoon Gert made a mountain of sandwiches for the crowd she knew would turn up at 17 Sussex Street, win or lose, once the outcome was known. Again the *Globe* photographer happened to be in the Frost kitchen to show her at work and the man of the house appreciatively sampling her wares.[29] No one understood better than Frost the political value of these common touches. After supper he went over to his committee rooms to await the results. As they began to come in, first in a trickle, then in a torrent of good news, it became clear that his party had scored a triumph of unprecedented dimensions. Its share of the popular vote was slightly less than in Howard Ferguson's landslides of the 1920s but its share of seats was the highest ever. It had captured seventy-nine, the Liberals eight, the CCF only two. One of those two was Ontario riding, where Walter Thomson ran a dismal third. Jolliffe was a casualty also, losing more narrowly in York South, and so was A.A. MacLeod of the Labour Progressives. Frost rather regretted this last, even though the seat had been taken by a Tory. He liked MacLeod, whose wit had often enlivened proceedings in the House and whose remarks there, while often reflecting an ideology to which Frost was unalterably opposed, were usually pointed and effectively stated. Thus the premier was the sole party leader returned, trouncing his young Liberal opponent by nearly ten thousand votes. The Tories gave up only one seat, Stormont, while capturing eighteen from the Liberals and eight from the CCF. As usual there were wide discrepancies between the popular vote and seats won (Conservatives got less than half of all the votes) and on that basis both opposition parties would be badly underrepresented in the new House. Even so, there was no denying the astonishing one-sidedness of the outcome. Frost was not less surprised than others. 'I had hoped that we might win around sixty seats,' he wrote, 'but that we would win seventy-nine was far beyond anything I had thought of even in my wildest imagination.'[30]

One explanation of the sweep was that Frost had managed to separate many non-Conservatives from their allegiance by appealing to them as premier of all the people, one who was above narrow partisanship and who offered the only realistic alternative to the irresponsible, demagogic Thomson. They had been lured like moths to the candle by the beckoning light in his window. A Toronto lawyer and Liberal defector wrote to him: 'I am afraid you are developing a dangerous habit of persuading Liberals to vote conservative. I confess to being a not unwilling victim.'[31]

Renegade Liberals there were, but no mass desertion from the party occurred. Its popular vote was larger by more than 36,000 than in 1948 and its share of the total rose by nearly 2 per cent. The real loser was the CCF, whose vote declined by nearly 127,000, its portion of the whole by about 7.5 per cent. How was one to explain the collapse of a movement that less than a decade before had appeared to be riding the crest of an irresistible wave? Perhaps good times were a detriment to it and perhaps, too, Jolliffe had not regained the credibility lost in the gestapo fiasco. But why had the party done so much worse than in 1948, when the economy was generally buoyant and the gestapo affair even fresher in people's minds?

Writing from his home in Hamilton to old friends in Saskatchewan, Milton Campbell, at one time a Progressive MP and afterwards a supporter of the CCF, tried to supply the answer. He thought that on the whole the Frost government had been a good one, with 'the most progressive legislation in Ontario's history' to its credit. It would in any event have been returned with a comfortable majority, but things were stirred up by Thomson and 'the scurrilous propaganda' of the Toronto Star, which 'so disgusted thousands of non-P.C.'s that they voted for the government in protest.' But something more than fear of a Thomson victory must account for the near annihilation of the CCF. Like the good old western agrarian he was, Campbell found it in the CCF's identification as the political arm of the industrial unions affiliated with the CIO. That alarmed many voters outside the labour movement and within it produced a result opposite to the one hoped for. Many union members, Campbell believed, were disposed to back the CCF but not at the behest of their leaders. 'Those leaders are about as anti-democratic as I have ever seen. The men don't dare oppose

them in meeting so they take it out on them when they get behind
the curtain to mark their ballots.' Thus the paradox that in Hamilton, the most unionized city in Canada, the Tories had won all
the seats with good majorities.[32]

Frost wanted his administration to be seen as non-partisan and
for all the people, but partisan feeling reigned supreme on election
night in the crowded, stuffy Tory committee rooms in Lindsay and
also outside, where an overflow gathered in a cold, windswept rain
to share in the excitement. As each bit of good news was announced, cheers went up, the loudest greeting word of Thomson's
personal defeat. Frost, gratified though he was, did not join in the
boisterous celebration. Ralph Hyman, observing the scene for the
Globe and Mail, discerned a growing thoughtfulness in the premier's expression as he pondered the results and scribbled some
notes for the few words he was about to address to the people of
Ontario over the radio. Later, his face solemn, he mounted a chair
and offered a brief impromptu speech to those pressed together in
the jam-packed room. 'There was no exultation,' Hyman reported,
'no gloating over the stunning defeat of the opposition candidates.
It was Les Frost speaking to his friends and neighbours ... There
was a deep silence as he spoke to those with whom he had lived
and worked and told them that what he wanted now more than
ever was the kind of unity that would enable him to do a good job
for Ontario and for Canada.'

As he stepped down from his perch, a deafening roar filled the
room and people surged forward to shake his hand or slap him on
the back. At that moment a fire engine siren was heard outside.
'Rain or no rain, I guess I'll have to ride on that wagon,' said Frost.
Donning a fireman's hat, he climbed aboard, grinning from ear to
ear. The engine moved off, bell clanging and siren wailing, followed
by horn-tooting cars filled with joyous Tories. Through the town's
main streets the procession rolled, arriving finally at the Frost
residence. Everyone went inside to savour the sweet taste of success
and all those sandwiches and gallons of coffee Gertrude had prepared.[33] Having his friends to the house was the way Frost liked
best to celebrate a happy occasion. What could be happier than
this one? He had sought his mandate and the voters had obliged
with a decisiveness undreamed of. Now the people of the province,
and many beyond, would watch with interest to see what use he
would make of it.

11

A Big View of the Future

Not long after the 1951 triumph, Frost promised an old friend to 'continue along the same lines and give a good, down-to-earth administration.'[1] As far as it went, this accurately described his course following the election. There was no shift in direction, nor was one to be expected; the lack of his own mandate from the voters had not inhibited him after succeeding Kennedy in departing from precedent and going his own way, as witness his overture to the federal government. The fact was, though, that important innovations and major developments were in preparation that went far beyond good down-to-earth-administration. Of the former, the introduction of a metropolitan form of government for the Toronto area was the most striking. Among the latter, the St Lawrence Seaway and power development and a natural gas pipeline from Alberta, which Frost while electioneering had undertaken to strive for, were especially noteworthy. And of course the slow, stately progress towards a tax accord with Ottawa was certain to continue. No one of these was on the verge of being achieved in the fall of 1951, but the complex plans and negotiations were going ahead.

Regarding the tax matter, there was no outward indication by Frost when the new legislature met in February 1952 that an agreement with Ottawa was any closer than it had been a year earlier. In the throne speech debate he reiterated at length the familiar contention that Ontario was doing better by collecting its own monies than it would under any terms so far offered by the St Laurent cabinet. Farquhar Oliver, thanks to Thomson's personal defeat still leading the Liberals in the House and now, as well, leader of the official opposition, chastised the premier for preaching co-operation with Ottawa and at the same time rejecting all its tax rental proposals. 'It is our desire to be co-operative,' replied Frost. 'We want to be understanding in what we do, and we hope that the Federal administration ... will be mindful of our problems.' All federal offers had been and would be considered intensively, but it would be foolish to take a premature plunge. 'We have gained a great deal by not rushing in and suspending our tax powers.'[2]

Nothing had changed when Frost brought down the budget a few weeks later. In its general outline it was virtually a carbon copy of previous ones, with a comfortable surplus and a modest one in prospect for the coming twelve months without new or increased taxes. An important new departure would allow municipalities to tax government and Hydro properties within their boundaries. A substantial boost in their regular subsidies from the treasury would further assist hard-pressed local governments, and a record $100 million for such major needs as education, hospitals, and roads was promised. The provincially supported universities, which Frost described as 'not only the centre of things cultural, but ... also the main spring of scientific and health research which is fundamental to Ontario's progress and betterment,' would receive special capital grants as well as larger operating funds. In the light of all this, what need of renting taxes? Frost emphasized that he was not closing the door on that, but for now the province would continue on its own.

But a general must guard his flanks. The budget speech contained a passage apparently designed to provide a justification for a reversal of Ontario's traditional preference for going its own way. 'In these times of sudden and unpredictable change, we dare not fail to recognize our responsibilities as the largest and most prosperous of all the provinces ... We must ... ever be mindful ... that the prosperity of Canada is all of one piece – indivisible. We cannot morally or wisely grasp prosperity with one hand and with the other strive to impede the progress of our brother Canadians in other provinces. As Ontario prospers, so must Canada prosper.'[3] The beauty of these words was that they could be read in two ways. If Ottawa came forth with a satisfactory offer, its acceptance could be deemed necessary for the indivisible prosperity of the country and Ontario be seen to subordinate its selfish interests to the common good. On the other hand, if there were no acceptable proposal, the maintenance of the status quo could be defended on the ground that what was best for Ontario was best for Canada.

Because the 1947 agreement embracing all save Quebec and Ontario would expire at the end of March 1952, negotiations for its renewal had been going on for some time. Little doubt existed that the central government would be able to retain those already in the corral, but whether it would round up the two hold-outs was far less certain. Douglas Abbott had tried in January by offering a significant modification of the basis on which rental payments would be computed, but so far Duplessis and Frost had eluded capture. For all the latter's agreeable language and his evident disposition to join if the price were right, he was proving to be a hard bargainer. Duplessis appeared to lack the inclination altogether, whatever the terms might be.

When the House was about to be prorogued in 1952, Farquhar Oliver moved a non-confidence motion criticizing the government for its failure to initiate further discussions with Ottawa. Speaking to this, Frost admitted that the federal offer of 1950 and Abbott's revision thereof early in 1952 afforded 'the fundamentals ... to make a reasonable deal ...' In addition, the St Laurent government had removed an aggravation by abandoning one by one its minor direct taxes on gasoline, natural gas, electricity, amusements, and pari-mutuel betting. The chief difficulty was 'the fashion of those who look at Federal-Provincial Relations to take Ontario as the standard, and ... grade everything from that ... The formula is always worked out on the basis of grading the other provinces up to Ontario ... they have invariably under-estimated, not only Ontario's needs, but ... the potentialities of what they are trying to wrest from us.'

That was the key point. No formula yet devised for calculating rentals, perhaps none capable of being devised, could accurately reflect potential tax yields in a period of burgeoning growth, even with an escalator clause to take care of increases in population and the value of goods and services produced. That being so, was there not a risk of sacrificing prospective revenue for provincial coffers? 'Should we gamble with the potentialities of Ontario, should we gamble with the future of Ontario,' by embracing an agreement which might generate a lot less income than taxes gathered by the province itself? That was the agonizing question.

Furthermore, renting tax fields was wrong in principle; on that Frost claimed to be still of the same mind. It was true that the West and the Maritimes had benefited from doing so but 'the whole trend ought to be on the part of the Federal Government to get these provinces out of these deals as soon as possible, and to get them on their own feet and to levy their own taxes.' Subsidies by one level of government to another were not the answer.[4]

One might have gathered from Frost's comments in the House

that a tax accord with Ottawa was still in the distance, even though the fundamentals of one were there. A resolution of the impasse was, however, not far off. In June, Abbott announced to the House of Commons the new terms being offered. There proved to be, in fact, nothing altogether new about them. The guaranteed annual minimum rents, essentially those offered at the 1950 conference, were a good deal higher than under the old agreements. Equally attractive was the change Abbott had proposed at the start of 1952; that the *per annum* rent might at the option of a province be determined by the ratio of gross national product and provincial population in the base year of 1948 to the size of these in the year immediately preceding payment, rather than to their average in the three preceding years. In other words, the amount would be derived from only the most recent available data. Since population and production were both rapidly rising, nowhere more so than in Ontario, that would produce larger payments for taxes surrendered than under the old formula.

How much larger? Finance Department officials concluded that Ontario would get approximately $137 million, more than $35 million above the new guaranteed minimum, assuming that the province vacated all three major direct tax fields. Abbott said nothing about the possibility of any being jointly occupied.[5] This was an important sticking point at Queen's Park, where it was still strongly held that retention of succession duties was vital to the provincial interest. It appeared no more likely than ever that Ottawa would cease imposing them, but perhaps a continuation of joint occupancy could be agreed to. Discussions about that and some other matters continued until at long last, at the end of August, all differences were resolved. Abbott and Frost met in the former's office to initial a settlement and then summoned reporters to announce the good news.

Stressing that neither government surrendered any of its constitutional powers – a declaration Frost evidently thought necessary to reassure those who might fear he had sold out – the document provided that for the next five years Ontario would rent personal and corporation income taxes. Both governments would go on collecting death duties, but Ottawa would deduct from payments for the other two fields the credits it allowed estates for duties paid to Ontario. The tax rate on corporations would be reduced by 2 per cent and they would be relieved of a pair of provincial nuisance taxes, one on their paid-up capital, the other on each place of business they operated. Certain other existing provisions were considered part of the agreement: abandonment by the federal government of the minor taxes already mentioned; and acceptance of provincial royalties and other imposts on logging and mining operations as deductible expenses for income tax purposes. The net annual gain in revenue to Ontario over what it would take in from its own income and corporation taxes was roughly estimated at $25 million. Frost presently announced that the bulk of this would go to highway construction and improvement.[6]

For all its spokesmen's talk about provincial financial autonomy and of money being raised by the government that spent it, the truth now appeared to be that Ontario had simply been waiting for the pot to be sweetened sufficiently. Moreover, Frost had attached great significance to the two central provinces acting in concert and had warned of the dire consequences of Quebec's fiscal isolation. Now the concert was over as far as a united stand on tax rentals was concerned. Duplessis, deciding that Quebec should not 'sell its pottage for a mess of birthright,' as someone expressed it, rejected these latest terms as he had all others.[7] Reacting to Ontario's decision, he declared: 'We shall never sign the death warrant of the province of Quebec.'[8]

Although understanding the political reasons for Duplessis's stand, Frost no doubt thought that comment extreme, and rightly so. But his own acceptance of the kind of settlement he had professed to regard as wrong in principle was grudging and unenthusiastic. It was strictly temporary, he insisted in a special legislative session called to approve it in October, not to be regarded as an adequate solution of problems caused by the limited taxing powers of the two lower levels of government. He repeated what he had said in a prepared statement when the pact was announced: there should be a thorough review of the Canadian tax system. To that end, the dormant committee of technical experts set up at the 1945–6 dominion-provincial conference should be revived, to examine the distribution of taxes, revenues, and functions among governments and to suggest 'fiscal measures that will best promote good government at all levels.'[9]

The opposition parties were, if anything, more pleased by the turn of events than Frost seemed to be. Oliver welcomed the premier's belated 'conversion' and Jolliffe, still leading the CCF from outside the House, wondered aloud why it had taken all this time to conclude the long tug-of-war.[10] For better or worse, Ontario's resistance to renting its taxes, begun flamboyantly by Hepburn and continued stubbornly by Drew, had been first moderated and then brought to an end by Frost. Doubtless there would continue to be disagreements between Ottawa and Toronto over administration of the pact, the determination of payments and so on, and if the province became dissatisfied it would be free to break away at the end of five years. But for the time being, presumably to the relief of all concerned, the issue was settled.

No sooner had the legislature approved the tax deal than Frost warned Ontario municipalities not to expect a windfall from it; they should concentrate on cutting their own expenses.[11] This might seem a hard-hearted attitude to the plight of many of them, which he fully comprehended. But he knew that some of them were misrepresenting their financial position in the hope of wangling additional funds from the senior governments. Some evidence of this was found in four resolutions addressed to Prime Minister St Laurent in the fall of 1952 by the Association of Ontario Mayors and Reeves. These complained that measures in force to assist the unemployed and to stimulate employment were inadequate, resulting in demands for welfare payments of a magnitude unbearable to municipalities whose revenue, it was repeatedly asserted, came almost exclusively from taxation of real property. St Laurent sent Frost a copy of the resolutions and of his reply, which clearly exposed their logical inconsistencies and factual errors. They showed, Frost observed to one of his senior officials, 'the exaggeration which is used in some cases ... it tends to weaken the cause.' Municipal spokesmen would make more headway by acknowledging that greatly augmented grants now received from the province materially mitigated their problems.[12] There was room for further improvement, of course, but subsidies, like other expenditures, had to be limited. The alternative was new or higher taxes, which might discourage investment, impede development, and thus bar the door to the bright future Frost saw beckoning.

Like his counterparts in other times and places, he found the financial needs of municipalities a staple of his diet as premier and provincial treasurer. The vitality of local government was too important not to be seriously addressed when threatened, as Frost believed it was in some localities. Rather than allow matters to drift, solutions must be sought if municipalities were not to be forever mendicants camped on the doorstep of Queen's Park. He lost little time in commencing the search. Well over a year before accepting the tax deal with Ottawa, he instituted a comprehensive inquiry into provincial-municipal financial relations by a special committee chaired by the provincial statistician, Harold Chater.[13]

Four of its nine members would be named by the municipal associations, the remainder by the government. The scope of the investigation was to be extremely broad: 'all matters relating to municipal finance, the responsibilities of municipalities, possible additional tax sources and a division of responsibilities.' Small wonder that when Chater was asked by a fellow public servant whether the committee had any terms of reference, the answer was no. That apparently did not bother officials of the municipal bodies. They expressed appreciation of Frost's 'practical approach to the knotty problems facing the municipalities.' In keeping with the breadth of its mandate and the complexity of the subject before it, the committee developed an elaborate organizational structure consisting of a secretariat, consultants, an editorial staff, legal counsel, and no fewer than twelve sub-committees. A royal commission could have done no better.

Setting up the committee was easy enough; getting it to move along with reasonable despatch was more difficult. One impediment was that in certain instances the municipal people disregarded Frost's advice that for the sake of continuity permanent officials rather than elected councillors be chosen as members. When the committee had existed for about six months, he was annoyed to be airily informed by the secretary of the Mayors and Reeves Association that, as neither its representative nor alternate any longer occupied the elective office held when appointed, they would have to be replaced by the two other elected persons whom the association now nominated. 'May I point out to you,' Frost replied with a trace of testiness, 'that it is not in order to change personnel now. If this ... became the practice, the Committee could never complete its work.' It would be intolerable to lose members just as they were learning the ropes and to begin educating their successors from scratch.[14]

More serious was the committee's uncertainty as to what it was expected to do. A good start was made on gathering statistical data, but sooner or later it would have to be determined what these added up to, what new policy directions, if any, should be recommended. Although Frost had stressed repeatedly that the committee's labours would probably extend over a period of years – indeed, he had suggested that it might become a permanent body – he was a little uncomfortable when the House met in 1952 over the lack thus far of even a progress report. Nearly eighteen months after the committee's birth, Chater informed Frost that 'we have come to the point where a definite decision will have to be made as to the direction we are to follow in our work.' He had been trying to impress on the committee that 'there is need for municipal reform ... Some, however, do not seem to be conscious of this.'[15]

In early 1953 the committee presented a brief interim report. Its mere four pages proposed unconditional grants by the province in place of some existing subventions – a reform advocated for some time by the municipal associations and more than once suggested to Chater by Frost as worth considering. Legislation giving it effect was presently introduced, the complexity of which suggests that it was in the making before the committee was formally heard from.

In his extensive remarks on this enactment, Bill 81, Frost was at unsurprising pains to contrast the generosity of Conservative governments since 1943, while assuming a greater share of obligations formerly municipal, with the parsimony of their predecessors. When he became treasurer in 1943, said Frost, the total of all grants to municipalities, including those for school and hospital boards, was $18 million; in 1952–3 they came to $120 million, 40 per cent of all provincial revenues. In the Liberal regime's last year, local governments were given about $3.5 million for road building and maintenance; the current figure was more than $28.5 million. The increase to that figure over the preceding year exceeded the total the stingy Liberals had offered in 1943. Farquhar Oliver, 'who would mount his charger and put on his breastplate and all the rest of it and go out and fight the battle of the municipalities,' should bear all this in mind. 'I am quite safe in saying that there is not in Canada, indeed I doubt if there is in America, any Government which has done for its municipalities what this Government has done over ... the last nine years.'[16]

It was all the more pleasant to dilate on Tory open-handedness when he was about to announce more generous treatment still. True, under the new dispensation certain grants would be terminated. In 1949 the standard one mill subsidy paid annually to all local governments since 1937 had been abandoned and replaced by sums for specific purposes. These earmarked subsidies, Frost conceded in 1953, had not worked satisfactorily, being widely resented as inequitable and an infringement on the municipalities' surviving power to make their own decisions. They would now be replaced by unconditional grants and in this 'we are breaking new ground in Canada.'[17]

The grants were of varying size *per capita* in proportion to population, with municipalities grouped in categories on that basis. While there were no strings attached, it was hoped at Queen's Park that they would be applied to the cost of social welfare and thus contribute to keeping property taxes down. As such costs, like those of local government generally, were much higher *per capita* in big urban centres, it was only just that these receive proportionately more. Under the existing system municipalities with the same population might receive markedly different amounts; under the new one those disparities would disappear. In the aggregate, the new grants would total in the first year, 1954, about $12 million, roughly three and one-half times the ones they were replacing. All municipalities would get more than before, as Frost illustrated with numerous examples, but that the scheme was less than perfect he admitted. 'I do not want for a moment to say to the House that the population factor basis is entirely fair, but there is no basis one can arrive at that is more fair.' No local government would get less and a number of glaring anomalies would disappear.[18]

Harold Chater had argued the need for wholesale municipal reorganization in the form of regional government. Nothing came of that at the time but something akin to it was in the making for Toronto and its suburbs. Bill 81 went through its passage in tandem with a companion, Bill 80, the Metropolitan Toronto Act. Respecting municipal affairs, nothing was of more concern in the early 1950s than the structure of government in the greater Toronto area. Not a new issue by any means,[19] this was on a different plane altogether from the complaints and pleas for help by local politicians that customarily reached Frost's desk. The steady growth of that urban concentration had earlier led to the successive annexations by the city of newly settled adjacent suburbs, but in time Toronto lost interest in further extending its boundaries; providing services to newly acquired districts was placing too severe a burden on its ratepayers.

The result was the appearance of twelve more or less urbanized villages, towns, and townships, contiguous to but administratively separate from the city. They differed greatly in area and population, all were inhabited in the main by people working in Toronto, and few had significant revenue sources other than residential property. They were constituent parts of York County, which Reeve Gardiner of Forest Hill complained gave 'few and inconsequential services.'[20] With growing populations, they found it increasingly burdensome to furnish the amenities expected of municipal governments. By the end of the Second World War they formed a galaxy of disparate units with widely varying tax rates and levels of service. In a socio-economic sense they were elements in a single urban community. Legally and administratively each was a distinct entity trying to look after its own needs, although some had bilateral agreements with the city or each other for provision of specified services.

Near the end of 1949 the Toronto and York Planning Board under Frederick Gardiner's chairmanship formally recommended amalgamation, excluding the lakeshore towns of Long Branch, New Toronto, and Mimico and the still largely rural townships of Scarborough and Etobicoke. Frost, while sceptical about the feasibility of total unification, was fully seized by the time he became premier of the need for change. He also knew that the situation would have to be handled with kid gloves. It was far too sensitive to be left entirely to the Ontario Municipal Board, whose chairman, Lorne Cumming, was not noted for tact or diplomacy. In any case the board's powers, while wide and including the right to define municipal boundaries, did not seem to extend to ordering the kind of reconstitution of the greater Toronto area that appeared to be called for and would require provincial legislation. As Frost saw it, far better to prepare the ground by consultation with municipal leaders than to proceed at once by administrative fiat or legislative enactment in an enterprise so potentially explosive and fraught with political hazards.

His insistence on consultation disappointed Gardiner but the latter grudgingly accepted – indeed, had no choice but to accept – Frost's plan to convene a meeting of the mayors and reeves of all thirteen municipalities. The municipal leaders met in the cabinet room at Queen's Park with Frost in the chair. Making liberal use of his favourite adjective, Frost outlined the problems that had to be faced if the 'great future' of this 'great area,' incontestably 'one of the world's greatest city and urban areas,' was to be fully achieved. Certain needs demanded immediate attention: arterial roads to move traffic between the city and its suburbs; adequate water supply and sewage disposal for municipalities without direct access to Lake Ontario; a unified urban transit system; a more equitable distribution of commercial and industrial assessment to reduce disparities in property taxes; better organized police and fire protection for the whole area; and co-ordinated overall planning to meet present and future requirements. The ultimate need, though, was for 'a big view of the future ... of the challenges and opportunities presented to this very important part of Canada ...' The objective must be 'a municipal set-up which is going to give the people the very best living conditions obtainable.' There were bound to be 'issues concerning local interest. I ask you all, however, to raise your sights and look at the needs and possibilities of this great area whose interests after all are inseparable.'[21]

When Frost finished speaking a general discussion ensued. It was anything but conclusive. Some professed general satisfaction with things as they were, most were concerned about the financial implications of reorganization, and a few wanted to know the direction in which the government thought they should move. Although intimating that some kind of borough system merited consideration, Frost refused to be drawn out on this. They should themselves try to discover the best solution. At length his suggestion that they comprise a continuing committee for this purpose with an outside chairman was accepted and they retired to his office to decide who the chairman should be. Their choice, a member of the bench, proved to be unavailable and the committee was chaired by a senior officer of the Department of Municipal Affairs, A.E.K. Bunnell, then and afterwards an advocate of full amalgamation.[22]

Not long after the cabinet room meeting, the Toronto city council, urged on by Gardiner who appeared as a witness before it, voted by a large majority to endorse amalgamation and to petition the Municipal Board to bring it about. That was distinctly a minority point of view in the Bunnell committee; only Mimico, which had its own application before the OMB for a joint management board to administer shared services, showed qualified support for Toronto's position. In a series of meetings the other suburbs presented their arguments against and their alternatives to amalgamation, embodying, Bunnell told Frost, 'all the old lumber, the very features that ... have created the present situation.'[23] Meanwhile, Frost was endeavouring, as he informed an Etobicoke Conservative opposing amalgamation, 'to maintain an attitude of reasonable neutrality.'[24] To do otherwise when the city was firmly on one side and the suburbs almost wholly united in opposition would be foolhardy, the more so because the division was mirrored in Frost's caucus and among other Tories, some of them municipal politicians directly concerned. Because as matters stood consensus was clearly unattainable, one could only allow the OMB to consider the applications before it and trust that ultimately a reasonable compromise would be found. Frost was ready to work behind the scenes to help make that happen.

The Municipal Board hearings opened in June in the legislative chamber, surroundings suited to the importance of the subject, and continued with some interruptions for a year. A long parade of

witnesses marched in to address the board and be questioned by a
battery of lawyers representing all parties to the inquiry. The proponents of amalgamation, among whom Gardiner was prominent
and who were supported by the three Toronto newspapers, made
their case and were followed by one after another of the suburban
leaders for the other side. During the hearings, and for many
months thereafter while the board prepared its report, Frost and
other ministers were in steady contact with chairman Cumming, so
much so that Gardiner's biographer concludes that 'the cabinet ...
was for all intents and purposes the coauthor of the report.'[25] Some
had a darker suspicion that the cabinet had in effect dictated the
findings of the OMB, ostensibly an independent body. Allan Grossman, a Toronto alderman and president of the St Paul's Progressive
Conservative Association, claimed in writing to Frost to '*know* that
the vast majority of the people in the city and suburbs favour amalgamation,' as he did. He thought it obvious from its report that the
OMB was of the same mind 'but ... appeared to be hesitant for some
reason to recommend it.' Presumably the reason must be the
overriding wish of the government, which in effect meant Frost.

The latter skirted that issue in his reply. 'I think you will agree
that if the City of Toronto had done what was necessary years ago
in progressive annexations ... this situation would not exist ... the
failure to take action on the part of many governments has further
complicated the problem. Shortly after taking office in 1950 [*sic*] I
intiated action, and I intend to do the very best I can and abide by
the results.'[26] Those results might not please Grossman but, notwithstanding his reading of public opinion, there was abundant
evidence in the news reaching Frost that unification was widely
opposed. Although the cabinet did not simply dictate the report,
some of whose proposals were either rejected or materially modified in the ensuing legislation, the board was by no means left
entirely alone to make up its mind.

The close collaboration between the Municipal Board chairman,
Lorne Cumming, and the cabinet explains why, only a month after
the OMB report was made public in January 1953, Frost was able
to introduce in the House a measure giving parts of it effect, the
enormous and highly complicated Bill 80 with its more than two
hundred sections.[27]

The report proposed and the legislation created a confederal
form of government, a new Municipality of Metropolitan Toronto
between which and the thirteen constituent entities power would
be divided. The make-up of the 'Metro' council and how its mem-

bers were to be selected were among the most hotly debated issues. The result was a compromise favoured by Frost (it would have not been adopted otherwise) as an imperfect but best available option. The council would comprise all the suburban mayors and reeves, and from Toronto the mayor, the two members of Board of Control with the largest vote in the latest election, and the alderman standing highest in the polls in each of the nine wards. Its first chairman was to be appointed by the cabinet for an interim period of less than two years; thereafter the council would elect its chairman from among themselves or from outside.[28]

Bill 80 was given a mixed reception but on the whole a less hostile one than had greeted the Cumming report, especially in Toronto. The support of its mayor, Allan Lamport, who had a flair for being obstreperous (and was a Liberal to boot), would be the key. Allan Grossman became convinced, once the terms of the bill were known, that Frost had taken the precaution of applying his persuasive talents to bring Lamport around. Pushing ahead with the Metro plan, Grossman added admiringly, 'was a very courageous act on the part of the Premier. Practically everybody was in favour of amalgamation, including the city papers. It took guts when you had 22 members of a 23 member City Council opposed violently, but the Premier just went ahead and did it.'[29] The three Toronto dailies were not quite as one regarding the bill. All had indeed supported amalgamation and been very critical of the OMB submission, but when it came to Bill 80 there was some divergence. The Toronto *Telegram* approved of it without serious demur. The *Globe and Mail* and the *Star*, in unaccustomed agreement, were more critical. They saw it as an improvement on the Cumming plan but had serious objections. The *Globe* conceded that it at least had the virtue of not erecting obstacles to amalgamation and it deserved a fair trial; the *Star* thought the reorganization, while not without attractions, 'too big and too quick,' likely to cause higher taxes and a regrettable subordination of the city's true interests to those of the region as a whole.[30]

In the House there was surprisingly little commotion, no doubt partly because all but one of the MPPs from the area affected were Conservatives. Some of them moved a series of minor amendments, which were passed without division. To counter the natural suspicion that these had been not only agreed to but prompted by the cabinet, one of the Toronto Tories, W.J. Stewart of Parkdale, declared with some heat that 'never was any amendment handed to me pre-arranged by the Government, for our consumption. We experienced no curtailment, either by the hon. Prime Minister or any hon. Minister at all. We had an absolutely free hand.'[31] No doubt, but one may hazard the guess that had those gentlemen shown a disposition to tear at the vitals of the bill, their freedom would have been curtailed abruptly. Neither the small Liberal rump nor the even tinier CCF remnant attempted that kind of onslaught. The only sustained opposition was mounted by J.B. Salsberg, but his solitariness was shown by his inability to find a seconder for a motion that the bill be given the six months' hoist.[32]

One important decision remained to be announced when Bill 80 passed its third reading on 2 April. Who was to be the first Metro chairman? Various possibilities were speculated about in the press and some of these, including Lamport and Cumming, were seriously considered by the cabinet. But Frost, shortly after release of the OMB report, decided on Fred Gardiner, whose association with him, and with his brother Cecil until the latter's death, had been so long and so close. Much more than friendship recommended Gardiner to the premier. No one had taken a livelier interest in the future of greater Toronto. He was, of course, known to favour amalgamation but, even so, had greeted Cumming's report as 'a thoroughly sensible and practical alternative.'[33]

So Frost, asking him to come to his office for a chat, not only offered him the position but practically demanded that he take it. Gardiner protested that his large law practice would not permit him to shoulder so mammoth an additional task. Frost, smiling, looked him in the eye and said, 'You thought a hell of a lot about my law practice when you were urging me to allow my name to stand for leader.'[34] There was no denying that and, moved by his fondness for the premier, and no doubt by the allurements of a fresh challenge, Gardiner after some hesitation agreed to serve until 1955.[35] In fact he stayed on much longer and became known as the 'Big Daddy' of Metro, the form and structure of which, he grew to believe, were after all more fitting than amalgamation would have been. A year after accepting the offer, he wrote to Frost: 'While I supported amalgamation you convinced me that the metropolitan form of government is a more appropriate answer to the problems involved and I am now satisfied you were right.'[36]

In making his case for better financial treatment by Ottawa, Frost emphasized again and again that rapid urban development imposed obligations on Ontario, unmatched anywhere in Canada, for facilities and services, many of which local governments were expected to supply. But there was more to this than the provision of such good things as schools, roads, transit systems and social services. Among the dark consequences of development was serious pollution of water and air. The more people moved into the province, the more acute became the difficulty of disposing of their sewage and supplying them with drinkable water. The more old industries expanded their operations and new ones appeared, the more toxic waste was dumped into rivers and lakes or spewed into the atmosphere. Widespread awareness of pollution was relatively new in Canada. The subject had not closely impinged on the consciousness of governments or the public, but scientists working in the field and some amateur environmentalists had long known of the danger. The minister of health, Mackinnon Phillips, warned Frost: 'We are receiving complaints continually about water pollution, and this Department as well as the Government is being criticized strongly for not taking more definite action to correct this situation. I regard this problem of pollution as a most urgent one.'

Responding to the mounting alarm and calls for action, in the summer of 1953 the government created a Pollution Control Board headed by Dr A.E. Berry, an official of the Department of Health. The board reported that municipalities claimed to be unable to finance construction of sewage treatment plants and trunk sewers; it recommended that the province offer to pay in the course of a decade one-quarter of the estimated $113 million total cost. Frost was indignant and demanded more information. 'I must admit,' he wrote, 'that I am ... bewildered by a recommendation that the province should pay 25% and the municipalities 75%. What business is it of the ... board to make any recommendations in this regard? As a matter of fact the province has no fiscal responsibility, unless we are prepared to accept responsibility in all cases of pollution.' Asked for more information by W.M. McIntyre on the premier's behalf, Berry obliged and added an explanation of his board's suggestion. McIntyre noted on Berry's letter: 'NOT TO BE QUOTED. PM says to let this matter stand. Province cannot embark on any grandiose scheme of this character. Local municipalities create these problems and primarily responsible for their solution.'[37]

Frost was not going to get his government off the hook quite that easily. As both the Pollution Control Board and a memorandum prepared for him in the spring of 1954 pointed out, one complicating factor was that the problem was especially acute in the Windsor and Sarnia areas, where Canadian pollution of boundary waters, in the American view, violated a 1909 treaty between the two countries. It was true, the memorandum agreed, that sewage and waste disposal was primarily a municipal responsibility and a section of the Public Health Act empowered the province to compel local governments to accept it. But 'this Section has not been fully enforced since Government policy is somewhat obscure. As a result, municipalities quite capable of bearing the cost of required sewage plants, are delaying construction in order to discover what assistance the Ontario Government may give and to use [their own] money for more attractive vote-catching projects.' But that was not the whole picture. The pollution of water from discharge of untreated sewage was a serious health problem and diminished the recreational enjoyment of lakes and rivers, a point that ought to appeal to an outdoorsman like Frost. Since the public at large was affected, was it not reasonable to use provincial funds to assist municipalities unable to afford treatment facilities? Perhaps, the memorandum suggested, the two senior governments might share the cost of municipal debentures for sewage treatment plants where boundary waters were affected, while the province might do so alone for the protection of inland waterways. And the relevant section of the Public Health Act should be enforced.[38]

Months passed without action on these recommendations, but in the fall of 1954 the pressure on Frost mounted. Phillips sent him a memorandum, marking it 'urgent & important,' reporting that Michigan was threatening legal action if Ontario failed to take remedial steps and had brought its complaint before the International Joint Commission. The Sarnia area was the chief culprit, both respecting industrial waste, in particular from oil refineries, and raw sewage from the city. The industrial waste problem was on the way to being solved but not so the condition of discharged sewage. Port Huron across the St Clair River from Sarnia was operating a treatment plant and Michigan was compelling other cities to do the same. But Sarnia protested that it could not afford such a facility. 'This situation,' wrote Phillips, 'calls for definite action if considerable embarrassment is to be avoided.' It should be definitely decided what the border municipalities were to be required to do and how whatever they did was to be paid for. 'It is believed that none of these will be prepared to undertake these expenditures unless pressure is applied by the province or unless financial assistance is given.'

Frost remained adamant. 'May I point out,' he replied, 'that sewage disposal is surely one of the fields which is purely municipal. There is no possible justification for giving Sarnia ... assistance unless we are prepared to do that for every municipality in the province having sewage problems ... That is their job, and I think all ... should be facing up to the fact that they cannot pollute our waters.' As for industries discharging waste, 'it is simply indefensible ... It is unthinkable that they should be discharging these into the boundary or other waters ... and the practice should cease. Please advise.' Phillips tried to lower the temperature in answering this. It had been made clear to municipalities that they were responsible. His object in writing had simply been to apprise Frost that Michigan threatened litigation. 'I wanted you to have the facts so that you would be prepared to deal with the situation, should it arise.'[39]

A few days later Frost received a solemn letter from Prime Minister St Laurent, reminding him of the Boundary Waters Treaty and of American complaints, and mentioning that General A.G.L. McNaughton, chairman of the Canadian section of the International Joint Commission, had reported that 'the discharge of municipal sewage and waste in Ontario continues to cause anxiety.' Failure to correct this 'would naturally have serious repercussions on Canada's relations with the United States.' What steps, St Laurent wished to know, was Ontario taking 'for the abatement of the pollution of boundary waters through municipal waste and sewage'? After a lapse of more than a month, Frost replied. The subject had been under continuing study for some time, he assured the prime minister, but there was no quick or easy solution. The financial stringency of the 1930s, followed by the wartime unavailability of funds for such purposes, had prevented many municipalities from acquiring adequate sewage treatment means, so there was a lot of catching up to do. But 'it is evident that it is the industrial development which has brought with it a concentration of urban population which is ... the main source of the pollution. This emphasizes a point I have made on occasions at Federal-Provincial conferences that a province with a relatively large volume of industrial development requires substantially greater revenues to meet the ... costs of pollution and traffic congestion and other problems in the fields of health and welfare than one which does not experience it ... For this reason, I firmly believe that the abatement of pollution should be considered as part of the broader Federal-Provincial fiscal problem.'

Even so, much progress had been made. It was now five years since Ontario established its Municipal Improvement Corporation to lend local governments money for construction of waterworks and sewage disposal plants; the number of the latter had increased by 50 per cent. 'Today this Province has twice as many plants for complete treatment as all the rest of Canada.' The problem along the international boundary was especially severe for certain good reasons. 'Many industrial plants find it advantageous, owing to their heavy consumption of water or the availability of shipping facilities, to locate near the boundary waters, and ... these plants draw other feeder industries to the same locality.' An example was the federally owned Polymer Corporation at Sarnia which had attracted oil refineries and chemical plants. Some of these discharged toxic substances directly into the St Clair River or into the city sewer system and, while progress had been made in getting them to clean up their operations, 'the overall picture [is] less satisfactory than might be desired.' And of course new industry attracted more people to the area, adding to the difficulty of treating and disposing of human waste. 'We recognize the gravity of the pollution problem and the necessity for finding a solution. We are advising the municipalities concerned that it is imperative for remedial measures to be adopted. The Province, on its part, will continue to review the situation and assist where it is able.'

St Laurent's response, as E.J. Young remarked to Frost, indicated that he 'apparently docs not think your letter ... covers his request.' The prime minister inquired again what specifically the Ontario government was doing in conjunction with the municipalities concerned to abate pollution of boundary waters by municipal sewage and waste. He rejected unequivocally Frost's suggestion that anti-pollution costs be factored into the federal-provincial fiscal equation. Only a small number of local governments were involved in the boundary waters problem and their needs could be met by a relatively insignificant expenditure of provincial funds. Ottawa could not consider subsidizing some communities for this purpose when it could not agree to do the same for all. Of course this was precisely Frost's objection to singling out certain municipalities for provincial assistance. He made that clear in responding to St Laurent's letter, two months after receiving it, adding that, after all, a lot of the pollution of Ontario origin which eventually found its way into boundary waters came from sources far removed from them, so that it was impossible to separate municipalities into categories on the basis of their proximity to the border. But as to what Ontario was actually doing, all he could say was that pressure was being exerted on municipal governments.[40]

In fact, however, something more than that was in the making when this exchange of letters ended. In the spring of 1955 the government appointed an Ontario Water Resources and Supply Committee chaired by A.M. Snider, president of Sunshine Waterloo Company Limited, with a mandate to investigate all matters pertaining to the amplitude and purity of the province's water supplies, to recommend whatever legislation it deemed necessary for adequate control of water resources, and to estimate the cost of assuring the people of Ontario a reliable supply of good-quality water. Snider was a bit perturbed by an intimation as the committee was being formed that Frost might soon relinquish direct control over it to one of his colleagues, 'as I feel that we can do more effective work under your guidance.' Snider need not worry, the premier assured him. 'May I point out that even if the same were assigned to a Government Department that [sic] still it would come under my general direction on a policy basis because it is a new and important undertaking which will involve very substantial commitments.'

In 1957 the committee was transformed by statute into the Ontario Water Resources Commission, with Snider as chairman. The machinery was now in place for a more organized attack on pollution, of water at least, and Frost wrote to Snider, 'I am anxious that the Water Resources Commission under your direction not only have the opportunity, but that it will make an outstanding contribution to our life.'[41] As the cliché has it, however, it was only the end of the beginning. The beginning of the end of water pollution was still too distant for the human eye to see.

Although the knotty environmental issue was already on his plate, in his March 1954 budget speech Frost, looking back over the past decade, felt able to claim that 'they have ... been years of more concentrated growth and progress than this province has seen in any other corresponding period of its history.' To prove this, he offered a long recital, of the kind to which members of the House and the public were by now accustomed, of things accomplished, of projects going on, of new undertakings planned and hoped for.

It was an impressive catalogue. Whether one considered population, production, highway construction, electric power output and distribution, or house and apartment building, the record was one of unparalleled expansion. Provincial aid to municipalities and to education at all stages was at a record level, and there had been marked improvements in public health facilities and social services. The long feud with Ottawa over taxing powers had been settled more or less satisfactorily, for now at least, and the two governments were administering in a reasonably amicable way a variety of shared-cost programs. The enormous increase in provincial public expenditure had been matched by a growth of revenue without higher taxation, while the net per capita debt, thanks to prudent management, had been much reduced. Thus the high credit rating of Ontario was unimpaired, allowing it to borrow for capital projects at relatively low cost. Inflation, a cause of concern in recent years, had given way to stable prices, enhancing real income growth and benefiting the public purse.

On the other side of the ledger, Frost conceded, a few soft spots were visible, small blemishes on the bright canvas he was painting. Demand for some manufactured goods was slack, resulting in larger than normal unemployment in places. Agricultural income was somewhat depressed, the gold mining industry was in the doldrums, and housing construction still lagged behind need. Earnest attention must be given to these problems but in Frost's mind they did not seriously detract from the onward and upward march of Ontario's economy, or from the improved quality of life enjoyed by most of her people. There was, however, another worrisome feature, of increasing urgency and in the early 1950s seldom absent from his thoughts or from the minds of his senior advisers. Ironically, it was caused by the very material expansion of which he was so proud, and by technological advances which promised a glowing future. The unexampled growth of population and the quickening pace of economic activity created a seemingly insatiable demand for energy which existing supplies would not indefinitely satisfy.

Expanding the supply of two sources, electricity and natural gas, was thought to be of particular importance in meeting future needs, although oil and coal, especially the former, were very much in the picture. Since the end of the war, the Hydro-Electric Power Commission had been energetically building additional hydro and thermal generating capacity. In addition, a massive project had been begun to convert an area covering most of southern Ontario from 25-cycle to 60-cycle power; when completed this would permit the integration of the entire system with those of neighbouring provinces and states into a single power grid for the Great Lakes–St Lawrence River basin. In the light of these developments and of purchase agreements with other producers, Frost had thought himself able by 1950 to declare Ontario's electric power shortage, a troubling reality for years past, at an end. But that pronouncement soon proved premature. Demand for electricity continued to rise rapidly and further sources would have to be found. Faith was now pinned largely on harnessing power from the International Rapids section of the St Lawrence, in conjunction with construction of a deep waterway. Frost was an unquestioning believer in the need for a seaway; as well as going far to satisfy Hydro's pressing requirements, it would make Ontario's ports accessible to ocean shipping and infuse huge amounts of money into the provincial economy. Equally vital was laying a pipeline from Alberta to southern Ontario to meet the growing demand for natural gas. In his 1954 budget speech he expressed confidence that work on both these undertakings would commence that year. In the case of the seaway his confidence was justified; the pipeline was another matter altogether.[42]

Like all his predecessors from James P. Whitney on, Frost necessarily paid much attention to the affairs of Ontario Hydro, which, he once remarked, had grown 'so large and extensive that it provided the life blood of the Province.'[43] A significant proportion of his vast correspondence was devoted to its activities, with officials concerning policy, or with disgruntled citizens nursing grievances, real or imagined, against the utility. What it did impinged directly on virtually everyone and, although it was more or less autonomous in its day-to-day management, the cabinet bore unavoidable responsibility for its actions. For this reason the relationship between it and the government was of great importance to Frost, as was the recognition by Hydro of the supreme necessity of good public relations.

The problem was how to reconcile Hydro's desirable operational freedom from political interference with defence of the public interest, not to mention the interests of the Conservative party. It was a problem inherent in all crown corporations, but not all affected the lives of so many people as directly as Hydro, or were as indispensable to the economic well-being of the province. In the final analysis, control had to reside in the elected authorities. 'The original conception of Hydro was that it was independent of Government,' wrote Frost. 'On the other hand, in practice ... it virtually has to be a Government Department. The Chairman in theory represents only the Commission. In practice, however, he must be the Government's right hand in relation to Hydro matters. I know that this interposes a problem of administration and creates anomalies.'[44]

One anomaly was that Frost was not above stepping in and making decisions on comparatively minor matters that the Hydro management might have been expected to look after. For instance, he wrote to George Challies, cabinet representative on the Hydro Commission: 'Please carry out the following: ... John McMechan is to be appointed to the Toronto Hydro in place of Loftus Reid. This appointment I believe is made by Hydro. Therefore, the Chairman can make the announcement at the beginning of the week.' So clear was it made to the chairman, Robert Saunders, that movements of the 'right hand' must be controlled by the head that Saunders evidently thought it wise to notify Frost early in 1953 that he planned to take a holiday; it is fair to add, however, that the two were in close consultation on important policy questions at the time. 'Your holiday is quite in order,' Saunders was graciously informed.[45]

For some time it had been the practice to maintain liaison between government and utility by appointing a minister without portfolio a vice-chairman of Hydro. In the early years of the Frost government that office was filled by Challies, probably the best informed member of the legislature on Hydro matters. Without questioning his competence, for which he had high regard, Frost thought that something more was needed. His objective was less to curtail Hydro's autonomy, such as it was, than to afford the appearance of its accountability to the public and of public participation in broad policy decisions. The people as 'shareholders' were surely entitled to more direct representation in its governing councils. Soon after becoming premier, Frost began to discuss his ideas with Saunders, whom Drew had appointed Hydro chairman in 1948. Saunders was a go-getter who liked making decisions, an achiever enthusiastically committed to seeing Hydro become bigger and better, in particular to building installations required to meet the growing demand for power.

Frost liked Saunders and admired the energy and devotion he brought to his tasks. At the same time, he had some misgivings about an attitude the chairman displayed at times – perhaps an occupational hazard of those filling the post – that Hydro was pretty much a law unto itself. Frost frequently found it necessary to remind Saunders that this was not so, that as a publicly owned enterprise his agency was but one element, a vitally important one of course, in a larger scheme of things. As he pointed out à propos of Hydro's capital funding, these 'borrowings ... are done on the guarantee and, therefore, on the credit of the Province and we have to take the same into our fiscal picture.' Liaison must be improved so as to avoid direct competition between government and utility in a limited capital market. Saunders agreed (he could hardly do other) but, not having to keep political considerations in mind, was rather inclined when it came to big things to go full steam ahead and damn the torpedoes. To provide a brake and facilitate 'a rational dealing with Hydro problems as they affect the Government,' Frost created a small committee of senior Treasury and Hydro officials to co-ordinate the raising of capital and to consider the implications of Hydro's plans from the standpoint of general public policy.[46]

No less important than preventing conflict between the capital financing of the two institutions was the need to combat a public perception of extravagance in Hydro's operations. Saunders had also to be reminded of the virtues of economy. 'I am now beginning,' Frost told him on one occasion, 'to get reactions from our Members around the country' to a recent rate increase which in the case of Lindsay amounted to over 22 per cent. Saunders might adopt and publicize some economy moves. 'It would not be well to let the public feel that there are extravagances in Hydro, and of course it must be remembered that with all of the vast sums we are spending people do not appreciate that these come from capital.'[47]

The importance of countering the impression that Hydro was a ravaging monster beyond the reach of democratic control preoccupied Frost when he put in writing to Saunders some thoughts about policy-making becoming more consultative. In 1947 the Power Commission Act had been amended to authorize enlargement of the commission from three to nine members, but as yet this had not been done. Frost proposed to carry out the enlargement but in a way different from the one originally intended. He had consulted a number of large corporations, he informed Saunders, and found that all made a functional distinction between a full board of directors and the executive committee. A board concerned itself solely with broad policy questions and left management of the enterprise and the power to make executive decisions to a committee. Perhaps an arrangement like this would be appropriate for Hydro. Nine full-time commissioners, as envisaged in 1947, would be too unwieldy an executive body but it was advisable to have an advisory board. 'The efficiency which comes from a very small group ... should be maintained, but we should get the advantage of a broader representation.' The present commissioners would continue to perform executive and management functions but meet once a month or so with a group representing 'the North, agriculture, labour, municipalities, the home, industry and commerce generally ... Such a body would provide a good sounding board ... and would make the people feel that the Commission itself was not autocratic but was representative of the people.' Would Saunders please let him have his reaction to the plan at once, along with any suggestions he cared to offer?[48]

Saunders may have thought that the advisory board would be an unmitigated nuisance, but he was scarcely in a position to say so. Instead he accepted, even praised, the idea. He had, though, some suggestions of his own, in particular respecting the office he currently held. Although the 'original and present provisions allow, and in fact presume, that the Chairman has other interests and earning power,' he should devote his entire time to the job, as indeed its magnitude required. Moreover, for the sake of continuity the 'Chairmanship of Hydro must not be exposed to any elective political interests' or 'subjected to the whims or patronage of any political party.' The post should be held during good behaviour instead of at pleasure, except for compulsory retirement at age sixty-five. The appointment 'should parallel that ... of a Supreme Court Judge ... There is no talk of ... making a Judgeship ... subject to the vagaries of each Administration.' And the chairman should be accorded the pension and other benefits of Hydro's salaried employees generally.[49]

All this may have been more than Frost had bargained for, especially as to security of tenure. One could not bind a future government or foresee altered circumstances. It might be undesirable to change the occupant with every new administration, to treat the post as another patronage plum, but that was an unavoidable risk. Consequently, preferring apparently not to reject Saunders's proposed change flatly, Frost equivocated while remaining determined to carry out the one he wanted. In 1951 the Ontario Hydro-Electric Advisory Council was duly constituted with members representing the diverse interests he had mentioned.

It cannot be said that it was a great success or had much impact, although exactly what it was supposed to do was never very clear. Initially Frost was optimistic about its effectiveness. 'Public relations have been improved immeasurably,' he enthused. But it seems fair to conclude that the council was largely window-dressing. Late in 1958, a few months after becoming the cabinet member of the Hydro Commission, Robert Macaulay confessed to Frost that he had been unaware of the advisory council's existence until he came across some questions asked in the House years before. At that time the opposition, he found, appeared to be interested only in the salaries paid its members and had not 'the slightest interest in what the Council did, why it existed or if it fulfilled any useful function.'[50]

One of the projects Frost had originally proposed that Saunders bring before the advisory council was the desirability or otherwise of proceeding with the St Lawrence power development. Both men were already fully committed to this and a contrary opinion from the council would not have changed their minds. Projected as early as 1913 by Adam Beck, founder of Ontario Hydro, the St Lawrence Seaway and power scheme had been much talked about in Canada and the United States since the early 1920s but not a great deal had been done about it.[51] In 1932 the two countries concluded a St Lawrence Deep Waterways Treaty. This was quickly approved by the Canadian Parliament but failed to be ratified by the American Senate. A second pact, the St Lawrence Basin Agreement of 1941, was also rejected. Opposition was not wholly lacking in Canada either. Mitch Hepburn, following his spectacular victory in 1934, affirmed on behalf of Ontario that there was and would be no need of St Lawrence power other than what could be bought if required from existing installations in Quebec. Sentiment in the latter province appeared to range from indifference to hostility. In any event, the great depression was bound to put a damper on such grandiose plans, while the war that followed, although intensifying energy requirements, created more pressing needs that ruled out for the present the huge public investment the project would entail.

By the late 1940s, however, the situation had changed dramatically. The post-war boom further increased demand for electricity in both Ontario and New York State. In 1950 the need was no longer in question, nor was the unflagging enthusiasm with which Robert Saunders regarded the project. Shortly after becoming Hydro chairman, he flew over the International Rapids section on an inspection trip and resolved both to harness the rapids and never to make a speech without stressing the urgent need of doing so.[52]

Frost fully agreed with that: in fact he declared publicly that Canada should go it alone and assured an audience in Kingston that 'the seaway is as certain as the rising of the sun.'[53] He gladly entered into discussions with the federal government, assisted by Saunders, Challies, and senior officials of his own and of Hydro, about sharing of responsibilities and costs. Hammering out an agreement, begun by officials and completed by the politicians, took a lot of hard bargaining. Nevertheless, an agreement between federal and provincial governments was signed towards the end of 1951 and when the House next met Frost introduced a bill giving it effect. It was complex but, in broad terms, Ontario would build the necessary dams and powerhouse, while Ottawa would dig the navigation channel and construct the locks.

As for electric power, Frost stressed that there was no room for debate about Ontario's and New York's need of the more than two million horsepower that would be generated. 'The fact that we have hour after hour great quantities of water pouring down to the ocean, making no contribution to electrical energy to this great part of the continent is something which cannot be explained away.' There was no other practicable means of sufficiently raising output, certainly not nuclear power, which the experts assured him could provide within 'measurable time' only a partial answer and at much greater cost than exploiting the St Lawrence rapids. The cost of Ontario's share of construction, estimated by Frost at about $250 million, would be no problem. The province could borrow the money on reasonable terms, just as it had financed projects worth roughly $700 million in the last half-dozen years. 'We have the need for the power; we have engineering ability ... second to none in the world, and we can do the job.' And yes, do it without the Americans. 'Since the commencement of history, we have been prepared to "paddle our own canoe", and go it alone.'[54]

The bill passed without a recorded vote, only J.B. Salsberg voicing some reservations, and so did a complementary one, sponsored by Challies, authorizing the Hydro Commission to proceed with construction. At the same time, the House of Commons unanimously approved two measures of its own, one giving the go-ahead to build the navigation works in the Canadian portion of the river, the other empowering Hydro to commence its job in concert with whatever body the United States might designate to undertake the same work on the American side. Respecting power as distinct from navigation, joint Canadian-American action was necessary if for no other reason than that it was impossible to dam only half the river. In the following year, 1953, the New York State Power Authority was licensed for this purpose and, the required consent of the International Joint Commission to go ahead having been obtained, the way seemed clear at last to get on with an enterprise about which there had been so much ink spilled for more than three decades.

Meanwhile, the idea of an all-Canadian seaway was going by the boards. Despite St Laurent's declaration of independence from the United States, his government persisted in trying to bring the

Americans into the scheme. That was not altogether surprising since without them the cost to Canada would be more than quadrupled.[55] When the 1951 agreement between Canada and Ontario was signed in St Laurent's office, Frost remarked jocularly on the heat of the powerful lights set up for television cameras. 'Let's hope,' the prime minister rejoined, 'that the result of this may not only be heat on us but that the heat will be applied elsewhere.' The agreement, he went on, assumed that the 'seaway would be all-Canadian. But the door is still open for the United States to come in.'[56] Congress eventually relented and in the spring of 1954 Eisenhower signed a bill committing his country to the partnership.

By mid 1954, then, Ontario's need for more hydro-electric energy was on the way to being met, at least for some years to come. But, important though electricity was, that would fall far short of meeting total foreseeable energy requirements. More was needed in the way of fossil fuels, especially natural gas, to heat buildings, operate machinery and, not least, to run Hydro's new thermal generating plants more economically. Frost had already encountered a shortage of gas in southwestern Ontario as minister of mines in 1947, and had had to patch together an ad hoc solution to that problem. His 1947 conversations with N.E. Tanner of Alberta had brought out the idea of a pipeline from the prairies to southern Ontario as a possible answer. But that had seemed to be, not a 'pipe dream' exactly, but something for the rather distant future, and for the following few years it had been put aside for another day.

By the early 1950s Frost was convinced that the day for the pipeline was at hand. Early in 1951, with the Korean War raging and defence production again a high priority, he was reminded by his mines minister, Welland Gemmell, of what he already knew very well: that 'practically all industrial plants throughout southwestern Ontario utilize gas, and since many of these plants produce materials of war, it is essential that their fuel supply be protected.' Because the province's own gas fields were depleted, Gemmell thought the province would need to negotiate for large supplies of natural gas from the United States. In consultation with the gas companies, his department had drafted legislation giving them the right to expropriate private land on which to lay their distribution lines in anticipation of an augmented flow from Texas. The industry, with Gemmell's support, wanted this approved by cabinet and legislature. But Frost was not going to be hurried into anything of that sort. The subject should be thoroughly discussed with members of the caucus, and Gemmell should meet all the Tory MPPs whose ridings would be affected.

The political danger of antagonizing property owners, in particular farmers, by giving gas companies power to expropriate was cause for concern; but far more disturbing to Frost was the assumption of the companies and the minister that there would be continued dependence on American gas. Frost saw at least two serious objections to this. First, since domestic requirements in the United States would inevitably take precedence, the supply might be interrupted at any time. And importing gas from the south instead of from Alberta, he pointed out to Gemmell, would rule out the benefits an all-Canadian line from the west would bring, especially to the Lakehead, Sault Ste Marie, Sudbury, and North Bay. 'They would be on the direct line and we would be able to take care of them incidental with our extensions to the south.' Gemmell had forwarded a recommendation from Ontario's fuel controller, A.E. Crozier, that the government be neutral as between reliance on Texas or Alberta. Frost understood very well that there were occasions for neutrality but did not think this one of them. 'I must admit that if there is sufficient gas in the Alberta and western areas to justify it ... the all Canadian plan has many attractions to me.'[57] But, could and would Alberta supply enough gas to serve the Ontario market? Who would construct the trunk line from the west and how would it be financed? And was the St Laurent cabinet prepared to play its necessary co-ordinating role? 'We have to have an integrating force,' wrote Frost, 'and this has to be found in the Federal Government. If [it] was not whole-heartedly in favour we could get nowhere.'[58] Obviously, though, the gas itself was the first requirement. Initial estimates of Alberta's reserves, which further exploration was to prove far too modest, made the Manning government cautious and very much aware of the objections of various groups who feared either deprivation or competition if export on a large scale were allowed. At the same time, Alberta was being pressed by C.D. Howe, now minister of trade and commerce, to permit export – but to the northwestern United States rather than central Canada. His attitude to the trans-Canada concept was not as yet altogether promising. He still seemed to believe that importing Texas gas into Ontario and Quebec, as a *quid pro quo* for sending the Alberta product to the American northwest, would be more feasible and economical than building a line across the Pre-Cambrian Shield.

The Shield, in fact, appeared to most experts an insuperable barrier, as it had to many when the first Canadian railway to the Pacific had been projected eighty years earlier. There was, however, one important exception. Clint Murchison, a Texas oil and gas entrepreneur, created Trans-Canada Pipe Lines Limited, a subsidiary of his Canadian Delhi Oils Limited, for the express purpose of promoting and then laying an all-Canadian line. He was convinced that this was practicable from an engineering standpoint and was equally sure that, given raw material and markets, it could be successful. On that subject Murchison was a man after Leslie Frost's own heart, but when he began talking it up to his friend Howe, the latter reacted sceptically. 'Mr. Murchison,' he is said to have inquired, 'have you ever travelled over the Canadian shield? I come from there. It is a little more rugged and a lot colder than Texas.'[59]

To Howe and many others, a rival proposal for disposing of Alberta's surplus gas, if it were to be moved east at all, at first glance seemed more realistic. This was promoted by a Canadian company, Western Pipe Lines, and called for construction of a line to Winnipeg and thence south to the American border, whence it would be carried for sale in Minneapolis–St Paul and the surrounding area. That would be immensely easier and less costly, and a quick, adequate return on the investment far more certain. From Frost's point of view this plan, of course, had nothing to recommend it. Ontario would be left permanently dependent on uncertain supplies from Texas and the northern part of the province would be bypassed. He therefore set out to persuade the federal government not to permit the shipment of Alberta gas across the international boundary until it was definite that Ontario's needs would be met from that source.

Murchison and his group were undeterred by Howe's doubts and the widely favourable reception at first accorded the Western Pipe Lines proposition. In the summer of 1952 Trans-Canada Pipe Lines sent an emissary on a tour of northern Ontario cities to drum up support. His remarks before the Port Arthur Industrial Committee were reported to Frost by George Wardrope, the city's MPP. The company had applied for a licence to build a line, once Alberta had issued an export permit, to Regina, Brandon, Winnipeg, and the Lakehead, thence east and south to Toronto and on to Montreal. Financing the original capital outlay of $250 million had been arranged in the United States but Canadian investors would be given the first chance to subscribe. The total investment would grow to $1 billion in a decade and the volume delivered from 200 million to 500 million cubic feet daily. Gas would be brought to city limits along the way; it would be up to each municipality to provide its own distribution system. 'Our Industrial Committee are giving full support to the proposition,' Wardrope wrote, 'and if you have anything you would like me to know or do, please advise me.' Frost answered that the key figure was Howe. 'You might care to write to him urging this on him.'[60] Howe was the federal member of Parliament for Port Arthur and the two men were well acquainted. Wardrope sent him Frost's letter and in due course received a reply which he promptly forwarded to the premier. Howe wrote that he had 'already expressed to the Alberta Government my wish that the trans-Canada pipeline receive a permit [to carry gas out of the province]. I have discussed the matter with Mr. Frost and his technical men and have received their agreement to cooperate in every way. I believe that Mr. Frost is organizing support from cities throughout Ontario, which will be helpful.'[61]

It was not to be expected that Frost would rely very much on the lobbying of interested back-benchers or be content to sit on the sidelines while others made the plays. He wanted to be in the game, carrying the ball and scoring points. But the pivotal player was indubitably the federal minister, whose letter to Wardrope simply confirmed other evidence that, as Frost assured Wardrope, 'we can count Mr. Howe on our side.'[62] The evidence came largely from a series of meetings and of missions by his mines minister and Fuel Controller Crozier initiated by the premier in the late spring of 1952. He had two objectives in view: to advance the all-Canadian project and to explore the chances of bringing the two rival companies together in one common venture.[63] Both proposed a line to Winnipeg. Would it be possible to make it large enough, assuming sufficient gas and export permits from Edmonton and Ottawa, to supply both the Minnesota market, as Western Pipe Lines intended, and central Canada in accordance with the plans of Murchison's company?

As Frost remarked with reference to the St Lawrence development, he always looked for areas of agreement; an either-or choice between mutually exclusive alternatives did not appeal to him. Accordingly, in the presence of Crozier and Phillip T. Kelly, who had succeeded Gemmell as minister of mines, Frost met in his office with representatives of Wood, Gundy, one of the investment firms associated with Western Pipe Lines, who undertook to look into the practicability of amalgamation. Ten days later Murchison was at Queen's Park to outline his proposal of a thirty-inch pipe from Alberta to Ontario. Whether union with his rival was discussed the record does not show, but if the sole topic of conversation was the merit of his project, Murchison was preaching to the converted.

A week after that visit, Kelly and Crozier set off on a junket across western Canada to canvass the situation with provincial governments and other interested parties. They found ministers in the prairie provinces unopposed in principle to an all-Canadian route but unanimous that a comprehensive national fuels policy must be formulated before any new pipelines were laid. Nathan Tanner in Edmonton assured them that, should Social Credit be returned in the impending provincial election, the needed export permit would be granted. To whom he was not prepared to say. Alberta would not decide that until it knew whether an acceptable national policy on fuels would be arrived at. Tanner said that he would be glad to see Howe about this and he advised his visitors that 'Ontario should without further delay, discuss the matter of the markets for Western Canadian gas with Mr. Howe and at the same time, determine whether [it] should be exported to the United States or to Eastern Canada.'

Tanner apparently did not mention a third option, that it be exported to both. That would be the basis of the hoped-for union of the two companies but until the federal government made up its mind on policy, any movement in that direction was unlikely. On their way west Kelly and Crozier had a long session in Winnipeg with representatives of Western Pipe Lines, who threw cold water on Murchison's plans as not economically viable. They professed disbelief, which Kelly assured them was mistaken, that gas utilities in the central provinces would pay Trans-Canada's estimated price of fifty to sixty cents per million cubic feet. On their return journey the travellers stopped again in Winnipeg and heard the result of Western's promised inquiry into amalgamation: that 'it would not be economically feasible to join the two proposals and that each one should stand on its own.'

Back in Toronto, Kelly and Crozier briefed Frost on the results of their trip and then flew to Ottawa, no doubt with careful instructions from their chief, for a meeting with Howe, to whom they gave the same briefing. Howe told them that he would give full support to the pipeline from Alberta to central Canada and that Ontario and Quebec should not rely on an uninterrupted supply from the United States. He would try to dissuade the Federal Power Commission in Washington from allowing Consumers' Gas of Toronto to import Texas gas. Were the company permitted to do so, it might not be possible to justify an all-Canadian line. And he would shortly visit Premier Manning to discuss export of natural gas to central Canada. News of these statements could only encourage Frost's hope that events would move as he wanted them to, as did Howe's letter to Wardrope the following month.

So by midsummer of 1952 things appeared to be moving along in fairly good order, despite the unwillingness thus far of Western to join forces with Trans-Canada. Tanner had given assurance that Alberta would allow export and Howe had committed himself privately to the all-Canadian concept. He also informed Ernest Manning and Frost at the ceremonial opening of an oil refinery at Sarnia in September that, as he subsequently wrote to Manning, 'government policy would not permit export [to the United States] unless prior provision is made for serving Ontario and Quebec.' He believed that the solution to the problem would be to combine the two projects. He reiterated these views as government policy when Parliament met early in 1953. This was greeted favourably by all parties in the House of Commons, save for some Alberta MPs. More significant was its impact on Western Pipe Lines, which began to revise its proposal so as to allow for extension of its line to Ontario and Quebec a few years after first delivery to Manitoba and Minnesota.[64]

Howe's announcement covered exports from Canada southward but what about movement in the opposite direction? Not the least important of the assurances he gave Kelly and Crozier was that he would have representations made in Washington against the Consumers' Gas plan to supply the Toronto area from Texas. Tennessee Gas Transmission Company had applied to the Federal Power Commission to sell to Consumers' and, as Kelly pointed out to Frost, the volume would be approximately one-third of the total anticipated delivery to the central provinces by Trans-Canada. Consumers' made no secret of its opposition to Murchison's ambitions and attempted, with the support of Mayor Lamport of Toronto, to muster public opinion through full-page newspaper advertisements. The other large gas utilities were equally unimpressed. 'They have shown little interest,' Kelly remarked, 'in the proposal to pipe Alberta gas to Eastern Canada and ... without their support the undertaking might fail.'[65]

This attitude was indeed troubling. Early in October 1952, at Frost's behest, his friend, the financier E.W. Bickle, convened a meeting in the cabinet room in the hope of uniting Consumers' and the rival pipeline companies behind the plan to which Howe and Frost were now alike committed. In attendance were Frost and Chester Walters, still deputy treasurer, Phillip Kelly, Clint Murchison, two spokesmen for the Wood, Gundy–Western Pipe Lines interests, and Colonel A.L. Bishop, president of Consumers' Gas, who was probably in a position to speak for the other utilities as well. 'The meeting was not successful,' Frost recalled some years later. 'The Gas Companies were not thinking along the lines of bringing gas from Western Canada.' That was an understatement for Colonel Bishop actually walked out of the meeting in disagreement, while the would-be pipeline builders were still bent on going their separate ways.[66]

It was clear that Consumers' would buy its supply from Texas sooner or later, the Federal Power Commission willing, unless an all-Canadian alternative were forced upon it. It was thus imperative to press forward with that alternative. Also, Kelly argued, consideration should be given to piping gas to Toronto from the comparatively close at hand (but depleted) fields in southwestern Ontario as an interim source. This would cost less delivered than the American product and help to tide Consumers' over until Alberta gas was available. Meanwhile, Ontario should do what it could to have the Tennessee Transmission application rejected.[67] With that end in view, Frost wrote to Howe early in May 1953 to say that past experience in importing gas from Texas was not reassuring. 'Ontario and Canada are at the end of any United States gas line and it is usual for us to take what is left over.' Canada ought to develop its resources for its own use.[68]

With pipeline matters still in a very unsettled state, Frost sailed for England to attend the coronation of Queen Elizabeth II in early June. Shortly after he left home, St Laurent decided to go to the country on 10 August. Frost now found himself in a somewhat awkward situation, one that he knew would arise and that he was prepared for. He realized, of course, that Drew and the federal party wanted him to play an active part in the campaign and encourage his followers to do likewise. Many true-blue Ontario Tories might be indignant if he failed to help in a forceful manner. On the other hand, he had become accustomed to working constructively with the federal government and was on friendly terms with some of its members – the prime minister himself, but in particular with Howe and Robert Winters, minister of resources and development. With such great objectives as the seaway and the pipeline being jointly and harmoniously pursued, Frost had no wish to damage those relationships by actively getting behind what he regarded as the forlorn electoral prospects of the federal Conservatives. He did not doubt that Drew was as much in favour of the seaway and a pipeline as he was but, in the unlikely event of a change of government at Ottawa, a period of unsettlement would ensue and impede the orderly progress being made. This might be especially harmful to negotiations about the pipeline, which were at a delicate, crucial stage, and to the success of which he thought Howe was virtually indispensable. Moreover, Frost had gone out of his way to attract Ontario Liberals to 'the people's party.' Why run the risk of alienating them by partisan meddling in national politics for the sake of a hopeless cause? So, convinced that there was not the slightest chance of a Tory victory whatever he might do, and not wanting to antagonize those in the St Laurent administration with whom he not only had to work but enjoyed working, Frost remained almost entirely on the sidelines in 1953.

The election produced another dismal defeat for the Conservatives, though not quite as bad as that of 1949. According to some, the blame belonged largely to Frost, whose aloofness had been very noticeable. The veteran journalist John A. Stevenson reported in *Saturday Night* that the federal Conservatives were 'aggrieved by what they regard as the passivity of Mr. Frost and his colleagues.' They believed that had he shown more vigour in support of Drew, 'there would have been a much different story to tell about the result in Ontario.'[69] But Frost thought them entirely wrong. 'I think the course we took ... was the right one,' he wrote. 'Another course would not have bettered the Federal showing and indeed might have weakened it. Our job is to do our work in this Province and to strengthen the Progressive Conservative Party by meeting our obligations here.'[70]

Although Frost's inaction was among the factors mentioned in explaining this latest Tory débâcle, the real scapegoat, in the time-honoured tradition of the Conservative party, was the national leader, who had now led it to two overwhelming defeats. Inevitably talk now began to be heard about the need to replace Drew, and Frost's name was among those figuring in this minor agitation. The *Victoria Daily Times*, for one, arguing that Drew had had his chance and failed, suggested that the saviour might be the current premier of Ontario. He 'seems to possess those qualities of good sense, sober judgment and tolerance which the Canadian people demand in national leaders. He is free of those spectacular histrionics and flaming passions which the people distrust.'[71] And so he was, no doubt about it. But he was also free of such ambitions, content where he was, with things going nicely his way in a milieu he thoroughly understood. Unlike Drew earlier, he did not yearn to rise to a higher sphere.

As Frost sat out the closing stage of the federal campaign at Pleasant Point, there was a flurry of rather frantic activity in connection with the Tennessee Transmission–Consumers' Gas affair. It was caused by the long awaited decision at the end of July by the Alberta Oil and Gas Conservation Board to allow export to central Canada if Ontario and Quebec utilities gave assurance that adequate markets existed, a condition that could not be met if the Toronto market were lost to Texas. Upon learning of this, Ross Tolmie, the Trans-Canada Pipe Lines' solicitor, fired off a telegram to Phillip Kelly from Calgary, where he had discussed the situation with Howe. It was now urgent that Frost ask the Department of External Affairs 'to indicate officially in Washington that you do not want Texas gas to come in to Toronto.' This would 'receive immediate action plus backing of Ottawa.'[72] Tolmie could not be charged with letting grass grow under his feet. The day after sending his wire, he flew to Toronto and went to see Kelly. Together they repaired to the premier's office, where Kelly, prompted by Tolmie, dictated a memorandum to Colonel Young, who wrote it down in longhand before having it transmitted to Pleasant Point.

Hon. P. Kelly & Mr. Tolmie   31/7/53

URGENT

1. In March 1949 the Dominion Government at the request of Ontario made representations before the FPC at Washington that Ontario urgently needed American gas and that there was no alternative supply in Canada and that [it would be] a friendly act to allow American gas to come into Ontario. The application was not entertained – but *this is the only Ontario representation or request before the FPC* at the present time.

Mr. Howe does not consider our letter of May 5th a specific request to stop the import of Texas gas.

He has stated to Mr. Tolmie in Calgary July 30th that he will have External Affairs make a specific request to Washington to deny any export of gas into *Ontario* if Mr. Frost requests that this be done.[73]

A few days later Tolmie and his partner, W.D. Herridge, were back to find out whether Frost had answered. Upon being told that he had not, they agreed to return in a couple of hours to learn the result of another message Young undertook to send to Pleasant Point. The word they got was that Frost had only promised to telephone his instructions to Young the following day. This made them want to go up to see Frost themselves, Young noted, 'but I discouraged the idea, so they returned to Ottawa.'[74] That was prudent advice; Frost's severe displeasure and profane vocabulary would certainly have been fully vented had the much prized privacy of Pleasant Point been violated.

Before the premier got around to telephoning Young on 5 August, Fuel Controller Crozier informed Young that the views of the Ontario government would have to be made known in Washington the following day, when the FPC was scheduled to meet. Young asked Crozier to draft the desired message and this was read over the telephone to Frost, who ordered it telegraphed to Howe. It asked the latter to take steps to have the FPC decision postponed 'until it is finally determined whether it is economically feasible to bring Alberta gas to Ontario.'[75] Frost had little doubt by then that it would be, but he cautiously left the door ajar in case the scheme he favoured should break down and Texas have to be the supplier after all.

His telegram and related efforts by Howe and Murchison to influence the Federal Power Commission were to no avail. On 28 August the FPC authorized Tennessee Transmission to export gas at Niagara for sale to Consumers' Gas. Although a disappointment to those who had counted on the opposite result, this was not the end of the matter by any means. President Eisenhower would have to sign an executive order giving effect to the decision and Kelly reported his understanding that, on the strength of representations to be made by Howe, the president would not do so. Crozier thought further intervention by Ontario might strengthen Howe's hand and drafted another letter for Frost to sign. 'I want to stress to you,' it concluded, 'that, despite the recent developments in Washington, there has been no change in the policy of the Ontario Government.'[76]

That government held a trump card which might help defeat the Tennessee-Consumers' contract. A pipeline to Toronto would be required from the proposed entry at Niagara and this must cross land under the jurisdiction of the Niagara Parks Commission, whose consent would have to be obtained. In the fear that consent might be denied on orders from Queen's Park, Mayor Lamport wrote to Frost in mid September, urging that it be given and emphasizing the importance to the city of allowing Consumers' to proceed with its plans. Replying to this, Frost made no mention of the Niagara Parks aspect but simply reaffirmed his conviction that the answer for Toronto and the rest of the province – and for all of Canada when it came to that – was to be found in reliance on western gas. 'I know you will agree ... that we should take a big view in connection with the possibilities of our country.'[77]

As it happened, the solution to the Consumers' Gas matter lay elsewhere than in submissions to the White House or the veto power of the Niagara Parks Commission. The fertile brain of Ross Tolmie supplied a way out: Ottawa could use the Navigable Waters Protection Act. The astonished and angry proprietors of Toronto's gas utility were informed that the turbulent waters below the Falls must be protected for navigation, which would rule out crossing them with a pipeline. The federal government then introduced legislation requiring a licence for all future imports of natural gas. No safer wager could be imagined than that Consumers' would be granted no such licence.

Meanwhile, Howe kept up his efforts to arrange a marriage of Western and Trans-Canada, each of which continued to pursue its ambitions in arguments before the Alberta Conservation Board about who should receive the coveted export permit. Those proceedings were bound to be fruitless, for Howe and Premier Manning had agreed that a wedding must occur before either government made a final licensing decision. Under inexorable pressure from Ottawa and Edmonton, matters at last came to a head toward the end of 1953. Manning met with Howe and St Laurent late in November, agreed to release enough gas to a single merged company to supply central Canada and the Minnesota market, and promptly so informed the two applicants. Telling Frost of this, Manning wrote: 'The Prime Minister has offered the complete co-operation of the Federal Government in an effort to roll these two projects into one ... I have assured him and the applicants that if this is accomplished on a basis that will permit satisfactory prices to Alberta producers and ensure that the project can be finances [sic] ... the permit will be issued without delay.'[78]

Frost was not at all surprised, shortly after this welcome news arrived, to learn that Howe had assigned the task of bringing the two companies together and working out an application to the Conservation Board for approval of a single, properly financed project. Howe intended to call the antagonists to his office early in January to work out an agreement. Once that was done, two of the three major requirements – availability of gas and construction of the trunk line – would have been arranged. But the third – marketing the product in Ontario – was no less important, because until the demand for the fuel and the facilities to distribute it were guaranteed, the Conservation Board would not release it and financing the main line would be in jeopardy. Howe suggested that Frost was 'the logical person' to assume responsibility for marketing and that Ontario Hydro was 'an organization capable of handling the marketing problem efficiently.' There were other ways of doing this 'but from your point of view I would think that this is the simplest.'[79] It was not as simple as Howe thought. Hydro had no experience in selling anything other than electricity, a competing energy source, and the private gas utilities, which had such experience, could hardly be left out of the picture.

Nevertheless, anticipating that Ontario would have to create its own marketing system, in which he thought Hydro would probably have a role, Frost had already acted. He created an 'investigating committee' chaired by Dana Porter, with Robert Saunders and officials from the departments of Mines and Planning and Development as members. 'From the standpoint of Hydro,' he told Porter, 'it scems to me that the gas problem is inseparable from theirs ... As a matter of fact, natural gas is power, and it must supplement our other power sources. If we allow it to grow up in competing systems it might not be to our advantage. I am sure it wouldn't.' Alluding to an issue that was to be much discussed during the next few years, he went on: 'I am not so sure that when all of this affair is sorted out ... the Dominion Government will not be the builders of the transmission pipelines. I may be entirely wrong about this but in a matter so vital to our country, close Dominion control is inevitable and it is only a short step to complete ownership.'[80] That, however, was for the future. In the meantime Porter's committee could start devising a scheme of distribution and sale for the day when laying the main line would finally go ahead.

That it would appeared certain when Howe succeeded early in 1954 in forcing the two companies to merge under a board of directors representing all interested parties, among them the major consuming provinces, Ontario and Quebec. Frost's man was E.W. Bickle, while Maurice Duplessis's proxy was his personal lawyer, Edouard Asselin. As its chairman and chief executive officer, the board presently elected N.E. Tanner, who had earlier left the Alberta cabinet to return to private life. At long last, after all the delays, convolutions, and uncertainties, the stage seemed set for the denouement of the drama and Frost therefore felt confident in his 1954 budget speech prediction that construction would commence that year. But a final act, rising to a tumultuous climax that none could foresee, had yet to be played out.

Human Betterment

In his first budget speech Frost had declared 'a happy and healthy people' to be among the objectives of government planning. On reflection, he would no doubt have granted that the pursuit of happiness and health was an unending quest in which many were bound to be disappointed, and that there were strict limits to what the state could do in assisting it. Yet he strongly believed that government must strive, to the extent of its power and with its foundation stone the economic growth that made all things more possible, to promote human betterment. This meant not only the physical and mental fitness of individuals but the collective well-being of the body politic. A healthy society needed full employment, adequate housing, good education, and some protection for those disadvantaged by class, sex, religion, or race. It demanded, too, safeguards for established moral values. To a degree, government had a duty to protect people from their own failings, without intruding unduly into their private lives. Within the limits of political and fiscal prudence, the goal of human betterment must be striven for.

Using the power and purse of the state to help bestow good health upon the people became an aspect of policy that loomed larger while Frost was in office, and afterwards, than he could have dreamt of in 1944 when he mentioned it casually as one of the fundamental purposes of planning. Who could have foreseen then that a preoccupation with bodily health, already much in evidence, would grow into the unhealthy obsession which in the opinion of some it became? Fear that its price might spiral ever upward, jeopardizing his cherished balanced budgets or requiring the higher taxes he so wished to avoid, was one reason why Frost was at first sceptical about a government-operated health insurance scheme for

Ontario, whether limited to payment of hospital bills or including medical charges as well. He had, it was true, good private reasons of his own to appreciate the importance of physical health; his old war wound still troubled him, especially when he was tired, contributing to his inability to sleep soundly and occasionally flaring up badly enough to require hospital treatment. He knew that but for his personal policy with a commercial insurer those visits would have noticeably depleted his pocketbook.

Walter Thomson's heart-rending revelations in the 1951 election were not needed to make Frost aware that more severely ill people might – in many cases did – suffer catastrophic expense. At first he was inclined to think that the solution lay in somehow extending private insurance coverage to more of the population. In time, his ear cocked as always to the winds of public opinion, he changed his mind and became a leading advocate of public hospital insurance, keeping his gaze fixed, however, on the danger of excessively escalating costs. The result was a policy which, it has been aptly said, reflected 'an amalgam of financial realities, organizational limitations, interest group pressures, political rivalry, federal-provincial gamesmanship, and, perhaps most important, a concept of what Mr. Frost called simply, "human betterment." '[1]

In 1945 the Mackenzie King government, as part of its grand design of post-war reconstruction, had proposed a national health insurance program. Nothing came of that because it was contingent upon acceptance by the provinces of the accompanying tax rental arrangement. For some time thereafter Ottawa showed no interest in a new initiative in that direction, although it offered grants to help develop health care facilities. Undaunted by the failure of the 1945 plan and the federal retreat from the field, Saskatchewan's new CCF government introduced its own hospital insurance plan in 1946 and two years later British Columbia followed suit. By 1950 Alberta and Newfoundland – the latter bringing its unique system with it into Confederation – had more limited schemes offering hospital coverage to a portion of their people. Of the remaining six provinces, Ontario and Quebec obviously held the key, for a truly national program would be impossible without them. Frost found himself under mounting pressure to get on the health insurance bandwagon.

He was not one to be rushed prematurely into something whose implications, financial and other, were both highly complex and uncertain, nor was he inclined to follow Saskatchewan's lead in going it alone without federal money. He believed that it would be imprudent to proceed until Ontario's hospitals, starved for funds during depression and war, were expanded sufficiently to accommodate the influx of patients which insurance coverage for all could be expected to bring. Under his direction, both before and after he became premier, provincial grants to hospitals for both capital expansion and maintenance had risen greatly. There was still a long road to travel, however, before facilities would be adequate to cope with a markedly heavier demand. In the fall of 1951 Frost set out his general view of the matter to George Gathercole, upon whose counsel he was to depend heavily on this subject. 'The basic consideration,' he wrote, 'is hospital beds and maintenance ... Any hospitalization plan immediately puts thousands of people in hospitals for troubles which ordinarily they would tend at home ... We have tackled our problem from the bottom which I think is right. All of our energies have been devoted to providing more beds for hospitals ... it is idle to talk about a state hospital plan which will call for arbitrary and compulsory payments for services which it may not be possible for the state to give because of the lack of hospital accommodation.'[2]

His initial preference for relying on private agencies, with public assistance for the indigent, accorded with the views of the Canadian Medical Association, the Canadian Hospital Association, and, not surprisingly, the commercial insurance industry. They were also shared by his minister of Health, Dr Mackinnon Phillips, who was asked by Frost late in 1951 to have his officials canvass the subject and report as soon as possible. 'I doubt very much,' Phillips wrote, 'if the result of this survey will be known for probably a month or so, but, speaking confidentially; it seems to me that a great deal of pressure would have to be brought to bear before I could recommend saddling this Province with a Government sponsored insurance scheme. It would cost about $90,000,000 a year if this Province's commitments were similar to those of the two Provinces in the West.'[3]

As time went by, Frost began to see the matter in a different light. Progress in constructing new hospitals and enlarging old ones was bringing closer the day when a shortage of beds would not be the obstacle it had been. Announcement by the St Laurent government in its 1953 election platform of willingness to assist an insurance program when most of the provinces were ready to go ahead put the onus on the provinces to take the lead. On the surface this seemed to promise what for Frost was a *sine qua non*, the eventual availability of federal funds. But it was not yet clear how much money might be forthcoming or how many provinces Ottawa would require to join in. Relying heavily on Gathercole more than on Phillips and his people, Frost began the accumulation of a mountain of statistical data and expert opinion necessary to create, administer, and estimate the cost of universal coverage. At Gathercole's suggestion, Malcolm G. Taylor, a recognized authority, was retained as a consultant and in the spring of 1954 was asked to prepare a comprehensive analysis with the help of the senior economist on Gathercole's staff.[4]

Taylor's report, submitted later that year, both substantiated Frost's belief that the amount of hospital accommodation was not yet up to the required level and cast doubt on the validity of his fears about the comparative cost of state-run insurance plans. Taylor found that the ratio of beds to population, owing to unavoidable neglect before 1945 and to rapid population growth since, still fell considerably below the generally accepted standard. The only provinces meeting the standard were the three most westerly ones where public insurance in some form was in effect. At the same time the operating expenses of hospitals had grown dramatically in recent years; in spite of sharply increased provincial and municipal grants, many of them were incurring large and growing deficits. Significantly, however, costs per patient day had risen no more in Saskatchewan, and in British Columbia less, than in Ontario. Two-thirds of Ontarians, Taylor found, were insured by private agencies, mostly in employer-operated plans with payroll deduction of premiums. The largest of the private insurers was Blue Cross, a subsidiary of the Ontario Hospital Association, but various insurance companies and co-operatives also offered coverage. Their overhead costs were much higher than those of Saskatchewan's public, compulsory system. Not only were one-third of the people without insurance of any kind, but there were marked disparities in the protection afforded by these private policies, all of which set limits on benefits. The effect of such limits, Taylor wrote later, 'was that those most in need of an insuring or budgeting system, but outside its protection, were the chronically ill, the less physically robust, the low income groups, and the aged. And of course even those with some coverage could through serious illness or injury find their protection minimal.'[5]

The Taylor report provided an informative, thought-provoking basis for further consideration, but much more groundwork had to be done. Many uncertainties remained, which Frost, ever the cautious reformer, would insist on having cleared up as far as possible before going ahead. What would the other provinces do, especially Quebec? How much financial support, if any, would Ottawa offer, and with what stipulations? What were the costs likely to be and how should Ontario finance its share? What mechanism would need to be devised to administer the program? How would hospital administrators, medical professionals, and private insurers react to a compulsory plan operated by the state? And would the Tory caucus, Conservatives generally, and beyond them the public at large take kindly to assumption by government of that power? By the end of 1954 another general election lay not far ahead. Both major opposition parties, especially the CCF, could be expected to make hospital insurance an issue, as they had the last time. The new CCF leader, Donald MacDonald, lost no opportunity to preach that gospel and to hold the Saskatchewan plan up admiringly as the model Ontario should follow.

In 1951 the opposition had got nowhere with prepaid hospital care as an election issue. Whether the voters were now ready to embrace it had to be of paramount importance to Frost. Neither that nor the other questions on his mind would be answered to his satisfaction without extensive consultation, careful soundings, and additional study. 'For if a Health Plan is not to create as many difficulties and inequities as it solves,' he told the House in 1955, 'it must be soundly based and planned ... There is no magic way of creating an elaborate system of hospital and medical insurance services without providing the services and paying for them. I think we have to be practical and reasonable people and face that ... if there are to be more services ... of course, we – and by "we" I mean the people of Ontario – must be prepared to pay for them.'[6]

Paying for them would be no small task. Assuming no rise in hospital maintenance expenses or professional fees, the minimum cost of full medical care for Ontario would be in the neighbourhood of $190 million annually, and over $112 million for hospital care alone. Should federal help not materialize, Ontarians would have to shoulder a sizeable annual premium and a 3 per cent retail sales tax, as well, perhaps, as hospital admission and per diem charges. These were the hard truths of which everyone should be aware. For all that, though, 'the question is not ... whether health insurance will come. The question is simply – when is the right time for it, and how will it be taken care of and financed.'[7]

In giving this carefully hedged commitment, Frost had concluded that the moment was at hand for Ontario to lead by making an important move. A federal-provincial meeting was to convene in a few weeks to set the agenda of a full conference the following autumn. He decided that national health insurance must be on the agenda; this would reveal where Ottawa and the other provinces stood. This resolve was stiffened by a statement attributed to J.W. Pickersgill, one of St Laurent's ministers, that there could be no national plan without a change of government at Queen's Park. Pickersgill's explanation that he had called only for a change of attitude by the Ontario government did little to assuage Frost's ire. He was determined to demonstrate that if anyone was dragging his feet, it was not he.[8]

Frost arrived in Ottawa for the preparatory meeting with the biggest delegation: ten ministers, a dozen senior officials, and five expert outside advisers. The turnout from Quebec was disquieting: three ministers and no one else accompanied Duplessis. Did that ·and the brevity of his remarks bespeak a calculated indifference to the proceedings? He was genial, however, and promised to be co-operative so as to show that 'I am certainly not the ogre I am represented to be in certain quarters.' He thought the forthcoming conference should be limited to a few very clearly defined topics if it were to succeed. Frost had mentioned a considerable number, too many, Duplessis implied. 'Of course I know,' he said slyly, 'that my friend Mr. Frost is not going to have an election this year, and did not make a speech in view of an election – I know that very well.'[9]

In opening the meeting, St Laurent anticipated and agreed with Duplessis's contention that the scope of the conference should be strictly limited. He had only two subjects to suggest: the future of federal-provincial fiscal relations, and measures for assisting jobless workers not covered by unemployment insurance.

Frost challenged the notion of a narrow agenda. The conference, he said, 'will consider, and I am sure, pass upon many important matters ... We come here not in any dogmatic sense. I quite realize that in this broad country, problems vary and the emphasis natu-rally changes, and our agenda should be broad enough to include the pressing problems of all.' He suggested six topics, among them the pair St Laurent had referred to. Of the other four, health insurance was the most significant. 'It is,' he asserted, 'generally recognized that any health insurance plan of a broad nature should have both federal and provincial participation.' The subject should be thoroughly examined for answers to several questions, not the least of which was 'in what manner and under what conditions a health plan could be proceeded with in stages in accordance with the medical and hospital organization and the financial position of each province.' He added, 'I think we have learned in these conferences that the provinces cannot all be put into one mould. Canada is just not made that way.' Health insurance should be on the agenda, 'with a view to producing a sound, workable plan with which we could proceed.'[10]

Reactions to this were mixed. Except for the premiers of the three westernmost provinces, all ignored the suggestion entirely. None of those three would be averse to federal aid in financing, and in Alberta's case expanding, existing hospital insurance plans, although Ernest Manning voiced misgivings about the probable cost. Malcolm Taylor, present as one of Frost's advisers, observed divergent responses by St Laurent and his health minister, Paul Martin: some alarm on the former's part and quiet satisfaction on Martin's face. At an *in camera* meeting the next day, Taylor noted, 'the constraints of speaking for the public record were removed. Only the formal overlay of parliamentary courtesy thinly veiled the tough political battle being waged as Mr. Frost pressed (with the support of [T.C.] Douglas and [W.A.C.] Bennett) and Mr. St. Laurent resisted.'[11] Finally the prime minister conceded that health insurance should be on the agenda, but only under the more non-committal heading of 'Health and Welfare Services,' along with fiscal relations, public investment, and resource development, and Frost's proposed continuing committee of experts.

Thus a start was made along a road which would lead, first, to a national hospital insurance system two years later, and eventually to a complete medical care package in 1968, seven years after Frost's retirement. His carefully qualified prophecy that 'in the fullness of time on a gradual basis it will come' was fulfilled to the letter. As that preliminary agenda-setting session ended and the Ontario delegation packed their bags for home, he was satisfied that the door was now open.

These first, tentative steps towards national health insurance could be considered the result in part of Frost's willingness to undertake some major projects together with the federal government. The same was true of another subject no less vital to human health and happiness: housing. Here, even before the tax rental deal was worked out, a breakthrough of sorts took place, one of the first signs of the friendlier relationship that distinguished most of the St Laurent–Frost era from that of Drew and Mackenzie King. Housing became a principal part of the rapidly widening spectrum of state activity and engaged Frost's close personal attention. Traditionally individuals had been expected for the most part to look after their own needs for shelter. Public housing ventures had long been advocated by urban reformers and embarked upon here and there, usually under municipal auspices, but this was a relatively new field for senior governments.[12] In recent years, however, largely as a result of the depression, insistence had mounted that Ottawa and the provinces address more actively the pressing shortage of low-cost housing in the country.

During the war the federal government had responded in a limited way by having erected a number of modest homes, chiefly in communities with an influx of war production workers. But its most important initiatives were the National Housing Act of 1944 and creation of Central Mortgage and Housing Corporation to encourage purchase of new houses of acceptable quality with long-term, federally guaranteed mortgages at fixed interest rates. In 1948 the Ontario government, believing that NHA loans were too small, began advancing second mortgage funds in order to reduce down payments. Thanks to these measures and other favourable circumstances, the late 1940s saw house-building in the province at an all-time high. It was not enough, however. With one major exception – the Regent Park rental housing redevelopment in Toronto, being done with some financial help from the province – the emphasis had been on single-family dwellings for purchase. An evident need existed for inexpensive rental accommodation, especially in large urban centres undergoing rapid growth – a need which private developers were unable or unwilling to satisfy and which senior governments had long been loath to tackle.

Housing was one of the first major subjects to which Frost directed his attention after becoming premier. He was prompted to do so by a friendly overture in July 1949 from the federal minister of reconstruction and supply, Robert Winters, who wrote on proposals for subsidized housing. This elicited a cordial response from Frost. Upon learning that Winters was to visit Toronto on 8 August and would gladly attend a meeting at Queen's Park, Frost, vacationing at Pleasant Point, scribbled a letter to his deputy minister in the premier's office, Lorne McDonald, instructing that certain preparations be made forthwith. 'I have been turning over in my mind the housing problem,' he wrote. 'The conference of the 8th will be important.' McDonald should show this letter to Deputy Treasurer Walters 'and arrange for an intensive study' by officials at Treasury, Municipal Affairs, and Planning and Development.

'My idea will be to take as much of the burden from the province and municipalities as possible. What I can do will depend on the negotiations. The more we know of the problem the better.'

Specifically he wanted to know, among other things, how much Ontario had paid out in second mortgage loans, in subsidies for serviced land assembly, and in assisting the Regent Park project. 'I want to put as little more in as possible. I want the Dominion to do this.' And what were other provinces doing about subsidized housing? McDonald should have the Treasury car pick Frost up at Lindsay at 7:00 a.m. on the 8th, allowing him to be in his office by 9:00 to 'meet with our experts so I will be ready for Winters later in the morning ... Housing is #1 priority. Get all information and studies possible.' A couple of days later Frost added an after-thought. McDonald should have the provincial statistician, Harold Chater, ascertain as nearly as he could the housing needs of the province, especially in the big cities, under three categories: for purchase under the National Housing Act; for slum clearance after the fashion of Regent Park; and for *low-rental housing which we are presently subsidizing and which I assume the Dominion will subsidize. Important.'* Figures showing total dwelling construction in the past few years 'would also be interesting. Get Chater and his organization into high on this.' McDonald did as ordered. 'I think everything is pretty well under control here,' he assured Frost, 'and I hope that you are able to relax completely at your cottage.' But this was followed to Pleasant Point almost at once by a cautionary note. McDonald, Walters, Chater, Gathercole, and Arthur Bunnell of Planning and Development had put their heads together and 'will have some thoughts to express to you on Monday morning' before Winters arrived. Meanwhile, Frost should know that in their judgment, while the current rate of house-building by the private sector 'is really not far short of the requirements,' a move 'into low rental housing on any sort of a subsidy basis is an extremely dangerous venture, particularly for the Province.'[13]

The upshot of the Winters-Frost discussion and of talks Winters and David Mansur, president of Central Mortgage and Housing, had with other provincial leaders was a plan for a housing partnership between the two levels of government. Its terms, evidently framed in their essentials at the 8 August meeting, pretty well satisfied Frost's desire for more federal money. After consulting the other premiers, Winters told Frost he would shortly announce legislation authorizing Ottawa to make agreements with provincial governments for publicly assisted housing projects. These could take any or all of three forms: serviced land assembly for use by private builders; construction with government funds of moderately priced houses for direct sale to individual buyers; and publicly financed rental accommodation to be under local management when completed. 'The other provinces,' Winters wrote, 'agreed with you in favouring the first two forms' and that 'if public rental projects are necessary, they might better proceed at a later date.' The federal government, however, would join in projects of this sort should any province so desire.

Winters then turned to financial arrangements. It was hoped that all projects would be self-liquidating and costs incurred would be a charge against them. Ottawa would furnish 75 per cent of the capital, a province the remainder. It was for each province to decide whether participating municipalities should defray a portion of its contribution. Local governments would receive a grant in lieu of taxes. The scheme was sufficiently flexible to ensure assistance only where there was genuine need. 'Care will be exercized to see that the operations of the senior governments ... supplement rather than replace the activity of private endeavour upon which we place the greatest reliance for a high volume of house building.'

So far, so good from Frost's perspective and there was another feature, for which he had pressed in his talk with Winters, that pleased him especially. The National Housing Act would be amended to increase the maximum loan to buyers, thus obviating the need for Ontario's second mortgage advances. These had worked less well than hoped for. About $13 million had been disbursed, facilitating a great many purchases, but Frost was sure that a lot of contractors took advantage of the chance to inflate their prices by the amount of the loan. They had thereby enhanced their profits but also increased the risk of default by purchasers. Ottawa would now bear sole responsibility for controlling such practices; shortly after Winters announced the shared-cost program in the Commons, Ontario ceased accepting second mortgage applications.[14]

The outbreak of the Korean War in 1950 put a severe crimp in activity under this promising venture in federal-provincial co-operation. Credit restrictions reduced the availability of mortgage money and construction materials were diverted from civilian to war purposes. The supply of new housing slumped while the demand went on growing. Especially acute was the need for more rental space, which all governments had agreed they would prefer not to subsidize for the time being, if ever. Winters, though, had left the door open for federal participation in that kind of project and early in 1951 the Frost government, overcoming its reluctance, decided to formulate a proposal for joint action. Arthur Bunnell was asked to prepare an analysis and recommendations.

Bunnell proposed that Ottawa should be invited to join in erecting five thousand houses, to be apportioned roughly on the basis of population among Toronto, Hamilton, Ottawa, Windsor, London, and lesser centres. Three-quarters of the cost might be borne by the dominion and the balance equally shared by the province and participating municipalities. The houses, all to be equipped with stoves and refrigerators, ought to be rented or sold for amounts sufficient to recover the entire capital investment; should that prove impossible, annual subsidies would be required. Central Mortgage and Housing would be responsible for design and construction of the units but, once they were up, the program should be administered by local housing authorities.[15]

Having studied Bunnell's submission, Frost and Griesinger agreed that the former should telephone Winters to broach the plan. Winters was 'favourably disposed,' Frost reported to Griesinger. 'I think it looks like a deal. Please keep after it to the very limit.'[16] Griesinger did so. After officials had worked out the details, he sent to Winters a formal proposal of the scheme agreed upon. In essence his letter echoed Bunnell's recommendations, but a few important changes were made. There was no reference to selling any of the dwellings and it was specified that they would be for low and middle income families with children. The municipal share of the outlay was reduced from 12.5 to 7.5 per cent, roughly the cost of providing local services, the province to add the difference to its share. Municipalities wishing to take part would have to stipulate the number and type of units desired, the location of available land, the cost of acquiring and servicing it, and the adequacy of school facilities in the project area.[17] Winters accepted the plan and the way was cleared for action.

Frost unveiled the project at the Canadian Federation of Mayors and Municipalities' annual convention at London in mid June. But if he had expected his proposals to be greeted with a unanimous accolade of thankful praise, he was to be disappointed, for a bloc of dissident mayors took shape the very next day. It was headed by Edward Sargent of Owen Sound, president of the Ontario Mayors and Reeves Association, and Arthur Reaume of Windsor. They had four main objections: five thousand houses were too few (Frost's assurance that the number could be enlarged was conveniently ignored) and they were to be apportioned according to population instead of need; municipalities had not been consulted but presented with a take-it-leave-it proposition; the province should pay its full 25 per cent share and not saddle local governments with part of it; and the Frost administration was shirking its responsibility by forcing municipalities to choose the location and occupants of the housing. Reaume claimed that Windsor had been promised one thousand instead of the three hundred it was now being offered. There were other complainants. Controller Charlotte Whitton, stormy petrel of Ottawa civic politics, lamented that the policy would do little for those most needing help, low-income couples with children. The Toronto area was to get two-fifths of all units built but some spokesmen for Toronto itself denied that it would benefit because it had run out of building sites. It needed more redevelopment of existing residential districts. 'Why should our people,' one of those gentlemen grumbled, overlooking the fact that all lots would be serviced, 'have to go away out in the middle of a field with nothing but a septic tank?' On the other hand, officials from Toronto suburbs, where land was to be had, were more favourably impressed. Toronto might worry about urban blight and the exodus of people but suburban leaders were inclined to rejoice at the prospect of their own urban sprawl. After all, was not growth what everyone should want?

No sooner was Frost back in his office than he received a resolution from the Windsor Board of Control protesting the city's meagre share and the requirement that it contribute to the capital cost. Frost gave this the back of his hand. When Reaume himself carried on the attack, Frost told him: 'The Ontario Government, of course, has to regard the whole housing situation in Ontario and what can be done must be distributed with some equality.' Scarcity of materials imposed for the present unavoidable limits to the number of units. In the meantime, Windsor had 'the opportunity to get 300. Let us go ahead and do it and then see how much we can extend this by good, reasonable co-operation on all levels of government.' Windsor wanted to co-operate and get started, Reaume answered, but 'we are waiting for someone from the Province to say "go," or at least give some direction.'[18]

Of course there had already been a 'go' signal, both in Frost's statement at London and in a letter from Griesinger to municipalities with at least five thousand inhabitants, explaining the policy and inviting applications.[19] The following year the minister was able to report a good deal of progress to the legislature. Rental accommodation projects were under way or had been approved in five centres, including Hamilton and Windsor of the chief cities, while land assembly for housing was going on in six others, among them Ottawa and London. A half dozen places were undertaking combined assembly and construction, negotiations were at an advanced stage with seven more and preliminary discussions were taking place with others still. Under none of these categories did Griesinger mention Toronto or any of its suburbs. Elsewhere, however, well over one thousand units had been contracted for or would shortly be. In addition, some alterations in policy would be made to meet particular needs and objections. Even Arthur Reaume, doing double duty in representing Essex North at Queen's Park while remaining Windsor's mayor, was pleased by these changes. Municipalities would be relieved of their 7.5 per cent of both capital costs and operating losses but in return might have to accept grants less than in full lieu of taxes as originally promised. Because some families in dire need of shelter could not afford the rents being charged, rent for some of the units would be geared to income. A further innovation, presumably designed to meet Toronto's particular difficulty, would allow the province to expropriate land in one municipality needed for housing by an adjacent one, and the Planning Act would be amended to facilitate the launching of urban redevelopment projects.[20]

All of this seemed to show a promising start and ensuing years to some extent bore out the promise. In 1954 William Warrender, who had taken over from Griesinger at Planning and Development, informed the House that to date land assembly to provide in all about ten thousand serviced lots had been arranged or was being negotiated with thirty-one municipalities, including North York, Etobicoke, and Scarborough in Metropolitan Toronto. Rental housing programs under the federal-provincial partnership totalling nearly two thousand units had been or were being worked out with thirty-four municipalities. Additionally, in concert with Ottawa, the province was preparing to finance an extension of the Regent Park redevelopment which would add almost one thousand subsidized rental units. Up to the end of 1953 the provincial treasury had expended close to $4 million on these various undertakings and the amount was expected to exceed $9 million.[21] Presenting his 1954 budget, Frost announced that the preceding year had seen all records surpassed for housing construction, both privately financed and publicly assisted. Since 1944 a grand total of 250,000 houses had been erected, space for about one million people. Frost confidently predicted that new records would be set in 1954.[22] They would need to be for all indicators pointed to a steadily rising demand and to continuing insistence on the duty of the state to help satisfy it.

No less important for human betterment than health and housing, and unlike them not a relative newcomer to provincial responsibility, was education. Possibly excepting liquor control, no field of policy had caused more emotion-laden controversy, generation after generation. In the early 1950s, however, once the flurry over the Hope Commission's proposals affecting separate schools died away, discussion of educational policy had less to do with sectarian and language rights. Rather, the emphasis now was on the tasks of expanding and paying for an increasingly elaborate and expensive system serving a rapidly growing clientele, with more children staying longer in school than ever before. There was, it is true, an undercurrent of demand, not yet of the proportions it later assumed, for provincial funding of separate schools through grade thirteen, to which Frost was strongly opposed, and for their share of business school taxes which Mitchell Hepburn had unsuccessfully ventured to secure for them two decades earlier. But for the most part preoccupation was with the nuts and bolts of school construction, teacher training and recruitment and, in Frost's mind, finding the wherewithal to pay for it all. There was also a great deal of argument about the quality of schooling, largely given focus by Hilda Neatby's 1953 critique of progressive educational theory and practice, *So Little for the Mind*. Frost appears not to have been caught up in that debate and when the following year he observed in the House that 'Education continues to be, again, our most pressing problem,' he undoubtedly had in mind not its quality but its cost.[23]

The best vote-getter of George Drew's election platform in 1943 had been the seemingly open-ended guarantee to 'assume 50 per cent of the school tax now charged against real estate.' It was up to Frost as the new treasurer to find the means of making good on the undertaking and at first he dipped into existing and prospective budgetary surpluses for the money. Of course that stop-gap could not be relied upon indefinitely. With the help of V.K. Greer, chief inspector of Ontario schools, Frost worked out a new grant structure which, far from remitting 50 per cent of taxes levied by each school board, paid half of 'approved' costs for the province as a whole. Under this formula, provincial subsidies varied among and between urban and rural education boards, public and separate, not exclusively on the basis of school population or the amount of property assessment, but partly with regard to need. The aim was to lessen disparities between the superior facilities the wealthier urban areas could afford and the comparatively meagre ones provided by those less affluent. The result was that when the measure was first applied, urban districts received from 30 to 60 per cent and rural districts from 50 to 90 per cent of approved costs.[24]

Years later, recalling the purpose and effect of these reforms, Frost used his own constituency to illustrate. 'In Haliburton County ... there were no separate schools but all of the schools were poor. Therefore, their grants were very greatly augmented. In the Town of Lindsay the public schools were all relatively wealthy on an assessment per pupil basis, while the Roman Catholic Separate Schools would have virtually no corporate assessment and would be relatively poor,' making them eligible for proportionately higher grants. The result as he saw it in retrospect, perhaps too optimistically, was that 'people no longer walked on the opposite sides of the street. They all became friends again. It also meant the practical application of equality of opportunity.' Such equality was further enhanced by the gradual elimination of one-room, one-teacher rural schoolhouses, so as to bring children from a wider area together in bigger, modern, better staffed and better equipped schools 'where a child in the country area had just as fine opportunity as the child from the largest ... urban community.'[25]

That may have overstated the truth but Frost's satisfaction was by no means unjustified. Neither was his pride in the far more generous amounts given under his direction to a school system undergoing rapid growth, not only in size but, he was convinced, in quality. The increase in outlays for education after the Tories took office was certainly impressive in simple dollar terms. In 1943, total spending on education by the Treasury was about $15.6 million, not quite 15 per cent of all provincial net ordinary expenditure. By 1954 the sum had grown to roughly $91.5 million, about 23 per cent of disbursements and more than two-thirds the size of the whole Ontario budget on ordinary account in 1943. Moreover, the 1954 payments were supplemented by special grants of four dollars per pupil, which amounted in all to nearly $3.5 million.[26]

And yet, great though these sums were, all this was not enough in the opinion of some, as the price of building, equipping, staffing, and operating schools went on escalating, and with it the tax burden on real estate. Grants by the province rose year by year but the scope of approved costs became more limited, being altered in

1953, for example, to exclude building of gymnasiums and auditoriums. This put a crimp in the plans of some school boards, requiring them either to forego certain hoped-for amenities or to raise taxes in order to obtain them.

Narrowing the scope of approved costs, along with the steady inflation of expenses, meant that provincial grants, despite rising in amount, declined as a percentage of total costs. By 1954, according to calculations by the Ontario School Trustees' Association, the province was contributing on the average 40 per cent or less of total funding at the elementary and secondary levels, instead of the 50 per cent the Ontario government had promised. This complaint and others of like tenor reached Dunlop's desk, who now drafted a reply for the premier's approval. Its gist was that the 50 per cent promise 'was carried out as long as that was possible but the arrangement was not intended to be a perpetual one nor could it be so ... Would the Association require the Government to pay half the cost, no matter how extravagant some School Boards might be? Not all, not many, but some Boards are, in my opinion, inclined to be somewhat extravagant in more ways than one.'[27]

Frost may well have agreed with that opinion, but he did not think Dunlop's draft 'quite accurate' in conveying the purport of Drew's pledge.

Eleven years ago the promise was made to pay 50 per cent of the cost of education, and as a result in 1945 the school grants were raised from approximately $8 million a year to $25 million a year which carried out that promise. That as a matter of fact was 50 per cent of the cost premised upon the conditions under which the promise was made. Since that time school grants have gone up from $25 million approximately to considerably over $60 million. In other words, the Government not only made a promise to pay 50 per cent of the cost of education as it was in 1943 but is paying nearly two and a half times as much.[28]

That put a quite different face on the matter. Drew had in mind, it now transpired, only the immediate, not the more distant, future. This interpretation was a somewhat inglorious escape from a commitment offered without any such qualification, but also without sufficient study of its possible long-term implications for a future none could foresee.

There was, of course, a higher level of education which the provincial government was obliged to support. When the Drew ministry took office, and for some time thereafter, there were three publicly supported universities. The University of Toronto, much the largest and most widely renowned, was considered 'the provincial university' and received the most generous government financial support. Queen's and the University of Western Ontario seem to have been looked upon as 'provincial' in a different sense and complaints about their too miserly treatment were by no means unheard of in Kingston and London. McMaster and the University of Ottawa were ineligible for government grants because of their Baptist and Roman Catholic affiliations respectively, although it was found possible before very long to assist the former expressly for instruction in the sciences and the latter for training in medicine. Also ineligible were several other church-related institutions across the province. Carleton College in Ottawa, concentrating on adult education, aspired to university status, which it achieved in 1952, and being non-sectarian was entitled to public funds. So were the Ryerson Institute of Technology, established in 1948, the Ontario College of Education, and the Ontario College of Art. The agricultural and veterinary colleges at Guelph were supported through the Department of Agriculture.[29]

In contrast to the curricular control of the elementary and secondary schools by the Department of Education, and the administrative authority it shared with locally elected boards, the provincially supported universities made their own decisions and went their own ways with little or no direction from Queen's Park and little attention by the general public. Yearly, cap in hand, they presented their requests for funds, with more or less complete explanations of their hopes and plans, and each year the government decided what it would let them have. This ad hoc, unsystematic process provoked some criticism from the universities. By the mid 1950s government grants, mostly from the province, furnished more than half of their income,[30] but their academic decisions, the tunes they played, were called, not by those who largely paid the pipers, but by the pipers themselves.

Their financial requirements paled to insignificance beside those of elementary and secondary schools, and their enrolments fell off early in the decade with the departure of the throng of war veterans who had taken advantage of federal underwriting to secure a degree. Frost began to fear, however, that if the university system expanded and broadened its horizons by adding to the range of teaching and research, a needless, costly duplication of effort might result. As with the schools, ways and means of funding preoccupied him, but he took a livelier interest in what the universities were doing than in what was going on at the lower rungs of the educational ladder. Respecting scholarly expertise and lacking the marked disdain of some politicians for the 'eggheads' of the ivory tower, he attached much importance to the work of the universities, especially in research. Some of that, it was true, seemed arcane to put it mildly, with little or no bearing on the real world, but he was content to leave its worthwhileness for the academics themselves to judge. On the other hand, much of it could be of immense utility in assisting economic development, thus indirectly promoting human betterment, and also in furnishing government with well-informed guidance about the myriad problems of an ever more complex society. Frost cheerfully raided the campuses from time to time to enlist intellectuals in the service of the state.

Nevertheless, while the importance of the universities was beyond dispute and their autonomy deserving of respect, some means needed to be found of assuring that the public funds they received were used in the most efficient manner attainable. And, as some of their spokesmen were urging, a more orderly method of allotting government grants was desirable. This need was heightened when the St Laurent government decided to act on a recommendation of the Royal Commission on National Development in the Arts, Letters and Sciences that it make annual grants to universities. Each province accepting these was to apportion the money among recipients deemed eligible by Ottawa and undertake not to reduce its own subventions. Although it meant intrusion into a field of provincial jurisdiction, and was rejected by Quebec on that ground, the move was welcomed at Queen's Park, where a willingness to have Ottawa share costs on an equitable basis was seldom hard to find. Ontario's brief to the commission, like others, had proposed it.

Soon after the commission was created in 1949, its chairman, Vincent Massey, invited submissions from provincial governments. Frost referred this to Dana Porter, who responded after consulting his officials with a few suggestions of what a brief from the Department of Education might contain. Porter was distinctly lukewarm about the commission's general mandate. 'The present tendency to look to the Federal Government for indefinite sources of easy money for projects of all kinds is fundamentally unsound ... The large [federal] surpluses of recent years have resulted in a false perspective. The Arts and Sciences might be much better off in the long run if the main financial objective of governments was to reduce taxes rather than to finance what might merely become marginal activities.' Frost agreed with that but also with Porter's opinion that federal money would, however, be well spent in supporting post-secondary education. It was undesirable, wrote Frost, 'that our representations to the Commission should assume the form of asking for money,' but there were 'very definite possibilities that the Federal Government might be interested in more bursaries, grants to universities and, in particular, to research.' In the meantime, he had had a telephone chat with Massey. Having preliminary, informal chats about important subjects with other key players before irrevocably committing anything to paper was always Frost's preferred mode of operation.[31]

Although federal funds for universities were welcome, the responsibility for apportioning them complicated the already bothersome problem of how much provincial money the universities should be given in the aggregate and severally. Frost concluded that expert guidance from outside the civil service would help in making the right decisions and deflecting complaints, as well as in guarding against wasteful duplication. In the summer of 1951 he sounded out Dr R.C. Wallace, a respected scientist shortly to retire as principal of Queen's University, about becoming the government's adviser on university affairs. The objective he had in mind was 'a little more co- ordination' so that each university could devote itself to certain specialties and undue duplication be avoided. 'I think that we could get better value for our dollars ... I do not want to introduce anything in the way of regimentation ... it could be done by understanding and co-operation.' Wallace could be helpful, too, in advising about the apportionment of federal money, especially in countering what Frost wanted to discourage, the expectation of church-related, provincially unsupported institutions that they would share in federal grants.[32]

That was not, however, the way the matter was seen in Ottawa. Frost notified Porter, who agreed that it was a somewhat embarrassing complication, of his discovery that the federal list of eligible recipients in Ontario included 'a number which do not come into our grant system at all. To that extent the Federal grants do transgress our discretion in the matter of education.' Ontario supported seven institutions, the federal list included twenty-seven, among them the federated denominational colleges of the University of Toronto 'who can complain that they receive nothing from us ... The Quebec people may have their point that this is an interference with education. As a matter of fact, these Federal grants are going to increase the urge that some of the bodies receiving [them] be raised to university status with us. This may be all to the good but it is undeniable that our hand is forced.'[33]

It was characteristic of Frost to seek one knowledgeable individual in the person of Wallace rather than set up an elaborate, bureaucratically organized apparatus as was done at a later date when, of course, the complexities of the university system were vastly greater. It was also typical that he made his move without, apparently, bothering to consult the minister of education. In fact it was a fortnight after Wallace had been approached, and a week after one of Porter's officials, the chief director of education, J.G. Althouse, had been informed, that Porter himself was told of Frost's overture and asked for his views. Porter, evidently not put out by the die having been cast without his knowledge, agreed that Wallace should be retained.[34] Wallace was duly appointed and continued to function, though with increasing difficulty because of ill health, until shortly before his death in 1955.

In the spring of 1952 Frost reminded him of the need, in Wallace's words, to avoid 'an expansion which would necessitate new support from the Government if that expansion does not seem to be necessary and if the work is already taken care of in a sister institution.' Wallace advised that existing facilities for professional training were sufficient but that all universities must continue to offer a well-rounded education in the humanities and the natural and social sciences. He concluded: 'For the population of Ontario there are adequate university facilities at the present time. There may not be adequate funds to meet their needs in the future.'[35]

Wallace's function was to help set the size of annual legislative grants and divide the new federal subsidies. Presumably his presence simplified the task somewhat, although Frost later remarked that he had been too gentle to crack the whip over the universities. Adopting a self-denying ordinance, Wallace did not presume to include the University of Toronto in his detailed recommendations. That institution, he explained to Frost, 'has provincial responsibilities which the other universities do not need to assume ... It is a very large organization, the Governors have always approached you as Premier direct, and I felt that it would not be advantageous to project myself in any sense directly into picture.' So where the major entity was concerned, he simply suggested 'something of the order of size' of its grants, 'making clear that any such statement ... should be given limited significance.'[36] That Toronto's pre-eminence entitled it to special treatment accorded with Frost's own view. He had a close and agreeable relationship with the chairman of its board, Eric Phillips, whom he frequently consulted about university affairs and who might not take kindly to having to approach the government through the retired principal of a rival institution. Thus the University of Toronto maintained its direct access to the premier.

The sums asked for by all the universities rose each year and Wallace may have deserved part of the credit (or blame in not cracking the whip) for the province's greater generosity following his appointment. For the first few years after the advent of the Conservatives, grants declined from the 1943-4 figure of about $3.4 million but then began to rise. By 1954-5 they were double that amount. As a proportion of total outlays for education, however, they fell off sharply, a reflection of the dramatic growth in spending on elementary and secondary schooling.[37] Even so, the fortunes of the universities, considering the substantially enlarged assistance by Queen's Park in dollar amounts and the federal grants (in 1955 nearly $6 million in Ontario),[38] were much improved over what they had been in less bountiful times. No doubt some university leaders thought the government still too niggardly, that Frost's well-known frugality was being carried too far. Others, however, were pleased to count their blessings and hope for still better things to come. Wallace assured Frost that 'the heads of the universities seem to have been very happy overall in the action that the Government has taken.' Naturally many of their 'plans and hopes for the future ... remain unfulfilled. Some may be ill conceived. But it is better to plan, even ambitiously, than not to plan at all.'[39]

Frost was by no means averse to ambitious planning; a lot of it in other fields went on with his encouragement. For some reason, though, he was convinced, for all his high regard for many academics and the importance he attached to education generally, that the universities, despite their as yet comparatively modest needs, must be held under a tight rein. Typically indifferent to abstract, theoretical issues, he seems not to have concerned himself with how holding a tight rein could not but help lead to the regimentation he wished to avoid. Probably he trusted his favourite recipe of goodwill and common sense to solve that difficulty should it arise. But if he thought that in the first half of the 1950s, a period of consolidation and modest growth, the university system threatened to get out of hand, he had not seen anything yet.

13

A Moral and Sober People

Public health, housing, and education were among the fields in which government was increasingly expected to assume new or enlarged responsibility for the common good. But the health of the body politic also demanded that the state not neglect its traditional preventive and punitive roles against practices flouting generally shared standards of morality. These included such familiar evils as drunkenness, gambling, and prostitution. And there was another festering sore requiring treatment – discrimination on the grounds of race, religion, or sex. Discrimination, not the easiest thing to define, was certainly nothing new. That governments had a duty to identify, discourage, and punish it was, however, still a comparatively novel idea in the 1950s and, as the future was to show, one with wide-ranging implications.

Frost believed that all these evils called for vigilance and action by those charged with maintaining public order, not out of narrow, puritanical censoriousness but because a healthy society depended upon the sober, industrious, decent majority being protected against the canker of the dissolute or bigoted few. As he commented to the general secretary of the Ontario Temperance Federation, 'one thing all good people are agreed upon is that we want decency and cleanness in the life of our province ... Our policy is a moral and sober people ... and to strive for a solution of these problems, many of which are old and ... complicated by the days in which we live.'[1] As always, stating the objective was easy enough, finding ways of reaching it much more difficult. Trying to pursue the middle course, Frost inevitably found his measures attacked by some for going too far and by others for not going far enough.

Of the many policy issues to which he devoted close attention, none was more persistent, baffling, or aggravating than regulating the liquor trade. There must have been times when he wished that the cause of temperance, so dear to his parents, had triumphed for all time. Prohibition, however, had been tried and in his judgment been proved an impracticable failure. Since the other extreme – leaving the trade to unfettered private enterprise – was equally out of the question, far beyond the tolerance of the public and of Frost himself, the state had to intervene. It must retain its monopoly of selling bottled spirits in government stores, which caused no particular trouble except in the minds of prohibitionists and brought in a very tidy revenue. It must also continue to license, inspect, and control premises where intoxicants were sold by the glass. It was here that the most bothersome problems arose.

Sales of potable alcohol had risen greatly in recent years, their dollar value, according to figures Frost cited in the House, having more than doubled between 1944 and 1949. In part, of course, inflation, higher taxes, and especially immigration and population growth had caused that but unquestionably *per capita* consumption had increased.

In any event, because of his strong feelings about liquor-related abuses, Frost paid close attention to the work of Ontario's Liquor Licence Board. Although he had a lot of respect for its chairman, Judge Walter Robb, he was less than fully satisifed with the way in which it functioned. Complaints about its decisions formed a significant proportion of his mail. He learned from the Board of Stewards of Carman Memorial United Church in Toronto, for example, that because of 'the moral irresponsibility which appears to motivate the policy of the Liquor Licence Board,' there were now within easy walking distance of the church and of three nearby schools three night spots selling liquor until 2 a.m., two hotels dispensing it until midnight, a retail wine store, and a government liquor store.[2] Frost grew accustomed to such messages, for instance this from the chairman of the United Church Toronto Conference Committee on Evangelism and Social Service: 'The entertainment on liquor premises is the most vicious evil of the present liquor system ... Some proprietors of cocktail bars have encouraged the most vulgar type of entertainment. Some of the jokes, songs and actions have been a thousand times worse than anything I heard in the trenches in World War I.'[3] The indignant cleric had been doing his field research!

Closely related to the allegedly too liberal dispensing of licences and too lax enforcement of liquor regulations was the prostitution openly practised in some licensed establishments, most notoriously in the Jarvis-Dundas-Sherbourne district of Toronto. The oldest profession had long flourished there and was thunderously denounced from the pulpit of Jarvis Street Baptist Church by the Reverend T.T. Shields, with almost as much righteous fury as he directed against popery. There were, though, indications in the early 1950s that it was becoming more flagrant in some of the steamier watering holes. In 1953 the *Telegram* ran a series of stories exposing the situation. Having read these, Frost discussed their contents with the paper's proprietor, John Bassett, and with Judge Robb. Controlling vice was the job of the police, he admitted to the latter, but 'the conditions in some of the places they are policing are deplorable.' The Licence Board ought to respond to the *Telegram*'s exposé by cracking down. Its inspectors, if left too long on the same beat, perhaps tended 'to overlook the strict enforcement of the law.' Robb would be well advised 'to import two or three inspectors [from elsewhere] to Toronto ... Would you let me know.'[4]

He had impressed upon Robb, Frost assured Bassett, 'that this situation must be tightened everywhere, not only on Jarvis Street, but throughout the Province.' Earlier he had tried to bring home to people in the hotel business their 'duty to ... keep their premises clean and decent and free from conditions which would bring discredit upon them or upon the Province.' Clearly some of them were unwilling to do so.[5] It was for Robb's staff to patrol the area and clean it up, but how? Robb brought in inspectors from outside the city, telling them individually that their 'instructions were from me, and myself alone, and were not being given through the Chief Inspector, and that I was desirous of nobody at all knowing what was being done.' Despite these precautions, it was apparently realized that the heat was on, with the result that the imported inspectors found 'generally speaking ... a semblance of fair supervision.' Their observations nonetheless bore out some of the complaints, both as to liquor violations and prostitution. One of them recounted that on leaving a certain hotel he was accosted by a girl who suggested a later rendezvouz inside. Asked what he should do if she was not there when he arrived, she said, 'Just ask the doorman or any of the waiters where Kay is.' The upshot of this special surveillance was that four of the more disreputable establishments were summoned to show cause why their liquor licences should not be suspended or revoked.[6]

These disturbing signs of the rebirth of Sodom and Gomorrah in the fair city of Toronto troubled Frost greatly. He was not inclined, however, to blame it on the Licence Board's moral irresponsibility, but on an overworked board. Shortly after becoming premier, he had sent Robb a long letter detailing proposals for structural changes. These would have created a more elaborate apparatus, with a general manager making licensing decisions, subject to review by board members, and presiding with a clearly defined chain of command over a hierarchy of inspectors.[7] Robb was not the kind willingly to surrender his powers and nothing much seems to have come of the suggestions. Frost's interest in the prickly subject was undiminished, however, and he continued to ply Robb, and various chief commissioners of the Liquor Control Board with comments, questions, advice, and instructions, mostly directed at the need to encourage sobriety and seemly behaviour.

When the Licence Board was created, Robb had been asked by Attorney General Blackwell to become its chairman and, after ascertaining from Ottawa that there was no objection to a federally appointed judge doing so, had agreed on condition that there be no interference by politicians. 'I'll stand between you and the politicians,' Blackwell promised him. It was not, however, quite so straightforward. Robb recalled that he saw a lot of Frost 'and Alex McKenzie ... in Alex's room at the Royal York, oh, probably twice a month, discussing different facets of liquor legislation, my views ... his views. Alex was just a listener, he was a wonder.' It is hard to believe that individual applications did not sometimes figure in these conversations but in any event the judge admitted that 'there was pressure applied indirectly, let me put it that way, to have me do certain things which did bother me. In some cases I was well aware ... that it might be the Prime Minister [Frost] who wanted that, and I had to do a lot of convincing to do what I thought I should do.'[8]

Although Frost was chiefly interested in the board's general policy, he found time to attend to particular administrative decisions or licence applications, either to put in a good word for an applicant or to argue that approval be denied. Hugh Latimer tells of one disappointed applicant who, being acquainted with the premier, implored him to intercede on his behalf. Frost telephoned Robb at his house to ask about the case. 'If you say so, I will grant the licence in the morning,' the judge told him, 'but you will have my resignation at the same time.' Frost replied, 'Judge, it is your ball game and you play it your way.'[9] But the indirect pressure Robb felt was certainly exerted on occasion. A different leader might have thought it beneath him to stoop to the level of individual cases. It would have been simpler to deflect the incessant importunities by applicants and their opponents to others, while concentrating on more elevated topics of general significance. Frost, however, understood how important decisions about liquor licences were to petitioners on both sides of the issue. They raised emotions, as did the manner in which drinking premises were run, in a way that dominion-provincial relations would never do.

Frost became personally upset about one request in particular. When the Lindsay branch of the Canadian Legion asked permission to sell intoxicants in its quarters along Sussex Street from his house, he exclaimed 'My God, no ... We're not going to have liquor down there.'[10] No doubt he knew that Gertrude would make his life miserable if that happened and, while he always wanted to do his best for veterans, in this case the need for domestic tranquillity overrode his solicitude. On the other hand Frost went to bat for the Twentieth Battalion Club in Toronto, veterans of his old unit. It had moved to new premises on Willcocks Street, where it had spent $25,000 on improvements, and applied for a transfer of the licence held in its former club house nearby. Judge Robb turned it down because the neighbours objected. What more natural than to appeal to the premier, who by good fortune happened to be one of themselves? Willcocks Street in Toronto was a long way from Sussex Street in Lindsay and Frost was sympathetic. He put it to Arthur Welsh, the LCBO commissioner: 'After all, if the location is satisfactory and they are good people, why not go ahead and get it cleared up without causing further irritation with them?'[11] It was no mystery what Robb meant by indirect pressure.

Frost turned aside many of the countless seekers of help by explaining that licensing decisions were made by the politically independent Licence Board. Others he felt obliged for reasons of his own, usually political, to handle differently. The more aggressive of them simply refused to be put off and kept on badgering him. This was understandable because, as Robb put it, licences 'were so valuable. God they were valuable. There's money in this liquor business.'[12] And they usually enlisted the support of people in the Conservative party whom Frost felt unable to ignore. Thus he sometimes became enmeshed in wrangles which, however important to those directly affected and possibly of some slight political consequence, were trivial compared to his larger responsibilities.

In the course of a long speech to the House in 1951 concerning proposed amendments to the Liquor Licence Act, Frost dipped into the history of liquor control in Ontario and offered some general observations about the drink problem and how to deal with it.

He denied that someone like himself, 'brought up in an old Scotch home in Orillia, where liquor was completely taboo – completely,' could favour wide open sale, as alleged by some. He also categorically contradicted suspicions, which may have been partly fed by knowledge of Robb's meetings with him and McKenzie, that there was systematic 'tollgating' of the traffic, that successful applicants were expected to contribute to Tory party coffers. 'There are no toll gates operated by this government,' he declared, 'there never have been and there are none now ... licenses may have been granted through error of judgment by the Board' but not out of 'favouritism or political consideration.'[13] Looking back, Judge Robb agreed, especially as to accusations that Harry Price, the party treasurer, had extracted payments from licence holders. 'Harry Price was honest,' said Robb. 'If he wanted to get money from you for the party, he would have told you just exactly what he wanted, why he wanted it, and you would have given it to him or you wouldn't.'[14]

Frost emphasized the need in awarding licences to keep in mind the wide variety of attitudes and circumstances in a vast province like Ontario with its many diversities. Of course there was little disagreement about some objectives, 'decency and moderation, the elimination of drunkenness, help for the unfortunate alcoholic, the protection of youth and good, honest law enforcement.' Irreconcilable differences of opinion existed, however, within and between localities. It would be forever impossible to satisfy everyone, but the principle of local autonomy must be adhered to as fully as could be. That there were limits to this Frost recognized. Uniformity of administration was essential and it would be quite impracticable, for instance, to confer on each city and county control over licensing and regulation within its borders. But what might be tolerable in a large city like Toronto, though not to all Torontonians, would never be countenanced in, say, Lindsay, Brockville, or Owen Sound. The present amendments sought to strengthen the local option power and to discourage unsuitable licence applications. This might at least curtail the undesirable proliferation of drinking outlets.[15]

Another question about liquor which called for Frost's attention almost from the day he assumed the premiership was whether the producers of alcoholic drinks should have the right to advertise themselves and their wares. His personal opinion was as clear-cut as the attitude of Calvin Coolidge's parson towards sin: he was against it. As he once wrote to a small-town clergyman, 'I think my views in connection with liquor advertising are very well known. I do not like the same, and I think all things being equal, we could well do without this type of publicity.'[16] As usual, things were not equal and advertising in one form or another had arrived to stay. Ontario law forbade all types of it not authorized by the Liquor Control Board. The print media were permitted to publish institutional or public interest advertisements by breweries, distilleries, and wineries, but nothing explicitly promoting their products. The broadcast media, mainly radio but after 1950 also television, fared even worse. The CBC, at that time the regulator of all broadcasting in Canada, had lifted its ban on institutional advertising but provinces had the power to prohibit it, which in Ontario the Liquor Control Board did. Understandably, the private radio stations were aggrieved by being treated differently from newspapers and magazines, and the solicitor for some of them, Joseph Sedgwick, engaged in a protracted correspondence with Frost in an effort to have the anomaly removed.

There was a distinct air of make-believe about the ban on product advertising over the air waves. Periodicals published in jurisdictions with less stringent rules circulated freely in the province, unashamedly touting the merits of this or that brand. American radio stations beamed beer commercials (some by Canadian companies) into Ontario homes, and owners of television sets within viewing distance of Buffalo or Detroit enjoyed the same dubious advantage. Meanwhile, domestic commercial broadcasters ground their teeth as they thought of advertising dollars denied them flowing across the border. The print media suffered in the same way, as companies increasingly spent their budgets in periodicals published where they were allowed to hawk their wares. This was illustrated for Frost by his friend Floyd Chalmers of Maclean-Hunter. Chalmers had learned that a major distillery was cancelling its institutional advertising in *Maclean's*, at a loss of $25,000 a year to the magazine. 'The obvious place for them to spend this money,' he wrote, 'will be in Reader's Digest and Time, which already get a substantial part of their product advertising ... These two publications cut deeply into the market for magazines produced and published in Ontario.' The result would be 'not only loss of employment by printers, paper makers etc. in this Province, but ... a weakening of the influence of magazines edited in Canada by Canadians for Canadians.'[17] Frost saw the difficulty but could not agree that it was time for a change.

Along with drunkenness, public indecency, and vice, the premier worrried much about some forms of gambling. He was especially exercised about its growing prevalence at harness racing meets and by the fear that it might come increasingly under the control of dangerous foreign elements. The criminal code regulated gambling but the province had authority over race-track operations. It was therefore able to act, and demands that it do so were not lacking. Frost had little in the way of personal experience to guide him. He was neither a habitué of the tracks nor a gambling man, and had had little to do with horses since he had driven Prince, the family steed, into downtown Orillia to pick up his father after work. He did, though, know a thing or two about pressure group politics. With the thoroughbred racing fraternity an interested party in the background, the conflicting pressures now came from the harness horsemen ranged against the forces waging war on sin in all its forms. These were spearheaded by the Protestant churches, one of whose leading spokesmen informed the premier, 'We regard gambling as a grave menace to the moral and economic welfare of our people.'[18] Instinctively Frost sought a compromise, some way of putting a damper on gambling without harming the legitimate interests of the standardbred racing community. In the result he failed to satisfy fully the anti-gamblers, which was indeed beyond the constitutional power of a province, and aroused lively resentment among many engaged in the sport, some of them his friends and followers.

Breeding and racing harness horses was an enjoyable, and sometimes profitable, sideline for many farmers and small-town folk throughout Ontario. Attendance at standardbred meets, often a feature of county fairs, was a very popular recreation. Although especially favoured in the smaller centres, it was found also in the major cities, where in some cases it competed with thoroughbred racing for the patronage – and the wagers – of the public. Frost was surprised and bothered to discover that betting on harness horses took place, not only through pari-mutuel wickets at some of the tracks, but also and more widely through bookmakers. Under the pari-mutuel system, all the wagers formed a pool which, after deducting taxes and the operator's share, was divided among those who had backed the right horses. The bookies, plying their trade either at the tracks or in offices and small shops, and using telephone and telegraph lines over which the federal government had exclusive jurisdiction, enjoyed the advantages of little or no overhead and practical exemption from taxation. They were thus well placed to compete for the betting dollar, the more so for those located off the track because so many betters were prevented by their work from attending the races. In Frost's eyes the bookmaker was an abomination. Inasmuch as race track betting was both legal and under Ottawa's jurisdiction, he pointed out to the Reverend J.R. Mutchmor of the United Church who wanted the vice stopped altogether, the province was powerless to stop it. He would, however, welcome any means of restricting it to the pari-mutuel method. That would eliminate 'elements which have been in many particulars lawless' and were beyond the reach of the provincial levy on pari-mutuel wagers. 'I can see no logic in imposing a tax on the pari-mutuel type of betting and having the bookmaking type go free.'[19]

What could be done to limit the growing volume of race-track gambling, if not to stamp out the elusive but legal bookmakers? A statute creating a quasi-independent Ontario Racing Commission to regulate both kinds of horse racing was enacted in 1950. The Commission had no direct control over gambling, of course, but was empowered to set standards for the operation of tracks, including the number of days and the hours during which racing could take place. As with other such bodies, Frost did not hesitate to intervene in its affairs with his own overriding authority when he perceived a need to do so.

When, for example he considered that night racing would bring swarms of shady operators to the tracks and be a magnet for powerful gambling rings controlled in the United States, he promptly issued a press release in which first singular pronouns were conspicuous.

I am interested in encouraging the breeders of either thoroughbred or standard-bred horses and I am anxious to give them any legitimate assistance I can. My strong objection to night racing in the Toronto area, however, lies in the fact that promoters of this type of racing are primarily interested in pari-mutuel betting and wider gambling facilities in this province.

They are not so much interested in the breeding of horses as in the returns from mass gambling. This sort of thing introduces an extended form of mass gambling and the government is not going to allow it.

The interdiction of night racing brought a distinctly mixed reaction. As was to be expected, anti-gambling bodies such as the Canadian Council of Churches welcomed it, as did some newspapers. The *Globe and Mail* found in Frost's statement 'a constructive attitude' and suggested that if night racing with pari-mutuels gained a secure foothold in the big cities, in many smaller places the sport would suffer 'under the conditions of near-monopoly which it seems certain would follow.'[20] There was, indeed, an air of finality to the premier's declaration which the harness racing people were not going to take lying down. They were outraged by the decision and dismissed the *Globe and Mail*'s opinion as a reflection of the close ties between George McCullagh and powerful figures in thorough-bred racing circles who feared that night racing of the other sort would lure away some of their customers.

Frost was unmoved by the fierce protests on this subject from some of his supporters, persisting in his contention that the real danger lay in mass gambling and high pressure American methods. The danger was demonstrated, he thought, by revelations of the situation in Windsor and Toronto. The Windsor police commission had been investigating the problem, with particular attention to control of gambling from across the river in Detroit. Concluding that the local authorities were unable by themselves to deal with this, Frost announced in the spring of 1950 that the full power of the provincial police would, as one newspaper story put it, 'be directed toward eliminating evil in the Border City.' He would welcome any probe on either side of the border that would wipe out bookmaking, gambling and the attendant evils of prostitution, dope peddling, high-grading of gold, and smuggling. 'We do not intend to permit Ontario to become the base of operation of lawless U.S. elements' or let them operate in Ontario.[21] That American-controlled syndicates *were* operating in Toronto, however, was shortly revealed by its mayor and police chief in a report which, the *Globe and Mail* editorialized, afforded 'sufficient warrant for extreme measures to suppress the sources of gangsterism.' One desirable step had already been taken, forbidding night harness racing in Toronto. Protection of the betting public was not the only issue. 'Much more important is the protection of the whole community from the other forms of crime and filth' that fed on organized gambling. Frost agreed and stated that the OPP and the Toronto police would combine forces in an all-out war on gambling racketeers.[22]

The premier could not fail to appreciate, however, the political risk pointed out by many party members of stubbornly insisting on afternoon hours. A compromise was in order and perhaps it lay in allowing twilight racing, as advocated by influential harness horsemen such as Earl Rowe after racing under lights was ruled out.

The long summer evenings would enable race-goers to get to the track after work for at least part of the card and place their wagers in good clean sunlight rather than the shadowy glow of the lamps. In the belief that this would satisfy Frost, plans were made to have the Thorncliffe track, newly renovated and complete with flood-lights just in case, begin its weekday races at five o'clock in the afternoon, with the last one to be run under natural light. But one slight hitch appeared when the Racing Commission, with Frost's approval if not at his direction, decreed a seven o'clock curfew at all the major tracks. Thorncliffe thus had to revise its arrangements, moving the starting hour forward to 4:15 p.m. This was far less satisfactory to the horsemen than the ten o'clock closing they had originally hoped for, and did not even embrace the full twilight period. Whether such a crumb of nourishment would increase the clientele without attracting the much feared American gambling mobsters, as the dark night hours allegedly would, remained to be seen. As for the warnings reaching Frost of dire political penalties, the great Tory election sweep the following year showed that harness horsemen and their spectators were too few, too forgetful or uncaring, or too mollified by twilight racing to sound the death knell of the Conservative party. But if Frost believed he had heard the last of the night racing agitation, he was mistaken.

The standardbred horsemen complained of being discriminated against by a government favouring their thoroughbred racing rivals and allowing other sports to be played at night. Frost refused to take that seriously. There were other kinds of discrimination, real rather than imagined and far more troubling to him, against which he proposed to act. In 1951 the House passed two bills in which he took a particular interest and whose enactment made him especially proud. Ostensibly they emanated from the Labour Department but Frost did more talking about them than anyone else on the government side. In fact he introduced one of them, an Act to Promote Fair Employment Practices in Ontario, and it was he who explained at length the principles and intent of the other, an Act to Ensure Fair Remuneration for Female Employees. In speaking of the Fair Practices bill,[23] he alluded to the history of anti-discriminatory legislation in Ontario going back to 1944. In that year, with all parties in accord, the Racial Discrimination Act had been passed. It banned discriminatory signs and advertising on the ground of race or creed and was the first of its kind in Canada. In 1950 there were two more enactments, one outlawing racial or religious discrimination in the sale of property, the other (an amendment to the Labour Relations Act) forbidding it in collective bargaining agreements.

All this legislation had won general approval in the House and the press, but the bill relating to the disposal of real estate aroused the hostility of some people as an unwarranted infringement of property owners' rights. Frost's sometime fishing companion, Judge J.A. McGibbon of Lindsay, fired off a broadside of a letter to the premier, displaying deplorable want of high-minded judicial detachment and a strong dose of the very bigotry the measure was intended to combat. 'Surely,' McGibbon exploded, 'we have not arrived at this stage of life where the Government is going to take it upon itself to dictate to whom I must sell property, and whom I must have as my next door neighbour. I do not want a coon or any Jew squatting beside me, and I know way down in your heart you do not.' Frost must agree (he did not, of course) that someone setting up a new subdivision should be free 'to debar all but Anglo-Saxons. Nobody would be interested in any property if they felt that a Jew or coon could come in and buy a lot in a strictly residential area.' The reply to this outburst was even-tempered but firm. Frost happened to have at hand a resolution of the General Synod of the Anglican Church, of which McGibbon was a member, calling for a more sweeping law against discrimination in covenants. 'I know you will be greatly interested in the position of your church,' he remarked. The new law did not compel anyone to do anything; like many laws, it simply prohibited certain actions. 'My position is this, that we do not need legislation saying that people must do things because I think we are a broad, tolerant people ... This argument is completely defeated as long as persons can point to things that are very definitely discriminatory such as covenants, signs, etc. These ... are unnecessary and outdated in the days in which we live.'[24]

Frost elaborated on this last point in speaking to the House on the Fair Employment Practices bill, putting it in the context of developments on the world stage. Civil rights legislation, he declared, was one of the great tests of democracy by which those professing their belief in democratic values 'will be judged by millions of people throughout the world who are engaged ... in the racial and political revolutions of our century ... Some day historians will record these days in which we live as days of great and fundamental changes in the thinking of mankind.' In Canada, Frost pointed out, Parliament was constitutionally debarred from enacting civil rights laws. That left it up to the provinces and Ontario was showing the way. An obligation existed to honour the United Nations Universal Declaration of Human Rights, but equally 'there is an obligation to ourselves ... All men, of whatever race, colour or creed, must be accorded equity and the fundamental rights of the human person ... Mr. Speaker, our people believe in these things. They subscribe to these principles ... While this Act is, in a sense, pioneering in Canada, we believe that it is a sane and practical approach to the problem.'

No doubt the approach was as sane and practical as could be devised for tackling the vexing question of what constituted discrimination, determining when it had been committed, and protecting those who believed themselves its victims. The bill made it illegal to deny employment or to discriminate against any employee for racial or religious reasons. It created mechanisms for conciliation of disputes and prescribed penalties as a last resort. 'It puts sanctions in the background,' Frost explained. 'We believe that our people as a whole want this legislation ... we have laid the ground ·where people of good will can come together if there are differences and solve them ... and penalties will be reserved for the flagrant violations which we here hope – and I think with some confidence – will seldom if ever happen in this province of ours.'[25]

The other innovative measure of 1951, concerning fair remuneration for female workers, was sponsored by the minister of labour, Charles Daley, but Frost undertook to explain its meaning and purpose.[26] It had no forerunner, as far as he knew, in Canada or the British Commonwealth. Some American states had laws on the subject but for the most part they were merely declaratory, with no teeth. A major exception was New York, whose statute provided means for its enforcement and had been closely followed in drafting the Ontario bill. The key provision in the Ontario law stipulated that no female employee should be paid less than a male 'for the same work done in the same establishment.' Not only was inferior pay unjust to women in these circumstances, it also gave them an unfair advantage in seeking employment with companies trying to cut down labour costs. Thus both sexes had something to gain from the legislation.

Restricting its application to the same work in the same establishment was necessary, Frost argued, if the law was to have practical effect. Wage and salary levels for comparable work varied widely in the province and, for that matter, even within a locality and a single industry. While it was right and practicable within bounds to order equal pay for equal work, prescribing equal pay for work of equal value was out of the question. It was impossible 'to decide what degree of similarity is required in order that workmen in two employments may be described as equal or unequal.' How and by whom could it be determined what 'jobs of different description, even within one industry, can be assigned to common grades,' to say nothing of making comparisons 'across the frontiers of industries'? The only workable solution was the one adopted in the bill.

This one small step for womankind was not greeted by the opposition, especially the CCF, with the gratitude Frost thought it deserved. He rose to conclude debate on second reading, he said with mock sorrow, 'under a deep burden of disappointment, because I thought that finally we had introduced a Bill here which would meet with the unanimous and enthusiastic support of the Opposition.' Instead, led by the CCF's redoubtable Agnes Macphail, they had offered only grudging approval hedged by petty objections. The government, they asserted, had dragged its feet and now, having finally decided to move, had presented a bill good as far as it went but too restricted, too narrow in application. A truly satisfactory measure could, however, scarcely be expected from the Conservatives, so timid on social issues of this kind. That was too much for Frost. What party, he demanded, had brought in votes for women, their right to sit in the legislature and on juries, and their entitlement to a minimum wage? Why, none other than the Conservative party. 'Yes. Before the C.C.F. Party was thought of. And I would like to say, Mr. Speaker, that this [Conservative] Party will be here giving progressive legislation to Canada and ... Ontario long after the C.C.F. Party is completely forgotten.' He had 'never looked upon our Opposition as our enemy; I always thought they were people who had gone astray a little and I always had the light in the window over here for them ... But now I have doubts as to being able to win them away from the error of their ways.' Nonetheless, he predicted, 'when the chips are down, there will not be one of them that will oppose this Bill ... which is a good Bill.' And so it turned out. Efforts to amend the measure having failed, it was passed unanimously.[27]

One more piece of legislation in this field was approved during Frost's first full term as premier. It resulted from numerous complaints of discrimination against minority groups, blacks and Jews in particular, in public accommodation and housing. This was brought to a head largely by the situation in the southwestern Ontario town of Dresden. Its considerable black population, descended from escaped American slaves brought to that terminus of the underground railway a century earlier, objected to being denied service in the town's two restaurants. This made Dresden, said the spokesmen for a delegation meeting with Frost in 1954, the only town in Ontario where a colored person cannot buy a sandwich or a cup of coffee.' Such practices, replied Frost, were 'a blot on our good name.'[28]

The government's response was to replace the 1944 statute with a more far-reaching one, the Fair Accommodation Practices Act, which Frost presented to the House in 1954. The bill forbade denial of services, facilities, or accommodation because of race, creed, colour, nationality, ancestry, or place of origin wherever 'the public is customarily admitted.' Those who felt aggrieved by violation of these terms could complain to the minister of labour.[29]

Passing a law is one thing, enforcing it quite another. The new one was presently tested by the prearranged strategy of two blacks and a Chinese Canadian, none a Dresdenite, who entered one of the by now notorious restaurants and were denied service. Daley reacted angrily, not to this refusal but to the victims having deliberately provoked it in an effort to foment social unrest. Frost had some sympathy with that viewpoint. Nevertheless, he took the incident more seriously than his colleague. Illegal discrimination was clearly being practised 'and I think for the good of the Province and the community it should be cleared up.' At that Daley changed his tune, announcing that any formal complaint would be investigated and, if necessary, charges laid. Before long complaints against both offending restaurants were lodged, prosecutions undertaken, and the two obstreperous proprietors convicted in magistrate's court.

Their convictions, though, were soon overturned by a county court judge in a decision Frost thought absurd but, because of an anomaly in the Summary Convictions Act (soon removed), an appeal from it was found to be impossible.[30] So the first case under the new law ended rather ignominiously for those who had counted on it as a weapon. Frost was certain that the blame lay, not in the statute, but in its faulty interpretation by a judge. He remained confident that in the future it would fare better in the courts and that thanks to it and other laws on the general subject, as well as to the underlying common sense of the people, the Ontario body politic would be less and less afflicted by irrational prejudice.

14

Thunder on the Left

In addressing the various issues surveyed in the preceding several chapters, the Frost government met with neither unqualified success nor universal acclaim – no government is that fortunate – but it had built a record of accomplishment in which some pride could be taken. By the time Frost was ready to seek a renewal of his mandate in 1955, his government appeared to enjoy a measure of popularity and public satisfaction which any democratically elected administration might well envy. The generally prevailing prosperity assisted in this, of course. But so did the conscientious devotion to the public interest exemplified by Frost himself and for the most part by his ministers, who knew they would not be long tolerated if they showed themselves careless in that respect. The development of a cadre of able, hard-working senior civil servants, a mandarinate less prominent and celebrated than its federal counterpart but much in evidence nonetheless, was increasingly an asset in both the formulation and administration of policy. Frost's generally sunny, ingratiating ways in meeting the public, managing the House, and dealing with friend and foe alike – not to mention his knack for finding a sure-footed way through the minefields in his path – also accounted for the seeming lack of widespread discontent with his regime.

It could not be denied, however, that some discontent existed. Some troubling problems remained far from solved. Frost, in a speech in the House in 1954, offered the prescription of 'flexibility and adaptability to changing conditions. We should recognize that in a dynamic economy, adjustment in industry and employment is the normal process by which production is adapted to demand. If normal influences fail, there is a variety of measures that will be brought into play to cushion the downward swing.'[1] This assurance, easy to give, was cold comfort to those, working people especially, who stood to suffer the dislocations that such adjustment in industry and employment would inescapably bring. Adaptability might be a virtue from the perspective of Queen's Park, but practising it was not easy. Nowhere was this truer than in the depressed gold mining industry of northern Ontario. Its chronic ailments led to serious labour unrest and to disaffection among the miners and their union leaders with the performance of the Frost government. Nor was this the only segment of labour with which the premier found himself at odds. The movement as a whole, at any rate some of its spokesmen if not always its general membership, was the one major entity, other than the opposition parties, to mount sustained criticism of a ministry freer from it than most. In sections of the work force, judging by the pronouncements of union leaders, unhappiness was conspicuously present.

Frost's first run-in with organized labour arose, not from any specific government measure or from the problems of the gold mines, but out of his response to a significant court decision affecting the powers of an administrative tribunal, the Ontario Labour Relations Board. Such bodies, executive agents of the crown but some performing quasi-judicial functions, were proliferating rapidly in Ontario and elsewhere. Some were merely advisory, but others wielded seemingly absolute decision-making authority. The Labour Relations Board had been created in 1944, as the provinces prepared to resume their normal jurisdiction over industrial relations with the forthcoming end of Ottawa's wartime pre-emption of that field. One duty of the board was to grant or refuse the certification of unions as bargaining agents. It appeared to enjoy untrammelled power. In the words of the governing statute, 'the orders, decisions and rulings of the Board shall be final and shall not be questioned or reviewed nor shall any proceeding before the Board be removed, nor shall the Board be restrained ... by any court.' To laymen unversed in the arcane intricacies of the common law, that seemed as plain as words could be.

In the summer of 1950 the board certified the Toronto Newspaper Guild as bargaining agent for the *Globe and Mail*'s circulation department. Dissatisfied with the way in which this had been done, the company applied to the Ontario Supreme Court for *certiorari*, a common law writ, recourse to which was expressly forbidden by the Labour Relations Act. If granted, this would nullify the decision complained of. Although within the bounds of belief that the newspaper's motive was to prevent unionization of the employees concerned, its counsel argued, not that certification should have been denied, but that the board's proceedings had been improperly conducted. For one thing, it had neglected to hold a supervised vote of the employees by secret ballot. The company, it was additionally alleged, had been unlawfully denied the right to cross-examine witnesses and to elicit information about the true desire of its workers. Mr Justice Gale, who heard the application, in effect sided with the company, without questioning the right of the legislature to bestow summary powers on administrative bodies. Citing Magna Charta as well as more recent precedents, he ruled that the statutory prohibition of appeal from the board's conclusions 'will not expel the right of this court to review and set aside proceedings in an inferior tribunal where there has been a substantial failure to follow the dictates of essential justice.' The legal authorities, he found, 'point irresistibly to the conclusion that inferior courts are not sheltered by no-*certiorari* provisions where there has been an abuse of jurisidiction in the form of a denial of substantial justice.' Since such had occurred in a matter vitally affecting it, the *Globe and Mail* was entitled to the remedy of *certiorari*.[2] So much for the theoretical omnipotence of legislatures.

The Gale judgment proved to be a cat among the pigeons. Cries of outrage rose from labour spokesmen, accompanied by demands that the government defend its own legislation by having the board launch an appeal. At that time there were two large labour federations in the province: the Ontario Provincial Federation of Labour, whose ties were with the Trades and Labour Congress of Canada and through it with the AF of L in the United States; and the Ontario Federation of Labour, affiliated with the Canadian Congress of Labour and the CIO. Although the Newspaper Guild's connections were with the latter, the loudest voice in early attacks on the judgment belonged to Russell Harvey, who represented the AF of L in Ontario and was a member of the Labour Relations Board. The Gale decision, he declared, 'strikes at the very roots of the labor movement ... It is up to us to fight this as a means of indicating that we, the common people, are the final arbiters of justice.'[3] The only legal way to fight it was by appeal to a higher court. When it became clear that the government did not intend to do so, the Guild took its case to the Ontario Court of Appeal and then to the Supreme Court of Canada, both of which upheld Justice Gale.

Shortly after the first appeal was entered, Frost issued a lengthy statement. One might have looked to Attorney General Porter or

Labour Minister Daley to speak on this subject, but on matters of real moment Frost preferred to do that himself. Moreover, although he had confidence in Daley, whom he once described as 'the most outstanding Labour Minister in Canada, and probably ... the most outstanding that has ever been in Canada,'[4] he knew his colleague disapproved of the Gale judgment and might make a more controversial utterance than was desirable. A month after publication of Frost's statement, which carefully avoided argument about the case itself, Daley was reported in the press as disagreeing that 'the board's action was questionable ... he felt the board had acted fairly and properly in certifying the Toronto Newspaper Guild on the evidence before it.' The *Globe and Mail* was quick to charge that this comment was itself improper, since the case was *sub judice*, and Frost probably agreed. Indeed, it may be reasonable, though perhaps uncharitable, to suspect that he withheld his own remarks until the issue was again before the courts so as to be precluded from giving an opinion about its merits. Better to avoid antagonizing either party to the dispute, and confine oneself to the general question of the relationship between the legislature's power to make law and the right of the courts to judge the manner in which enactments were administered.

His own and other governments were very much alive to this question, he wrote. 'In the complex society and days in which we live the administrative Boards with powers of adjudication are necessary. Administrative matters cannot be thrown into the Courts. Matters have to be determined quickly and efficiently and indeed without appeal.' There were, however, 'grounds for concern as to the effect of such widespread powers upon the rights of the individual. After all, our democracy has been built upon the freedom of individuals, and we all view with concern things which tend to take away from the rights of individuals.' But how to reconcile these rights with the need for prompt, decisive action? There was no fully satisfactory answer. Frost could only express hope that boards and commissions would always deal fairly with those affected by their decisions. 'I am satisfied that the Legislature in giving broad, non-appealable powers ... have [sic] done so with the understanding that there would always be a full and complete hearing and fair trial of the issues and that there should be the fullest opportunity of presenting all sides of the case.' He thought this had happened in the vast majority of instances. 'According to their own lights,' quasi-judicial bodies had 'endeavoured to be fair and just, and after all they are human beings and with arbitrary powers they may be inclined sometimes to err.'[5] In that event a reference to the courts could not rightly be objected to.

Presumably the aim of Frost's statement, with its pious hopes and assurances, was to appeal to all fair-minded people and quiet the clamour provoked by Justice Gale. The result fell short. The *Globe and Mail*, from which he was not accustomed to severe criticism, objected to his assertion that boards and commissions 'of necessity and by reason of the days in which we live have to have summary and non-appealable powers.' Nor would it suffice to be guaranteed a full hearing and a fair trial. 'The denial of justice could be in the decision itself,' a fact Frost had failed to face.[6] Labour's spokesmen were likewise unmollified. A.F. MacArthur, president of the Ontario Provincial Federation of Labour, found serious flaws in the province's labour law, despite many urgings to the cabinet to have them removed. 'In the light of the Gale decision,' he said, 'we are wondering if the [Labour Relations] act is doing what it was supposed to do – encourage sound, responsible trade unionism, or is it being used as a deterrent to the trade union movement?'[7]

Having read this and other outbursts of union leaders in the press, Frost may well have been bemused at being assured by Russell Harvey, a union member of the OLRB, that they should not be construed as an attack on the government or its legislation. Rather, they must be seen as a tactical move in the bitter rivalry between those, centred in the CCL-CIO wing (including the CCF and Labour-Progressive party which wanted to politicize the union movement), and those like himself who adhered to the AF of L view that labour should remain non-political and non-partisan. The unions he represented were entirely 'in support of Government policy on this legislation which was perfectly obvious from the start.'[8] Apparently one was supposed to conclude from this improbable disclaimer that Harvey and his friends were not the demons of the *Globe and Mail*'s imagining, but steadfast allies of a government which happened to find itself caught in the internecine rivalries of union politics.

Anger at the government's refusal to appeal the Gale judgment was also vented by a delegation from the OFL headed by its president, George Burt, at a meeting with the premier it had requested. The encounter, to which Frost thoughtfully invited the press, became most unpleasant. They found him unyielding. Doubtless he did not improve their temper by remarking that some of them were of a different political stripe from him and that labour made a mistake in tying itself to any political party. Regarding the authority of government boards, so Frost was reported, 'he had sympathy with the individual, big and little.' Surely 'it was unthinkable that the decisions of a board, holding arbitrary powers, should be un-reviewable even if it had departed from the fundamentals of justice ... No legislation can be insulated totally against court applications and I do not think you gentlemen would think it should be.'[9]

The brief read by George Burt at that meeting also dealt with a strike in the Timmins area launched about three weeks earlier by the United Steelworkers against Hollinger Consolidated, Ontario's largest gold mining operation.[10] Like all gold producers in Canada, and in the rest of the world for that matter, Hollinger was beset by the difficulties of a stagnant industry. Working gold mines in the province had declined in number by nearly half since 1941, as had the size of their work force. The value of gold output had dropped by almost 40 per cent and fewer than half of the mines still operating earned appreciable taxable income.[11] The underlying problems were a limited demand for the metal and, more important, that its price was fixed by international agreement at $35 U.S. per ounce. This precluded the mining companies from compensating for rising costs in an inflationary period by jacking up the price of their product. An effort to curb costs resulted in badly depressed wage levels for those still employed. Of course the ripple effect had a severe impact on those communities in northern Ontario which depended heavily on the mines for their very existence.

The main issues in dispute at Hollinger were wages and union security, which meant chiefly compulsory check-off of union dues. A *Globe and Mail* reporter sent to Timmins was assured by the townsfolk that the miners were earning too little to support their families adequately. Even if the men got what they were asking, their incomes would still be far below those earned in other sectors of the mining industry. This was borne out by Dominion Bureau of Statistics data cited by the paper's Ottawa correspondent.[12] The company, which had offered an eight cents hourly increase, stubbornly protested that, failing a change in the world price of gold, it could not afford the thirteen cents the union was after. A petition asking for a higher price circulated in Timmins and by early August 1951 had ten thousand signatures.

Early action was necessary if Timmins were not to become little more than a ghost town. Its economy was very badly affected, with the workers' already meagre purchasing power much diminished and many of them leaving to find jobs elsewhere, which the healthy demand for labour made relatively easy. In fact, the powerful Steelworkers' leader C.H. Millard, threatened to move the Hollinger miners *en masse* to steel mills and other mines with which his union had contracts. The town's mayor besought Frost to do something, but all he could offer was the facilities of the Labour Department to bring the two sides together. There was one abortive attempt to do that. A few days before Frost's heated exchange with the OFL delegation, it was reported that Hollinger had turned down, while the union had accepted, a compromise worked out by Daley and Louis Fine, his chief conciliation officer. This called for return to work while wages and fringe benefits were negotiated, with a vote to be taken once they were settled on whether the miners wanted a voluntary, revocable check-off. The company would be obliged to grant it if at least 60 per cent were in favour. This was the basis of an agreement reached shortly afterward with another company, Preston East Dome Mines, but Hollinger would have none of it and there seemed no way to change its mind. Alarmed by Millard's threat, the mayor telegraphed Hollinger's president, Jules Timmins, pressing him to visit the town bearing his name and help settle the dispute. Timmins declined, saying that until the union dropped its demand for a check-off there could be no settlement.[13]

Faced with this intransigence, the labour leaders argued for an amendment to the Labour Relations Act making union security obligatory. This was proposed to Frost by the OFL delegation as a means of ending the strike and avoiding others. He was unimpressed, maintaining that this, like others, was a subject for collective bargaining. 'Surely you, Mr. Burt, would not suggest ... legislation to settle individual strikes?' It was an awkward question, the true answer to which may have been that it would all depend on what the legislation contained. But Frost's attitude to this, like his refusal to appeal the Gale judgment, struck union spokesmen as an evasion of responsibility. Indeed, they found another, sinister connection between the two issues. Evidently alluding to the well known close association of George McCullagh with important figures in the northern Ontario mining business, Cleve Kidd, secretary-treasurer of the OFL, declared: 'It is rather peculiar that the same people involved in the Gale decision are involved in Hollinger – the gold mining interests.' McCullagh's paper, he pointed out, was printing vicious editorials about union security and attacking Daley for his temerity in objecting to Gale's ruling. 'Is this government by newspapers or by the people? Is it what the Globe and Mail wants, or what the people want?'[14]

Frost knew that an acceptable compromise must be found to avoid prolonged deadlock. 'It seems to me,' he wrote to Daley, 'that we might feel out the management as to the best that could be done in the wage end of things, which might put us in a position to then approach the Union with a view to dropping the checkoff demand. Please treat all this as highly confidential.' He added, probably with his stint as mines minister in mind, 'I may say that I have a considerable acquaintance with some of the Hollinger people and perhaps that could be used to advantage.'[15] An even bolder move was suggested in mid August by Pat Conroy, secretary-treasurer of the Canadian Congress of Labour. He proposed that the premier personally arbitrate the check-off issue and that both sides agree to accept his decision. He was sure, Conroy told a large Timmins audience, that Hollinger would accept the premier as arbitrator.[16]

As Conroy tacitly admitted, it was surprising to find a union official advocating binding arbitration, a way of settling disputes for which Frost himself had no use. For other reasons, too, the suggestion did not appeal to him. Personal diplomacy had its uses when practised discreetly, but dictating a settlement of so controversial an issue in the full glare of publicity was not his way of doing things. Better by far to prepare the ground quietly behind the scenes along the lines mentioned to Daley, with a nudge here, a cajolery there, gently persuading until resistance broke down sufficiently to bring the two sides face to face in a conciliation proceeding with real hope of success. By the time Conroy's letter reached him, this process showed signs of bearing fruit and he telegraphed in reply: 'I am sure that the best service that can be rendered is to make it possible for these parties to come together. I am optimistic enough to believe that the individuals involved, who are all Canadian citizens, can arrive at a settlement which will get them back to work.' He was therefore urging them to return to the bargaining table with Louis Fine, and presently negotiations were resumed.

After four days' discussion, and seven weeks after the strike began, agreement was reached, news that touched off the most festive celebration in Timmins since V-E Day. Hollinger discovered that it could afford the thirteen cents pay hike after all and conceded some other benefits, notably a company pension plan. It also promised not to discriminate against any employee because of the strike.

The union agreed to forego the checkoff and was offered space on company premises to make its collection of dues more efficient. As so often in such disputes, an outsider might have been excused for wondering why it had not been possible long since to arrive at these terms, which the miners promptly approved overwhelmingly in a standing vote.[17]

The Hollinger strike proved to be only a foretaste of more serious, and at times violent, strife in the Porcupine district near Timmins two years later. Nor were the gold mines the only centres in 1953 of strike action and passionately antagonistic labour relations. The inter-city trucking industry of southwestern Ontario, far more vital to the provincial economy, was racked by a bitter struggle by certain locals of the Teamsters' Brotherhood to win improved wages and shorter working hours. In part this was also a contest between rival factions for domination of the union, which imparted to it the particularly vicious quality of fratricidal warfare. For truckers as well as gold miners, the summer of 1953 was truly the season of discontent.

Trouble in the north began in mid July with action against three junior gold producers, one of which, Broulan Reef, also worked four other small properties on behalf of their owners. There was fear that this would set off a chain reaction of strikes against the rest of the mines in the area, including the two biggest, Hollinger and McIntyre Porcupine. Contract talks between Broulan Reef and the Steelworkers union had been in progress for months to no avail, with wages, hours of work, and union security the chief issues, and the dispute had recently come under arbitration. This led the mine manager to denounce the strike as illegal, while the union accused him of trying to destroy it by intimidating its members. Picket lines went up under the gaze of OPP officers. Meanwhile, all concerned watched nervously for the spark that might not only disturb the peace but ignite a wholesale walkout of the more than five thousand miners in the district.[18]

On 24 July word spread among the strikers that a day earlier the Broulan management had contrived to spirit twenty-five strikebreakers into the mine. There followed a scene that might have been contrived in Hollywood for a grade B movie. A group of about thirty picketers entered the Broulan property, while their colleagues barred the way to three OPP inspectors. As the officers engaged in extended conversation with the picketers, Arnold Peters, vice-president of the Porcupine Labour Council and CCF candidate in the forthcoming federal election, was heard to shout from the edge of the crowd, 'I want twenty more men inside the mine right away.' While the police watched, a number of picketers got into cars and sped off towards the mine. For half an hour a pitched battle raged in and around the mine buildings between the invading picketers and the 'scabs' inside, the gladiators wielding baseball bats, mining steels, picks and boards with protruding nails. Most of the outnumbered defenders were captured one by one, roughed up and transported some miles away, where they were abandoned on the roadside to ponder their folly. The union disclaimed responsibility for the onslaught, the success of which depended on keeping the police off the property, but as the *Globe and Mail* reporter saw it, the attack seemed to be planned and co-ordinated with military precision.[19]

Things took an even nastier turn a few days later when it was learned that the mine manager, on the grounds that the police could not or would not control the situation, had issued shotguns and ammunition to the scabs who had avoided capture, with instructions to 'shoot to maim' in the event of another invasion. The crown attorney in Timmins was immediately instructed to order him to disarm his troops.

Settling the strike was less simple. All the government felt able to do was continue efforts to bring the disputants together in negotiation. It had also to consider what action to take concerning the *mêlée* of 24 July. It was being pressed to crack down by prosecuting the lawbreakers and sending large police reinforcements to the scene. Frost conferred with senior officials in the attorney general's department, with Roland Michener, the company's Toronto solicitor, and by telephone with Daley and George Doucett. It was quickly agreed that despatching a large body of police 'would only invite additional difficulties and the force should be reasonably reinforced by 25 ... men.' It was also decided that the crown attorney should lay charges after carefully considering evidence of police officers present during the fracas, and that Frost would issue a statement explaining the law about picketing and violence arising therefrom.[20] It was a moderate response, too much so to suit the management of Broulan Reef, which wanted more police and more uncompromising enforcement of the law. Nor was the company willing to act on the suggestion of C.H. Millard, with which Michener agreed: that the union would call off its pickets if the company suspended operations pending the outcome of scheduled talks in Toronto between the two parties, over which the invaluable Louis Fine would preside.[21]

Fine proposed withdrawal of pickets and suspension of work in the mine while negotiations continued under Labour Department auspices. The union accepted this but Broulan declined to cease operations. It did consent to take part in further talks but two more violent incidents between strikers and company employees caused it to back out.

Serious though the disturbances at Broulan Reef were, and alarming though the danger that they would mushroom into a general work stoppage with ugly confrontations at other mines, unrest in the Timmins area for a time took a back seat to what was happening on the highways of southwestern Ontario. The violence and destruction arising from the truckers' strike were more visible and closer to home in the major population centres west of Toronto, while the impact of the walkout was felt more directly than the comparatively insignificant effects of an interruption in gold production at a few small faraway mines.

Trouble with the truckers appeared to owe its origins as much to an intra-union struggle for power as to disputes with the employers. An indication of this was the dismissal in mid July of A.F. MacArthur as Canadian representative of the International Brotherhood of Teamsters, an AF of L affiliate. MacArthur was known as a moderate who regarded striking as a last resort and who had favoured the settlement which the Toronto Teamsters' local had recently concluded with the companies. One of those said to be hostile to him was James Hoffa, a vice-president of the brotherhood who controlled its operations in the Detroit district. Hoffa was believed to control as well the Windsor local through its president, I.M. (Casey) Dodds, and to be ambitious to extend his sway across the province. Wilfred List, the *Globe and Mail*'s well-informed labour reporter, came to the conclusion that Hoffa was the key figure in decisions being made by the Windsor local and its counterpart in Hamilton, the third of the three representing drivers in southwestern and central Ontario. Both rejected the agreement accepted in Toronto and prepared to pull their members off the roads. The harried labour minister, now threatened with a shut-down of much of the vital trucking industry in the south, took the only path open to him, telegraphing Dodds and the trucking association that the strike could be averted and inviting them to meet in his office on 20 July. Both sides accepted but that did not prevent a walkout. Dodds informed the employers that a strike would begin at midnight on 19 July and turned down Daley's plea that it be postponed pending the meeting with the excuse that it was too late to call it off.[22]

By the time the meeting took place it was estimated that three-quarters of the inter-urban truck traffic in southern Ontario had ground to a halt. Scores of trucks westward bound from Toronto were turned back by flying squads of picketers roaming the highways in cars in an effort to close entry to the towns and cities along the way. Other pickets were set up at company premises. The union announced that it would concentrate on effecting a total blockade of Hamilton, and assigned four men in each of four cars to seal off the main entrances to the city. Frost then warned that the criminal code would be strictly enforced to prevent highway picketing and police were mustered in strength to do so, which brought complaints that they were being used as strikebreakers. Denying this categorically, Frost replied to one of the objectors that 'if for no other reason than for public safety it is quite impossible to allow the picketing of provincial roads ... I think you will see the difficulty. Unauthorized road blocks would create traffic blocks which almost inevitably would lead to accidents, and furthermore, the practice of chasing trucks and overtaking them at high speeds on the highways is ... so contrary to just ordinary common sense.'[23]

The blockade was cancelled for the time being but ordinary common sense seemed in short supply as intimidation and violence became more common. Tires were slashed, sulphur was poured into gasoline tanks. One frightened non-striking driver, rolling along near Clappison's Corners at 1:30 in the morning, had his cab struck by four bullets. In another incident at about the same time, five picketers wheeled their car across the highway at Burlington Beach in the path of a truck convoy, disconnected the tractor from the trailer of the lead unit and collapsed its 15-ton load of steel pipes. The police then swung into action in the best tradition of cinematic drama, arresting the intrepid five after hot pursuit across a nearby field. On 24 July, the day of the Broulan Reef set-to, things went from bad to worse on the highways. Striking drivers assaulted non-strikers and damaged their trucks and loads. Men were dragged from their rigs to be beaten by roving picketers, and one was burned about the face and hands when a Molotov cocktail was tossed into his cab.[24]

The police, unable to be everywhere at once, could not prevent such acts or apprehend all their perpetrators, so the crown attorney in Kitchener, apparently on his own initiative, advised companies in the area to provide their drivers with an armed companion. With a man riding shotgun, as on the stagecoaches of the old wild West, there was no telling what might happen if it led to retaliation rather than deterrence. The long stalemate being predicted by Hoffa might turn into a bloodbath. Demands were heard that the Frost government act decisively to restore order but what it could do, aside from further augmenting police patrols, was less than obvious. To one of Frost's sanguine outlook, his faith in conciliation and consensus rather than draconian measures of repression and control, it was a painfully vexing problem. Perhaps another appeal for goodwill, decency, and respect for law, qualities he thought so deeply rooted in Ontario society, would have a salutary effect. On 30 July he issued such a statement.

The moment was opportune, it began, to remind everyone that violence by or to picketers was unlawful. 'Not only intimidation by picketers or others, but the arming of guards ... can both lead to the gravest consequences.' Force must only be used 'to a sufficient degree to protect oneself from injury and no further.' If the criminal law needed changing, it should be changed by Parliament. 'That is the democratic procedure. There is no excuse for any of us to violate the laws because we do not like them or even for an object which we consider worthy.' The police should be assisted, not obstructed. 'It is their duty to enforce the law and it is our duty to help them because the laws are ours.'[25]

Frost's admonitions appeared to have little effect. Two weeks after the statement appeared, a fierce fight broke out at Kitchener as picketers tried to stop drivers from leaving the terminal of a firm that had agreed to union demands and was not being struck. The city police became involved, using bare fists (their chief was knocked down and taken to hospital) as strikers clambered over the trucks, kicking in windshields and trying to prevent the rigs from starting out for Hamilton. The convoy finally got under way and was escorted to its destination by the OPP, only to find an almost total blockade of Hamilton now in effect. Police cruisers were patrolling the outskirts to assure safe passage for trucks en route between Toronto and Niagara.

So it went day after day, one incident following another, while anxious consultations continued at Queen's Park about how to end the disorder. The *Globe and Mail* repeatedly urged decertification of the Teamsters' Brotherhood, and four trucking companies applied to the Labour Relations Board to have that done. But decertification was too drastic to suit Frost, for the time being anyway. He still preferred negotiation.

Finally, union and company representatives met with Daley and Fine to seek a solution. The talks were held in a closely guarded room, it was reported, and among those present was Hoffa, who announced that without a quick settlement the union would undertake 'new economic action.' This was interpreted by the president of the Toronto Teamsters local, who objected to the presence of a foreign intruder and promised to protect his local autonomy from encroachment by Hoffa, as a threat to bottle up Toronto drivers by blockading roads around the city. Suspicion of Hoffa's ambitions was not, of course, confined to his antagonists in the brotherhood. One Toronto businessman complained to Frost:

We happen to be living in the piping times of peace, yet we witness convoys accompanied by armed O.P.P. against unruly elements of labour unions led by a foreigner ... When strikes are confronted [sic] by merely a power-hungry segment of unions it is time that your cabinet do something with the foreign element in particular.

This current Truckers' dispute ... is an effort by James Hoffa, a foreigner from Detroit, to become the power in Ontario.

Many of us employ labor and ... are not in any way opposed to unions but we do not believe that labor should become a political entity nor that Canadian unions should be dominated by foreigners like Hoffa.

Frost coolly replied that the issue was not as clear-cut as the complainant believed.

The difficulties in this matter, of course, can be over-simplified. For a great many years, almost generations, there have been international unions operating in this country. For instance most of the railway unions are international and have been since the beginning of things. On the other hand, the same thing applies to business. Many of the largest corporations in this country are representative of interests from elsewhere and in many cases the presidents and executive officers reside in other countries and notably in the United States.

You will readily see the difficulty. I have heard discussions many times in the past concerning the international character of unions and objection has been taken because of what you refer to as foreign direction ... On the other hand, you will readily see that there is a very quick answer for the same condition applies to business and industry.

Relative to a tyranny on the part of labour or anyone else or unruly or unlawful elements, I quite agree ... that our people are opposed to this sort of thing ... May I point out to you that while we have difficulties, that [sic] these ... only occur in a very small percentage of cases. The public hears of the cases in which there are difficulties and ... strikes, but nothing of the literally thousands of cases which are amicably settled because of good collective bargaining arrangements.[26]

James Hoffa and the baneful foreign domination he personified to many were not the only targets of those who were appalled by the chaos of the truckers' strike. The government was severely censured for its allegedly too timid response to the situation. 'The law has been brazenly flouted,' declaimed the *Financial Post*. 'Hoodlumism has triumphed. After one or two feeble, verbal protests, the authorities meekly stepped aside and let union strong-arm squads take over ... Orderly, decent society has received a jolting setback in Ontario. Ontario's Government has made a miserable showing in this matter. There are times when government must not take the easy course. This was one such occasion.'

Indeed, the law *had* been flouted, personal injuries suffered and property damaged or destroyed. These were evils not to be taken lightly. But short of calling in the military in aid of the civil power, which Frost would have abhorred, old soldier though he was, it was not clear what more the government could do. Its critics had nothing feasible to suggest other than union decertification, which would have been more a punishment than prevention, and possibly provocative in effect. Complaints about failing to enforce the law overlooked the practical difficulty of doing so. As it was, the government, caught in a familiar crossfire from opposing positions, was being accused by some of allowing the provincial police to be used as strikebreakers.

As August neared its end the union exerted additional pressure by moving to shut off the extensive traffic between the Niagara peninsula and Toronto, which with police assistance had continued to flow during the strike. Pickets were mounted in all the important urban centres of the peninsula in the hope that their drivers, represented by the Toronto local, would respect the lines. This proved to be an effective lever in fresh negotiations that opened at Queen's Park. At Daley's urging, Hoffa agreed to withdraw the pickets for thirty-six hours, and trucks moved again, but when two days of talks brought no progress, the union prepared to reimpose the blockade. With that looming, the discussions suddenly reached their denouement on 27 August in a settlement of all issues, overwhelmingly approved at once by members of the Hamilton local and shortly afterwards in Windsor. It was a compromise, worked out and promoted by Daley and his officials, but generally favourable to the employees.[27]

The strikers' satisfaction with the outcome was not shared by the Toronto local's president, who denounced the settlement as 'the most colossal bungle in the history of Canadian labor.' That could be dismissed as sour grapes, inasmuch as his own men had long since accepted less attractive terms, but it was evident that it would take some time for the strikers to make up wages lost during their six weeks off the job. The agreement was no more welcome to those who thought it a sell-out to the union. The *Globe and Mail* grumpily accused Daley of having made 'a "settlement" – behind closed doors – with a Detroit mobster who has treated the laws of this Province and Dominion with undisguised contempt; and with Windsor and Hamilton union leaders who have grossly abused their license to organize and bargain collectively.' The minister, it charged, had repeatedly appeased the unions in helping to settle disputes. 'In short, he makes employers accept compulsory arbitration, with himself acting as the arbitrator.'[28] That was palpable nonsense, merely demonstrating that, although George McCullagh had died in 1952, his spirit still infused the editorial page of his newspaper, at least where industrial relations were concerned. The criticism was directed implicitly at the premier as well as Daley, for the two had been in close consultation throughout the strike and no important initiative was taken without Frost's concurrence. He looked on the settlement as a reasonable one the companies could well afford. But whether one liked its terms or not, it had one great virtue: the long, hot summer on the highways was over.

Not so in the Timmins district, where Broulan Reef was still strife-torn and strikes or lockouts continued at other mines. On 19 August the home of a Broulan shift boss was demolished by a dynamite charge, in response, so it was said, to certain union leaders being subpoenaed to appear before Chief Justice J.C. McRuer of the Ontario Supreme Court in connection with illegal picketing. When McRuer ordered early in September that the crown enforce an injunction restraining picketing, an attempt was made to burn down the mine's shaft-house. Two men, one an officer of the Steelworkers, were charged with attempted arson and attempted murder following a gunfight with police in the bush. In view of these happenings, it was not surprising that Millard's published assurance in a letter to Frost, that union members had been instructed to avoid incidents at all cost, was greeted with widespread scepticism. That there would be more incidents was generally taken for granted. In fact Don Delaplante, reporting to the *Globe and Mail* from Timmins shortly after the gunfight, wrote that 'Labour Day finds Broulan Reef Mine more resembling a plantation in Kenya surrounded by Mau Mau terrorists than a Canadian gold mine. Armed guards, pistols strapped to their hips, and squads of provincial police officers ... patrolled the bushland property.' The police were still showing restraint, however. When it was complained that all roads connecting the different mines had been closed by picketers to everyone except strikers and union officials, they admitted being aware of this illegal action but explained that 'their orders from government sources specify only to put down violence when it occurs.'[29]

At this juncture Millard sent Frost a proposal, coupled with a thinly veiled threat of escalation failing a prompt settlement. He wrote that it was apparent that the disputes are not with individual mines. Rather, the issue was 'between the mining industry as a whole and their employees who seek wages and security long since granted by the great majority of employers.' This being so, 'it seems inevitable that the strikes will spread to other mines where conciliation has been completed or union agreements are reaching their termination dates.' The only way to prevent this was 'by high level discussions with the industry as a whole.' Frost should convene such a meeting, at which his presence 'would compel both parties to approach their problems in a spirit of urgency and the knowledge that inflexible viewpoints are not good for the industry, its workers or the country.'

Frost did not think well of the suggestion. He replied that the dispute was of no concern to those engaged in other types of mining and to call them in would not accomplish anything. Gold mining was in a depressed state because the price of the commodity was fixed while the cost of producing it was constantly rising. 'Many mines are undoubtedly operating out of a sense of obligation to their employees and to the municipalities in which they are located.' The services of the Labour Department were always available and Millard might do well to ask Daley to call a meeting of the union and the mines concerned. Millard was unimpressed. Most of the conciliation boards which had tried to mediate the various disputes, he pointed out, had concluded that wage increases and the check-off of dues were justified. As always, though, the union stood ready to meet the mine operators, as municipal leaders in Timmins and the surrounding area were also urging, whenever 'the Minister could persuade them to meet us.'[30]

It was true that local officials, spurred by the prospect that the union would shortly strike the two largest employers, Hollinger and McIntyre Porcupine, were pressing the government to act. On 16 September Mayor Wilfred Spooner of Timmins requested in a telegram that Frost call the disputants together to arrange for binding arbitration and thus avert a disaster to the community. A short time later Spooner and the reeves of neighbouring townships came to Toronto to put their case to Daley and the premier. The latter, however, would have none of binding arbitration. Voluntary arbitration was quite in order and was provided for in the law, but organized labour and most on the management side objected to compulsion, and with good reason. Compulsory arbitration would be fine 'if you could obtain an all-understanding arbitrator who would have to have the wisdom of Solomon. I have never yet been able to find him.'[31] The only sound way to settle labour disputes was by collective bargaining, not by government intervention.

Leaving things alone, while reiterating that Labour department services were available whenever the parties were ready to negotiate, had been Frost's policy ever since the abortive effort to bring the union and Broulan Reef together in early August. His refusal to intervene more actively was denounced by Millard as a cowardly retreat, and he was accused by the CCF provincial executive of 'abetting the union-busting of piratical mining magnates' by his unwillingness to insert provision for the check-off into the Labour Relations Act, as had been done in six other provinces. Frost was thought to favour the check-off personally but to be averse at that stage to incurring the wrath of the mining companies by going so far. Much less ready was he to countenance a suggestion by the Ontario CCF's vice-president that the government take over the mines until the owners came to their senses.[32]

If only the two sides would show some common sense and start talking to each other, the government's posture of masterful inactivity might be vindicated. As summer gave way to autumn, no signs of that happening appeared. Instead the situation deteriorated as, fulfilling Millard's prophecy, first McIntyre and then Hollinger were hit by strikes. Not only that, most workers at Noranda Mines, the largest Canadian gold producer with its operations in northwestern Quebec but its head office in Toronto, had walked out in late August. With matters going from bad to worse, could the government any longer afford to sit on the sidelines and wait for the warriors to seek a truce? At the end of September it was decided that it could not. Daley invited the presidents of the three large companies to a meeting, presumably hoping to persuade them to give ground, and at the same time asked the Steelworkers to call off the Hollinger strike, an illegal one since the dispute had not been submitted to conciliation. Neither move succeeded. The walkout at Hollinger continued and the three 'piratical magnates' – J.Y. Murdoch of Noranda, Balmer Neilly of McIntyre, and Jules Timmins of Hollinger – seemed no more inclined to co operate, or to compromise on union security. After their session with Daley, Frost, and Dana Porter, Murdoch told reporters that he would never grant the check-off as long as he lived; it was clear that his confrères were of like mind. However, said Murdoch, he was willing to consider wage concessions.[33]

That was a seed which Frost thought might germinate and blossom under careful tending, even though for the moment the ground looked barren. En route to New York on a business trip a few weeks later, he dictated a letter to Daley. 'I have wondered,' he wrote, 'if there is something we could now do in the Timmins situation. At the present time it looks like a blank wall.' He understood that the mines were preparing to close shop entirely for the winter. He would be willing to meet with management again, if Daley thought it helpful, and perhaps now was the time for one of them to have a chat with Millard. 'If I did so, I would simply point out to him the facts of life and that there would be no loss of face if he were just to recognize the hard facts of the situation and make the best possible deal, hoping that [a rise in] the price of gold or some other thing would enter into the matter ultimately and enable a better agreement.' Something less than the whole loaf the union was after, he continued, betraying impatience with the mine operators, was all that could be gained at present from 'an industry which obviously does not care to co-operate.' Now was the moment for 'one more grand effort before the thing becomes so irrevocable that it would take some months to get the mines back into operation and maybe not before spring.'[34]

It was decided to concentrate on the Hollinger strike; a solution there might break the log-jam. In November Frost conferred separately with Millard and Jules Timmins, and later in the month a series of meetings between the premier, Daley, Millard, and company officials took place, without the hoped-for result. Early in December the Steelworkers' general counsel, Arthur Goldberg, came up from Washington, which suggested that union headquarters wanted an end to the trouble. He accompanied Millard to a session with Timmins in Daley's office, shortly transferred to Frost's, the first face-to-face encounter of Millard and the president since their dispute began. Daley offered a plan providing for, among other things, a pay raise and a government-appointed fact-finding committee to inquire into the economics of the gold mining industry, but not for the check-off of dues. The union accepted this but after an interval Timmins turned it down, stating his willingness to consider wage concessions but objecting to other features. After pondering this decision for a week, the union gave in and the Hollinger strike came to an end on 22 December, affording the miners a crumb of satisfaction – a five cents hourly raise for the eighteen months' duration of the contract – with which to celebrate Christmas. Millard was bitterly disappointed by the failure to obtain union security and in his anger blamed Frost for allowing the company to dictate the terms. It was clear that the Steelworkers would redouble efforts to have the check-off made obligatory.[35]

During the first several weeks of 1954 almost all the remaining northern Ontario mine disputes were settled, on terms similar to those accepted at Hollinger. The government had attempted throughout to act as a neutral referee, to make sure that the game was played according to the rules and from time to time prodding the players to get on with it. Some players complained that it showed insufficient backbone in enforcing the rules, while others wanted it to amend them while the game was in progress by embodying the check-off of union dues in the labour law. There was no doubt that it had the power to do so, although a special session of the legislature would have been needed to make the change apply to the current strife. But Frost clung to the conviction (such it was and not a craven knuckling under to the hard-nosed, intransigent mine operators) that union security, like other issues, was best left to collective bargaining. Unfortunately for the union, the time was not propitious for extracting a concession from a depressed industry whose proprietors regarded it as the devil's mischief, and one to which union officials attached far more significance than most of the rank and file appeared to. To the latter, traditional bread-and-butter issues were of more pressing importance. These were among the facts of life which Frost had said he would try to impress upon Millard, but only the crucible of hard experience would bring them home to a man convinced that the employers were bent on breaking the union. That settlements had at last been reached Frost took as vindication of his faith that in the end common sense would prevail, and of his belief that labour disputes must be resolved by the disputants, not by government fiat.

Renewing the Mandate

As the time approached for another appeal to the voters, to be expected in 1955, Frost was well aware that dissatisfaction with the record of his administration was not confined to organized labour. The temperance lobby continued to bewail the too liberal licensing and too lax supervision of drinking places, and harness horsemen were said to be awaiting the chance to demonstrate their resentment of discriminatory treatment. Opponents of separate schools were unhappy with the cavalier dismissal of certain of the Hope Commission's central recommendations. Dissatisfaction with the metropolitan experiment survived among some in Toronto who continued to prefer outright amalgamation, while civic leaders in some, perhaps most, other municipalities were unconvinced that their expanded grants from Queen's Park amounted to all that the province could and should do for them. Inevitably, too, many individuals felt aggrieved by particular decisions of government departments or agencies affecting their personal interests. Even 'the people's party' could not please all the people all the time.

There was much on the opposite side of the ledger, however. Good times prevailed and this was reflected in the healthy state of public finances, made still healthier, at whatever cost to Ontario's fiscal autonomy, by the tax deal with Ottawa. Public money was being spent on more projects and services than ever before, without higher taxes or dangerously increased borrowing. The St Lawrence Seaway and power development were under construction and at least a little movement had been made towards building the gas pipeline from Alberta. The evil of discrimination had been attacked by various measures, and some progress was to be seen in equipping towns and cities with low-cost rental housing. There was agreement to consider a national health care plan, probably limited at first to pre-paid hospitalization, but capable of expansion into a comprehensive medical insurance system.

The outlook from the Tory standpoint was improved by the weakness of the opposition parties. They were handicapped by their small numbers in the House, it is true, although the solitary J.B. Salsberg was perhaps the most effective, certainly the most doggedly persistent, critic of the government. It was an unenviable task to conduct an opposition in prosperous times, especially against a chief target so impervious, so adept at turning aside their thrusts, calming agitation and fostering the impression that, on the whole, the universe was unfolding as it should. The image Frost enjoyed, assiduously cultivated but far from undeserved, of a dutiful public servant striving at all times to promote the public good, tended to make their attacks seem petty, wilful, unwarranted. His performance rating, had the polls later devised to measure such things been in use at the time, would have been high. There was, though, another kind of poll between general elections by which to gauge this – an unbroken winning streak in by-elections. From Drew's accession in 1943 to Frost's retirement in 1961, the Tories came out on top in all twenty-four contested, a record without parallel.[1]

The failure of Frost's opponents to make more headway had other causes; their own ineptitude was partly to blame. Farquhar Oliver, first elected to the legislature in 1926 when Frost was still an obscure small town lawyer, had been Liberal House leader since 1948. Shortly after the 1954 legislative session, at a convention where the disappointingly small attendance bespoke the party's low morale, he was chosen its leader, which in effect he had been for some time, in place of the ill-starred Walter Thomson. Experienced, personally estimable and an eloquent speaker, he lacked the inclination for sustained, concentrated effort, the drive and energy, the 'fire in the belly' needed by an opposition leader facing so formidable an adversary. The CCF suffered from Edward Jolliffe's loss of his seat in 1951, which relegated him to the House gallery to direct his tiny remnant on the floor. Donald MacDonald, his successor two years later, had the same disadvantage at first, preferring to avoid a by-election in an inhospitable riding and to await a general election before seeking a seat. Should he win one, he appeared likely to instill new vitality into his followers. He gave the impression of being a tireless scrapper at home in the trenches of bare-knuckle politics, a different breed of man from the slightly aloof and reserved Jolliffe. But for now the CCF, like the Liberals, seemed not to threaten the Conservative hegemony.

Neither gained the political mileage hoped for from the one turn of events deserving the name of scandal, in the Department of Highways, that troubled Frost during his first full term as premier. Highway construction and improvement was one of the most important activities of government, and the single most expensive, as motor vehicle registrations rose by leaps and bounds, more than doubling in the decade after 1943 and by the mid 1950s approximating 1.5 million. Good roads were essential to serve a burgeoning industrial economy, to encourage tourism, and to accommodate a more and more mobile citizenry. Technological advances as well as the higher density of traffic necessitated not only more but better highways. What had sufficed for the Model A and its contemporaries, or even for their ante-bellum successors, would hardly do for the bigger, faster, more elaborate post-war cars or for the semi-trailer juggernauts hauling a growing share of an ever-mounting volume of goods. For convenient, comfortable, safe, and economical transportation, roads must be re-engineered, widened, paved, and extended into areas where modern roads had hitherto been virtually unknown.

The war, by diverting funds to more urgent uses, had interrupted progress in highway building; there was much ground to be made up. These needs were reflected in the budgets of the Highways Department which, in line with a five-year plan adopted in 1949, rose dramatically. Taking account both of work contracted for by the department and provincial road grants to municipalities, some $150 million was being spent annually on construction and maintenance, more than the total budget in 1952. Frost was at once proud of and slightly disturbed by these escalating outlays. 'I have felt for some time,' he wrote to the provincial auditor, Harvey Cotnam, 'that the Department of Highways were building up a very expensive standard of road construction which we might be justified in lowering very considerably with a view to creating the road and gradually building it up to a higher standard over a period of years ... I look at some road construction in the province and really it does look on the extravagant side, but ... I may be quite wrong.'[2]

Notable among the many projects completed or under way were a four-lane divided throughway that would eventually extend from Windsor to the Quebec border, a high-level bridge – the Burlington Skyway – to remove an aggravating bottleneck at the entrance to

Hamilton harbour, and the Ontario section of the Trans-Canada Highway, being carried out through a federal-provincial shared cost agreement. In 1953 Cotnam's office discovered serious irregularities, chiefly related to that enterprise, in the accounts of the Fort William division of the Highways Department. Cotnam immediately investigated and some employees were suspended, among them the chief engineer who ranked only below the deputy minister. Evidence was found engineering plans had been tempered with, records changed, and charges listed for materials not used and work not done. The crown's law officers having studied the evidence, a few department employees and contracting firms were charged with criminal offences. That was not the end of it. The government retained J.D. Woods and Gordon, management consultants, to assist Cotnam and, in the words of highways minister George Doucett's instructions, 'to recommend such improvements in the organization and administrative practices ... which may be found necessary to meet the growing volume of work done in this department.'

Improvements certainly were called for, and not only at the Lakehead. The disease appeared to be assuming epidemic proportions as symptoms of corruption were exposed in the Kenora, Blind River, and Huntsville divisions. A team of officials sent to look into suspected misconduct around Blind River, where there were stories of provincial equipment being privately sold and of falsified billings, found things not altogether as they should be. One small nugget of information dredged up was that department workmen had undertaken without permission to grade the town of Thessalon's streets, of course using Department of Highways machines. For this service they received cheques payable to them personally, instead of to the province as regulations required, signed by the mayor and the pastor of the Church of Pilgrim's Progress, who happened to be town clerk. The two admitted that the system seemed funny to them but, the price being right, they went along with it. Meanwhile, the federal minister of public works, Robert Winters, announced that Ottawa would dispense no more funds for Trans-Canada Highway work in the Lakehead region until satisfied that the money was being properly spent, and stressed that Ontario was exclusively responsible for administering construction.[3]

That a well-organized swindle had apparently been operating in northern Ontario was naturally seized upon by the opposition parties as a stick with which to flail the government. Speaking in the 1954 throne speech debate, Oliver conceded that in any large department lavishly spending public money there was bound to be the odd miscreant. There would probably always be 'the penny chiseler ... who sees an opportunity to get a little of something for nothing.' But the facts thus far disclosed seemed to indicate graft on a large scale. The government's response had not gone far enough. J.D. Woods and Gordon's mandate extended only to investigation of specific irregularities in the Fort William division. Moreover, those consultants 'are appointed by the government, they report back to the government, and ... members of this House are dependent upon the government to divulge to the full the extent of that report.' The best way of getting to the bottom of things would be a royal commission to receive evidence under oath and hold public hearings. Failing that, a select committee of the House should be appointed to examine the evidence at leisure once the session was over.[4]

A few days earlier, Frost had argued that the proper forum for the problem was the Public Accounts Committee. The opposition disagreed, not without reason. Standing committees ceased to function when the House was prorogued. Members of that particular one had much else to concern themselves with and were expected to attend meetings of other committees as well. Furthermore, how much latitude could any public inquiry have now that the preferring of charges had rendered the matter *sub judice*? Did the privileges of the House extend to its committees and immunize their members from contempt of court citations when accused persons were awaiting trial? Because trials were impending, ministers and public servants such as Cotnam refused to say anything about the substance of the allegations. What hope did that leave the Public Accounts Committee of getting at the truth?

Denying any desire to limit its inquiry, Frost equivocated about whether *sub judice* issues would be out of bounds. 'I think the situation is this: questions which are ... before the courts, I think by all the rules, bar references outside of this House.' Talking about them in public might 'be considered ... in contempt of court. Whether that extends to the House, where we are privileged, is another question. I would like to reserve the answer.' But did the immunity of MPPs extend to the proceedings of committees? 'I rather take the view,' said Frost, 'that perhaps it might not be *sub judice* if referred to a Committee of the House. Then it comes down to a question of good sense and good judgment as to whether any investigation would be prejudicial to the trial of any individual.' Opposition members were not satisfied. 'I may not be as good a lawyer as the hon. Prime Minister,' said Oliver, a farmer from Grey County, 'but I think I can see what is coming ... Not only will the Committee be handicapped, but this was indeed an astute political move' to lay charges and then hand the matter over to a standing committee. Frost was 'putting through a smart political move by which he will successfully smother the work before the Committee and will prevent the Committee from doing the job it is appointed to do.' Clearly a select committee was needed to sit between sessions after the trials had been held.

Frost was indignant. Did Oliver, he retorted with an air of injured innocence, really 'want to argue that as Prime Minister of this province, I desire to stand here and withhold information from the people of this province until these cases have gone through the courts? I certainly do not ... we want to meet this thing head on and deal with it in a businesslike way.' What would be the effect of resorting to the select committee advocated by Oliver, who 'is going around this country talking about disclosures, and saying a number of things which I can assure him will bear a great deal of correction'? It might take years, there might even be appeals to the Supreme Court of Canada, before the cases were finally disposed of, while the committeemen cooled their heels waiting for the inhibitions of *sub judice* to disappear. That would never satisfy public opinion.[5]

In view of Frost's resistance to going beyond the standing committee, the news he sprang on the House immediately after his budget speech a few weeks later caused much surprise and vindicated some of the opposition's arguments. It had thus far not proved practicable, he explained, to have Cotnam or anyone from Woods, Gordon appear before the Public Accounts Committee and, as the session would end in about three weeks, there would not be time for it to undertake the careful study required. 'In order not to take from Parliament – the peoples' [*sic*] representatives – the right of full disclosure to which they are entitled,' he would propose a select committee with sweeping powers. He had rid his mind of doubts about such a body's immunity from contempt of court citations. 'I am not one who believes a committee of the Legislature is bound by the *sub judice* rule. It is only bound by the limitation of good sense, judgment and fair play. Parliament is supreme in these matters.'[6] It was only right to have the issue dealt with by MPPS, rather than by a judicial inquiry for which Oliver had unsuccessfully moved the day before. And of course, though Frost naturally refrained from mentioning this, a committee would be dominated by the governing party, an advantage not lightly to be thrown away.

Chaired by Kelso Roberts, the select committee of eleven members (including from the opposition Oliver, Grummett, and Albert Wren, Liberal-Labour MPP for Kenora) began their deliberations in the middle of April. The inclusion of Wren was appropriate. Representing one of the districts being investigated, he had been the most vocal critic of the department and its minister, subjecting Doucett to close questioning about its tendering methods and other practices. Having intimated that he could bring important witnesses with damaging testimony before the committee, he would now have a chance to put his evidence where his mouth was. Unless he really had significant revelations, however, it was uncertain what the committee could add to the findings of the provincial auditor and the consultants, whose reports it had before it. Normally an inquiry into a situation of this kind would seek to ascertain whether there was guilt and, if it was thought so, to recommend what if any charges should be laid. In this instance, however, legal proceedings were already under way. But the hearings would at least give the public airing which not only the opposition but the newspapers and even some Tory back-benchers were demanding.

By the time the committee presented majority and minority reports in February 1955, after travelling extensively and questioning numerous witnesses, the trials of the accused contracting firms and individuals were over and other significant events had occurred. Three companies were fined an aggregate of over $200,000 and made restitution totalling about $550,000. Certain men, one an inspector in the federal Public Works department, another the divisional engineer at Fort William, were convicted and given short jail terms or fines or both. C.H. Nelson, the department of highways' chief engineer, was committed to stand trial for fraud but died in a drowning accident before his case was heard and without having appeared before the committee. In addition, the deputy minister of highways, J.D. Millar, was transferred to the Department of Public Works in the same capacity and George Doucett resigned his portfolio a few weeks before the committee reported. In a letter to Frost, he stated: 'An elected representative charged with operation of a Government Department must accept full responsibility for that Department. The recent disclosures of irregularities ... have given me great concern, and in the circumstances I ask you to relieve me.'[7] In his place Frost chose James N. Allan, whom Doucett in his failed attempt to oust Alex McKenzie had tried to make party president in 1949. Having been very active in the Good Roads Association, Allan seemed a logical choice.

Doucett's departure was unavoidable in Frost's judgment, although probably he did not have to demand it.[8] The interests of party and government, not to mention the conventions of responsible government, dictated that the minister pay this price. His loss was a blow in some ways. He had thrown his influential support behind Frost for the leadership, had been designated deputy premier with a seat beside his chief in the House, and was generally recognized as the most senior minister next to the leader. Even more of a blow, however, was Doucett's having allowed conditions in his department to get into such a mess, and also that he had failed to level with Frost about the situation. The latter confided to Hugh Latimer that he 'didn't know from one day to the next once that thing broke' what would come out, because 'I couldn't get anything out of Doucett.' He was so incensed with this 'broken reed' for, as he said, having taken 'ten years off my life' that the very mention of Doucett's name in later years caused him to 'blow his top.'[9] It was not a happy parting of the ways.

In presenting his majority report to the House, Kelso Roberts spoke for two hours, recounting the committee's work, the findings of its Conservative members, and the outcome of the trials.[10] It was well known that the committee had led a troubled existence, especially in the later stages. Disagreements centred mainly on what witnesses should be called, what questions might be put to them, and what conclusions and recommendations would be proper. It had been agreed after a wrangle while the trials were yet to be finished that questions possibly prejudicial to the accused should not be asked, but more difficulty arose over the selection of witnesses. Attorney General Dana Porter, a committee member, exercised the right, presumably with Frost's consent if not at his direction, of deciding which public servants should be allowed to appear. On one occasion this provoked a squabble between him and Roberts over the failure of some senior Highways officials to turn up at a meeting in Fort William. More acrimony was caused as the committee prepared to end its labours, when its two Liberal members requested that certain persons who had testified at the trials be summoned. Roberts refused to subpoena them unless he could be convinced that they were able to add materially to their earlier testimony. He did, though, offer to find out whether they wished to be heard, thus embracing the surprising notion that it was for potential witnesses to decide, rather than the committee

itself. Understandably, the three opposition committeemen stren-
uously objected, walking out of the meeting when Roberts announced his decision, and staying away from the subsequent one
where they had intended to examine the witnesses concerned. They
also declared that they would write their own report.

It is unlikely that the refusal to call those people or the non-
attendance of the officials at Fort William made a material difference to the contents of the reports, which were not entirely at odds
with each other. Wren's most sensational allegation was that Doucett had not paid for work done on his own property by employees
of a contractor, H.J. McFarland, with whom his department did a
lot of business. Wren's demand that Doucett be cited for perjury
for having denied this to the committee came to nothing. Nor did
the fact that the charge was shown to be groundless lead Wren to
resign his seat, as might have been expected. The committee as a
whole agreed, however, that some of the more serious claims by
him and others were valid, that 'very bad practices,' as the majority
put it, had been found. In some cases there had been insufficient
pre-engineering before inviting tenders, with resulting large cost
overruns. Indeed, there was every reason to believe that contractors
as a matter of course underbid in the hope of landing the job, in
the certainty that they would be paid enough to cover their costs
and earn a profit. There must henceforth be guarantees that contracts would be honoured as to price, that those awarded them
were qualified to do the work, and that they would perform it
promptly. If a section of road was reclassified to a higher standard,
if it became part of the Trans-Canada Highway, for example, the
original contract should be replaced by one more realistic as to
probable costs, instead of continuing under the old one. Tenders
should be opened in public, not in the minister's office as Doucett
had done, and full information concerning the low bid be given to
all competitors. There had been inadequate inspection, especially
around the Lakehead, by head office Highways people and that
laxity had allowed the problems to assume larger dimensions than
they need have. All of this was largely an echo of submissions by
the provincial auditor and Woods, Gordon, and caused little disagreement in the committee.

When it came to assigning blame, recommending other reforms,
and carrying the investigation further, government and opposition
members parted company. The majority decided that Doucett and
Millar neither knew of nor profited from the corruption and refrained from censuring them, presumably believing that the min-

ister's resignation and his deputy's transfer to another department were punishment enough. The main culprit singled out was the deceased chief engineer, Nelson, who was judged to have been aware of what was going on and derelict in his duty to stop it. The Tories on the committee concluded that the reorganization of the department under new management, the fact that most reforms called for had been carried out, and the opinion of Cotnam – a universally respected public servant of unquestioned integrity – that further inquiries and prosecutions were unnecessary, meant that all was now well in the Department of Highways. The minority dissented, crying 'Whitewash!' They wanted the investigation continued by royal commission. In an apparent attempt to implicate Frost directly, not in wrongdoing but in administrative inefficiency, they proposed a reorganization of the Treasury Department, as well as modernization of government auditing procedures. The practice of promising roads here and there for political gain, but without proper engineering data and in ignorance of costs, should be discontinued – a revolutionary suggestion that would have ended one of the most time-honoured customs of democratic politics. In addition, department heads and civil servants should be prohibited from accepting gifts from or having private dealings with persons or companies doing business with the government. But most of all, the three opposition members wanted the probe pursued further, to the utmost limits. More evil remained to be exposed, they were convinced; justice had not been fully done by a few jail terms and fines and by collecting restitution.[11]

In concluding his protracted presentation of the majority findings in the House, Kelso Roberts credited Cotnam and Frost with extinguishing the 'fire' in the department of Highways and predicted smooth sailing ahead in road-building and the administration of public affairs generally. There was anything but in the ensuing debate before crowded galleries, one of the stormiest in years, as members, their voices rising, hurled taunts across the aisle while the Speaker, M.C. Davies, valiantly tried to maintain decorum. The dialogue may have added little to an understanding of the subject, but it showed that Frost was no mean debater when the occasion arose. By the time he finished speaking Frost had placed the opposition leader more on the defensive than he was himself. A year earlier, he admitted, the Highways affair had caused him the gravest concern. Now that the nature and extent of the difficulties were known, these had proved to be far less serious than opposition spokesmen, their friends in the press, and the minority committee report would have it believed. One thing the report called for, he noted, was a reorganization of his own department. 'With all the able men I have around me in the Treasury Department – I would say the outstanding stars in the civil service of this country – I do not think there could be anything required there.' The minority had also objected to promising roads for political gain, mentioning that Frost had done so in a speech at Atikokan during the 1951 campaign. He was unrepentant. 'Mr. Speaker, I plead guilty ... the road is there and being used ... I have made further promises. We are going to extend that road to Fort Frances.'[12]

Not least of the unfounded allegations were, in Frost's view, the bloated estimates of what the Highways Department's failings had cost the taxpayers. Various figures were bandied about but he dismissed them as no less absurd than all the talk about improper political interference, wholesale conniving in graft, and the rest of it. Ontario had one major unsettled claim against a contractor and its bonding company amounting to less than $1.5 million. This was being negotiated, he explained in concluding his speech, and he expected it to be settled satisfactorily. There had been no dishonest conduct in this case, the firm having got into difficulties through no fault of its own and requiring help from the government to meet the claims of its workers and sub-contractors.

Roberts had spoken of a fire in the Department of Highways. How serious had it really been? Perhaps something more than the localized, readily contained and quickly extinguished brush blaze, as it was painted on the government side, but a great deal less than the roaring inferno of corruption imagined by some on the opposition benches. One thing was clear, although this would be admitted more grudgingly by some than by others: Frost had practised damage control with great adroitness by recognizing that something was amiss and taking steps at once to deal with it. His opponents would undoubtedly try to capitalize on the affair in the forthcoming election. Let them try. His defences were ready and the means for a counter-attack at hand if needed. He did not fear to leave the final verdict to the voters.

That verdict was not to be long delayed. At a gathering of party faithful at London, Frost announced a general election for 9 June. The news was greeted with tremendous acclaim. Even the rather surprising results of a Gallup poll released a couple of days later did not dampen the enthusiasm. These showed the Tories supported by 29 per cent of decided voters, only four points ahead of the Grits, and the CCF with 12 per cent. More than one-third of all voters were said to be undecided.[13] Once the campaign warmed up, the organization got into high gear and Frost took to the hustings, 'Old Man Ontario,' as he fondly called the province, would awaken and do the right thing. So Conservatives from Kenora to Cornwall confidently believed.

The party apparatus was ready for a contest, of course; it was always ready. Although constituency conventions made the final choice of candidates, party headquarters could do much behind the scenes to identify suitable persons and persuade them to stand for nomination. To some extent riding executives were relied on for help in this, but equally telling, often more so, was the judgment of Alex McKenzie and Hugh Latimer. In his extensive travels around Ontario Latimer met and talked with a great many people, always with an eye to discovering those who might ably carry the party standard. These were not necessarily members of riding executives, or even known as active Tories, but leaders in the community 'successful in their line of business who were not looking for patronage or an appointment,' someone without a partisan background who 'would cut across party lines and ... appeal to the moderate Liberal.' Having found such persons, Latimer always tried to have them meet McKenzie and Frost when in Toronto, often discreetly without even the knowledge of the local executive.[14]

Hardly less important than finding the right person was the timing of his nomination. Although it might appear that the party was lagging behind its rivals, McKenzie and Latimer were opposed to doing this too early, since 'a strong candidate is always a busy man ... and every day is receiving good publicity as an active man in the public eye ... He can go places, attend functions and funerals and so forth and ingratiate himself in many ways to the public.' But some one already nominated 'is a target for criticism ... and there is always attached an ulterior motive in everything he says, every place he goes and everything he does. Invariably the person ... anxious for an early nomination is a weak candidate and the better known he becomes the more obvious are his weaknesses.'

No candidate, however attractive, could succeed without a smoothly working local organization, effective party publicity and, of course, money. Headquarters did its best to make sure that the party was everywhere represented by trustworthy people, poll chairmen above all, and that there was no relaxation of effort. 'A dedicated and alert poll chairman is worth his weight in gold,' Latimer observed, largely because in having much to say about the selection of enumerators, deputy returning officers and poll clerks 'he makes sure they are deserving and ... will produce the maximum effort and goodwill. The naming of the right people can alone mean 15 to 20 votes per poll. On the other hand, a selfish poll chairman can cost us that many votes by naming himself or members of his family to these positions.' Responsibility for advertising and other publicity was in charge of Harry Robbins at headquarters and the McKim Advertising Company was employed to prepare and distribute the material. Emphasis was placed less on the merits of the Progressive Conservative than of the Frost government for, as Latimer remembered, this 'had a far greater appeal to the moderate Liberal ... there was magic in the Frost name.'

Raising money was primarily the task of E.W. Bickle, whom Drew had made party treasurer and who continued in that post under Frost, assisted by Harry Price. When Bickle's health began to fail in the later Frost years, Price took over as treasurer and did an equally efficient job of gathering in 'the needful.' As the time for a general election was approaching, McKenzie advised Bickle of the total needed. Once candidates were nominated, he met with them individually in his office or his room at the Royal York to decide upon their requirements, jotting down riding by riding in a little black book the amount agreed upon and the date on which each instalment was to be remitted. The money, on the average between seven and eight thousand dollars for a constituency, was sent by registered mail to the candidates or their agents. There were almost daily postings. Latimer, who doubled as bank messenger, had the task of visiting Bickle's place of business to pick up the funds, in one hundred dollar bills, that McKenzie had advised were required for that day's despatch. There he would be met by a somewhat dour official whose only comment as he handed over the package was, 'Here is another pound of butter.' On occasion the 'pounds' were overweight. One day the parcel contained $80,000 and Latimer recalled: 'As I walked rather hurriedly up Bay Street to Mr. McKenzie's office ... I must confess that my heart was pounding and I had a feeling that I was being followed and expected to be pounced on any minute.' Additional allotments might be made as the campaign went on to ridings where there was a stiff fight and sometimes candidates who found that they needed less than their original share returned the surplus.[15] Where the funds came from was for Bickle and Price to know. Who got how much was McKenzie's business.

Following his election announcement at London, Frost retreated to Pleasant Point to 'putter around,' he told a reporter, 'cook beans and generally take advantage of the good weather.'[16] The respite did not last long. Two evenings later he was in Brampton at Tom Kennedy's nomination meeting, setting the predictable tone of his campaign: he would run on his record. Stressing the familiar theme of fiscal responsibility, which ruled out costly pledges, he said: 'I do not come here tonight competing in promises. Anybody can outpromise me. I come here with ... accomplishments and great policies actually in operation.'[17] What those were he proceeded to relate. Farquhar Oliver, in contrast, felt himself under no such constraints. He promised, among other things, a judicial inquiry into administration of the Highways Department, greater assistance to municipalities for road-building, unemployment relief and housing land assembly, higher old age pensions for the needy, a joint federal-provincial health care plan, increased grants for low income rental housing and for hospital construction, and a boost of ten dollars in the existing education subsidy of sixteen dollars per pupil.[18] Responding to this, Frost remarked that the three-quarters of the Liberal promises he had had time to study would cost the Treasury about $250 million. Clearly higher taxes would be unavoidable. Among those on the platform as he voiced that warning, at the North York nominating convention, were Chief Alonzo Big Canoe and another Ojibway from the reservation on Lake Simcoe's Georgina Island. This gave Frost a chance to mention that Ontario's Indians would vote for the first time in this election because the Progressive Conservative party had spearheaded the attack on discrimination.[19]

Although the Liberals and CCF had their own programs, both concentrated on the alleged sins of the Frost government. Among these, they claimed, was its failure to provide effectively for conservation of natural resources, to end a serious shortage of trained teachers, to assure an adequate supply of housing, and to rescue municipalities from their increasingly precarious financial position. And the Frost administration was not only inept and lethargic but fundamentally corrupt, riddled by the cancerous abuse of patronage, complacent in the settled conviction that what was best for the Conservative party was best for Ontario. At the CCF nomination meeting for Victoria-Haliburton, Donald MacDonald, being on Frost's own turf, carefully distinguished between the Tory party and its leader. The premier, he generously admitted, was justly admired for his devotion to public service and his personal integrity, but could not control, much less eliminate, 'the rotten practices of

the Tory machine as it absorbs more and more of public administration for its own purposes.'

Frost took notice of this comment a few nights later at the Gate-
way Theatre in Lindsay, where it took exactly one minute to open
nominations for the Conservative candidacy, acclaim him and close
nominations. There was no need, he said, to remove 'the mantle
from my poor inadequate self to cover the people of my party.'
MacDonald's reference to him had been kind 'but a kindly reference that slanders my party is no kindness to me.' He was not going
to reply with slander, though. 'My course and my chart will be to
talk business to the people of Ontario. A greater Ontario and a
greater Canada is my platform, in the main.' The formality of naming him standard-bearer disposed of, Frost and his wife moved to
the theatre lobby to greet people as they filed out, standing near
billboards advertising current and coming attractions with fittingly
adversarial titles, 'Battle of Rogue River' and 'No Holds Barred.'[20]

The subject probably on MacDonald's mind when he inveighed
against 'rotten practices,' in addition to the highways scandal which
figured large in his and more especially Oliver's electioneering, was
the much publicized Dempsey affair.[21] This titillating little sensation went far to enliven what without it might have been a rather
dull election. As the politicians were unlimbering their big oratorical guns, it was revealed that James Dempsey, Tory MPP for Renfrew South since 1945 and recently renominated, had failed to
report on his tax returns substantial donations for his 1951 campaign from long-time friend James Drohan, a lumberman of Barry's
Bay. These were said to be in return for Dempsey's help in obtaining a timber licence for Drohan. Dempsey was a colourful, almost
legendary figure, widely known and immensely popular in the
Ottawa Valley. A rough and ready, big-hearted Irishman, a hard
drinker in his earlier days, he was at one time regarded as the
champion fist-fighter of the Valley. There were tales of many prolonged bouts of which he bore visible scars, including a missing ear
bitten off by a rival pugilist. At Queen's Park he became known as
a faithful back-bencher devoted to the interests of his constituents,
one unlikely to rock the party boat.

It was severely rocked, however, once Drohan's beneficence and
Dempsey's failure to report it became public knowledge. Frost
informed Dempsey at the first opportunity that, as he had been
given no acceptable explanation, he no longer had his blessing. The
Tories of Renfrew South, however, gave the premier the back of
their hands by nominating Dempsey again at a second convention,

this time as an independent Progressive Conservative, with a tremendous display of support. Talk of running an official candidate against him was silenced by a discussion between local party officials and McKenzie, who had consulted Frost about this. It would be best to leave Dempsey alone, rather than risk an ignominious defeat and a split Tory vote which might hand Renfrew South to the Grits. That presumably was the very result that J.J. McCann, who sat for the same district in the federal Parliament, and who had alerted Frost to Dempsey's misdeed, was hoping for.

There was one other constituency, in addition to Renfrew South, in which a more than usually interesting situation existed in 1955. Joseph Salsberg had represented Toronto St Andrew for the past dozen years and, since A.A. MacLeod's defeat in 1951, had been the solitary Communist spokesman in the House. He had successfully cultivated the loyalty of the large immigrant population in his riding and was especially admired in the numerous Jewish community, probably less because of than despite his Marxist identity. St Andrew had become a kind of Salsberg fiefdom in which he enjoyed a devotion more marked than was accorded most MPPs. In 1951, however, while avoiding the rebuff that befell MacLeod, he found his customary comfortable margin of victory considerably reduced. By 1955 there were those convinced that he could be beaten. This was decidedly the opinion of Allan Grossman, who secured the Conservative nomination and set about to topple the local hero from his pedestal.

Grossman was, as his biographer has called him, an 'unlikely Tory' in the Ontario of the 1950s.[22] The son of an immigrant Jewish peddler, he had been brought into the Conservative party more by way of certain friendships he had formed than through philosophy or conviction, a fact that did not necessarily set him apart from many others in all parties. Involving himself in local activities and organizations, he became widely and favourably known in his part of Toronto, so much so that in 1950 he was elected one of the two aldermen for Ward 4, narrowly beating a communist for second place. With an emotional hatred of communism, Grossman decided five years later to take on Salsberg and rid the legislature of its remaining red blot. There ensued a peculiarly fierce and vicious struggle, waged by Grossman and his supporters with little or no direct help from his leader or other party notables. More than once he may have wished for a dash of the inveterate anti-communism of George Drew.

Another sidelight on the Toronto campaign came from the up-and-coming incumbent in Riverdale, aggressive young Bob Macaulay. A week before polling day he fired off a steamy expostulation to Alex McKenzie:

Is it not possible to stop the McKim Advertising Company from sending me all this crap in the mail every day? We are nearly being pushed out of the back door by piles of paper and other useless twaddle. As I have said on many occasions, I would far rather have the tremendous amount of money that all of this represents to use in my Riding where I need it. I cannot use ninety-nine pictures of Mr. Frost of the dimensions of 76 feet by 38 yards. However, the despatch of this useless nonsense I suppose makes everybody down-town feel that they are earning their fabulous salaries. As far as I am concerned, they are so far removed from the people who count at Election times that they might as well be in Siberia.

I cannot be in my Committee Rooms on Monday when the Prime Minister arrives – there is not a vote in it but I do ask you to give him my very best wishes. The real machinery of our campaign will be here in the Committee Rooms, consisting of five women and they will greet the Prime Minister. The balance of our workers are out on the streets, where they should be.[23]

That sounded as though Frost would not need to tarry long in Riverdale.

Outside of Renfrew South and St Andrew with their special enlivening circumstances, the 1955 election was a rather humdrum affair. William Kinmond of the *Globe and Mail*, following Frost around on much of his arduous travel to the usual luncheons, teas, garden parties, dinners, and speeches in school auditoriums, concluded that the voters were 'suffering from a bad case of handsittingonitis.'[24] He had observed that with some exceptions crowds were small, not only for Frost but for Oliver and Mac-Donald. Audiences seemed to lack enthusiasm, to be less exuberant than one might expect of bands of partisans gathered to hear their leaders. Frost did encounter one bit of excitement, a hostile reception at Windsor by members of the United Auto Workers' political action group supporting the CCF, who picketed the high school where he was to speak, jeered the preliminary speakers, heckled the premier, and shouted at him when he left. As a precaution against possible trouble, he was escorted into the hall by several policemen, who then stationed themselves in the gallery behind the

hecklers. Nothing untoward happened, however, no scuffles or fis-
ticuffs.[25] But even that little bit of tumult was exceptional in a
contest that induced more yawns than spine-tingling fervour.

The leaders, of course, did their best to rouse the faithful and
attract new recruits. The Tories used radio and television extensively to reach an audience that might never turn out to a political
meeting. Frost made his TV debut in a rather unlikely centre, Sault
Ste Marie, and went before the cameras in several other places.
But these appearances were a far cry from the slick party commercials of a later day, being simply the 'talking heads' of the
premier and a group of ministers expounding and defending government policy. One marked contrast with 1951 was found in
Frost's stump speeches. Where before he had studiously ignored
Walter Thomson, never mentioning his name, this time, with mixed
sarcasm and anger, he repeatedly attacked Farquhar Oliver, in particular what he was saying about the Highways matter. There was
a distinct dissimilarity in the platform styles of the two men. Oliver,
wrote Kinmond, could speak for two hours without notes and seemingly without effort, 'ranging from a confidential tone of voice to a
bellow that can be heard for blocks.' Frost, while equally voluble,
'seldom raises his voice above conversation level.'[26]

Oliver had cause to feel frustrated. Not only had he to grapple
with the personification of 'Old Man Ontario,' as Frost was becoming, a rival with the image of a wise, benign, and approachable
father figure, but he had to do so with less money than the Tories
and a much inferior organization. This last contrast was illustrated
by the ways in which his and Frost's tours were handled. Oliver
usually travelled by himself, driving his own car or making solitary
journeys by train and plane to his next destination. According to
Kinmond, whose paper sent him to cover part of the odyssey, Oliver
would more often than not arrive unheralded to sit in an hotel
room until some local Liberal came to pick him up. And the party's
staff work left much to be desired. He was not informed until his
arrival in Thorold, for example, that the scheduled garden party
had been cancelled and no one had informed the Welland newspaper that he was to speak there later the same day. And Frost?
He enjoyed the luxury of a chauffeur and was accompanied everywhere by cabinet secretary Malcolm McIntyre and another officer,
although their presence was mostly to help him keep abreast of
government business as he moved about. The three were preceded
by an advertising agency man whose job was to line up the premier's
radio and television appearances. Upon arriving at a scheduled

stop, Frost would be greeted by a band of supporters and escorted to where he was going in a manner befitting so important an event. For the most part his itinerary was adhered to with well co-ordinated precision.[27]

Accompanied by Gertrude, Frost wound up his campaigning at Oshawa on 7 June. They attended yet another garden party, the premier exuding confidence all around, and in the evening he delivered his final speech in the Masonic Hall. It was not only the shortest but, Kinmond thought, the best of them all, with no recrimination against his opponents but, as usual, breathing optimism about the future of Ontario and Canada. After that meeting the Frosts repaired to Lindsay. The local Conservative candidate was on the road at 7.30 the next morning to call on as many of his constituents as he could. He made it clear to reporters that he did not want to be followed on this foray, but one of them caught up with him late in the afternoon at a field day in Little Britain, watching a baseball game. On election day he motored around some more of the riding, 'hauled in a few votes,' as he told Ralph Hyman of the *Globe and Mail*, 'and talked to my wife.'[28] In the evening he was at his committee rooms to await the returns. As they trickled in from all over Ontario, it soon began to look as though another Tory landslide was in the making, and so it proved. Its full dimensions were not yet known when, abiding by the Victoria tradition, the fire engine siren sounded outside and Frost climbed aboard to be carried, a procession of celebrants in his wake, home to Sussex Street and the refreshments Gert had once again prepared. It was a replay of 1951 but, in contrast to the subdued and sober air with which he had received the good news then, this time he was exultant, no doubt in part because the scandal-mongering of his opponents was being repudiated. When someone asked if the huge majority his party was certain to have was not a little too lopsided, Frost replied: 'I handled it before, didn't I? I stimulated the individual thinking and actions of the members and I used the capabilities of everyone. I'll do the same thing again.'[29] Perhaps not all the back-benchers in the old House would agree that their capabilities had been so fully utilized, but who could quarrel with a leader whose very name seemed synonymous with success?

As always, the measure of success was the complexion of the new House. Through redistribution it would have eight more seats than the last one, ninety-eight in all. The Conservatives captured eighty-four, including Renfrew South where the 'independent' Dempsey was returned with a reduced majority, and St Andrew, won by Allan

Grossman with a plurality of over seven hundred votes. Dempsey did not live long to savour his vindication, for a few months later the man who had never been sick a day in his life suffered a fatal heart seizure at the Walker House Hotel in Toronto. Grossman was more fortunate, destined to be a cabinet minister in the closing phase of the Frost regime and in that of Frost's successor, John Robarts. By giving the Tories 85 per cent of the seats, the voters left precious little room for the other parties. The Liberals took eleven ridings in all, counting Kenora where Albert Wren was again elected on the Liberal-Labour ticket. With the exception of that one and Stormont, they were all in the old Clear Grit stronghold of southwestern Ontario. The CCF came out of it with only three seats, a severe disappointment. MacDonald recaptured E.B. Jolliffe's old bailiwick of York South from the Conservatives but W.J. Grummett, their House leader before dissolution, lost in Cochrane South. The other two CCF victories were both in labour-intensive districts, Oshawa and Wentworth East.

The new majority was the second biggest in Ontario's history, exceeded only by Howard Ferguson's sweep of a larger House in 1929. Voter turnout was relatively low, the smallest percentage since 1943, bearing out Kinmond's observation about the apathy of the electorate. One crumb of comfort for the Liberals was that alone of the parties they received more votes than in 1951, and thus a higher proportion of a smaller total. The Conservatives' share remained about the same, slightly less than half of the aggregate, while the CCF's declined. Frost himself was given nearly two thousand fewer votes than the last time and a lessened majority in Victoria-Haliburton. Of course, he had been able to devote little personal attention to it and doubtless many who favoured him stayed home in the belief that his re-election was a foregone conclusion.[30]

The Laird of Lindsay, as A.A. MacLeod had christened him, was still the undisputed ruler of all he surveyed, in the province at large as in his own territory. He had managed to persuade enough of the people that steady as she goes was the best course for Ontario. Some thought this the hypnotic magic of 'the great tranquillizer,' with his gift for obscuring the defects of a tired, corrupt, and inefficient administration. But scandals, unless of truly alarming proportions and proved by irrefutable evidence (not the case in 1955), do not usually overturn governments. With good times, with a government that had much to its credit, and the promise of more of the same under the leadership of a man for all seasons, there was no overpowering urge to make a change.

16

Speaking up for Ontario

Although he neither claimed nor deserved entire credit for it, the lopsided result of the 1955 election offered additional proof that Leslie Frost was a politician to the manner born, ideally suited to his time and place. Few premiers of Ontario, certainly none since Howard Ferguson, had so dominated the political life of the province. Even the irrepressible Hepburn in his heyday had not matched Frost's mastery of public business, capacity for sustained, concentrated work, and sureness of political touch. Few had so completely overshadowed their cabinet colleagues to the point where the government often seemed virtually a one-man show, relegating most of them (by 1955 Dana Porter was the major exception) to a comparative and, some observers might have unkindly suggested, well-merited obscurity.

Their insignificance should not, though, be exaggerated. It was true that the premier grew accustomed to having his own way on matters of consequence; in effect his word was law. But however great Frost's pre-eminence, however often he interrupted or sidelined ministers during discussions in the House, or bypassed them by communicating directly with their senior officials, he relied on them to keep their departments in good order (as George Doucett lamentably had not), suggest policy initiatives, and offer advice about both the public and the party interest. And the low profile with which most of them had to be content was in part simply the fate of provincial ministers generally, even within their own spheres. There have been among them few counterparts anywhere of the numerous federal ministers who attained marked prominence in their own right by dealing with more dramatic, seemingly more important, and always better publicized affairs.

The cabinet Frost led to the polls in 1955 included a number of men who had fought the preceding election in the same posts, but several changes had taken place in the interim. Before being replaced at Highways by James Allan, Doucett had relinquished his other portfolio, Public Works, to a newcomer, Fletcher Thomas. Soon Thomas, an Elgin County farmer, was moved to Agriculture to replace the venerable Tom Kennedy, who retired, and was followed at Public Works by William Griesinger, whose place in Planning and Development was given to a second new man, W.K. Warrender of Hamilton. A further round of musical chairs saw Welland Gemmell, Frost's successor as mines minister, move to Lands and Forests in place of Harold Scott, who remained in the cabinet without portfolio. The Department of Mines was taken over by P.T. Kelly and, upon Gemmell's untimely death in 1954, Lands and Forests passed to another northerner, Clare Mapledoram. Subsequently, Porter handed over Education to W.J. Dunlop, Arthur Welsh retired as provincial secretary in favour of W.M. Nickle of Kingston, and William Hamilton was appointed without portfolio. When George Challies retired before the 1955 election to become chairman of the St Lawrence Parks Commission, Hamilton took over as vice-chairman of Hydro. For the rest, the status quo prevailed. Frost remained treasurer and Porter attorney general. Charles Daley was a fixture at Labour and George Dunbar continued to preside, somewhat uncertainly, over Municipal Affairs. Others retaining the offices they had held for the past four years or longer were William Goodfellow in Public Welfare, Mackinnon Phillips in Health, John Foote in Reform Institutions and, most inconspicuous of ministers in the least conspicuous department, Louis Cecile in Travel and Publicity. Of the whole roster, only Hamilton was a casualty in the election, losing in Wellington South.

For some time before voting day, Frost had considered further cabinet changes but decided to stand pat until after it passed. When it came, the shuffle consisted mostly of moving incumbents around, but some of the reassignments were important. Most noteworthy was Frost's surrender of the treasury to Porter, by then closest to and more relied on by him than any other colleague. In announcing the reorganization, Frost pointed with pride, to the surprise of no one, at the flourishing state of Ontario's finances and to the fact that the Treasury was a more efficient, smoothly functioning organism than he had found upon taking charge of it in 1943. He singled out for special mention creation of the economics branch under the invaluable George Gathercole. This had given him what he wanted, 'a periscope to see where we were going and there isn't any better economics branch in Canada, including the federal Government.' That may have been a bit of hyperbole but there was no denying that the level of professional expertise in financial planning and management had risen greatly in the past dozen years.

Admitting that he was sorry to leave the office, Frost made it clear that he would remain very much in the picture as a member of Treasury Board. No one who knew him would harbour the slightest doubt of that or anticipate, as long as he headed the government, any marked change of direction under whatever treasurer. But the province's finances had become so large, the department's operations so complex, that they required a minister free to give them his undivided attention. The *Globe and Mail* agreed, deeming it fortunate that the premier would now have more time to confer with his colleagues, as well as to 'see more of his backbenchers and pick out from among them those best fitted to carry on the good work.'[1] The implications were plain: Frost had been taking too much on himself and his latest readjustment had not gone as far as it might have in replacing dead wood with living timber.

The new attorney general was A. Kelso Roberts, whose advancement increased Metropolitan Toronto's numerically meagre representation by 50 per cent. First elected in 1943, Roberts had retired from provincial politics five years later and considered running federally. Instead he resurfaced in 1949 as an aspirant for the Ontario party leadership. The sensation he caused at the convention by breaking ranks over the Charitable Gifts Act cast him again into the shadows, from which he emerged as the victorious candidate in Toronto St Patrick in 1951. His subsequent work as an MPP, especially as chairman of the select committee on highways irregularities, had evidently overcome any lingering resentment of his indiscretion in 1949. The other new man in the cabinet was Bryan Cathcart of Lambton West, who took over from Cecile at Travel and Publicity. Cecile in turn was assigned to Public Welfare in place of Goodfellow, who assumed Dunbar's job at Municipal Affairs. Dunbar, seventy-seven years old and in frail health, was given the less onerous portfolio of provincial secretary. His predecessor there, Nickle, was promoted to Planning and Development, and Warrender was moved into the vacancy as vice-chairman of Hydro created by William Hamilton's defeat. One change that might have been looked for was not made – the replacement of John Foote at Reform Institutions. Foote, awarded the Victoria Cross as a chaplain in the war, was seriously ill with a heart condition. But it was felt, a press report had it, that 'the Premier would hesitate to make any change here as long as the minister is ill.'[2] That might smack of kicking a man when he was down and impede the hoped for recovery. Frost would want to do that to a war veteran least of all.

All the appointments he was announcing, the premier claimed, would assist in stimulating sound development and productivity, 'the greatest contribution we can make to Canada and the standard of living of our people.' In light of that, particular significance was seen in Nickle's move to Planning and Development. 'He should pump some badly needed energy into that department,' the *Globe and Mail* predicted. 'As Provincial Secretary, he established an excellent reputation for making decisions and getting results.' None would question his public spirit, energy, willingness to take action, and impatience with red tape. Like his father, however, the crusty attorney general with whom Frost had had a disagreement over the McGaughey murder case thirty years before, Billy Nickle had a rather prickly personality. Some mistrusted his judgment and feared that he might be a loose cannon. As Robert Macaulay had written to Frost in applauding Nickle's earlier elevation to the cabinet, he 'is a very strong man with a great deal of ability, and no one with a lot of energy is not at times a little difficult to handle (not saying of course that Bill *ever* would be difficult to handle) but I am sure if he ever was you are just the fellow to do it.'[3] Whatever qualms one might feel, Nickle's brand of decisiveness might help the department in which he now found himself live up to its name more impressively than in the past, although major decisions would without doubt continue to be made in the premier's office.

The prospects for continued development – the magic word of the 1950s – appeared bright as Frost and his revamped cabinet faced the future. One reason for optimism was that C.D. Howe was known to be beavering away at his current big project, getting the natural gas pipeline from Alberta built and operating; when he set his sights on having something done, the odds were good that it would be. In Frost's opinion, none of Howe's previous accomplishments could surpass in importance success in this venture, at least from the standpoint of Ontario's growth and prosperity. Of course, there were bound to be setbacks and delays before the gas began to flow. Frost's prediction in his 1954 budget speech that construction would begin that year had proved unfounded and Trans-Canada Pipe Lines Limited was in serious financial straits, unable to secure the capital investment required to proceed. For many months complicated negotiations had been going on among the federal government, the Bank of Canada and numerous private interests in an effort to resolve the difficulty.[4]

The Ontario government was not directly involved in all this and could do little more than watch hopefully from the sidelines, offering some suggestions and ready to help if it could. It may be, as the Toronto *Telegram* thought, that theoretically Frost would have preferred 'that the whole pipeline be financed with private money, as a straight business venture, without any form of Government aid.'[5] But theoretical preferences had to make way for reality. He was still of the opinion that on the purely practical grounds of moving forward with certainty it would be better if the entire line were built with public funds and operated as a publicly owned utility, rather than rely on private enterprise with unsure financial resources. Had that been done, the federal government would have avoided some unforeseen pitfalls, although other troubles might have arisen.

Frost got nowhere with the public ownership option in a conversation with the prime minister a few weeks prior to the federal-provincial conference of October 1955. It was very clear that the federal ministers had 'no preference in principle for public ownership,' as St Laurent later told Premier Douglas of Saskatchewan, who favoured it for reasons more ideological than Frost's. Even less inclined in that direction were Alberta's Social Credit government, which controlled the gas supply, and the various private companies by now involved. In addition, Frost got the impression that the prime minister wanted to avoid antagonizing Howe, whose earlier recommendation that the log-jam be broken by a government guarantee of Trans-Canada Pipe Lines' bonds had been turned down in cabinet. He had often thought, Frost wrote, that 'perhaps in a sense this was an abdication of responsibility on the part of Mr. St. Laurent, who was then quite up in years.'[6]

Howe's new approach directly affected Ontario and consisted of another means of bringing public financial support to bear. A major difficulty in attracting private investment was that the line must lie wholly within Canada and therefore traverse northwestern Ontario where relatively little revenue would be generated. The idea was to create a crown corporation, Northern Ontario Pipe Line, to which Ottawa and the province would both subscribe capital and which would build the section from the Manitoba border to Kapuskasing. The section would then be leased to Trans-Canada to operate in conjunction with the rest of the system. All this would be conditional on the company's demonstrating by 1 May 1956 that it was assured of sufficient private capital to build the balance of the line.

St Laurent and Howe discussed this proposition with Frost and Dana Porter at the October conference. According to Frost's handwritten (and not easily decipherable) notes of the conversation, he and Porter expressed 'misgivings about Trans-Canada's personnel & organization,' pointed to the uncertainty of private financing, and predicted that the company would not meet the 1 May deadline. 'We are satisfied T.C. will fall down,' the notes read, 'and Fed Govt should now consider that eventuality.' Ontario preferred a government-built line all the way from the gas fields. The Canadian people would be enthusiastic over this and 'not question our putting money in.' The federal ministers were adamant. Government ownership was quite impracticable, given the attitude of the Alberta government if for no other reason, and in any case the complications of arranging it would cause further long delay. Trans-Canada Pipe Lines was the only possible instrument if laying the pipe was to begin in the summer of 1956, as Howe was determined it should and Frost certainly desired. As he explained to Robert Macaulay, while the province faced no energy shortage at the moment, by 'about 1960 we are going to feel the pinch and from then on [new] power supplies are going to be increasingly necessary.' Time was of the essence. The trunk line into the Ontario market could be built quite quickly, but constructing the distribution network to make the gas usable would take longer. Work on that would not start until the main line was assured. 'The sooner it is here the better and it would be folly to lose the construction year of 1956.' After their discussion with St Laurent and Howe, Frost and Porter concluded that the private ownership proposal was the only feasible one. They would have to back it therefore, not because they liked it but, as Frost put it bluntly to Macaulay, because they had to.[7]

Thereupon a contract between the federal government and Trans-Canada, setting forth the terms under which the northern Ontario portion would be laid and leased to the company, was drawn and sent to Queen's Park for consideration. An exchange of letters between Howe and Porter defined the terms of the agreement between the two governments.[8] Money to cover one-third of the total cost, but not to exceed $35 million, would be supplied by Ontario, the balance by Ottawa. The crown corporation would pay interest on these advances and its total net earnings would go towards repayment of the principal. Ontario would not have to remit any of its share until satisfied that Trans-Canada was in a position to build and operate the rest of the line. In announcing the agreement and publishing the Howe-Porter correspondence, Frost asserted that 'the reasons for concurring in the arrangements made are overwhelming.'[9]

The legislature seemed to agree, for in February 1956 it unanimously approved Ontario's participation. Howe claimed part of the credit. 'Between Frost and myself,' he wrote to President Tanner of Trans-Canada, 'we were able to get a unanimous vote in the Ontario house.' The unanimity was, however, misleading. It came after a spirited debate in which Donald MacDonald in particular raised a number of serious objections which he was willing to put aside when voting only because there appeared to be no other way of bringing natural gas to northern Ontario. Frost's own speech in the debate was less than unreservedly enthusiastic. It reflected the doubts about Trans-Canada's capabilities that he and Porter had conveyed to St Laurent and Howe, but concluded in effect that, considering how things were rather than how one might like them to be, the plan offered the best obtainable way of getting the pipeline. The staunchly Conservative *Telegram* disagreed. Frost ought to have 'insisted on a completely Government-owned pipeline,' it declared, 'so that Ontario's interests may be better protected, and Canadian taxpayers might have a far better chance for their money.' But Frost, only one player in the game, was in no position to insist on that. As he pointed out in the House, Alberta had the gas and rejected public in favour of private enterprise. 'The people of Alberta can run their own affairs. That is their business. We may be strongly in favour of public ownership here, and be very sympathetic to the idea – and, as a matter of fact, we are – but because we are, we should not insist that another province ... accept that view.'[10]

Donald MacDonald was incensed by Howe's misrepresentation of the Ontario vote. He contemplated putting a resolution on the order paper affirming that, notwithstanding the vote, 'this Legislature wishes to go on record as favouring public ownership of the trans-Canada line.' His plan was to send this in advance to Frost, with a covering letter, and to release both resolution and letter to the press. Knowing that the premier would have to oppose the resolution, MacDonald thought the CCF might benefit from 'the profound embarrassment that Frost's confirmation of support for the existing plan would create in the Tory party,' whose federal wing was on the other side. In the end, MacDonald's federal colleagues dissuaded him from this course.[11]

Although he seems not to have been bothered by it himself, Frost would have welcomed an end to whatever awkwardness the division on this issue between federal and provincial Conservatives was causing. But to end it the Ottawa Tories would have to give ground, he would not. He wished they would 'hammer their case' on the federal government's foolishness in refusing to countenance public construction and ownership. 'As I read the news reports, however, they criticize the Trans-Canada Pipeline arrangement, but provide no alternative.' He was under no illusion that he could influence them, or that they would grasp the compelling reasons to concur in what, like it or not, was the only practicable course if public ownership was ruled out. Aware that there would be resistance to the measure, he telephoned Howe immediately after the legislature voted, urging him to have it passed quickly.[12] Little did he imagine what an extraordinary expedient the St Laurent cabinet would adopt to achieve that, even though it was all too clear that Howe's bill would have no quick or easy passage. More than that, Trans-Canada was still bedevilled by the scepticism of investors, which even the prospect of the taxpayers footing the bill for the northern Ontario line did not dissipate.

With the passing weeks it became obvious that, as Frost had foreseen, the company would fail to meet its 1 May deadline for demonstrating sufficient financing. Trans-Canada was prepared to wait longer, to postpone construction for another year if necessary, until the American market was opened. That did not satisfy Howe. Persisting in his determination to have the prairie section begun and if possible completed during the coming summer, he proposed, and Ontario agreed to, an extension of the deadline to the fall, and a short-term federal loan to the company of $80 million to enable it to get started. St Laurent telephoned Frost to sound him out about the extension. The premier, according to his scribbled notes of the conversation, assured him that 'I will stand with you Northern Ont pipe line ... we will amend the agreement ... & take a chance.' But referring to the system as a whole, he had one last, fruitless go at the idea of making it a public enterprise: 'Perhaps none of my business ... I would build it yourself.'[13]

Trans-Canada graciously agreed to accept the loan but notified Howe that unless Parliament authorized it no later than 7 June, completion of the western section that year could not be guaranteed. It was now early May. To speed things up, an unprecedented method was devised to have adopted without delay the bill approving the loan and creating and funding the crown corporation, Northern Ontario Pipe Line. Closure would be imposed in the House of Commons and in committee, not to bring prolonged debate to an end as in its previous applications, but to prevent debate altogether. This was a sure-fire way of winning the immediate battle; the federal cabinet seemed blissfully unsuspecting that it might lose them the war.

The misuse of closure provoked one of the stormiest rows ever in the Commons, as those who did it must have expected. This tended to obscure the substantive criticisms of the policy, as distinct from the method of ramming it through, which its opponents, both Conservative and CCF (Social Credit MPs supported the Liberals), had begun to voice weeks before the gag was applied. Frost's comment some years after the event that it 'was not the content of the bill itself ... not what was done but how it was done,' overlooked certain facts. It was true that there were no changes in Howe's plan – the obedient Liberal majority saw to that – but there were objections, to some extent blunted by Howe's repeated reminder that the Conservative premier of Ontario backed the scheme. Among these were that Trans-Canada had come under American control; that Trans-Canada would be handed the line across northern Ontario at no capital cost to itself; that a large sum was to be loaned to a company whose precarious financial condition made its repayment doubtful and a costly bail-out at further public expense a distinct possibility. And of course the promised success of the venture was predicated upon access to the United States market (not necessarily desirable from the Canadian standpoint, in the opinion of some), of which there was no assurance. But for all that, it was the rape of Parliament, once it began to happen through the draconian use of closure, that most aroused the fury of the opposition and of much of the press. In the tumultuous scenes that rocked the House of Commons day after day, Howe was largely discredited, St Laurent's credibility as prime minister and leader of the country was severely harmed, a hitherto respected Speaker of the Commons was ruined, and the stage was being set, though other factors significantly contributed to this, for a stunning upset in the next federal election.[14]

Frost watched these proceedings, especially the fulminations of Conservative MPs, with a jaundiced eye. Although he said nothing about it publicly at the time, presumably thinking it none of his business and not wanting to make an unfortunate situation worse, he admitted later that the improper use of closure was a 'real affront to Parliament.'[15] He was not much impressed, however, by the complaints of the Ottawa opposition about the proposed loan to Trans-Canada. One of these, the much advertised danger of American control, he had already dispelled to his own satisfaction in the legislature. Whatever proportion of the shares Canadians might own, 'the fact of the matter is that the construction is in Canada, wholly within the jurisdiction of our country, and is subject to the legislative enactments not only of the Government of Canada, but of the provinces through which it passes. That in itself is the real essential of control.' The development of Canada had always depended on foreign capital and it still did.[16] The end was what mattered. The method the federal government employed for giving effect to its policy was not his concern.

His attitude angered many federal Conservatives. He was taken severely to task by the *Ottawa Journal*, presided over by that ardent and eloquent upholder of the Tory cause, Grattan O'Leary. Frost was 'in the position of silently condoning the murder of reasonable parliamentary discussion in 1956 so that Ontario may get natural gas possibly needed in 1960. Hardly an enviable position for a parliamentarian trained in British traditions of discussion and debate.' John A. Stevenson, writing in *Saturday Night*, pointed out that Frost's stand would make it 'extremely difficult for Mr. Drew to appeal for votes in Ontario in the next election on the ground that the Government's policy about the pipeline has been a calamitous blunder.' It was therefore to be expected that Drew and his friends would 'feel deeply aggrieved over Mr. Frost's partnership in the project, and they make no bones about branding him a false and disloyal ingrate.' Ingrate? According to Stevenson, Drew had made Frost his successor as premier and was now being repaid by the desertion of his protégé. Furthermore, Stevenson continued in his fanciful reconstruction of the past, Frost was really paying off a debt to Howe for having denied Farquhar Oliver the help of the federal Liberal machine in the last provincial election. Not only so, 'Mr. Frost, intent chiefly upon preserving his own ascendancy in the provincial sphere, is trying to keep the allegiance of the numerous Liberal voters who have been supporting him.'[17]

In any event, Howe's bill having been jammed through Parliament, the way was cleared to advance the loan and create the crown corporation. Construction was soon started and was finished by October 1958 with the arrival of Alberta gas in Toronto and Montreal. In time Trans-Canada Pipe Lines became a great success. Best of all from Frost's viewpoint, an ample supply of nature's wonder fuel could now be counted on, both for the established and growing market of southern Ontario and for promoting development in the north. Little did he suspect that distributing natural gas there would before long embroil his government in another scandal and that his talent for damage control would again be put to the test.

As Frost well knew, economic growth generated not only material benefits, among them increased revenue for the provincial treasury, but attendant costs with a significant impact on public finance. One had only to measure the comparatively vast outlays by Ontario on both capital and ordinary account, and itemize the varied activities of provincial and local governments in the 1950s, to grasp something of the contrast with a decade or so earlier when the Tories had returned to power. How well Ontario was able to meet its mounting obligations depended much on the effects of the tax rental agreement. Frost had always looked upon it as a stopgap awaiting a more satisfactory solution and, three years after signing it, remained convinced that it denied his province its due. The agreement would expire in 1957, negotiations for a new one would shortly begin, and he was intent on getting a better deal.

With the usual large entourage, including for the first time the president of one of the municipal associations, Frost set up shop in Ottawa for the federal-provincial conference in early October 1955. Tax-sharing headed the agenda. The prime minister began his opening remarks with an optimistic assessment of the state of the country. He stressed the heavy demands on the national government, but he recognized that 'the Canadian people demand more of their provincial governments and ... municipalities' without direct federal participation. It was 'these competing demands for expenditures which lie at the centre of the problems we must consider.'[18] How true!

St Laurent acknowledged the lack of universal satisfaction with the present tax-sharing system, and he outlined the type of plan he and his colleagues were inclined to favour. First, each province would have the right to levy any or all of the three major direct taxes. That was already being done by some. Secondly, an annual equalization grant might be paid to any province needing it to bring its revenues up to some defined minimum, whether it rented its tax fields or not. And perhaps there would have to be a stabilization guarantee to ensure that no province would find its combined income from those fields, rented out or retained, and from equalization payments, falling below a specified floor because of worsening economic conditions. These measures might help to 'ensure that there will not be any first-class or any second-class kind of Canadian citizen.'[19]

Ontario, said Frost, did not come with a dogmatic attitude. 'We recognize and support the fundamental principles of Confederation, but beyond this we have not come to this conference with rigid conceptions or fixed demands.' Ontario, like all provinces, had problems and needs that must be addressed; this the existing division of tax money did not do in a realistic way. That the prime minister's suggestions failed to touch the heart of the matter Frost made clear by virtually ignoring them in his remarks, except to say that he did not object to equalization grants if their amounts were 'determined in the light of sound principles. While giving assistance to the receiving provinces, they should not be such as to destroy enterprise and productivity in the province from which the revenue is taken.' Half of all federal government receipts from direct taxation were earned by the productive enterprise of Ontario, and a substantial portion of that depended on or was directly derived from spending by the province and its local governments. Currently this came to more than $700 million, including, for instance, half the Canadian cost of the St Lawrence Seaway and power development.

Creating facilities for a rapidly mounting population and expanding industry – schools, universities, hospitals, highways, water and sewage disposal works, and many others – was a serious drain on provincial and local coffers, and had lagged behind the need.

The 'realistic part of the national tax dollar' was not to be defined 'by tying our requirements to a national average' but by more fully 'relating them to the productivity of the province and the revenues arising therefrom.' Ontario had never conceded that the rental agreement entered into in 1952 'was fair or realistic in a peacetime economy ... nor in fact were we asked to concede that.' Its unfairness was shown, Frost argued, coming to the nub of the matter, by the fact that Ontario received for leasing personal income taxes an amount 'based upon only one-nineteenth of the Federal government's take from this field.' Similarly, the rent for corporation taxes was but one-sixth of their total, the balance going to Ottawa. But it would not suffice 'merely to consider the amount of ... tax arising from a province ... It would be more proper to consider the net position which, of course, would involve not only the revenues arising but also the obligations imposed.' From that standpoint, 15 per cent of both those taxes 'would be more in line with reality and with the problems devolving upon the province and its municipalities.'[20] This position having been staked out, it was clear that a lot of hard bargaining would have to occur before a new, and undoubtedly imperfect, resolution of this perennial issue would be found. For now it was simply agreed that Ottawa would in due course advance a definite proposal.

Frost and Porter reiterated Ontario's stand in a discussion with the prime minister in December. In a letter to St Laurent, Frost summarized what he had said: 'I am frankly fearful that in making adjustments with the other nine provinces Ontario's position may be lost sight of. I am one of those who feel that an adjustment is desirable because of the uneven distribution of taxing sources. On the other hand, care must be taken that this does not develop into an attitude of how little can be left with Ontario and how much can be given to the other provinces.' Ontario must not be 'frozen into a completely unrealistic position. This would be unfair to this Province, which, because of its concentration of industry and income, earns the adjustment payments made to the others and has to bear all the incidence of costs which run with concentration of industry.'[21]

Nevertheless, early in 1956 St Laurent unveiled proposals which in Frost's judgment were quite inadequate. Equalization grants would be paid according to a formula which, it transpired, would make every province except Ontario a beneficiary.[22] Frost promptly informed the prime minister, 'that a formula that provides a special payment to all ... except Ontario fails to meet the special needs of this Province.'[23] It was beginning to look as though the Ottawa-Toronto détente, so central to his strategy in governing, was in some danger.

The federal-provincial conference reconvened in March. The Premier repeated his by now familiar contentions and his claim as 'an absolute need' to the 15 per cent of the income tax yield. He also asserted again that Ottawa should cease levying succession duties altogether and that Ontario was not as well off compared to others as some people believed.

My concern must be for the needs of Ontario. Taking a strictly realistic view of our needs, Ontario should have at least $100 million more from these three main tax fields [income and corporate taxes and estate duties], the returns from which are based upon the earnings and production of our province. Our problems come from production and so should our revenues. It is not fair that Ontario should be driven into a position where she would have to resort to regressive taxation [e.g., a retail sales tax] to pay the bills that progressive taxation should pay. If we are driven to this, our competitive position vis-à-vis producers in the United States and other lands will inevitably be weakened. Development and production from Ontario will be hampered. Not only the people of Ontario, but the people of all provinces would suffer in consequence. It is of major importance ... to all provinces, and to Canada, that Ontario be placed in a financial position where business costs can be kept at internationally competitive levels and there be full incentive to development. Any other course would be blind and unrealistic.

The formula for tax sharing, then, denied Ontario her due; the formula for adjustment grants placed her in a different category from all others. Consider the case of Quebec, with which Ontario had much in common. Under the federal formula, Quebec would receive an annual adjustment grant of over $40 million. 'I have no doubt she needs this additional money and can put it to good use, but, if this is the federal assessment of Quebec's needs, how much greater it should be for Ontario in the light of our larger population and industrial structure' and all their attendant costs. 'I am not complaining about the recognition the Federal Government is giving to nine of our provinces, but I represent the tenth ... She undoubtedly has to help carry the load for the others and I am here to present her case and to speak up for her.'[24]

His voice did not seem to be heard where it counted. In July further representations and yet another conference having failed to change its mind, the federal government introduced a bill embodying its offer. In response, Frost issued a press release which restated the case he had tried to make privately with St Laurent. It pointed out that the British North America Act gave the central and provincial governments equal powers of direct taxation but that Ontario, far from insisting on her entitlement to half of the proceeds from the most lucrative tax fields, was seeking only a modest 15 per cent. This would not be a 'cost' to the federal treasury, as Finance Minister Walter Harris termed it, 'It is merely giving us a portion of what is our own.' Anyway, Ottawa could afford to be more generous, with its budgetary surplus estimated at $500 million for the current fiscal year. What Ontario was seeking, not on its own behalf alone but for all provinces, would amount to only about one-half of that.[25] Subsequently, Frost held a news conference at which, without raising his voice or losing his temper, he let fly at the St Laurent regime more outspokenly than ever before. 'It seems peculiar,' he said, 'that after months of debate on every conceivable subject, this important matter should be presented in the final, tired, ragged moments of Parliament.'

For their part, the newspapers proved less interested in the merits of Frost's case than in what his language suggested about his political intentions. His statement was widely interpreted as a declaration of war and the *Telegram* took it that he would 'intervene actively in the next federal election.' Credence was thought to be given this by the testimony of federal ministers that at a meeting in March he had denounced the tax proposals in a manner reminiscent of Mitch Hepburn at his worst – most damning of indictments – and by the fact that he and Drew had recently been seen lunching together. That was considered significant in view of their cool relationship. Frost tried to play the speculation down at his press conference. 'It is all pure nonsense that Drew and I have been at loggerheads. I don't know how many times I have had dinner with Drew.' Furthermore, the persistent rumours that he had ambitions in national politics were wholly unfounded. 'I have no intention of seeking the Federal leadership or of going to Ottawa in any capacity.'[26] This was undoubtedly true, but his get-together with Drew was probably more of a portent than he cared to admit.

Until now Frost had placed little reliance on the federal Tories for help in the tax-sharing dispute. After the October conference the year before, Drew had written to him that he found the situation 'more difficult to understand from outside than ... on any earlier occasion.' He added with a touch of plaintiveness, 'I shall look forward to a chance to sit down and go over all the details with you in surroundings that will leave us free to talk them over in the way we used to in the past.'[27] At that stage, however, Frost thought it better not to make the issue a subject of partisan debate at Ottawa, counting on his amicable relations with the federal cabinet and his powers of persuasion to reach a satisfactory outcome. Moreover, the anger said to have been caused by his divergence from the Ottawa Conservatives over the pipeline did not make it easier, had he so desired, to do battle together over taxes. And his virtual abstention from the two most recent national elections had hardly endeared him to Drew and his followers. Even so, Drew would certainly welcome his aid in a contest expected in 1957. Like almost everyone at that time, Frost was inclined to think another Liberal victory a certainty. He hoped, however, that Conservative representation from Ontario would be significantly increased. Were such gains made with his and the provincial party's help, they would be seen as Ontario's answer to what he regarded as the pigheadedness of the St Laurent government.

That was for the future; the present required a decision about whether to accept or reject, in whole or in part, the deal offered by Ottawa. The 1956 throne speech contained no inkling of the government's intention. It made extended reference to the subject and, rather unusually, devoted several paragraphs to criticizing the offer. Its treasury 'filled to overflowing,' the federal government was able to finance all its ordinary and capital expenditures out of current revenues and retire some of its debt. 'The paradox of declining federal debt and rising provincial and municipal debt cannot be accepted with equanimity.' Additional funds must be found for the two lower levels of government and that meant one of two things – higher provincial taxes or a better fiscal deal.[28]

Since St Laurent and Harris refused to budge, Dana Porter had no option in bringing down his budget but to announce various tax increases, painful for an administration that for years had prided itself on holding taxes steady. They did not affect personal income; that field would be rented for a further five years in return for 10 per cent of its yield in Ontario. The province would revive its corporation income tax at the rate of 11 per cent, most of which would be deductible from federal tax, continue to impose its own succession duties, and both reintroduce some previously discontinued levies and raise others. The fault was Ottawa's, Porter stressed, but at least he had not had to resort to the retail sales tax found in five other provinces.[29] But how long could that line be held and still more tax hikes be averted in view of the ever mounting costs of government and the absence of an equitable tax sharing system? More and more, the key to the dilemma appeared to lie in the approaching federal election and the prospect of rebuking the Liberals in the way they would understand best. Ontario might then receive the justice thus far denied.

As Frost saw things, human betterment for Ontarians depended at bottom on a thriving provincial economy; hence the importance of, among other things, ample, inexpensive energy and a realistic division of tax spoils between the senior governments. Otherwise, the most desired social program, health insurance, could not be afforded. He was committed to help in its establishment if financially acceptable ways of doing so could be found, but was by no means ready to cast aside restraints and push full steam ahead. That would entail risks which no prudent insurer would willingly assume. Shortly in advance of the federal-provincial conference he wrote to St Laurent confidentially, enclosing a copy of what he intended to say on the topic and sounding a typically cautionary note. 'It is very easy to agree upon the general principle that there should be hospital and health insurance. The implementation, however, is very difficult and everything I have seen suggests extreme care and caution.' Financing such a program entailed the risk of 'adding costs to our products – because taxation has that effect – and making it more difficult for us to compete in the markets of the world.' So one must progress in stages. For instance, any plan should at first be mandatory for payroll employees but voluntary for the self-employed, and then step by step be made mandatory for the latter. 'This, in brief, is our proposal.'[30]

Opening the conference, St Laurent emphasized that health care was squarely within provincial jurisdiction. Federal assistance might be justified in plans designed and administered by the provinces, provided that 'it can reasonably be shown that the national rather than merely ... local sectional interest is thereby being served.' If 'a substantial majority of provincial governments, representing a substantial majority of the Canadian people,' were prepared to adopt their own schemes, Ottawa would be willing to give technical and financial support. To tax the whole population for the benefit of a minority would be unwarranted. The stages by which a full program of health insurance could eventually exist should be carefully considered. Perhaps the first need was continued effort to add to the number and quality of hospitals and other facilities, before moving in turn to payment for diagnostic services, to hospital insurance and ultimately, perhaps, to coverage for medical care.[31]

Frost would have been among the last to dispute the importance of provincial rights, but he at once warned against letting each province go its own way. There must be a concerted, though not necessarily uniform, approach 'and it should be brought out into the open and placed before this conference for study and action. If this is not done, we can look forward to more misunderstanding and confusion.' Governments might create a 'hodge-podge that no one will be able to disentangle; and a national health plan will never be achieved simply because of the impossibility of finding common ground upon which to act. A few years more and an integrated plan becomes an impossibility.' On the other hand, there could be a common objective without a common approach. Ontario had prepared a number of study documents but was 'prepared to consider the proposals from others that we would consider more desirable than our own.'[32] As always, consensus was the goal.

Ontario's study papers,[33] the only concrete analysis and suggestions put on the table for discussion, had been drafted by Malcolm Taylor, again present as an adviser, as were this time an official of the Ontario Hospital Association and the executive director of Blue Cross. They were framed with definite objectives in mind: to meet hospitalization costs more fully for the whole population while discouraging needless use of hospital services available more economically elsewhere; to eliminate as far as possible distinctions in administering and paying for acute, convalescent, and chronic care, as well as treatment for mental illness and tuberculosis; and to satisfy as fully as could be 'the aspirations of the people in this area of need, consistent with the prudent use of public funds' and with the least attainable disturbance of 'existing patterns of practice and insurance arrangements.'

The strategy in Toronto was to devise a system at once best for Ontario but suitable for a majority of the provinces and therefore acceptable to Ottawa. Because of uncertainty about the terms of new tax rentals yet to be negotiated, the five components of Ontario's draft plan were presented as separate entities, any or all of which a province might adopt according to its circumstances. To seek acceptance of an indivisible package might prevent all progress. The five entities were diagnostic services; home care; assistance in meeting extraordinary hospital charges for a stay of, say, more than fifty days when private insurance benefits were exhausted; maternity and post-natal care; and for those provinces in a position to establish it, a comprehensive hospital services program. It was assumed that the first four of these would be administered by government, the last (favoured by Ontario) either through commercial companies or Blue Cross, by a government agency, or a combination of both. Ontario believed that the federal government should pay 60 per cent of total costs, as it had undertaken to do in its stillborn health insurance proposals of 1945. The provincial share should be met as fully as possible by individual premiums and perhaps by small user fees, with supplementary payments by the Treasury.[34]

Watching the proceedings, Taylor observed that Frost's statement and the study papers had an electrifying effect at the conference.[35] Spokesmen for provinces with some type of public hospital insurance already in effect reacted approvingly, though with some reservations about particulars. But Duplessis ignored the subject entirely in his remarks and the remaining premiers cautiously made their commitment to any plan conditional on sufficiently generous tax rentals. The upshot, suggested by Frost and doubtless all that could be hoped for at that stage, was agreement to have a committee comprising two ministers and two deputy ministers from each of the eleven governments conduct intensive studies and report later.

Although wheels were starting to turn a little faster, the road ahead was full of potholes. Early in 1956, while the joint committee was meeting and after persistent prodding by the minister of national health, Paul Martin, a hesitant federal cabinet presented its insurance proposal. The three most westerly provinces soon accepted it but the others held back. Ontario, convinced that public insurance in some form was definitely in the cards, referred the subject for study to the standing committee on health and presently formed a Hospital Services Commission chaired by A.J. Swanson, former administrator of Toronto Western Hospital. One of its major functions would be to take charge of preparations and to operate the plan when it came into effect, which in Frost's opinion could be no sooner than the beginning of 1959.

Meanwhile, much had yet to be settled. The federal offer was not seen at Queen's Park as an unmixed blessing, differing significantly as it did from what Ontario had put forward. In making Ottawa's participation dependent upon agreement by the provinces to a number of conditions, it seemed to flout the prime minister's disclaimer a few months earlier of any desire to trespass on provincial jurisdiction. One especially troublesome sticking point was that Ottawa evidently intended to construe its demand that coverage be universally available to mean no payment of the federal share until that was achieved. It was generally agreed that absolute universality was unattainable, but it appeared that Ottawa would demand 85 or 90 per cent enrolment.[36]

Frost preferred that to start with enrolment be required of payroll employees generally but be voluntary for the self-employed, increasing numbers of whom, he believed, would choose to join until coverage was virtually universal. Malcolm Taylor has remarked on the paradox of 'a province insisting on a voluntary plan notwithstanding the fact that it was the failure of the voluntary approach that had made a government plan necessary.'[37] But to

Frost the voluntary system, under which nearly three-quarters of Ontarians had some protection, had not failed; it was merely inadequate by itself in not meeting the needs of some people or insuring against contingencies such as protracted illness with catastrophic financial impact. Moreover, he was advocating only a partly voluntary arrangement under which compulsion could be extended if, as, and when advisable. On this point he explained: 'The definition of "universally available" will necessarily have to be very elastic ... whether we would make [enrolment] mandatory to various classes and sections of our people would have to be entirely within the judgment of the [Hospital Services] Commission. Nevertheless, it would be available to everyone.'[38]

As with any insurance, spreading the risk over the largest possible number of policy-holders was desirable. But in this case, Frost feared, encouraging or even requiring people to join could have unwelcome financial results. No one thought that premiums would fully cover the province's share of costs, so the higher the enrolment and thus the probable demand for services, the greater might be the need for subsidies from the public purse. This would damage provincial finances, necessitating ever higher taxes, risking ever larger deficits, and damping down investment and development. If in the future – and Frost was always looking ahead – medical were added to hospital coverage, as was to be expected, the danger would be vastly compounded. It was therefore vital to keep costs down by restricting coverage to basic diagnostic and ward care, discouraging frivolous use of the system, and, for the time being at least, allowing people in a position to do so to take care of some or all of their hospital bills privately. So, having pressed Ottawa to move on health insurance, Frost sought a compromise that would limit public expenditure while overcoming weaknesses in the voluntary method, and incidentally to some extent appease the private insurers such as Blue Cross who feared their almost total exclusion from the business.

This was derided by some as falling between two stools. The provincial CCF, at one with its national counterpart, demanded a plan on the Saskatchewan model, universal and compulsory. Others contended that government did not belong in the insurance business at all. 'The Conservative Party will never be elected to power by trying to out-do the C.C.F.,' grumbled an official of a large insurance company. He must have been thinking of some other jurisdiction than Ontario, where the party had such a tight grip on power and a policy falling well short of what the CCF was pushing for.[39] A rather more philosophical objection, which apparently Frost either did not fully grasp or thought unworthy of serious consideration, was raised by a Woodstock lawyer. While agreeing that the needy should be financially assisted to obtain health care, he was alarmed by the rate at which individual freedom was being narrowed 'by Government planners who believe in the planned state with its consequent regimentation.' It was morally wrong for a government to decree 'compliance with its mandates on this private matter' of whether to have health insurance and 'the citizen who would oppose such arbitrary exercise of power, would in the opinion of many, be performing a patriotic duty.'

In a brief reply, Frost explained that Ontario was seeking 'basic public ward care coverage for every citizen on an insurance basis. It would spread the incidence of sickness, including catastrophic incidence, over the insured population which we would hope to make a very large number indeed. At the same time there is a very large field in which the private insurance companies would operate.' His correspondent was unwilling to let the matter rest there. The point he had tried to make was that meddlesome compulsion, the 'trend towards regimentation of the people,' was inimical to liberty. Frost was unimpressed by this, if not mystified, and ignored the argument in his answer. He did not intend to bring in anything that would 'be insupportable by our people' or subject them to 'unjust burdens of taxation.' Private companies would remain in the field but could not supply the basic coverage at moderate cost to which all citizens were entitled. He was confident that the policy settled on 'carries with it the overwhelming convictions of our people.'[40] So much for libertarian individualism.

In the prolonged discussions at Queen's Park and the negotiations with Ottawa, lasting more than a year following announcement of the federal offer,[41] Ontario bowed to the inevitable respecting some features it disliked. But the definition of 'universally available' remained very much in dispute, as did whether Ottawa should relax the stipulation of no federal contributions until at least six provinces containing a majority of Canadians had signed on. Frost gave an undertaking that the Hospital Commission would bend every effort to secure 85 or 90 per cent enrolment but, while professing faith in eventual success, refused to guarantee this level by the time the plan began operating. As for the requirement of majorities, it made participation by either Ontario or Quebec essential and, since Maurice Duplessis would probably be the last to mount the bandwagon, if he ever did, action by Ontario was crucially important. In that sense, Frost was in the driver's seat, the more so because he would not have to face his voters for another three or four years, unlike St Laurent, who was expected to go to the polls in the spring of 1957. A perception that the latter was setting too stringent conditions or dragging his feet, as was being charged in some quarters, would be to his disadvantage with an electorate encouraged by countless speeches and other publicity to expect the early arrival of 'free' hospital care. Frost, stressing the need for prompt action, kept urging the prime minister to bend somewhat on the two major outstanding disagreements. An accord could then be reached and, once that happened, at least some of the remaining provinces, waiting to see what the biggest of all was going to do, would fall in line.

At length there was a slight bending. In February 1957 St Laurent accepted as sufficient, though no doubt with misgivings, Frost's promise of serious efforts to achieve universality once the plan became operative. The federal cabinet, reversing itself, also decided to introduce legislation before the election authorizing contributions to provincial insurance schemes, even though as yet fewer than six provinces were committed to participation. When a province had agreed with Ottawa about specific regulations, funding would be available once its plan was in effect. The federal bill sponsored by Paul Martin, exultant over the imminent fruition of a policy for which he had striven so hard, was passed unanimously by both the Commons and Senate, to the accompaniment of loud cheers and desk thumpings. Meanwhile, complementary legislation had been approved by the Ontario House, so the way was clear to work out detailed terms and conditions. That would take several weeks and, it turned out, was still in progress when the federal election took place in June. Frost's determination to intervene in that contest, caused by the outcome of the tax-sharing controversy, was not diminished by his dissatisfaction with some aspects of Liberal policy on hospital insurance. Conservative spokesmen in Ottawa had voiced the same objections. If the election resulted as he hoped, perhaps some modifications would be possible.

Wonders from the West

According to one explanation of Frost's departure in 1957 from his customary hands-off attitude to federal politics, he 'simply climbed on the anti-government bandwagon.'[1] The fact is that he had made up his mind to join the battle against the government long before there was a bandwagon, when almost everyone would have wagered on another Liberal victory. A different view is that his Conservative partisanship reasserted itself, causing him to desert 'the path of true statesmanship.'[2] If the mark of statesmanship was willingness to co-operate with a Liberal government under any and all circumstances, it had become clear well before the end of 1956 that Frost was headed for a fall from grace. But partisanship had little or nothing to do with it. He remained ready to work with a national government of whatever stripe so long as its policies served the vital needs of Ontario. He could only trust that a Tory cabinet, if such came about, would show itself more understanding of those needs, more open to persuasion, than the incumbents had lately proved to be. He was going to do what he could to administer a telling rebuke to St Laurent and his colleagues; if a change of government resulted, so be it.

His resolve to throw himself and his organization into the fight was formed before it was known that he would be campaigning with a new national leader. Exhausted and in unsatisfactory health as the autumn of 1956 neared, George Drew announced his retirement, and preparations were set afoot for a convention in December. At once Frost's name began to figure in speculation about who would take over, but again he categorically ruled this out. To a correspondent who thought him the man of the hour he wrote: 'It is always the job of the head of a provincial administration to look after the interests of his own province ... I think you will agree that it is pretty difficult to relinquish this role. The history of such changes is not an encouraging one. Provincial leaders who have gone into the federal field have almost invariably not been successful or have not accomplished any outstanding success.'[3]

Whether he could have been the exception, have triumphed where John Bracken and George Drew had not, was thus left for idle conjecture. The mantle would be donned by someone else, probably one of the prominent MPs expected to be contenders. But who should it be? Evidently Frost had little trouble in making up his mind. Upon learning of Drew's decision, he telephoned Hugh Latimer from Lindsay to come to the Royal York for breakfast the next morning. Latimer found the premier at his customary table with the usual galaxy of cabinet ministers. 'I want to speak to you for a moment,' he was told, and the two walked out to the lobby, Frost so preoccupied with what was on his mind that he carried his table napkin with him. He said, 'Hugh, John Diefenbaker is the man that I think should take Drew's place.'

Latimer had experienced what struck him as Diefenbaker's prima donna behaviour in a number of federal by-elections at which the man from Prince Albert was much in demand as a speaker. Latimer began to object to Diefenbaker's 'impossible temperament' but Frost cut him off sharply. 'Listen, Diefenbaker is the man that can win the next election and I want you to go and see Alex in hospital and tell him what I think and let me know what he says.' McKenzie, recuperating from a heart attack, had his own misgivings, especially about whether Diefenbaker could handle the pressures of leadership, but agreed the risk must be run. Despite his faults, from a political standpoint he was the best of the prospective candidates.[4] Others in addition to McKenzie shared Frost's opinion. Among them were one of his closest confidants, Oakley Dalgleish of the *Globe and Mail*, who looked on Diefenbaker as the only valid choice, and Garfield Case, a well-known Ontario Tory and former MP, who thought that 'if we can persuade Johnny to accept the responsibility, we have a real chance of winning the next heat.'[5] Inasmuch as Diefenbaker had already tried twice for the leadership, in 1942 and 1948, it seemed improbable that much persuasion would be required.

In fact, well before the convention scheduled for Ottawa in mid December, he was in the field along with the two others most often mentioned, Donald Fleming and Davie Fulton. When the convention met, Frost was backing him without publicizing his preference. He spoke briefly to the gathering but non-committally about the merits of the three aspirants, lauding them all as 'great and worthy Canadians.' When Diefenbaker in his nomination speech declared it his aim to make the Progressive Conservatives 'the people's party,' Frost's certainty that he was 'by all odds the outstanding candidate' must not have been lessened. Thanks in part to 'the support of the immensely powerful Ontario Conservative organization,' Frost wrote in retrospect, Diefenbaker's victory was assured.[6] It was, in truth, a triumphal march, his votes on the first ballot far outnumbering those for Fleming and Fulton combined, though with very noticeable objections to him in the Quebec delegation. Despite that sour note, Frost was content in the belief that a new day of promise for the party had dawned. If that promise were fulfilled, perhaps Ontario's financial needs would receive a more sympathetic hearing.

At any rate, Diefenbaker's election clearly presaged important changes in the party, and a fortnight after that event Frost received a communication that may have given him slight pause concerning the bent of the new chief and his cohorts. Shortly after Christmas, Alvin Hamilton, Saskatchewan Conservative leader, sent Frost a 'Declaration of Principles' for the party which he had drafted and then polished with the help of Roland Michener, now a Toronto MP, and Gurney Evans, a Manitoba MLA. This rather lengthy endorsement of motherhood was not objectionable to Frost, but his reply to Hamilton was brief and deflating. 'I have a good deal of doubt as to the wisdom or the practicability of any such thing. Canada is a very large country and in such an undertaking you would have the inevitable request ... for the inclusion of things of local importance ... It is very difficult to make such a statement without creating possible misunderstanding.'[7]

One of Diefenbaker's early actions after becoming leader seemed to indicate a readiness to rely on Frost and the Ontario party apparatus. As always, success in at least one of the large central provinces was a prerequisite of victory and, since no one expected the Tories to breach the Liberals' Quebec fortress, Ontario was the key. Soon after the convention, Diefenbaker met with Frost and McKenzie to tell them that organization in Ontario for the forthcoming election was entirely in their hands. It surprised McKenzie to be given carte blanche but he energetically set about marshalling his forces.[8] Later, when the provincial House was sitting, Frost agreed that Diefenbaker could meet the caucus, and a luncheon was arranged. The federal leader's arrival at Queen's Park was noticed by the press, and when he and Frost emerged from the latter's office on their way to lunch, arm in arm and smiling broadly, the photographers caught the moment in pictures widely published across the country. That should have been an ominous signal to the Liberals of trouble ahead, but as yet they were blissfully unsuspecting of what was in store.

The election was called for 10 June. As the campaign warmed up, an inspired Diefenbaker addressed large, growingly receptive crowds with evangelical fervour, excoriating the Grits as a discredited band of tired old men like 'Uncle Louis' St Laurent, natural-born despots like C.D. Howe, or woeful incompetents like most of the rest. In his own less dramatic way Frost made it abundantly clear in his numerous platform appearances, sometimes in the company of Diefenbaker, that at this crossroads in Canadian history the duty of the voters was to change the government. He dwelt in his speeches almost exclusively on what in his mind was the over-riding issue for Ontario, tax-sharing.

In his appearances, among them at Midland, Barrie, Port Hope, Toronto, and Hamilton and at a press conference, Frost reiterated and developed this theme. At Midland, turning to Diefenbaker behind him on the platform, he said: 'There is only one man who can find that just solution [of the tax-sharing problem] for the little men and the little women of Canada.' At Barrie, after greeting by name at the door nearly every one of a crowd that filled the Odd Fellows Hall, he defended himself against the charge that he had not been partisan enough in past federal elections. His concern had been to spearhead the development of Ontario rather than to seek mere party advantage. Even now he was 'not here for the purpose of taking political sides. I'm here because this province, our people and our municipalities face staggering problems.' He had always tried to deal fairly with Ottawa but never had any of the fifty Liberal MPs from Ontario spoken up in defence of the province's position. They and their leaders had a lesson to learn. 'When I listen to some of the things that Canada is doing for people overseas,' remarked Frost in words presently denounced as shameful parochialism by Donald MacDonald, 'I can't help thinking that perhaps the politicians might spend a little time at home here in Canada learning about the problems of the little people who have to pay the bills.'

Frost's prominence on the hustings was widely remarked upon, and not only in Ontario. Hugh Latimer, who served as advance man for Diefenbaker's cross-country travels, sensed an optimistic feeling among Conservatives wherever he went that the all-out effort of Frost, then at the height of his power and popularity, 'would ensure a sweep of Ontario.'[9] The significance of this factor was not lost on St Laurent and his advisers. Increasingly in his speeches the prime minister dwelt on the danger of an alleged conspiracy between Diefenbaker and Frost to enrich Ontario at the expense of other provinces. What the government of Ontario was demanding, he kept repeating, could not be given without a substantial increase in federal taxes and he suspected that this was what Frost wanted for the sole reason that it would give him more money to spend. Frost ridiculed the conspiracy theory. 'Mr. St. Laurent has completely missed the point of the argument advanced by Ontario and some of the other provinces ... The tactics of the federal Liberals are to set province against province – to divide and rule.'

The premier's public role in the campaign ended as it began with an introduction of Diefenbaker, this time at the final rally in Hamilton three days before the poll. It is obligatory in Canadian politics to present the leader of any major party, as he did on this occasion, as the next head of whatever government he or she seeks to head.[10] This time Frost's ritual words proved prophetic. The Conservatives took 112 seats, a modest plurality, though with a slightly smaller share of the popular vote than the Liberals, who were reduced to 105 seats from the 171 given them in 1953. The CCF captured twenty-five ridings, a gain of two, and Social Credit representation rose to nineteen, up by four. That the Tories more than doubled their numbers in the House of Commons was widely attributed to the magic of John Diefenbaker. Not only did he show himself to be a wonderfully effective campaigner in exploiting widespread disenchantment with the existing regime, the cult of personality arrived with a vengeance in Canada in that election. Frost himself, whatever reservations he may have entertained privately, heaped praise on the leader as the author of victory. 'The success of the Conservative cause,' he wrote, 'I think can be all summed up in the dynamic personality and leadership of John Diefenbaker.'[11]

Of the sixty-eight seats lost by the Liberals, twenty-nine were in Ontario and all but three of these were Conservative gains. The Liberal popular vote there dropped by nearly one-tenth, while the Tories' rose by 8.5 per cent.[12] Both of these percentages were surpassed in a few other provinces with comparatively small representation but, because of its size, the turnover in Ontario was of decisive importance. Could this be ascribed mainly to Diefenbaker's charisma, to an irresistible urge to 'follow John'? That seems unlikely. The transformation into a Conservative bastion of the three prairie provinces, where his populist proclivities might have been expected to be most attractive, was yet to happen. Thus, on the morrow of the election, Toronto's *Telegram*, in a lead editorial entitled 'Ontario the Key to Victory,' declared: 'John Diefenbaker rightly proclaimed a date with destiny. In this Province, Hon. Leslie Frost made it good. The Ontario Premier emerges from this latest triumph an extraordinary political figure in the national scene.'[13] That was an over-simplification, of course, but there can be little doubt that Frost's intervention and the work of his organization in contributing to the selection of good candidates, helping to supply the sinews of war, and getting out the vote had much to do with the result in Ontario. In Diefenbaker's judgment, 'No man in public life did more than [Frost] for the Conservative Party in that election ... from the very beginning of the campaign, it was Frost who said, "We're going to win." '[14] Watching from the sidelines, George Drew may well have reflected ruefully on the advantage thus enjoyed by his successor and the indifference with which Frost and the provincial party had reacted to his own pressing need in 1953.

Looking back in disillusionment on his close and sometimes troubled relationship with Diefenbaker later, Frost confessed that he found the man 'an exceedingly complex character and personality. It is difficult to make an assessment ... My judgment will not be those of others.' He remembered something his father, a Lowland Scot, had often said about the mystic quality of the Highlanders, from whom Diefenbaker was descended on his mother's side. 'I felt that this strain has been very evident in John Diefenbaker's life.' Moreover, the Highlander 'is firm in his allegiance and unwavering in his support but he is capable of intense likes and dislikes, of brooding over injustices and differences and ... sometimes of unreasoning ... hatreds.' Diefenbaker, noted Frost, was a great admirer of Sir John A. Macdonald, a Lowlander by birth, and liked 'to feel that there were great similarities between himself and John A.' That was not so. 'Diefenbaker is an incomparable platform man, John A. was not. John A. was an incomparable manager of men. Diefenbaker is not. Diefenbaker is the incomparable sole operator and lone wolf.' Macdonald knew how 'to keep together the diverse elements of a national party, a quality almost completely lacking in Diefenbaker.'[15] Whether or not it occurred to him, by these reckonings Frost was more in the Macdonald mould than was Diefenbaker.

Whatever the merits of his ethno-cultural interpretation, Frost was now going to have to lie in a bed he had helped make, to deal with a prime minister of very different temperament and manner from Louis St Laurent. Disenchantment was yet to arrive. And he would have to grow accustomed to the other new cabinet faces in Ottawa, most important from his standpoint Donald Fleming, who had been given the Finance portfolio. Would their being of his own party facilitate the resolution of issues important to Ontario, tax-sharing by far the most pressing? Frost had cause to hope for the best, or at least for something better. But one could not count on this in advance of the conference Diefenbaker had promised to call if and when he formed a government.

At the conference, which convened in late November, Diefenbaker's original intention was to make the provinces a definite tax offer in fulfilment of his campaign undertaking. He was dissuaded by Fleming, who argued that this would be attacked, not only by some provinces as inadequate, but by the Grits as presenting a take-it-or-leave-it proposition, the very thing of which they had been accused.[16] Thus in opening the conclave, the prime minister informed the premiers, 'We are not placing before you any rigid formulae. This conference was convened to seek your ideas and your proposals.'[17]

The premiers were happy to oblige. Having listened to them all, Donald Fleming thought that some had come up with proposals unheard previously, but Frost could not be accused of this. He reiterated his fundamental point: that existing fiscal arrangements denied provincial and local governments a share of the tax take commensurate with their rights and obligations. Yet Ottawa had consistently failed to recognize this and to adjust its policy accordingly. As a result, those governments were going further into debt to finance necessary projects, some of which should be paid for out of progressive taxation, chiefly on personal and corporate income. In the next twenty years Ontario would have to finance public capital investment of roughly $11 billion. As much of this as possible should come out of revenue, so as to limit the growth of public debt and maintain a favourable credit rating, but that would require correction of a fiscal system badly out of kilter. The 15-15-50 per cent of the direct tax fields he sought, said Frost, was the bare minimum to assure the future health of the provincial economy.[18]

Fleming's response lent no more credence than the prime minister's had to the spectre conjured up by the Liberals of a conspiracy between Diefenbaker and Frost. A quick calculation satisfied Fleming that all the propositions he had heard at that table would cost Ottawa more than $1.5 billion per annum, which it would be out of the question to grant. No effort should be made to arrive at definite conclusions then and there. Rather, the federal government would like to have from the provinces an assessment of all that had been proposed and an opinion about the priority to be accorded each suggestion. Frost was too much the realist to expect any better result than this at the conference itself, but he may have thought to himself that, while the federal actors had changed, the script remained pretty much the same. He was running out of patience with ever more discussion and delay, with assessment and reconsideration. It was time for a little *realpolitik*. He was going to collect some political debts by exerting the kind of pressure that every politician understood.

A fortnight after the conference, following a long private conversation between them, Frost wrote confidentially to the prime minister, restating his position but suggesting a possible compromise. The 15-15-50 formula was essential to Ontario 'if we are not to be overwhelmed.' Since this presented a problem for the federal government, he was willing to discuss progressive hikes in provincial tax shares until the desired proportions were achieved by, say, 1961–2. This would still leave Ontario short of funds but might be a way out. 'Some of our friends seem to think that the ... revenue Ontario receives from the 10-9-50 formula is a net revenue. It is no such thing.' All of it had to be passed on to municipalities to keep them afloat.

Frost knew that enlarging the abatements for the two kinds of income tax, personal and corporate, would create some difficulty for Ottawa respecting equalization payments. Their size was partly based on the proceeds under the abatements to the two highest tax-earning provinces, Ontario and British Columbia. Indeed the 10-9-50 formula 'was established in accordance with the principle of squeezing down Ontario to the point where the Federal Government was not giving too much by way of equalization to the other provinces. Members of the former Federal Government repeatedly admitted to me that this was their approach.' A solution might lie in retaining the existing formula for equalization purposes, with some supplementary subsidies. Extra assistance could be given any province in real need, along the lines of the special grants-in-aid for the Atlantic region which Diefenbaker had announced at the conference.[19]

Fleming, perhaps unaware of this discussion between his chief and Frost, thought the conference had relaxed provincial pressure on the national treasury. His eyes would soon be opened. 'There was one wise old political owl,' he wrote in his memoirs, 'who did not intend to be put off.' In mid January 1958, Frost sent George Gathercole to see Fleming to press for a progressive upward adjustment of the formula towards 15-15-50 during the next four years. 'As an interim measure for the fiscal year 1958-59 he demanded a move to either 10-10-50 or 13-9-50, preferably the latter ... Then came the sting; if his proposal were not met he [Frost] would find it difficult to assist in a general election campaign as he had in 1957.' Moreover, a mere 'statement of intent by the federal government would not suffice. If this was not political blackmail it was at least a very cold-blooded ultimatum of a political ally at a critical point of time.' As another election was expected soon, it was certainly timely. The Diefenbaker cabinet yielded. A week after Gathercole's mission the premiers were informed by telegram that the apportionment would be 13-9-50 for 1958–9.[20]

The second Diefenbaker election was not long in coming. Having been promised a first instalment of the larger tax share he so desired, Frost had no excuse for staying out of the fray and he did not. However, the federal party was no longer as reliant on the Ontario organization as it had been in 1957; now they had set up their own machinery. Indeed, Diefenbaker not only thought the provincial apparatus expendable; he now seemed to be insufficiently appreciative of its services in 1957, and especially of its chief, McKenzie. The over-confident Liberals had neglected to fill a number of Senate vacancies, one of them in Ontario. Many Tories believed that this should go to McKenzie. This was urged upon Diefenbaker but he was determined to appoint his friend William Brunt. Not only was McKenzie passed over, to the intense annoyance of those who thought it both unjust and a serious political mistake, the prime minister did not even bother to speak to him for over five months after the 1957 election, either to thank him for his work or to explain why he wanted Brunt to have the seat. Latimer was certain that the offer would have been declined but that McKenzie felt badly over being ignored by the man whose selection as leader and triumph over the Grits he had done much to bring about. Despite any chagrin over this, though, he and his people did not avoid the new election. They were active without being the directing force, Latimer for one again serving as Diefenbaker's advance man and witnessing on all hands a political hysteria and adulation of the Leader such as he had never seen before.[21]

Like his organization, Frost was not as much in evidence this time, although his desire for a Conservative win had not diminished. With Diefenbaker riding so high, there seemed less need of his prominence on the hustings. The campaign coincided with a legislative session where, as always, Frost was regularly in attendance and much to the fore in debate, in part because Dana Porter had become chief justice of Ontario and the premier had resumed the Treasury portfolio. He did, though, join Diefenbaker at a couple of gatherings in Toronto, one of them a giant reception at Exhibition Park, and near the close of the campaign they were together again for meetings in Renfrew County where hard-fought struggles were going on.[22]

That Frost was relatively inconspicuous and the provincial organization no longer in charge did not harm Tory fortunes in Ontario, where the party gained six additional seats. In the country at large the election produced a tremendous sweep, with 208 of the 265 ridings returning Conservatives. No fewer than fifty of these were in Quebec, an extraordinary result given the historic weakness of the party there. It was a personal triumph of unprecedented proportions for Diefenbaker, whose dramatic platform style, messianic fervour, and talk of a national vision seemed to grip the popular imagination even more than in 1957. Was he a man who could stand such success or would it spoil him by further inflating an already oversized ego? Some sceptical Conservatives feared the worst, since his self-esteem had obviously, and understandably, risen sharply after the turn-around the year before.

In the aftermath of the 1958 landslide, Frost ventured to offer some advice to Diefenbaker, hoping to encourage calm deliberation now that the excitement of the battle was past. He shared the counsel Mackenzie King had offered him in 1950 about the importance of rest and relaxation. The Chief should take three months off, 'collect around him the very best opinion possible ... converse with leaders of political, business and academic life in Canada, and build up an organization of people and thought, that would enable him to make a thorough assessment of the problems of Canada and the policies to meet them. John listened to me with kindness and patience and then proceeded to make plans for a trip around the world with his brother, Elmer.' As Frost expected, he observed Diefenbaker on his return from this junket to be worn out and weary. It was not, he thought, an auspicious beginning to what could be a time of great accomplishment, and his disappointment was to be deepened by a number of subsequent events.[23]

One of the most surprising (and surprised) Liberal casualties of the 1957 election had been C.D. Howe, who lost his Port Arthur seat in a stunning upset. After the dust settled, Frost dropped a few lines to Howe expressing 'admiration for your very many accomplishments and my thanks for my relationships with you which I think have been very happy.' Howe returned his own thanks to 'My dear Les.' He was leaving public life with no regrets, glad to be spared a period in opposition. The two of them had cause for satisfaction in what they had achieved together. 'I have always felt that you and I could co-operate in the interests of Canada and your Province, and that has been my experience. Whatever may have been said about the pipeline, you and I know that it had to be built and without delay.'[24] Frost also knew that putting down the pipe from Alberta to Kapuskasing was but the beginning. There would have to be distribution networks to serve consumers. In the most thickly populated parts of the province, in and around Toronto and in the southwest, such facilities already existed, controlled chiefly by two large utilities, Consumers' Gas and Union Gas. But in northern Ontario the field was open for development.

This presented a wondrous opportunity for entrepreneurs and promoters to form companies, line up customers, and raise capital by selling stocks and other securities to investors eager to be in on the bonanza. Some would have preferred a public system comparable to Ontario Hydro from which municipally owned utilities could buy gas in bulk for resale to customers. Frost claimed to have been quite favourable to the idea at one time. But he found that in this case there was no enthusiasm for the public distribution of natural gas. In southern Ontario, in fact, most existing municipally owned gas systems had been sold to private concerns. Doubtless to most other communities, short of funds and with restricted borrowing powers, it appeared simpler and more economical to strike a bargain on acceptable terms with companies that could demonstrate the requisite expertise and access to capital. That being so, the private sector was left to meet the need under the regulatory authority of the Ontario Securities Commission and the Ontario Fuel Board.

What became the most notorious of the new enterprises was the Northern Ontario Natural Gas Company Limited commonly known as NONG and not to be confused with the crown corporation of similar name formed to construct the line eastward from the Manitoba border. Incorporated in 1954, it had an initial authorized capital of four thousand no par value shares with a maximum aggregate valuation of $40,000. Its original directors, who bought small amounts of stock for cash at four dollars per share, were Ralph K. Farris, president, C. Spencer Clark, and Gordon McLean, a nephew of Phillip T. Kelly who at about the same time became minister of mines in the Frost cabinet. The company proceeded to contract with Trans-Canada Pipe Lines for a supply of gas and, as a prerequisite of further financing to meet its estimated construction and early operating costs of $24 million, to secure franchises in a number of municipalities stretching in a vast arc from Kenora in the far northwest to Orillia. Thanks to two stock splits in 1955 and 1956, authorized by the provincial secretary's department, of one hundred for one and then of five for one, the holdings of the first investors and other insiders who had bought in grew five hundredfold. Farris's original seventy-five shares, for example, ballooned to 37,500 which, at his investment of $300, amounted to four-fifths of a cent each. These fortunate few gentlemen stood to make handsome, not to say unconscionable, profits, non-taxable if treated as capital gains, if the shares appreciated greatly, which they did. Some, including part of the promoters' holdings, were sold on the unlisted market, presumably for a lot more than those bargain prices, before the stock was listed in 1957, and an issue to be disposed of by underwriters in Canada and the United States was announced.

Some months earlier, Frost had instructed his ministers in writing not to invest in any natural gas company and to divest themselves of all such holdings. Subsequently he had Malcolm McIntyre, the cabinet secretary, remind each minister of this personally. The action was prompted by news of a forthcoming issue of Trans-Canada Pipe Lines debentures and common stock, but the prohibition was not restricted to them. With the province committed to help finance building the northern Ontario main line, which would benefit not only Trans-Canada but ancillary distribution companies, it was important to avoid a conflict of interest on the part of cabinet members. Had Frost's injunction been obeyed to the letter by all concerned, he would have been spared much anxiety and embarrassment. Other aspects of the situation, too, worried him, as they did Attorney General Roberts. Having read in the press about the activities of NONG, including the stock splits, in the spring of 1957 Roberts asked the chairman of the Securities Commission, O.E. Lennox, for a report. Lennox's reply, to the effect that the company and its proprietors had stayed within the law, ended with the curious statement that the profits accruing to promoters and other insiders 'would not have been permitted if ... the exceptional public demand accompanied by a scarcity of stock being made available for the market' could have been anticipated.[25] This did not satisfy Roberts, who in a long memorandum to Frost complained that more justification of the stock splits should have been demanded than the perfunctory claim that they were 'necessary and expedient in the interests of the company.' The whole situation, he warned, 'appears to me to create something highly undesirable from the public standpoint [and] fraught with serious political implications.'[26]

Donald MacDonald, who had been preparing for a major attack by assiduously reading press accounts and interviewing many people in the north, raised the subject when the Mines Department estimates were being considered by the House in 1958.[27] Having discovered a lot of smoke, he was sure that there must be a fire. He began by pointing to two aspects: the means by which NONG had appeased objections to its absorption of a rival company, Twin City Gas, which had beaten it for a number of franchises between Dryden and Geraldton; and the fact, which he found surprising, that none of the northern municipalities had chosen to set up its own gas utility. In both matters he suspected sinister influences which ought to be investigated by a royal commission. He hinted darkly, without naming names or making an actual charge, that 'behind the scenes, the financial boys got into operation' and sold NONG stock to northerners at fire sale prices, among them, he implied, some local politicians. This was done both to silence objections to the Twin City takeover and to discourage resort to municipal ownership. It explained why Frost was able to say that there had been no request that the Fuel Board review the franchises: men 'who might have been making the demand were in on the bonanza.' MacDonald wanted to know who owned all the shares resulting from the splits before NONG's stock was listed. Frost's claim that they were all named in the company's prospectus was too absurd to believe.

This brought MacDonald to the case of Phillip T. Kelly, who had resigned as mines minister in July 1957 and later as MPP.

Now, I want to bring this a little bit closer to home ... All across this province last summer, questions were being raised, and it is an open secret around Queen's Park, and northern Ontario, that one of the hon. Ministers in this cabinet was involved in the pipe line profiteering. In fact, so much so, that eventually the hon. Prime Minister had a show down with him and he was dismissed.

HON. MR. FROST: I did no such thing.

MR. MacDONALD: The hon. Prime Minister did no such thing?

HON. MR. FROST: No, sir.

MR. MacDONALD: Can he tell us, then, why he was dismissed?

HON. MR. FROST: Let the hon. member go ahead, and I will tell him.

MR. MacDONALD: Oh, well now, here is once when I would be glad to give the hon. Prime Minister the floor. Actually, the fact of the matter is that the former Minister of Mines in this province (Mr. Kelly) was involved in this pipe line profiteering, just like R.K. Farris and everybody else. It is all very fine for the hon. Prime Minister merely to dismiss the man. The fact ... is that, in so doing, he has not cleaned up the mess, he has just tried to cover it up ... it is currently said all across this province that the former Minister of Mines was involved in this pipe line profiteering ... I challenge this government ... to establish a Royal commission ... In this way, we will find out just exactly who got these shares, and to what extent any hon. member of the government, happened to be involved in it too.

Later that afternoon, Frost undertook to supply some of the facts in order to dispel what he alleged were misapprehensions spread by the CCF leader, 'a master of insinuation and innuendo, which is always based on this "somebody said so-and-so" and "they said that" and so on.' He reviewed the history of how Alberta gas came to Ontario, the creation of NONG, its acquisition of control of Twin City, and the essentials of government policy, including his instruction to ministers about personal investment and divestment. He then turned to the Kelly matter. The minister's resignation was voluntary and had nothing to do with NONG or any other gas company. It was well known that Kelly wanted to run in the next federal election, not likely to be long in coming given the minority position of the Diefenbaker ministry. The subject of NONG shares had not arisen in discussions with Kelly, who as far as he was aware, said Frost, like all others had complied with his directions. This did not square with Frost's later recollection that Kelly 'said to me quite voluntarily that he had no interest in Northern Ontario Natural Gas Company.'[28] Indeed, the assurance at the time that they had not discussed the subject and that Kelly had retired of his own volition was widely disbelieved, not only by MacDonald and his friends. Unnamed sources at Queen's Park told a *Globe and Mail* reporter that the resignation, once the premier learned that Kelly's original investment 'had increased by 500 times, was a cut and dried affair.' In this version, Frost 'had Mr. Kelly's resignation already typed out for him ... It was simply a case of Mr. Kelly reading the letter and signing it.'[29]

Interviewed at his home in Smooth Rock Falls, Kelly threatened to sue MacDonald if he repeated his allegations outside of the House. 'I have never been a stockholder in any of the gas line companies,' he said, 'because at the time of the Trans-Canada pipeline deal the premier said he did not want any of us in it.' Frost knew the reason for his resignation. 'I couldn't consistently interest myself in an Ontario iron ore company and be minister of mines.'[30] But MacDonald had not contented himself with aspersions on Kelly. He had, Frost charged, on the basis of nothing more than hearsay, impugned the honesty of municipal officials in the north by implying that none had asked for a rehearing regarding the NONG–Twin City merger because they 'had been bribed and had received considerations, and that is what he said.'

MR. MacDONALD: I did not say anything like that at all.
HON. MR. FROST: I would say to the hon. member ...
MR. MacDONALD: Just a minute now. I rise on a question of privilege ...
HON. MR. FROST: No, no, just wait a minute.
MR. MacDONALD: ... I was referring specifically to the area under Twin City Gas between Dryden and Geraldton. To confuse it from Kenora to Orillia is a deliberate confusion.
HON. MR. FROST: All right, then, I will take his own words then, from Dryden through to Nipigon [sic], there the officials were bribed, there the officials ... did not make any application for a re-hearing of this matter because they received something under the table ...

I would say to the hon. member ... that if he wants to make a charge like that against municipal officials, let him come here and name the time and place. I would say it is an unseemly thing to do, a cowardly thing in fact to do, to say to these municipal officials that ... they are corrupt and that they do not fulfill their duty.

These heated exchanges, which ended with MacDonald accusing Frost of twisting his words, were resumed the following day, the former trying in particular to find out who had acquired all the split shares not accounted for in the company's prospectus. Among the few holders listed there was a certain Mr McLean, not otherwise identified. Who was McLean? Frost denied knowing who he was, other than one of NONG's promoters, but implied that that was immaterial. The House should concentrate on something more disturbing, MacDonald's 'outburst' the day before when he had called into question the honour of municipal councillors and others in the north, and of the government itself. MacDonald's remark,

'Now, if the government has nothing to hide, let them not hide it,' meant in other words, Frost alleged angrily, that 'You people sitting over there ... are a bunch of crooks and ... your hands are dripping with corruption.' To MacDonald's objection that he had said nothing of the sort Frost rejoined, 'Now that is what he means.' The exaggeration was patent but understandable. Imputations of dishonesty not confined to 'the financial boys' of NONG and related interests but embracing both unidentified residents of the north and, by implication, the Frost administration were liberally sprinkled throughout MacDonald's discourse. It was not surprising that Frost, who set great store by his own probity and by extension that of his government, was incensed.

MacDonald's persistent queries provoked Kelly into revealing what must have been fairly common knowledge among interested people, that the Mr McLean mentioned was his nephew. Although he had no stock in NONG himself, he explained, 'his family connection was one of the main reasons for his resignation as Mines Minister.'[31] MacDonald wondered whether the premier had not learned this at the time. Frost repeated that he had not, nor had he known until now that Kelly was McLean's uncle. Before long it came out that Kelly's denial of personal interest in Northern Ontario Natural Gas was untrue, that there was more to his relationship with it than his family connection. Early in May some startling news broke. Frost was in Lindsay for a relaxing weekend (he thought) after being up north campaigning in a by-election to fill Kelly's Cochrane North seat. Despite his claims to the contrary, it now turned out that Kelly was and had long been a stockholder in NONG, having taken over half of nephew McLean's stake, and had, he admitted, made a great deal of money from disposing of shares he controlled. That was not all. Blaik Kirby of the *Toronto Star*, having gone through NONG's shareholder list, reported that it included the names of numerous elected officials in northern Ontario towns, all of whom 'deny that they got the stock as a "bribe." They say it was issued to them at market price because the gas company felt there should be some local ownership of the utility.' Also on the list were newly elected Liberal leader, John Wintermeyer, and the minister of public works, William Griesinger, who explained that he had purchased shares in the fall of 1956 and had disposed of them in July of the following year, realizing 'a small profit.' These revelations, MacDonald proclaimed acidly, had but one meaning: 'Obviously the premier did not know what was going on in his own cabinet, and his verbal assurances were therefore worthless.'[32]

This exposure led to Griesinger's resignation from the government two days later. He sold his stock, he wrote to Frost, 'when I was advised of your directive ... I did not, as some have stated, hold the stock for several months. The sale was proximate to the time I was advised of your directive.' Presumably he meant advised by Malcolm McIntyre at Frost's behest, but 'reminded' would have been more accurate. Griesinger held his shares for two months after the original instruction went out in May 1957, but Frost did not make an issue of that in his written acknowledgment of the resignation. 'Many will feel that you have gone beyond the reasonable requirements,' he replied. But 'public life is, and must be, inexorable in its insistence that the standards be high, even unreasonably high.'[33]

All this news brought prompt declarations by Kelso Roberts that there would be, not a royal commission (Frost had ruled that out in the House) but an investigation that 'will spare no one,' and by the premier that he would conduct one of his own. A few days later Roberts announced an inquiry by a three-man board consisting of Gordon Ford, QC, and two staff members of the Securities Commission. Thereupon Frost received the resignation of another minister, Clare Mapledoram of Lands and Forests, in a letter explaining how he (the same was true of Griesinger) had been ushered into the ranks of NONG shareholders by Kelly. The story illustrated, as Frost years later wrote, that Kelly 'had a propensity for talking to people and giving them "hot tips" in one line or another. This was a matter of great dissatisfaction to me and I specifically warned Kelly that he was not to do this, that it was not in the tradition of the Minister of the Crown.'[34]

Evidently the habit could not be shaken. In 1956 Kelly tipped off Griesinger and Mapledoram about a supposedly good prospect, a copper mining venture in Quebec. Both invested in it and lost their money. Hoping to make amends for his bad advice, Kelly then recommended that they buy some of the NONG shares he controlled and both did so, Mapledoram through his brother-in-law with whom he shared the equity. When the stock was listed on the market, he bought additional shares shortly after Frost issued his instruction to ministers. This was an inadvertence, he assured his leader, caused either by oversight or by ignorance of the directive owing to his absence while campaigning in the 1957 federal election. Like Griesinger, Mapledoram unloaded his stock in July of that year and so did his brother-in-law. 'I can assure you,' he told Frost, 'that my connection with the shares of this company arose completely innocently under the above circumstances. I had no dealings with the management ... My dealings were entirely with Mr. Kelly on a friendly basis.' He trusted Frost would recognize 'that I in no way intended, or in fact did use, my connection with the government and knowledge of the things in which the government is engaged for my personal profit.' Frost accepted that in his answer, not sent until the investigation wound up in July when the resignation took effect, and described Mapledoram's actions as mere 'indiscretions.'[35] But much as he regretted losing him and Griesinger – unlike Kelly whose departure he found a relief – the reputation of his administration required that they be let go.

John Wintermeyer had also been persuaded by Kelly to invest in Northern Ontario Natural Gas. He had represented Waterloo North since 1955 and had succeeded Farquhar Oliver as Liberal leader less than a month before these disclosures in the spring of 1958. Frost was sorry that the NONG affair had embarrassed this new man facing him across the aisle, whom he liked and to whom, following the Liberal convention, he took the trouble to wire congratulations, typically adding his best regards to Mrs Wintermeyer and the family. 'The job that I have ahead is a difficult one,' responded Wintermeyer, understating the obvious. 'I will pursue it in the same devoted manner that you have so eminently pursued your work. My hope is that I can emulate some of the outstanding characteristics of mind and heart that you have shared with the people of Ontario.'[36] The job was not made easier by the fact that, thanks to Kelly, Wintermeyer too had been a victim of the failed copper mine. Hoping to recoup his loss and again relying on Kelly's judgment, he bought some shares in NONG through his bank, unaware that they happened to be part of Kelly's supply. Upon being elected party leader, he sold them, along with his other stocks, and this transaction happened to coincide with the launching of the investigation. 'I acknowledge this human indiscretion,' Wintermeyer said to the House in 1959. 'But I am thankful that it came early in my political career as a hard and helpful lesson.'[37] In addition to the three MPPs, two officials of a local improvement district in the north, old friends and associates of Kelly, purchased stock from him. Other than these instances, the board of inquiry brought to light no improper distribution of shares among provincial and municipal politicians or public servants prior to the public offering.[38] Charges would be laid, Roberts announced, against the company, its president, and executive vice-president.

The widespread corruption to which MacDonald had pointed

with alarm appeared in the light of the inquiry to have been much less in evidence than he thought. Nothing daunted, however, he returned to the natural gas fray when the House convened in 1959. The investigation, he believed, had been insufficiently rigorous and had left unanswered some important questions, among them the identity of those to whom Continental Investment Corporation, a Vancouver brokerage, had disposed of its large block of shares. MacDonald suspected that these had gone to municipal officials to help them see the wisdom of awarding franchises to NONG, a suspicion not lessened by the refusal of Convesto's president, who could not be subpoenaed, to appear at the inquiry.

The commissioners' findings, based largely on examination of numerous witnesses, were tabled, as was the voluminous transcript of the testimony. Both MacDonald and Wintermeyer sought to exploit this material as best they could. The debate began calmly enough, with a brief statement by Roberts reviewing the inquiry, but soon degenerated into an unedifying dogfight.[39] MacDonald devoted a good deal of uncomplimentary attention to Wintermeyer's investment in NONG, and that of Griesinger and Mapledoram, but both opposition leaders found particular interest in the testimony by and about A.D. McKenzie. Here was something, they thought, Wintermeyer expressing himself in less categorical and censorious language, that betrayed an improper relationship between the company and the government, or at any rate the governing party.

In December 1954, after having previously refused employment as NONG's solicitor, McKenzie accepted Farris's invitation, suggested by Kelly, to act as its general counsel and adviser for an annual retainer of six thousand dollars. He served for a year, receiving as part of his fee fifteen hundred shares valued at one dollar each, a portion of which he subsequently sold at a substantial profit.[40] On his advice the company employed the firm of McCarthy and McCarthy to do its legal business in Ontario, including its incorporation. McKenzie evidently did none of its legal work and never, for example, represented it before the Fuel Board in connection with franchises. But legal work as such was not what was wanted of him; the company hoped to benefit from his intimate knowledge of a province about which, Farris acknowledged, he and his associates (all westerners) were quite ignorant. In December 1955 McKenzie relinquished his post, informing Farris that this was advisable 'in view of the political position that I occupy in the Progressive Conservative Party, and ... the fact that the Party forms the Government to-day in Ontario and has entered into arrangements with the Dominion Government in connection with the financing problems relative to the building of the [main] line.'[41]

MacDonald interpreted McKenzie's advisory role as putting 'the strangers who headed Northern Ontario Natural Gas Company in touch with the right people all throughout the province ... The picture now becomes clear. The services of top men in the Tory party were available to Northern Ontario Natural Gas – Mr. Kelly from within the Cabinet and Mr. McKenzie from the top echelons of the Tory party. The shocking thing is that those services were available for a return that made each a much richer man.' There had been a lot of talk, continued MacDonald, who had indulged in some of it himself, 'about possible bribery through stock distribution to persons ... in a position to influence the delivery of franchises ... This ... misses the real point, for ... on most occasions ... bribery would not be needed. Enough other pressures and influences, through the Tory machine, had been brought to bear to make certain that Northern Ontario Natural Gas achieved its objective of securing all the franchises.'

It was no more possible to disprove these insinuations of improper political influence than for MacDonald to prove them, although he spent a lot of time in the House in trying, on the basis of quite strong circumstantial evidence, to establish a *prima facie* case to be settled conclusively only by a judicial inquiry. MacDonald argued that the three investigators had not questioned McKenzie as closely as they should have. 'His key position in both Northern Ontario Natural Gas and the Tory party, in light of everything else now known, makes it obviously necessary that the full details of Mr. McKenzie's contribution be sought.' But it was one thing to recognize the value of his advice and quite another to imply that he had improperly exerted political pressure on northern municipalities in the interests of NONG. After all, as even MacDonald agreed, the purpose of the company – to bring natural gas to northern customers – was laudable.

At this point, an exchange of heavy verbal fire took place, with Frost's temper exploding as it rarely did in the House. Under goading by MacDonald, Frost momentarily lost his tranquillity, telling him to keep his trap shut, not to sit there 'and chitter like a pig in a trough ... let him keep quiet and we will get along better. I am not through with him yet. Let him yammer away, and get down into the sewer and get himself covered with it.'

When the raucous din accompanying this little scene had abated,

Frost went on to defend McKenzie. As a lawyer he was entitled to practise as he pleased and not a tittle of evidence showed him to have acted with impropriety on behalf of NONG. In surrendering his retainer when it was known that Ontario would help finance construction of the trunk line in the north, he had fully satisfied all ethical requirements.

The day after this tangle with MacDonald, Frost apologized. The story went that he was scolded by Gertrude for some of his language. There was no jocular reference in his apology to any such wifely remonstrance. 'Last night I was extremely irritated,' he said, 'I am very sorry if I made references to my hon. friend or anybody else which may not have been in accordance with parliamentary procedure. But I would say, sir, I did that under very extreme provocation.' MacDonald's aspersions had cast doubt on the honour of people both within and beyond the legislature, arousing suspicions without substantiation. 'I think the time has arrived that this sort of thing should cease entirely. I do not like to see the dignity of this House affected by the use of language which is un-parliamentary, and if I have used language which is ... I am quite willing ... to withdraw those things, and ... to apologize. I think that is going a long way.'[42]

This contrition, however, in no way altered his disgust with MacDonald's methods. No doubt the CCF, and the Liberals too, would try to make the NONG affair a major issue in the next election but Frost was not much alarmed by that. Scandal-mongering more often than not failed to influence voters in the way intended. MacDonald himself remarked years later on the 'old political proverb that says you can't sling dirt without losing ground and I became persuaded that in politics so-called scandal-mongering isn't a good vote getter. People said, "Well, good old Leslie Frost – he's got a den of thieves around him but he is the only man who can clean it up." So back he would go.'[43] In the spring of 1959 it would not be long before it was known whether in that respect history had repeated itself.

Of course, Frost would not have agreed that he was surrounded by a den of thieves, nor was there good reason to believe that most people thought he was. He did not approve of how NONG's promoters had conducted themselves in the early stages, of the stock-splitting, and the outrageous profits made by a privileged few who had invested very little of their own money. Insofar as any discredit had been brought on the government, he thought Kelly was to blame. Mapledoram and Griesinger had been foolish to get mixed up in it and remiss in retaining their shares after being told to get rid of them. Kelly's sins were of a different order of magnitude. Frost was reminded of all this in the summer of 1972 when he was approached for an interview by a nephew of Kelly (not Gordon McLean), who proposed to write a book exonerating his uncle, with whose blessing the project was being undertaken. After a year's research, the nephew had reached the conclusion that 'the only thing Kelly can be chided for is his lack of political astuteness and too much talking to the press. The image he left the legislature with is unjustly tarnished as you can well understand.' Frost understood no such thing. 'The Gas affair and your uncle,' he replied, 'caused me more anxiety and distress than any other incident in my long public life.'[44]

In Frost's opinion, Kelly should have promptly declared his interest in NONG and resigned his portfolio. Instead, he had not only discredited himself by belatedly recanting earlier denials of such interest but 'destroyed the public life of three very fine men – Greisinger [sic], Mapledoram and Wintermeyer. About this I have always felt very badly.' He recalled that 'some of my colleagues, quite a large section of the business world, and probably Griesinger and Mapledoram thought that I dealt harshly with them in accepting their resignations.'[45] That was hardly surprising if, as Frost insisted, they were entirely innocent. In the absence of guilt, why the punishment of resigning? Frost's view that it was for voters to judge them if they presented themselves for re-election was not convincing in view of the fact that his letting them go either implied some kind of guilt or applied 'unreasonable standards,' as he put it in his letter to Griesinger. Both men were defeated in the general election later in 1959, despite Frost's taking to the hustings on their behalf. That may have been the democratic way of deciding; that it was a just manner in which to seal the fate of two men whom their leader depicted as innocent victims of the nefarious Kelly was a good deal less certain.

Getting on with Dief

The natural gas scandal was not the only vexing political problem Frost had to face. He found himself increasingly preoccupied in the late 1950s with federal policy as it affected the provincial economy. Close attention to that was nothing new, of course; ever since 1949 the quest for a more equitable tax-sharing arrangement had headed his priorities. The Diefenbaker government, even if under some political duress, had taken one promising step towards fiscal justice by conceding a larger share of personal income taxes. Frost trusted that this was but the first of successive steps whose necessity he spared no effort in impressing on the prime minister. It was not easy to get this and other messages through Diefenbaker's head. 'He had much of the Prairie suspicion and perhaps dislike for things that emanated from Ontario and from the financial world,' Frost reflected in looking back. Diefenbaker referred to himself as a prairie lawyer. 'Unfortunately from a standpoint of business administration and knowledge of the economics of the country, he never seemed to emerge from that status.'[1]

As well as policy issues, there were personal and political grounds for Frost's mounting disillusionment with Diefenbaker. According to Latimer, he was angered by Diefenbaker's failure to consult him on decisions affecting Ontario, in the apparent belief that it was no longer necessary to cultivate his goodwill. Frost 'would learn of judicial appointments and the like by reading the morning Globe and Mail' and 'didn't hesitate to make it clear to his friends that he resented very much the treatment he was receiving.' So annoyed was he that he was determined not to attend the 1959 annual meeting of the federal party, which alarmed McKenzie, ever the faithful party servant. McKenzie asked Latimer to accompany him to Frost's office, saying that 'we have simply got to get him to change his mind. Support for Diefenbaker was already on the decline and it was vital that Mr. Frost attend and show his support.' They spent nearly an hour arguing with him. When Frost was disturbed or annoyed he could be exceptionally fluent in the use of profanity and this meeting was certainly one of those times. He asserted that Diefenbaker's arrogance was losing him support all across Canada and asked, 'Why in hell should I go down there as window dressing for him?' In the end, persuaded that his absence would cause speculation and do neither of them any good, he relented.[2]

Believing the prime minister to be badly in need of wisdom, Frost freely tendered advice and was annoyed to find it ignored or rejected, as often happened. The welcome concession about personal income tax, however, raised hopes and there would be no relaxation of the effort to assure that they were not too long deferred. Frost was sometimes more appalled by decisions of the Diefenbaker government than he had usually been when dealing with Louis St Laurent, C.D. Howe, and Robert Winters, until he became fed up with their intransigence over tax-sharing. There may have been second thoughts at times about having helped to replace them with the regime of the turbulent 'Highlander' from Prince Albert. But the party tie and his contribution to the victory entitled him, he thought, to counsel Diefenbaker more than he had St Laurent, although the latter may not have noticed any particular inhibition in that regard.

Tax-sharing was by no means the only major federal policy that worried him. Almost equally important to the provincial economy and public finance, perhaps in some ways more so, was the operation of the banking system, in particular the course being followed by the Bank of Canada under James Coyne, who had succeeded Graham Towers as governor in 1955. Under Coyne's direction the bank, to the dissatisfaction of Frost and many others in all political parties, appeared wedded to tight money with relatively high interest rates and, as was widely thought, a Canadian dollar overvalued in relation to its American counterpart. In correspondence and conversations with both Diefenbaker and Coyne, Frost battled against current monetary management, which struck him as inimical to the interests of the country as a whole and as crimping Ontario's development. It was all the more inappropriate in the economic downturn making itself felt in 1957, when the economy, he believed, needed stimulus, not stringency. The governor's refusal to admit that it was time to press the gas pedal instead of the brake, and his failure, in Frost's eyes, to provide coherent leadership to financial institutions, eventually convinced the premier that Coyne should be replaced.

There was no doubt that economic conditions were deteriorating before the Diefenbaker government took office in the spring of 1957. About that time George Gathercole sent a lengthy assessment of the situation to Dana Porter shortly before Porter's retirement from the cabinet.

Gathercole pointed out: 'As the economic picture is now changing [for the worse], a reversal in the Bank of Canada's tight money policy may be required ... Signs are multiplying that if the policy of credit restrictions is not moribund, it soon will be.' More and more soft spots were appearing in the North American economy. Profits were falling off, unemployment was up from the year before and would be even worse during the coming winter. Capital investment was flattening out and prices of industrial stock shares had declined by 13 per cent in the past two months. The gross national product for 1957 was expected to be only 2 or 3 per cent higher than in 1956, in contrast to increases in each of the two preceding years of about 10 per cent. The Canadian dollar was at a premium over the American, damaging the country's export trade and exposing Canadian producers to intensified foreign competition in the domestic market. Still, while Canada was facing many problems, the economic outlook as a whole, Gathercole concluded, was not discouraging. 'The slow down in some sectors and the stock market decline, if moderate, will be conducive to stability and strength ... We should strive to avoid pessimism, for a widespread melancholia which contracts spending and investment could bring on a depression.'[3]

A man of Frost's sanguine temperament needed no admonitions about the dangers of melancholia, but he could not afford to view the situation with the disinterested eye of the economist. He had always to be alive to political ramifications and the most visible, socially destructive, and potentially damaging feature of the economic malaise was the rising unemployment to which Gathercole alluded. Early in November, with demands mounting in municipal councils, labour bodies, and the press that the province act to reduce unemployment, Frost summoned a number of his ministers and their deputies to 'a round table talk,' as he called it, to consider what might be done and to get organized planning started. Various possibilities were canvassed, among them some offered by the Premier. More public works might be undertaken in wintertime to lessen high seasonal unemployment and in some hard-hit areas invited rather than tendered bids might be resorted to. Possibly extra money could be found to subsidize municipal works and measures be devised to stimulate activity in the private sector, for example in housing. And it would be well to have a continuing committee of ministers and officials 'that could be prepared to deal with unemployment matters and ... have plans on the shelf that could be used if necessary.' In the meantime those in attendance should formulate specific plans for consideration in advance of the forthcoming federal-provincial conference. It was clear, Frost emphasized, that as with so many subjects much depended on federal action. Ottawa should be pressed to assume fuller responsibility for unemployed employables, to modify the tight money policy and to offer more generous unemployment insurance benefits. The ability of a province to cope by itself with a difficulty of this magnitude was severely limited.[4]

Some things Ontario could do on its own, although they were palliatives that did not touch the causes of the disease. Early in 1958 Ray Farrell, who had moved from Gathercole's staff to become Frost's executive assistant following E.J. Young's sudden death, summed up in a memorandum to the premier what was being done. More generous special grants to municipalities reduced from 40 to 20 per cent their share of relief costs for jobless workers who were either ineligible for unemployment insurance or had exhausted their benefits. Renovations and additions to a number of provincially owned buildings in the Toronto area were being or would soon be carried out. The province was continuing to assist in construction of public housing, in conjunction with federal and municipal governments, and along with Ottawa had recently raised its grants to hospitals with the effect of increasing the number of available jobs. Moreover, Queen's Park would shortly offer to pay half the cost of approved make-work municipal projects for repairing and renovating buidings, overhauling equipment, installing sidewalks and sewers, and for maintenance and outdoor work. To encourage local authorities to undertake these projects during the winter the grants would have a spring cut-off date. Farrell also reported on means adopted by the Saskatchewan government to stimulate winter work under a scheme inaugurated by Ottawa a few years earlier. In promoting its 'Do It Now' campaign, Saskatchewan was enlisting the co-operation, not only of municipalities, but of trade unions, contractors, women's organizations and churches to publicize advantages of wintertime work. On Farrell's memorandum Frost wrote, 'This is a good idea – why *not us*.'[5]

Who should pay for direct relief to unemployed employables had been a bone of contention between the two senior levels of government for some time. Ontario held that the unemployables were its problem, the unemployed employables were the problem of the federal government, as recommended by the Rowell-Sirois Commission. But the policy of the St Laurent regime, embodied in the Unemployment Assistance Act of 1956, was very different, asking 'us to look after our share of the problem and ... to share 50-50 with them in taking care of their share ... I argued at Ottawa that if we were to take care of 50 per cent of their load they should take care of 50 per cent of ours' or, failing that, pay a lump sum roughly equivalent to half the cost of relief for unemployables.[6] Getting nowhere with that proposal, he had decided that Ontario, unlike some other provinces, would not subscribe to a cost-sharing agreement under the terms offered. He hoped that the Diefenbaker government would be more generous and shortly after it was installed he set out, working in the first instance through his minister of public welfare, Louis Cecile, to secure better terms.

On Frost's instructions, Cecile and his deputy minister met in late July with the federal minister of labour, Michael Starr, and A.J. Brooks, acting minister of national health and welfare. Cecile and Band were accompanied by cabinet secretary McIntyre, who the next day wrote an account of the discussion to Frost. Cecile and his deputy had made a forceful presentation and had agreed to back it up with a written submission. McIntyre trusted that the new 'ins' at Ottawa would 'not – in the belief that they are in office only on "borrowed time" – fail to grapple with problems such as this' and would 'rid themselves of the holdover bad thinking that proposals by Ontario are advanced solely for Ontario's benefit and detrimental to the rest of Canada. The old-guard members of the Civil Service could be filling the minds of the new Ministers with this sort of thinking.'[7]

Yet before long, as Frost (having temporarily put back on the Treasurer's cap), was pleased to mention while presenting his budget in 1958, the new deal he had hoped for was struck, at least in part. The Diefenbaker government abolished the differentiation between employables and unemployables, would henceforth assume half the cost of direct relief for all jobless, and made a modest improvement in unemployment insurance benefits. A joint public works program specifically designed to take people off the relief rolls had yet to be organized. In the meantime Ontario had an experimental emergency plan of its own, arising out of the deliberations Frost had set in motion in the fall of 1957, under which Queen's Park contributed 70 per cent of the wage bill on approved projects and municipalities the remainder.[8] Before 1958 was out a new federal-provincial public works plan was announced, intended to ameliorate winter unemployment in areas where the jobless rate was high. In essence the senior governments would pay 75 per cent of labour charges on approved municipal works, with Ottawa furnishing two-thirds of that proportion and in addition subsidizing certain provincial projects. Machinery had been created to integrate the work of the seven provincial departments directly involved in administering and implementing the plan, and to co-ordinate federal and provincial participation. The plan appeared, at any rate on paper, to involve a very large works program. There were bound to be countless headaches in administering it, as in any scheme involving three levels of government and any number of people with special ambitions, axes to grind, particular interests to serve, and scores to settle. It did, however, seem to belie McIntyre's sardonic comment to Frost after meeting with the two federal ministers in the summer of 1957 that 'the opinions you had expressed about Ottawa co-operation were just as real today as they were, regardless of who held office.'[9]

In bringing down the last of his budgets, Frost departed from precedent in not reading the usual prepared text full of facts and figures. Instead, he delivered a discursive, reminiscent, and rather self-satisfied extemporaneous speech. It encapsulated the main features of the budget but dwelt more on the growth of the provincial economy, on the ever more generous provision by Conservative governments since 1943 for, among other expanding needs, education, health, welfare, highways, and municipal government, and on the rosy prospects for even greater development. The one serious blemish on the picture he drew was the unemployment rate, but on that score he was able to say that, not only were measures in operation to lower it, but with a rapidly growing population and labour force, 58,000 more people were gainfully employed than a year earlier. His peroration, called for 'all our courage, our enthusiasm and our energy for the great and inspiring task which is before us.'[10]

During 1958 economic conditions began to improve, lending credence to Frost's characteristic optimism. Unemployment, however, remained high and early in 1959 the federal government took a sudden, drastic action which overnight severely worsened the jobless rate in the greater Toronto area, indeed beyond it. Some years previously, the St Laurent government had contracted for the design and manufacture of an all-weather jet interceptor by the British firm A.V. Roe's Canadian subsidiary at Malton.[11] The aircraft that resulted, the Arrow, was by common consent a superb piece of machinery, superior for the moment to anything else of its kind in the world, but the cost of developing it and of turning out the first few units was staggering, far exceeding estimates.

Disturbed by mounting costs and by fears that rapid technological advances might make the aircraft obsolete before it got into full production, the Liberal government began to reconsider its commitment. As political prudence ruled out cancelling the contracts until after the next election, it merely began cutting back on the scale of the project.

Their unexpected loss of office in 1957 freed the Liberals from having to back out. Inheriting this hot potato, the Diefenbaker cabinet dithered and delayed accepting the inevitable. Frost, who was very concerned about the effects of closing down operations employing many thousands of people, was aware by September 1958 that in all probability the Arrow would be terminated sooner or later and had urged upon Ottawa the importance of making advance plans for alternative work at the plant. But when and how the termination would take place he did not know, nor was he either consulted or informed before it happened.

Indeed, the day before the axe fell, the premier reiterated the importance of advance planning: 'The decision in this matter has momentous effects on a large number of municipalities and their residents in this area, and I strongly counsel an unhurried decision which provides a reasonable substitute program which will take care of the problems of the municipalities and thousands of individuals who are the innocent victims of incorrect decisions by the Canadian Government in the year [sic] prior to June 1957.'[12] It was too late. Sitting in the legislature the following day, 20 February 1959, 'Black Friday' as it became known to Avro workers, Frost was handed a note bearing the startling news that the Arrow contract had been cancelled and that all work on it was to cease immediately. He was not outraged by the cancellation, recognizing that it had to come, but he also recognized that how things are done is no less important than what is done. 'The decision to terminate ... was completely sound,' he wrote later, 'but its execution was really indescribable.' It 'was the beginning of the decline of the Diefenbaker government. The method adopted completely lost the confidence of business and industry. In a space of some ten months, the overwhelming vote of confidence of March 1958 was completely lost.'[13]

The method was certainly draconian. Instead of a phased reduction of activity being arranged, the whole operation was brought to a grinding halt and the entire work force thrown out on the street not only with initially severe consequences for them but with a depressing ripple effect on all those sub-contractors and service industries which depended on doing business with Avro and its employees. Nor did the federal government appear to have made any concrete plans for alternative lines of production by Avro. This manner of proceeding provoked bitter denunciations of the government.

From Frost's point of view, why the deed had been executed in this deplorable fashion was of less consequence than what might be done to pick up the pieces. On the day following the bad news from Ottawa, he sent another telegram to the prime minister: 'While the Arrow decision is important the primary problem is what is to be done as a result, on this depends public reaction. All expect collaboration of Industry and Governments.'[14] What means could be found to soften the blow for the employees and to prevent the loss, probably to the United States, of the highly trained professional and technical experts whom Avro had assembled? One had also to consider the serious impact on a number of municipalities, notably Toronto Township in which the two plants were located, in lost taxes and payroll spending, as well as increased relief and welfare costs.

In his first statement to the House about the Arrow affair, Frost noted that defence production was, of course, solely within federal jurisdiction and Ontario had never been consulted about contracts with Avro. The province and certain local governments were, however, deeply involved. They had made large commitments in good faith for schools, roads, sewers, waterworks and housing projects to serve the company and its employees. Moreover, they had to be 'very much concerned with the plight ... of thousands of individuals who have been brought together to service this defence project ... In this regard, the Canadian government has a very definite responsibility and one which cannot be answered merely by a change of policy.' On the following Monday, having consulted with the federal ministry and the company, Frost made a somewhat more extended reference to the subject. Avro's suggestion that it be allowed to diversify and get away from exclusive reliance on defence contracts he thought deserved careful attention. Ontario stood ready to help in any way it could and, ever hopeful, he concluded that 'Canadian commonsense can come into the picture, and ... that industry can be rehabilitated.'[15]

Limited as its jurisdiction was, there was little the provincial government could do directly, other than furnish succour to affected municipalities, try to create employment with stepped-up public works, and devise plans for social assistance to those who still had not found other work when their severance pay and unemployment insurance benefits were exhausted. Beyond that, Frost could and did continue to encourage a 'commonsense reappraisal' which would lead to a more gradual dismantling of the Arrow program and discovery of other uses for Avro and Orenda. In doing so, he sought advice from a number of people, among them the much respected J. Grant Glassco of the Clarkson, Gordon firm who was very familiar with the companies' operations, and on the basis of their counsel persisted in a fruitless attempt to have the federal ministers alter their position.

As the spring of 1959 approached, the attitude of the Diefenbaker government was of less immediate importance to Frost than the standing of his own regime; he had decided to go once more to the electoral well in June. One had to hope that there would be no serious political fallout for the provincial Conservatives, no guilt by association, from the Arrow débâcle. In making clear his concern over its regrettable ramifications and his efforts to organize remedial measures, Frost had tried to protect his flanks by disassociating himself from Ottawa's action without resorting to explicit public condemnation of it. In any event, conditions on the whole seemed propitious for another appeal to the voters. The provincial economy had picked up steam, enabling Frost to dwell on his favourite theme of further development and ever greater prosperity. The hospital insurance plan, for which he was entitled to claim some of the credit, was in operation. Alberta natural gas was flowing in Ontario. The St Lawrence Seaway would shortly open and already power from the related hydro-electric installations was on stream. All in all, he thought, there was a record of solid achievement to fall back upon, as well as the generally very high esteem which he personally still enjoyed and the continuing weakness of the opposition.

In addition, his cabinet had been considerably refurbished since the last election. The opposition could not claim that it was simply the same old tired gang. There had been a few unlooked for alterations in its makeup following the shuffle in the summer of 1955. Fletcher Thomas's death in 1956 led to his replacement at Agriculture by William Goodfellow and W.K. Warrender took over Goodfellow's post in Municipal Affairs. In 1957 J.W. Spooner of Cochrane South entered the cabinet as minister of mines in place of the departed Kelly, and so did T.R. Connell (Hamilton-Wentworth), without portfolio and as second vice-chairman of Hydro. The following year Connell made two moves, first into Reform Institutions to fill a gap left by the ailing John Foote's resignation, and then to Public Works. At that point Reform Institutions was assigned to another newcomer, George Wardrope from Port Arthur.

In the course of 1958 Frost made further substantial changes, partly to appease a group of restive back-benchers disgruntled by his failure to advance them. Four of them entered initially without portfolio: John Yaremko and Robert Macaulay, both from Toronto (Macaulay took over Connell's position at Hydro as well), John P. Robarts from London, and John Root of Wellington-Dufferin. Matthew Dymond, a physician representing Ontario riding, was given the new Department of Transport but later in the year assumed the onerous Health portfolio from Mackinnon Phillips, who had held it since he became provincial secretary, succeeding the venerable George Dunbar, now an octogenarian, who retired. Spooner's shift to Lands and Forests opened a vacancy in Mines which was filled by James Maloney from Renfrew. Frederick Cass of Grenville-Dundas took over Highways from James Allan, who moved to the Treasury following Frost's interim stint in his old department. Finally, in the spring of 1959, while the election campaign was in full swing, the outspoken, irrepressible Macaulay, retaining his post at Hydro, was put in charge of the new Department of Energy Resources, the first in Canada; it was fitting that it have so energetic a minister. Ironically, one of only two new arrivals left without a portfolio before the election was the one destined to take Frost's place, but John Robarts's day would come before long.

These extensive changes since late in 1957 brought ten fresh faces to the council table and one result, as the *Globe and Mail* noted approvingly with particular reference to Macaulay's appointment,[16] was to give the cabinet a much more youthful complexion. Connell, Dymond, Spooner, Cass, Yaremko, and Robarts were all in their forties, Macaulay still in his thirties. It almost looked as though Frost, realizing that his own retirement could not be very far off, had decided that the next generation from among whom his successor might well come must be given their chance. At any rate, so much younger blood could not help but have a rejuvenating effect.

Announcing the election, Frost issued a thirty-one-page 'report to the people' outlining every basic step in government policy since 1949. He noted with satisfaction that Ontario's rate of growth in the past decade had been double that of the United States as a whole; his economic creed had been and still was 'More people, more industry, more jobs, more wages, more opportunity and from these, more productivity and revenues to do the job.'[17] The election trail, travelled doggedly by the three party leaders in abnormally hot spring weather, began for Frost at Strathroy early in May and, as always, led him into all corners of the province. Approaching his sixty-fourth birthday and still troubled by his old war wound when fatigued, he must have found the rigours of electioneering wearisome at times. But if so, he showed no signs of it with his broad smile, his outstretched hand, his knack for greeting people with some remembered contact from the past or a gracious word of recognition. He played to the hilt his role as wise but humble guardian of the public interest, 'like a kindly canon beaming over his parish,' as one description had it. He was not the dictator and one-man government his opponents persisted in picturing, he told those attending a large reception for Gertrude and him in Toronto. 'I come to you as Leslie Frost the man – with no trappings of office – just as a servant of the people of Ontario.' One newsman amused himself at that function by counting hands and reported that the premier had shaken 775 of them in 55 minutes, 'his greatest hand-shaking marathon to date.'[18]

Standing on his record and offering more of the same in even greater abundance, Frost seldom deigned to respond to what Wintermeyer and MacDonald were saying; he had no time 'to talk about the other fellow,' he told one audience, and was devoting all his energy 'to the great tasks to which I am turning my hand ... I must confess to you I haven't been too political in my outlook. I have been too busy looking after human betterment.' But on occasion he did react. Speaking at Galt, he was so riled by something MacDonald had said that he tore into him 'for 15 blast-filled minutes,' so one listener described it, as a 'reckless, glib, ridiculous and absurd man with no logic and a disregard for truth.'[19] The opposition leaders relied heavily on repeating that it was time for a change from a government grown arrogant, careless, and corrupt –

so corrupt, MacDonald charged, that it was 'willing to sacrifice the public welfare to the greedy drive for private profits.'[20] Frost spurned MacDonald's suggestion, agreed to by Wintermeyer, that as the three of them would be in or near Sudbury on a certain day, they should meet there to debate the public business. Why would a crafty fox, running well ahead of the pack, permit the baying hounds to gain ground?

Such a debate might have enlivened what proved to be on the whole a dull and listless campaign. Opinions differed about who or what was responsible for the prevailing apathy. Not surprisingly, the *Globe and Mail* blamed the opposition parties. Wintermeyer was not living up to expectations and neither he nor MacDonald was mounting an effective attack on the government or giving voters a clear idea of what they would do in office or how their policies would differ from those now in effect. 'In the CCF's case we are not surprised. Socialism is a spent force in Canada generally, and in Ontario particularly ... The Liberals' failure to provide a vigorous alternative to the Frost regime is less excusable. Here is a party which has played a great role in Ontario's history, and which ought to be playing one today.' But lacking constructive policies different from the government's, the paper predicted, the Liberals would find their 'biggest television campaign ever undertaken by a political party in Canada' of no avail.[21]

While it was generally agreed that the campaign was lacklustre, not all stood with the *Globe and Mail* in blaming the government's opponents. The *Ottawa Citizen* thought that it was caused by the 'great tranquillizer' with his 'complacent self-righteousness.' Frost, it rightly pointed out on the day before polling, had offered not a single new proposal or reform, being content to stand on what his government had accomplished and the assurance that it would go on moving in the same direction. Only the opposition had made any real effort to debate the issues.[22] Furthermore, in standing on his record the premier was sometimes inclined to exaggerate. In a speech at Hamilton he gave his government credit for the Seaway, 'a fact after 40 years of frustration because your government spearheaded its building' by goading Ottawa into action. While he had persistently prodded to get it started, the lion's share of the credit lay elsewhere. Nor was he accurate in claiming that Ontario had paid half of the Canadian costs of the project. As the *Toronto Star* was quick to point out, the province had shared equally with New York State in paying for the power development but had contributed no money to construction of the seaway itself.[23] But like the press generally, neither the *Star* nor the *Citizen* urged a change of government. The former hoped for a strong protest vote but felt unable to give a blanket endorsement to either the Liberals or the CCF. The Liberal party 'with its present leadership and program' was no more liberal than the Frost Conservatives; the CCF had an attractive program but its promise to finance it largely by taxing business would 'put a severe damper on industrial development.' The *Citizen*, although it mildly praised the Liberals, endorsed no party, leaving it to the voters to make up their own minds.[24]

The opposition parties finished campaigning with a flourish at Massey Hall. The Grits' turn came first. Before a boisterous crowd of twelve hundred, making a deafening din, 'The Liberal Follies of 1959 played Massey Hall last night,' the *Telegram* reported satirically, 'Dancing girls pranced to a 15 piece band and drum majorettes of all shapes and sizes leaped to political slogans.' All twenty candidates in Toronto and the Yorks were seated on stage, 'coated with confetti' and resembling 'bridegrooms at a burlesque show.' As each candidate was introduced, 'Miss Look Forward' pinned a red carnation to his lapel (in the case of one, to her dress), while balloons popped and confetti showered down. An Italian tenor sang 'Sunny Italy' as some present held up placards reading 'Votate Liberale.' Not all the Liberal follies were portrayed at that meeting, Frost remarked the next day in Oshawa, for if all Wintermeyer's promises were carried out, the province would be bankrupt. The next night the CCF attracted a crowd more than half again as large, in fact the biggest any party had in the campaign, and entertained them with an orchestra twice the size of the Liberals' measly fifteen. A cavalcade of cars arrived at the door, each bearing a candidate for Toronto and the Yorks, and when MacDonald came down the aisle, last of all, 'the audience rose to its feet and made the ornate ceiling quiver to the cheers.'[25]

The Tories had made no ceilings quiver nor, as far as the record shows, had they produced a single dancing girl. Frost was unconcerned; hoopla did not win elections. The day before polling he made his customary last-minute informal tour of his own riding, to which he had been able to devote little attention in recent weeks but which only an astounding upset could wrest from him. There was no such surprise but, sitting in his steamy, crowded committee rooms on election night as returns from across the province came in, he could see that the tremendous sweep of 1955 was not going to be matched. Both opposition parties were making gains but far from enough to prevent a decisive pro-Frost result. The Liberals doubled their representation to twenty-two and the CCF added two seats to its previous three. These losses left the Conservatives with seventy-one of the ninety-eight seats, as so often for the winning party quite out of proportion to its 46 per cent of the popular vote. Both the other parties could once again justly claim, although it would have been dismissed by the Tories as sour grapes, that in this respect the electoral system worked very much against them.

To the accompaniment of discordant tuning by a girls' band lined up outside the committee rooms to lead a victory parade, Frost announced the victory and then invited all present to celebrate with Gertrude and him at a reception in the Odd Fellows Hall. The old master's last electoral hurrah was to be marked in a more commodious if less welcoming place than 17 Sussex Street, and without the sandwiches and coffee that Gert had generously prepared for all comers on other election nights. But that in no way dampened the joy of winning, the warmth of fellowship, the fond memories of triumphs past, and expectations of sunny political weather still ahead.

On the whole such expectations seemed justified, despite the net loss of thirteen seats. True, fewer than half of the people, in the smallest turnout of eligible voters since 1943, had supported Conservatives, but their share of the vote was virtually unchanged from 1955. The losses were scattered across the province, save in the stronghold of eastern Ontario where the Tory grip on all seats except Stormont was unshaken. Three northern ridings were surrendered to the Liberals, as were two in Windsor, while a pair in the Hamilton district slipped away, one of them to the CCF. Two others, Grey South and Niagara Falls, were historically Liberal and their capture by the Conservatives in 1955 had been something of an aberration. Most unexpected, perhaps, was the loss of five seats in Toronto and the Yorks, where, but for York South, the Tories had made a clean sweep four years earlier. Of course no one could tell what lay ahead, what effect a serious economic downturn, say, would have on the party's fortunes or what might happen when Frost disappeared from the scene. He was unquestionably the party's major drawing card and whether any possible successor would be able to match his performance was certainly open to doubt. But for now the slippage in seats won did not seem cause for serious concern as Conservatives in Lindsay and throughout Ontario rejoiced.

Even had Frost wanted to be more specific about concrete issues on the hustings, the one uppermost in his mind, federal fiscal and monetary policy, would not have had much of an airing. Party loyalty did impose some constraints and he had no wish to campaign against the Diefenbaker government. He did, however, serve notice, as though any were needed, that he was not yet satisfied with the division of tax revenues. A week before the voting in Ontario, Diefenbaker informed the Commons that a thorough study of the responsibilities of all levels of government in relation to their revenue sources would shortly get under way. This announcement, for which the *Globe and Mail* gave Frost much of the credit, was an encouraging sign inasmuch as he had been advocating such a reassessment for years.[26]

In his mind its purpose was, as he had always seen it, to increase provincial income so as to remove or at least lessen the disparity between resources and responsibilities. But the time was not opportune for that. Gone were the days when he had been able to contrast the fat federal surplus with the mounting debts of provinces and municipalities. The federal government now had its own large deficits and was scrambling to finance them. 'I would have been very happy had I been able to play Santa Claus,' Donald Fleming recalled in his memoirs, 'but circumstances never permitted me to assume that role. The would-be Santa was kept busy scraping the bottom of the barrel to find cash to pay the never-ending bills.'[27]

Frost was not convinced that Ottawa's financial cupboard was as bare as Fleming pretended. He had undertaken to give Diefenbaker a lesson on the meaning of deficit shortly before Fleming brought down his 1958 budget, presumably to show that the federal treasury was in better shape than it might seem. Naturally, his advice had not been sought 'but having constructed a dozen Budgets myself, I have some little experience.' Ottawa's longstanding accounting practice of lumping current and capital expenditures together in reporting surpluses or deficits distorted the meaning of 'deficit.' It set 'a very high standard ... that Ontario has not been able to attain except on very few occasions. The municipalities ... have never been able to do this, and I expect they never will. They amortize and set up sinking funds and other provisions to take care of their capital expenditures over a period of years.' He was not suggesting that the system be changed but the difference between ordinary and capital spending should be explained. 'I do not imagine that the [federal] Government will have a very serious deficit on ordinary account. In all probability there may be a surplus ... I do not think the deficit should be magnified and distorted.'[28] To

Fleming, however, it was no distortion to point to the inescapable fact that Ottawa was very hard pressed for funds.

A plenary conference of first ministers in 1959 had been expected. Instead, Fleming's preference for a meeting of provincial treasurers and himself, to be held in camera with no verbatim record kept, was agreed to, and they got together in Ottawa a few weeks after the Ontario election. The premiers were welcome to attend – three of them also held the treasury portfolio in any case – and Duplessis was one of the others who did, his last appearance at a federal-provincial gathering before his sudden death a couple of months later. Frost stayed away, both in July and when the deliberations were resumed in October. He was content to let James Allan speak for Ontario, of course under his instructions and in language of which he approved. He and Fleming, though, did have what the latter considered 'a useful talk' in advance of the first meeting. Frost, as Fleming understood him, 'agreed that it was not practicable to consider a large increase in payments to the provinces at once and that what was needed was a comprehensive study of the entire field of federal-provincial fiscal relations.'[29]

Commencing that study was considered the primary purpose of bringing the treasurers to Ottawa, but Frost was not quite as willing as Fleming seemed to think to put aside his desire for more money. Allan's formal statements on both occasions, drafted by Gathercole and approved by Frost, emphasized Ontario's pressing need for more money. Echoing what Frost had argued on many occasions, Allan pointed to the province's expanding industry and rapidly growing population (caused partly by a birth rate among the highest in the world) as proof that more generous treatment was deserved.[30]

Fleming's response, approved by the Diefenbaker cabinet, was that the provinces would have to find some other way to satisfy their needs than dipping deeper into the federal purse. Their increased share of personal income taxes previously granted would be extended to the expiry of the current rental agreements at the end of March 1962. There would be no other change in the tax-sharing formula before then. The next plenary conference of first ministers would be put off until 1960. Fleming understood the disappointment of some provincial spokesmen at these decisions but doubted that 'they were greatly surprised after the ungarnished account I had given them of the state of the federal Treasury.'[31]

Frost was probably not surprised that the additional $100 million he equated with 'rough justice' was not going to be forthcoming.

While hoping for something more, he had never expected to get it all at once and he could be patient. But in the meantime there was a new feature of Ottawa's policy, a means of finding more money for itself, that aroused his ire. A new issue of Canada Savings Bonds was to be offered in the fall. Frost learned that the limit on individual purchases, until then five thousand dollars, was to be doubled; he objected to this but his remonstrances to Fleming were of no avail. Having got nowhere with the minister of finance, he turned to the prime minister: 'Our money comes from the private investors not from the banks,' he explained. In the past the market for Savings Bonds had been in an 'area which we did not touch – that of what might be termed the pay-roll investor.' For this kind of buyer '$10,000 is a high limit ... but if you go beyond that it seriously impairs, and in fact could disintegrate, the bond market which is in a highly unsatisfactory condition right now. I want to impress upon you this point of view. If we cannot sell our bonds, and we are pretty much in that position ... we have to curtail our program in a very substantial way.' Frost professed confidence that Diefenbaker would 'give this your deepest thought and consideration and I hope action favourable to us provincially.'[32]

Instead, two days after that was written the maximum was doubled again, to twenty thousand dollars. Frost was incensed and drafted a passage to be included in Allan's statement at the forthcoming October meeting. Ontario took 'the strongest possible objection' to quadrupling the maximum purchase. This policy would irreparably damage the ability of provinces and municipalities to obtain 'the social capital which is so necessary to the development of this great country.'[33] By the time Allan spoke, the Savings Bonds had been on sale for a month. He might as well have saved his breath.

To regret over lack of further improvement in tax sharing (tempered by the promised review of the whole subject), and to annoyance over the Savings Bonds matter, was added Frost's continuing dissatisfaction with the policies of the Bank of Canada and their effect on the financing of public undertakings. He was inclined to blame James Coyne and so were many others. Donald Fleming found himself defending the governor against some of his colleagues, including the prime minister, who thought that Coyne should be dismissed.[34] Frost agreed with this but not because he shared the conviction Diefenbaker characteristically came to, that Coyne, scion of a prominent Liberal family, was bent on sabotaging his government and bringing it to its knees. The governor might be wrong-headed, as Frost believed he was, without necessarily being driven by such a sinister political motive.

During 1959 Frost began protesting to Diefenbaker, a receptive listener on this subject, against Coyne's approach to managing monetary affairs, which in his judgment contributed to excessive interest rates, an overvalued dollar, and a general want of confidence in the economy by the business world. There was 'a policy of drift which leads to disorderliness. My dealings over many long years with the banks and financial institutions have shown that they are like all human beings – they require strong and positive leadership.' The contrast with how things used to be was striking. 'Over very many years Graham Towers built up a feeling of positive leadership and confidence in the financial fraternity. This ... has deteriorated very greatly under the Chairmanship of the present Governor ... Should the whole economy of this country be dependent upon the unrestricted and uncontrolled decisions of one man?'[35]

Several days later Frost and Gathercole met with representatives of banks and investment firms to discuss the situation. Frost then telephoned Diefenbaker, jotting notes as he talked. 'Essential problem is one of confidence & leadership – rests with yourself. Nothing is insurmountable now but it could be insurmountable. Not so much what is done ... How it is done ... Why not discuss with Ed [Bickle]' and Neil McKinnon of the Canadian Bank of Commerce? '... get him on your side get banks on your side ... Coyne impossible – all depends on the hand at the throttle.'[36] Gathercole drafted a summary of the conversation with the financial people. All, including Bickle and W.P. Scott of Wood Gundy, had agreed that the absence of positive leadership by the bank had created uncertainty and confusion in the financial community. Although inflation was a danger, 'present Bank of Canada policy tends to get out of touch with reality. Corrective measures are adopted too late and then applied too rigidly.' And something more than credit restraint was needed to control inflation. 'The Government of Canada should make clear its own policy and supplement monetary restrictions by fiscal measures including an effective pruning of its own expenditures to avoid competing with other buyers and forcing up prices.'[37]

Fortified by this support from the financial world, Frost continued exerting pressure on Diefenbaker not to let the matter drift. 'It may be impossible to get another Graham Towers,' he wrote, but 'people are ready for reasonable, considerate action.' Since 'the Statute makes it pretty difficult to change the present appointment,' what might be done short of removing Coyne? A recent meeting of the governor with some investment men about which Frost had been told indicated that action was imperative. 'He seemed ... entirely pleased and satisfied and ... oblivious of the difficulties of the present situation which, for a person closely in touch with the matter, can only be a subject of the greatest concern.'[38] Because he knew Diefenbaker's political instincts to be more acute than his understanding of high finance, Frost added a warning about the electoral consequences of inaction: 'History has indicated that hard ... times invariably follow tight money and ... that John Public blames that on the Government in power. In my estimation, this was the greatest single contributing factor to the change of Government in 1956 [sic] and it can very easily be the cause of a similar change in the future ... The fact that there is a lot of similarity today is great food for thought.'[39] Thus, presently Frost offered another suggestion, an inquiry by a small committee of well-informed, impartial persons (he mentioned names in business, academe, and the judiciary) into the functions and operations of the central bank.[40]

While the prime minister was being plied with all this advice, in the fall of 1959 Coyne commenced giving a series of addresses which, as they unfolded, did nothing to improve tempers at Queen's Park. Recognizing, as all did, the inseparable relationship of fiscal and monetary policy, he undertook to instruct the country on the virtues of restraint and retrenchment. After one of his speeches, at Toronto in mid December, he called on Frost and gave him a copy, remarking as he left that its recipient 'probably would not like the contents.' That was true; it afforded no light, Frost told Diefenbaker.[41] The speech, and in particular Coyne's remark to Frost that the provinces and municipalities were spending too much, led to an exchange of correspondence which, while friendly, produced no meeting of minds. Frost began by reminding the Governor, needlessly no doubt, of the demands placed on provincial finances by the expansion of Ontario since the war.

As I see Canada in the last forty years of the Twentieth Century, we have unparalleled opportunities and indeed obligations. In the world of today we cannot sit down and leave our mighty areas undeveloped. We have to go ahead. I might point out that in Ontario, while we have invested enormous sums of money, actually speaking from a standpoint of social services, we have been pretty economical. Some people say too much so. On the other hand, we have felt that we should invest our dollars in development, and in creating development we, of course, have created problems for ourselves ... Frankly, we can cut down very radically in our expenditures, but it is going to be at the expense of the expansion of this province and ... this country, and the question your speech seems to bring to me is ... whether you think this should be done. We can effect this almost immediately. We can cut down on hydro expansions, highway expansions. We can let municipal requirements such as sewers, water, schools ... go further into arrears ... I cannot believe that this is right. It seems to me that dollars we invest in these things today are going to be productive of immense profits for this country in years to come.[42]

Frost sent Diefenbaker an excerpt from his letter with the comment, 'Perhaps this represents what you call "the Toronto point of view" of which I happen to be a part.' The next day he added: 'My feeling is that Mr. Coyne's outlook is dismal, unimaginative and, as a matter of fact, unworkable ... it is the direct opposite of what I have been ... advocating and doing these past nearly eleven years ... It seems to me that either he is wrong or I am all wrong and it is this point which gravely worries me.'[43] Coyne left no doubt in his reply about who he thought was wrong. He appreciated the need for large capital expenditure but 'the question must always be asked "How large?" ... The country as a whole has for at least four years been living far beyond its means. I think that to continue on this course would be imprudent and dangerous.' Governments and their agencies should voluntarily moderate 'their expenditures, and particularly their borrowings.' Moreover, and this reflected his concern about the magnitude of foreign investment in government securities, 'borrowing programmes should be considered, and if necessary revised, in the light of availability of funds in Canada.'[44]

Of course, saying these things was easy for one who did not have to fight elections, face an opposition in the legislature, or subject himself to incessant badgering by municipal politicians, school trustees, health care practitioners, and so on *ad infinitum*. Coyne's pronouncements and particularly a speech in Winnipeg entitled 'Living within our Means' struck some people (but not Frost) as presumptuous. To the increasing embarrassment and displeasure of the Diefenbaker government, Coyne continued delivering speeches throughout 1960 until Fleming asked him to desist. Coyne did so but this did not forestall his removal before his term expired.[45] The issue provoking the final rupture was an increase in his pension, approved by the bank's directors without the knowledge of the government. The whole matter soon turned into a frightful public row as the governor, not the kind of man to go quietly under those circumstances, launched a media campaign to vindicate himself. A bill was then drafted declaring the governorship vacant and was passed after rancorous debate, but without giving Coyne a chance to appear before a standing committee of the Commons where the Conservatives, of course, would have a commanding majority. He was given that chance by the Liberal-dominated Senate, where the bill underwent committee hearings. The committee, enjoying the unaccustomed glare of wide, even sensational, publicity, vindicated Coyne, who had exploited his day in court brilliantly and now submitted his resignation.

Who should take his place? Before a decision was reached, Diefenbaker consulted Frost, who replied that he had made 'a number of private enquiries ... and I give you this rough outline for consideration as I promised to do.' If Louis Rasminsky, Fleming's first choice, were appointed, 'he would have to rid himself of some of the top organization.' But Frost, admitting that Rasminsky was able, was not sure that he should be chosen. 'He perhaps has the disadvantage that his background is rather academic and has not been associated with the actual practical workings of the monetary system ... Nevertheless he has a good reputation if he has the ability to give the matter the new lead which is very necessary indeed.' There were, however, alternatives worth considering. Frost mentioned six men, with one exception all from the business community. The exception was John J. Deutsch, 'with whose abilities you are very familiar. He of course is an academic man.'[46]

Rasminsky was offered and accepted the position, which did not displease Frost. But, while recognizing the difficulties the Diefenbaker cabinet had faced in first dealing with and then disposing of Coyne, he was not impressed by the way in which the affair had been handled. He was especially aghast at the decision not to refer the bill vacating the governorship to a Commons committee. Frost would have agreed with Paul Martin's conclusion that 'the whole Coyne affair laid the foundations for the fall of the ... Diefenbaker government.'[47] But he would have coupled with it the Arrow fiasco and a devaluation of the dollar too long delayed until the spring of 1962. In each case the federal regime had done the right thing but at the wrong time and in a maladroit way.

Recurrences

Two weeks after the 1959 election, Frost and his wife were present at a memorable occasion, the official opening of the St Lawrence Seaway by President Eisenhower and Her Majesty the Queen, then on a tour of Canada with Prince Philip. Many dignitaries from both countries were on hand for the festivities but, as the Canadian role in the seaway itself was a federal undertaking, the Frosts were less to the fore than the Diefenbakers and their party. The premier could reflect with some satisfaction on his part in encouraging the St Laurent government to get on with the job, indeed to make it a purely Canadian project, and was confident that the advent of deep draft vessels would greatly benefit Ontario. But the ceremony, for all the presence of heads of state, the attendant social functions, the speeches full of glowing tributes and platitudes about hands across the border, was something of an anticlimax as far as Ontario's major interest in the enterprise was concerned. For it was the power development, not the seaway as such, that seemed to Frost the most valuable outcome.

St Lawrence power had come on stream for Ontario Hydro a year previously, at the beginning of July 1958, when the first two turbines turned over following a ceremonial inauguration on Dominion Day. It was a gala occasion. Frost was one of the luncheon speakers at this event. Naturally he praised the exemplary cooperation of the two agencies, Ontario Hydro and the New York State Power Authority, the skill of the engineers, and the performance of the many construction workers. But he went beyond that in the euphoria of the moment to hold forth, in what he called a ninety-first birthday lift for the Canadian ego, about the desirability of an all-Canadian seaway. This was practicable, he claimed, and 'he wanted to see a stream of traffic moving down the Canadian side of the river.' The people of Cornwall must have been pleased to hear this because 'the Seaway City' was in effect being bypassed by the route along the south channel.[1] But had the Diefenbaker cabinet decided to embark on a project of that magnitude, James Coyne would have become even more dyspeptic about the profligacy of governments.

The man presiding on Ontario's behalf over those Dominion Day festivities was James S. Duncan, whom Frost had appointed chairman of the Hydro Commission two years earlier. Duncan came to the position with a distinguished background in business and public service, as president of the Massey-Harris Company and during the war as an acting deputy minister of defence for air with responsibility for organizing the Commonwealth Air Training Plan. A widely travelled, multilingual, and cultivated cosmopolitan, he had earned in both those capacities an international reputation. Frost respected Duncan highly and was pleased that he had agreed to take on the Hydro chairmanship.

There was one minor but visible embarrassment for Frost when, the big moment for the Ontario delegation at the seaway opening, the Queen visited the Robert H. Saunders–St Lawrence generating station to unveil a plaque to international friendship. The Hydro Commission had chosen a Toronto artist, Harold Town, to paint a large mural for the reception building. This decision had generated complaints from traditional painters and their supporters, which Frost feared might produce a public furore. Charged with this concern, Duncan agreed that Town's mural would be controversial: 'But I would rather be controversial for being a little ahead of the parade than ... by putting a mural into the most modern engineering surroundings in Canada which belonged to the period when power was derived from the water wheel.'[2]

Admitting his own lack of artistic qualifications, Frost did not demand that the mural be replaced but he asked Robert Macaulay, the Hydro vice-chairman, to discuss with Duncan whether 'Hydro's choice of a subject could be fortified by the opinion of some outstanding artists and also the editorial comments thereon.'[3] In forming his misgivings about the mural, Frost seems to have relied, as he often did, on his subjective and almost instinctive feeling for the sensibilities of the people. But this time he was needlessly apprehensive. Judging by the only test that really mattered politically – the result of the general election soon to come – most voters, if they had heard or cared about the mural, seemed able to take Town's creation in their stride.

Because so much of the public credit stood behind Hydro, and because its contribution to the lifeblood of the provincial economy was of crucial importance, concern about its health, its development, and its relationship to the government as well as its public relations, was never far from Frost's mind. As he put the matter in the House, although electric power furnished only one-tenth of the energy consumed in the province, it had made a 'fundamental and far-reaching vital contribution to the development of industry, in the extension of labour-saving devices and indeed, to our rising living standards.'[4] Accordingly, in his argument with James Coyne about the inescapable obligations of the province, its agencies and municipalities, he set the capital requirements of Hydro, roughly estimated at $3 billion over the next fifteen to twenty years, at the top of his list, along with an equal sum that would have to be found for highways.[5] The vast St Lawrence development and the various other new generating stations Hydro had constructed since the war by no means satisfied its need for capital investment.[6]

The magnitude of Hydro's operations and its financial requirements made its relationship to the government vitally significant. Not only was payment of interest and principal on its borrowings guaranteed by the province, its service affected virtually everyone and thus had, since it was publicly owned, inescapable political implications. So had the fact that it was in essence in partnership with the municipalities. It was incessantly subjected to complaints and demands by its customers, backed up by their elected representatives, and although it was supposed to be free from political interference in its day-to-day operations, in the nature of things some of that kind of pressure was unavoidable. The Hydro chairman dealt directly with the Premier – neither Frost nor Duncan would have had it otherwise – but for years a cabinet minister had sat on the Hydro Commission as second vice-chairman. His job was to provide liaison between it and the government and MPPs, and to transmit information and representations back and forth. This arrangement, to which he had evidently given a good deal of thought, was not pleasing to Duncan.[7]

Duncan's disapproval of the role of the second vice-chairman, which did not impress Frost, was as nothing compared to his misgivings over creation of the Department of Energy Resources in 1959 and possibly over the identity of its first minister. Robert Macaulay was an activist who had versed himself in energy matters, not the sort who would be content merely to provide linkage, and Duncan seems to have feared that he would now have to serve two masters, indeed that his direct access to the premier might be endangered.

At Frost's request, Macaulay assured Duncan that 'The successful partnership of the Province, the Commission and the Municipalities will continue undisturbed, unaltered and untouched in any way.' Duncan was not satisfied. Quoting from the throne speech, he wrote: 'It is obvious that any department which is set up to deal "comprehensively with Hydro" or which would "determine the most economic use of power sources" and "deal with the vast financial problems involved in the development of Hydro" would be actually controlling Hydro and by no stretch of the imagination could it be said that such an arrangement would leave Hydro's present relationship undisturbed, unaltered and untouched.' The only way to preserve the status quo would be 'to exclude Hydro completely from the responsibilities of the Ministry of Energy.'

Two other features of the proposed new dispensation bothered Duncan. First, in his opinion, the province should stay out of the development of nuclear energy. The federal government should bear the responsibility and cost for that, as he had argued in recent discussions with Gordon Churchill, the federal minister concerned, and the head of Atomic Energy of Canada. 'Ottawa agreed finally. They would love to see Ontario getting into this field, but they will expect Ontario to pick up their [its?] share of the chips.' The other thing that disquieted Duncan was the intended resurrection of the Hydro Advisory Council.[8] That body, first appointed nearly a decade earlier at the insistence of Frost, had proved to be no more than window dressing.

In introducing a bill establishing the Department of Energy Resources, Frost sought to allay Duncan's concerns. He stressed that it was not intended to change the relationship of Hydro and the government in any way. The purpose was, rather, to secure the means of developing a coherent, co-ordinated policy in the energy field where a greater diversity of supply than formerly was meeting a vastly expanded demand. In the past fifteen years, he pointed out, the population of Ontario had grown by nearly half but energy consumption had almost doubled and would probably triple in the next twenty years. Coal, largely imported from the United States, had formerly been the predominant energy source, but at present oil, natural gas, and electricity supplied two-thirds of the demand.

Now there was an important new element in the picture, Ontario's huge reserves of uranium, the fuel for nuclear power. In this field the governments of Canada and Ontario had heavy investments and commitments, and the development of uranium for domestic purposes was extremely valuable. His government had 'never regarded uranium simply as a "defence" material. We have regarded it as a source of power, as a source of healing, and as an energy source for improving and bettering the standard of living of our people.' Frost waxed almost rhapsodic as he contemplated the unlimited uses of uranium. Not only could it become for Hydro an invaluable fuel for generating electricity, but 'I would hope and believe that 5 years from now it may be, with the advances of science, that uranium will be used to perhaps run refrigerators. I do not know. It may be used to run motor cars ... and I think that there is a tremendous future in the great uranium industry. I think it opened up completely new vistas to the people of this country and indeed to the people of the world.' In the mean time Ontario Hydro was working with Atomic Energy of Canada on a small demonstration power plant on the Ottawa River, while research and planning were in progress for a larger, full-fledged nuclear power installation.[9] Ontario was poised to take off on the nuclear power route. Frost had no way of foretelling what a stormy political issue that was destined to become.

Hydro's affairs, and energy policy generally, were among the most important, but only two of a seemingly endless variety of subjects that kept cropping up to demand Frost's attention throughout his years as premier. Some of them seemed incapable of final, satisfactory resolution, dogging him and remaining controversial during his later years in office as he began to contemplate retirement. Life would have been a lot simpler (and duller) without such good old stand-bys as the liquor traffic and night harness racing to worry about. What would he have done without municipal problems, housing needs, health care, and any number of other matters great and small, to pile his desk with paper, beset him with delegations, and take him to an endless succession of meetings? And, needless to say, federal-provincial relations were always there in the background to furrow his brow and sometimes test his temper over the operation of shared cost programs and the division of the fiscal pie. His interest in all these things was unabated, his willingness to cope with them undiminished, as he marked completion of a decade at the helm.

Frost's stubbornness about night racing surprised many of his political supporters and brought him a lot of 'flak,' but the issue had been resolved to his satisfaction in 1950 with a compromise:

'twilight' harness racing would be permitted with a 7.00 p.m. curfew. Devotees of the sport later caused the closing time to be extended to 8:30 – still early enough to catch the summer evening twilight – but they persisted in demanding a 10.30 deadline. In the spring of 1959 the Canadian Standard Bred Horse Society, headed by Earl Rowe, submitted a brief containing numerous reasons for granting this further concession. That led to extensive consultations and correspondence, the net result of which was to demonstrate that Frost's talent for stonewalling was no less marked than his ability to make things happen. Racing under lights as such was not what bothered him, he wrote. 'What I do not like is the fact that our own Canadian breeders and a large number of our people should be taken to town in a very big way from a betting standpoint.' In the end, however, it was decided that the Attorney General's Department would conduct an inquiry into gambling in Ontario. Until that was completed, which proved to be after Frost's retirement, the status quo would be undisturbed.[10]

Frost, who, despite his commitment to promote economic growth, remained an exemplar of the values of small-town Ontario, believed that the moral quality of Ontario life demanded vigilance against abuses of the liquor control system, against careless licensing, violations of the law, and excessive advertising of the product. He wrote to one of his back-benchers in 1959 that he hesitated 'to remove restraints in this day and generation when I am inclined to think that people drink certainly as much as is good for them, and in very many cases too much. We are engaged in a great struggle for the maintenance of our way of life ... I feel that restraints in personal conduct and habits are all to be desired.'[11]

The amount of time and attention Frost devoted to the particulars of controlling the liquor trade was quite remarkable, no less so as the close of his premiership approached than previously. It did not match as a preoccupation such fundamentally important subjects as economic development, energy supply, or federal-provincial tax-sharing but it was not very far behind. He was still receiving complaints about lax enforcement of the regulations and worrying, among other things, about inspectors becoming too friendly with those they were supposed to police. Where alcoholic drinks could be supplied was also a subject of continuing concern.[12]

Frost looked upon liquor policy as his own special responsibility. His approach to product advertising was the aspect of the whole vexing subject most in his mind in the few years before his retirement. He was looking for a compromise that would appease the temperance forces, not antagonize the industry and the media unduly, and accord as far as possible with his judgment of what was best for Ontario. 'Frankly,' he wrote to one cleric who demanded that the province be insulated from the blandishments of the trade, 'if I could eliminate liquor advertising I would do so. Unfortunately I am unable.' And he remarked to his old prohibitionist friend Harold Hale in 1957 that thus far 'I have held the line but it may be that I am like King Canute.' That comparison would have seemed apt to the *Globe and Mail*'s Oakley Dalgleish, to whom Frost sent one of Hale's expostulations on the subject. He commented that 'like the Government, Mr. Hale resides in the past, which, in his case, is understandable.' Hale's views had 'absolutely no relationship to the present since, I think you will agree, it is impossible to retrace our steps.'[13]

Frost had no wish for so forward-looking a government as his to be seen as living in the past. But he thought it was out of the question to open the door wide, as in Quebec and Newfoundland, where there were few restrictions. The diversity of provincial policies ruled out the national advertising code advocated by some, so Ontario would have to frame its own. Once it was known that this would happen, it followed inevitably that Frost would not want for advice on what the code should contain.[14] Having made the resulting document public at the end of May, he wrote to Harold Hale: 'I do not want you to be too disturbed about my move in connection with liquor advertising.' It was designed 'to bring about very great betterments, including the elimination of bottles, glasses, drinking scenes and family scenes with which this Province is being deluged.' He had consulted 'all sorts of people, including church groups. I think this will be an improvement, although I must admit I do not like liquor advertising in any form.'[15]

In announcing the code, he issued a long statement explaining the situation. To keep out advertising from beyond the province was impossible and to maintain the existing stringent restrictions might in some ways be harmful. Ontario was the chief publishing centre in Canada. Some of that concentration had already been lost because of the existing code. The thousands of skilled workers in the industry 'have their homes and their roots in Ontario, and it is quite understandable that they and their unions should be in opposition to the present arrangement.' The rules must be relaxed somewhat but with strict controls. Transgressors who persisted in publishing elsewhere for circulation in Ontario advertisements of a type not allowed by the new code should be told that the Liquor Control Board 'might feel that it was undesirable to ... handle their products.' But Frost doubted that this would be necessary. The code would not go into effect for another two or three months; before it did, 'there will have to be amendments and changes made to ... conform to the varying conditions with which we are faced ... after consultation with the advertising agencies and publications concerned.'[16]

Unquestionably the industry would want changes. The size and frequency of both public service messages and product advertisements in the print media were strictly limited, as was the creative freedom of artists and copy writers. For instance, while labels might be printed, they 'shall not be presented in any way that can indicate the shape of a bottle.' Brand preference promotion was permissible but nothing 'encouraging the use of alcohol per se,' and everything 'must be within the limits of good taste.' On public transportation vehicles and subway platforms, only public service notices of limited number and size would be allowed, with no identification other than the corporate name. The use of Canadian radio and television, over which the province had no jurisdiction, must conform to a directive of the Board of Broadcast Governors, which the Diefenbaker government had created as the regulatory agency in place of the CBC. This allowed sponsorship of programs but no product promotion of any kind.[17] Touching all bases, the Ontario code also either forbade or limited use of outdoor signs, company vehicles, premiums and giveaways, educational films, pamphlets, direct mail, trophies and prizes. Only the awarding of bursaries, scholarships, and scholastic prizes escaped restriction.

One central difficulty with which none of all this came to grips was the bugbear of advertising over American radio and television stations with an Ontario audience. The solution was a policy which might have seemed to some Americans an unwarranted intrusion in their affairs. In October 1960, after discussions with the brewers, W.H. Collings, now chief commissioner of the board, issued a set of rules. Canadian breweries and wine producers would be permitted to sponsor one hour of programs weekly over American border stations reaching into Ontario. Their commercials must contain no reference to Canada or Ontario. 'The showing of containers, packages, bottles, glasses or the pouring of beer is forbidden.' Collings summoned representatives of the three big brewing concerns, Canadian Breweries, Molson's, and Labatt's, to his office to give them this directive. 'I might say,' he informed Frost, 'that they were not altogether too happy and it is quite possible we may be hearing further from them.'[18]

Not only from them. Strong industry objections were matched by anger in temperance circles. The Reverend J.R. Mutchmor, an indefatigable crusader as secretary of the United Church's Board of Evangelism and Social Service, had got the impression, he told Frost, that advertising of beer and wine over border stations across the line would be stopped. It now transpired that it would not be. He had telephoned Collings about this and there had been a 'heated and hectic' argument. Unless he had misunderstood this new policy, Mutchmor threatened, 'I must speak about it in Church meetings.' Frost answered with less than full candour that he was 'not familiar with the points you raise ... I shall be very glad to look into the same ... and perhaps you ... with Mr. Collings and myself, can have a discussion about the same.'[19] Yes, perhaps.

Some publishers also complained about the code. Partly for technical reasons connected with layout and printing, they disliked in particular limits on the size and frequency of advertisements, and they suggested some relaxation. For the most part, though, their objections were moderate and coupled with approval of the aims the code was intended to achieve.[20] By far the most critical was Frost's good friend Oakley Dalgleish. Enclosing some tear sheets from the *New Yorker*, he wrote: 'Why in the world should reputable firms be barred from developing advertising of this high quality by a silly restriction against bottles, especially when they are used in such a discreet way?' That was only one of several complaints Dalgleish had. For all the talk of consultation, he fumed, it was evident that 'we are now to have the so-called draft code imposed on us as a fait accompli. For reasons which you must well understand, this I cannot accept.'[21]

Faced with sometimes conflicting objections from socio-moral reformers like Mutchmor, publicists like Dalgleish, and marketers in the breweries, Frost accepted a few minor modifications but otherwise stuck to his guns. He thought the new code an entirely reasonable compromise. Doors could seldom be slammed shut. One had to run the risk in leaving them ajar that they might be forced open ever wider and evils one had hoped to evade be allowed in. That was to happen after Frost's departure from the scene with liquor advertising, as with the proliferation of licensed premises. But in 1960 he was content that the regulations he and his associates had fashioned, even if they did not dispose of the issue for all time, would at least afford some protection to the people of Ontario from the excesses he so deplored.

Bowing Out

During his final years in office, Frost, aged sixty-five in 1960, remained no less on top of things, unflagging in his care for a wide variety of large issues and small details alike. As ever, his attention was divided between the activities of his own government and national policies which impinged on the vital interests of Ontario. Of these latter, how the tax pie was cut remained paramount but others took up much of his time, in particular the Bank of Canada's stand on interest rates, valuation of the dollar, and the size of foreign investment. Obviously, when it came to federal action, unwise though some of Ottawa's decisions might seem, he could only advise and did so freely, at times gratuitously. But at home he made his will prevail, as far as financial and political considerations permitted.

One major field of provincial policy that engrossed him in the last phase of his premiership was education, which he said in his 1958 budget speech 'has been for more than a decade, Ontario's most absorbing problem.'[1] How to pay for an educational system that seemed to grow exponentially was a perpetual concern, one of his favourite illustrations of why Ontario simply had to have more money from a grudging federal government. The effort to make grants for education more equitable from the standpoint of need had brought widespread though far from complete satisfaction among hard-pressed school boards and municipal ratepayers. However forthcoming the provincial treasury, costs kept on rising and the government was constantly subjected to demands for still greater generosity. But these had always been a staple in the diet of provincial politicians and Frost would have looked for two moons in the sky had they ceased.

Two elements in the educational picture – the position of sepa-rate schools and expansion of post- secondary education – were of special significance in the late fifties and early sixties, and indeed continued to receive Frost's attention after his retirement. One of the leading church figures who complained of justice denied to the Roman Catholics was Bishop John C. Cody of London, who ad-dressed frequent pleas to the premier for redress. Congratulating Frost on the 1955 election victory, Cody wrote: 'With my finger on the pulse of our Catholic people, this is the term in which they will expect something more definite to be done to remove the financial disabilities which through obsolete legislation still so obviously hamper them in the field of education. As you know, the advent of so many immigrants has made action in this matter even more imperative than heretofore.'[2]

Two years later Cody renewed his call, larding it with a good deal of flattery while permitting himself an implied warning. Before Frost's next appeal to the people, 'the long pent-up pressures for the revamping of school legislation are inevitably going to reach a climax ... There can be no mistaking the temper and groans of Separate School supporters,' not all of whom were 'as keenly aware as I am of your deep sense of justice which is the basic explanation of the growing atmosphere of general good will which has happily characterized your administration of provincial affairs.' Supporters of Catholic schools, 'more numerous and better organized than ever before, are literally unable to endure any longer their litany of disabilities.' But they were coming to see 'that what militates against the public schools militates also against the separate schools and vice versa. This is the sound basis upon which your expected reforms repose: justice to all, respect and love for all, equal op-portunity for all.'

Frost agreed that there was a lot of groaning, but pointed out to Cody that much of it came from those whose taxes went to public and secondary schools. 'Indeed, in some ways the last two are more vocal because there are more of them.' The need was for a system of grants with 'a greater relationship to assessment than ever be-fore. One of our problems is that with the disparity of assessments in Ontario we have to create an equalized assessment of our own, which is not an easy matter.' For that purpose a new approach to school grants was being prepared for presentation in 1958. During the next fifteen or twenty years, Ontario's school population was going to double and finding the money to educate it was the heart of the matter. 'Please do not feel that my urgings for a better tax arrangement at Ottawa are founded in politics. They are founded in the sheer stark necessities of the situation.'[3]

Low property assessment relative to expenditure by separate school boards was most acute in Metropolitan Toronto, especially the central city. Large numbers of Roman Catholic immigrants were occupying multiple family dwellings, and in effect were paying no school taxes. The board there was proposing to discontinue kindergartens and to refuse admittance to all those not on the tax roll as separate school supporters. One school, illustrative of others, had an average of forty-nine pupils per classroom. The board was having to add thirty-five portable classrooms to its existing eighty-nine to accommodate the rapidly rising numbers, and was projecting in addition 114 new regular rooms at a cost of over $2 million. Nearly 15 per cent of its current income was going to be required. Along with its unfavourable ratio of revenue to assessment, the central city area was handicapped by capital grants from the province which under the existing system were proportionately lower than for the suburbs and for many other parts of the province. All in all, redress was sorely needed.[4]

In an effort to meet difficulties such as these without confining the solution to separate schools, Frost announced in 1958–9 that provincial assistance to local education would amount to about $133 million, an increase of 64 per cent in the last two years. In an effort to equalize grants, recourse was being had to a 'growth-need factor.' Frost shied away from trying to explain this, remembering, he said, the time in the Hepburn days when Harry Nixon was presenting Education estimates in the minister's absence. 'Somebody asked him to explain the grant system, and he said that he could not explain it to save his life. I must say that, likewise, I do not profess to be a great expert in these matters.'

The minister of education, W.J. Dunlop, did his best to clarify, although even his fairly simple elucidation made the premier's uncertainty wholly understandable. One of the main purposes of past reforms had been to overcome the disadvantage of rural areas with low property assessments by recognizing need as one of the criteria in determining grants. But new disparities had arisen, affecting particular urban areas where rapid growth put excessive strains on the resources of school boards. Part of the solution would be found in a uniform property assessment for school purposes across Ontario, very difficult to achieve but being worked out by officials in his department and in Municipal Affairs. But even that would not solve the problems of some urban districts whose assessments would be relatively low no matter what the standard. To help them, the growth-need factor was being introduced. It would recognize the specific requirements of school boards with quickly rising school enrolments, and provide them with more provincial assistance.[5]

In sum, the chief elements of the policy were augmented grants, equalization of real property assessment for education taxes, and special assistance where population pressures created a need for extraordinary expenditure. More than the wisdom of Solomon would be needed to work it all out in a reasonably equitable manner and only the naive would expect everyone to be satisfied. Bishop Cody, however, was pleased. 'Congratulations are certainly in order,' he enthused. The new approach 'ably tackles the heart of the problems. Once again you and your colleagues have justified the confidence placed in you by the citizens of Ontario and merited a special blessing from on high.'[6]

Others saw it in a decidedly different light; from their perspective, the bishop's satisfaction was amply warranted but it was gained at too high a cost. In a long brief, the Public School Trustees Association of Ontario objected that, while confessional schools had hitherto received less than their due, the new plan would put them in 'an unreasonably favourable position ... The balance will be tilted so greatly in [their] favour ... that dissatisfaction and discord will prevail throughout the province ... If a disproportionate share of the total provincial grant is given to Separate Schools, the extra amount must [be] taken from what would [otherwise] have been paid towards the support of Public Schools. The net effect is a double levy on the Public School supporters.' This might well be unconstitutional, the brief contended. In any event, 'the action of the government is indefensible. Favouritism is very definitely shown, and at the expense – literally as well as figuratively – of those discriminated against, namely, the Public School supporters.'[7]

There was some rather strong language in this presentation but it was the soul of sweet, moderate reason compared to one that Frost and all other MPPs received from the grand masters of the Provincial Grand Orange Lodges of Ontario East and West. They were still seething over the government's failure to implement the Hope Commission report. And the Orangemen had other grievances. For example, public school grants had risen less in proportion than those to separate schools. In many supposedly public schools in northern Ontario, regulations were habitually flouted: 'catechism is taught; crucifix on walls; R.C. "holy days" observed;

nuns teach in garb; etc. ... the Government seems to be unable –
or unwilling – to enforce its own regulations to protect the children
of Protestant parents attending these *Public Schools inspected by
Roman Catholic inspectors.*' The politicians were reminded of some
history. 'The reaction in 1936 to Hepburn's placating Separate
school voters with public school dollars should stand as a warning
that public school supporters are capable of similar action to safeguard their interests.' The spirit of the East Hastings by-election,
which in fact the document invoked, was not dead, it seemed.[8]

Probably Frost would have been astonished had the new grants
policy satisfied the Orangemen, of whom he was nominally one;
many of them would never rest content until separate schools were
no more. But in all likelihood he was undismayed by the threat of
political reprisal, which the 1959 election showed to have been a
hollow one. He was quite certain that his latest reform of school
grants had brought general satisfaction, above all to Roman Catholics, ironically in such a way, he thought, as to turn many of them
away from their own school system. Drafting a memorandum on
educational matters in the year before his death, he wrote: 'There
has been a very tremendous change in the viewpoint of Roman
Catholic Separate School supporters. Now that the old grievances
and gripes have been removed, Roman Catholic supporters themselves are questioning as to whether or not their children should
not [*sic*] be educated with other children. The old fervour coming
from people who felt they had an injustice' had gone and they 'are
in very many cases turning to the Public Schools.' This was very
welcome to Frost, an example of people ceasing to 'walk on opposite sides of the street.'

But not everything was settled by any means. As the 1960s
dawned, the agitation for full provincial funding of separate secondary schools through grade thirteen began to pick up steam.
Frost was dead set against that. Non-Catholic private high schools
would demand the same treatment and the public secondary system, 'built at very great expense to the Province, would be deprived
in very many cases of substantial support at the municipal ... level.'
The assertion of some that Catholic high schools had a constitutional right to full funding he dismissed as without foundation. He
was not to survive long enough to see that opinion overturned.[9]

If anything, post-secondary education preoccupied him in the few
years before he left office even more than the elementary and
secondary levels. He had always been interested in what the universities were doing, especially in harnessing some of their research

in the service of the state. And, although its financial requirements were modest compared to those of the lower elements in the system, the academic community seemed to have discovered money, to be no longer content to live in genteel poverty. Frost worried that university costs might get out of hand unless means were found of rationalizing and co-ordinating activities to eliminate needless duplication. By the mid 1950s, however, he had come to realize that there would have to be a very substantial expansion of universities, either in their number, the size of existing ones, or both. As he put it to Arnold Edinborough, then editor of the *Kingston Whig-Standard*, 'In its briefest terms the problem is simply this: – Today with seven universities we have an enrolment of about 21,000 students. Twenty years from now, with the very great increase in school enrolment together with the fact that more pupils are taking an interest in university education, we shall have an enrolment of about 90,000 ... The great question is how this will be taken care of ... This is the formidable problem which concerns our people – in my judgment the most difficult ... of any with which this province is confronted ... a tremendous problem, so large that it is almost of crises [*sic*] proportions.'[10]

In the summer of 1958 Frost put down some thoughts about the problem and how to meet the cost of solving it in a letter to his provincial treasurer, Allan. Formerly, he wrote, it had been 'understood that the universities financed themselves and that we merely helped them out.' Now that understanding had been replaced by a very different viewpoint, the universities had been 'coming to us demanding money as a matter of right ... If we were to do everything the universities wanted us to do there would be no money for anything else ... On the other hand, I think we have to agree that the requirements of university training, particularly specialist training, is [*sic*] very much more pressing now than it was a dozen years ago.' Developing the country required doing 'our best to extend university training and education, provided it is not done wastefully and ... is directed to achieve the very best results.' It was desirable to discourage 'society education in universities ... I think it should be based upon utility and the training of the best minds and aptitudes ... we should cut off all of the funny frills ... and get down to essentials.'[11]

There were four possible answers to the 'great question' Frost had mentioned to Edinborough and each of them proved to be part of the solution: expansion of existing universities; the partial or total secularization of church-affiliated institutions, which would make them eligible for government grants and encourage their growth; the development of specialized schools such as the agricultural and veterinary colleges at Guelph into full-fledged universities; and the creation of wholly new ones.[12] Frost distinctly preferred the first of these options, along with greater co-ordination to lessen duplication, and was content that a degree of secularization at McMaster and the University of Ottawa had entitled them to public funds for medical and scientific education. The fully public institutions – Toronto, Western, Queen's, and Carleton – were prepared to grow up to a point, but if his estimate of future enrolment was correct, the number of universities would have to rise. Indeed, before very long he had to revise the projected figures upwards. 'Our university enrolment fifteen years ago was 13,000,' he told a federal-provincial conference in 1960. 'This fall it will be nearly 31,000. By the end of the 1960's [it] will be in excess of 65,000 and by 1980 more than 120,000 – and some of the university men tell me that even this projection is too modest.'[13] Pressure for expansion was mounting as public- spirited groups organized to bring the higher learning to their communities. Behind all these efforts was a body of opinion that could not be ignored.

The outcome in the late 1950s was the appearance of five additional publicly funded post-secondary institutions, at Windsor, Sudbury, Waterloo, the Toronto area, and the Lakehead. (The last of these did not formally receive university standing until 1962 after its nucleus, Lakehead College of Arts, Science and Technology, had offered university courses for several years.) The most complicated to arrange, and in some ways the most controversial, was the one for Metropolitan Toronto, alone among the five in not growing out of an existing entity. Partly because it directly affected the University of Toronto, whose special status set it apart as more equal than the others, this establishment, to be called York, probably received more attention from Frost than the other four combined.

The movement to create York University got started in the mid 1950s and soon was in charge of a committee of prominent businessmen headed by Air Marshal W.A. Curtis, vice-chairman of A.V. Roe & Company.[14] There was some disposition in University of Toronto circles to look askance at the project, the success of which might result in competition for students and dilution of government funding. In response to an inquiry from Mayor Nathan Phillips of Toronto in 1958, Eric Phillips of the University of Toronto explained that his institution had embarked on an expansion plan which was expected to give it an enrolment of twenty-five thousand by 1968, approximately double the current number. He saw 'no reason to expect us to be unable to deal with the numbers of students seeking admission in this area within the next ten years.' He added: 'No adequate university, worthy of the name, can spring full blown from the longing or the earnestness of any one group, no matter how well informed, nor how sincere their intentions.' Nevertheless, while the efforts of the York committee might be premature, Phillips did not rule out the future need for a second university. He sent Frost a copy of his letter to the mayor, commenting: 'I would not take any negative stand that would appear to be opposed to the worthy ideas of this new group ... but if ... they are asking for immediate financial support, I would think their whole planning needs a re-appraisal ... I for one think that we should take a very cold look at the realism of the proposals of any such group in terms of what we already have and to what we are already committed.'[15]

Notwithstanding Eric Phillips's reservations, Frost encouraged the York group to proceed with their plans but without promising government financial support. He did not think well of their request for a capital grant to assist in purchasing land for a campus and warned Beverley Lewis, MPP for the district in which the hoped-for land was situated, against 'any commitments that the Province will contribute to them 200 acres of land or any other amount.' To tie up public funds in land for that purpose would be unproductive 'at this time when money is scarce.' What funds could be spared must be made to 'count in the places that we can get the quickest and most effective results ... We would prefer to put money into buildings that would produce students in a short period of time.' The York promoters 'might very well go out and raise the money to buy the land they want, or buy less expensive land, and we will assist in the building when that time comes. I know you will see the point.'[16]

In 1959 York University received its charter, acquired temporary quarters pro tem on the downtown campus of the University of Toronto, appointed as its first president Murray Ross, a vice-president of the University of Toronto and, unlike some of his colleagues, an enthusiastic proponent of the new school, and worked out a transitional affiliation agreement with its temporary host. A board of governors was constituted to replace Curtis's provisional board. It was headed by Robert Winters, who following the demise of the St Laurent regime had become prominent in the business community, especially as chairman of Rio Tinto Mines. Having had many dealings with Winters while the latter was a federal minister, Frost knew him well and liked him; he thought York fortunate to have secured his services. But the appointment was not so well regarded, or so Frost thought, by John Diefenbaker, to whose notice it came. Winters, he pointed out to Frost, 'is also the Chairman of the Board of Directors of the Liberal Union, and I have before me a letter over his signature in which he advises that "Representatives of the Liberal Party would be calling in a few days on a matter of urgent importance to the Party, both federally and provincially, in Ontario" ... Have you got any idea what this is all about?'

Frost assumed that the prime minister was registering an objection to Winters as chairman of the York board. He replied: 'Mr. Winters is, of course, a Liberal. He was a member of the late Government.' Neither of these observations would take Diefenbaker by surprise. There followed an account of the trouble the Curtis committee had had in getting off the ground, of what Frost had done to help resolve the difficulties, and of the arrangements made with the University of Toronto regarding accommodation and affiliation. These had the approbation of the academics and the University of Toronto board, 'of which our friend Ed Bickle is a member, and he strongly advocated the solution.' Although governors of the University of Toronto were appointed by the cabinet, it had no such powers in the case of York. In announcing the selection of Winters as chairman, Frost had merely registered a decision made by others. 'Mr. Winters has now chosen seven or eight members of the [new] Board without consulting me, but incidentally they are all my friends. Some are Grits and some are Tories. A few more Grits makes little difference to me because I have dozens of them in my retinue anyway ... The Provincial Party is very largely different than the Federal Party. Our supporters in many cases are not the same. One draws support where the other does not and vice versa. It has ever been thus and ever will be ... I expect that Mr. Winters will remain a Liberal. About that I have no illusions.'

This was all very interesting, Diefenbaker responded in effect, but what was Winters up to, 'federally and *provincially,*' with the Liberal Union? Frost left the question unanswered: 'I admit to you that perhaps I have some strange friends. They include the gentleman you mention [Winters], Walter Gordon, Dr. [W.A.] Mackintosh, Ray Lawson and a whole lot of others. I do not know that I

can change my ways and perhaps they just have to be tolerated.'
Two minds having thus met in close communion, this correspondence about the York chairmanship (or was it the Liberal Union?)
came to a close.[17]

Although Frost expressed confidence that the arrangements regarding York had met with general approval, disquiet remained at
the University of Toronto. In the spring of 1961, Eric Phillips suggested to Frost that they get together to discuss various matters,
including York University. He was sure that 'York are off on the
wrong foot, although I well understand the essential requirement
of enthusiasm on the part of the new group if they are to get
anywhere. As I have told you several times, I am convinced that
their plans are too big and too grand for practical accomplishment
within the short period they apparently have in mind.' Frost agreed
to the meeting, no doubt hoping to calm Phillips's fear that his
university's allegedly too meagre government grants would be further dissipated by the demands of its young rival.[18]

There was no doubt that the appearance of the new universities
placed additional strain on the provincial treasury and complicated
the already troublesome task of apportioning grants. After the
death of R.C. Wallace in 1955, the job of advising the government
on that subject was assigned to J.G. Althouse, chief director of
education. When Althouse himself died the following year, Frost
created a committee consisting of Dana Porter as chairman, education minister Dunlop, and officials from their departments to
carry on the advisory work. Upon becoming chief justice of Ontario
in 1958, Porter agreed to stay on for the time being as what Frost
called 'university co-ordinator'[19] but subsequently his committee
was reconstituted and formalized as the Committee on University
Affairs, chaired by Althouse's successor, C.F. Cannon. Neither the
way in which it conducted its business nor its recommendations and
funding decisions earned many accolades from the academic community. Queen's and Western Ontario, in particular, complained
that they were discriminated against.[20]

The committee got off to a bad start with the University of Toronto as well when late in 1958 Dunlop addressed a letter to its
president, Claude Bissell, requesting detailed financial and enrolment figures and announcing that the university might be visited
by the committee's chairman, and its part-time adviser, Dr Samuel
Beatty (who also happened to be the university's chancellor) 'to
discuss new situations. Of course, if you wish, arrangements may
be made for you and members of your Board or Staff to discuss all

matters with the Committee in my Department.' Presumably the same letter was sent to all presidents but the provincial university was not accustomed to being treated like the others. Bissell referred the letter to Phillips, who sent a copy to Frost accompanied by his own angry remonstrance.

The letter should have been addressed to him as chairman of the board, he asserted. 'Rightly or wrongly, for at least the last twelve years, the established pattern has left the Chairman as the sole source of communication with the Government on matters pertaining to administration and finance. I can see no good reason to depart from this pattern which I admit is not, as far as I know, the pattern pertaining at other universities.' He had always discussed things with the premier in person and had not dreamed that setting up the committee 'would result in the Minister of Education being the point of communication with the Government on matters affecting policy.' Furthermore, Beatty's appointment as adviser was extraordinary in view of his position as chancellor. 'I suggest that it is an altogether improper appointment and one which contains the certain seeds of controversy.' Dunlop's 'suggestion that Dr. Beatty may wish to visit our University ... is so fantastic as to suggest that there is some serious lack of understanding between us.'[21]

By now Frost was well accustomed to such little storms, arising from every quarter of the compass, and he at once set about to calm the waters. Dunlop had 'obviously got off the wrong foot,' an opinion probably expressed privately in stronger language, 'but to an extent it is excusable in that Toronto is the only university with that particular set-up.' Frost directed the committee to meet with Phillips and Bissell. Dunlop would have a 'frank discussion' with Beatty and keep Frost informed of developments. Soon Beatty informed the minister that the university board had considered the case and the arrangement had been 'squared' with Phillips. Therefore Beatty would like to carry on in his advisory capacity.[22] This suited Frost, whose idea it had apparently been that he be asked to serve.

Like many of its sister institutions, the University of Toronto was dissatisfied with the size of provincial grants. In the spring of 1960 Phillips despatched a long letter complaining about the discrepancy between what had been asked for in maintenance and capital subsidies and what had been forthcoming. For 1960–1 the shortfall was nearly $3 million. Not only would this reduction, as Phillips chose to term it, create serious operating difficulties, 'the methods by which the reduced grant has been determined gives [sic] rise to real apprehension as to the future of the University.' Frost referred the letter to George Gathercole and instructed him to meet with Phillips to try to straighten things out.

In a typically detailed and cogent report to the premier about the meeting, at which he was accompanied by several other officials and Phillips by Bissell and the university's administrative vice-president, Gathercole pointed out that the university's maintenance grants had nearly doubled in the past five years. For 1960–1 it had originally requested 40 per cent more than it received for the preceding year, which had struck the Committee on University Affairs as excessive. Since then the university had scaled down its request by effecting various economies but Gathercole saw danger in overdoing retrenchment. It was imperative that all the post-secondary institutions grow, and to 'a moderate degree stockpiling staff in advance of needs may be necessary.' In view of the demands which such growth would impose on the provincial treasury, 'the need for economy has to be constantly stressed. On the other hand, it would be unfortunate if our program was so stringent as to create an atmosphere of uncertainty and militated against long term planning.' Having weighed these considerations, Gathercole outlined a number of options: various combinations of higher tuition fees, increased government grants, and short-term borrowing by the university to cover possible deficits.

On the capital side, the university was asking for more than $11 million, part of it to make up the difference, as Phillips saw it, between what it had been promised and had received for the past three years. It was suggested to Phillips and Bissell that so large an increase 'was from budgetary and other points of view fraught with the greatest difficulty. Consideration had to be given to the grants payable to other universities as well as the unbalancing effect on the Province's own budget.'[23] Being no stranger to the imperatives of compromise, Frost would willingly accept more discussion, while being well aware that the University of Toronto would not, any more than the others, be fully satisfied with what it was found possible to do.

A few months before this latest of Phillips's many pleas for more money, William Dunlop, in failing health and weary of holding one of the most onerous portfolios in the government since 1951, retired. As his successor, Frost chose John Robarts, whose work for the past year on various committees, and especially as a member of the Ontario Water Resources Commission, had caught the premier's eye. With his somewhat strait-laced outlook, Frost was inclined to look askance at Robarts's rather flamboyant lifestyle, but those habits had not seemed to interfere with the effective performance of his public duties. Perhaps this younger, more vigorous man would free him from so much involvement with the department's affairs. But of course Frost was certain to keep a close eye on any department spending that much money and administering so important an aspect of policy, no matter who was minister. Although not a shining star in the House or at the cabinet table, Robarts seemed to possess a lot of the good, pragmatic common sense that Frost admired and his performance as minister of education would add greatly to his reputation.[24]

There were to be only a few more changes in the cabinet before Frost stepped down. In the spring of 1960 Mackinnon Phillips resigned and was succeeded as provincial secretary by John Yaremko, who remained also minister of transport. Six months later, however, the latter post was assumed by a newcomer, Leslie Rowntree of York West, and at the same time two new ministers without portfolio were added – Allan Grossman, who had wrested Toronto St Andrew from Joe Salsberg, and W.A. Stewart from Middlesex North. Grossman was the first Jew to sit in a Tory cabinet and, his biographer writes, during the Frost regime 'Jews and Tories began to feel comfortable together.' He had no official duties but he 'knew that Frost expected him to advance the party's interest in the Jewish community.'[25] Yaremko had much the same function among the Ukrainians, and perhaps other ethnic groups, to help the party shed its image as the exclusive preserve of the old Wasp society.

Those final ministerial changes were still to come as Frost headed for Ottawa in late July 1960 for yet another dominion-provincial conference. (The Diefenbaker government had restored 'Dominion' in place of 'federal.') It was to consider a lengthy agenda headed as usual by tax-sharing arrangements. The prime minister offered no specific proposals and made the wholly safe prediction that one or more additional conferences would be needed to work out a replacement for the tax rental agreements due to expire in 1962. The premiers responded each with his own variation of the same old tune: they wanted more money. For his part, Frost delivered what was in all essentials the speech he had given on previous such occasions and before other audiences, stressing the burdensome obligations of provincial and municipal governments and the injustice of the existing division of direct tax revenues. Justice to Ontario, whence the bulk of revenue to finance them came, required steady progress towards giving the provinces half the proceeds from personal and corporate income taxes. Failing this solution, much preferred by Frost, the federal government should initiate a constitutional amendment permitting an indirect provincial sales tax.[26]

Faced with its own serious financial problems, the Diefenbaker government was understandably averse to reducing its tax share to the extent desired by Ontario. Donald Fleming wrote later that the demand for half the yield of the three fields 'was an utterly preposterous claim and was not taken seriously.'[27] In private conversations during the conference, Diefenbaker evidently chided Frost for far exceeding his earlier demand for a 15-15-50 per cent share. Upon returning to Toronto, Frost sent the prime minister a copy of his speech at the Massey Hall rally in the spring of 1957, pointing out that it contained a claim to 50 per cent of each, to be achieved over a period of years. This was what he had asked for, too, at the 1955 federal-provincial conference, as he had in the one just concluded. 'There is no difference in my stand now and then.' Diefenbaker, he added diplomatically, had 'handled the Conference excellently. It is a difficult task but you used tact and patience, and everything worked out well.'[28]

One pleasant feature of the conference, to Frost, was the demeanour of Jean Lesage, who had recently become premier of Quebec upon the collapse of the Union Nationale following the deaths in rapid succession of Maurice Duplessis and his successor, Paul Sauvé. 'Lesage seems to be a very personable, well-informed man,' Frost told Dana Porter. 'His attitude is very much different than that which we became used to. This, of course, is not in any way disrespectful to Maurice who was a very great man in his own right, but it is a very complete change of atmosphere and approach.' Frost was agreeably surprised when Lesage brought up the desirability of patriating the British North America Act, efforts to do which had thus far been abortive thanks partly to Duplessis's insistence on the right to veto amendments to certain sections of the act. Frost had agreed to exchange views on the subject with Lesage and wanted Porter to refresh his memory about the position Ontario had taken in the past. 'You will remember ... my visit to Maurice's suite which he terminated with the statement "When I die I do not want them to spit on my coffin." '[29] Lesage seemed to have no such fear, but would he really prove to be more flexible than Duplessis?

Another project Lesage had in mind was to convene a provincial conference in Quebec City before the end of 1960, which Diefenbaker would be invited to attend as an observer, not a participant. Was Lesage out to duplicate the performance of another Liberal Quebec premier, Honoré Mercier, who had staged such a gathering in 1887 at which most of the premiers had ganged up on Sir John A. Macdonald? When Lesage broached the subject to him informally at the federal-provincial conference, Frost's comment was, as Lesage recalled it, 'All right, Jean, as long as we restrict our meetings to provincial matters ... there must not be any ganging up on Ottawa.' Such a get-together might foster provincial collegiality and, he told the House, was 'something that I have favoured for a great many years and as a matter of fact have endeavoured to bring about. But sometimes invitations from Ontario are not as acceptable as they are from some of the other provinces.'[30] He accepted Lesage's invitation, remarking that it might lead to the formation of a body similar to the American Council of States and adding: 'Our principal objective ... must be to strengthen the provincial level of government which still suffers from the wartime concentration of powers in federal hands.'[31] The meeting took place early in December in the very room where Mercier had held his conclave, without Diefenbaker but with a federal official observing and Frost presiding at Lesage's suggestion, as Oliver Mowat had in 1887. It was agreed to make it an annual event, with the next one in Charlottetown. No concerted onslaught on the federal government occurred. Although some unidentified premiers were thought to believe that 'the meetings should be used as a means of enabling the provinces to reach unanimous agreement on their stand in relation to fiscal and other problems involving the Federal Government, this idea was firmly quashed.' Nor was progress made respecting patriation, the time for which lay more than twenty years in the future.[32]

If Frost entertained any hope that the Diefenbaker cabinet would move boldly towards 50-50-50, he was disabused of it when the dominion-provincial conference reconvened *in camera* in October. Diefenbaker surprised the premiers by proposing that tax rentals be ended altogether and that Ottawa reduce its major direct taxes by the amount of the existing abatements, that is, 13 and 9 per cent for personal income and corporation taxes respectively and 50 per cent for succession duties. In other words, the provinces would be able to levy up to those limits without subjecting their people to double taxation. Equalization payments would be continued for a further five years but only at their current levels. Frost was not averse to abolishing tax rentals, far from it, but the present abatements fell so short of what he wanted that a refusal to adjust them would represent outright rejection of his claims. Was it for this that he had helped oust the Liberals in 1957? Of course any province would be free to tax corporate and personal incomes at rates above the abatements but, as Frost had said at the July meeting, 'in practice they cannot. The hard inescapable fact is that with [combined federal and provincial] corporation income tax now at 52 per cent in Ontario, 2 per cent above the Canadian average, and personal income tax at virtually a peacetime high, these taxes are at levels that cannot be increased without serious effects on the ability and the willingness of our people to work and save.'33 His reply to Diefenbaker now, however, was said to have been mild compared to some others. The die had not yet been finally cast.

On the second day of the resumed conference word leaked out of a possible compromise. Ottawa might consider a 15-15-50 formula, long since suggested by Frost as a first step towards the ultimate goal, provided that Ontario could rustle up provincial agreement to the freezing of equalization payments. That would take some doing. Naturally, none of the recipients wanted it and Lesage was reported to be the big obstacle, although he favoured the more generous division of tax money. So did Frost, of course; it might obviate the need for a retail sales tax. He was certain that a provincial sales tax in any form, direct or indirect, while undoubtedly lucrative, would be regressive, costly to administer, and widely unpopular, a much inferior substitute for a fair share of the major direct fields.34

The premiers went home to mull over the federal proposition before the conference met again in February 1961. When it did, Diefenbaker announced what his government was going to do, and in effect ruled out changes of substance in it. Tax rentals would be ended and Ottawa would increase abatements for the major direct taxes in stages over five years, on personal income, for example, from the current 13 per cent to 20 per cent by 1967. This would afford Ontario roughly $18 million of additional revenue in the first year, assuming the continuance of existing tax rates, and a similarly modest increase from the corporation tax. Equalization payments would continue but be calculated differently, in a way advantageous to some provinces but not to others and with Ontario still left out. A stabilization formula would prevent a greater than 5 per cent reduction of revenue for any province and all could set their own taxes below, at or above the abatement levels as they chose.

Donald Fleming has described the federal offer as the most generous ever made. The premiers of Quebec, New Brunswick, Saskatchewan, and British Columbia, however, were strongly critical in talking to reporters, while others, with the notable exception of Frost, said they were more or less satisfied. He was said to be almost indifferent, although he did allow himself to protest that the plan was very far removed from the province's requirements, an understatement if ever there was one, given his estimate of requirements.[35] Fleming found him unhelpful, 'notwithstanding the encouragement he had given us beforehand to believe that he would support our package.'[36] It is not easy to imagine Frost intending such encouragement. For several years he had claimed that Ontario needed an additional $100 million and had recently increased that amount by 50 per cent. The figure may have been in part a bargaining chip but, if so, he had got much the worst of the bargain. After all the conferences over so many years, all the speeches and letters, all the face-to-face discussions with federal politicians of both parties, his quest for what he saw as fiscal justice for Ontario had ended in failure. The retail sales tax, to which he had often expressed an aversion, now seemed unavoidable. When Allan presented his 1961 budget it included a 3 per cent levy. He pointed out that seven provinces, to say nothing of thirty-four American states, were already taxing retail sales, that a number of goods would be exempt, and that $150 million of annual revenue would be generated. Ottawa having shirked its duty, Ontario consumers would have to take up the slack.[37]

Disappointment over this outcome may have been among the factors reinforcing Frost's determination in the spring of 1961 to retire before the year was out. He had, however, made plans a good deal earlier to do so. Shortly after the 1959 provincial election, A.D. McKenzie told Hugh Latimer that the premier had confided in him his intention to step aside in a couple of years and that he, McKenzie, would resign the party presidency at the same time. In May 1960, however, McKenzie died suddenly from a heart seizure and Latimer had the task in the early hours of the morning to telephone the bad news to Frost in Lindsay. 'Hugh,' said Frost, 'this is a dark day for the Tory Party and I have lost my political right arm.' The two of them visited the funeral parlour the next evening and on their way back to the Royal York, Frost asked Latimer to take over as chairman of organization, saying, 'You know the way we have worked together and as long as I am around I don't want someone around who will disturb our way of doing things.'[38]

McKenzie and Latimer had discussed who should succeed the former as president and they agreed on Elmer Bell, an Exeter lawyer and a vice-president of the party, 'an able person with sound judgment and an unassuming person which appealed to Mr. McKenzie.' Upon the latter's death, Latimer so advised Frost, who was agreeable. Frost had not the slightest objection to Bell but without McKenzie things would never be the same again, even with the ever dependable Latimer in charge of organization. He had grown so accustomed to his almost daily confabs with McKenzie at the Royal York, had come to rely so implicitly on his advice and judgment, that no one, however well qualified, could entirely fill the void. Thus the loss of McKenzie must have made the prospect of retirement easier to face.

There were, however, more compelling reasons for him to step aside than McKenzie's death or discomfiture over the result of the tax-sharing dispute. He was sixty-five years old and did not want to run the risk of his death leaving the party in a leaderless state, as had happened when Sir John A. Macdonald and, more recently, Maurice Duplessis died. If he stayed on to fight another election, perhaps in 1963, he would, assuming victory, be expected to remain in office for another couple of years after that, by which time he would be in his seventies.

A political party, he went on, should refresh itself with new leadership at regular intervals and there were several younger men well qualified to take his place. 'He said,' as Latimer recalled the conversation, 'that in the light of time there were some positions that he had taken that should be changed.' A new man 'could divorce himself from unpopular things of the Frost government and literally be a new government.' He admitted that it was not an easy decision to make. What did Latimer think? 'I told him that if I allowed my emotions to govern my thinking I would say it was the end of our party but I did think his reasoning was sound.'[39] Later on Frost asked Latimer to come to Pleasant Point to consider how and when the decision should be announced. Press speculation had been sparked, as he expected, by a passage in his speech at Sir John A. Macdonald's graveside at Cataraqui Cemetery in Kingston. John A's death had 'created a great void in Canadian political life which took some years to fill, in the country, and many years within his own Party. Looking back in the light of history I think we can say it is a mistake not to recognize the physical frailty and limitations of a human being. And not to recognize that the building of leadership is a constant process.' A reporter called him about the bearing of this on his own future and he said jokingly that his wife made the decisions and he would have to consult her. Gertrude herself was questioned by a newsman about her husband's possible retirement and her response was that 'it is news to me, I think it is just wishful thinking. Of course I would appreciate him having an easier time.'[40]

It was decided that he would first notify the cabinet and then send a formal letter to Elmer Bell, who was by now aware of his intention. During a cabinet meeting at the end of June, he told his colleagues that he was going to retire and that they should 'consider the matter.'[41] His letter to Bell tactfully omitted age as a reason, since it was rumoured that James Allan, older than he, hoped to succeed him. After pointing out that he had been premier longer than anyone else save Sir Oliver Mowat, he wrote that 'it is time to reassess the leadership of the Party with a view to the development of the very great talent it possesses. It would be best to elect a new leader 'at a time when the Party is in power, when it is strong and when its prospects are bright ... The strengthening of the Party, the development of talent and the maintenance of its vigour are the basic reasons for the decision.'[42] Bell at once issued a press release, to which Frost's letter was appended, announcing a meeting to decide the time and place of a leadership convention.

Once the news was made public, Frost began to receive a steady stream of letters, almost all regretful and warmly appreciative of his service. The press reacted in much the same way, with a few exceptions. The *Toronto Star* gave the story only modest front-page coverage, under the respectful heading 'Grand Old Man Frost to Retire,' and refrained altogether from editorial comment. Its attention was concentrated on the birth of the New Democratic party then taking place and the selection of T.C. Douglas as its leader. At the other extreme, the *Telegram*, like the good Tory paper it was, gave the story front-page play under a headline of blockbuster size, 'Frost to Ottawa?' Rumours about that were again rife and the paper predicted that he would become government leader in the Senate with a seat in the Diefenbaker cabinet. The whole of one inside page was given over to stories about Frost's record and speculation about his successor. Editorially, the paper declared that his career had 'touched and changed the life of Ontario in countless ways,' and we 'will not, in our time, see his like again.'

The reaction of Toronto's third daily paper lay between the casual indifference of the *Star* and the *Telegram*'s glowing tribute. Frost's announcement got a big play as the *Globe and Mail*'s lead story but the editorial notice of it was surprisingly restrained, considering that Oakley Dalgleish was closer to Frost than any other editor or publisher. It merely referred to what were considered two of his most striking characteristics: devotion to the province and the Conservative party and intense orderliness, exemplified by his careful arrangements for the succession.[43]

Who the new man would be was the burning question. There was no shortage of ambition to assume the crown; when the convention opened in Varsity Arena in October, seven candidates were in the field, all but one cabinet ministers: James Allan, Matthew Dymond, John Robarts, Kelso Roberts, Robert Macaulay, and George Wardrope. The seventh was A.M. Downer, a former Speaker of the House. It was generally agreed that the real race was between Allan, Roberts, Macaulay, and Robarts. Frost regretted Allan's entry, not because he lacked regard for the man but because he thought him too old and better able to serve as the sheet anchor of the new administration. Frost kept his preference to himself, except to say to some of his close confidants that either Macaulay or Robarts should top the poll. Harry Price thought that, like Fred Gardiner and Oakley Dalgleish, he at first leaned towards Macaulay but later came around to Price's view that Robarts would be the better choice. Allan Grossman suspected as the leadership campaign went on that Frost, while carefully avoiding any public indication of his wishes, was quietly lining up support for Robarts behind the scenes. In any event, Robarts led throughout in the voting, with Roberts and Macaulay next, but he was not elected until the sixth ballot after Macaulay withdrew and joined the Robarts camp.[44]

This climax had been preceded on the convention's first evening by a rousing tribute to Frost which went on for nearly three hours before about twenty-five hundred noisy delegates and party supporters. The premier and Gertrude were led onto the stage by three skirling pipers (how often that had happened!) and then the band of the Governor General's Horse Guards broke into 'For He's a Jolly Good Fellow.' Compliments rained upon his head in a flow of oratory and Gertrude's grand-nephew, Bobby Beal, presented him with a gift on behalf of the Progressive Conservative party, the keys to a new station wagon. Frost, in a relaxed, reflective mood, spoke reminiscently for forty minutes, recalling the names of many with whom he had been associated over the years – among them Drew, Kennedy, Dunbar, J.M. Macdonnell, McKenzie, E.W. Bickle – and not forgetting to mention two recently deceased friends,

James Maloney, a colleague, and Harry Nixon, for so long an MPP, briefly premier, an adversary with whom Frost had always enjoyed tilting lances and sharing a love of the parliamentary scene. Naturally Frost called for a closing of ranks behind the new leader and promised that his advice would be available if and when requested. No less naturally, he urged his listeners to look forward, to create a future for the party and the province even greater than the recent past.

Indeed it was a jolly good fellow whom they were saluting that evening but, as they all knew, he was much more than that: a superbly competent leader ideally suited to his time and place; a consummate manager of men and balancer of forces, whose retentive mind was steeped in both the broad outlines and the manifold details of the public business; one eager to listen and learn, willing to compromise but unafraid to decide and, with very rare exceptions, to take responsibility for his decisions; above all, perhaps, a man deeply, genuinely committed to public service, whose forceful personality, engaging ways, enormous energy and buoyant spirit were devoted with a whole heart, not alone to keeping 'the people's party' in power, but to making it an agent of the common good. The exercise of power brought him untold satisfaction but he did not value power for its own sake. His would be an exceptionally hard act to follow.

The Laird of Lindsay

The new government was sworn in on 8 November. Having been so much in the public eye, so long engrossed in affairs of state, accustomed to giving directions and having them obeyed, Leslie Frost would have found a rocking chair retirement unbearable. He was given an office in the legislative building and a few years later Donald MacDonald encountered him in a corridor. 'You know, Donald,' said Frost, 'when I come in here, I don't feel at home. Things have so changed.' MacDonald reflected, 'For a man who had literally ruled Queen's Park for twelve years, it was a little sad.'[1] But for now, Frost did not feel at all sad. His concern with public issues was as lively as ever, his energy scarcely if at all impaired. So without having to search for them, he found a number of activities to engage his mind. Some of these sprang from long-standing interests, for example in education and the history of Ontario; others came his way because of the position he had occupied and the respect in which he was held. With him, he once remarked, it was not so much retirement as a change of occupation. There was nothing new, however, about one of his occupations after 8 November – to serve in every way he could the fortunes of the Conservative party. On the day of his retirement he promised Diefenbaker: 'I just want to say that my interest in the grand old Party will remain as active as ever ... To the Party I have devoted most of the active years of my life. This I propose to do in the future ... I am interested in your success and the Party's success. It will be a pleasure always to give my aid and support.'[2]

But would this extend to accepting a federal appointment of some kind? Diefenbaker, not for the first time, was pressing him to do so. On various occasions Frost had declined a portfolio and leadership in the Senate. A few weeks before the change of government in Ontario, the two men talked over the prime minister's latest proposal, that Frost become ambassador to Washington or, failing that, a senator without leadership duties. After consulting Gertrude, whose marked aversion was probably little greater than his own, he rejected both suggestions, the second more equivocally than the first. It would be a signal honour, he assured Diefenbaker, to occupy such an important position as ambassador. 'There are very many aspects which are of great personal interest and attraction to me. On the other hand, as you know, there are a lot of considerations,' first among them 'what I owe my wife after twenty-five years of pretty rugged experience here. I am anxious that she should be happy and while I know that she would accept any assignment without complaint ... I always have this in my mind.' He added: 'It is pretty difficult to make ourselves over and we therefore both feel that someone of personality but less rebellious to what I have termed social rigidities would do better.'

In addition, it would be a terrible wrench to uproot themselves 'from the Ontario scene, with which we are so familiar.' And it would remove Frost from the place where he could be most useful. 'I have had a great deal to do with the rebuilding of our Party from the shambles of twenty-five years ago to its present strength ... Perhaps it is here I could make the best contribution in helping yourself, the new leader here and the Party.' A Senate seat 'might provide the best avenue of doing things' but, at the same time, 'the greatest care and consideration would have to be given to those others who have given long and good service.'[3]

After the 1962 federal election – a setback of epic dimensions which reduced his government to a minority in the House of Commons – Diefenbaker prepared to shuffle the cabinet and invited Frost to become minister of finance. Donald Fleming was to take over Justice, replacing Davie Fulton, who would be moved to Public Works. The matter was canvassed at least twice by telephone. Frost jotted down his objections, not mentioning that joining the crew of what seemed to be a badly leaking craft was less than entrancing: 'Don't want to! What does this involve ... recrossing the Rubicon ... Entering an unfamiliar field with all hazards. Provincially opening the riding of Victoria [which Frost still held] ... abandoning the provincial field in advisory capacity (Robarts shadow cabinet) ... Directorships business arrangements new life ... moving to Ottawa ... an anti-climax. Can one come back (*lightweight*) at my time – in the *Heavyweight*. Where can I do any good?'[4] Diefenbaker gave up and appointed George Nowlan in Fleming's place at Finance.

To Diefenbaker's disappointment, he also turned down yet another offer of a Senate seat. When asked about the latest rumour that her husband would be going to Ottawa, Gertrude was said to have told a reporter, 'I won't let him ... he's had his time for politics.' Upon hearing of this, Frost laughed and said, 'Well, she's the boss and I'd better listen to her. Whatever she says, that's official.'5

Although his wife may have thought that he had served his time in politics, Frost, while spurning office, made good on his undertaking to give such assistance to the federal party as he could both before and after the reverse of 1962. He took it upon himself particularly to offer advice to the prime minister in an attempted salvage operation. Donning the mantle of elder statesman, he spoke out of the ripe experience and wisdom of one with twelve years of effective governance behind him and an unbroken record of smashing electoral success. The situation called above all, he thought, for a clear statement of the government's philosophy, of the direction in which it wished to lead the nation. 'Speaking of political philosophy,' he observed to Diefenbaker, 'I have always found that the best approaches were first founded on good business and then on dressing them up in a most attractive form and placing them in the political shop window. Basically however, it is good business and the ultimate appeal to logic that really counts.'6 In February Frost sent off a five-page letter outlining his ideas and invoking the spirit of Diefenbaker's hero, Sir John A. Macdonald.

In general terms I believe that Canada needs a blueprint for the future which will be understanding, confident and objective. Today the minds of people are perplexed as to the future of our country in these changing days ... A comprehensive statement of policy after the fashion of John A's national policy is needed. This could be given in perhaps a series of statements but then all tied together into one ... manifesto. There is a parallel today to John A's day. In 1877 certainly the winds of change were blowing much as today. The minds of people were perplexed. John A. sensed this and had a series of great picnics and made statements ... from which evolved the national policy, a political philosophy which pretty much dominated the scene for nearly fifty years ... My suggestion is that you prepare such a statement ... and fit into the same the multitude of worthwhile things this government has done to carry out its purpose ... I am afraid the effect of these things is going to be lost unless they are part of a composite picture of policy ... As John A. led our people into national policy in the 70's, so must we lead them into new conditions and markets in the 60's.

But beyond that was one great underlying truth, the gospel Frost had preached for many years.

This country simply has to grow and expand ... If Canadians are going to be permitted to develop this huge country they have to get down and make all sorts of sacrifices to do it. This is the inspiring task once our people get the determination. This means that we have to take big chances. Certainly we have to bring more people to this country. Canadians cannot pull themselves up with their own bootstraps. We have to raise our sights and take the chances that are involved in bringing here fine people from elsewhere, with all of their skills and creative capacity. One of our assets today is the work being done by new Canadians. If we have growth, development and expansion, we have an expanding economy and upon these things we can soundly build and provide for better standards of living. That is why I feel that upon these points hangs all the law of the prophets.

The kind of manifesto needed could only be prepared by Diefenbaker and his advisers, of course, but Frost offered some advice reflecting his own experience and way of doing things.

In my day my manifestos and statements of policy were based, as yours will be, upon consultation and opinion from the best I could draw from everywhere. I drew people to help me and advise me in connection with industry, expansion, education, the problems of business big and little, hospital insurance and a host of other things, without regard to their political affiliations. I always bore in mind the fact that there are not enough Tories in Ontario to elect a Conservative government. They provide a great nucleus, but one has to go out into the highways and byways and get people, regardless of previous political ... background. Many of my best supporters were people who had voted the other way a few years before ... I am satisfied that the other parties are not overlooking this angle either here in Ontario or in Canada. I would not underestimate the capacity of the Liberal brain trust or that of the N.D.P. Both have people of great capacity and I do not think they will overlook the general point of view which I have raised here. The government in power, however, has a tremendous advantage. It can translate into action things that the others talk about.[7]

Diefenbaker expressed thanks for all this. 'I think your ideas are excellent and the suggestions are of such a nature that I will gather together a number of the Ministers tomorrow to discuss the question at length.'[8] Frost was then asked to draft the kind of manifesto he had in mind and a screed of fourteen foolscap pages went to Diefenbaker late in March.[9]

Very little use was made of the manifesto which Frost had been at such pains to produce. 'I am going to say that Diefenbaker paid attention to this,' he wrote to Wallace McCutcheon nearly a year later, 'but his conception of putting it before the people was terribly faulty.' The prime minister had delivered without a text a rambling and a disappointing policy pronouncement in a campaign speech at London but it 'was ninety minutes in duration and went completely over the heads of the press and the people.'[10]

In the aftermath of the 1962 federal Conservative reverse, Frost attempted to encourage Diefenbaker and did not relax his efforts to get him back on the right track. 'In the present crises [sic], if the Government is to survive, then it depends upon yourself. The people are looking to someone big enough and strong enough to do the job. This all presents a great opportunity for you ... in the present impasse, cabinet and its members are of lesser importance and the Prime Minister himself is all important. He has to call the tune ... If his call and leadership is [sic] sound and inspiring, all levels of our people will uphold his hand. No Party dare challenge it. You are the one on whom the Government will stand or fall ... This is the real control and mainspring of Government.'[11]

To overcome, in particular, the business community's lack of confidence in the Diefenbaker government, Frost and Oakley Dalgleish hatched a plan to have Wallace McCutcheon brought into the cabinet. They were sure this step would go far to enlist business support in view of his prominence as an associate of E.P. Taylor, J.A. McDougald, and Eric Phillips in the Argus Corporation. McCutcheon was agreeable and willing to resign his many directorships but Diefenbaker, with his ingrained suspicion of Bay Street tycoons, was unenthusiastic. In the end, however, he agreed and McCutcheon was appointed to the Senate and as a minister without portfolio.[12]

The presence of McCutcheon did not have the desired effect. As Frost admitted, McCutcheon 'really had no aptitude for things political. His life was entirely in a financial and corporate world and like C.D. Howe, he had little patience for the processes of democracy ... Instead of relating the government to the financial world the converse was largely the result.' Moreover, he managed to antagonize Dalgleish. This was one reason, in Frost's opinion, along with 'Dalgleish's complete frustration with either the inability or disinclination of Diefenbaker and his administration to get down to the problems economic and others which were plaguing Canada,' why the *Globe and Mail* came out against the Conservatives in the 1963 election.

Frost refused to follow suit and campaigned for Diefenbaker, introducing him at meetings and speaking on his behalf over the radio and on the hustings. He himself thus alienated Dalgleish, a great personal friend, who 'thought I should have supported the Globe & Mail stand ... I could not bring myself to do this and I know that Dalgleish was deeply hurt.'[13] That sorely troubled Frost but he was determined that no one would be able to accuse him of being aloof or indifferent, much less of jumping ship. Hence, in addition to speaking on Diefenbaker's behalf, the Ontario elder statesman continued to ply him and his aides with advice about broad strategy and particular tactics.

It was to no avail. Despite Diefenbaker's skilful oratory, Liberal ineptitude, and Frost's advice, the election on 8 April produced a plurality of seats for the Liberals. Two nights later Frost and Diefenbaker talked at length on the telephone, canvassing the Chief's options. One was that he remain in office and meet the new House of Commons in the hope that the minor parties with the balance of power would sustain him. Frost, who had not yet run out of advice, thought this would be unwise. Diefenbaker should announce his resignation in words devoid of 'recrimination, philosophical and good-humoured and, above all, full of optimism for the future of our Country.'[14] The prime minister, in fact, shortly surrendered office.

With his party out of power federally after the spring of 1963, and his patience with Diefenbaker wearing thin, Frost's contacts with the Chief diminished in number and he began to share the growing belief that a change in federal leadership was required. He was urged by some to say so to Diefenbaker himself, but he was not confident of his influence with Diefenbaker. 'I cannot say that I ever enjoyed his real confidence,' he wrote later. 'He had I think an underlying suspicion of everybody excepting his wife and the Almighty. I always felt that I was included in the great majority.'[15] In any event, Frost shrank at that stage from taking a step which would in all likelihood lead to his estrangement from a man whose good qualities he had admired, whatever his defects.

Nevertheless, like many others in the party, by 1966 Frost had made up his mind that there must be a new leader. 'It seems to me that Diefenbaker has outlived his usefullness [*sic*],' he wrote to

Ray Milner in Edmonton, adding an astounding claim: 'Of course I never did have any confidence in him as the Party Leader ... I refused point blank to support him for the Leadership.' Never? Had Frost forgotten the conversation at the Royal York ten years earlier when he had brushed aside Latimer's objections and insisted that Diefenbaker was the man who could win the next election? Had he not meant all those complimentary introductions, all the speeches, all the letters and conversations in which he had encouraged and praised the man? Now he could find little good to say of him. 'He was certainly a thorn in the side of the various temporary Leaders and of George Drew. I think it is a sound principal [sic] – if he can't be a good follower, he can't be a good leader! Anyway he has established the truth of that principal as far as he is concerned.' At the same time, Frost remained dubious about the wisdom of pressing the case against the Chief at the 1966 general meeting of the party: 'Perhaps the harm done to us would be as great as waiting things out ... Diefenbaker has intense loyalties and if these are not carried in behind the new leader, whoever he may be, he is going to have a pretty difficult time. It will be hard to compete with Diefenbaker in colour.'[16]

He thus summed up his own judgment shortly after Diefenbaker's ignominious exit from the leadership: 'We have to set out to rebuild the party. It had become sort of a cult ... around the figure of one person. This is totally ... wrong. We have to get down and be the people's party ... Our past leader had very many attributes in opposition but none in government ... He could be admired as a first class fighting man but is not a man who could lead the country in these difficult days.'[17] Frost was convinced that the new leader, Robert Stanfield, was such a man, and also one to rid the nation of a 'weak, vacillating, directionless government.'[18]

When it became known that Frost would retire from office in November 1961, he began to receive invitations to join the boards of numerous companies, large and small. A few he regretfully declined, including the Bank of Nova Scotia, Chartered Trust Company, and National Trust Company. Others he gladly accepted. Among these were offers from radio station CKLY in Lindsay, the Victoria and Grey Trust Company (whose president, former Finance Minister Walter Harris, was an old political adversary), the Bank of Montreal (of which Frost was made a vice-president in 1964), Massey-Ferguson Limited, the Canada Life Assurance Company, Lever Brothers Limited, and Trans-Canada Airlines. Knowing of the close relationship between the Bank of Montreal and Canadian Pacific Railways, which had its own ambitious airline subsidiary, upon accepting the TCA directorship he wrote to Arnold Hart, president of the bank, 'I hope that the C.P.R. people will not feel that I am in any way preconceived in my ideas because ... I am quite independent.'[19] So he was, and also very conscientious about his directorial duties.

Frost had always cultivated the image of the unpretentious, down-to-earth small-town lawyer, epitomized by the remark he was said to have made at a federal-provincial conference: 'Well, Mr. Chairman, I look at this matter from the standpoint of the barber chair in Lindsay.' It was not a false image by any means. He lived comfortably but simply and without great wealth, his maximum salary as premier being sixteen thousand dollars in addition to his stipend as an MPP. That his psyche was deeply rooted in the values, attitudes, and customs of non-urban central Ontario there could be no doubt. But that was only one side of his make-up. He admired successful businessmen, enjoyed their company, and courted their confidence. As the head of an operation which, he often pointed out, was itself very big business, he had had a lot to do with them, believed that he thoroughly comprehended their problems and needs, and counted many among his friends. Sitting down in corporate boardrooms, he had no cause to feel out of place, a stranger in an alien world. He took naturally to this milieu, confident that he knew what was going on and understood sound business practice, that his opinions merited attention, and that as sage adviser he had a valuable contribution to make. He was not the kind to be content with attending board meetings and collecting his director's fees.

Probably none of his directorships brought Frost greater satisfaction or was taken more seriously by him than that of the Bank of Montreal, whose long history and important role in the development of the country gave it a special place in the annals of Canadian banking. Finance, after all, had been his prime concern during his whole public career. He therefore took an especially keen interest in the bank's affairs, warning of pitfalls and pointing to the path he thought it should follow. A letter in 1965 to its general manager is illustrative. 'Our bank,' it ran, 'has a great background both in accomplishment and goodwill. All that is necessary is to keep it equated with a fast changing country and world. We are fortunate that we have young men in the higher command.' While it would be wrong merely to copy competitors, 'in my experience it is not a bad thing to look at what the other fellow is doing ... They might have some good ideas.' Top executives should not be 'so loaded down with detailed work that they cannot see the woods for the forest [sic].' Operations in the Toronto area needed reappraisal. 'I think the Montrealers are inclined to overlook the vast implications of Ontario business and the tremendous competition ... which exists there ... If there is anything I can do to help I would be delighted.'[20]

Frost was ever alert to any step that might benefit the bank. In the spring of 1966 he wrote to Arnold Hart: 'Apropos conversation yesterday, just looking at things I was concerned lest Charles Bronfman be drawn too closely to Toronto Dominion. I imagine that Charles is naturally enough his father's successor and the latter having reached the magic number, the son becomes of interest. If ... you think he is the man [for the Bank of Montreal board], I would certainly tape him down. Really what you need is representation from a powerful Hebrew connection. I know of no family hierarchy which is more powerful.'[21] Frost of course was acquainted with the patriarch of the hierarchy – with whom was he not? – and one day he dropped a line to 'Dear Sam' in Mexico City. He and Gertrude were going to be there 'in connection with some undertakings of Massey-Ferguson Limited ... This has to do with the introducing of a great new line of machinery.' They would like to drop in on Bronfman and his wife. Whether the visit would be purely social or have some business purpose Frost did not say but probably in his mind those elements would be combined.[22]

Being a director of Trans-Canada Airlines brought him an invitation from the federal minister of transport to be aboard its inaugural flight to Moscow in the fall of 1966. At first he was uncertain about going. 'It does disrupt my plans badly,' he told Hart. 'On the other hand, there are pressures to go. Seemingly I am the only one on the other side of the [political] fence insofar as Ontario is concerned.' He finally decided to go on the junket and one of the other passengers was Senator Heath Macquarrie, who observed Frost in action. 'He played Red Square and the streets of Moscow, Leningrad and Kiev as if he were in Lindsay or Orillia. I recall his delight in teasing the Russian kids who at the time were on a kick for ball point pens. Frost used to give them at first some of the Russian manufactured types, needless to say the youngsters didn't really want the domestic product. All the way with all the people he met he exuded warmth, goodwill and a certainty that he really was glad to be there and to be with them.'[23]

Another of Frost's reasons for not wanting to move to Ottawa was that it would mean abandoning the provincial scene and his role as a member of Robarts's 'shadow cabinet.' He described his relationship to the new regime to James Armstrong, Ontario's agent general in London: 'I do not desire to interfere in the deci-sions of the government. I am glad to give advice and help where I can. At the same time my position must be definitely on the sidelines and I in no way want to press my point of view, which could be an embarrassment to the administration.'[24] Concerning many matters – hospital and medical insurance, separate schools, university policy and federal-provincial relations, to name but a few – Robarts did frequently tap Frost's almost infinite capacity for dispensing advice.

Acceptance of a federal appointment would also require resignation from the Committee on University Affairs, where Frost had taken the new premier's place. He attached real importance to this one remaining visible public duty. In 1960 the committee had been enlarged to add three men from outside government, Floyd Chalmers, R.W. Mitchell, and Senator T. D'Arcy Leonard. Upon joining them and the others, Frost probably became, thanks to his prestige, experience, and force of personality, its dominant member. The job of the committee, he believed, was to represent universities and government to each other. Their relationship was the central, underlying issue: how to avoid undue government interference in university activities while recognizing the inescapable responsibility of government for the way in which public funds were spent. There is little doubt that Frost thought the latter need the more pressing of the two. On at least one occasion, though, he complained that the government had made an important (and unwise) decision affecting the universities without seeking the committee's advice and had thereby raised 'a serious question as to the independence of the committee.'[25]

In 1966 he crystallized his thoughts on the proper relationship between the universities and the government in a letter to James L. Cooper, who had succeeded Dalgleish as publisher and editor of the *Globe and Mail*. 'One of the great problems to-day is that the universities have found a completely new well of money in government grants. At the same time they want, with no doubt good reason, to preserve their autonomy. The combination of these two, in my judgment, is leading to all sorts of ridiculous excesses of expenditures ... I think the universities,' he went on, 'have to submit to some form of government direction in relation to the type of work in which they engage; for instance if we take ... say Guelph and Waterloo, they shouldn't both embark on extensive studies say in business administration' and thus 'avoid expensive duplication of staff and everything else.'[26]

But how to rationalize? That was the conundrum, still unsolved long after Frost disappeared from the Committee on University Affairs. The committee, with its purely advisory, non-executive status, could not do so. In 1962 the committee, at Frost's urging, called together the university presidents with the object, as he put it, of obtaining 'co-operation and the attainment of objectives and goals which really did not appear to be possible in dealing with the universities piecemeal.'[27] The presidents agreed to form a committee of themselves and to undertake a comprehensive study of the future of higher education in Ontario.[28] The onus of planning, collectively instead of individually in the time-honoured way, was thus placed on the universities.

As always in the past, there remained, however, perennial dissatisfaction on the campuses with decisions by Queen's Park, usually arising from recommendations of the Committee on University Affairs. This annoyed Frost intensely. In 1963 he replied at length, and with some heat, to a report by the presidents' committee and an accompanying letter from Claude Bissell of the University of Toronto. 'I must say,' he wrote, 'that the Committee was concerned because anyone reading your letter or the report and not knowing the background might be completely misled ... I am afraid that both your letter and the report would appear to be critical of the Committee and the Government. I am quite sure that this is not your intention ... The increase in university grants has been greater percentage-wise than, I think, in any other field of education.'

Moreover, neither the report nor Bissell's letter acknowledged what had been done to encourage graduate studies for the training of university teachers, the importance of which Frost recognized despite his scepticism about the need for much of it in liberal arts subjects. A graduate fellowship program had been introduced and additional funds made available to eight universities to expand their graduate work. 'Our thought at the time, which seems to have escaped those who wrote the report in question, was that ... teaching staff were of the most primary importance and that, while we might get along with temporary accommodation, we could not get along without this [sic] trained personnel.' There were other regrettable omissions from the report which added to the distortions in the picture it drew. 'I think we all have to have regard for the position of our Country and Province in relation to the dollars that are available to do the things we have to do.' If Bissell shared what has been described as the view of academics 'that ageing politicians, civil servants, and businessmen were not the best exponents of university interests,' Frost's letter must not have altered it.[29]

Notwithstanding his resentment at the failure to appreciate the efforts of the committee, Frost retained his customary optimism that things would work out for the best. In a letter to Robarts early in 1966, after cautioning the premier not to let himself, respecting medicare, 'be power played into some extravagant plan at the present time in the light of all the obligations you are going to have to meet in the province,' he added: 'We finished up the consideration of the University's [sic] proposals today ... I must say I was greatly impressed by the way the University Affairs Committee took hold of things. The academics were really very realistic and reasonable, and they are fine fellows to work with.'[30]

Before long he was given the opportunity to work more closely with the 'fine fellows' of a particular university, one to which he became closely attached and in which he took a special interest, partly because it would serve his own section of the province. In 1967 Frost became chancellor of Trent, which had opened its doors three years previously and occupied a fine site astride the Otonabee River at Peterborough. Like all the positions he had ever held, Frost regarded this one as a job with important duties and responsibilities in guiding the development of the institution, not as a ceremonial and honorific sinecure. He took a special interest in Trent's becoming an important centre of Canadian studies. He and Gertrude established a fund to assist in that and the bulk of his estate was bequeathed to it, including much of his memorabilia and a valuable collection of his papers, mostly relating to the times before and after his years in government.

In addition to the state and the universities, there was a third great institution, the church, about which Frost was much concerned in the later years of his life, not as so often in the past regarding its role in education or its campaigns against vice and drunkenness, but in a more personal way. He had been a faithful member of the United Church of Canada since its birth in 1925 and was in regular attendance at Cambridge Street United Church when he was able to be in Lindsay on a Sunday. From 1937 to 1942 he had been chairman of its committee of stewards[31] and thereafter, while too involved in public affairs to take much part in its activities, he attached real importance to his church membership.

By the 1960s, however, indeed earlier, he had become dissatisfied with what he viewed as the church's increasing secularization, the tendency of its official publication, the *United Church Observer*, and of some of its ministers to concern themselves with the things of the world rather than of the spirit, even to the point of taking positions on controversial political issues. 'Since union,' he wrote to one of them, 'my wife and I have endeavoured to make the United Church of Canada our spiritual home and I must say to you sometimes somewhat dispairingly [*sic*].' His disquiet led him into extensive correspondence with a number of church officials, including the editor of the *Observer*, A.C. Forrest, and Frost's old friendly critic about liquor policy in particular, the Reverend J.R. Mutchmor, who was now (1963) moderator of the church. Frost was annoyed, for instance, by an article in the magazine on defence policy and nuclear arms at a time when the Diefenbaker government was fighting for its life in 1963. 'There is,' he told Forrest, 'a very definite place for the church in great moral issues but ... the church cannot afford to get off its pedestal ... to get mixed up in politics as such ... I think you were getting away from the moral issue when you say "When the Minister of External Affairs sits on one side of the fence and the Minister of National Defence on the other and the Prime Minister on the top of the fence, it is confusing to ordinary people." This seems to me to be politics and ... adds more confusion to the church membership, some elements of which are probably irritated ... a church paper is different from all others.'

Frost thought his own minister at Cambridge Street was guilty of the same fault. One Monday in April 1963, he wrote to his sister-in-law Roberta: 'Coming down on the train [to Toronto] this morning I was thinking of yesterday and I thought I would drop you a line to get the matter off my mind. As you know, for some very considerable time past, Gertrude and I have had our doubts about the United Church being our spiritual home. Frankly, I thought I was overcoming this matter. Now we are back in turmoil.' He had gone to church expecting a sermon on a biblical subject 'and instead of that I got what seemed to be a very largely irrelevant reference to nuclear warfare, which I must admit left me cold ... I am an old front line soldier. The heart rending story of the young officer, who very probably has never seen a shot fired in anger and never likely will, turning grey and aged over the fact that his squadron was not equipped with nuclear missiles simply did not click with me ... I think the most charitable explanation of what was said yesterday was that it was exceedingly bad judgment and timing.' But Frost seemed to realize that he was swimming against an overwhelming tide. 'Perhaps my wife and I and a lot of others who would like to make the United Church our anchorage and spiritual home are just simply out of date and would do better to go elsewhere to find answers.' That did not happen. The Frosts remained in the fold and both were buried from Cambridge Street United.[32]

In the midst of all his activities, public and private, Frost found time to write two books, both historical and both labours of love. He had long been a history buff, interesting himself, even while immersed in complicated affairs of state, in aspects of the past that intrigued him. These were both numerous and diverse. He was fascinated by the history of Huronia, devoting much effort by reading and field work of his own to determining, for example, Champlain's route to Lake Couchiching and the location of Cahigue. He was surprised to discover that the people of Nova Scotia were largely unaware of the connection with Upper Canada of Thomas Chandler Haliburton, after whom Haliburton County was named. In 1959 he was at great pains to learn about the fate of the Tolpuddle Martyrs, especially those who settled in Canada, before unveiling a plaque to their memory near London. Was MPP or MLA the proper designation for members of the Ontario legislature? Frost favoured the former, for historical reasons which he was glad to explain to various friends and correspondents, some of whom were under a misapprehension on that score. And of course he had a personal interest in the Great War of 1914, including the career of the inimitable Sam Hughes. In 1965 he delivered a paper to Lindsay's 20 Club, still going strong after more than seventy-five years, in which he spoke up for a man whose faults he recognized but who he believed had never received his due.[33] The work of the Ontario Archaeological and Historic Sites Board attracted his consistent interest and support. On his initiative the Ontario Series of the Champlain Society publications was launched with government financial support, the completion of its successive volumes, beginning with Edwin C. Guillet's *The Valley of the Trent*, bringing him untold pleasure. As he put it, 'I am most anxious that more stress should be laid on the history of our province and country and that public interest should be created. We are a young country and we have yet to develop a sense of history which is so important.'[34]

His own first book, *Fighting Men*, appeared in 1967, a personal centennial project. Despite the rather harrowing outcome of his overseas military career, interest in soldiering, acquired as a youngster in Orillia, had never left him. Nor had admiration, affection, and solicitude for those who had served in the most hazardous of professions. Shortly before writing the preface to *Fighting Men*, he flew to London, England, on Bank of Montreal business, after which he attended a Lever Brothers meeting in Brussels. It was arranged that he take a side trip to the battlefields and, on behalf of the Ontario government, lay a wreath at the Vimy Memorial on the fiftieth anniversary of that memorable Canadian engagement. Typically, he asked two other Ontario veterans to assist him, one of them his old company commander from the 20th Battalion. 'The Vimy visit is really incidental to what I am doing,' he wrote in notifying Ontario's agent general in London of these plans. But as he was being driven, through the courtesy of Lever Brothers, around the old battlefields of the Arras-Cambrai-Mons region before going to Vimy Ridge, vivid memories of the heroic exploits of the Canadian Corps and his own minor role in them must have been rekindled in his mind.[35]

His book, dedicated to the Orillia community, concentrated on one small aspect of Canada's part in the war, the story of the First Simcoe Regiment and of those who served in it, although he did permit himself many reflections on the wider story of how the war was fought, in some ways mis-fought. He had tried without success, he explained in the preface, to find someone better qualified in historical training and literary skill to write it. So he had done it himself, trying 'to make this story grassroots and intimate.'[36] He was too modest. While in no sense a major work of military history, its pages reflect a painstaking effort to reconstruct a bit of the past and to bring it alive, not only for the people of Orillia and Simcoe County but for a wider audience of Canadians.

Frost's other book, *Forgotten Pathways of the Trent*, was published in 1973. This slim, attractively produced volume was part of a broader study, supported by the Canada Council, of Indian history and Indian-white relationships. His assignment, he wrote, 'related particularly to the trading habits of the Mississaugas and their predecessors, the Hurons and the Iroquois, in the days of the French Regime and of the succeeding English period up to the first days of the settlement of the Valley of the Trent.' The description in a foreword by his friend Malcolm Montgomery, himself an authority on native studies, of the book's gist and significance cannot be improved upon.

The author's conclusion that there were three principal routes of access into the Trent waterway is interesting, especially his hypothesis that the

Iroquois assault on Huronia came through the Trent and not over the Toronto Carrying Place as is sometimes presumed. Because of his research, it is likely that the Scugog, the Rice Lake Carrying Place and the Trent River itself will be drawn more into the ambit of consideration of future scholars than has been the case until this time. Mr. Frost has shrewdly presented his evidence by means of early maps, traveller's accounts and fairly reliable local historians. To these he has added his personal observations which are considerable. He personally traversed and intimately knew the portages and areas of which he has written. His plea for the protection of nature and the environment is a point well taken and demonstrates the breadth of his vision ... Throughout his life Leslie Frost sought to stimulate an ever growing interest in the history of Ontario and Canada. Even if there are those who do not agree with his conclusions, this in itself will spark lively controversy over our history and this is something he would have liked to bring about.[37]

Midway between the publication of his two books, Frost was stricken by a grievous loss that darkened his remaining days. In the fall of 1970 Gertrude entered the Toronto General Hospital for a gall bladder operation. Hugh Latimer went to see her; he was shocked by her desperately ill appearance and found later that she had terminal cancer. With difficulty she said to him, 'Hugh, things haven't turned out as I had hoped. I need your prayers.' After a few moments he made to leave. She took his hand and said, 'Kiss me, Hugh.' He did and left the room shaken, certain that he would not see her again. Soon she was removed to the hospital in Lindsay, where she died on 2 December. Latimer had seen a great deal of the Frosts together over the years and to him they always behaved like honeymooners. Often Leslie had joked publicly about his wife's supposed dominance over him and there was no doubt of her strong will and equally strong opinions. Sometimes when Latimer was with them and the two men were discussing a political problem caused by someone getting out of line, Gertrude would interrupt 'and express her views quite vehemently and say what she would do if she were dealing with them and it would be quite drastic action that she would suggest. Mr. Frost would smile and say that it would be a rough government if Gertrude was running the show.' Whenever Frost and Latimer were together on the campaign trail, the former would invariably call home before breakfast and then relate her opinions on current affairs.[38]

And now this vibrant partner, so devoted, generous, intelligent, and such stimulating company, was gone from Frost's life. He grieved but, being the kind of man he was, kept himself busy with his still lively interest in public affairs, with the life of Trent University, and with writing his little book on the Trent Valley. Solace was found, too, in the companionship of Roberta Frost, of Gertrude's nephew Jack Beal and his wife Eileen, and of Roberta's daughter Marjorie Porter, who lived not far from Lindsay. And there were friends who came to see him, either in town or at his cherished Pleasant Point retreat, which over the years he and Gertrude had enlarged and improved. He might take them out in his powerful outboard motor boat to scud over the waters of Sturgeon Lake, while Frost waved to other cottagers and regaled his passengers with tales of those who had summered in this place or that and of the history of the area.

But he was not to have long to make the best of things in these ways. Each winter after Gertrude's death he took a trip south, accompanied by the Beals. Late in 1972 he arranged for them to spend three weeks in Florida in the coming January but as the time approached he was feeling far from well. He attributed this to one of the periodic flare-ups of his war wound and checked into the Toronto General Hospital to have it treated. His physician told him there was no need to cancel the Florida plans but, once there, Frost continued to feel very unwell, so much so that he telephoned the doctor and made an appointment for the day after his return. Following a series of x-rays and other tests, the doctor called Eileen Beal at the Royal York, where she and her uncle had been staying while the tests went on, to tell her that the diagnosis was cancer. At that moment Frost entered her room, spoke to the doctor, and learned that he must enter the hospital a few days later. He was determined, however, to go back to Lindsay until then, saying to Eileen as he prepared to check out of the hotel, 'Well come on, little one, we better get this show on the road.'

Latimer, who had seen him at George Drew's funeral in early January and for the first time noticed that Frost, his face drawn, was showing his age, visited him in the hospital. He seemed comfortable and in no pain but, without knowing the nature of his illness, Latimer had the uneasy feeling that he was slipping and would not recover. Presently he was sent home on medication, which at first he refused to take because it made him feel worse and would not do any good anyway. That was true; he was simply fading away in a process that medical science could not arrest.[39] On the morning of 4 May he died.

The funeral took place three days later at Cambridge Street

United Church, packed full with many standing in the lobby and listening through open doors. Outside a large crowd gathered. An assemblage of dignitaries was on hand, headed by Governor General Roland Michener, Frost's onetime colleague in the Drew cabinet, and Lieutenant-Governor Ross Macdonald. John Diefenbaker was there, as were Earl Rowe, Premier William Davis, James Allan, Robert Nixon, the provincial Liberal leader, and Donald MacDonald, representing the NDP. Most of the Davis cabinet turned out, along with a large number of MPPs. And of course the faithful, conscientious Latimer was present, deservedly one of the honorary pallbearers. But for the most part the church was filled with ordinary folk from the town and a wide area around, the people with whom Frost had striven to identify himself and his party and in whose good, sound common sense he had steadfastly believed.

It was a short, simple service with no eulogy, as he had requested. When it was over, the casket, draped in Ontario's provincial flag on which Frost's medals lay upon a purple cushion, was carried to the hearse by members of the Queen's York Rangers. Then the cortège moved off slowly along the so familiar streets now lined with silent onlookers, many of them children released from school for the afternoon, come to say a final, respectful goodbye to an exceptional man. Reaching the cemetery on the edge of town, the hearse stopped near the freshly dug grave next to Gertrude's. As a gusty breeze rustled the leaves of the great, still surviving elms, in a brief burial service the mortal remains of the Laird of Lindsay were committed to the earth beside the Scugog River, in his own corner of the Old Ontario he had known and loved so well.

Appendix: The Frost Ministry

Premier and president of the council	Leslie Frost	4 May 1949–8 Nov. 1961
Provincial secretary and registrar	Arthur Welsh	4 May 1949–30 Jan. 1955
	W.M. Nickle	30 Jan. 1955–17 Aug. 1955
	G.H. Dunbar	17 Aug. 1955–22 Dec. 1958
	Mackinnon Phillips	22 Dec. 1958–15 May 1960
	John Yaremko	26 May 1960–27 Jan. 1961
Provincial secretary and minister of citizenship	John Yaremko	27 Jan. 1961–8 Nov. 1961
Treasurer of Ontario	Leslie Frost	4 May 1949–17 Aug. 1955 3 Feb. 1958–28 April 1958
	Dana Porter	17 Aug. 1955–30 Jan. 1958
	J.N. Allan	28 April 1958–8 Nov. 1961
Minister of agriculture	T.L. Kennedy	4 May 1949–20 Jan. 1953
	F.S. Thomas	20 Jan. 1953–1 Aug. 1956
	William Goodfellow	1 Aug. 1956–8 Nov. 1961
Attorney general	Dana Porter	4 May 1949–17 Aug. 1955
	A.K. Roberts	17 Aug. 1955–8 Nov. 1961
Minister of education	Dana Porter	4 May 1949–2 Oct. 1951
	W.J. Dunlop	2 Oct. 1951–17 Dec. 1959
	John Robarts	17 Dec. 1959–8 Nov. 1961
Minister of energy resources	R.W. Macaulay	5 May 1959–8 Nov. 1961
Minister of health	R.T. Kelley	4 May 1949–8 Aug. 1950
	Mackinnon Phillips	8 Aug. 1950–22 Dec. 1958
	M.B. Dymond	22 Dec. 1958–8 Nov. 1961

Minister of highways	G.H. Doucett	4 May 1949–5 Jan. 1955
	J.N. Allan	5 Jan. 1955–28 April 1958
	F.M. Cass	28 April 1958–8 Nov. 1961
Minister of labour	Charles Daley	4 May 1949–8 Nov. 1961
Minister of lands and forests	H.R. Scott	4 May 1949–3 June 1952
	W.A. Gemmell	3 June 1952–18 June 1954
	Clare Mapledoram	7 July 1954–4 July 1958
	J.W. Spooner	23 July 1958–8 Nov. 1961
Minister of mines	W.S. Gemmell	4 May 1949–3 June 1952
	P.T. Kelly	3 June 1952–18 July 1957
	J.W. Spooner	18 July 1957–22 Dec. 1958
	J.A. Maloney	22 Dec. 1958–8 Nov. 1961
Minister of municipal affairs	G.H. Dunbar	4 May 1949–17 Aug. 1955
	William Goodfellow	17 Aug. 1955–1 Nov. 1956
	William Warrender	1 Nov. 1956–8 Nov. 1961
Minister of planning and development	William Griesinger	4 May 1949–20 Jan. 1953
	William Warrender	20 Jan. 1953–17 Aug. 1955
	W.M. Nickle	17 Aug. 1955–8 Nov. 1961
Minister of public welfare	William Goodfellow	4 May 1949–17 Aug. 1955
	L.P. Cecile	17 Aug. 1955–8 Nov. 1961
Minister of public works	G.H. Doucett	4 May 1949–2 Oct. 1951
	F.S. Thomas	2 Oct. 1951–20 Jan. 1953
	William Griesinger	20 Jan. 1953–6 May 1958
	J.N. Allan	14 May 1958–22 Dec. 1958
	Ray Connell	22 Dec. 1958–8 Nov. 1961
Minister of reform institutions	G.H. Dunbar	4 May 1949–15 July 1949
	William Hamilton	15 July 1949–16 Nov. 1950
	J.W. Foote	16 Nov. 1950–18 July 1957
	M.B. Dymond	18 July 1957–28 April 1958
	Ray Connell	28 April 1958–22 Dec. 1958
	G.C. Wardrope	22 Dec. 1958–8 Nov. 1961
Minister of transport	J.N. Allan	26 June 1957–28 April 1958
	M.B. Dymond	28 April 1958–22 Dec. 1958
	John Yaremko	22 Dec. 1958–21 Nov. 1960
	Leslie Rowntree	21 Nov. 1960–8 Nov. 1961
Minister of travel and publicity	L.P. Cecile	4 May 1949–17 Aug. 1955
	Bryan Cathcart	17 Aug. 1955–8 Nov. 1961
Minister without portfolio	G.H. Challies	4 May 1949–17 Aug. 1955
	R.T. Kelley	8 Aug. 1950–18 Jan. 1952
	William Hamilton	16 Nov. 1950–17 Aug. 1955
	H.R. Scott	3 June 1952–28 April 1958
	William Warrender	17 Aug. 1955–1 Nov. 1956

Ray Connell	1 Nov. 1956–28 April 1958
John Yaremko	28 April 1958–22 Dec. 1958
R.W. Macaulay	26 May 1958–5 May 1959
John Robarts	22 Dec. 1958–17 Dec. 1959
John Root	22 Dec. 1958–8 Nov. 1961
W.J. Dunlop	17 Dec. 1959–21 Nov. 1960
Allan Grossman	21 Nov. 1960–8 Nov. 1961
W.A. Stewart	21 Nov. 1960–8 Nov. 1961

SOURCE: *Legislators and Legislatures in Ontario: A Reference Guide*, compiled and edited by Debra Forman (Toronto 1984), vol. I: xl–xlii

Notes

The major collection of Leslie Frost's papers is in the Archives of Ontario (AO), Record Group 3. Unless otherwise indicated, all citations of RG3 refer to those papers. They are divided into three main categories, each identified in the notes as follows: I – general correspondence; II – correspondence, subject files; and III – riding and personal correspondence. The box in which a file cited resides is identified by arabic numerals, followed by the title of the file.

Use has also been made of a smaller but valuable body of Leslie Frost papers (LMF) and Cecil Frost papers (CGF) in the Trent University Archives (TUA), of some Frost family papers in the Orillia Public Library (OPL), of the Treasury Department Papers (RG6) in the Archives of Ontario, and of certain collections in the Queen's University Archives (QUA).

CHAPTER I: GROWING UP IN MARIPOSA

1 The foregoing is based on a letter to LMF from his Aunt Emily and a report of a speech to the Orillia Kiwanis Club by his father. RG3, III, 18, 'Historical Sites & Matters,' Mrs J.C. Swallow to LMF, n.d. [received 27 Sept. 1948]; OPL, W.S. Frost scrapbook, unidentified clipping probably from the *Packet and Times*, Orillia, Nov. 1930. Apparently having forgotten the letter from his aunt, Leslie Frost had it firmly fixed in his mind that his grandparents arrived in Orillia on the day the Dominion was born, and this coincidence evidently pleased him. He gave his version in various places, including a memorandum prepared for the author about his paternal ancestry. Mrs Swallow's testimony to the contrary is, however, corroborated by her brother's Kiwanis Club speech. See also interview with Leslie Frost by Peter Oliver and Roger Graham (hereafter Oliver-Graham), 10 Nov. 1972: 2, and OPL, W.S. Frost scrapbook, explanatory notes by LMF.

2 TUA, LMF, LMF to C.B. Janes, 8 Sept. 1943; Oliver-Graham, 4. See Herbert P. Wood, *They Blazed the Trail: An Account of the Adventures of Seven Early-*

day Officers of the Salvation Army in the Canadian Territory from 1882 to 1910 (Canada and Bermuda n.d.), chap. I; Robert Sandall, *The History of the Salvation Army*, II (London 1950), 225. Neither of these works mentions Margaret Barker's career in the Army. Nor does *The Lady with the Other Lamp: The Story of Blanche Read Johnston*, as told to Mary Morgan Dean (Toronto 1919), although Mrs Johnston, Blanche Goodall as she had been, and Margaret were friends.

3 Memorandum by LMF for the author; Oliver-Graham, 13; OPL, W.S. Frost scrapbook, notes by LMF, 221

4 Oliver-Graham, 20. William Frost recorded in his Bible the date and exact minute of birth of his three sons, with a verse from scripture for each. The entry for Leslie read: 'Leslie Miscampbell Frost, born at twenty-five minutes past 9 in the evening, Friday, Sept. 20, 1895. But my God shall supply all your needs according to His riches in glory by Christ Jesus. Phil. 4–19.' Frost's birthplace at the corner of Mississaga and Wyandotte streets still stands, and is now a duplex.

5 Oliver-Graham, 7

6 See ibid., 6; Hugh Latimer, 'Political Reminiscences,' 356. Mr Latimer's unpublished recollections of his career as a Conservative party organizer, which brought him into close and frequent contact with Leslie Frost, are in the Archives of Ontario.

7 Oliver-Graham, 23

8 Ibid., 17–18

9 Ibid., 19

10 Memorandum by LMF for the author; RG3, III, 29, 'Frost, Leslie M. – 1951,' LMF to C.H. Hale, 9 July 1951

11 Oliver-Graham, 116; *Globe and Mail*, 2 May 1949

12 Memorandum by LMF for the author; TUA, LMF, scrapbook 'LMF – CGF 11935–47,' 22, group photograph of YMCA basketball team; RG3, III, 59, 'Frost, Hon. L.M. 1958,' unidentified clipping [Orillia *Packet and Times*, 1958?]; Dorothy Swallow to the author, 12 Aug. 1980

13 Oliver-Graham, 24

14 Floyd S. Chalmers, *Both Sides of the Street* (Toronto 1983), 14

15 RG3, I, 3, 'Alcoholism Research Foundation,' LMF to Ben H. Spence, 13 Jan. 1959

16 Oliver-Graham, 25

17 Frost was reminded of this decades later when the Toronto *Evening Telegram* published a picture of Cecil and him in military uniform, Cecil with bugle in hand, on their way to summer cadet camp at Niagara-on-the-Lake in 1913. He sent a framed print of this to the neighbour, still living in the same house, with a note recalling the bugling and offering a belated apology. She responded with a picture of her married daughter who had

been a baby in her pram on the porch next door at the time. The incident illustrates Frost's remarkable gift for attending to such minor acts of thoughtfulness when so many weightier matters were on his mind. *Telegram*, 15 Jan. 1959; RG3, III, 66, 'Flag – Red Ensign – 1959,' LMF to Mrs A.M. Dunn, 4 Feb. 1959; Mrs Dunn to LMF, 21 Feb. 1959

18 Leslie M. Frost, *Fighting Men* (Toronto 1967), 23–4; memorandum by LMF for the author

19 Frost, *Fighting Men*, 16–17; Oliver-Graham, 30

20 Ibid., 'Memorandum Concerning the Military Service of Frost Family and with Particular Relationship to Leslie Miscampbell Frost and Cecil Gray Frost' [hereafter 'Military Service Memo'], May 1972: 4. LMF was its author. The bible is in TUA.

21 Ibid., item 1, LMF to Sadie Barker, 11 Aug. 1915

22 Ibid., 'Military Service Memo,' 4–5; memorandum by LMF for the author, 6

23 Memorandum by LMF for the author, 6–7; Oliver-Graham, 53

24 Frost, *Fighting Men*, 55–6

25 TUA, Wartime & Military Letters [hereafter LMF], WML, item 22, LMF, Nov. 26, 1916. All these letters from Leslie and Cecil were to William and Margaret Frost unless indicated.

26 Ibid., item 18, LMF, 17 Nov. 1916

27 Frost, *Fighting Men*, 89–91

28 TUA, LMF, WML, item 21, LMF, 17 Nov. 1916

29 Ibid., item 22, LMF, 26 Nov. 1916

30 Ibid., item 24, LMF, 7 Dec. 1916

31 Ibid., item 28, LMF, 25 Dec. 1916

32 Ibid., item 37, CGF, 2 Feb. 1917

33 Ibid., item 42, LMF, 3 March 1917

34 Ibid., item 45, LMF, 31 March 1917

35 Ibid., item 47, LMF, 7 Apr. 1917; item 56, LMF, 5 May 1917

36 Ibid. The Ontario Liberal party had officially embraced female suffrage shortly before the 1917 legislative session. It became law after a sudden change of heart by the Conservative government of Sir William Hearst during the session.

37 Ibid., item 65, LMF, 4 June 1917

38 Ibid., item 66, LMF, 10 June 1917

39 Ibid., item 73, LMF, 19 July 1917

40 Ibid., item 75, LMF, 30 July 1917

41 Ibid., notes accompanying item 83, LMF, 19 Aug. 1917. For a detailed account of the battalion's role at Hill 70 and throughout the war, see D.J. Corrigall, *The History of the Twentieth Canadian Battalion (Central Ontario Regiment) Canadian Expeditionary Force in the Great War, 1914–1918* (Toronto 1925).

42 Quoted in John Swettenham, *To Seize the Victory: The Canadian Corps in World War I* (Toronto 1965), 178
43 TUA, LMF, WML, item 81, LMF, 15 Aug. 1917
44 Ibid., item 83, LMF, 19 Aug. 1917
45 Ibid., item 84, LMF, 27 Aug. 1917
46 Dorothy Swallow to the author, 16 July 1980
47 TUA, LMF, WML, notes accompanying item 90, LMF, 20 Sept. 1917; memorandum by LMF for the author, 8
48 TUA. LMF, WML, item 86, LMF, 16 Sept. 1917
49 TUA, LMF, WML, item 102, LMF, 2 Dec. 1917
50 Ibid., item 113, LMF, 14 Feb. 1918
51 Ibid., item 88, LMF, 16 Sept. 1917
52 Ibid., item 105, LMF, 12 Dec. 1917
53 Ibid., item 108, LMF, 4 Jan. 1918
54 Ibid., item 121, LMF, 11 Mar. 1918
55 Oliver-Graham, 49
56 TUA, LMF, WML, 'Military Service Memo,' 6–7
57 Ibid., item 131, E.E. Pugsley to Mr and Mrs Frost, 1 Apr. 1918
58 Ibid., item 137, LMF, 21 Apr. 1918
59 Ibid., item 151, War Office to W.S. Frost, 30 July 1918, cable; item 152, Mrs Peuchen to Dr Ardagh, 1 Aug. 1918, cable
60 Ibid., item 149, LMF, 30 June 1918.

CHAPTER 2: LIVING BY THE LAW IN LINDSAY

1 Oliver-Graham, 54
2 CGF to LMF, 12 May 1921, in possession of Mrs Marjorie Porter
3 TUA, LMF, WML, item 173, LMF, 26 Nov. 1920; Dorothy Swallow to the author, 12 Aug. 1980
4 *Watchman-Warder* (Lindsay), 21 July 1921
5 RG3, III, 21, 'Frost, Hon. L.M. (Personal) '49,' LMF to G.H. Wilson, 30 May 1949; Marjorie Porter to the author, 3 Aug. 1980; *Telegram* (Toronto), 4 May 1949
6 Alan Capon, *Historic Lindsay* (Belleville 1974), 37–8
7 Watson Kirkconnell, *County of Victoria Centennial History*, 2nd ed. (Lindsay 1967), 114; *Canada Year Book 1924* (Ottawa 1925), 424
8 *Lindsay Past and Present: Souvenir of Old Home Week, June 28th–July 5th 1924* (n.p., n.d.)
9 *Packet*, 20 Oct. 1921
10 TUA, LMF, box 1, folder 2, handwritten memorandum by LMF
11 Ibid., letterbook 1, LMF to Finlayson, 23 July 1923

12 *Lindsay Past and Present*; Marjorie Porter to the author, 29 Mar. 1981; OHSS
 oral history, Jack and Eileen Beal interview, 3–4
13 *Lindsay Past and Present*
14 TUA, LMF, scrapbooks, vol. 4: 1
15 OHSS oral history, Marjorie Porter interview, 15–16
16 Ibid.
17 Ibid., 8–9
18 TUA, LMF, 'F.W. McGaughey (murder trial),' LMF to Lapointe, 21 Nov.
 1924
19 Ibid., LMF to Dr Edward Ryan, 6 Aug. 1924
20 Ibid., LMF to W.F. Nickle, 19 Aug. 1924; Nickle to LMF, 21 Aug. 1924
21 Ibid., letterbook 2, memorandum on the M'Naghten rules
22 *Daily Post* (Lindsay), 3 Oct. 1924
23 TUA, LMF, box 123, folder 1, LMF to Bradford, 4 Oct. 1924; Bradford to
 LMF, 6 Oct. 1924
24 Ibid., LMF to Ryan, 25 Oct. 1924
25 Ibid., LMF to Pardee, 30 Oct. 1924; Pardee to LMF, 31 Oct. 1924
26 Ibid., Ryan to LMF, 19 Dec. 1924; LMF to Ryan, 10 Dec. 1924
27 Ibid., box 100, folder 2, '20 Club – Modern Criminology,' 22
28 Ibid., letterbook 3, CGF to G.W.H. Millican, 13 Mar., 11 Apr. 1931
29 Ibid., CGF to Finlayson, 22 Feb. 1927, 26 Sept. 1929
30 TUA, LMF, box 1, folder 7, 'Provincial Election 1926,' handwritten
 memorandum by LMF and notes for a speech
31 Ibid., folder 10, 'Provincial Election 1929,' handwritten memorandum by
 LMF and notes for a speech
32 OHSS oral history, Marjorie Porter interview, 9; Marjorie Porter to the
 author, 18 Aug. 1980

CHAPTER 3: LOW TIDE FOR THE 'GOVERNMENT PARTY'

1 Neil McKenty, *Mitch Hepburn* (Toronto 1967), 38
2 *Lindsay Daily Post*, 1 May 1934
3 Ibid., 25 May 1934
4 TUA, LMF, vol. 2, folder 3, 'Provincial Election 1934,' handwritten note by
 LMF. The following description, except where otherwise indicated, is drawn
 from these notes Frost used for his standard campaign speech.
5 *Post*, 25 May 1934
6 TUA, LMF, vol. 2, folder 3, Henry to LMF, 20 June 1934
7 *Lindsay Daily Post*, 2 Jan. 1936
8 *Telegram*, 29 May 1936
9 Ibid., 7 May 1936

10 McKenty, *Hepburn*, 84
11 Ibid., 82–3; Hugh D. Latimer, 'Political Reminiscences,' 10. I am grateful to Mr Latimer and to Professor Peter Oliver for furnishing me with a copy of this document; *Telegram*, 10 Dec. 1936.
12 The forthcoming biography of Hepburn by John Saywell will undoubtedly throw additonal light on this episode. On McCullagh's role in Canadian affairs, see Brian J. Young, 'C. George McCullagh and the Leadership League' (MA thesis, Queen's University 1964).
13 Numerous authors have written about this subject. The fullest treatment is in James A. Pendergest, 'Labour and Politics in Oshawa and District, 1938–1943' (MA thesis, Queen's University 1973). See also Irving Abella's 'Oshawa 1937' in the volume edited by him, *On Strike: Six Key Labour Struggles in Canada, 1919–1949* (Toronto 1975); the same author's *Nationalism, Communism and Canadian Labour: The C.I.O., the Communist Party and the Canadian Congress of Labour* (Toronto 1973), chap. 1. Professor Saywell's biography will include a major revision of these accounts of the strike [Eds].
14 OHSS oral history, Rowe interview, 20. Senator Arthur Meighen did not agree.
15 Quoted in McKenty, *Hepburn*, 123
16 OHSS oral history, Rowe interview, 19, 21
17 TUA, CGF, box 1, folder 3, 'Hon Earl Rowe states our Party's stand on Labour'
18 Ibid., CGF to officers of all riding associations in Ontario, 13 May 1937
19 *Lindsay Post*, 16 June 1937
20 OHSS oral history, Rowe interview, 21
21 TUA, LMF, box 3, folder 1, LMF to 'Dear Friend,' 28 Aug. 1937
22 OHSS oral history, Jack and Eileen Beal interview
23 *Lindsay Post*, 2 Oct. 1937
24 Ibid., 4 Oct. 1937
25 TUA, CGF, box 1, folder 4, '1937 Campaign and the Conservative Party,' CGF to Rowe, 10 Dec. 1936. (emphasis in original)
26 TUA, CGF, box 1, folder 5, 'Letters Following the 1937 Provincial Election,' F.D.L. Smith to CGF, 13 Oct. 1937
27 Ibid., W. Flavelle to CGF, 14 Oct. 1937
28 The foregoing is derived from the *Telegram*, 23, 25, and 26 Oct. 1937, and the *Globe and Mail*, 26 Oct. 1937.
29 Ibid., 23 Nov. 1937
30 TUA, LMF, vol. 16, folder 7, Hepburn to LMF, n.d. This file contains a copy of the speech, which was reported in the *Globe and Mail*, 4 Mar 1938, and more fully in the *Lindsay Post*, 4, 11 Mar. 1938.
31 *Globe and Mail*, 15 Mar. 1938
32 Ibid., 4 Mar. 1938

33 The foregoing is derived from various news items in ibid., 22 July 1938.

34 Ibid., 3 Mar. 1938

35 On the Bren gun controversy, see C.P. Stacey, *The Military Problems of Canada* (Toronto 1940), 128–33; the same author's *Arms, Men and Governments: The War Policies of Canada 1939–1945* (Ottawa 1970), 498–9; H. Blair Neatby, *William Lyon Mackenzie King, 1932–1939; The Prism of Unity* (Toronto 1976), 278–81.

36 TUA, CGF, vol. I, folder 6, Walker to CGF, 8 Nov. 1938

37 Ibid., Macdonnell to CGF, 15 Nov. 1938

38 *Globe and Mail*, 10 Dec. 1938

CHAPTER 4: A PRIVATE IN THE RANKS

1 On the King-Hepburn feud, see Neil McKenty, *Mitch Hepburn* (Toronto 1967), chaps. 3, 9–15; H. Blair Neatby, *William Lyon Mackenzie King, 1932–1939: The Prism of Unity* (Toronto 1976), chaps. 13–14; Christopher Armstrong, *The Politics of Federalism: Ontario's Relations With the Federal Government, 1867–1942* (Toronto 1981), chaps. 9–10; Reginald Whitaker, *The Government Party: Organizing and Financing the Liberal Party of Canada 1930–58* (Toronto 1977), chap. 8.

2 RG3, III, 25, '1950, Frost, Leslie M.,' John Dibblee to LMF, 16 Feb. 1950

3 *Globe and Mail* and *Lindsay Post*, 5 Apr. 1939

4 TUA, LMF, vol. 3, folder 6

5 McKenty, *Hepburn*, 199–203

6 TUA, LMF, vol. 15, folder 13, LMF to A.W.R. Sinclair, 23 Sept. 1939 (personal)

7 *Globe and Mail*, 11 Jan. 1940

8 TUA, LMF, letterbook 8, LMF to C.H. Hale, 10 Feb. 1942

9 Ibid., LMF to J.A. McGibbon, 15 Sept. 1942. Frost added that this was not the only legal work he did gratis. Since his election to the legislature he had 'made it a point never to charge anyone in connection with any business arising out of Ontario Government matters such as Old Age Pensions and Mothers' Allowances, or the other innumerable provincial matters in which people find themselves in difficulty.'

10 Frost had apparently forgotten the woeful shortage of rifles when he had commanded C Company in Orillia in 1916.

11 *Globe and Mail*, 18 Jan. 1940; McKenty, *Hepburn*, 209

12 On the state of the party at that time, see J.L. Granatstein, *The Politics of Survival: The Conservative Party of Canada, 1939–1945* (Toronto 1967), chap. 3.

13 TUA, LMF, vol. 3, folder 7, C.N. Gordon to LMF, 29 Apr. 1940 (personal and confidential); LMF to Gordon, 3 May 1940 (private and confidential)

14 Ibid., LMF to Drew, 20 June 1940
15 Ibid., CGF, vol. 2, folder 3, Drew to CGF, 25 June 1940; CGF to Drew, 26 July 1940; folder 2, Minutes of Ontario Conservative Association executive meeting, 17 Oct. 1940
16 Ibid., LMF, vol. 3, folder 7, LMF to Drew, 12 June 1940
17 Ibid.; *Globe and Mail*, 5 June 1940; McKenty, *Hepburn*, 220
18 TUA, LMF, vol. 3, folder 7, LMF to Drew, 12, 20 June 1940
19 Ibid., vol. 81, folder 5, Drew to LMF, 11 Aug. 1941
20 Jonathan Manthorpe, *The Power and the Tories: Ontario Politics – 1943 to the Present* (Toronto 1974), 41
21 TUA, LMF, letterbook 7, LMF to R.J. Smith, 8 Sept. 1941 (personal)
22 Ibid., LMF to A.W. Gamble, 31 Jan. 1942
23 Ibid., LMF to Drew, 14 Jan. 1941 (personal)
24 TUA, LMF, letterbook 7, LMF to Drew, 8 Jan. 1941 (personal)
25 Ibid., LMF to Drew, 15 Jan. 1941 (personal)
26 *Globe and Mail*, 16 Jan. 1941
27 Ibid., 22 Jan. 1941
28 Ibid., 6 Mar. 1941
29 OHSS oral history, George Gathercole interview, 10 Aug. 1976, 12. I am indebted to Mr Gathercole for allowing me to use the valuable material in his series of interviews, of which this is the first.
30 RG3, II, 37, 'Treasury – Citizens' Research 1940 Budget, 1939, 1941,' R.C. Berkinshaw to LMF, 1 Dec. 1939; LMF to Berkinshaw, 6 Dec. 1939; George Gathercole to LMF, 19 Dec. 1939
31 TUA, LMF, letterbook 7, LMF to Hale, 10 Feb. 1941
32 *Watchman-Warder*, 19 Mar. 1941. A draft of this piece, partly in Frost's handwriting, is in RG3, II, 37, 'Elections – Campaign 1943.' It may have been initially drafted by Gertrude Frost's nephew, Jack Beal, who frequently wrote editorials for the paper at Frost's behest. OHSS oral history, Jack and Eileen Beal interview, 6
33 A copy of this manuscript with emendations in Frost's handwriting is in RG3, II, 37, 'Treasury – Budget Real Estate 1941.'
34 Armstrong, *Politics of Federalism*, 230–2. For a comprehensive history of the tax rental issue, see R.M. Burns, *The Acceptable Mean: The Tax Rental Agreements, 1941–1962* (Toronto 1980).
35 TUA, LMF, letterbook 7, LMF to Challies, 28 May 1941
36 Ibid., vol. 4, folder 1, LMF to Drew, 5 Sept. 1941
37 *Globe and Mail*, 26 Mar. 1942

CHAPTER 5: SOMETHING TO FIGHT AND CHEER FOR

1 TUA, LMF, letterbook 7, LMF to Hale, 4 Feb. 1942
2 Ibid., letterbook 8, LMF to Hale, 7 July 1942

3 Ibid., LMF to Drew, 15 July 1942
4 'Can We Return to Freedom?' (11 July); 'A Conservative Party is Essential to Canada' (18 July); 'The Conservatives and a New National Policy' (25 July)
5 TUA, LMF, letterbook 8, LMF to Drew, 29 July 1942 (private and confidential)
6 Ibid., vol. 15, folder 13, Drew to LMF, 1 Aug. 1942
7 Ibid., letterbook 7, LMF to Hale, 10 Feb. 1942
8 TUA, LMF, letterbook 8, LMF to Hale, 14 Sept. 1942
9 *Globe and Mail*, 25 June 1942; TUA, CGF, vol. 2, folder 2, CGF to Drew, 25 June 1942
10 TUA, LMF, letterbook 8, LMF to Hale, 7 July 1942
11 J.W. Pickersgill, *The Mackenzie King Record*, vol. 1 (Toronto 1960), 404. A copy of Drew's letter to King is in TUA, LMF, vol. 4, folder 1.
12 See, for example, QUA, Herbert A. Bruce Papers, Bruce to R.B. Hanson, 22 Aug. 1942.
13 TUA, CGF, vol. 2, folder 5, Macdonnell to LMF, 11 July [1967]. For a detailed discussion of the Port Hope conference, see J.L. Granatstein, *The Politics of Survival: The Conservative Party of Canada, 1939–1945* (Toronto 1967), 125–35.
14 TUA, LMF, letterbook 8, LMF to Hale, 14 Sept. 1942
15 Ibid., vol. 81, folder 5, Drew to LMF, 26 Sept. 1942; LMF to Drew, 28 Sept. 1942; Drew to LMF, 5 Oct. 1942. See also Neil McKenty, *Mitch Hepburn* (Toronto 1967), 247–9; Ivan Avakumovic, *The Communist Party in Canada: A History* (Toronto 1975), 142, 151.
16 TUA, LMF, vol. 101, folder 3
17 Ibid., vol. 17, folder 1, LMF to Hepburn, 22 Oct. 1942 (personal). For the circumstances surrounding and the reasons for the resignation, see McKenty, *Hepburn*, 250ff.
18 *Globe and Mail*, 2 Feb. 1942, 20 Mar. 1941
19 TUA, LMF, vol. 17, folder 1, LMF to Conant, 22 Oct. 1942 (personal)
20 Ibid., letterbook 8, LMF to Challies, 30 Oct. 1942
21 *Globe and Mail*, 30 Nov. 1942; TUA, LMF, letterbook 8, LMF to Drew, 1 Dec. 1942
22 On Bracken's candidacy and the Winnipeg convention, see Granatstein, *Politics of Survival*, 139–50; John Kendle, *John Bracken: A Political Biography* (Toronto 1979), chap. 12; Roger Graham, *Arthur Meighen, a Biography*, 3 (Toronto 1965), 138–51.
23 *Globe and Mail*, 1 July 1943
24 *Star*, 10 July 10, 1943
25 Timothy J. Colton, *Big Daddy: Frederick G. Gardiner and the Building of Metropolitan Toronto* (Toronto 1980), 36; OHSS oral history, Gardiner interview, 88. That Drew framed the platform himself without much

consultation has been confirmed for the author by the Right Hon. Roland Michener, active in the party's progressive wing at the time, and by Hugh Latimer who, although absent on military service when the 1943 election took place, subsequently acquired a close knowledge of the party's affairs and of its principal figures.

26 It might have differed in one respect. Shortly before Drew summarized his program over the radio, Frost advised him on the strength of soundings taken at recent political meetings to give defence of provincial rights and of the individual against federal regulatory power a prominent place in the election manifesto. 'I believe that rightly handled a storm could be raised which would turn this [Nixon] government out of office without any other issue' (TUA, LMF, letterbook 8, LMF to Drew, 26 June 1943 (personal). The platform made some mention of these matters but less stress was placed on them than Frost seems to have thought desirable.

27 *Globe and Mail*, 10 July 1943

28 OHSS oral history, Hugh Latimer interview, 16 June 1972, 1–2; Hugh D. Latimer, 'Political Reminiscences,' 74ff

29 TUA, LMF, vol. 4, folder 3, typed statement presumably intended as a press release

30 Ibid., letterbook 8, LMF to Clayton Hodgson, 24 July 1943

31 Ibid., LMF to McAlpine, 20 July 1943

32 Ibid., LMF to Gardiner, 7 Aug. 1943

33 The foregoing is derived from Legislative Assembly of Ontario, *Returns from the Record of the General Election* (1943), and *Globe and Mail*, 5 Aug. 1943.

34 TUA, LMF, letterbook 8, LMF to Drew, 5 Aug. 1943

35 RG3, III, 29, 'Frost, Leslie M. – 1951,' LMF to H.B. Neal, 27 Oct. 1951

36 *Globe and Mail*, 18 Aug. 1943: Ontario, *Legislative Assembly Debates* (hereafter *Debates*), 1949: 864

37 TUA, LMF, scrapbooks, vol. 2, 1935–47, unidentified clipping

CHAPTER 6: RESISTING THE CENTRALIST TIDE

1 *Globe and Mail*, 9 Oct. 1943

2 Ibid., 5, 13 Nov. 1943; Timothy J. Colton, *Big Daddy: Frederick G. Gardiner and the Building of Metropolitan Toronto* (Toronto 1980), 36

3 OHSS oral history, Gathercole interview, 8

4 RG6, 1-2, 39, 'Budget Speech, 1944,' LMF to Walters, 1 Feb. 1944

5 *Globe and Mail*, 27 Nov. 1943

6 AO, Legislative Assembly newspaper hansard, 17 Mar. 1944. There is no attribution to specific newspapers of the clippings comprising this collection, which one must rely upon in the unfortunate absence at that time of an official verbatim report.

7 QUA, Principals' Papers, LMF to Wallace, 28 Jan. 1944; Wallace to LMF, 7 Feb. 1944. I am indebted to Prof. F.W. Gibson for calling this correspondence to my attention.

8 RG3, II, 3, 'Dom-Prov Conference on Various Subjects 1943–45,' memorandum by LMF, May 1963

9 Ibid.; and 'Dom.-Prov. – Negotiations Concerning Reciprocal Agreements, 1944, 1945,' in particular, Stuart Garson to LMF, 19 Dec. 1944; LMF to Garson, 4 Jan. 1945; Garson to LMF, 7 Feb. 1945. See also Robert Bothwell, Ian Drummond, and John English, *Canada since 1945: Power, Politics and Provincialism* (Toronto 1981), 98.

10 *Globe and Mail*, 20, 21 Jan. 1944

11 RG6, I-2, 39, LMF to Walters, 1 Feb. 1944

12 Newspaper hansard, 17, 24 Mar. 1944

13 *Globe and Mail*, 17 Mar. 1944

14 Drew to King, 6 Jan. 1944. Copies of this letter and of those cited below to which it gave rise, in which Frost also participated, are in RG3, II, 3, 'Dom.-Prov. Conference 1945 (I).'

15 Canada, *House of Commons Debates* (hereafter *Commons Debates*), 1944–45: 4

16 King to Drew, 13 Jan., 28 Feb. 1944

17 Drew to King, 14 Mar. 1944. On the genesis and eventual demise of this abortive plan, see Robert Bothwell, 'The Health of the Common People' in John English and J.O. Stubbs, eds, *Mackenzie King: Widening the Debate* (Toronto 1977).

18 LMF to King, 21 Sept. 1944

19 *Commons Debates*, 1944: 6502

20 Drew to King, 14 Feb. 1945, telegram; A.D.P. Heeney to Drew, 22 Feb. 1945

21 According to Gerald Caplan, who got it from Larry Zolf, who got it from Harry Nixon, Drew told Nixon that, in Caplan's paraphrase, he 'did not intend to have Ontario pay for Quebec's prolific procreation.' Gerald L. Caplan, *The Dilemma of Canadian Socialism: The CCF in Ontario* (Toronto 1973), 139, 153, n.24

22 J.L. Granatstein, *Canada's War: The Politics of the Mackenzie King Government, 1939–1945* (Toronto 1975), 285. Drew had probably read a memorandum prepared for Frost by Chester Walters which pointed out that Ontario would contribute about half of the estimated $200 million initial annual cost of the plan. According to Walters, if the lost tax fields were regained, Ontario could on its own not only provide more generous family allowances but greatly increase payments to municipalities for education and other purposes, expand health services, enlarge its projected highway building program, and have left over $12 million with which to reduce the

net provincial debt. RG3, II, 3, 'Dom.-Prov. Conference 1945 (II),' Walters to LMF, 31 July 1944 (confidential)

23 Neil McKenty, *Mitch Hepburn* (Toronto 1967), 269, 71; David Lewis, *The Good Fight: Political Memoirs 1909–1958* (Toronto 1981), 264–5

24 Newspaper hansard, 10 Mar. 1945

25 For evidence of this from Drew's own papers, see Lewis, *The Good Fight*, 276ff.

26 TUA, LMF, vol. 3, folder 6

27 *Toronto Star*, 5 June 1945

28 TUA, LMF, vol. 3, folder 6, LMF to McKenzie, 5 June 1945 (personal)

29 RG3, II, 'Dom.-Prov. Conference 1945 (III),' LMF to Drew, handwritten draft telegram, n.d. [Nov. 1944]; Drew to LMF, 18 Nov. 1944 (telegram)

30 Ibid., 4, 'Dom.-Prov. – General Files 1942–46 (III),' 'Memorandum ... 4 July 1945' (private & confidential)

31 Ibid., 3, 'Dom-Prov Conferences on Various Subjects 1943–45,' memorandum by LMF, May 1963

32 For a useful discussion of the conference and Ontario's role in it, see Marc J. Gotlieb, 'George Drew and the Dominion-Provincial Conference on Reconstruction of 1945–6,' *Canadian Historical Review* (March 1985): 27–47.

33 *Dominion-Provincial Conference (1945): Dominion and Provincial Submissions and Plenary Conference Discussions* (Ottawa 1946), 7 (hereafter cited as *Conference 1945*)

34 Ibid., 10–12

35 Ibid., 118

36 Donald Creighton, *The Forked Road: Canada 1939–1957* (Toronto 1976), 108–9

37 *Conference 1945*, 227

38 Ibid., 237–8

39 Bothwell et al., *Canada Since 1945*, 95

40 *Conference 1945*, 239–48

CHAPTER 7: RESOLVING PROBLEMS OLD AND NEW

1 Newspaper hansard, 29 Mar. 1946

2 RG3, III, II, 'Liquor Licensing Act,' I, T.B. Bridle to Drew, 2 Apr. 1946 (copy)

3 Ibid., LMF to Gordon Smyth, 31 Oct. 1946 (personal)

4 OHSS oral history, George Gathercole interview, 35

5 RG3, III, II, 'Liquor Licensing,' LMF to C.D. Cross, March 29, 1946 (personal); RG6, I-2, 48, 'Liquor Control Board, 1946–7,' LMF to Mrs George Challies, 29 Mar. 1946

6 RG3, III, II, 'Liquor Licensing,' LMF to Cross, 29 Mar. 1946 (personal)

7 Newspaper hansard, 21 Mar. 1946

8 RG3, II, 4, 'Dom-Prov Conference Letters & Memos 1946–1947,' LMF to Drew, 15 July 1946 (private and confidential)

9 *Commons Debates*, 1946: 2909–11

10 RG3, II, 4, 'Dom-Prov Conference Letters & Memos 1946–1947,' LMF to Bracken, 4 July 1946 (two letters, one confidential); LMF to Macdonnell, 4 July 1946 (personal)

11 *Commons Debates*, 1946: 3225, 3602, 3740–1

12 The minister of Justice, Louis St Laurent, had recently moved a resolution asking the British Parliament to amend the BNA Act so as to change the method of determining the number of seats allotted to each province in the House of Commons. He denied that the provinces had a right to be consulted about this, asserting that legally, though not by accepted convention, Parliament could even petition unilaterally for amendments to section 133, which guaranteed certain fundamental language rights. He explicitly stated, however, that such unilateral power did not extend to subjects under provincial jurisdiction. See *Commons Debates*, 1946: 22621; RG3, II, 4, 'Dom.-Prov. – Correspondence, Drew-Frost 1946,' Drew to LMF, 9 July 1946.

13 Ibid., 'Dom-Prov Conference Letters & Memos 1946–1947,' LMF to Drew, 15 July 1946 (private and confidential)

14 J.W. Pickersgill and D.F. Forster, eds, *The Mackenzie King Record*, vol. 4 (Toronto 1970), 7

15 See RG3, II, 5, 'Dom.-Prov. Conference, Discussions and Memos, 1947,' LMF to Drew, 15 Jan. 1947 (confidential)

16 Ibid., LMF to Drew, 28 Jan. 1947 (emphasis in original)

17 Ibid., document bearing notation 'These were LMF's views as transmitted to Geo Drew in 1947' (emphasis in original)

18 See *Montreal Star*, 15 Feb. 1947; RG6, I-2, 41, 'Dom-Prov Relations, 1947,' Macdonnell to LMF, Feb. (?) 1947; LMF to Macdonnell, 21 Feb. 1947.

19 *Debates*, 1947: 773–9

20 Ibid., 71, 85–8

21 Ibid., 1948: 624ff

22 RG3, II, 27, 'Natural Gas Situation 1947, 1948 (III),' LMF to Howe, 9 Sept. 1947; Howe to LMF, 17 Sept. 1947

23 Ibid., LMF to T. Weir, 10 Sept. 1947; Weir to LMF, 16 Sept. 1947; LMF to Weir, 5 Nov. 1947; Weir to LMF, 15 Nov. 1947

24 Ibid., LMF to Howe, 10 Sept. 1947; Howe to LMF, 18 Sept. 1947. See William Kilbourn, *Pipeline: Trans-Canada and the Great Debate, a History of Business and Politics* (Toronto 1970), 13ff.

25 *Globe and Mail*, 19 May 1948

26 RG3, III, 14, 'Frost, Hon. Leslie M.,' LMF to A.M. Mahaffy, 28 May 1947; 25, 'Leslie M. Frost – Personal,' LMF to G.B. Frost, 18 Feb. 1948; II, 15, 'Frost, C.G. (Lindsay), 1947,' LMF to J.C. Ferguson, 18 Aug. 1947; LMF to G.B. Frost, 5 Nov. 1947; I, 160, 'Queen's Counsel (Appointments) 1956–7,' LMF to Harold Scott, 6 Dec. 1956; OHSS oral history, Marjorie Porter interview, 10–11

27 On the events leading to Bracken's resignation, see John Kendle, *Bracken: A Political Biography* (Toronto 1979), 234–5.

28 *Debates*, 1948: 1244ff

29 RG3, III, 18, 'Frost, Hon. L.M.,' LMF to C.H. Hale, 29 June 1948 (personal)

30 *Packet and Times*, 23 Sept. 1948

31 RG3, III, 18, 'Frost, Hon. L.M.,' LMF to Geo. G. Johnston, 16 Aug. 1948

32 *Globe and Mail*, 4, 5 Oct. 1948; *Star*, 6 Oct. 1948

33 *Debates*, 1949: 13

34 Ibid., 111–12

CHAPTER 8: FRONT AND CENTRE

1 *Telegram* (Toronto), 27 Apr. 1949

2 RG3, T.L. Kennedy Papers, general correspondence, box 2, 'Mancross, Mr. Park – M.P.,' Kennedy to LMF, 6 Dec. 1948

3 *Debates*, 1949: 543ff

4 Ibid., 1335–9

5 *Star*, 26 Mar. 1949

6 Quoted in ibid., 1 Apr. 1949

7 Quoted in *Debates*, 1949: 1629

8 *Time*, 11 Apr. 1949, 21

9 Quoted in *Debates*, 1949: 1629

10 A. Kelso Roberts, 'The Member for Saint Patrick: Thirty Years of Ontario Political Action' (Toronto: private edition, 1969), 52

11 TUA, LMF, outgoing letters, LMF to Malcolm McIntyre, 28 Oct. 1965

12 RG6, I-2, 40, 'Charitable Gifts Act – Corresp. etc.,' LMF to Walters, 5 Nov. 1948

13 Ibid., W.C. Browning et al. to Walters, 16 Nov. 1948; LMF to Walters, 17 Nov. 1948

14 Ross Harkness, *J.E. Atkinson of the Star* (Toronto 1963), 350–1

15 The foregoing is drawn from *Debates*, 1949: 1619ff, 2092–5

16 TUA, LMF, outgoing letters, LMF to Malcolm McIntyre, 28 Oct. 1965

17 For Jolliffe's speech see *Debates*, 1949: 1627ff, 1855ff

18 Ibid., 2093–5

19 *Telegram*, 17 Feb. 1949; *London Free Press*, 20 Apr. 1949

20 Verbatim report of the convention supplied to the author by Hugh Latimer, I

21 RG3, III, 18, 'Frost, Hon. L.M.,' LMF to Hale, 29 Oct. 1948 (personal)

22 *Globe and Mail*, 16 Feb. 1949

23 TUA, LMF, vol. 4, folder I

24 Ibid., vol. 2, folder 8

25 RG6, I-2, 43, 'Frost, L.M. Re: Convention, April 1949,' draft of sketch to be used 'exactly as written,' accompanying LMF to Frank Hawthorne, 19 Apr. 1949

26 Ibid., vol. 5, folder I; ibid., handwritten note by LMF headed 'after convention'

27 Verbatim report of convention, 41

28 Margaret Aitken, 'Between You and Me,' *Telegram*, 6 Oct. 1948

29 *Globe and Mail*, 21, 25, 26 Apr. 1949; *Port Arthur Chronicle* (CP despatch), 22 Apr. 1949; *Galt Reporter*, 25 Apr. 1949; *Owen Sound Daily Sun-Times* (CP despatch), 27 Apr. 1949; *Ontario Intelligencer*, Belleville, 28 Apr. 1949

30 This story was recounted to the author by Maloney's brother, the late Arthur Maloney, QC.

31 Verbatim report of convention, 50–2

32 TUA, LMF, vol. 4, folder I

33 *Kitchener Record* (CP despatch), 23 Apr. 1949; *Owen Sound Daily Sun-Times* (CP despatch), 27 Apr. 1949; *Telegram*, 27 Apr. 1949

34 *Toronto Star*, 27 Apr. 1949; *London Free Press*, 28 Apr. 1949

35 Transcript supplied to the author by Hugh Latimer

36 RG6, I-2, 448, 'Legislature, 1948–49,' Blackwell to LMF, 29 Apr. 1949; LMF to Blackwell, 2 May 1949

37 *Globe and Mail*, 2, 5 May 1949

CHAPTER 9: NEW DIRECTIONS

I RG3, I, 151, 'Prime Minister's Office'; OHSS oral history, Irene Beatty interview, II July 1974, 272–8; Hugh Latimer, 'Political Reminiscences,' 118; author's interview, Ray Farrell, 20 Aug. 1979

2 Hugh Latimer to author, 28 July 1983

3 *Toronto Star*, 24 June 1949

4 RG3, II, 5, 'Dom.-Prov. – St. Laurent Corresp. 1949,' memorandum by LMF, 1963

5 Ibid., LMF to St Laurent, 30 June 1949

6 Ibid., memorandum by LMF, 1963

7 Ibid., LMF to St Laurent, 12 Sept. 1949 (personal)

8 Ibid., 100, 'McCl-McCz,' folder I, McCullagh to LMF, 12 Apr. 1951 (personal); LMF to McCullagh, 19 Apr. 1951 (personal)

9 Ibid., II, 5, 'B.N.A. Act (Amending),' Drew to LMF, 15 Oct. 1949
(confidential)
10 Ibid., LMF to Drew, 15 Oct. 1949 (confidential)
11 Latimer, 'Reminiscences,' 69–70; memorandum by Latimer for the author
12 *Toronto Star*, 21 Oct. 1949
13 Ibid., 20 Oct. 1949. See also Timothy J. Colton, *Big Daddy: Frederick G.
Gardiner and the Building of Metropolitan Toronto* (Toronto 1980), 36–8.
14 RG3, II, 40, 'White, James M.P.P., Kenora,' White to LMF, 26 Oct. 1949
(personal and confidential)
15 Ibid., 31, 'Progressive Conservative Organization Policy 1949, 1950,' White to
LMF, 3 Jan. 1950 (personal and confidential)
16 Ibid., III, 23, '1949 Patronage,' LMF to Doucett, 24 June 1949 (private and
confidential); Doucett to LMF, 20 July 1949; Rex Boice to LMF, 7 Sept. 1949
17 Ibid., I, 212, 'Win-Wa,' folder I, 'Eric' to LMF, 19 Oct. 1949, with notations
by LMF and E.J. Young
18 OHSS oral history, Irene Beatty interview, 54
19 Memorandum by Hugh Latimer for the author; Latimer to the author,
28 July 1983
20 Latimer, 'Reminiscences,' 57
21 J.N. Allan to W.T. Robb, 13 Nov. 1949, copy supplied by Hugh Latimer;
Latimer to the author, 1 Aug. 1983
22 Latimer, 'Reminiscences,' 55–6
23 Edgecombe to W.T. Robb, 21 Nov. 1949; Allan to Robb, 13 Nov. 1949
(copies supplied by Hugh Latimer)
24 *Globe and Mail*, 23 July 1983. In his memoirs, *Life of the Party* (Toronto
1988), published after the late Professor Graham had completed his
manuscript, Goodman stated: 'On the night before the annual meeting
started, when Frost and McKenzie were in Frost's room at the Royal York
Hotel, Frost said, "Alex, it would be a great shame if after all your service
to the party, you were to be defeated for the presidency. Don't you think
that you should consider withdrawing?" McKenzie retorted, "If those
bastards are going to take over the party, they're going to have to do it by
defeating me in a vote and not by me walking away" ' (p. 58) [Eds].
25 *Globe and Mail*, 7 Nov. 1949; *Toronto Star*, 8 Nov. 1949
26 Latimer, 'Reminiscences,' 59–61
27 Ibid., 62–3
28 Allan to Robb, 13 Nov. 1949 (copy supplied by Hugh Latimer)
29 RG3, III, 23, '1949 Political Matters,' LMF to Hamilton, 8 Dec. 1949, and
accompanying memorandum
30 Minutes of Executive Committee meeting, 2 Oct. 1950, supplied by Hugh
Latimer; Latimer to the author, 20 Sept. 1983; Hamilton to the author, 29
Sept. 1983

31 RG3, II, 28, 'Progressive Conservative Annual Meeting 1950,' letter signed by LMF, 25 Oct. 1950
32 Ibid., letter signed by Latimer, 1 Nov. 1950
33 Latimer, 'Reminiscences,' 74–5

CHAPTER 10: GROWING PAINS

1 Peter Oliver, *Unlikely Tory: The Life and Politics of Allan Grossman* (Toronto 1985), 31–2
2 *Debates*, 1951, vol. 43: C13–14, DD1, DD3–6
3 RG3, I, 23, 'Cathcart, Bryan, M.P.P.,' Cathcart to LMF, 12 Apr. 1950
4 *Debates*, 1951, vol. 5: F10
5 RG3, II, 33, 'Throne Speech – Leaders' Day Speeches 1951,' speech by LMF, 7 Nov. 1950
6 RG6, 1-2, 56, 'Statistics & Research Bureau, 1951–54,' LMF to Chater, 23 July 1951
7 RG3, I, 36, 'Dom.-Prov. Relations, 1949–50,' 'Memorandum Relative to Province of Ontario in Dominion-Provincial Relations'
8 Ibid., with revised figures and accompanying explanatory note marked 'Secret'
9 *Proceedings of the Conference of Federal and Provincial Governments, December 4–7, 1950* (Ottawa 1953), 18–24
10 Ibid., 142, 145–6
11 *Globe and Mail*, 8 Dec. 1950
12 *Debates*, 1951, vol. 24: 8, 44–6
13 RG3, II, 6, 'Dom.-Prov. Conference, Abbott, Hon. Douglas, Aug. 1951,' LMF to Abbott, 23 Aug. 1951 (personal and confidential); draft statement, 17 Aug. 1951 (secret); Abbott to LMF, 18 Aug. 1951 (personal and confidential)
14 RG3, III, 33, '1951 – Election Correspondence,' folder 4, LMF to Herbert Irvine, 4 Dec. 1951
15 *Report of the Royal Commission on Education in Ontario* (Toronto 1950)
16 *Globe and Mail*, 22 Dec. 1950
17 RG3, III, 29, 'Frost, Leslie M. – 1951,' LMF to Hale, 12 June 1951
18 *Debates*, 1951, vol. 5: E9-10, F1-3
19 *Globe and Mail*, 5 Oct. 1951; *Canadian Forum*, Nov. 1951
20 *Globe and Mail*, 13 Oct. 1951
21 RG3, II, 12, 'Elections – Campaign Miscellaneous 1951'
22 RG3, II, 12, 'Elections – Provincial General 1951'; *Globe and Mail*, 21 Nov. 1951
23 *Globe and Mail*, 30 Oct., 7 Nov. 1951
24 Ibid., 23 Oct., 12 Nov. 1951
25 Ibid., 21 Nov. 1951

26 'The Grits Write off Ontario,' *Maclean's*, 15 Nov. 1951
27 *Toronto Star*, 6, 13 Nov. 1951
28 Ibid., 21 Nov. 1951
29 *Globe and Mail*, 23 Nov. 1951
30 RG3, III, 33, '1951 – Election Correspondence,' folder 4, LMF to Herbert Irvine, 4 Dec. 1951
31 Ibid., folder 2, H.R. Frost to LMF, 23 Nov. 1951
32 Saskatchewan Provincial Archives, John and Gertrude Telford Papers, Campbell to Mr and Mrs Telford, 23 Nov. 1951. The late Professor L.H. Thomas kindly furnished me with a copy of this letter to his parents-in-law.
33 *Globe and Mail*, 23 Nov. 1951

CHAPTER II: A BIG VIEW OF THE FUTURE

1 RG3, III, 33, '11951 – Election Correspondence,' folder 4, LMF to Herbert Irvine, 4 Dec. 1951
2 *Debates*, 1952, vol. 6: E7-13
3 *Globe and Mail*, 21 Mar. 1952
4 *Debates*, 1952, vol. 36: E7ff
5 *Commons Debates*, 1952: 3548–51
6 *Globe and Mail*, 30 Aug. 1952
7 R.M. Burns, 'Recent Developments in Federal-Provincial Fiscal Arrangements in Canada,' *National Tax Journal* XV, no 3 (Sept. 1962), 228
8 Quoted in *Commons Debates*, 1952–3, 700.
9 *Globe and Mail*, 30 Aug., 22 Oct. 1952
10 Ibid., 30 Aug. 1952
11 Ibid., 23 Oct. 1952
12 RG3, I, 155, 'Provincial-Municipal Relations Committee 1951,' Seely Eakins to St Laurent, 23 Sept. 1952, with accompanying resolutions (copies); St Laurent to Eakins, 23 Oct. 1952, with accompanying memorandum (copies); St Laurent to LMF, 23 Oct. 1952; LMF to H.J. Chater, 24 Oct. 1952
13 Ibid., 'Address by Hon. L.M. Frost ... May 31, 1951 ...,' in which he announced this initiative; see also LMF to Chater, 14 June 1951; Chater to LMF, 20 June 1951.
14 Ibid., Seely Eakins to LMF, 21 Jan. 1952; LMF to Eakins, 31 Jan. 1952
15 RG3, I, 155, 'Provincial-Municipal Relations Committee 1951,' Chater to LMF, 13 Nov. 1952
16 *Debates*, 1953, vol. 6: DII, E9–10; vol. 10: DI
17 Ibid., 1953, vol. 30: E10
18 For Frost's explanation and defence of the new grant structure, see ibid., vol. 10: C12ff; vol. 30: E6ff.

19 For its background and the process leading to its resolution, see Timothy J. Colton, *Big Daddy: Frederick G. Gardiner and the Building of Metropolitan Toronto* (Toronto 1980), chap. 3, on which the following paragraphs largely rely.

20 Ibid., 55

21 RG3, I, 149, 'Toronto Metro. Re: F.G. Gardiner, chairman 1950–55,' 'Proceedings at a Special Meeting of the Mayors and Reeves of the ... Toronto area'

22 See ibid., 195, 'Toronto, Metropolitan & W.J. Stewart,' Bunnell to LMF, 23 Jan. 1957.

23 Colton, *Big Daddy*, 65

24 RG3, I, 193, 'Toronto. Metropolitan Area Amalgamation. Genl. Corresp.,' LMF to E.J. Savage, 24 Mar. 1950

25 Colton, *Big Daddy*, 71

26 RG3, I, 59, 'Grossman, Allan, MPP,' Grossman to LMF, 4 Feb. 1953 (private and confidential); LMF to Grossman, 9 Feb. 1953 (private and confidential)

27 See in this connection *Debates*, 1953, vol. 10: B9; OHSS oral history, Gathercole interview, 36–7.

28 The OMB recommended a small body selected by constituent municipal councils, with the possibility of direct election later. Gathercole, in contrast, favoured a true federal system with the popular election by proportional representation of councillors in Metropolitan wards cutting across existing boundaries. See RG3, II, 36, 'Municipality of Metro. Toronto Miscellaneous Papers 1953,' Gathercole to LMF, 30 Jan. 1953 (confidential).

29 Peter Oliver, *Unlikely Tory: The Life and Politics of Allan Grossman* (Toronto 1985), 56

30 *Globe and Mail*, 26, 27 Feb. 1953; *Toronto Star*, 26 Feb. 1953

31 *Debates*, 1953, vol. 30: DD5

32 Ibid., vol. 35: F7

33 Colton, *Big Daddy*, 73

34 Latimer, 'Reminiscences,' 329–30

35 Colton, *Big Daddy*, 73

36 RG3, I, 194, 'Toronto Metro. Re: F.G. Gardiner, chairman 1950–5,' Gardiner to LMF, 24 Feb. 1954 (personal and confidential)

37 RG3, I, 148, 'Pollution of Border Waters 1945–53,' Phillips to E.J. Young, 2 July 1953; LMF to Young, 29 July 1953; McIntyre to Berry, 12 Aug. 1953; Berry to McIntyre, 13 Aug. 1953

38 Ibid., 'Pollution of Boundary Waters (Agreement between Canada and U.S.),' memorandum by D.J. Collins, 5 April 1954

39 Ibid., Phillips to LMF, 4 Nov. 1954; LMF to Phillips, 10 Nov. 1954; Phillips to LMF, 12 Nov. 1954

40 Ibid., St Laurent to LMF, 16 Nov. 1954; LMF to St Laurent, 23 Dec. 1954; St Laurent to LMF, 24 Mar. 1955; memorandum by E.J. Young, 22 Apr. 1955; LMF to St Laurent, 24 May 1955

41 Ibid., 209, LMF to Snider, 25 May 1955; Snider to LMF, 28 July 1955; LMF to Snider, 9 Aug. 1955; McIntyre to LMF, 4 Feb. 1957; McIntyre to Dana Porter, 5 Feb. 1957; LMF to Snider, 3 Apr. 1957

42 *Debates*, 1954: 490ff

43 RG3, I, 73, 'Hydro Advisory Council ... Frost,' LMF to Saunders, 15 Nov. 1950

44 Ibid., 22, 'Cas,' LMF to Garfield Case, 9 Oct. 1951 (personal)

45 Ibid., 74, 'H.E.P.C. – Saunders,' folder 2, LMF to Challies, 30 Oct. 1953; Saunders to LMF, 19 Feb. 1953; LMF to Saunders, 26 Feb. 1953

46 RG6, 1-2, 46, 'Hydro 1948–54,' LMF to Saunders, 23 Apr. 1953; Saunders to LMF, 23 Apr. 1953; LMF to Chester Walters, 27 Apr. 1953

47 RG3, I, 74, 'H.E.P.C. Chairman R.H. Saunders,' LMF to Saunders, 26 Jan. 1953 (personal and confidential)

48 Ibid., 73, 'Hydro Advisory Council ... Frost,' LMF to Saunders, 15 Nov. 1950

49 Ibid., 11, 18, 'H.E.P.C. – Hydro Advisory Committee, 1950, 1951,' Saunders to LMF, 22 Nov. 1950 (personal and confidential)

50 Ibid., Macaulay to LMF, 8 Oct. 1958

51 For its history, see William R. Willoughby, *The St. Lawrence Waterway: A Study in Politics and Diplomacy* (Madison, Wis. 1961).

52 Lionel Chevrier, *The St. Lawrence Seaway* (Toronto 1959), 30

53 Kingston *Whig-Standard*, 2 Aug. 1951

54 *Debates*, 1952, vol. 10: A2-B9

55 Willoughby *St. Lawrence Waterway*, 233

56 *Globe and Mail*, 4 Dec. 1951

57 RG3, I, 93, Gemmell to LMF, 30 Jan. 1951; LMF to Gemmell, 7 Feb. 1951; 116, 'Natural Gas,' LMF to Gemmell, 2 Oct. 1951

58 Ibid., LMF to G.C. Wardrope, 28 July 1952

59 William Kilbourn, *Pipeline* (Toronto 1970), 27. The reader is referred to this work for a comprehensive history of the pipeline.

60 RG3, I, 116, 'Natural Gas,' Wardrope to LMF, 18 July 1952; LMF to Wardrope, 28 July 1952

61 Ibid., 208, 'Wan-War,' folder 1, Howe to Wardrope, 12 Aug. 1952 (confidential); Wardrope to LMF, 18 Aug. 1952 (confidential)

62 Ibid., LMF to Wardrope, 25 Aug. 1952

63 These discussions were summarized in a memorandum by Crozier, from which the following information and quotations are derived. Ibid., Crozier to P.T. Kelly, 13 Aug. 1952

64 Kilbourn, *Pipeline*, 35–7

65 RG3, I, 116, 'Natural Gas,' Kelly to LMF, 16 Feb. 1953

66 TUA, LMF, vol. 7, folder 17, memorandum by LMF, n.d.; folder 1, W.M. McIntyre to LMF, 28 May 1956, with marginal notes by LMF. Frost claimed that this meeting was 'the actual genesis of what is now the Trans Canada Pipe Line and the opening of the markets of Central Canada to gas from Western Canada.' There had been 'vague discussions' previously but 'the first official meeting' was the one chaired by Bickle in October 1952. How an unsuccessful discussion could have had such seminal significance he did not explain.

67 RG3, 1, 116, 'Natural Gas,' Kelly to LMF, 16 March 1953

68 Ibid., LMF to Howe, 5 May 1953 (confidential)

69 *Saturday Night*, 5 Sept. 1953: 10

70 RG3, 1, 120, 'Nickle, W.M., LMF to Nickle, 9 Sept. 1953

71 *Victoria Daily Times*, 15 Aug. 1953

72 RG3, 1, 'Natural Gas,' telegram conveyed in Kelly to LMF, 30 July 1953

73 Ibid., memorandum signed by Kelly

74 Ibid., memorandum by E.J. Young, 'Re Alberta Gas Controversy'

75 Ibid., LMF to Howe, 5 Aug. 1953 (telegram)

76 Ibid., Crozier to Kelly, 4 Sept. 1953; Kelly to LMF, 4 Sept. 1953; LMF to Howe, 4 Sept. 1953

77 Ibid., Lamport to LMF, 16 Sept. 1953; LMF to Lamport, 30 Sept. 1953

78 RG3, 1, 116, 'Natural Gas,' Manning to LMF, 4 Dec. 1953, accompanied by copy of Manning to St Laurent, 3 Dec. 1953

79 Ibid., Howe to LMF, 14 Dec. 1953

80 Ibid., 7, 'Attorney General, Dept. of 1948–1956,' LMF to Porter, 8 Dec. 1953

CHAPTER 12: HUMAN BETTERMENT

1 Malcolm G. Taylor, *Health Insurance and Canadian Public Policy: The Seven Decisions that Created the Canadian Health Insurance System* (Montreal 1978), 110. The following pages rely heavily on this valuable work.

2 RG3, 1, 64, 'Health Insurance,' folder 2, LMF to Gathercole, 9 Oct. 1951

3 Ibid., 6, 'Associated Medical Services,' Phillips to E.J. Young, 8 Jan. 1952

4 Taylor, *Health Insurance*, 108–9

5 Ibid., 115

6 *Debates*, 1955: 1143–4, 1147. Frost's remarks were based on a statement Gathercole drafted for him to read. In places Frost departed from and enlarged upon it in his somewhat more discursive style. Gathercole's text is in RG3, 1, 64, 'Health Insurance,' folder 2.

7 *Debates*, 1955: 1147

8 Taylor, *Health Insurance*, 125

9 *Federal-Provincial Conference 1955: Preliminary Meeting* (Ottawa 1955), 22–3

10 Ibid., 16, 18–19

11 Taylor, *Health Insurance*, 106, 126

12 What may have been their earliest joint venture was initiated by the Union Government in 1919 as part of its post-war reconstruction plans. Sponsored by Newton Rowell, chairman of a cabinet subcommittee on housing, it greatly enlarged funds earmarked for loans to municipalities (for constitutional reasons transmitted via provincial governments) to build houses for low-income families. Although Ottawa intended to control operation of this venture, in Ontario, where the Hearst government was developing a housing policy of its own, Rowell was forced to compromise and allow the province more discretion in administering it than he wished. See Margaret Prang, *N.W. Rowell: Ontario Nationalist* (Toronto 1975), 295–6.

13 RG3, I, 72, 'Housing Federal & Provincial,' LMF to McDonald, Saturday a.m. [30 July 1949]; Monday a.m. [1 Aug. 1949]; McDonald to LMF, 2 and 4 Aug. 1949 (Frost's emphasis)

14 Ibid., Winters to LMF, 13 Sept. 1949 (confidential); 'Brief record of the meeting on Housing ... September 8, 1949'; 'Short notes on the special meeting ... September 28, 1949'; LMF to Griesinger, 14 Nov. 1949

15 Ibid., II, 18, 'Housing – Mayors & Reeves 1951,' Bunnell to Griesinger, 8 May 1951 (copy). The speed with which events moved suggests that Bunnell's memorandum was not the origin of the plan, although its language might indicate otherwise, but simply spelled out a policy already determined. Of course he may have been instrumental in setting its broad outlines.

16 Ibid., III, outgoing 1945–62, LMF to Griesinger, 10 May 1951

17 Ibid., II, 18, 'Housing – Mayors & Reeves 1951,' Griesinger to LMF, 14 May 1951; Griesinger to Winters, 7 June 1951

18 RG3, I, 213, 'Windsor, City of, genl. Corresp.,' W. Steward to LMF, 14 June 1951; C.V. Waters to LMF, 20 June 1951; LMF to Waters, 25 June 1951; Reaume to LMF, 29 June 1951; LMF to Reaume, 5 July 1951; Reaume to LMF, 8 July 1951

19 Ibid., Griesinger to municipal clerks, 20 June 1951

20 *Debates*, 1952, vol. 34: C4ff

21 Ibid., 1954: 1031–2

22 Ibid., 496

23 Ibid., 494. For a survey of developments in elementary and secondary education during the Drew and Frost periods, see Robert M. Stamp, *The Schools of Ontario, 1876–1976* (Toronto 1982), chap. 9.

24 Ibid., 185

25 TUA, LMF, vol. 12, folder 9, 'Memorandum by L.M.F. Concerning Separate Roman Catholic Elementary Schools,' 1972, 4–5

26 *Ontario Public Accounts*, 1943–4: C10; 1954–55, II, C30-1

27 RG, I, 43, 'Education, Minister of,' quoted in Dunlop to LMF, 1 Mar. 1954.

28 Ibid., LMF to Dunlop, 8 Mar. 1954

29 For a useful extended account of the relationship between universities and government under Drew and his Conservative successors, see Paul Axelrod, *Scholars and Dollars: Politics, Economics, and the Universities of Ontario 1945–1980* (Toronto 1982)
30 Ibid., 258–9
31 RG3, I, 171, 'Royal Commission on National Development in the Arts, Letters & Sciences,' Massey to LMF, 8 Sept. 1949; Porter to LMF, 23 Sept. 1949; LMF to Porter, 28 Sept. 1949
32 Ibid., 161, 'Queen's University,' LMF to Wallace, 25 June 1951
33 Ibid., 203, 'Universities – Federal Grants,' LMF to Porter, 1 Nov. 1956; Porter to LMF, 2 Nov. 1956
34 Ibid., 161, 'Queen's University,' Wallace to LMF, 27 June 1951; LMF to Althouse, 29 June 1951; Althouse to LMF, 4 July 1951; LMF to Porter, 11 July 1951; Porter to LMF, 20 July 1951
35 Axelrod, *Scholars and Dollars*, 82–3
36 RG3, I, 208, 'Wallace, Dr. R.C.,' Wallace to LMF, 31 Dec. 1954
37 In 1943–4 the province's contribution to the universities was nearly 22 per cent of its net ordinary expenditure on education and slightly above 3 per cent of its total disbursements; by 1954–5 the corresponding figures were 7.5 and 1.3 per cent. Beginning in 1951–2, annual capital grants were also paid, but three years later the operating and capital sums together came to only about 14 per cent of the provincial budget for education and about 3 per cent of all ordinary expenditure. These data are derived from *Ontario Public Accounts*, 1943–4 *et seq.*
38 Axelrod, *Scholars and Dollars*, 258
39 RG3, I, 208, 'Wallace, Dr. R.C.,' Wallace to LMF, 31 Dec. 1954

CHAPTER 13: A MORAL AND SOBER PEOPLE

1 RG3, I, 139, 'Ont. Temperance Federation,' folder 2, LMF to Albert Johnson, 18 Oct. 1951
2 RG3, II, 23, 'Liquor Control IV Personal and Confidential 1950,' A.E. Morgan to LMF, 5 Oct. 1950
3 Ibid., I, 95, 'L.C.B.O. Genl. Corresp.,' folder 2, F.W.L. Brailey to LMF, 25 Sept. 1953
4 Ibid., III, outgoing 1945–62, LMF to Robb, 15 Sept. 1953
5 Ibid., I, 96, L.L.B.O. Genl. Corresp.,' LMF to Bassett, 21 Sept. 1953 (confidential)
6 Ibid., 95, 'L.C.B.O. Genl. Corresp.,' folder 2, Robb to LMF, 1 Oct. 1953 (strictly private and confidential)
7 Ibid., III, outgoing 1945–62, LMF to Robb, 7 July 1949
8 OHSS oral history, Robb interview, 29–30, 131

9 Hugh Latimer, 'Political Reminiscences,' 106
10 OHSS oral history, Robb interview, 31
11 RG3, I, 199, 'Twentieth Battalion Club,' LMF to Arthur Welsh, 3 Feb. 1950
12 OHSS oral history, Robb interview, 36
13 *Debates*, 1951, vol. 20: B5, B13
14 OHSS oral history, Robb interview, 57
15 For this speech, see *Debates*, 1951, vol. 20: B4ff.
16 RG3, I, 95, 'L.C.B.O. Advertising of Liquor,' LMF to J.R. Watt, 7 Jan. 1950
17 Ibid., II, 23, 'Liquor Control IV 1950,' Chalmers to LMF, 7 Sept. 1950 (personal)
18 RG3, 162, 'Racing, Night Harness,' folder I, W.J. Gallagher to LMF, 27 May 1950
19 Ibid., Mutchmor to Porter, 28 Apr. 1950; LMF to Mutchmor, 5 May 1950
20 *Globe and Mail*, 4, 6 Feb. 1950
21 Ibid., 28 Apr. 1950
22 Ibid., 1 June 1950
23 *Debates*, 1951, vol. II: 43–5; vol. 29: A5ff. For an extended treatment of policy respecting discrimination during the Drew and Frost regimes, see John C. Bagnall, 'The Ontario Conservatives and the Development of Anti-Discrimination Policy, 1944 to 1962' (MA thesis, Queen's University 1984).
24 RG3, III, 25, '1950 Frost, Leslie M.,' McGibbon to LMF, 17 Feb. 1950; LMF to McGibbon, 21 Feb. 1950
25 *Debates*, 1951, vol. 29: A10–11
26 Ibid., vol. 28: D1ff
27 Ibid., vol. 29: H8ff. Frost's memory was at fault about women on juries, brought in by the Hepburn government with some bipartisan support.
28 Bagnall, 'Anti-Discrimination Policy,' 301–2
29 *Debates*, 1954: 874
30 Bagnall, 'Anti-Discrimination Policy,' 325–32

CHAPTER 14: THUNDER ON THE LEFT

1 *Debates*, 1954: 490–1
2 *Globe and Mail*, 2 June 1951; A.W.R. Carrothers, *Collective Bargaining Law in Canada* (Toronto 1965), 141
3 *Globe and Mail*, 9 June 1951
4 RG3, I, 150, 'Press Gallery,' LMF to Don O'Hearn, 4 Feb. 1954
5 RG3, II, 19, 'Labour Relations – Globe & Mail, 1950, 1951,' statement by LMF, 18 June 1951
6 *Globe and Mail*, 19 June 1951
7 Ibid., 6 July 1951

8 RG3, II, 19, 'Labour Relations – Globe & Mail, 1950, 1951,' Harvey to LMF, 18 July 1951

9 *Globe and Mail*, 28 July 1951

10 The mines in the Timmins district had formerly been deemed within the jurisdiction of the International Union of Mine, Mill and Smelter Workers, another CCL-CIO affiliate. In the climax of a bitter struggle against it by those objecting to its domination by communists, largely led by the Steelworkers union which was eager to supplant it in the gold mines and elsewhere, Mine-Mill was expelled from the CCL in 1949. Not all locals accepted this decision. Some remained loyal to Mine-Mill, while others, including the Hollinger local, cast in their lot with the Steelworkers. For a detailed account of these events see Irving Martin Abella, *Nationalism, Communism and Canadian Labour* (Toronto 1975), chap. 6.

11 RG6, I-2, 53, 'Provincial Treasurer, 1952–53,' P.T. Kelly to LMF, 12 Nov. 1952; *Debates* 1954: 647

12 *Globe and Mail*, 12 July 1951

13 Ibid., 17, 31 July, 1 Aug. 1951

14 Ibid., 18 July 1951

15 RG3, I, 70, 'Hollinger Gold Mines,' LMF to Daley, 7 Aug. 1951 (personal and confidential)

16 Ibid., Conroy to LMF, 18 Aug. 1951

17 Ibid., LMF to Conroy, 22 Aug. 1951 (draft telegram with emendations in LMF's handwriting); *Globe and Mail*, 24, 31 Aug., 1 Sept. 1951

18 Ibid., 14, 17 July 1953; RG3, II, 19, 'Labour Relations – Timmins Strike 1953,' memorandum by E.J. Young, 24 July 1953

19 *Globe and Mail*, 25 July 1953

20 RG3, II, 19, 'Labour Relations – Timmins Strike 1953,' 'Memorandum of Meeting, July 24, 1953 ...'

21 Ibid., Millard to LMF, 24 July 1953 (telegram)

22 *Globe and Mail*, 16, 17, 18, 20, 29 July 1953

23 RG3, I, 100, 'McCa-McCk,' A.L. McCallion to LMF, 21 July 1953; LMF to McCallion, 27 July 1953

24 *Globe and Mail*, 21, 22, 23, 25 July 1953

25 RG3, I, 199, 'Truckers' & Miners' Strikes: Letters received re and Law Observance,' Statement by Frost, 30 July 1953

26 Ibid., 20, 21, 22, 25 Aug. 1953; RG3, I, 199, 'Truckers' & Miners' Strikes: Letters received ...,' R.W. Smith to LMF, 31 Aug. 1953; LMF to Smith, 2 Sept. 1953

27 *Globe and Mail*, 26, 27, 28 Aug. 1953

28 Ibid., 29 Aug. 1953

29 Ibid., 7 Sept. 1953

30 RG3, II, 19, 'Labour Relations – Timmins Strike 1953,' Millard to LMF, 4 Sept. 1953; LMF to Millard, 9 Sept. 1953; I, IIO, C.H. Millard,' Millard to LMF, 22 Sept. 1953
31 Ibid., 174, 'Sal-Saq,' LMF to B.K. Sandwell, 30 Oct. 1953
32 Ibid., 120, 'Nov-Nt,' Ken Hansen to LMF, 4 Oct. 1953, LMF to Hansen, 13 Oct. 1953 (personal and confidential)
33 *Globe and Mail*, 30 Sept. 1953
34 RG3, I, 87, 'Labour, Dept. of: Minister's File – Hon C. Daley,' LMF to Daley, 19 Oct. 1953 (personal and confidential)
35 *Globe and Mail*, 22, 26 Nov, 2, 3, 5, II, 14, 15, 23 Dec. 1953

CHAPTER 15: RENEWING THE MANDATE

1 See Hugh D. Latimer, 'Political Reminiscences,' 242ff, for descriptions of his *modus operandi* on the scene in influencing the choice of a by-election candidate and tactfully guiding the local party apparatus.
2 RG3, I, 155, 'Provincial Auditor (Harvey Cotnam),' LMF to Cotnam, 7 Oct. 1953 (personal)
3 *Globe and Mail*, 21, 22 Jan. 1954
4 *Debates*, 1954: 102–3
5 Ibid., 32–3, 35–6
6 Ibid., 505
7 Quoted in Kelso Roberts, 'Member for Saint Patrick: Thirty Years of Ontario Political Action' (private edition 1969), 77
8 Hugh Latimer to the author, 22 Dec. 1985
9 Author's interview of Hugh Latimer, 18–19
10 *Debates*, 1955: 159ff. For his briefer retrospective account, see 'Member for Saint Patrick,' chap. II.
11 *Globe and Mail*, 18 Feb. 1955
12 *Debates*, 1955: 187–8, 205ff
13 *Toronto Star*, 2 May 1955. For an extended discussion of the election, see M.C. Havey, 'The Ontario Election of 1955' (Master's essay, University of Waterloo 1984). I am obliged to Ms. Havey for allowing me to read her paper.
14 Latimer, 'Reminiscences,' 83–6
15 Ibid., 94–8
16 *Globe and Mail*, 2 May 1955
17 Ibid., 3 May 1955
18 Ibid., 5 May 1955
19 Ibid., 12 May 1955
20 Ibid., 10, 13 May 1955

21 The following account of this episode is based on: RG3, II, 7, 'Dom-Prov Conf April 1955,' memorandum by LMF, 'The Dempsey Incident,' n.d.; Latimer, 'Reminiscences,' 210–25; Havey, 'Election of 1955,' 41–3; *Globe and Mail*, 7, 10, 11, 12, 16, 18 May 1955.

22 See Peter Oliver, *Unlikely Tory: The Life and Politics of Allan Grossman* (Toronto 1985), especially chap. 4 on which the following paragraphs are based.

23 Macaulay to McKenzie, 2 June 1955, copy supplied by Hugh Latimer

24 *Globe and Mail*, 3 June 1955

25 Ibid., 24 May 1955

26 Ibid., 3 June 1955

27 Ibid.

28 Ibid., 8, 9, 10 June 1955

29 Ibid., 10 June 1955

30 The foregoing data are derived from *Ontario Sessional Papers*, 1952, 1956, 'Returns from the Records of the ... General Election ...'

CHAPTER 16: SPEAKING UP FOR ONTARIO

1 *Globe and Mail*, 18 Aug. 1955

2 Ibid., 17 Aug. 1955. Mr Foote outlived Frost by many years.

3 *Globe and Mail*, 18 Aug. 1955; RG3, I, 104, 'Macaulay, R.W.,' Macaulay to LMF, 24 Jan. 1955

4 For these negotiations see William Kilbourn, *Pipeline* (Toronto 1970), chap. 6.

5 *Telegram*, 17 March 1956

6 RG3, I, 176, 'Saskatchewan,' Douglas to St Laurent, 29 Nov. 1955 (copy); St Laurent to Douglas, 9 Dec. 1955 (copy); TUA, LMF, vol. 7, folder I, undated memorandum by LMF

7 Ibid., handwritten notes by LMF headed 'St. Laurent Howe Porter conference October 1955'; undated memorandum by LMF; RG3, I, 104, 'Macaulay, R.W.,' LMF to Macaulay, 25 May 1956

8 See TUA, LMF, vol. 7, folder I, for drafts of the letters, both with emendations in Frost's handwriting incorporated in the final version of each, and for two reports by Clarkson, Gordon.

9 Ibid., press release, 23 Nov. 1955

10 Kilbourn, *Pipeline*, 100; *Debates*, 1956: 385ff; *Telegram*, 17 Mar. 1956

11 QUA, Donald C. MacDonald Papers, draft resolution; MacDonald to LMF, undated draft; MacDonald to Ingle, 19 Mar. 1956; Ingle to MacDonald, 22 Mar. 1956

12 TUA, LMF, vol. 7, folder I, memorandum by LMF; RG3, I, 104, 'Macaulay, R.W.,' LMF to Macaulay, 25 May 1956

13 TUA, LMF, vol. 7, folder 1, handwritten notes by LMF headed '8 May 1956 St. Laurent conversation'

14 For the great pipeline debate, see Kilbourn, *Pipeline*, chap. 9; Robert Bothwell and William Kilbourn, *C.D. Howe, a Biography* (Toronto 1979), chap. 18; Dale Thomson, *St. Laurent* (Toronto 1967), chap. 14. A less dispassionate journalistic account is in Judith Robinson, *This Is on the House* (Toronto 1957), chap. 9.

15 TUA, LMF, vol. 7, folder 1, memorandum by LMF

16 *Debates*, 1956: 392

17 *Ottawa Journal*, 26 May 1956; *Saturday Night*, 9 June 1956

18 *Proceedings of the Federal-Provincial Conference ... October 3, 1955* (Ottawa 1955), 8

19 Ibid., 16–18

20 Ibid., 18–21

21 RG3, II, 8, 'Dom Prov St. Laurent Dec 12, 1955,' LMF to St Laurent, 14 Dec. 1955

22 RG3, I, 38, 'Dom-Prov Financial Proposals of 1956,' St. Laurent to LMF, 6 June 1956

23 Ibid., 36, 'Dominion Govt – Hon L. St. Laurent,' LMF to St Laurent, 22 Feb. 1956

24 Ibid., 38, 'Dom-Prov Conf. Statement LMF March 9, 1956'

25 Ibid., II, 8, 'Dom-Prov Conference July II, 1956,' press release, 18 July 1956

26 *Globe and Mail*, 19 July 1956

27 RG3, I, 39, 'Drew, Hon. George A.,' Drew to LMF, 17 Oct. 1955

28 *Debates*, 1957: 5

29 Ibid., 535–8

30 RG3, I, 36, 'Dominion Govt. – Hon. L. St. Laurent,' LMF to St Laurent, 27 Sept. 1955 (personal and confidential)

31 *Proceedings of the Federal-Provincial Conference ... October 3, 1955*, 9–11

32 Ibid., 24–6

33 Ibid., Appendix D

34 Malcolm G. Taylor, *Health Insurance and Canadian Public Policy* (Montreal 1978), 128–30; *Proceedings ... October 3, 1955*, 26 and Appendix D

35 Taylor, *Health Insurance*, 131

36 Ibid., 217–19

37 Ibid., 221

38 RG3, I, 130, 'Ont. Hospital Services Comm'n – General,' folder 1, LMF to Gathercole, 28 Sept. 1956 (personal)

39 Ibid., 151, 'Pri-Pt,' folder 2, W.P. Kilbride to H.J. Price, MPP, 1 Mar. 1956 (copy)

40 Ibid., 64, 'Hospital Insurance in Ont ... Letters re,' T.V. McManamy to LMF, 8 Feb. 1957; LMF to McManamy, 12 Feb. 1957; McManamy to LMF, 21 Mar. 1957; LMF to McManamy, 28 Mar. 1957

41 For a good narrative of these negotiations see Taylor, *Health Insurance*, 218ff. For the extensive correspondence between Frost and St Laurent and Martin, see RG3, I, 65, 'Health – Health Insurance – Hospital Care (Special File).'

CHAPTER 17: WONDERS FROM THE WEST

1 J. Murray Beck, *Pendulum of Power: Canada's Federal Elections* (Scarborough 1968), 303

2 Robert Bothwell, Ian Drummond, and John English, *Canada since 1945: Power, Politics, and Provincialism* (Toronto 1981), 192

3 RG3, I, 62, 'Hea-Hek,' LMF to W.C. Heine, 16 Oct. 1956

4 Hugh Latimer, 'Political Reminiscences,' 136–7

5 TUA, LMF, vol. II, folder I, 'The Diefenbaker Days,' 4; RG3, I, 23, 'Cas,' Case to LMF, 24 Sept. 1956

6 *Globe and Mail*, 14, 15 Dec. 1956; TUA, LMF, vol. II, folder I, 'The Diefenbaker Days,' 5

7 See on this matter, RG3, I, 60, 'Hamilton,' Hamilton to LMF, 27 Dec. 1956, with 'A Declaration of Principles'; memo by Young, 2 Jan. 1957; LMF to Hamilton, 7 Jan. 1957; Hamilton to LMF, 15 Jan. 1957.

8 Latimer, 'Reminiscences,' 140–1. For an informed insider's account of organizational preparations and activities, see these and the ensuing pages of this work.

9 Ibid., 151. The text of Frost's Barrie speech is in RG, II, 14, 'Elections-Federal-Barrie-Midland, 1957.' For newspaper reports see the *Globe and Mail*, 11, 22 May 1957. His response to St Laurent is in ibid., 23, 24 May 1957.

10 RG3, II, 14, 'Elections – Federal Hamilton 1957'

11 QUA, Herbert A. Bruce Papers, box 3, LMF to Bruce, 4 July 1957; RG3, I, 23, 'Challies, George H.,' LMF to Challies, 18 June 1957

12 Howard A. Scarrow, *Canada Votes: A Handbook of Federal and Provincial Elections* (New Orleans 1962), 146, 162–4

13 *Telegram*, 11 June 1957

14 John G. Diefenbaker, *One Canada: The Years of Achievement 1957–1962* (Toronto 1976), 29

15 TUA, LMF, vol. II, folder I, 'The Diefenbaker Days,' 2–4

16 Donald M. Fleming, *So Very Near: The Rising Years* (Toronto 1985), 420

17 *Dominion-Provincial Conference 1957* (Ottawa 1958), 8

18 Ibid., 13–19

19 RG3, I, 35, 'Diefenbaker, John,' LMF to Diefenbaker, 10 Dec. 1957 (private and confidential)

20 Fleming, *Rising Years*, 423

21 Latimer, 'Reminiscences,' 160–1

22 *Globe and Mail*, 20, 29 Mar. 1958
23 RG3, II, 58, 'Diefenbaker, Rt. Hon. John 1958,' LMF to Diefenbaker, 8 Apr. 1958; TUA, LMF, vol. II, folder I, 'The Diefenbaker Days,' 7
24 RG3, I, 71, 'Hor-Ht,' LMF to Howe, 18 June 1957; Howe to LMF, 19 June 1957
25 Ibid., 7, 'Attorney-Genl. Dept of Att-Genl.,' Roberts to Lennox, 12 June 1957 (copy); Lennox to Roberts, 17 June 1957 (copy)
26 Ibid., Roberts to LMF, 17 June 1957 (private and confidential). For Roberts' narrative of his part in the NONG affair, see his 'Member for Saint Patrick,' chap. 13.
27 Except as otherwise indicated, the following paragraphs are based on *Debates*, 1958: 668–79, 695–703, 745. For MacDonald's account of the NONG scandal, see his memoirs, *The Happy Warrior* (Toronto 1988), 75–90. I wish to thank him for allowing me to consult his memoirs in advance of their publication.
28 TUA, LMF, vol. 7, folder 17, 'Memo – 29th August, 1972,' 5
29 *Globe and Mail*, 5 July 1958
30 Ibid., 12 Mar. 1958
31 *Telegram*, 12 Mar. 1958
32 *Globe and Mail*, 5, 6 May 1958
33 TUA, LMF, vol. 7, folder 17, Griesinger to LMF, 5 May 1958; LMF to Griesinger, 6 May 1958
34 Ibid., 'Memo – 29th August, 1972,' 4
35 Ibid., Mapledoram to LMF, 16 May 1958; LMF to Mapledoram, 2 July 1958
36 RG3, I, 214, 'Wintermeyer, John MPP,' LMF to Wintermeyer, 20 Apr. 1958 (telegram); Wintermeyer to LMF, 22 Apr. 1958
37 *Debates*, 1959: 91
38 TUA, LMF, vol. 7, folder II, press release by Roberts, 4 July 1958; folder 17, 'Memo – 29th August, 1972,' 4. The inquiry report was published in the *Globe and Mail*, 13 Feb. 1959. One notable municipal politician later implicated in the NONG stock distribution was Leo Landreville, mayor of Sudbury when the franchise there was granted, who as a result of his involvement lost his seat on the bench to which he had subsequently been appointed. In the House on 18 Mar. 1959, MacDonald mentioned Landreville as a prominent advocate of awarding the Sudbury franchise to NONG, without explicitly alleging that the mayor had been a recipient of shares. 'It is not my function,' said MacDonald, 'to name any names at this point. It is the responsibility of a properly constituted judicial body.' *Debates*, 1959: 1346
39 Ibid., 1317–59
40 *Globe and Mail*, 13 Feb. 1959
41 Quoted in *Debates*, 1959: 1357

42 Ibid., 1368
43 OHSS oral history, Donald MacDonald interview, 11
44 TUA, LMF, vol. 7, folder 17, Peter Quinn to LMF, n.d.; LMF to Quinn, 21 July 1972
45 Ibid., 'Memo – 29th August 1972,' 1–2, 6

CHAPTER 18: GETTING ON WITH DIEF

1 TUA, LMF, vol. 11, folder 1, undated memorandum by LMF, 'The Diefenbaker Days,' 14
2 Hugh Latimer, 'Political Reminiscences,' 161–2
3 RG3, I, II, 'Bickle, E.W.,' Gathercole to Porter, 28 Sept. 1957
4 Ibid., 203, 'Unemployment Situation & Works Measures,' 'Meeting of Steering Committee on Unemployment'
5 Ibid., 201, 'Unemployment Situation – General,' Farrell to LMF, 29 Jan. 1958; 203, 'Unemployment Situation & Works Measures,' Farrell to LMF, 7 Feb. 1058; 87, 'Labour, Dept. of, Genl. Corresp.,' Farrell to LMF, 2 Jan. 1958
6 Ibid., 201, 'Unemployment Situation Re: Employable Unemployed,' LMF to McIntyre, 7 Aug. 1957
7 Ibid., McIntyre to LMF, 27 July 1957
8 Debates, 1958: 382–3
9 RG3, I, 201, 'Unemployment Situation Re: Employable Unemployed,' McIntyre to LMF, 27 July 1957
10 Debates, 1958: 379ff
11 See James Dow, The Arrow (Toronto 1979) and, for a brief history of the project, J.L. Granatstein, Canada 1957–1967: The Years of Uncertainty and Innovation (Toronto 1986), 105–9. Greig Stewart, Shutting down the National Dream: A.V. Roe and the Tragedy of the AVRO Arrow (Toronto 1988) should be noted as well [Eds].
12 RG3, III, 80, 'Diefenbaker, John 1961,' LMF to Diefenbaker, 19 Feb. 1959 (telegram)
13 'Diefenbaker Days,' 8, 10
14 RG3, III, 80, 'Diefenbaker, John 1961,' LMF to Diefenbaker, 21 Feb. 1959 (telegram)
15 Debates, 1959: 505–6, 530–2
16 Globe and Mail, 7 May 1959
17 Ibid., 5 May 1959
18 Ibid., 22 May, 5 June 1959
19 Ibid., 28 May 1959
20 Telegram, 3 June 1959
21 Globe and Mail, 19 May, 3 June 1959

22 *Ottawa Citizen*, 10 June 1959
23 *Toronto Star*, 6 June 1959
24 Ibid.; *Ottawa Citizen*, 10 June 1959
25 *Telegram*, 9, 10 June 1959
26 *Globe and Mail*, 4 June 1959
27 Donald M. Fleming, *So Very Near: The Summit Years* (Toronto 1985), 67
28 RG3, III, 58, 'Diefenbaker, Rt. Hon. John 1958,' LMF to Diefenbaker, 10 June 1958 (personal and confidential)
29 Fleming, *Summit Years*, 62
30 RG3, III, 65, 'Dominion-Provincial Conference 1959,' 'Statement by the Honourable James N. Allan'
31 Fleming, *Summit Years*, 65
32 RG3, III, 80, 'Diefenbaker, John 1961,' LMF to Diefenbaker, 11 Sept. 1959 (personal)
33 Ibid., 65, 'Dominion-Provincial Conference 1959,' memorandum by LMF with covering letter LMF to Gathercole, 14 Oct. 1959
34 Fleming, *Summit Years*, 67–8
35 TUA, LMF, vol. II, folder 6, LMF to Diefenbaker, 20 Aug. 1959 (personal and confidential)
36 Ibid., 'Notes on conversation with Diefenbaker Aug 26/59'
37 Ibid., Gathercole to LMF, 28 Aug. 1959, with accompanying memorandum
38 RG3, III, 80, 'Diefenbaker, John 1961,' LMF to Diefenbaker, 23 Sept. 1959
39 Ibid., LMF to Diefenbaker, 6 Oct. 1959 (personal)
40 TUA, LMF, vol. II, folder 7, LMF to Diefenbaker, 6 Nov. 1959 (personal and confidential)
41 RG3, III, 73, 'J.E. Coyne 1959,' 'Credit and Capital,' speech by J.E. Coyne, Toronto, 14 Dec. 1959; LMF to Diefenbaker, 17 Dec. 1959 (personal and confidential); LMF to Oakley Dalgleish, 19 Jan. 1960 (personal)
42 TUA, LMF, vol. II, folder 7, LMF to Coyne, 16 Dec. 1959. Frost later asked Coyne to correct his oversight in not marking this personal and confidential.
43 Ibid., LMF to Diefenbaker, 10, 17 Dec. 1959 (both personal and confidential)
44 Ibid., Coyne to LMF, 7 Jan. 1960
45 For Fleming's account of the Coyne affair, see his *Summit Years*, chap. 79. A more disinterested narrative is in Granatstein, *Canada 1957–1967*, chap. 4.
46 TUA, LMF, vol. II, folder 8, LMF to Diefenbaker, 21 July, 1961 (personal and confidential)
47 Quoted in Granatstein, *Canada 1957–1967*, 78

CHAPTER 19: RECURRENCES

1 See Merrill Denison, *The People's Power* (Toronto 1960), 265–6; *Globe and Mail*, 2 July 1958.

2 See RG3, I, 76, 'H.E.P.C. Re: Hydro Mural,' Roy Greenaway to LMF, n.d;
  Farrell to Duncan, 20 June 1958 (confidential), Duncan to Farrell, 26 June
  1958.

3 Ibid., LMF to Macaulay, 2 Mar. 1959

4 *Debates*, 1959: 1062

5 TUA, LMF, vol. II, folder 7, LMF to Coyne, 16 Dec. 1959

6 For these other post-war developments see Denison, *People's Power*,
  chap. 25.

7 RG3, I, 74, 'H.E.P.C. J.S. Duncan, 1956–58,' Duncan to LMF, 26 Aug. 1958,
  with accompanying draft paragraphs

8 RG3, I, 75, 'H.E.P.C. J.S. Duncan, 1959–61,' Duncan to Macaulay, 16 Feb.
  1959 (confidential, copy, and covering letter, Duncan to LMF, 17 Feb. 1959,
  strictly confidential); LMF to Duncan, 19 Feb. 1959

9 *Debates*, 1959: 1062–3

10 RG3, I, 199, 'Trotting Ass'n, Canadian,' Ray Farrell to LMF, 31 Mar. 1959;
   Farrell to Bigelow, 1 Apr. 1959 (confidential); Farrell to LMF, 28 Apr., 6, 8
   May 1959; 87, 'Labour, Dept. of Hon. Chas. Daley, Personal,' LMF to Daley,
   24 Aug. 1960

11 Ibid., 91, 'Lau-Ld,' folder I, LMF to Allan Lawrence, 15 Jan. 1959

12 Ibid., 153, 'P.C. Assoc. Ontario Ass'n, A.D. McKenzie, President,' LMF to
   McKenzie, 3 Feb. 1956

13 Ibid., 95, 'L.C.B.O. Advertising of Liquor,' LMF to J.R. Watt, 7 Jan. 1958;
   LMF to Hale, 10 Dec. 1957; Dalgleish to LMF, 16 Dec. 1957 (personal)

14 Among those sharing their wisdom with Frost was Charlotte Whitton, who
   drew on her expertise in social policy to compose a nine-page memorandum
   proposing, among other things, a small body, 'The Supervisors of the
   Advertising of Alcoholic Beverages,' and a large, representative
   'Consultative Panel' to decide on the suitability of proposed material. With a
   good deal else on his mind, Frost seems not to have paid this the attention
   Miss Whitton thought it merited, indeed not to have acknowledged it, and
   she reacted with a mild rebuke bearing neither salutation nor signature:
   'Et tu! Brute! I thought I would get a call at least. Eh bien!' Ibid., II, 23,
   'Liquor Control II 1960 Personal & Confidential,' Whitton to LMF, 21 Mar.
   1960, with accompanying 'Confidential Memorandum re Supervision of
   Advertising in Ontario'; Whitton to LMF, n.d.

15 Ibid., LMF to Hale, 1 June 1960 (personal and confidential)

16 Ibid., 'Memorandum ... Concerning Liquor Advertising,' 26 May 1960
   (secret, marked 'Draft only')

17 Frost thought strict enforcement of this restriction important enough to
   warrant complaining to Andrew Stewart, chairman of the Board of
   Broadcast Governors, about a TV commercial on the CBC network. 'I have
   had numerous enquiries concerning the same. Many have taken it as a label
   on a bottle held close to the camera so that the label would show. In any

event, it is a label which has been bent to indicate the shape of a bottle or a can.' Ibid., 'Liquor Control I 1957–60 Personal and Confidential,' LMF to Stewart, 24 Aug. 1960

18 Ibid., Collings to John Labatt Ltd., 25 Oct. 1960; Collings to LMF, 26 Oct. 1960

19 Ibid., Ian Dowie to Collings, II Nov. 1960 (copy); Mutchmor to LMF, 18 Nov. 1960; LMF to Mutchmor, 23 Nov. 1960

20 Ibid., 'Liquor Control II 1960 Personal & Confidential,' for example: John Bassett to LMF, 3 June 1960 (personal and secret); Floyd Chalmers to LMF, 3 June 1960; Arthur Ford to LMF, 8 June 1960

21 Ibid., Dalgleish to LMF, 17 June 1960 (personal); memorandum by Cooper, 14 June 1960; Dalgleish to LMF, 16, 20 June 1960 (personal)

CHAPTER 20: BOWING OUT

1 *Debates*, 1958: 393

2 RG3, I, 28, 'COA-COF,' Cody to LMF, II June 1955

3 Ibid., Cody to LMF, 23 Mar. 1957; LMF to Cody, 27 Mar. 1957

4 Ibid., 195, 'Toronto – Metropolitan Area Re: Separate School Problem (Confidential),' D.J. Collins to LMF, 3 May 1957 (confidential)

5 *Debates*, 1958: 384–6, 393–7

6 RG3, I, 28, COA-COF,' Cody to LMF, 13 Mar. 1958

7 Ibid., 157, 'Public Schools Situation,' draft brief of Public Schools Trustees Association of Ontario,' n.d. [Jan. 1959]

8 Ibid., 'An Open Letter to Members of the Ontario Legislature,' signed by A.F. Mills and D.P. Rowland, 29 Jan. 1959

9 TUA, LMF, vol. 12, folder 9, 'Memorandum by L.M.F. Concerning Separate Roman Catholic Elementary Schools'

10 RG3, outgoing correspondence, LMF to Edinborough, 16 Oct. 1956

11 Ibid., I, 204, 'University of Toronto Genl. Corresp.,' LMF to Allan, II Aug. 1958

12 Paul Axelrod, *Scholars and Dollars: Politics, Economics, and the Universities of Ontario* (Toronto 1982), 55. The reader is referred to this work, especially chaps. 3 and 4, for a fuller account of university expansion in the last phase of the Frost period.

13 *Dominion-Provincial Conference 1960, Ottawa, July 25th, 26th and 27th, 1960* (Ottawa 1960), 20

14 On its genesis and development, see Axelrod, *Scholars and Dollars*, 63ff.

15 RG3, I, 205, 'University of Toronto Board of Governors, Chancellor and Staff,' Eric Phillips to Nathan Phillips, 28 Aug. 1958 (personal, copy); Eric Phillips to LMF, 28 Aug. 1958 (personal)

16 Ibid., 94, 'Lewis,' LMF to Lewis, 6 Feb. 1959 (personal and confidential)

17 Ibid., III, 80, 'Diefenbaker, John 1961,' Diefenbaker to LMF, 5 Dec. 1959 (private and confidential); LMF to Diefenbaker, 8 Dec. 1959 (private and confidential); Diefenbaker to LMF, 14 Dec. 1959 (personal and confidential); LMF to Diefenbaker, 16 Dec. 1959 (personal and confidential). Evidently this last letter was not sent. The original, on letterhead and marked 'File,' is in Frost's papers.

18 Ibid., I, 205, 'University of Toronto Board of Governors, Chancellor and Staff,' Phillips to LMF, 8 Apr. 1961; LMF to Phillips, 1 May 1961

19 Ibid., 204, 'University of Toronto Genl. Corresp.,' LMF to J.N. Allan, 11 Aug. 1958

20 On Queen's justifiable complaints, see Frederick W. Gibson, *Queen's University*, vol. II 1917–1961, *To Serve and Yet Be Free* (Kingston and Montreal 1983), 362ff.

21 RG3, I, 205, 'University of Toronto Board of Governors, Chancellor and Staff,' Dunlop to Bissell, 6 Nov. 1958 (copy); Phillips to LMF, 12 Nov. 1958 (personal)

22 Ibid., LMF to Phillips, 18 Nov. 1958 (personal); Cannon to Ray Farrell, 25 Nov. 1958; Dunlop to LMF, 2 Dec. 1958

23 Ibid., Phillips to LMF, 20 May 1960; Gathercole to LMF, 7 June 1960

24 On Robarts as education minister, see A.K. McDougall, *John Robarts: His Life and Government* (Toronto 1986), 53–7.

25 Peter Oliver, *Unlikely Tory: The Life and Politics of Allan Grossman* (Toronto 1985), 118

26 *Dominion-Provincial Conference 1960*, 15ff

27 Donald M. Fleming, *So Very Near: The Summit Years* (Toronto 1985), 279

28 RG3, III, 80, 'Dominion-Provincial Conference 1960–61,' LMF to Diefenbaker, 28 July 1960

29 Ibid., LMF to Porter, 28 July 1960 (personal and confidential)

30 Dale C. Thomson, *Jean Lesage and the Quiet Revolution* (Toronto 1984), 335; *Debates*, 1960: 145

31 RG3, I, 38, 'Dom-Prov. [sic] Premiers' Conf. Quebec Conf. Dec 1–2/60,' LMF to Lesage, 15 Nov. 1960

32 *Globe and Mail*, 2 Dec. 1960

33 *Dominion-Provincial Conference 1960*, 22

34 *Globe and Mail*, 27, 28, 29 Oct. 1960

35 Ibid., 24 Feb. 1961

36 Fleming, *Summit Years*, 279

37 *Debates*, 1961: 1972–3

38 Hugh Latimer, 'Political Reminiscences,' 109–11, 113-16

39 Memorandum by Hugh Latimer for the author

40 Quoted in Latimer, 'Reminiscences,' 316, 319

41 Oliver, *Unlikely Tory*, 118

42 RG3, I, 54, 'Frost, Hon. L.M. Re: Retirement,' LMF to Bell, 31 July 1961

43 *Toronto Star*, 3 Aug. 1961; *Telegram*, 3 Aug. 1961; *Globe and Mail*, 4 Aug. 1961

44 Latimer, 'Reminiscences,' 413, 419–20; Oliver, *Unlikely Tory*, 119; McDougall, *Robarts*, chap. 5

CHAPTER 21: THE LAIRD OF LINDSAY

1 Donald MacDonald, *The Happy Warrior: Political Memoirs* (Toronto 1988), 350

2 TUA, LMF, vol. II, folder 8, LMF to Diefenbaker, 8 Nov. 1961 (personal)

3 Ibid., LMF to Diefenbaker, 7 Oct. 1961 (personal)

4 Ibid., folder 9, notes in LMF's handwriting

5 Ibid., Diefenbaker to LMF, 7 Oct. 1962; *Globe and Mail*, 5 May 1963

6 TUA, LMF, vol. II, folder 9, LMF to Diefenbaker, 12 July 1962

7 Ibid., LMF to Diefenbaker, 19 Feb. 1962 (personal and confidential)

8 Ibid., Diefenbaker to LMF, 25 Feb. 1962 (personal and confidential)

9 Ibid., LMF to Diefenbaker, 23 Mar. 1962 (personal and confidential, second letter of that date, and accompanying confidential draft statement)

10 Ibid., outgoing letters, LMF to McCutcheon, 3 Jan. 1963 (personal and confidential)

11 Ibid., LMF to Diefenbaker, 12 July 1962

12 Ibid., folder 1, 'The Diefenbaker Days,' 13–14

13 Ibid., 14–18

14 Ibid., vol. II, folder 10, LMF to Diefenbaker, 11 Apr. 1963

15 Ibid., vol. 5, folder 14, incoming letters, Sullivan to LMF, 20 Jan. 1965 (personal and confidential and marked 'Please tear up'); outgoing letters, LMF to W.M. Nickle, 19 Sept. 1967

16 Ibid., outgoing letters, LMF to Milner, 26, 31 Oct. 1966

17 Ibid., LMF to Jean Wadds, 20 Sept. 1967

18 Ibid., LMF to Stanfield, 15 Nov. 1967 (personal), 1 Dec. 1967

19 Ibid., LMF to Hart, 2 Nov. 1962

20 Ibid., LMF to J.R. Walker, 5 May 1965 (personal). See also LMF to Arnold Hart, 26 Oct. 1966.

21 Ibid., LMF to Hart, 15 Apr. 1966 (confidential)

22 Ibid., LMF to Samuel Bronfman, 22 Jan. 1965

23 Ibid., LMF to Hart, 26 Oct. 1966; Macquarrie to the author, 1 Feb. 1985. I am grateful to Senator Macquarrie for acquainting me with this incident.

24 TUA, LMF, outgoing letters, LMF to Armstrong, 27 Mar. 1962 (personal and confidential). For illustrations of 'advice and help,' see numerous communications from Frost to the premier in ibid., and also in McDougall, *Robarts*.

25 Paul Axelrod, *Scholars and Dollars: Politics, Economics, and the Universities of Ontario* (Toronto 1982), 163

26 TUA, LMF, outgoing letters, LMF to Cooper, 4 Feb. 1966 (personal)

27 Ibid., LMF to Claude Bissell, 20 Nov. 1963

28 Axelrod, *Scholars and Dollars*, 93. The reader is referred to this and ensuing pages of this work for an account of subsequent events.

29 TUA, LMF, outgoing letters, LMF to Bissell, 20 Nov. 1963

30 Ibid., LMF to Robarts, 19 Jan. 1966

31 I am indebted to Mrs S. Wiltshire for this information.

32 TUA, LMF, outgoing letters, LMF to Forrest, 17 Apr. 1963; LMF to Roberta Frost, 1 Apr. 1963; LMF to H.E.D. Ashford, 24 June 1964

33 See, *inter alia*: RG3, 1, 18, 'Historic Sites & Matters,' T.F. McIlwraith to LMF, 21 Jan. 1948; LMF to McIlwraith, 27 Jan. 1948; McIlwraith to LMF, 9 Feb. 1948; 175, 'Sam Slick Sketches,' LMF to Watson Kirkconnell, 10 Aug. 1956; 192, 'Tolpuddle Martyrs'; TUA, LMF, outgoing letters, LMF to Fred Williams, 14 May 1941 (personal); LMF to John Bassett, 2 July 1965.

34 RG 3, 1, 16, 'Caa-Cal,' LMF to L.J. Cahaill, 1 Oct. 1953

35 Ibid., 18, 'Historic Sites & Matters,' LMF to J.S.P. Armstrong, 13 Mar. 1967

36 Leslie M. Frost, *Fighting Men* (Toronto 1967), vii–ix

37 Leslie M. Frost, *Forgotten Pathways of the Trent* (Don Mills 1973), 7–8

38 Hugh Latimer, 'Political Reminiscences,' 363–7

39 See ibid., 367-68; OHSS oral history, Jack and Eileen Beal interview, 23–4.

Picture Credits

Donald McKague, Toronto: Leslie Frost 1953 (frontispiece)
Elizabeth C. Frey, Toronto: Leslie Frost c. 1953
Walter Stewart, Lindsay: Gertrude Frost
H.R. Neibel, Orillia: William Sword Frost
Trent University Archives: Margaret Barker Frost; Grenville Frost; Leslie and
    Cecil Frost 1914; cottage at Pleasant Point; 17 Sussex Street North, Lindsay;
    meeting the people; Gertrude Frost and other Tory women; official opening
    of generating station 1958; election night in Lindsay
Ashley and Crippen, Toronto: Cecil Frost
Toronto *Star* newspaper service: Frost and Louis St Laurent
James Reidford, *Globe and Mail*: Frost meets the press
Ontario Ministry of Culture and Communications: Frost with Donald C.
    MacDonald; Frost unveils historical plaque at Port Carling

Index